DUBLIN CASTLE

From Fortress to Palace

To J.B. (Jack) Maguire

A pioneer researcher on Dublin Castle

Frontispiece An aerial view of Dublin Castle from the east taken in 2001. (NMS)

DUBLIN CASTLE

From Fortress to Palace

VOLUME 1
Vikings to Victorians:
a History of Dublin Castle to 1850

By

Seán Duffy, John Montague, Kevin Mulligan and Michael O'Neill

Executive Editors

Ann Lynch and Conleth Manning

NATIONAL MONUMENTS SERVICE

DUBLIN CASTLE
From Fortress to Palace

General Editors
Ann Lynch and Conleth Manning

VOLUME 1
Vikings to Victorians: a history of Dublin Castle to 1850
by Seán Duffy, John Montague, Kevin Mulligan
and Michael O'Neill

VOLUME 2
The Viking-Age Archaeology
by Ann Lynch, Conleth Manning and Ken Wiggins

VOLUME 3 (Parts 1 and 2)
The Medieval and Post-Medieval Archaeology
by Ann Lynch, Conleth Manning and Ken Wiggins

Published by National Monuments Service, Dublin,
on behalf of the Government of Ireland

Le ceannach díreach ó
FOILSEACHÁIN RIALTAIS,
BÓTHAR BHAILE UÍ BHEOLÁIN, BAILE ÁTHA CLIATH 8.
D08 XA06
(Teil: 046 942 3100 nó Riomhphost: publications@opw.ie)
nó trí aon díoltóir leabhar.

To be purchased from
GOVERNMENT PUBLICATIONS,
MOUNTSHANNON ROAD, DUBLIN 8.
D08 XA06
(Tel: 046 942 3100 or Email: publications@opw.ie)
or through any bookseller.

ISBN: 978-1-4468-8071-5

Designed by Caitlin Quinn and Claire Rubira,
Vermillion Design Consultants

Copy-edited by Editorial Solutions (Ireland) Limited

Printed by Colorman Ireland Ltd.

Print Project Manager: Marie Harpur

**An Roinn Tithíochta,
Rialtais Áitiúil agus Oidhreachta**
Department of Housing,
Local Government and Heritage

Contents

Réamhrá

Is séadchomhartha é Caisleán Bhaile Átha Cliath a léiríonn na castachtaí a bhaineann le stair na hÉireann, stair ar iomaí cor agus casadh a bhaineann léi, ar mhinic achrannach iad. Tógadh an caisleán ar bhunchloch Lochlannach agus tá coimpléasc an chaisleáin lárnach i stair na hÉireann ó bunaíodh é amach sa 12ú haois. Is ann a bhí an lárionad riaracháin ar an oileán nó gur tugadh an caisleán ar lámh do stát nuabhunaithe na hÉireann sa bhliain 1922 agus, dá bhrí sin bíonn cuimhne na ndaoine ar an gcaisleán dorcha agus gruama in amanna de bharr na staire sin. Bhain ról an chaisleáin ar feadh an chuid is mó de stair an chaisleáin le heisiamh agus le heisiachas; dún daingean, nó áit lenar bhain pribhléid gháifeach tráth níos déanaí dar le go leor daoine.

Ní mar a chéile ar chor ar bith atá ról Chaisleán Bhaile Átha Cliath i saol poiblí an Stáit le blianta beaga anuas. Tá ról lárnach fós ag an gCaisleán i bhfeidhmiú an Rialtais agus maidir leis an tuiscint atá againn ar ról na staire i dtaobh féiniúlacht a chruthú. Is ann a dhéantar Uachtaráin na hÉireann a oirniú, uachtaráin a thoghtar go díreach agus go saor, is ionad é ina mbíonn Stát ceannasach na hÉireann i mbun oibre lenár gcomhpháirtithe idirnáisiúnta ar mhaithe le leas na ndaoine uile. Is ann a fhógraítear cinntí daonlathacha na nDaoine i reifrinn shaora agus is ann a bhreithnítear saincheisteanna crua agus conspóideacha go poiblí ó am go chéile, róil riachtanacha i saol náisiúin atá ag éirí níos oscailte agus níos cuimsithí, saol ina dtugtar aird ar na saoránaigh go léir chomh maith leis an domhan níos leithne agus ina dtugtar aghaidh ar shaincheisteanna an lae mar dhaonlathas atá tagtha in inmhe.

Is saoráid Rialtais a fheidhmíonn é Caisleán Bhaile Átha Cliath óna leanann seirbhísí poiblí orthu ag cur réimse de phríomhsheirbhísí poiblí ar fáil. Maidir leis sin go léir, an obair nach dtugtar faoi deara chomh minic sin agus na himeachtaí móra a tharraingíonn caint sa nuacht araon, is faoi mhaoirseacht chúramach Oifig na nOibreacha Poiblí atá an caisleán bainistithe agus coinnithe. Trí sin a dhéanamh, agus trí infheistíocht leanúnach ón Stát chun coimpléasc an chaisleáin a chaomhnú, gheofar tuilleadh amach faoi thábhacht oidhreachta na réimse struchtúr, ó thréimhsí meánaoise go dtí tréimhsí níos nua-aimsire, atá mar chuid de shuíomh an chaisleáin, agus déanfar sin a chur ar fáil do shaoránaigh na tíre agus do chuairteoirí ó thar lear, cuairteoirí a gcuirimid céad míle fáilte rompu.

I bhfianaise ról comhaimseartha Chaisleán Bhaile Átha Cliath agus an teacht atá ag an bpobal ar oidhreacht an chaisleáin tá ról anois aige mar áit ionchuimsitheach agus uileghabhálach, agus beimid go léir ábalta machnamh i gcomhar a dhéanamh ar stair na hÉireann trí thuiscint a fháil ar oidhreacht an chaisleáin. Cuirfidh an foilseachán tábhachtach seo, an chéad fhoilseachán i sraith, go mór leis sin, ag tabhairt deis do chách torthaí dianscoláireachta príomhshaineolaithe a bhreathnú. Thug an cinneadh a rinneadh sna 1980idí saoráid chomhdhála shaintógtha fhorbairt ar láthair an chaisleáin chomh maith le hobair eile a rinneadh ag an am sin deis dúinn, trí thochailtí seandálaíochta a rinneadh go cumasach agus trí na torthaí dochreidte a bhí mar thoradh ar na tochailtí sin, tuiscint níos doimhne a fháil ar stair an chaisleáin agus ar stair na hÉireann. Tá ardmholadh le tabhairt do Sheirbhís na Séadchomharthaí Náisiúnta sa Roinn Tithíochta, Rialtais Áitiúil agus Oidhreachta le tacaíocht ó Oifig na nOibreacha Poiblí as na torthaí sin a chur os comhair pobal níos leithne trí chlár uaillmhianach agus cuimsitheach foilsithe. Is saothar mór scoláireachta an chéad imleabhar seo, ina ndírítear ar fhorbairt staire choimpléasc an caisleáin suas go dtí 1850, a chuireann cúlra tábhachtach ar fáil ar na tuarascálacha mionsonraithe a bheidh le teacht ar an obair sheandálaíochta.

De réir mar atá Caisleán Bhaile Átha Cliath i mbun leanúint de ról ríthábhachtach a ghlacadh i saol náisiúnta na hÉireann, agus muid ag ceiliúradh céad bliain ó thosaigh Stát na hÉireann á úsáid, tá an t-ádh orainn go léir go bhfuilimid ábalta sult a bhaint as, agus ní hamháin as an rochtain fhisiceach atá againn ar an gcaisleán ach as an rochtain chuimsitheach anois atá againn ar stair an chaisleáin. Le breis is míle bliain bhí Caisleán Bhaile Átha Cliath ina lárionad cumhachta agus ina shiombail den chumhacht in Éirinn. Daingean a bhí ann tráth ach is é pálás an phobail amach is amach anois é - agus na doirse oscailte don phobal le fada an lá. Tugann an stair iontach seo deis rochtana níos mó don phobail.

Micheál Martin

Micheál Martin, T.D.
Taoiseach

Foreword

Through the twists and often-turbulent turns of time, Dublin Castle stands as a monument to the complexities of Irish history. Built on Viking foundations, the castle complex has been central to the history of Ireland since its foundation in the late 12th century. The seat of administrative power on the island until its handover to the fledgling Irish state in 1922 has left the memory of the castle at times darkened by history and for many, its role during much of its existence is synonymous with exclusion and exclusivity; a fortress, or later a place of ostentatious privilege.

In more recent times the role of Dublin Castle in the public life of our State has been very different. It retains a pivotal role in the architecture of government and in our understanding of the role of history in forging identity. It is the place of inauguration of the directly and freely elected Presidents of Ireland, a venue where our sovereign State works with our international partners in the interests of all our peoples. It is a where the democratic decisions of the People in free referenda are announced and sometimes difficult and contentious issues are considered in public, all vital roles in the life of an ever more open and inclusive nation, concerned for all its citizens and the wider world and addressing the issues of the day as a mature democracy.

Dublin Castle is a working Government facility, from which many public servants continue to provide a range of core public services. In all this, both the lesser noticed but crucial work and the newsworthy events, through its careful stewardship the Office of Public Works has managed and maintained the castle. In doing so, and with continued and ongoing State investment in the conservation of the castle complex, the heritage importance of the range of structures, from medieval to modern dates, existing at the castle, is further revealed and made accessible to our citizens and our much welcomed visitors from overseas.

Dublin Castle's contemporary role and the public access to its heritage now casts it in the role of a place of inclusion and inclusivity, which through an understanding of its heritage allows us all to reflect together on Ireland's past. This important publication, the first in a series, will add greatly to this, providing access for all to consider the results of the deep scholarship of leading experts. The decision in the 1980s to develop a purpose built conference facility at the castle and other works at that time provided an opportunity, through expert archaeological excavations and the remarkable results they produced, to deepen our understanding of the history of the castle and Ireland. The National Monuments Service of the Department of Housing, Heritage and Local Government, with OPW support, is to be commended in bringing those results to a wide audience through an ambitious and comprehensive programme of publication. This first volume, focusing on the historical development of the castle complex to 1850, is a major piece of scholarship providing an important background to the detailed reports on archaeological work that will follow.

As Dublin Castle continues its vital role in our national life, celebrating a centenary of its use by the Irish State, we are all now fortunate to be able to enjoy not alone inclusive physical access to the castle but now also comprehensive access to its history. For over a millennium Dublin Castle was seat, centre, and symbol of power in this country. Once fortress, it is now truly the people's palace - portals long cast open to the public. This wonderful history gives even more of it to the public gaze.

Micheál Martin

Micheál Martin, T.D.
Taoiseach

Acknowledgements

The executive editors would like to acknowledge the following: Michael MacDonagh, Chief Archaeologist, National Monuments Service (NMS) and John Cahill, Mary Heffernan and Rosemary Collier of the Office of Public Works (OPW) for their unstinting support for this publication project and ongoing encouragement; John Lalor, Senior Photographer, Con Brogan, former Senior Photographer and Tony Roche of the NMS Photographic Unit for much assistance with the illustrations; Myles Campbell and William Derham (OPW), Dublin Castle for also assisting with illustrations and providing access to the castle; Nirvana Pitt, librarian and Elizabeth King, OPW Library, Trim, for providing many images; John Kirwan for sourcing images and obtaining permissions for publication; Conor McHale for producing Figs 1.1 to 1.3; Andrew Bonar Law for Fig. 3.44; John Goodall for Fig. 3.76; John O'Regan, Gandon Editions, for help in sourcing images; Jack (J.B.) Maguire for encouragement and sharing his knowledge of the castle; Aideen Ireland for help in trying to track down manuscript references in the National Archives of Ireland; Hugh Beckett of the Military Archives and the staff of the Royal Society of Antiquaries of Ireland and the National Library of Ireland for help with particular illustrations; Edward Bourke for facilitating access to the NMS archive; Ken Wiggins for accessing illustrations; the peer reviewers of the three sections and the reader of the overall text. Particular thanks are due to Sheelagh Hughes of Editorial Solutions Ireland Ltd for a difficult copyediting task, to Marie Harpur for her expert production management and to Caitlin Quinn and Claire Rubira of Vermillion Design Consultants for the stylish design.

John Kirwan, in sourcing many of the images and getting permissions, acknowledges the help of staff in various libraries and archives and in particular Colm O'Riordan of the Irish Architectural Archive, Joanne Carroll and James Harte of the National Library of Ireland, Susanna Feder of the Bridgeman Art Library, Dr Mary Clarke of Dublin City Library and Archives, Antoinette Prout of the Royal Irish Academy Library and Rosemary Ryan of Waterford Treasures.

Seán Duffy would like to acknowledge Dr Stuart Kinsella, for reading over and offering helpful comments on that portion of his text relating to the sixteenth century.

John Montague acknowledges the generous support of Eddie McParland, who made extended and important comments on early drafts of his text; Graham Hickey, Paul Ferguson, Sarah Gearty, Con Manning and Ann Lynch; Thaddeus Breen, whose research on Dublin Castle was an important resource; the work of Thérèse Robinson, whose PhD was a key source; Robin Usher, Patricia McCarthy, Colm Lennon, Freddie O'Dwyer, Aideen Ireland; the anonymous reader, whose welcome comments and suggestions expanded the scope of his research; Livia Hurley, the late Rolf Loeber, Paul Doyle and Seán Hughes of Trinity College Dublin Library; the staff of the Royal Irish Academy Library including Sophie Evans; the staff of the Dublin City Library and Archives including Mary Clark; the staff of the National Archives including Gregory O'Connor; the staff of the National Library Manuscript Department; all the staff of the Irish Architectural Archive; the staff of the British Library Manuscripts and Map Reading Rooms, and of the Bodleian Library, and finally his father-in-law, Godfrey O'Byrne and his wife Helen Montague.

Kevin Mulligan and Michael O'Neill would like to warmly thank the following for many kindnesses: Eddie McParland, Freddie O'Dwyer, Colm O'Riordan, Aideen Ireland, William Laffan and Tom Desmond; and to acknowledge and thank the following who provided much valuable assistance: Mary Heffernan and William Derham at Dublin Castle; Noel Collins and Emma Stevens of the OPW Library, Trim; Mary Clark and the staff of Dublin City Archive, Pearse Street Library; the staff of the Architectural Archive, the National Archives and of the Manuscript Department of the National Library of Ireland.

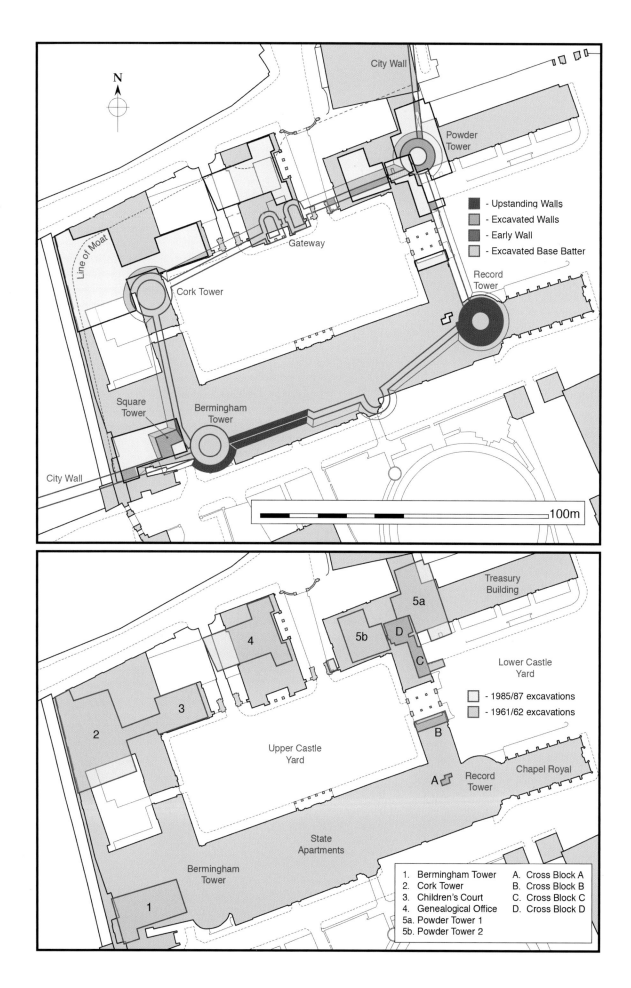

Introduction

Dublin Castle was the centre and symbol of English, and later British, royal and executive power in Ireland from the 1170s up until it was handed over to the Irish Provisional Government in 1922. There was a castle on the present site, possibly replacing a Hiberno-Scandinavian fortress, from the earliest days of the English/Anglo-Norman presence, but it was the large stone castle, built between 1204 and c. 1230, as a result of a mandate issued by King John, that endured throughout the remainder of the medieval period and up to the late seventeenth century. In plan, the castle was roughly rectangular with large circular towers at each corner and a gatehouse with rounded towers flanking the gateway on the long north side (Fig. 1). The gateway was accessed by a causeway and drawbridge across the wide deep moat. It was a fine example of medieval defensive architecture and one of the largest and strongest castles ever built in Ireland. In medieval times it contained, among other buildings, two large halls, accommodation for the chief governor of Ireland and his administration, a chapel, a mint, a prison and stores. Also, at times parliaments were held there and courts of law. New buildings were erected within the medieval defensive walls in the sixteenth and seventeenth centuries but by the later seventeenth century the medieval castle was regarded by those in power as an anachronism.

A fire in 1684 was the excuse and the catalyst for the drawing up of a grand design to replace the medieval castle with a palatial quadrangle of buildings. One part of the new building was erected in the late 1680s but the full quadrangle was not completed until the middle of the eighteenth century. Initially the two corner towers on the south side were retained, but in 1775 the Bermingham Tower at the south-west corner was rebuilt with thinner walls leaving the Record Tower, at the south-east corner, the only substantial and recognisable element of the medieval castle to survive, as it does to this day.

Opposite: Fig. 1 Plan of the present-day castle with the outline plan of the medieval castle superimposed in the upper image and the locations of the excavations shown in the lower image.

The south side of the quadrangle contains the state apartments including St Patrick's Hall. The chief governor of Ireland or viceroy held court here for social and ceremonial occasions. The other buildings in the quadrangle mostly contained government offices. Further offices, stables and the post-medieval chapel were in the Lower Yard accessed through an archway in the east block of the quadrangle, also known as the Cross Block. The post-medieval castle complex extended to the south with a garden, further offices and barracks (Fig. 2). Much eighteenth- and nineteenth-century Irish history is closely associated with the castle, which contained the offices of the Chief Secretary and other important government functionaries. It was seen by many as the centre of repressive foreign government in Ireland, where information, supplied by spies and informers, was held on dissidents who opposed British rule. It was also the ceremonial centre for the viceregal court and the Knights of St Patrick. Levees held in the state apartments were the high point of social life in Dublin for the gentry and aristocracy. Since the establishment of the Irish Free State in 1922, Dublin Castle has continued to house government offices, while the state apartments and, in particular, St Patrick's Hall are used for state occasions such as the inauguration of Presidents of Ireland and for receiving and entertaining foreign heads of state. The castle is used for international conferences and for European Union meetings and is now also a major visitor attraction.

The purpose of this volume is to provide an appropriate historical background to the report on archaeological excavations carried out at the castle between 1961 and 1987 (Fig. 1). The emphasis is very much on the physical development of the castle and its immediate environs up to 1850. While it does contain much general history, architectural history predominates, especially in the later period, over political, social or administrative history. The cut-off date of 1850 reflects the latest archaeology recorded and allows for an account of all the important historic buildings.

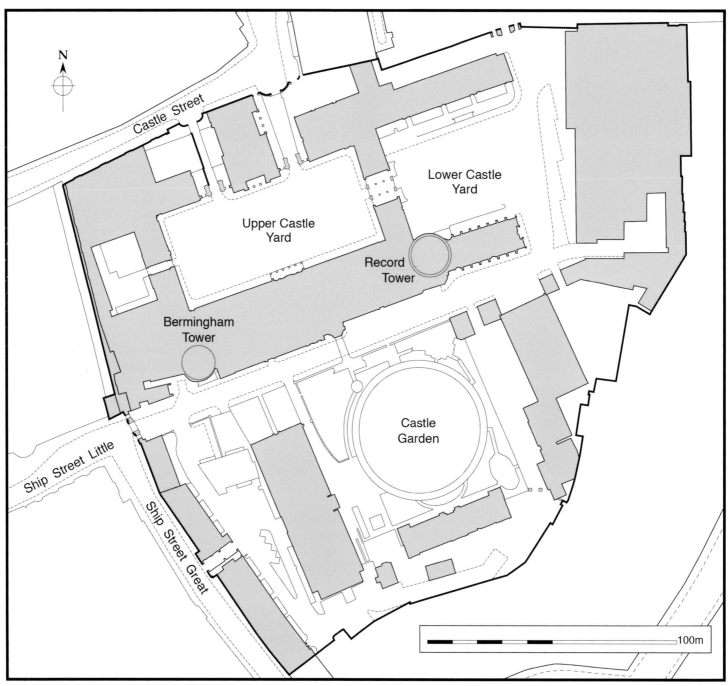

Fig. 2 A map of the present-day castle complex.

The archaeological excavations carried out by the National Monuments Service at Dublin Castle between 1961 and 1987 were all necessitated by building works (Fig. 1). When the Cross Block between the Upper and Lower Yards was demolished and rebuilt between 1961 and 1963, a small but important excavation was carried out under the direction of Marcus Ó hEochaidhe. As well as features of the medieval castle it uncovered pre-castle habitation deposits from the Hiberno-Scandinavian town. It was the first time these well-preserved deposits were archaeologically excavated in Dublin. The 1985–7 excavations, directed by

Ann Lynch and Conleth Manning, were necessitated by a major programme of new building and restoration works carried out in advance of the Irish Presidency of the European Union in 1990. These excavations, which were mostly confined to the north and west moat of the medieval castle, uncovered parts of the curtain wall and corner towers of the castle and the causeway leading to the gatehouse. Also uncovered were sections of the city wall at the south-west and north-east corners, where it crossed the moat to join the castle defences. As the castle was built in the south-east corner of the walled medieval town with the River

Poddle flowing along its south and east sides, the moat was designed to provide effective defence on the townward side. The excavations revealed it to be a formidable feature measuring almost 22m in width at the north-west corner with a maximum depth of c. 10m below contemporary ground level. Deposits had accumulated within the moat from the thirteenth century and, once the arches in the town wall were blocked up in the fourteenth century, it was used as a convenient dumping ground for refuse from the adjacent households. This continued until the seventeenth / eighteenth centuries when buildings began to encroach on the area. Most of the c. 200,000 artefacts recovered during the excavations were retrieved from the moat deposits. Ceramics form a large proportion of this material, but a wide variety of metal, bone and glass artefacts were also retrieved. The damp and waterlogged conditions in the moat also ensured the preservation of organic material such as leather, wood and textile.

Further information on the Hiberno-Scandinavian town was also recorded in the isolated areas where earlier deposits had survived the thirteenth-century building works. Outside the north-west corner of the moat, for example, traces of tenth- /eleventh-century house plots were still in situ while, encapsulated within the base of the north-east corner tower (the Powder Tower), the remains of defensive banks surrounding the Hiberno-Scandinavian town were revealed. These latter features together with part of the north curtain wall with a postern gate and part of the moat and city wall can be viewed by visitors to the castle in a specially designed undercroft.

This is volume 1 of a projected three-volume series on the 1961–1987 excavations. Volume 2 will be devoted to the pre-castle deposits, while volume 3, parts 1 and 2 will cover the archaeology of the medieval and post-medieval periods. This volume concentrates on the history of the castle and the site on which it was built from the earliest times up to 1850.

The long period of history covered in this volume, almost 1,100 years, has led to a number of authors being commissioned to produce the text. The differences between the sections in style and approach are largely the result of significant differences in the amount and nature of the records that survive between the medieval and post-medieval periods. The three parts should be seen as separate studies with some inevitable overlap of information.

Part 1 by Seán Duffy covers the period up to 1560 – some 800 years of the history of the site. The earliest reliable historical reference to settlement in the vicinity of the later castle is an annalistic reference in 790 to an ecclesiastical site called Duiblinn (dark pool), named after a tidal pool in the River Poddle, where the castle gardens are today. The same pool became the focus of a Viking *longphort* (ship encampment) established here according to the Irish annals in 841. By the early tenth century the focus of the

Scandinavian settlement had moved to the ridge between the Liffey and Poddle rivers and soon developed into a town surrounded by defences. By the eleventh century it is likely that there was a fortress of some sort within the town and this was probably on part of the present castle site. Dublin at this time, with its wide trading links, became the largest and richest town in Ireland, in all but name the capital of the country. Irish provincial kings and aspirants to the high kingship vied with each other for the privilege of controlling it.

After the capture of Dublin by the Anglo-Normans in 1170, Henry II came to Ireland and spent much of the winter of 1171–2 in Dublin. On leaving he gave the custody of Dublin to Hugh de Lacy and, according to Roger of Howden, ordered him to build a castle there. This reference to building a castle at Dublin has heretofore been overlooked. It may have been an enhancement of an older fortress and may have been, at least partially, an earth and timber castle. By the early thirteenth century this was not seen as strong and imposing enough and in 1204 King John issued an order for the building of a strong stone castle. This substantial roughly rectangular castle with large circular corner towers and a deep wide moat was constructed over the following decades and remained intact as the centre of royal power in Ireland up to the end of the seventeenth century. The somewhat patchy records up to 1560 document the erection of some new buildings within the castle but are characterised by frequent complaints about the buildings falling into disrepair and the carrying out of limited and often inadequate repairs. The castle suffered a period of neglect in the late fifteenth and early sixteenth centuries when the Fitzgerald earls of Kildare held great power in Ireland and often served as the king's deputy. Their fall in the 1530s spelled a new phase with the appointment of mostly English chief governors. From an architectural point of view the beginning of the post-medieval period at the castle was marked by the chief governorship in the 1560s and 1570s of Sir Henry Sidney, the father of the poet Philip Sidney. He carried out much building work within the castle thereby improving it as a residence for the chief governor.

Part 2 by John Montague, dealing with the period from 1560 to 1684, had somewhat fuller records to draw on as well the earliest maps of Dublin and surveys of the castle. Many of the chief governors during this period, especially in the early seventeenth century, erected new buildings at the castle, notably the long gallery erected by Lord Deputy Falkland in 1624, the large stable building built by Lord Deputy Wentworth in the 1630s outside the medieval castle to the east in the Lower or Stable Yard and the new lodgings built by Lord Deputy Essex in the 1670s. During this period, the chief governors were increasingly conscious of their position as the representative of the monarch in Ireland and developed the castle as a suitable viceregal court with emphasis on splendid furnishings and ceremony. From this period also we have the first detailed descriptions of the castle: the 1585 descriptive survey of the perimeter defences (Appendix 1) and Robert Ware's very informative description of the castle including the internal buildings in 1678 (Appendix 4). Ware's description indicates that there were some fine stately buildings within the castle, though they were built in a largely unplanned and haphazard fashion. Also, by this time the largest building within the castle, the great hall, originally built in 1245, had been destroyed by a fire in 1671.

By the early 1680s many people viewed the castle and its internal buildings as outmoded and inconvenient and were beginning to think of replacing it with a more up-to-date, palatial, commodious and purpose-built complex of buildings. The fire of 1684 and the blowing up of buildings around it to prevent the fire spreading provided the opportunity for the planning of new buildings to largely replace the medieval castle.

Part 3, authored by Kevin Mulligan and Michael O'Neill covers the period from 1684 to 1850. There is an abundance of documentary records, maps and images dealing with this period leading to a much fuller account of the history and development of the buildings of Dublin Castle than in the earlier parts. The initial eight decades from 1684 to 1850 saw the almost complete removal of the medieval castle and its replacement with the fine quadrangle of buildings that forms the present Upper Yard. This quadrangle, though partly planned immediately after the fire of 1684, took some 77 years to complete. Many additions and alterations were made to it over the years to suit its evolving role and the need for further office accommodation for the expanding administration. The Act of Union of 1801, which involved the abolition of the Irish parliament, made the castle the centre of all governmental power in Ireland. The new Chapel Royal symbolised this enhanced role of Dublin Castle. At the same time security concerns resulting especially from the Emmet rebellion of 1803 led to the purchase and demolition of private houses on the west and north-west perimeter of the castle and the erection of a massive boundary wall where they stood.

During the eighteenth and early nineteenth centuries, the greater castle complex was expanded to the east and south and further buildings were erected here including a military barracks in Ship Street Great and stables and other buildings in the Lower Yard. Many prominent architects were involved in designing new buildings at the castle during this period. The initial design concept for the Upper Yard was that of Surveyor General, William Robinson, soon after the fire of 1684. Other architects were involved over the following decades. The building of the Bedford Tower and flanking gateways in the centre of the north side between 1752 and 1761 completed the quadrangle. In the early nineteenth century, Francis Johnston, well known as the architect of the General Post Office in Dublin, played a major role in building works at Dublin Castle and, in particular, designed the Chapel Royal and refitted and heightened the adjoining Record Tower.

The eight appendices have been included to give readers a taste of the full text of these interesting surveys and descriptions of the castle dating between the late sixteenth century and the late eighteenth century. They reflect the changes that took place over this time and, in particular, the almost total replacement of the medieval castle with the fine quadrangle of buildings that surrounds the Upper Yard.

This is the first extended history to have been published of Dublin Castle and hopefully it will inspire further detailed research on other aspects of its history and on the period after 1850.

Ann Lynch and Conleth Manning

Frontispiece 1 The base of the Powder Tower during excavation in 1987 with the Record Tower in the background. (NMS)

Part 1: The Medieval Period
by Seán Duffy

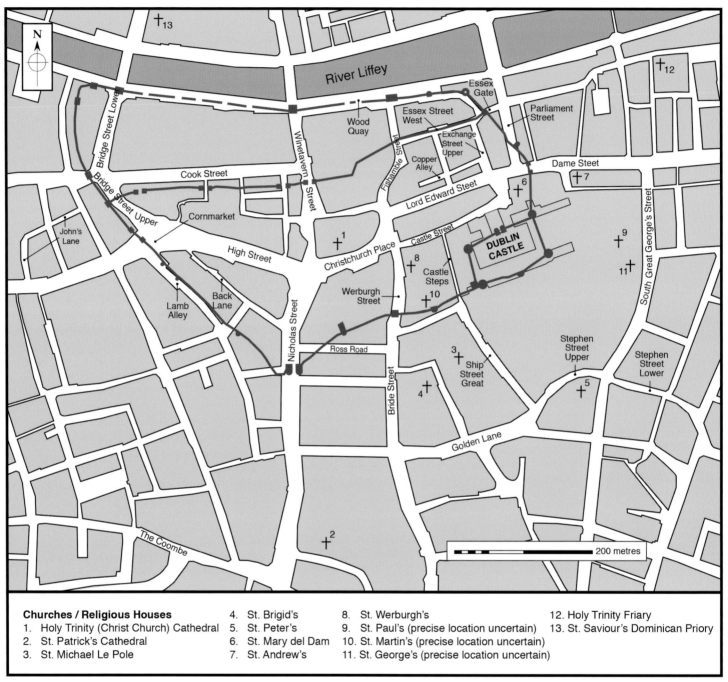

Fig. 1.1 A map of the centre of Dublin with the walls of the medieval castle and city superimposed and the churches and religious houses mentioned in the text marked.

Chapter 1.1

The Protohistory of the Castle of Dublin

When, in the summer of 1204, John, king of England and lord of Ireland, famously ordered the construction of the castle of Dublin, he did so because this, the most prestigious city of his Irish lordship, required such a fortification. But there had always been a fortification at Dublin for as long as there was something in need of fortifying.

The Early Christian presence in the vicinity

Dublin seems to have begun life as an ecclesiastical settlement although documentary traces of it are meagre indeed. The Annals of the Four Masters under the year AD 650(=656) record the death of a man called St Beraid, *abbas Duiblinne*, head of the church of Duiblinn (the latter being the Old Irish place-name from which the modern Dublin is derived). Unfortunately, the reference is unlikely to be an authentic historical record.[1] In addition, the Annals of Ulster note the death in AD 790 of a certain Siadal, *abbas Duiblinne*. If this is genuine, Siadal's church must have been a substantial settlement as his name occurs in a list of obits of some very important men, including four kings and nobles and two other men described as an *abbas*, respectively the heads of the great churches of Downpatrick and Glendalough. But where the church of Duiblinn was – assuming it ever existed – we cannot as yet say. Typically, such an eminent church site would have been surrounded by a *vallum*, a roughly circular bank-and-ditch or stone-wall enclosure with a diameter of up to 200m; some churches had two such concentric enclosures, the outer diameter being ordinarily up to 500m.[2] Fr Myles Ronan, writing back in 1940, noticed the oval curvature of the streets lying less than 200m south of Dublin Castle (Fig. 1.1) – those running from Stephen Street Lower to Stephen Street Upper, and perhaps to Whitefriar Street – and suggested that what he called a 'rath-like site' may once have occupied the location.[3]

Subsequently, Howard Clarke and others have speculated that this may reflect the outline of an ecclesiastical enclosure constituting the monastery of Duiblinn.[4] Unfortunately, extensive excavations within this area have yet to reveal early medieval activity.[5]

Just west of this, however, about 150m south-west of the castle, a large Early Christian cemetery has been discovered at the site of the medieval church of St Michael (Figs 1.1, 1.2); although precise dates for the burials have not been published,[6] an earlier excavation here produced features yielding a radiocarbon dating of AD 663–872 and a small number of artefacts of probable Early Christian date.[7] Further burials, dated to between the eighth and tenth centuries, found on the east side of Bride Street, have also been plausibly linked to St Michael's,[8] suggesting an extensive burial ground extending from Ship Street Great in the east to Bride Street in the west. This offers the prospect that St Michael's may represent the pre-Viking church of Duiblinn. Alternatively, it is worth bearing in mind that high-status Irish ecclesiastical centres frequently comprised a focal church and a number of satellite churches dedicated to other saints: at Armagh, for example, the church of St Patrick was ringed within a 400m diameter by others dedicated to St Brigid, St Colum Cille and Saints Peter and Paul.[9] St Michael's may therefore be one of a cluster of church sites in the vicinity over which the *abbas Duiblinne* presided, including St Patrick's, St Brigid's and St Peter's, all similarly within an arc having a diameter of 400m (Fig. 1.1).

The pool of Duiblinn

The term *Duiblinn* literally means 'black pool' and if there was an ecclesiastical settlement in the vicinity it presumably acquired the name from its proximity to such a feature (Fig. 1.3). When, as we shall presently discuss, Scandinavian incomers commandeered the location in the mid ninth

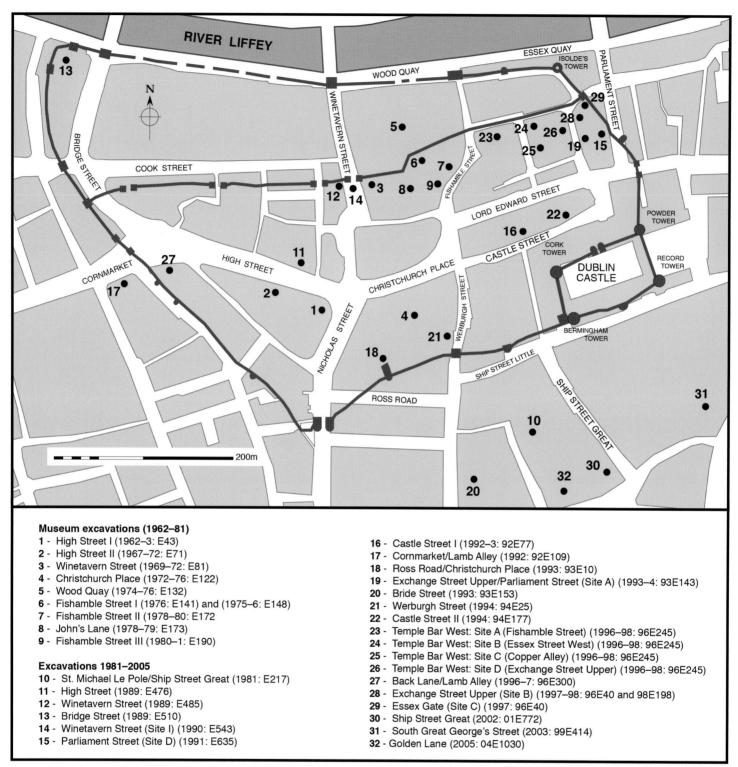

Museum excavations (1962–81)

1 - High Street I (1962–3: E43)
2 - High Street II (1967–72: E71)
3 - Winetavern Street (1969–72: E81)
4 - Christchurch Place (1972–76: E122)
5 - Wood Quay (1974–76: E132)
6 - Fishamble Street I (1976: E141) and (1975–6: E148)
7 - Fishamble Street II (1978–80: E172
8 - John's Lane (1978–79: E173)
9 - Fishamble Street III (1980–1: E190)

Excavations 1981–2005

10 - St. Michael Le Pole/Ship Street Great (1981: E217)
11 - High Street (1989: E476)
12 - Winetavern Street (1989: E485)
13 - Bridge Street (1989: E510)
14 - Winetavern Street (Site I) (1990: E543)
15 - Parliament Street (Site D) (1991: E635)

16 - Castle Street I (1992–3: 92E77)
17 - Cornmarket/Lamb Alley (1992: 92E109)
18 - Ross Road/Christchurch Place (1993: 93E10)
19 - Exchange Street Upper/Parliament Street (Site A) (1993–4: 93E143)
20 - Bride Street (1993: 93E153)
21 - Werburgh Street (1994: 94E25)
22 - Castle Street II (1994: 94E177)
23 - Temple Bar West: Site A (Fishamble Street) (1996–98: 96E245)
24 - Temple Bar West: Site B (Essex Street West) (1996–98: 96E245)
25 - Temple Bar West: Site C (Copper Alley) (1996–98: 96E245)
26 - Temple Bar West: Site D (Exchange Street Upper) (1996–98: 96E245)
27 - Back Lane/Lamb Alley (1996–7: 96E300)
28 - Exchange Street Upper (Site B) (1997–98: 96E40 and 98E198)
29 - Essex Gate (Site C) (1997: 96E40)
30 - Ship Street Great (2002: 01E772)
31 - South Great George's Street (2003: 99E414)
32 - Golden Lane (2005: 04E1030)

Fig. 1.2 A map of the centre of Dublin with the walls of the medieval castle and city superimposed and the locations of archaeological excavations marked.

century, we can expect them to have referred to the pool in Old Norse as a *pollr*. Needless to say, the lack of a written legacy from Norse Dublin means that they have left us no documentary trace of it but, in the aftermath of the English conquest of Dublin in 1170, this precise term regularly occurs in the much more extensive source material of the period.[10] It does not appear to be the English word 'pool' because, usually, English words are translated into Latin in texts written in the latter language whereas Old Norse words are left untranslated.

Let us look at some examples of this. We find, for example, the charter of Alexander of Chester issued not much more

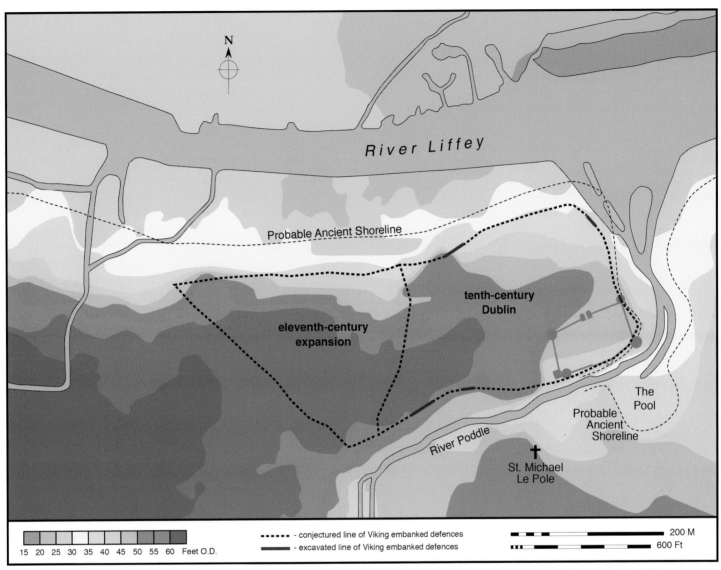

Fig. 1.3 Modern contour map of the vicinity of Dublin Castle showing the location of the pool, the likely two-phase development of the Viking-age town with its defences (after Halpin 2005) and the footprint of the later medieval castle. The outlines of the rivers Liffey and Poddle are as shown on Speed's map of 1610.

than a decade after the English takeover, granting to St Mary's Cistercian abbey 'certain land in the Poll (*terram quandam in Polla*)...opposite St Brigid's cemetery'.[11] He tells us that he holds the lands from a man called David of St Michael's, who presumably took his surname from the local parish. Similarly, around 1220, William of Worcester granted to Adam the Soapmaker his land lying on the north side of St Patrick's church, which 'stretches in the east towards the Poll (*tendit in orientem versus Pollo*)'.[12] And Gilbert fitz Daniel, a mid-thirteenth-century resident of the area, commissioned a seal on which he styled himself Gilbert de la Polle.[13]

This explains why, in later medieval references, St Michael's is styled the church of St Michael de Poll or de Polla or le Pole.[14] It was abutted to the west by the parish of St Brigid 'in the Pool' or 'of the Polle'.[15] Directly north of the latter, at the junction of Werburgh Street and Bride

Street, stood a mural gate into the medieval walled town called Pol/Poule/Poole Gate. Beside this, we find the Pol/Poll/Pole Mills on Pulle/Pol Street, now Ship Street Little.[16] Hence, in 1328, Thomas le Mareschal and his wife leased 'two water mills with the pond and land belonging thereto in the Polle, suburbs of Dublin, situate between the city wall on the north and the highway [Ship Street Little] on the south';[17] and in 1356 Sir Thomas de Asshebourn made a grant of 'lands in the Poll in the suburbs of Dublin, in the parish of St Brigid of the Poll, in the corner beyond the Poll Gate, on the cross ways, of which one goes towards St Brigid's church on the south, and the other towards the Poll mills on the east'.[18]

It is clear, therefore, that in the later Middle Ages this area directly to the south and south-west of the castle was known as the Poll and it is probable that the name preserves a trace of a Norse name given to it because of the presence of a pool nearby, presumably the same feature that had earlier given rise to the Irish name Duiblinn. It is not the case that Poll is merely a Norse version of the place-name Duiblinn since they retained this for their new settlement, referred to in the Anglo-Saxon chronicle in 937 as Difelin,[19] on coins produced in the town from the end of that century as Diflin or a variation thereof,[20] and in Icelandic skaldic verse of the mid eleventh century as Dyflinn.[21] Rather it appears that the Scandinavian colonists who, it seems, seized the ecclesiastical site at Duiblinn, adopted this latter as the name of their settlement, but separately referred to its eponymous pool as Pollr. And even as the pool tended to shrink or dry up over the centuries (though a remnant is still marked on the earliest Dublin map, that by John Speed published in 1610), memory of it remained in the place-name, the Poll. The archaeologist Linzi Simpson found the eastern rim of the pool in an extensive excavation on the western side of South Great George's Street[22] and it seems that the Poll place-name referred to an area stretching perhaps as far west as the River Poddle.

Of the latter it may be worth remarking that, in the late eighteenth century, it was still occasionally being called by its Irish name Sologh, Soulagh, or Sallagh (perhaps from salach ('dirty')) even though, by the late Middle Ages, English-speaking citizens of Dublin tended to call it the Podell or Puddell.[23] The latter is evidently the English word 'puddle' which – though nowadays of course a term for a small, shallow, temporary gathering of water caused as a rule by rainfall – had an original meaning defined by the Oxford English Dictionary as a 'pool of standing water, esp. a muddy or dirty one' (OED, s.v.). There is every reason to suppose, therefore, that the Poddle acquired its name as a calque or quasi-translation of its Irish predecessor, the Salach, the dirty or dark appearance of which is presumably also the origin of Duiblinn, the dark pool which the Poddle formed as it slowed in its approach to the Liffey just south of where the castle would be constructed. If the Poddle did indeed acquire its name because of its appearance as a muddy pool, this would explain the name applied to it in what appears to be its earliest surviving mention: in a property-deed from 1258, a plot of land is described as 'extending from the street to the Pool water' where the street in question appears to be Bride Street, in the east, and the Pool water the Poddle, to the west.[24]

The Scandinavian influx

The first trace in any western record of a Scandinavian piratical raid dates from 793 when the Irish-founded monastery at Lindisfarne in Northumbria was attacked by 'heathen men'.[25] Raiders attacked another North Sea monastery in the following year,[26] and by now the Irish world was aware of the new crisis, the Annals of Ulster

noting for 794: 'Devastation of all the islands of Britain by heathens'. If this refers to islands off Scotland's western coast, perhaps the raiders established a presence in some of these Hebridean islands and hence may have been able to venture further south in the following year, 795, when it seems their raids on Ireland began. In that year, Rechru was burned by the heathens and its shrines broken and plundered.[27] 'Rechru' is the Irish for both Rathlin island, off the Co. Antrim coast, and Lambay in the Irish Sea north of Dublin (Fig. 1.4) and so the raid might be on either. That it was the latter is suggested by the fact that a church on nearby Inis Pátraic (St Patrick's Island), just 10km to the north near Skerries, was also burned by the Vikings three years later, which might indicate that this part of the Irish Sea had become the focus of their ongoing attention.

The same 798 entry tells us that they 'took the cattle-tribute of the territories (borime na crích do breith)',[28] which surely involved more than the proverbial smash-and-grab raiding of churches we tend to think of in this very early stage of the Viking campaigns.[29] If there were Scandinavians in what is now north Co. Dublin in the late eighth century exacting tribute from its inhabitants, a tribute that was handed over in the form of cattle that needed to be housed and maintained prior to slaughter, one would have to assume that the Scandinavian newcomers had secured themselves a camp nearby and might be thinking of staying put.

This fits well with the latest archaeological evidence from Dublin, which throws into question the long-standing assumption that a Viking presence only came to be felt there in the 840s. In 2003 the skeletons of several Viking warriors – and evidence of habitation – were found about 100m south-east of where the castle was subsequently situated, at South Great George's Street, and have been shown by radiocarbon analysis to have a 95% probability of dating to between AD 670 and 880; also, another warrior excavated in 2002 in nearby Ship Street Great produced dates ranging between AD 665 and 865.[30] A number of other probable Viking burials have been found a little distance away at the rear of Golden Lane (and attached to the site of St Michael le Pole's church), the best preserved of which has dates ranging between AD 678 and 832.[31] These were formal burials of young warriors who seem to have met their deaths in conflict, and who were interred beside their camp on the banks of the black pool on the River Poddle near where it joins the Liffey (Figs 1.1, 1.3); it seems they occupied this camp and lived and died in its vicinity in the very earliest days of the Viking Age.

This early presence near where the castle would later be built should not surprise us. In 821 Scandinavian raiders plundered the Howth peninsula and 'carried off into captivity a great number of women';[32] such raids tended to be conducted by groups based in the region rather than being haphazard incursions from overseas. But proof of a

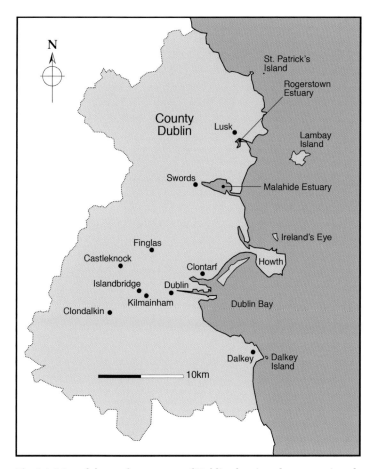

Fig. 1.4 Map of the modern county of Dublin showing places mentioned in the text.

'the first taking of Áth Cliath by heathens (*Cedgabail Atha Cliath o ghentibh*)'.[38] There is a tendency to assume that this is a retrospective insertion but – as with the same annalist's reference a decade later to the 'first burning of Emly by heathens (*Cédorgain Imlicch Iubair o gentibh*)' or the record in the Annals of Ulster in 836 of 'the first plundering of Southern Brega by heathens (*Prima praeda gentilium o Deisciurt Bregh*)' – it is more likely that he is simply calling our attention to the fact that this is the first time in living memory such a thing happened.

In the case of Dublin, the significance of the event is that – for the first time since the Viking incursions began – Áth Cliath, the strategic ford over the Liffey, had been captured by Scandinavians. The precise location of the Liffey ford at Áth Cliath remains elusive but for our purposes this is perhaps immaterial. Suffice to say that the seizure of the Liffey ford in 837 gave Scandinavians instant dominance in the area. It gave safe passage inland to a 60-vessel Viking fleet, which is reported as being on the Liffey that same year, ravaging the Liffey plain, 'both churches and fortresses and farmsteads (*eter cealla & dune & treba*)'.[39]

The text known as 'The Triads of Ireland' lists the island's three great fords as Áth Cliath on the Liffey, Áth Luain (Athlone) on the Shannon at the entrance to Lough Ree, and Áth Caille (probably Athlunkard), also on the Shannon just north of Limerick.[40] It is an interesting coincidence that, within seven years of their taking of Áth Cliath, Scandinavians had established a camp on Lough Ree and presumably therefore controlled Áth Luain, while archaeological investigations near Athlunkard (from Áth an longphoirt, 'ford of the ship-encampment') have revealed possible remains of a Viking camp on the site.[41] Similarly at Dublin, within four years the temporary advantage of taking the Liffey ford was converted to a longer-term presence when the annals for 841 report the existence of *longport oc Duiblinn* ('ship-encampment at Duiblinn').[42]

The term *longp(h)ort* has been much debated[43] but at its most basic was no doubt a term coined to describe the fortified camps the early Scandinavian ship-commanders established in Ireland to secure their vessels and men from counterattack. Initially, they were probably fortified enclosures on water, and hence perhaps the mention in 842 that there were 'heathens still *on* Duiblinn (*Geinnti for Duiblinn beos*)' – similar to the reference the previous year to 'heathens still on Lough Neagh (*Gennti for Loch Eachach beós*)'[44] – from which we might conclude that, if Duiblinn is the pool beside what would become Dublin Castle, this is precisely where the encampment was.

The camp's occupants must shortly, however, have dug themselves in nearby and perhaps it is these men who have left their imprint on Simpson's South Great George's Street site: besides five warrior burials, she found evidence of habitation, including flood-prevention trenches and the

Viking base in the vicinity only comes to light for the year 836: for the first time since the Viking campaigns began the annals name the location of one of their camps when they tell us that in this year the great monastery of Kildare was plundered by 'heathens from Inber Dée', which is probably Arklow.[33] By this stage there were undoubtedly other bases around the coast – and many more were soon to follow, including that at Dublin.

There must have been a base in the general Dublin Bay area (Fig. 1.4) by the mid to late 820s, from which Viking raiders sailed up the Rogerstown estuary in 827, attacked and burned the church of Lusk and invaded the territory of the Ciannachta to the north.[34] Ailbhe MacShamhráin noted the mention in the Martyrology of Óengus of the 'Foreigners of Inber Domnann', and although it is not possible to assign a date to this camp on the Malahide estuary,[35] it may account for an attack, dateable to the early 830s, on the church of Swords which lies at the estuary's landward end.[36]

The beginnings of a fortress at Dublin

The assault on Clondalkin in 833[37] suggests a presence on the Liffey, which is confirmed four years later when the annals known as *Chronicum Scotorum* inform us that 837 saw posts of a related palisade, an earthen bank, drainage ditches and gullies, domestic refuse pits, possible cultivation-furrows, post-holes, at least two open-air hearths, large numbers of iron nails (possibly ships' rivets), a drop-bearded axe-head, part of an iron shears, and two lead weights.[45] They were an active bunch wreaking devastation over a wide area. In the very year in which the Duiblinn longphort was established they led a plundering mission into the territory of the Southern Uí Néill and the Laigin as far as Slieve Bloom[46] – perhaps a single campaign heading directly west into south Meath/north Kildare and south Westmeath/north Offaly – a journey of about 100km in each direction, parts of which surely saw them quitting their river-borne vessels to advance overland, and hence perhaps the use of horses. They retraced their steps in the following year, this time heading slightly further west to Seir Kieran and on to Birr, and again in 845 when they established a dúnad – perhaps a fortified campaigning base of some kind – near Killeigh, Co. Offaly.[47] But again, surely, these expeditions were conducted overland to some extent and required substantial equine resources, so that we must imagine their Dublin command centre, near what would become the site of the castle, having the capacity to accommodate them.

The same follows for human resources. One source tells us that in 847 a battle was fought at a place called Carn Brammit – probably somewhere in south-west Leinster – between the rising king of Osraige, Cerball mac Dúngaile, and the Foreigners of Áth Cliath, at which 1,200 of the latter were slaughtered.[48] We can be sceptical about the figures involved but annals generally do not exhibit ludicrous exaggeration: still, even if in this instance we assume the number is inflated by a factor of, say, five and that the real figure is closer to 250, Dublin's standing army must already have been sizeable. Therefore, the encampment required to house them at Dublin was a major piece of infrastructure. This is all the more likely if another 1,200 Vikings said to have been killed in north Co. Dublin in the following year[49] hailed from the encampment at Duiblinn, which seems very likely. The man who triumphed over the latter was Tigernach mac Fócartai, the Southern Brega king of Lagore, and he was presumably following up an advantage secured in his 848 victory when, a year later, he joined forces with the king of Tara, Máel Sechnaill mac Máele Ruanaid, and together they recorded the first ever Irish assault on Dublin.[50] The word used to describe this raid is indred, which carries the same meaning as Latin vastatio (eDIL, s.v. 'indred'), meaning the devastating or laying waste of a place, and we can be sure that it came as a severe blow.

It is worth noting too that the annals describe this as Inredh Duiblinne, the laying waste, not of Áth Cliath, but of Duiblinn. From this point onwards annalists permanently cease to use the word Duiblinn to refer to the Scandinavian base at Dublin, and we may wonder whether or not – in the aftermath of the indred – a move might have been effected shifting the focus of the settlement away from the low ground of the Poddle valley south of the pool (Fig. 1.3) to the more defensive high ground to the north of what would be the site of the castle (a move that suggests itself on the basis of the early levels from Simpson's excavations in Temple Bar West).[51]

This was certainly a turbulent time for Dublin. In 851, the Dubgenti ('Dark Heathens') arrived at Áth Cliath, slaughtered the Finngaill ('Fair Foreigners'), and laid waste their longphort.[52] For present purposes, it does not matter greatly who these groups were or where they came from.[53] What matters is that the newcomers wreaked havoc on the existing camp at Dublin. They were also successful in establishing their own rule there and continued to supply its kings for generations to come.[54] The most dominant leader of Scandinavian forces in Ireland throughout the 850s and 860s was a man Irish sources call Amlaíb (perhaps from Old Norse Óláfr). Although he ranged widely throughout Ireland and indeed northern Britain,[55] Amlaíb seems to have been headquartered in Dublin, which already held primacy among the many Viking enclaves scattered around the country's coasts and inland waterways.

It is possible, though, that having acquired possession of Dublin in battle over his Norse predecessors in 851, Amlaíb abandoned it – as it was vulnerable to seaborne assault – in favour of a fortress in the interior, out of which he operated for up to fifteen years. Hence, we hear in 867 of the remarkable fact that Amlaíb had established a dún – presumably a substantial fortress – at or near the great church of Clondalkin more than 10km west of Dublin (and indeed more than 4km from the Liffey, though on the banks of its tributary, the Camac). Amlaíb had presumably seized the monastery and its lands and was developing a headquarters here with a view to making himself less vulnerable to maritime attack while at the same time securing a bridgehead for territorial expansion towards the west. But it came to nought in 867 when his dún at Clondalkin was burned to the ground by his Irish enemies and a hundred of his leading men were butchered there.[56] We can only assume that the Clondalkin experiment was abandoned at that stage because when next we hear of Amlaíb it is to the effect that he and his kinsman Ímar 'came again to Áth Cliath' with a fleet of 200 ships, having been on an expedition to northern Britain, 'bringing away with them in captivity to Ireland a great prey of Angles and Britons and Picts'.[57] It seems, therefore, that the Dublin encampment was back in use (if it had ever been otherwise) and was now home to an astonishingly large fleet and vast throngs of captives destined, no doubt, for the slave market.

Wherever in Dublin this Norse encampment was, it seems to have remained in uninterrupted occupation and operation for more than twenty years until, in 893, there was 'great dissention among the Foreigners of Áth Cliath, and they became dispersed'.[58] Another source says that they departed Ireland as a result,[59] though they returned a year later.[60] Even this resumption of occupancy was temporary, however, as in 902 a major assault on the naval camp at Dublin (*longport Átha Cliath*) was undertaken by the kings of Brega, to the north, and of Leinster, to the south, so that 'the Heathens were driven from Ireland'; they were forced to abandon a great number of ships, and 'escaped half dead after they had been wounded and broken'.[61] They seem initially to have taken refuge on the little island of Ireland's Eye north of Howth but here they were besieged by the Irish (*Cacht for Gallaibh Atha Cliath i n-Inis Mac Nessáin*) and presumably forced to abandon it too.[62]

There is in fact no documentary evidence for a Scandinavian presence at Dublin for the next fifteen years, although we should not assume that any members of Dublin's Scandinavian population other than its military and naval commanders had vacated the encampment, since Simpson's major archaeological excavations 200m north of where the castle would later be situated revealed no sign of a break in habitation in the period after 902.[63] It seems that, instead of Dublin lying waste in this interval, its control was assumed by the Irish, and so some aspects of life in the encampment endured. This is suggested by accounts of the Scandinavian reoccupation in 917: although one Irish annal merely reports that Sitriuc grandson of Ímar 'entered Dublin (*do tuidecht i n-Ath Cliath*)' in 917,[64] another has it that Dublin was 'forcibly taken by the Foreigners from the men of Ireland (*Gabáil Atha Cliath do Gallaibh ar hécin for feraib Erenn*)' immediately after Sitriuc's major victory over the king of Leinster at the battle of Cenn Fuait.[65] Hence it was the defeat and death of the king of Leinster at Sitriuc's hands that enabled the latter to descend on Dublin and recover it for his dynasty, perhaps by ousting an Irish overlord resident within the fortification.

It was a development undoubtedly perceived by the Irish as an urgent threat and heavy emphasis is placed by contemporary writers on both the impact of the Scandinavian restoration and the widespread and concerted Irish opposition they faced, led by the new king of Tara, Niall Glúndub. The latter, in fact, became the first king of Tara to die in battle with Vikings when he was unsuccessful in a critical confrontation with them at Cell Mo-Shamhóc (Islandbridge) in 919.[66] That said, the Irish gained some degree of revenge in the following year when the new king of Tara, Donnchad Donn, slaughtered them at the battle of Tigh-mic-nEthach in Co. Meath,[67] in the aftermath of which Sitriuc 'abandoned Áth Cliath through the power of God',[68] which may mean that the Irish reoccupied it although, within a year, it had been retaken by Sitriuc's kinsman Gofraid (*Gofraith ua h-Iomhair do ghabháil fosadh i n-Ath Cliath*).[69]

Gofraid's thirteen-year reign in Dublin must have seen substantial consolidation of the Scandinavian presence there, interrupted as it was by only one brief hiatus in 927

when he abandoned it – whether under duress or not we cannot tell – for a six-month period.[70] The aftermath of Gofraid's death saw the burning (*losccadh*) of Dublin by the king of Tara, Donnchad Donn, in 936[71] although the new Norse king of Dublin, Gofraid's son Amlaíb, was sufficiently strong in the following year to depart for England where he was one of the commanders on the losing side at the great battle of Brunanbuhr.[72] Returning to Dublin in 938, Amlaíb faced stern Irish opposition, the king of Tara and Southern Uí Néill overking, Donnchad Donn, being joined by the overking of the Northern Uí Néill, Muirchertach mac Néill, when they went 'fully assembled to lay siege to the Foreigners of Dublin so that they spoiled and plundered all that was under the dominion of the Foreigners from Áth Cliath to Áth Truisten' in Co. Kildare ('*do dhol go líonmhar lér-thionóilte do fhorbaissi for Ghallaibh Atha Cliath, co ro crechsatt & co ro crechsatt & co ro iondradhset ina m-boí fo mhámus Gall ó Ath Cliath co h-Ath Trusten*').[73] We are told that Amlaíb and the Foreigners deserted (*do dergu*) Dublin in the following year[74] but this too was short-lived as their new king crops up in the annals within a year and in 943 the king of Leinster met his death 'as he was plundering Dublin (*dia m-boí occ indreadh Atha Cliath*)'[75] while the Dublin army killed the man who seemed destined to be the next king of Tara, Muirchertach mac Néill, in a battle near Ardee that same year.[76]

The development of a dún

These events were the trigger for a major Irish offensive, so that in 944 we hear of 'the destruction of Dublin (*cosccradh Atha Cliath*)' by the kings of Brega and Leinster, and for once we get a bit of detail:

> The destruction (*cosccradh*) brought upon it was this, i.e. its houses, partitions, ships, and all other structures, were burned (*a tighe & a airbeadha, a longa & a cumhdaighe olchena do losccadh*); its women, boys, and common-folk (*a daesccar-sluaigh*) were carried into bondage (*do bhreith i n-daeire*), its men and warrior-folk (*a aes calma*) were killed. It was totally destroyed, both animals and humans, by killing and drowning, burning and capturing, excepting a small number who fled in a few ships, and reached Dalkey island (*i n-Delccinis*).[77]

Different descriptions of this event feature in other annals and the fact that this, the most detailed, occurs in just one, the Annals of the Four Masters, might call it into question; but it is, frankly, much more likely to be a genuine account than a late fabrication and is entirely plausible. It is also revealing. It contains the first mention in an Irish source of the houses of Viking Age Dublin and the reference to its *airbeadha* – an *airbe* is a hedge, fence, paling or animal-pen – can probably be taken to mean the post-and-wattle partitions between property plots so familiar to us from archaeological excavation in the Viking Age core of Dublin. The reference to women, children, and 'common-folk' is also unprecedented and it is clear that the writer is describing for us something which is no longer a military and naval camp – he is describing a town.

With this in mind it is worth pointing out that another account of this devastating onslaught on Dublin has it that 400 of its inhabitants were killed 'in the taking of the *dún* (*ag gabáil an duine*)',[78] the first time this word occurs in the Irish annals in regard to Dublin. There is a slightly earlier reference, in 937, to the effect that the Foreigners of Dublin temporarily 'left the *dúnad* (*do fhágbháil an dúnaidh*)'[79] but the term *dúnad* may not be quite the same thing (eDIL, s.v. 'dúnad'). In any event, the introduction into Irish sources by the mid tenth century of this word *dún*, to describe the Scandinavian settlement at Dublin, is a milestone development, and surely signals a major embellishment of its infrastructure.

The term *dún* tends to be translated as 'fort' or 'fortress' and in Old Irish sources is frequently applied to the fortified residence of a king or other dignitary (eDIL, s.v. 'dún'), and perhaps this is how it is intended here: the *dún* of Dublin may therefore be the fortress developed by its tenth-century kings. But *dún* also regularly occurs as a term for a town, and this seems to be what is intended in the case of Dublin. We see this, to pick one example, in the early twelfth-century poem known as *Senchas Gall Átha Cliath* where *dún* clearly means the city of Dublin. Hence, for example, it says 'There is another church in the *dún*/ it is the church of Brigit without malice (*atá cell oile 'sin dún*/ *is Cell Brigte can mírún*)',[80] this parish church being outside the fortress of Dublin, indeed outside the walls of Dublin, but nevertheless part of the town.

So what was emerging at Dublin in the mid tenth century was a settlement which is no longer referred to as a *longphort* because it has cast aside the sense of being a transient encampment, Irish sources instead applying to it a word, *dún*, that conveys the twin ideas of fortification and urbanization. Therefore, Dublin is a *dún* because major defensive fortifications are now in place, and it is a *dún* because within its fortifications live men, women and children – warriors and common-folk alike – dwelling in houses (*a tighe*) within defined property plots (*a airbeadha*). And this is remarkably borne out by the archaeological evidence which has found these houses, these property plots, the stone roads leading to and from them, and the embanked fortifications of the new town then starting to emerge.[81]

The Irish king who wreaked havoc at Dublin in 944, Congalach Cnogba of Brega, despoiled it again in 946[82] and in 948 he was victorious at the battle of Dublin (*Cath Atha Cliath*); he slew its ruler Blacaire grandson of Ímar, 1,600 of its inhabitants also being killed or captured.[83] We can take these numbers as generously inflated estimates but, even so, there can be little doubt that Dublin was now a settlement with many hundreds of inhabitants, many of whom perished in this instance. Likewise, there is presumably a basic truth to the claim that, in 951, when the Dublin army went on a massive raid to Kells and, basing itself on the monastic lands there, ravaged the nearby churches of Donaghpatrick, Ardbraccan, Dulane, Castlekieran, and Kilskeer, they came away from the campaign with 3,000 captives and a vast spoil of cattle and horses.[84] Of course we can insist that the totals are greatly exaggerated while accepting that the nascent *dún* of Dublin – based on the evidence of this expedition and many others like it – must have had the capacity for the reception of large numbers of transient guests, unwilling human detainees and purloined livestock alike.

The defences of the settlement were well illustrated in 980 at the time of the battle of Tara, at which Dublin's king Amlaíb Cúarán was comprehensively defeated by the new king of Tara, Máel Sechnaill mac Domnaill. In the battle's immediate aftermath, the latter descended upon the *dún* but was obliged to lay siege for three days and nights (*co tardsad forbais tri la & tri n-aidhchi forro*) before the Dubliners submitted. This suggests substantial if not insurmountable ramparts. Among the spoils of victory, besides 'jewels and goods (*co setaib & mainib*)', Máel Sechnaill acquired 2,000 cattle or, as one version has it, 2,000 people.[85]

We get a little more insight into the circumstances of the *dún* from Máel Sechnaill's next triumph over Dublin. In 989 he fought 'the battle of Dublin (*Cath Atha Cliath*)', killing many, and then followed it with a siege:

…and the siege of their *dún* (*forbuis in dúin forro*) afterwards for twenty nights, and during it they drank no water save brine (*connar' ibset uisce frissin acht sal*). Wherefore they gave him his full demand (*a óghriar fen*) so long as he should be king, and an ounce of gold for every *gardha* (*uinge óir gacha gardha*) on every Christmas Eve for ever.[86]

We can perhaps deduce from this important record that, having lost many men in a battle somewhere in the vicinity of Dublin, the Dublin forces retreated to the safety of the town defences – within the *dún* that is – only to find themselves blockaded by the king of Tara's men. Incarcerated within their *dún*, the townspeople, it would appear, had no access to fresh water and were therefore compelled to make do with saltwater from either the Liffey, which is tidal as far as Islandbridge, or the Poddle, which is tidal as far as the Cross Poddle on Patrick's Street. This suggests that there were no wells within the nascent town, which seems remarkable, although the elevation may have been an inhibiting factor. We know that there was a well in the Castle of Dublin in 1224[87] but perhaps this was only developed upon the castle's construction two decades earlier. We also know that an adequate supply of water to Dublin was not provided until the completion of the city watercourse and aqueduct in the mid thirteenth century, bringing water from as far away as the Dodder at Balrothery near Tallaght.[88] Perhaps, therefore, there is something to the annalist's account, the inhabitants of the *dún* being forced into submission for want of fresh water.

When they did submit to Máel Sechnaill, the Dubliners gave an undertaking to pay an annual tribute of an ounce of gold from every *gardha*. This is a borrowing from Old Norse *garðr*, a word which can mean a yard or other enclosed space, a court or courtyard, or a house or building in a town.[89] It has been doubted that this refers to a tax on the typical post-and-wattle property plots of Hiberno-Norse Dublin, on the assumption that if there were several hundred of the latter the amount payable would have been intolerably large.[90] But such sums are not unheard of in payments by the Hiberno-Norse (or Ostman) towns of Ireland to the Irish kings. Forty years later, the ransom paid by the Dubliners to secure the release of the king of Dublin's son included 60 ounces of gold and 60 ounces of pure silver, to say nothing of 1,200 cattle and 120 Welsh horses.[91] The tribute levied on Limerick in 1151 included 200 ounces of gold.[92] And a later siege of Dublin, in 1162, resulted in the Dubliners handing over 120 ounces of gold.[93]

More than likely, therefore, Máel Sechnaill did intend an annual imposition on each property plot in Dublin in the hope of raising, say, 200 ounces of gold (for as long as the Dubliners remained submissive) perhaps based on an existing system of taxation within the settlement. And it is possibly the case that all such plots were already laid out – it is certainly the case in Temple Bar West, for example, that Simpson's excavations found a remarkable continuity of property boundaries from the ninth to the thirteenth century[94]– otherwise, the development of a new one or the subdivision of an existing one would incur an additional tax.

But it is unlikely that Máel Sechnaill's onerous regime remained intact for long. Not long afterwards, the Dublin dynasty suffered a coup at the hands of Ímar, the Hiberno-Norse king of Waterford.[95] The head of the Dubliners was now Amlaíb Cúarán's son Sitriuc Silkenbeard, who expelled Ímar from Dublin in 993 along with 'the company of three ships (*lucht teora long*)', was himself expelled by Ímar a year later, but then finally got rid of the Waterford interloper in 995.[96] In this year Máel Sechnaill returned to Dublin, on which occasion he 'carried away by force' from the town the 'Ring of Þórir' and the 'Sword of Carlus'.[97] These objects, treasured possessions of the Dubliners, which possibly served as royal insignia,[98] must have been housed somewhere within the *dún*; one can only assume in a stronghold at its heart, perhaps within the grounds of what would become the site of the castle. It is a curious coincidence that this same year, 995, has been identified as the year in which Sitriuc Silkenbeard began minting silver pennies in Dublin,[99] and presumably

these too and the mint itself would require the security of a stronghold.

It is possible too that Máel Mórda, son of Murchad mac Finn, head of the Uí Fáeláin lineage of the Uí Dúnlainge overkings of Leinster, had established a residence at Dublin by this stage. His alliance with his sister's son, Sitriuc Silkenbeard (which memorably culminated in their defeat by Brian Bóraime at the battle of Clontarf in 1014) was such that it was Máel Mórda who in 995, apparently in Dublin, killed Ragnall, one of the Waterford dynasty who had been challenging Sitriuc,[100] and it was in Dublin that he killed one of his own Leinster rivals in the following year,[101] and it was also in Dublin that his son Bran was treacherously blinded by Sitriuc in 1018.[102] Máel Mórda was in Dublin too in 999 when Brian of Munster came marching towards the town, the result of which was the famous battle of Glenn Máma fought on 30 December of that year in which the Dublin and Leinster armies were slaughtered by the forces of Brian and Máel Sechnaill.

Immediately afterwards, Brian 'went to Dublin and remained there a whole week, and carried off its gold and its silver and many captives, and burned the fortress (& *cor' loisc in Dun*), and banished the king'.[103] Another account of this episode has the following:

> The despoiling of Áth Cliath and it was set fire to and burned (*Indred Átha Clíath & doud & a loscud*) by the men of Munster, and they beleaguered it (*forbas doib and*) on the Kalends of January [1 January 1000]; and they burned Caill Tomair as firewood (*do loscud doib do chonnud*); and the king of the Foreigners of Áth Cliath escaped from the battle (*asin chath*) to Ulaid, but found no protection for himself in Ireland until he handed over his hostages to Brian son of Cennétig; and Brian gave the *dún* to the Foreigners (*co tarat Brian a n-dún dona Gallaib*).[104]

It appears therefore that the Dubliners' rout at Glenn Máma had dreadful implications for the town itself, Brian Bóraime spending a week burning it to the ground – including Caill Tomair (the 'Wood of Þórir'), perhaps a sacred wood in the vicinity dedicated to the Norse god Thor – and requisitioning Dublin's assets, only handing back control of the town when its king, Sitriuc Silkenbeard, submitted to him as his overlord.

The text known as *Cogadh Gáedhel re Gallaibh* ('The War of the Irish with the Foreigners') also has an account of this which, like much it contains, shows some signs of elaboration. It may, therefore, tell us more about the state of Dublin at the time of its composition about a century later. Perhaps for this reason, it contains the first reference to Dublin as a *baile*, 'town', and the first reference to its *margadh*, 'market-place', a word borrowed from Old Norse:[105]

Brian at the time remained encamped in the town (*ro bai Brian ar sin a ffoslongport isin mbaile*) from Great Christmas to Little Christmas; he came then into the market-place and the whole *dún* was burned by them (*tanic iarsin isin margadh acus ro loisceadh an dún uile leó*), and they left not a treasure under ground that they did not discover.[106]

Not much can be deduced with certainty from this – at best it is an indication of what someone writing *c.* AD 1100 thought Dublin looked like a century earlier. But, giving it the benefit of the doubt, we might hazard a guess that Brian himself had camped outside the *dún* of Dublin and that the market-place was inside the *dún* and that some or all of the valuables Brian's army confiscated were monies and other valuables owned by the town's merchants and kept for safekeeping beneath the floors of their shops along the little streets of the *dún*'s market-place. These, of course, are the kinds of deposits which turn up in succeeding centuries as coin-hoards, a number of which have been found in the medieval core of Dublin.[107]

The thrashing they took at Brian's hands in the early days of 1000 was repeated five years later when the army of Southern Brega burned Dublin 'by stealth (*h-í taidhe*)', which may perhaps mean a night-time raid on the town.[108] And, if the *Cogadh* is to be believed, in 1013 in the prelude to the battle of Clontarf, Brian's son Murchad plundered Leinster, coming to Glendalough, and burning the province from there to Kilmainham, and to the *faithche* or green of Dublin. Brian joined him there, setting up camp at a place called Áth in Cháerthainn (unidentified but a ford on the Liffey or one of its tributaries), where he remained from the feast of St Ciarán (September 9) until Christmas, having 'made a siege and blockade around Dublin and an encampment there (*do ronsat forbasi ocus forcomet for Áth Cliath, ocus foslongport and*)'. It adds that neither the Norse nor the Leinstermen (who seem to have been holed up with them in Dublin) gave them a hostage or battle or peace-overture (*coma*), and therefore, when his provisions were exhausted, about Christmas, Brian retired home.[109] The failure of this lengthy siege – the generalities of which are confirmed by the annals[110] – is surely testimony to the strength of Dublin's defences at that point, and was the reason Brian led his final campaign the following spring, which culminated at Clontarf.

The battle of Clontarf might have begun as an expedition by Brian Bóraime to reclaim control of Dublin, but the town itself escaped assault. The *Cogadh* instead graphically – and no doubt fictionally – depicts the Dublin women and other non-combatants 'watching from the battlements of Dublin (*ac feithium ar scemlead Atha Cliath ed radairc*)' and seeing the sparks fly in the distance as metal struck upon metal among the armoured ranks fighting on the plain to their north-east.

It envisages too that King Sitriuc saw out the battle in the company of his wife, Brian's daughter, 'on the battlements of his palace (*ar scemled a grianan*)'.[111] If the latter refers to a castle within the *dún* of Dublin, it is the first such reference.

The *Cogadh* is, of course, a highly fictionalised account and, therefore, all this tells us is that the author imagined Sitriuc having a *grianán* complete with *sceimled*. Even then, both are notoriously difficult to define: the latter is a rarely encountered word which seems to mean a rooftop or battlement (*eDIL, s.v.*), while *grianán* frequently means a sunny chamber, a bower and perhaps a boudoir, and an upper room or balcony open to the sun (*eDIL, s.v.*). But it also occurs in numerous Irish place-names – the most famous being Grianán Ailigh in Inishowen – in contexts that suggest a royal residence, especially one on an elevated site.[112] It is just possible, therefore, that in mentioning the *grianán* of King Sitriuc, the *Cogadh*'s author is referring to a fortification within the *dún* of Dublin which existed in the writer's own day – perhaps on the site where the castle would later be constructed – and which he believed to have been the residence of Sitriuc at the time of Clontarf.

The *dún* after Clontarf

As stated above, the evidence would suggest that the term *dún* was applied, not to a fortress as such, but to the embanked and palisaded area – within which a fortress of sorts must have existed – which would later become the walled town. In the year after Clontarf, Máel Sechnaill, in seeking to reassert his claim to be king of Ireland, joined forces with the kings of the Northern Uí Néill and marched on Dublin. They

burned the *dún* and all of the houses from the *dún* outwards (*co ro loisccset an Dún & gach a raibhe ó Dún amach do thaighibh*).[113]

We must interpret this as meaning, not that they burned the fortress and the rest of the town, but that they burned both the town and the suburbs. We know from archaeological excavation that by this period, the early eleventh century, post-and-wattle houses of the Wallace typology were in existence well beyond the embanked town, including along the Coombe valley and even north of the Liffey in Oxmantown.[114]

Similarly, just over a decade later, when Brian Bóraime's son Donnchad also paraded to Dublin in his own bid for the high-kingship, we are told that

he himself spent three days in Dublin in peace, with his camp nearby the *dún* (*co rabe féin tri thrath i n-Áth Chliath i síd, & a longphort h-i farrad in dúine*),[115] from which it would seem, not so much that he was not inside the town and near a fortress within it, but that he camped outside but close to the town. Likewise, in 1052 the Leinster king, Diarmait mac Máele na mBó of Uí Chennselaig, – another province-king seeking dominance over Dublin – burned all Fine Gall from Dublin to the Delvin river but it was only after he 'had great conflicts around the *dún* (*co n-dernsat scaindreacha móra imon dún*)', in which many fell on both sides, that he forced the Ostman king of Dublin to abdicate and cede his kingship to him.[116] If these great struggles took place *imon dún*, around the *dún*, they were not in the little streets of the town around its castle, but in the town's immediate surroundings.

With Diarmait mac Máele na mBó's victory we enter a new era in Dublin's history. From this point onwards, until the Anglo-Norman invasion, its overkingship was always claimed by an Irish province-king in what was quite a complicated arrangement, sometimes involving several layers of power. At the apex of this structure there was at all times an Irish province-king who, as part of his bid to be high-king of all Ireland, claimed to be overking of Dublin and might stay in the city for extended periods of time; for instance, in 1111, Muirchertach Ua Briain of Munster spent the period from Michaelmas (September 29) until Christmas there.[117] On several occasions, overkings such as the latter appointed their favourite son to rule Dublin directly under them, and these princes, serving a kind of apprenticeship as regent under their father's supervision, ordinarily lived in the town.[118] But frequently too there was an internal Hiberno-Norse oligarch governing the city and these men also used the royal style. For example, Archbishop Lanfranc of Canterbury wrote to Dublin's Gofraid ua Ragnaill in 1074 and referred to this Ostman lord as a 'glorious king of Ireland',[119] despite the fact that Brian Boróime's grandson, Tairdelbach ua Briain of Munster, considered himself Dublin's overking and would, in the following year, banish Gofraid and set up his own son Muirchertach as king there.

Complicating matters further is the fact that dynasties within Leinster – deeming Dublin part of their province – sought to maintain a presence there (even when they were not contenders for the high-kingship of Ireland). More often than not, therefore, there was more than one royal figure claiming rights of kingship over Dublin and it is even possible (though perhaps unlikely) that two such claimants might simultaneously maintain a royal residence within the *dún*. Be that as it may, the location of this palace or these palaces remains impossible to identify.

Thus, after Diarmait mac Máele na mBó seized the kingship of Dublin in 1052 he appointed his son Murchad (eponymous ancestor of the MacMurroughs) to rule Dublin under him and the latter made the town his home. A charter granted by King John in 1202 to Christ Church cathedral in the city lists its early patrons and their grants, beginning with King Sitriuc who founded the cathedral around 1030; Murchad appears to be the second name on the list, having granted it Lambay Island and Portrane.[120] He died in Dublin in 1070 and, unusually, we are told that he was buried there (*sepultus est i n-Ath Cliath*).[121] An elegy for Murchad, which may be contemporaneous, has it:

> There is grief for a chief king at Dublin
> (*Cumha áird-righ i n-Ath Cliath*)…
> Empty is the *dún* (*Folamh an dún*) without [him]…
> Sorrowful every party in the *dún*
> (*Toirrseach cech drem isin dún*)
> For their chief, against whom no army prevailed.[122]

This evidence would tend to suggest that the Uí Chennselaig dynasty – having broken out of its south Leinster base to claim the overkingship of the entire province – was developing the makings of a provincial capital at Dublin.

Hence it was that when Tairdelbach ua Briain made his move for the high-kingship two years later in 1072 – marching on Dublin and claiming kingship over it – he took Murchad's cousin, Donnchad son of Domnall Remar mac Máele na mBó, prisoner in the town (*co tuc mc. n-Domnaill m. Maíl na m-Bó ra láim i n-Áth Cliath*).[123] The latter is the third patron of Christ Church listed in King John's 1202 confirmation charter, the man who granted it Clonkeen.[124] He obviously did so in his capacity as king of Dublin[125] and we can be fairly sure that he resided there in the royal palace. Yet the same source which tells us that Tairdelbach ua Briain took Donnchad prisoner at Dublin in 1072 adds almost immediately that among those who submitted to the Munster king was Gofraid ua Ragnaill, 'king of Dublin'. Perhaps Donnchad son of Domnall Remar was deposed by ua Briain, and Gofraid ua Ragnaill installed in his stead, but it is just possible that in 1072 both were claiming royal authority in Dublin simultaneously and both presumably living in formal residences there.

The situation is, however, made a little clearer by the events of 1075. In this single year, Dublin had three kings, but it appears that they ruled in quick succession. To begin with, Tairdelbach ua Briain overturned his earlier support for the Hiberno-Norse Gofraid and banished him overseas (probably to the satellite base Dublin's kings seem to have had on the Isle of Man). At this stage, it seems, a second member of the south Leinster dynasty of Uí Chennselaig – a son of the Murchad who had died as king of Dublin in 1070 – took over but died of 'three nights' illness',[126] at which point Tairdelbach installed his own son, the famous Muirchertach Ua Briain, as king. To judge from the annalist's statement that he 'was made king in Dublin (*do rioghadh a n-Ath Cliath*)',[127] Muirchertach was formally inaugurated as king in the town, presumably in the royal palace, or perhaps in the Thingmoot to the east of the *dún*.

It took a long time, though, for this Munster dominance to bed in. When Tairdelbach ua Briain died in 1086, Munster may have lost temporary control of Dublin to Donnchad son of Domnall Remar of Uí Chennselaig, though Muirchertach Ua Briain reclaimed command at the latter's death three years later.[128] Now, however, Muirchertach faced an Ostman challenge when, in 1091,[129] another Gofraid, the famous Gofraid Méranach, set himself up as king. The latter was a man with strong insular links, the founder of a dynasty that would dominate the Isle of Man and the Western Isles for generations,[130] and it would seem that his establishment in Dublin demanded a forceful response. The year 1094[131] was therefore a bloody one which saw a major offensive by Muirchertach against Dublin and the banishment of Gofraid and only at this point, we may surmise, did Munster's hegemony over Dublin begin to look secure.

All in all, the quarter of a century up to 1094 was a most unstable time in Dublin's history and it is hard to imagine any of its half-dozen transient masters presiding over a major programme of infrastructural investment in the *dún*. Insofar as we can tell – and it is a hazardous undertaking – some degree of stability was restored in 1094 after which the town enjoyed (if that is the correct word) two decades of uninterrupted Munster dominance. Perhaps it is to this period that we should date the start of the massive effort to enclose the town in curtain walls. It goes unmentioned in any documentary source, which is not particularly surprising; our main source for this period is the Irish annals and annals tend to record single events rather than drawn-out processes, whereas the walls would have taken shape only slowly. The walls – which are a massive edifice – required great communal effort, at enormous cost, under direction from an established leader or group. Their clear purpose was to protect the town from external threat and it is unlikely therefore that they would have been constructed at the behest of a short-lived, intrusive and unwelcome overlord in the absence of popular support. Consequently, as Dublin was extraordinarily turbulent in the period 1070–1094 and seems to have experienced another lengthy period of instability following the fall of Muirchertach Ua Briain in 1114, perhaps the most likely point at which the town walls of Dublin might have been begun is during the twenty or so years of his fixed rule following his 1094 overthrow of Gofraid Méranach.

There is one development more than any other which might have provided the impetus for the refortification of Dublin. King Magnus III of Norway (the famous *Magnús berfœttr* or 'Barelegs') made at least two western expeditions at the turn of the century,[132] Ireland getting off lightly on the first in 1098 – when the targets were the Western Isles, Man, and Britain's western seaboard from Galloway to Gwynedd – but not so the second. Almost all sources are agreed that the primary, or at least initial, objective of Magnus's 1102

campaign was Ireland, and the Irish annals indicate an assault or intended assault on Dublin from his Manx base, which required

> a hosting by the men of Ireland to Dublin to oppose Magnus and the Foreigners of Scandinavia who had come to invade Ireland (*Slóighedh fer n-Ereand co h-Ath Cliath i n-aghaidh Maghnusa & Gall Lochlainne tangattar d'iondradh Ereann*).[133]

This Irish show of opposition led by Muirchertach Ua Briain was enough to persuade King Magnus to agree to a year's peace, sealed by a marriage-alliance between his son and Muirchertach's daughter, and the whole emergency dissipated when the Norse king was slain on the coast of Ulster in the following year. But the threat he had posed might have been enough to stimulate a massive wall-building project at Dublin in its aftermath to prevent a recurrence.

The last days of the dún

We should not be surprised at a king like Muirchertach Ua Briain presiding over developments at Dublin. His family had long since directed affairs at Limerick, which was now his principal residence, being administered by a *rechtaire* ('steward', 'bailiff')[134] acting on his behalf especially during his many absences on campaign like, for instance, in 1111 when Muirchertach was in Dublin for the entire last quarter of the year.[135] But when serious illness struck in 1114 his hegemony collapsed amid internal feuding and external rebellion. He appointed his son Domnall Gerrlámach as king of Dublin[136] to face down a Leinster revolt, and this was initially successful when Domnall defeated the army of Leinster in the battle of Dublin, killing Donnchad mac Murchada, the king of Leinster.[137]

The latter, incidentally, was father of the famous Diarmait Mac Murchada (Fig. 1.5) who, according to Giraldus Cambrensis, ultimately got sweet revenge during Strongbow's conquest of Dublin in 1170, for one outrage in particular:

> For in the middle of a large building, where it was their custom to sit as if before the rostra in the forum (*In medio namque domus cuiusdam grandis, ubi tanquam in foro pro rostris sedere consueverant*), the citizens had buried his father, whom they had killed, along with a dog, thus adding insult to injury.[138]

If this story is true – and, although Giraldus was writing a full three-quarters of a century later, he had well-informed sources – this interment of Donnchad in unconsecrated ground must have occurred back in 1115, but it would seem unlikely that the large *domus* in which the citizens then gathered was Dublin's castle: if it was, we might have expected Giraldus to say so, and perhaps therefore it was the

ralem difficultatem induftria
plurimum 7 arte minunt;

Defcriptio ajurcharddie.

Erat autem Dermutr mr
ftate gñdir 7corpore p̄plo.
vir bellicof 7audar 7gente fua.
fr crebro continuoq; belli cla
more voce rautifona. Timen̄ a
cunctif cꝙ̄ alugi malenf. Ɏobi
lium oppreffor. humiliū erectoi.
Infeftuf fuif. Gros aliēuf. q̄an̄
omnium contrarip̄m. 7 ip̄e c̄er̄
omī. Rorbericuf aut mfifif ad
Scephainden nuntiuf. donatif
q̄ꞇ ꞇ modicuf taꞁ p̄miffuf cꝙ̄n pꞃo
miffif. ur a parria ꞇ c̄ꝫuf nulliꝰ
s uendicare porueraꞇ. cū patre 7
amore difcedec. uariif fuafir uer
biꞇ nec p̄fuafir. Ɏunctꞇ uo aꝺ aꞁ
charddien ouerfi ur mꝫercꞇenas

Fig. 1.5 Diarmait Mac Murchada. (NLI, MS 700)

Thingmoot where the city fathers deliberated[139] or, more likely, the guildhall of its merchants. Even though Dublin did not receive a charter formally authorizing it to have its own guilds until 1192, it is probable that its traders had organised themselves much earlier, as such associations had been common throughout western Europe from about 1000 and are well known in England after 1066.[140] As, throughout the eleventh century, Dublin's ruling elite had begun to abandon the hope of territorial acquisition but sought to maintain a dominant position through trade, it is likely that its merchants waxed as its military men waned (though there was doubtless a good deal of overlap between them) and the merchants may already have had a house (domus) in which they met and discussed their affairs. Perhaps, therefore, it was they who – having prospered under the light touch of Uí Briain overlordship for much of the previous generation – declared their repudiation of the king of Leinster's intrusion into their affairs by the contemptable way in which they treated his corpse.

In any event, Munster's triumph in 1115 was short-lived. Donnchad of Leinster was succeeded by his nephew who, two years later, also died in Dublin, apparently of natural causes.[141] It is certain that he was not merely passing through the town at the time of his demise but had set himself up

as its overking; this much is clear from the fact that he had been able to lead both the army of Leinster and Dublin into battle against the king of Meath that same year.[142] His death provided an opportunity for Domnall Gerrlámach Ua Briain to reassert his claim to kingship but by now the rising star of the Irish political scene, Tairdelbach Ua Conchobair of Connacht, had his eyes on this particular prize and in 1118 he marched on Dublin, laid it under siege (tria forbais), expelled Ua Briain, and assumed the kingship of Dublin himself (righe Gall do gabail dó).[143] It is difficult to know, though, what in practical terms Tairdelbach Ua Conchobair's 'kingship' of Dublin amounted to; he was busy on the national stage and could not be expected to manage Dublin's affairs directly. It is no great surprise, therefore, to discover from another source that he 'left Énna son of Donnchad under him in the kingship of Leinster and Dublin (do fag Enna mhac Donnchadha fri laimh fein a r(ighe) Laighean & Atha Cliath)'.[144] This was a son of the Donnchad who had been killed in the battle of Dublin in 1115 and ignominiously buried there; his son Énna was therefore now attempting to rule both Leinster and Dublin under Ua Conchobair's overlordship.

It was either Énna or Tairdelbach Ua Conchobair who, in 1121, wrote to Henry I of England notifying him that the Dubliners had elected a new bishop and requesting his consecration by the archbishop of Canterbury.[145] The letter was sent by a rex Hiberniae which of course must be Tairdelbach if we take it to mean 'the king of Ireland',[146] but may just mean 'a king of Ireland' and refer to Énna, in the same way that St Bernard of Clairvaux would later address his brother Diarmait Mac Murchada as 'glorious king of Ireland' even though he never held the high-kingship.[147] Be that as it may, we have the text of another letter sent to England at the same time and on the same subject, and issued in the name of 'all the burgesses of the city of Dublin (omnes burgenses Dublinae civitatis)'.[148] Perhaps these 'burgesses' authorised the dispatch of the letter at a meeting in the domus mentioned earlier. The word burgensis is of French origin and first occurs in England just thirty-five years earlier in the Domesday survey (DMLBS, s.v.); it can mean simply a town resident but usually refers to a member of a borough community, with rights and obligations, holding a burgage – a residential plot – by burgage tenure that typically involved a money rent to his lord.[149] Those Dubliners who described themselves thus in 1121 were undoubtedly the better-off town-dwellers and merchants, those who owned the narrow burgage plots that stretched backwards from the main streets of the town, comprising a house and garden and, at the front in many cases, a shop or tavern. They would have paid an annual rent for their tenement – what would later be called in Dublin, as it already was in England, landgable – and undoubtedly the sizeable sum thus raised ultimately found its way into the coffers of Dublin's new breed of Irish overlord such as Énna Mac Murchada of Leinster.

The latter, though – whose kingship of Leinster itself was as yet insecure – cannot have been in a position to govern Dublin directly and must generally have relied on a deputy. In this regard, we might note the death some few years later of a man called Torfind mac Turcaill, described as 'chief *óchtigern* of the Foreigners of Ireland'.[150] Literally meaning 'young lord', it has here a technical sense probably intended to convey his status as headman of the Ostmen below the rank of king (of Dublin), the latter title belonging at that point to Mac Murchada. From this point onwards the Mac Turcaill family are – apart from short intermissions – the ones who seem to be running things on the ground in Dublin (though always subject to an Irish overlord). Énna Mac Murchada continued to claim overlordship of Dublin and was confirmed in the role in 1125 when Tairdelbach Ua Conchobair – in his capacity as king of Ireland – went to Dublin 'and he was a night there, and gave the kingship of the Foreigners of Dublin to the king of Leinster (*co raibe aidche and, co tard righi Gall Atha Clíath do rig Laigen*)'.[151] But as soon as Énna died, in the following year, Tairdelbach returned to Dublin and installed his own son Conchobar as king.[152]

As with previous such incumbents, Conchobar Ua Conchobair was not a nominal king of Dublin, an absentee claiming merely titular authority. What little evidence we have suggests he took up residence there – presumably in a castle-like fortification – and hence the statement in one set of annals that within a year 'the Foreigners of Dublin rebelled against (*do inntogh ar*)' Tairdelbach, and his son Conchobar 'was driven out by them (*do dicur uatha*)'.[153] This involvement with Dublin since 1118, and the deployment of its castle in governing it, might perhaps have provided the spark for a new development in Irish castle construction which begins in Connacht in 1124 when Tairdelbach began building three separate castles, and more were to follow, which were of such new appearance that annalists coined new terms – *caisdeoil*, *caislén*, *caistél* – by which to describe them.[154]

Diarmait Mac Murchada (Fig. 1.5) was another Irish king who would build himself, at Ferns, a *caisteóil/caistiall* or *tech cloiche* ('stone house').[155] And after he had established himself in the kingship of Leinster, he can be seen, from 1134, commanding the forces of Dublin in his military campaigns.[156] We can therefore assume that he was claiming to be its king, though he cannot have been able to spend much time there and his rule over Dublin was never secure.

We now enter another extraordinarily turbulent period in Dublin's history. In the fifteen years between 1141 and 1156, the kingship of Dublin changed so frequently – sometimes annually – that it is hard to make sense of it. Mac Murchada's hold over Dublin was temporarily broken in 1141 following a major rebellion against him in Leinster and therefore, for the first time in a generation, a Munster army descended on the town, led by Muirchertach Ua Briain's nephew Conchobar na Cathrach Ua Briain, so that

'the Foreigners gave their kingship to him (*co t-tugsat Goill a ríghe dhó*)'[157] though he does not appear to have remained there very long and was dead within a year.

At this point, a Hebridean lord called Ottar son of mac Ottair 'took the headship and dominion of Dublin (*do gabháil chennais & forlamhais Atha Cliath*)'[158] although Ragnall Mac Turcaill was called king of Dublin in most annals when killed in battle in Meath in 1146[159] and it was members of the latter's family that murdered Ottar in 1148.[160] Mac Murchada may have resumed command briefly at that point[161] only to find a new Munster army led by Tairdelbach, another nephew of Muirchertach Ua Briain, storming the town in the following year, so that 'the Foreigners came into his house (*co t-tangattar Goill ina theach*)'.[162] This is a figurative term – it may not have required the town's leaders physically entering his 'house' at Dublin – which means that they submitted to him as their lord.[163] But this too proved ephemeral.

Already another claimant to the high-kingship of Ireland, in the person of Muirchertach Mac Lochlainn of Ailech, was beginning to make a mark and in 1154 he marched south 'and the Foreigners of Dublin gave their kingship to him (*do-ratsat Goill Atha Cliath a ríghe dhó*), and he gave the Foreigners 1,200 cows as their *túarastal*, after which he returned home'.[164] *Túarastal* is the ceremonial stipend paid by the overlord to his vassal and indicates the Dubliners' acceptance of Mac Lochlainn as their king. Since his home base was in north-west Ulster, Muirchertach was not likely to make frequent visits to Dublin but, as it happens, his right-hand man was Diarmait Mac Murchada and so we find the latter commanding the army of Dublin soon afterwards,[165] presumably acting as its king under Mac Lochlainn. The Mac Turcaill family were still dominant within the town, however, and their head, Bródar, was described as king of Dublin when he died in 1160.[166]

Perhaps it was the rebelliousness of the Meic Turcaill that motivated Muirchertach Mac Lochlainn to lead a vast army to Dublin in 1162 'to lay siege to the Foreigners (*d'forbais for Ghallaibh*)',[167] though one source claims he did so 'to take revenge on them for his wife and her violation',[168] whatever that may mean. He had little initial success and returned home leaving others to fight on his behalf, but eventually the Dubliners submitted, handing over 120 ounces of gold.[169] Another source reports at this point the 'despoiling of the Foreigners of Dublin (*Argain Gall Atha Cliath*)' by Diarmait Mac Murchada, as a result of which 'great power was obtained over them, such as was not obtained before for a long time'.[170] What this power – which lasted for four more years – may have involved we cannot say for lack of evidence. We know that Mac Murchada founded two religious houses in the town; perhaps they belong to this period and perhaps too, if he was in building mode, he may have strengthened further the town's defences and in particular its castle, possibly along the lines of his stone house at Ferns. And he, as overlord having the final say in such matters, may have been the one who authorised the Dublin fleet to take part in Somerled of Argyll's fatal invasion of Scotland in 1164[171] and Henry II's unsuccessful English campaign against the Welsh the following year.[172]

But within months, things changed dramatically again when the next claimant to the kingship of Ireland, Ruaidrí Ua Conchobair, marched with a vast army to Dublin, 'so that the Foreigners gave kingship to Ruaidrí and he gave 4,000 cows to the Foreigners (*co tucsat Gaill rige do Ruaídhri & co tuc-san da fiched cét bó do Gallaib*)';[173] the latter payment is again *túarastal* given to the Dubliners in acknowledgment of their subservience to their new overking. Having accepted Ua Conchobair as their lord, the Dubliners were now in rebellion against Mac Murchada, and marched with others of his opponents against him, demolishing his castle at Ferns, and banishing him overseas.[174]

The English conquest of Dublin

Ragnall Mac Turcaill's son Asgall now took over the governance of Dublin and it was he who faced Mac Murchada's wrath when, a full four years later, the latter had sufficient overseas muscle in his army – with his new son-in-law Strongbow (Fig. 1.6) at its head – to set about retrieving custody of Dublin. There are differing accounts of what transpired in the Irish annals and in Giraldus's *Expugnatio Hibernica* and the poem on the Anglo-Norman invasion which Orpen dubbed *The Song of Dermot and the Earl*.[175] Piecing them together, it seems that 'the citizens of Dublin called almost all the inhabitants of Ireland to help in its defence', blocking the approach routes. Ruaidrí Ua Conchobair assembled a great force and marched to within sight of the town, pitching camp on 'the green of Dublin (*co faichthi Atha Cliath*)' – *The Song of Dermot* has Clondalkin – where he spent three days and nights expecting a battle with Mac Murchada who had 'brought his army intact right up to the town walls (*ad urbis menia*)'.[176]

At this point, it seems, a lightning storm broke out and Dublin – the *dún* as the annals continue to call it – was set ablaze ('*cu fhaccadar in dun tre theinidh, i., teni dhi aitt*')[177] and was destroyed ('*cor' dithlaithrighedh h-e*').[178] The Irish annals report that the Dubliners then allowed Mac Murchada and his Anglo-Norman army to enter the town (which the Irish saw as disloyalty to Ruaidrí), having been given assurances that the citizens would be spared. Instead, though, the Anglo-Normans 'slaughtered them in the middle of their own *dún* (*ro chuirsett a n-ár ar lár a n-Dúine féin*), and carried off their cattle and goods', their king, Asgall Mac Turcaill, making good his escape.[179]

Giraldus does not shy away from the massacre perpetrated by his side, and nor does he deny that it followed the cynical termination of surrender negotiations that had been underway – the saintly archbishop of Dublin Lorcán Ua

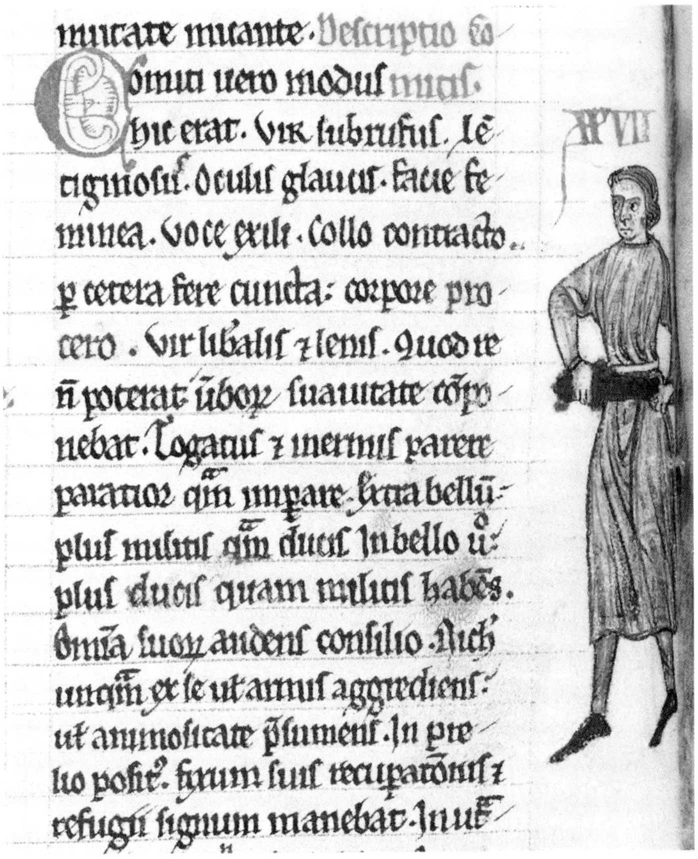

Fig. 1.6 Richard de Clare alias Strongbow. (NLI, MS 700)

Tuathail acting as mediator – when some younger members of the besieging army, led by Raymond le Gros and Miles de Cogan, made a two-pronged assault on the walls (*ad muros irruentes*) and overran the town. In that one impetuous charge, Dublin fell into Anglo-Norman hands and the castle of Dublin into ultimate English control, a control that was never again lost until 1922.

Securing English possession of the fortress

The conquest of the city of Dublin by the forces of Richard 'Strongbow' de Clare and his Irish father-in-law Diarmait Mac Murchada was an astonishing triumph. The contemporary English writer William of Newburgh says of Strongbow:

He decided that he must undertake a bold attack so as to become thereafter an object of fear to the barbarians, so he made a determined onslaught on Dublin, a maritime city which is the capital of all Ireland (*totius Hiberniae metropolim*), and which rivals our London in the merchandise and provisions handled in its very busy harbour. He stormed and captured it bravely and speedily, and compelled numerous people, even those quite far away, to come to terms with him since they were unnerved with fear.[180]

The fear was justified since Strongbow's army butchered and banished many of Dublin's citizens, but his triumph would be short-lived if he failed to hold onto it.

Hence, *The Song of Dermot and the Earl* tells us that, on 1 October 1170, Strongbow 'delivered the city into the custody of Miles (*A Miles ad…livré en guarde pur veir la cité*)'.[181] This was Miles de Cogan, who had spearheaded the English assault and whose appointment as *custos* is confirmed by Giraldus Cambrensis.[182] Miles was a soldier not an administrator, the *Song* calling him a *barun guerrer*, while the chronicler Roger Howden – who would have met de Cogan when he visited Dublin in the winter of 1171–2 – dubs him *vir bellicosus*.[183] In other words, this new post of keeper of Dublin was a military office and we can expect that de Cogan was headquartered in whatever stronghold its previous rulers occupied. We hear, for example, that in 1171 Miles had in his possession the hostages of at least one local king, Domnall Mac Gilla Mo-Cholmóc of Cuala.[184] They had been handed over as a guarantee of Domnall's loyalty to the new lord of Leinster, Strongbow, and were surely maintained in the stronghold of Dublin under Miles de Cogan's overall care.

The military side of Miles's role as governor of the city was apparent at that very point because he was facing a dire military threat. In May 1171, the ousted Hiberno-Norse king of Dublin, Asgall Mac Turcaill, launched an invasion of Dublin in the hope of driving out its English garrison. Up to one hundred shiploads of warriors landed, according to the *Song*, at the Steine, a strip of land running along the south bank of the Liffey at its lower reaches (perhaps in the area between modern College Street/Pearse Street and Townsend Street). Having set up camp there, they quickly marched up Hoggen Green (now College Green) and what became Dame Street, and attacked what Giraldus calls 'the walls at the eastern gate'.[185] Mac Turcaill knew better than anyone that breaking through that eastern gate, beside what is now City Hall on Cork Hill, would take him to within metres of his former fortress and probable victory in his objective. At a somewhat later date one accessed this eastern gate by crossing over a dam at the confluence of the Liffey and Poddle; this dam, which helped power watermills, gives us the names Dam(e) Street, Dam Gate, and the church of St Mary del Dam located just inside the gate (on the site of City Hall). There is, however, no evidence for its existence before *c.* 1215.[186]

The *Song* tells us that Miles de Cogan, being in charge of Dublin's defence, armed himself and his men and drew up outside the gate to defend the city, his archers and men-at-arms being dispatched to the walls to defend the battlements (*les kerneus*).[187] Giraldus tells us that Miles was forced back inside by the strength of the assault, and the town would have been lost had not de Cogan's brother Richard successfully attacked the Hiberno-Norse in the rear by making a sortie out 'the southern postern (*per posticam australem*)', though the *Song* has the western gate. The 'southern postern' is probably St Nicholas's Gate, while the western gate almost certainly refers to that which was soon afterwards replaced by the 'New Gate' at the Cornmarket.[188]

The invading army was heavily defeated; Mac Turcaill was captured at the seashore as he fled to his ship, brought back into the city to have his fate determined, and beheaded 'by order of Miles (*precepto Milonis*)', allegedly because of his defiant words while 'in the court in Miles's presence (*in curia coram Milone constitutus*)'.[189] We can take it that this court-martial, if we may call it that, occurred within the fortress. From the very outset of the English occupation of a fortress at Dublin, therefore, we see its multifaceted role as stronghold, prison and court.

It must have been after this disaster that Ruaidrí Ua Conchobair instigated his famous siege of Dublin. It is curious that, with a vast army at his disposal, Ruaidrí did not attempt to storm the town, which suggests that works to strengthen its defences had been undertaken by the new English garrison. Instead, a patient siege was initiated, the *Song* recording that Ua Conchobair himself camped his forces at Castleknock, that his northern ally, the king of Ulaid, set up camp at Clontarf, Ua Briain of Thomond at Kilmainham, and Murchad Mac Murchada (brother of the recently deceased king of Leinster, Diarmait Mac Murchada) at Dalkey, while Giraldus adds that thirty shiploads of warriors from the Isles sailed into the harbour of the Liffey and blockaded it.[190]

The beleaguerment lasted about two months, the Anglo-Norman inhabitants being confined within the walls, without access to provisions by either land or sea; the *Song* talks of food-shortages, a measure of barley selling for half a silver mark and wheat for twice that. Negotiations then ensued but eventually the besieged garrison decided to make a sortie, caught King Ruaidrí's forces unawares, and slew and plundered his army.[191] Again in this exploit, according to the *Song*, Miles de Cogan had been placed by Strongbow in the vanguard (*devant al frunt*), with sixty archers and a hundred foot-soldiers under him; it was he who led the charge directly north to Finglas, pouncing on the Irish bivouacs and killing over a hundred who were bathing at the time (perhaps in the Tolka). According to the *Song*, 'they found ample supplies for a year in the city: wheat flour and bacon; they had food in abundance'.[192]

This humiliation of King Ruaidrí Ua Conchobair did not prevent another Irish king, Tigernán Ua Ruairc of Bréifne, leading an army 'to expel the knights from Dublin', as the annals in MacCarthaigh's Book put it, some months later in September 1171. This initially saw the Dublin garrison defeated in battle at Kilmainham, Giraldus adding that the Irish then 'made a fierce attack on the walls and ditches (*muris et fossatis actiter insultant*)' of Dublin. But again it was Miles de Cogan who saved the day for the English, sallying forth from the town, surprising Ua Ruairc and a small troop of cavalry on the green to the west of the town, and inflicting heavy losses.[193]

Henry II's Dublin palace

By this stage, King Henry II of England (Fig. 1.7) – who had not licensed Strongbow's conquest of Dublin, to say nothing of his succession to the kingdom of Leinster following Diarmait Mac Murchada's death – was planning on coming to Ireland himself to take matters into his own hands. When the two men met in person to resolve their differences, probably in September 1171 at Newnham in Gloucestershire, Henry drove a very hard bargain; Strongbow was allowed to retain Leinster as a fief of the king of England, but Henry insisted that Dublin, 'the capital of the kingdom (*regni caput*)', along with its hinterland and the other coastal towns, including all castles, be handed over to himself.[194] It is from this moment we must regard Dublin as a royal city and its fortress as a royal castle.

Shortly afterwards, in mid October 1171, King Henry arrived in Ireland, staying for six months. Of this, he spent the period from 11 November until 1 March in Dublin.[195] There is no evidence, however, that he stayed in a fortress within the walled town. We know that, in advance of his expedition to Ireland, Henry ordered the repair of the royal pavilions (*pro reficiendis papilionibus*)[196] but if these are nothing more than tents they can only have seen occasional use in what was by all accounts a most harsh winter.

Fig. 1.7 Henry II. (NLI, MS 700)

Rather, as soon as he arrived in Dublin, Henry seems to have taken the unusual step – unusual enough for an eyewitness to record the fact in some detail – of ordering the 'kings and seniors of the land' to build, after the manner of that country, a royal palace for his use, which they made, marvellously we are told, out of wattle ('ibi construe fecit… *ad opus suum palatium regium, quod reges et ditiores terre mirifice construxerunt ad opus ejus per preceptum ipsius de virgis, ad morem patrie illius*'). There, on Christmas Day, he held a 'royal feast with the kings and seniors of Ireland (*in quo ipse regale festum in Natale Domini tenuit cum regibus et ditioribus Hibernie*)'.[197] The source is Roger of Howden, a royal clerk, author of the text known as *Gesta Henrici Regis* and of a later adaptation of it called his *Chronica*. Roger was a bureaucrat and diplomat involved on Irish affairs on King Henry's behalf (he is, for example, our sole source for the text of the Treaty of Windsor agreed between Henry and Ruaidrí Ua Conchobair in 1175) and was almost certainly in Ireland with Henry in 1171–2. This is why he is to be trusted on this Christmas Day feast (which Giraldus also mentions)[198] and why too he is able to record precisely the location of the palace; it was not inside the town walls but rather 'near the church of St Andrew the Apostle outside the city of Dublin (*juxta ecclesiam Sancti Andreae Apostoli extra civitatem Duvelinae*)'.

The latter church was situated only metres from the city's eastern gate in an extramural suburb mentioned earlier, called Thingmoot, a name indicating that it was where Dublin's Hiberno-Scandinavians had held their public assemblies presided over by their king and his fellow elite.[199] Presumably, therefore, Henry consciously built his palace on that very spot to enforce the point that he was now the Dubliners' king. Sure enough, the annals in Mac Carthaigh's Book confirm that the kings of Bréifne, Airgialla, and Ulaid 'came to the house of the king, to Dublin, and submitted to him (*do teacht gu teach an righ gu Baile Atha Cliath & umhaloid do tabhairt dó*)'.[200] Giraldus confirms the submission of two of these, and adds another four, concluding that at Christmas 'the princes of that land came to Dublin in great numbers to view the court (*ad curiam videndam*)', Howden also referring to the fact that Henry 'held his court (*tenuit curiam suam*)' at Dublin on Christmas Day.

Building the first English castle of Dublin

That Henry II seems to have lived at Dublin, for three months in a bleak winter, in a hastily constructed wattle longhouse – to have held court in it, to have received the submissions of the Irish kings in it, and to have feasted there on Christmas Day – is telling. Obviously it tells us that he had no particular fears for his safety outside Dublin's walls, but it must also suggest that, if there was a citadel of sorts within the walled town, it was not what Henry deemed a residence fit for a king. And surely this is the

Fig. 1.8 Hugh de Lacy. (NLI, MS 700)

reason for a little-known instruction that Henry left upon his departure from Ireland in April 1172. Having granted the kingdom of Meath to one of his followers, Hugh de Lacy (Fig. 1.8), Henry then 'handed over to him in custody the city of Dublin, and commanded him to build a castle in it (*tradidit ei in custodiam civitatem Duveline, et precepit in ea castellum firmari*)'.[201] So says Roger of Howden, who was probably there. He was a careful official recorder of proceedings and therefore we must believe that this instruction was issued, and hence that either there was no castle in Dublin at that point, or there was no castle fit for purpose.

And it seems the latter is the case. The *Song* claims that, at his departure from Ireland, 'the mighty king [Henry] then gave the custody of the city of Dublin and the castle (*le chastel*) and the keep (*le dongun*) to Baron Hugh de Lacy'.[202]

The *Song* was written at some point after 1176. It is a verse romance, which can be surprisingly accurate, but perhaps we should not take it too literally on this point. Elsewhere, for example, the author tells us that de Lacy built a motte at Trim but extensive archaeological excavations at Trim Castle found no trace of it (though the *Song's* author may have been referring to the ringwork which we know that de Lacy did certainly construct there).[203] Possibly, therefore, it is safer simply to assume that some sort of castle was already in existence at Dublin in 1172, ignoring the *Song's* specific detail that both a castle and a *donjun* or keep were to be found there, while giving greater weight to the testimony of Howden – an actual eyewitness – that part of the job entrusted to Hugh de Lacy as *custos* of Dublin was to build a new castle on the site.

The probability is, therefore, that de Lacy carried out this instruction and that at some point in or after 1172 extensive building works commenced at Dublin to remedy the deficiencies in the existing fortifications. He is unlikely to have overseen much of it in person, at least to begin with as, for several years after his appointment as *custos* of the city, he was more often than not absent from Ireland, and did not relocate to Ireland permanently until 1177.[204] Hugh de Lacy was, in fact, a castle-builder *par excellence* who put up, at Trim, what was probably the first great Anglo-Norman castle in Ireland.[205] Giraldus tells us that 'Hugh de Lacy, a man possessed of great honesty and good sense, admirably fortified both Leinster and Meath with castles', and adds that when, in 1181, he was replaced in office by John, the constable of Chester, and Richard de Pec, they

> joined with him in building a very large number of castles throughout Leinster. For hitherto very many castle had been built in Meath, but few in Leinster. So first of all a castle was built for Raymond [le Gros] at Fotharta Onolan, and another for his brother Griffin. The third castle was built at Tristerdermot in Uí Muireadhaigh for Walter de Ridelisford, the fourth for John de Clahull on the river Barrow not far from Leighlin, the fifth for John of Hereford at Collacht.[206]

It is interesting that Roger of Howden – who is more precise than Giraldus about people's job-descriptions – records that the constable of Chester and Richard le Pec had been sent to Ireland specifically 'to take custody of (*ad custodiendum*) the city of Dublin, which Hugh de Lacy had had the keeping of',[207] and so the fact that they set about building castles on their arrival suggests that castle construction was part of the responsibility of the *custos* of Dublin. Hence, Giraldus further recalls that when, by the winter of 1181–2, Hugh was reinstated, he

> built a very large number of castles. Among these is the castle he built for Meiler at Timahoe in the province of Laois…He also built a castle for Robert de Bigarz close by, in Uí Buidhe; a castle for Thomas of Flanders not far from there, in the furthest part of Uí Muireadhaigh…and a castle for Robert FitzRichard at Norrach. In Meath he built the castle of Clonard, the castle of Killare, a castle for Adam de Futepoi, another for Gilbert de Nugent and many others which it would be tedious to enumerate individually.[208]

And of course, as is well known, de Lacy met his death in 1186 while actually building a castle at Durrow; tradition has it that he was beheaded on site by an Irish worker he had been instructing on how to use a pickaxe.[209] It would seem extraordinary that a man who oversaw such a torrent

of castle building throughout the new English colony in Ireland would neglect the fortification of the one place entrusted to his keeping, Dublin.

Evidence of the first English castle

Evidence for the existence of the castle in the 1170s, while not plentiful, is solid and certain. Strongbow acted as Henry II's agent in Ireland for a two-and-a-half-year period from autumn 1173 until his death in April 1176 and issued a number of charters in this official capacity, and therefore dateable to that timeframe. One was a grant to a certain Aldred Gulafre and his heirs of a burgage (a property plot) '*infra castellum Duvelinie*'.[210] The word *infra* can mean 'within' or it can mean 'below' – in the sense of 'down from' – and in this instance perhaps the latter is intended but it is impossible to identify the precise location. The same grant also provided Aldred Gulafre with a further carucate of land elsewhere (approximately 120 acres), which he was to hold of Henry II and his heirs by the service of a knight, and nearly fifty years later an inquisition into this tenure provides the additional detail that the knight's service was to be provided 'at the castle of Dublin'.[211]

There are other instances of lands being tenable in return for military service payable at the castle, grants which seem to originate in these early days. For instance, in 1287, Hugh Tyrel, lord of Castleknock, stated that he held the latter in *capite* ('in chief', i.e., directly of the Crown) by the service of three knights with horses and arms, to be provided at the castle of Dublin when royal service was called, and 'that his ancestors had done so since time immemorial (*quam antecessores sui a tempore de quo non extat memoria fecerunt*)';[212] his original grant can be traced back to the 1170s.[213] In 1307 Robert Bagod showed that his ancestors had been enfeofffed of certain lands

> for the service of one man-at-arms at the castle of Dublin, which service his ancestors made from the beginning of the conquest of Ireland (*a primo conquestu Hiberniae*).[214]

And, while Strongbow was Henry II's agent in Ireland in 1173–6, he oversaw the grant of Bray to Walter de Ridelsford, which subsequently passed into the hands of Theobald Butler, who stated in 1290 that he held Bray

> by the service of providing an armoured horse at the gate of the castle of Dublin when the king's service is summoned (*par servise a trover un cheval covert de fer a la port du Chastel de Divelyn quant le servise le Rey est somuns*),[215]

and again this stipulation is likely to originate in the initial 1170s grant.

Also during the 1173–6 period, Strongbow made a grant to a certain Savaricus the Saddler, of Exeter, of a burgage in front of (*ante*) the church of St Mary (later known as St Mary's del Dam, on the site of the modern City Hall). The exact situation of the plot in question is described thus:

> …the front of the burgage he shall have in the route which is opposite the castle gate (*frontem burgagii habebit in ruta que est contra portam castelli*) as far as Blundell's land and extending in length, moreover, as much as the cemetery contains on that side of the road.[216]

The 'route' in question is Castle Street, the property being situated on its north side extending backwards towards the modern Lord Edward Street, and having as its eastern boundary the churchyard attached to St Mary's almost opposite the gate into the castle. This is presumably the same gate referred to in accounts of the assassination a year or two earlier of the king of Bréifne, Tigernán Ua Ruairc, which describe his body being brought to Dublin and the head 'raised over the door of the fortress (*in cenn do thogbail for dorus in Duine*), a sore, miserable sight for the Gael'.[217]

Very close by we find John de Clahull granting Geoffrey de Turville *unum mesuagium herbergatum*, possibly a warehouse, 'in the city of Dublin opposite the castle of Dublin (*in civitate Dublin, contra Dublinie Castellum*)',[218] and since it was witnessed by Philip de Barry (brother of Giraldus Cambrensis) who died *c*. 1200, it must date from before this point and before the famous instruction of King John in 1204 that a castle be built in Dublin.

The street of the castle is referred to in a number of other pre-1204 deeds. For instance, around 1200, Ralph the Clerk gave the canons of St Thomas's the rent from his property 'in the great street towards the castle (*in magni vico versus castellum*), namely, that which is between the land that was John the Archer's and the land of James the Tailor'.[219] And, around 1195, Ailred, prior and founder of the hospital of St John the Baptist, gave Hugh the Lorimer (or bridle-maker) and his heirs 'a fourth part of that half burgage which is between the land of William Brun and the land of William of Portbury in the great street towards the castle (*in magno vico versus Castellum*)'.[220]

One of the witnesses to his charter was the Savaricus granted a plot on that same street by Strongbow two decades earlier. Savaricus's occupation, saddler, and that of the recipient Hugh, a maker of bridle-bits and spurs, suggest the kind of craft activity underway in this area, no doubt profiting from the garrison quartered nearby. And it continued for generations. In 1266–7 we hear of Cecilia, widow of Richard the Lorimer, owing half a mark for the conveyance of 'land with buildings thereon in Castle Street'.[221] Indeed, that part of Castle Street became known as the Lormery (or *Lormeria*). Around 1233, the prior and convent of Holy Trinity at Christ Church gave to Robert Pollard 'land in the Lormery in Castle Street between the land which belonged to Gilbert de Livet and that which belonged to Audoen Brun'.[222] A list of the historical benefactors of Christ Church, compiled around 1285, mentions that 'Henry Peyntur, bequeathed 12s. rent in Castle Street, in the Lormery'.[223] And as late as 1326 John, son of Robert Bristol, granted to Adam Burnell 'land with buildings in *Lormeria*'.[224]

Another certain reference to the pre-1204 castle comes from a document issued at Dieppe on 18 October 1197, when the future King John, who was then lord of Ireland, granted the canons of St Thomas's the right to maintain a fishing-boat on the Liffey and also to receive 'a tenth of the salmon coming to my kitchen of the castle of Dublin (*decimam salmorium venientium ad quoquinam meam de castello Dublin*)'.[225] As lord of Ireland, John in effect owned the Liffey and its fishery (until he sold it to the city during the Magna Carta crisis) and employed bailiffs to manage it on his behalf; by the looks of things, these bailiffs played a role in provisioning the Dublin garrison, including supplying salmon to the castle's kitchen, an arrangement likely to have been in place since Dublin became a royal city in 1171.

Similarly, we later hear of a complaint by the citizens of Dublin that John had granted to St Thomas's a duty on beer which was levied in the city 'to the use of the constable of the castle of Dublin (*ad opus constabularii castri Dublin*)'. In other words, this duty (a portion of the produce) had previously gone to the constable but John gave it instead to St Thomas's. But the citizens complained that the constable was continuing to impose a duty, so that the city's brewers were paying on the double.[226] This complaint dates from 1234 and would not be relevant here were it not for the fact that two separate charters from John survive referring to this gift of his to the abbey, and both date from around the time of John's visit to Dublin in 1185.[227] Neither of these refers to the constable's claim to this beer-tax but, since this had preceded John's diversion of it to the abbey in the 1180s, this entitlement of the constable of the castle to a portion of the city's beer must be earlier still.

But perhaps the most revealing mention of the pre-1204 castle occurs in a legal case dating from 1200, although referring to events that occurred some years earlier. It concerns a dispute that had arisen between a certain William Brun (one of the new Anglo-Norman residents of Dublin) and a group of other new settlers in the town. William took his complaint to the court of the justiciar Peter Pipard (who was John's chief governor in Ireland in 1194) and he had William's opponents bound over to keep the peace towards him. Then, by order of the justiciar, William subsequently came to the castle of Dublin (*venit ad castellum de Diuelin*) – the implication appears to be that this is where the justiciar's court was sitting – but, upon leaving the castle, when William Brun was 'on the bridge (*et ipse esset super pontem*)', he saw his opponents in front of him including a man with a hatchet. The latter struck William, so that 'he fell into the castle ditch (*ita quod ipse cecidit in fossa castelli*)'. Although two of his party 'went down into the ditch to help their lord (*descenderent in fossam ut domino suo auxiliarentur*)', he was in fact mortally wounded and died three days later.[228]

It appears therefore that, even at that early date, the castle of Dublin was surrounded by a substantial ditch and that one entered the castle via a bridge or drawbridge over it. Within the castle itself, it appears, the chief governor of Ireland held court. But however impressive the pre-1204 castle was, it evidently remained sub-standard. England had a new king, John, a king very familiar with both Ireland in general and Dublin in particular, and under that new king Dublin would get itself a new castle.

Chapter 1.2
Building King John's Castle at Dublin

In 1204 the then justiciar, Meiler fitz Henry (Fig. 1.9), wrote to John, the lord of Ireland who was now king of England (Fig1.10), about the deficiencies of the existing castle. His communication does not survive but we do have John's response issued about the end of August that year. In it, he states that the justiciar had informed him that 'you have no place in which our treasure can be safely stored (non habuistis locum ubi thesaurus noster reponi possit)' and that for this and many other reasons a fortress (fortelicia) is necessary at Dublin.

Hence, the king ordered Meiler to build a castle (castellum) wherever seemed most suitable 'for the administration of justice in the city (ad urbem justiciandam) and, if necessary, its defence (defendendam)'. He was to make it as strong as possible (fortissimum poteritis), with 'good ditches and strong walls (cum bonis fossatis et fortibus muris)' but to 'build in the first place a tower (turrim) where later a castle (castellum) and a courtyard (baluum) and other fortifications (alia percunctoria)' could be added. The substantial sum of three hundred marks (£200) of the debt owed to the Crown by the baron of Kells-in-Ossory, Geoffrey fitz Robert, was to be spent on this tower. At the same time, letters patent were issued ordering the citizens of Dublin to fortify their city and, if they neglected to do so, the justiciar was to compel them.[229]

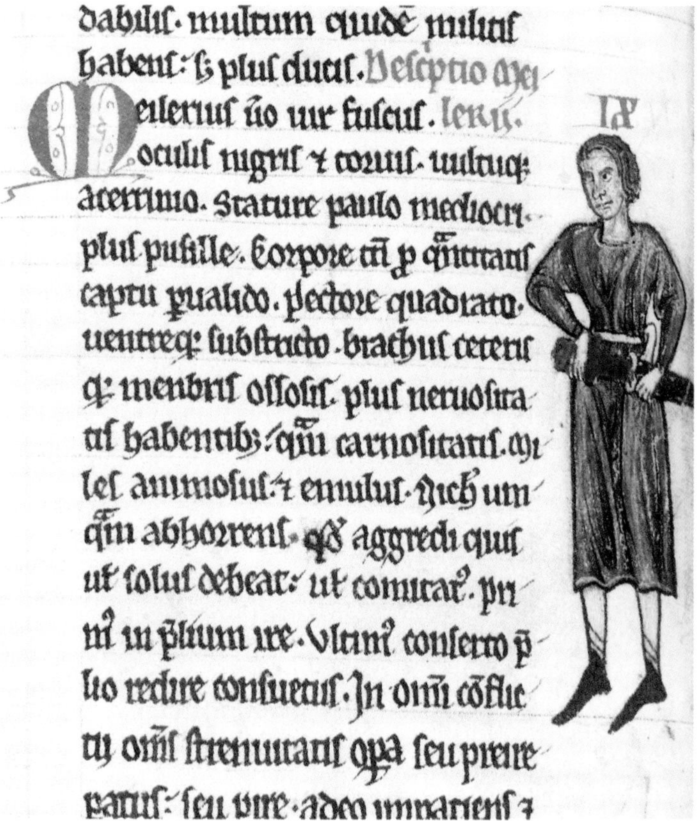

Fig. 1.9 Meiler fitz Henry. (NLI, MS 700)

Planning the new English castle of Dublin

Meiler fitz Henry, one of the most senior of the surviving adventurers from South Wales who had spearheaded the 1169 invasion of Ireland, remained as John's justiciar for the best part of four years following the issue of this instruction and it seems very unlikely that he would have ignored it. A hint that Meiler did indeed act on the 1204 mandate comes a full sixteen years later, when we find the citizens of Dublin agreeing to give the king what they call half the debt which Meiler owed them, the other half being kept back for further work on the fortification of the city.[230] The full story is hidden from us, but we can be certain that this refers back to Meiler's time as justiciar (1200–08) and concerns debts incurred in relation to the fortification of Dublin, almost certainly in implementation of King John's 1204 mandate.

The reference in the latter to the need for a secure place for the royal treasure may be significant because King John was contemplating an extensive reform of England's coinage at that point, a reform he undoubtedly intended extending to Ireland. The recoinage exercise culminated in the summer of 1205 in the establishment of a number of regional mints and exchanges (besides those already at London and Canterbury) at Bury St Edmunds, Winchester, Northampton, York, Chichester, Oxford and elsewhere.[231] Another, we may assume, was formalised at Dublin. In late May 1205, Robert de Vipont was paid his expenses for carrying 400 marks of 'Irish pennies (*denarii Hibernie*)' from Nottingham to Exeter[232] and Dolley and O'Sullivan have dated to this precise point the striking at Dublin for the first time of pennies and their fractions on which John is styled REX.[233] Sure enough, in March 1208, in a charter reconfirming William Marshal's tenure of the lordship of Leinster, John specifically excluded from the grant the city of Dublin and the mint (*moneta*).[234]

We can be fairly certain that this mint was located within the grounds of the castle of Dublin but there is limited evidence of progress on the building works that the 1204 mandate envisaged, perhaps because the justiciar, Meiler fitz Henry, spent much of his incumbency distracted by feuds with some of his fellow barons.[235] In March 1206, a full year and a half after the order was issued, King John sent Meiler a writ allowing him to distrain the lands and chattels of Geoffrey fitz Robert for his debts[236] which, if carried through, should have provided the funds, but our sources are silent. Instead, another year on, in February 1207, we find the king requesting the barons and knights of the lordships of both Meath and Leinster 'that for love of him they give an aid (*auxilium*) to the justiciar towards fortifying (*firmandam*) the king's city of Dublin'.[237] This means that they should provide emergency funding towards strengthening the city walls and defences, which surely was to progress in tandem with work on the castle – since the east and south range of the curtain walls of John's castle were in effect part of the city wall and would have to tie in with it – but still we lack evidence of direct action.

However, it is presumably not a coincidence that, on the very next day after these barons were asked to help with Dublin's fortification, we find our first reference in a generation to a constable of Dublin. On 22 February 1207 Eustace de Rupe, constable of Dublin, received from the king a grant of three carucates of land in the manor of Lusk; it was to be held at a yearly rent of sixty shillings, although later that year the terms were changed so that he held the land of the king in fee by the service of half a knight, to be rendered 'by guarding our city of Dublin (*ad custodiam civitatis nostre Dublinie*)'.[238] Incidentally, on the same day as the latter grant, one Jordan Locard was given Kilsallaghan,

Fig. 1.10 King John from the Waterford Charter Roll. (Waterford Museum of Treasures)

to hold of the king in fee, again 'by the service of one archer, to be rendered in guarding the king's city of Dublin'.[239] The new constable of the castle, Eustace de Rupe, seems to have been a member of the de la Roche family of Wexford and was probably a younger son of Robert fitz Godebert of Fernegenal, a Fleming from South Wales who had first settled in Ireland in 1167.[240] It is likely that he was appointed constable by the justiciar, Meiler fitz Henry – also an early arrival in Ireland from South Wales – and, if so, perhaps Eustace was the man on the ground building the new castle of Dublin for King John.

If these grants suggest the kind of heightened interest in defensive organisation that might come alongside a new castle for Dublin, still no trace of it is forthcoming. In fact, in April 1208, at a time when he was preparing to undertake an urgent expedition to Ireland, King John wrote to the archbishop of Dublin, John Cumin, stating that

we received yours concerning our Castle of Dublin,
how necessary and convenient it might be to us for our
Cyty of Dublin. Therefore, prepare all conveniences,
for we intend the next, by the assistance of Almighty
God and the Blessed Virgin, to visit you all, if we by
any other misfortunes be not hindered.[241]

Unfortunately, the letter survives only in a late translation but seems to indicate that Archbishop Cumin had written expressing the desire for a castle that had yet to be built ('how necessary and convenient it *might* be') and John urges him on with the task ('Therefore, prepare all conveniences') or at least wants him to put the existing structure in order.

Even this seems to have had no effect because, although John postponed his planned 1208 expedition and did not come to Dublin for another two years, there is no evidence that a new castle had materialised in the interval. That said, we should be careful in assuming that no progress had been made. There are very few records surviving from John's government in Ireland in this period but even the great parchment rolls that contain the records of John's chancery and exchequer of England – and which normally supply much of our information about developments at the castle of Dublin – are largely missing for a brief period between 1208 and 1212. We must, in some instances therefore, piece together an impression from the silence.

Hence it may be relevant that, like his father before him almost forty years earlier, John does not seem to have inhabited his castle when he visited Dublin in the summer of 1210. In fact, he spent very little time in the city. He had arrived there by 28 June but headed north on 30 June and did not return until 18 August, at which point he stayed only for a further six days.[242] The evidence seems to suggest that, while in Dublin, John opted to base himself in the abbey of St Thomas the Martyr, just west of the town, which his father had founded in the 1170s and of which he himself was a notable patron. There existed in the abbey 'a great Chambir calld the Kings chambir' (according to an account dated 1488).[243] This is presumably the 'chamber and an upper room and other buildings called the king's lodging' that we hear of at the time of St Thomas's dissolution under Henry VIII.[244] It is only in 1634 that it was described as 'Kinge John's chamber'.[245] Such late notices would be of questionable value were it not for the fact that a document exists in the register of St Thomas's which opens with these words: 'These were present in the hall of the lord king at St Thomas's (*Isti fuerunt presentes in aula domini regis apud Sanctum Thomam*)', a document which can be firmly dated to 1219.[246] If the hall acquired its name because a king had actually been in it and used it (and this can only be a surmise), the king in question cannot be Henry II since the abbey did not exist when he was in Dublin, and it surely therefore denotes John and may well allude to his centre of operations during his 1210 visit.

Commencing the new English castle

If Dublin was still lacking a castle capable of acting as a centre of government and royal residence, John is likely to have urged on the task of completing such a complex in 1210. He may even have left men to do this work, as we know (from surviving records of their expenses) that during his Irish expedition he employed quarrymen, ditchers, miners and carpenters, in works at the castles of Carrickfergus, Dundrum and Carlingford.[247] Presumably the Master Nicholas, 'carpenter', who was paid 15s. by John while at Dublin in the summer of 1210, was the French carpenter Master Nicholas de Andeli (who may have worked at Richard the Lionheart's great fortress of Château Gaillard in Normandy) who served both John and his son Henry III for a period of about forty years, and likewise the Master Osbert, 'quarryman', who was in Dublin with John is the man of the same name who worked for the king at the castles of Gloucester and Corfe.[248] These men must at least have been advising, if they were not overseeing work at the castle of Dublin in 1210.

Before that, at the beginning of 1209, Meiler fitz Henry's successor as justiciar, Bishop John de Gray of Norwich (a royal favourite), had arrived in Ireland and is credited by a contemporary chronicler with administrative and fiscal reforms,[249] but he was also a castle-builder. The Irish annals tell us that upon King John's departure from Ireland in August 1210, he 'left the governance of Ireland to the foreign bishop [de Gray] and told him to build three castles in Connacht (*adubairt fris trí caisléin do dhenam a Connachtaibh*)', whereupon, in that same year, he built the castle and bridge of Athlone.[250] Incidentally, another source tells us that when Richard de Tuit was deputizing for de Gray in the following year, he

founded a stone castle in Athlone, wherein there was
a tower of stone built, which soon after fell & killed
the said Richard Tuite with eight Englishmen there.[251]

This was a fate not unlike that which befell Hugh de Lacy in 1186, suggesting that these royal officers personally supervised the castle construction projects assigned to them.[252] Bishop de Gray also built, in 1212, a castle at Caoluisce, near Assaroe, and at Clones,[253] and in 1213 several more castles were erected or restored by him or following his orders, including Clonmacnoise, Durrow (originally built by de Lacy), Birr, Kinnitty, and Roscrea.[254] Orpen was perhaps right, therefore, in suspecting his involvement in the first phase of construction of the new castle of Dublin.[255]

This is borne out by one of our few financial accounts from this period of English rule in Ireland, the famous pipe roll 14 John, which records receipts and expenses for the period 1211–12 and, sure enough, includes the expenditure of 40 shillings (£2) for carriage of timber from Wicklow for works at the castle of Dublin, by order of the bishop of Norwich (*xl s. pro carriagio mairemii de Wikinglo ad opera castelli Dublinie per preceptum domini Norwicensis*).[256]

This is the first historical record of any work on the so-called 1204 castle. And it seems to have been tied in with a major project to fortify the city in general as we later hear that, during his justiciarship, de Gray had loaned 500 marks (just over £333) to the citizens for this purpose.[257]

By August 1213, de Gray had been succeeded as justiciar by the new archbishop of Dublin, Henry of London (Fig. 1.11), and he is the person usually associated with construction of the castle. An entry in the annals of Dublin under the year 1212, recording his appointment as archbishop, states that he was 'justiciar of Ireland and built the castle of Dublin (*et construxit castrum Dublin*)'[258] but it is a retrospective addition and can only tell us that that is how he was subsequently remembered. In that sense, the statement is not a great deal more credible than the remark of Richard Stanihurst, writing of Dublin in 1584, that

…in this city there is a very spacious castle, most beautiful to behold, and surrounded by a strong curtain wall of stone. This was built by Henry Launders who was once…archbishop of Dublin, a man outstanding in all manner of piety,[259]

or, for that matter, Sir James Ware's even later annals which have it that the castle was built in the year of Archbishop Henry's death (which Ware gives as 1220, recte 1228), adding 'I mean the Walls four square, or Quadrangle wise; but the four Turrets and the other [came?] afterwards'.[260] It should be pointed out that although all Ware's published works were in Latin, the particular statement quoted here appears in none of them, only in annals in English included in the volume entitled *The antiquities and history of Ireland by the Right Hon. Sir J. W. now first published in one volume in English*, prepared by his son Robert and published in 1705.[261] It is impossible to know on what he based the specific detail in this statement, to which we shall return.

What we can say is that Archbishop Henry carried on, from the moment he assumed the justiciarship, his predecessor's castle building programme throughout Ireland. A later inquisition on the subject of Roscrea Castle found that 'the [king's] council began to build a castle (*firmare castrum*) in the vill of Roscrea consisting of a motte and bretasch (*britagium*)', the same account adding:

Meanwhile Henry, archbishop of Dublin, came from England, as justiciar of Ireland, on behalf of King John, and coming to Roscrea found the council making the said motte and bretasch,[262]

another indication that John's chief ministers personally supervised his castellation strategy.

Archbishop Henry seems to have been given specific charge of the castle of Dublin shortly after this. When he arrived in Ireland as justiciar in August 1213, the castle was in the hands of a man called Thomas fitz Adam, an exchequer official responsible, among other things, for dispatching Irish revenues to the king in England.[263] Fitz Adam had possession of Dublin Castle in the same way that he was entrusted with various other estates or royal revenues. For example, he had custody of Trim Castle in 1215 and of Athlone Castle in 1223, was given, in 1218, joint-custody of all escheats falling into the king's hands, which included the temporalities of various vacant dioceses, and from 1219 had custody of the king's forests in Ireland.[264] It seems likely, therefore, that Bishop John de Gray had the keeping of the castle of Dublin until his retirement from Ireland in the spring of 1213, that custody was then temporarily passed onto Thomas fitz Adam, and finally on 13 November of that year King John issued an instruction to him to transfer 'custody of our castle of Dublin (*castri nostri Dublinie custodiendum*)' to Archbishop Henry.[265]

Fig. 1.11 Henry of London from the Waterford Charter Roll. (Waterford Museum of Treasures)

Major infrastructural works at the castle now proceeded under his supervision. Many years later, in 1230, the then king, Henry III, confirmed to the prior and canons of Holy Trinity at Christ Church a grant which, he tells us, had originally been made by his father King John,

> in compensation for damages which they incurred by the occupation of some of their buildings in the construction of the castle of Dublin (*per occupationem quorundam edificiorum suorum in constructione castri Dublinie*).[266]

A fortnight earlier Henry III had issued another charter, this time to the incumbent archbishop of Dublin, granting him in perpetuity the prebend of Tymon, Co. Dublin,

> which King John gave to Henry, then archbishop of the same province, in compensation of the damage done to the church of Dublin by the fortification of the castle in that city.[267]

Since John died in October 1216 this damage must have occurred before that point. Further detail on this latter grant comes in October 1217, when the king made a grant to Archbishop Henry of two carucates of land at Tymon to last until 1230, 'in compensation for those damages done to his churches outside (*extra*) Dublin, on the occasion of our castle of Dublin being fortified (*occasione castri nostri Dublinie firmati*)' from which the church of Dublin suffered a loss of up to £10 per annum.[268] This seems to suggest that the damage was well and truly done by this stage. Likewise, in August 1218 the justiciar was ordered to provide the archbishop's clerk, Geoffrey de Turville, with compensation in money for 'his land which he lost by the fortification of the castle of Dublin (*pro terra sua qui amisit per firmacionem castri Dublinie*)',[269] again an event which seems to have occurred quite some time earlier.

As to what these references tell us about the works at the castle, we can only conjecture. The priory of Holy Trinity had lost buildings to the new – presumably enlarged – castle, but it is not possible to identify their location. We might try to speculate about the site of properties in question based on their value, which other records tell us had yielded a rent of forty shillings per annum.[270] Around 1206, the priory had been granted a plot in St Werburgh's parish to the west of the castle, at a rent of 6s. 8d., and so the properties they lost were worth slightly more than six times this value and might therefore constitute the equivalent of up to six separate burgage plots. Likewise, around 1235 the priory gave away a plot in the Lormery in Castle Street which had a rent of 4s., a tenth of the value of those properties lost because

of the castle works. On the other hand, in 1230, when Adam fitz Simon's *stone* house in the city was granted to the priory, the rent was 20s., half of what they had lost to the castle.[271]

The rents of properties vary greatly, therefore, depending on various factors (including whether the lands had contained wooden or stone buildings, or any buildings at all). Hence, we simply cannot say for certain where or how large the premises were which were taken from Christ Church when the castle works were at their height, but we have to assume that several houses and their gardens were removed to complete the project, perhaps fronting onto either Castle Street or Werburgh Street and stretching back to an enlarged castle ditch (which we know to have been up to 22m wide and 10m deep at this precise point).[272]

As to Geoffrey de Turville – who, as we have seen, was also compensated for land lost – he was a cleric in the train of Archbishop Henry who would later become archdeacon of Dublin (and eventually bishop of Ossory); perhaps he had been assigned the care of a church in the vicinity of the castle and the land he had to forego because of the construction works may have been part of its grounds.

It is sometimes said that two churches, St Paul's and St Martin's, were demolished to make way for the castle,[273] but this does not appear to be so. Archbishop Henry did seemingly demote St Paul's (probably located in South Great George's Street) by uniting it with the parish church of St George and giving both over to the priory of All Hallows; by the end of the Middle Ages it was nothing more than a garden belonging to Christ Church.[274] But the fact is that it was apparently still standing *c.* 1230 and was occupied by a hermit in 1275.[275] Similarly, St Martin's was well and truly a going concern in 1220 when the archbishop, setting about elevating St Patrick's to cathedral status, appointed its first chancellor and gave him for his living the rich prebend of Finglas and the parish church of St Martin.[276] It seems to have continued to function as a parish church throughout the thirteenth century but is recorded as defunct in 1341,[277] having been merged with St Werburgh's, and 'few vestiges' remained in 1533,[278] even though, when Thomas de Castles was appointed as chancellor twenty years later his prebend still comprised 'Finglas, with St Martin's church in Dublin'.[279]

The latter record locates St Martin's church 'beside the walls and the Pole Mill in the south of the city (*juxta murum et molendinum de Pole in parte australi civitatis*)', which probably places it in the south-east corner of Werburgh Street, and it is possible therefore that lands to the rear of the church, backing onto the west ditch of the castle, were affected by the building works. If Geoffrey de Turville was, let us say, rector of St Martin's, this may be 'his land which he lost' because of the fortifications. We find a parallel for this a few years later, in 1225, when the abbey of St Thomas, just to the west of the city, was compensated for 'lands occupied by the fosse thrown up around the city of Dublin (*terris occupatis per fossatum levatum circa civitatem Dublinie*)'.[280]

The problem with identifying St Martin's as suffering at this juncture is, however, that Archbishop Henry was to be compensated for damage done to churches 'outside (*extra*)' Dublin, presumably, that is, outside the walls, whereas St Martin's was within. It is hard to pinpoint such an extramural church, and it is hard to see how any church outside the walls could have been damaged by the building of the castle. Now, it might be the case that what had happened was that cut-stone for the castle was plundered from unnamed ecclesiastical buildings within the diocese or, for example, that stone which the archbishop had acquired for what was to be his new cathedral church of St Patrick was requisitioned for the castle works. But the award of compensation in 1217 referred to losses by the church of up to £10 per annum.[281] This suggests an ongoing loss, such as the loss of rent. The most likely explanation, therefore, of the damage inflicted on the archdiocese by the fortifications is not that one or more churches were demolished to make way for the castle, but that a number of property plots were commandeered because they were in the way of the new expanded castle walls and ditch.

It is similarly difficult to date with absolute accuracy the intensive fortification phase. As we have seen, timber for it was being shipped from the port of Wicklow in 1211–12, and before his death in October 1216 King John was already paying out compensation for lands lost and churches impaired by the works. Archbishop Henry only had personal charge of the castle for a period of about eighteen months, until May 1215 when he left for England in the run-up to the meeting at Runnymede in June at which Magna Carta was issued and which he witnessed. Within a few months England was embroiled in a civil war and had been invaded by the French and it is hard to imagine work proceeding as normal at Dublin Castle in such circumstances.

Perhaps, therefore, we should envisage a period of sustained work taking place in the years before Archbishop Henry's departure from Ireland in May 1215, and something of a hiatus until his return two years later. This task may even have been a small part of the mission entrusted to him in April 1217 when it was announced that he would return to 'improve the state of our land of Ireland (*statusque terre nostre Hibernie emendacioni*)'.[282] Some weeks earlier a man called Master Odo de Havering was dispatched to Ireland, described by the government of the new king, Henry III, as *ingeniatorem nostrum*.[283] An *ingeniator* was an engineer or architect specifically involved with large-scale stone-construction projects[284] – he was a 'master' in the sense of being a master craftsman – and we may suspect that he was there to oversee works at the castle of Dublin.

As to the condition of the castle at this point, it may be unwise to read too much into a letter written by King John in September 1215. This instructed a number of prominent Dublin citizens to collect the massive sum of 4,000 marks from the king of Connacht, and another 4,000 marks of a fine imposed on the lord of Meath, Walter de Lacy. One would have expected such vast monies to be brought for safekeeping to the castle – after all, John had told us in 1204 that that was the castle's *raison d'être* – but instead, the king ordered them to deposit the funds in Christ Church adding that 'all other monies out of the king's manors and debts due to the king shall be deposited in the same place'.[285] This might mean that the castle was not sound; on the other hand, perhaps John – facing into war with his barons and the French – did not trust its keepers. The justiciar was now Geoffrey de Marisco, something of a law onto himself and unlikely to have been a careful steward of affairs relating to the castle. He was eventually called to England in 1220 and compelled to agree to strict terms of office. These stipulated that he 'maintain the custody of the king's land and castles', and 'appoint proper constables to keep the king's castles'; as regards the constables, 'they shall swear faithfully to keep them; if…the castles are withdrawn from the king, the constables shall surrender them to the latter…and the constables shall give into the hands of the archbishop [of Dublin] and of Earl William Marshal, their sons and daughters, or their nearest relations, as sureties, and shall make charters of faithful service to the king'.[286]

The 1224 inventory

This bespeaks a concern that England's Irish colony was vulnerable through misgovernment by royal ministers and an awareness that control of its castles was central to its security. De Marisco was dismissed in the following year and ordered to hand the castles over to Archbishop Henry, who was to replace him as justiciar[287] and the latter was in charge when the dispossessed earl of Ulster, Hugh II de Lacy, landed in Ireland in 1223 intent upon recapturing his lordship. His army marched 'almost as far as Dublin',[288] the city was put in readiness, and an inventory of the contents of the castle stores was produced which (though the surviving record is damaged) is our first detailed account of the castle's infrastructure. It contains references to eight separate rooms in one or more buildings – the castle prison, an alms hall, a workshop, a kitchen, a pantry, a buttery, a chamber, and then a chamber 'beyond the sheriff's chamber'.[289]

It goes without saying that the castle would have had a prison, but the only possession relating to the prison which the inventory recalls is a 'great chain to guard the prisoners'. Prisoners were maintained in a number of locations within the castle. As we shall see, about fifty years later we hear of monies spent by the constable 'in repairing the tower of the gate of that castle' which had been burned by inmates 'confined in the prison there'.[290] On the other hand, the earliest surviving plan of the castle – by a man called Wattson in 1606 – shows both a prison and a former prison occupying much of the north-west quadrant of the castle.[291] There was also a dungeon, located in the north-west tower.[292]

As to the kitchen, we have earlier seen references to it (in the form of royal grants assigning to it a portion of Liffey salmon and of beer brewed within the city), and in this period the pantry and buttery referred to would have been the storerooms for its food and drink respectively; the inventory records that the kitchen had a stock of 100 dishes which might give some idea of the numbers it typically fed. Where the thirteenth-century kitchen was we do not know. As discussed below, a new kitchen seems to have been built in 1228.[293] By the late sixteenth century it was located in the second storey of the Bermingham (or south-west) Tower[294] and seventeenth-century accounts and plans show its associated buildings and yard in the south-western corner of the quadrangle.[295]

In 1224 the castle also possessed 'one horse mill with harness, without horses' and so was presumably able to grind its own grain, and the 'new rope for the well' tells us

that this had been sunk within the precincts. It crops up again in the accounts for 1228 which record the expenditure of two shillings on a bucket for the well[296] but the latter may have been a feature of the castle for a long time previous because we hear in 1235 of the expenses for 'restoring the great well'.[297] No source indicates the location of the well but by far the most precise seventeenth-century plan of the castle, the 1673 Dartmouth plan (Fig. 1.12), probably undertaken by Surveyor General Sir William Robinson,[298] indicates an otherwise unexplained circular feature with a diameter of up to 2m in the yard nearest the kitchen (about midway between the Bermingham Tower and the castle's great hall).[299] It is possible that is the castle well.

The 1224 reference to an alms hall is curious. Almshouses were sometimes buildings used to accommodate the poor but could otherwise be a place from which alms were distributed, and this latter sense is presumably intended. A royal grant was made in 1244 'to cause the anchorite living in the church of St Mary del Dam to have three halfpence a day of the king's alms for her maintenance, with 10s. a year for her clothing', a donation she was still receiving thirty-five years later and which Henry III referred to in 1250 as the 'ancient alms of the king's predecessors'.[300] Since other

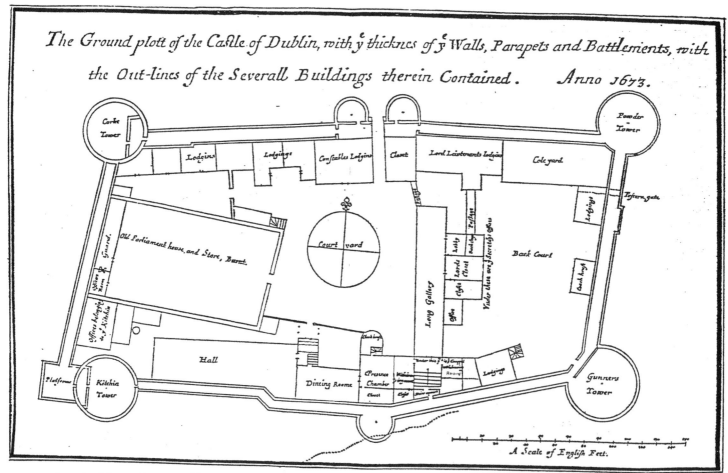

Fig. 1.12 Plan of Dublin Castle in 1673. (© Dartmouth Heirloom Trust and Staffordshire Record Office)

items in this grant pertain to the castle, it seems that this is where the alms were being dispensed (St Mary's being literally outside the castle gate). And the pipe roll of 1266–7 records together, as if they are connected, monies paid for the carriage of wine to Dublin Castle and the king's 20 marks per annum payment of alms to the canons of St Thomas's.[301] It seems likely, therefore, that the alms hall recorded in the 1224 inventory of the castle was a building or room for distributing alms to the poor and the church, perhaps manned by a full-time almoner. When King John was in Dublin in 1210, among his entourage was Brother Thomas the almoner who was given sizeable enough amounts of money to dispense as alms.[302]

There is one other possible explanation of the alms hall. Writing in 1589, the then lord deputy, Sir William Fitzwilliam said of the sons of Fiach McHugh O'Byrne, whom he had held in Dublin Castle as pledges for their father's good behaviour, that they 'were never kept by the alms of the gate, but maintained by their father'.[303] When a mass escape of prisoners occurred, he freely acknowledged some of those now at large were 'boys of ten, twelve or sixteen years or thereabouts, who were better at liberty with the others than lie in the grate to beg and starve'.[304] This indicates that castle authorities relied on public charity for maintenance of certain detainees in the castle. Richard Stanihurst, writing shortly beforehand, also states that the 'poore prisoners both of the Newgate [the town gaol] and the castell, with three or foure hospitals, are chieflie, if not onelie, relieued by the citizens'.[305] It is possible, therefore, that the alms hall mentioned in 1224 was the place from which such assistance was dispensed to prisoners. Only one item of contents was listed as being in this hall in 1224 – a 'great chest'.

There was also a great chest in a room described as the 'sheriff's chamber' and another in the chamber 'beyond' it, and we can assume that these chests were for the storage of money or documents. The sheriff was sheriff of the county of Dublin, its chief judicial and administrative officer, responsible for presiding over the county court, for summoning juries, handling prisoners, levying fines, executing writs, collecting the king's revenues in the form of rents from the royal manors, and so on. It appears that the county court met at the castle and prisoners to be arraigned before it or sentenced to imprisonment by it were placed in the castle's prison.

As to the castle's defences, the 1224 inventory tells us little. We are told that among its possessions was a great chain for the drawbridge (ad pontem turniz), which was obviously a feature of the defences already (and was also mentioned in a legal case relating to events in the 1190s, discussed earlier). The workshop which had, among its assets, three great hammers and an anvil may have been used in smithing to

do with the garrison's horses or armoury. One would have expected the castle to be well armed, but only one crossbow with a wheel (balissa ad troil) and one for the foot are recorded – although a healthy supply of 4,500 crossbow bolts was to hand – and there were also two mangonels (trebuchet-type engines used for catapulting missiles at enemy positions).

The 1224 inventory does not, of course, present a rounded image of the castle since it is concerned only with listing moveable goods, though even this aspect seems incomplete. To take some minor instances: it makes no mention of the bake-house of the castle, repairs to which were carried out in 1228;[306] and it makes no mention of the chapel, whereas the contents of the chapel of Athlone Castle are listed in the same inventory.[307] The castle certainly had a chapel already. In July of the following year the king nominated William de Radeclive as chaplain 'in our chapel of our castle of Dublin (in capella nostra in castro nostro Dublinie)', receiving yearly of the king's gift 50s. for his maintenance, the justiciar being ordered to pay this and to provide him with a vacant benefice worth 100s.[308] Now, William's appointment in 1225 might coincide with the chapel's construction[309] but since, exactly a decade later, monies had already been spent 'repairing the chapel',[310] perhaps it had been around for longer.

Completing the new castle of Dublin

It was noted above that Sir James Ware (or his son Robert) states the following:

> The same year that Henry Londreds died, being the Year 1220, the Castle of Dublin was builded, I mean the Walls four square, or Quadrangle wise; but the four Turrets and the other afterwards.[311]

He was referring to Archbishop Henry of London who in fact died in 1228, and of course it is entirely wrong to suggest that the castle went unbuilt until that date. Having said that, it is an extraordinary fact that for that very year we do find evidence, for the first time, of considerable expenditure at the castle, and, oddly enough, the expenditure is specifically on the very thing Ware tells us was not built in 1228, the towers. One wonders, therefore, whether it is just possible that his is a slightly corrupted rendering of a record of this very event.

The pipe roll for 1227–8 was destroyed in the bombardment of the Four Courts in 1922 and we are dependent on translated extracts from it that had managed to appear in print before that date.[312] These record a succession of itemised payments in relation to the works at the castle, including 24 marks to 'Walter the carpenter for construction of the towers of Dublin Castle', and of another £24 to him 'for making towers', and of £9. 19s. 4d. 'to the masons and other workmen making the towers', and the hefty payment of £88 12s. 2½d. 'for six loads of lead and the carriage thereof and converting it into gutters for the towers'. Obviously, if guttering was needed, the towers had by then reached their full height.

The Walter in question was no ordinary carpenter – the mere fact that his name is recorded is testament to that – and it is important to distinguish between a carpenter (*carpentarius*) and a joiner or other craftsman in wood, the *carpentarius* being for heavier and stronger work, such as construction of the framework of houses, ships, and so on (OED, s.v.). The Walter at work in the castle of Dublin in 1228 was therefore a master craftsman responsible for the timber components of the new towers (or for overseeing that work) and, as that record shows, alongside him there were teams of masons and other workmen involved in the laying of the blockwork, and others still who were taking what were obviously very substantial quantities of lead and rendering it into gutters for these new stone towers.

We do not know what towers were built at this point. The account makes such regular reference to 'towers', in the plural, that it is as if everyone reading knows about them and knows that several are being added. This might support Conleth Manning's suggestion that Meiler fitz Henry and his successors, in following the letter of King John's 1204 mandate, had built a single tower, and that the later building activity involved the addition of the other three corner towers of the quadrangle.[313] The gate house also had two substantial D-shaped projecting towers flanking it on either side and there was also a lesser mural tower on the southern curtain wall, called the 'midle towre on the sowth side' in Perrot's 1585 survey;[314] this may perhaps be the 'Privee Toure' mentioned in a document from 1433–4 (which would suggest it functioned in part at least as a latrine).[315]

Walter Harris, writing in the 1750s (and published posthumously in 1766), believed that in addition to the two corner towers on the south curtain wall, there were two intermediate towers:

> Between Birmingham-tower [southwest corner] and the wardrobe-tower [southeast corner] the courtin was interrupted by two other nameless towers, of much less dimensions than either of the former; one of which, together with a part of the courtin, has been taken down, as well to make room for other necessary buildings, as to give an entrance into the castle garden, contiguous to it. The stump of the other of those towers yet remains, and on it is erected an elegant polygonal apartment, which serves for a cabinet to the government.[316]

If the latter is on the site of the current octagonal tower on the south curtain, the other tower taken down to make way for a postern to the castle gardens (discussed further below)

may perhaps account for the peculiar kink in the south curtain almost midway between Bermingham Tower and the Middle Tower. But the fact that Perrot's survey knows nothing of this second intermediate tower would rather tell against it. That said, the surveyor was certainly conscious of some anomaly on this stretch of the wall, noting that

> over the gardin dore the wall is verie thinne and weke, by meanes ther hath bene, as I thinke, a murdringe hole and perculles, and nowe ther is none.[317]

Perhaps the machicolation and portcullis which the author speculated had previously been located there had in fact been a minor tower built as part of the thirteenth-century castle, removed to make way for a gate to the garden.

Be that as it may, if it is the case that a single tower was built in and after 1204 and the other towers added later, we do not know which came first. Manning suggests that the Bermingham Tower might have come as part of the initial phase.[318] As previously noted, in 1204 King John had been concerned to build a tower for the proper storage of treasure and, sure enough, as late as 1537 an instruction was issued that treasure and records were to be kept in the Bermingham Tower.[319] Having said that, the castle was in such disrepair at the time that the point of this instruction might be that *henceforth* valuables were to be stored there as being the least dilapidated, rather than it having always functioned as such. It was certainly constructed early in the castle project. The Lynch and Manning excavations, having exposed part of the thirteenth-century battered base of the Bermingham Tower and the curtain wall extending northwards from it, revealed at a distance of about 2m north of the tower a curved stretch of earlier masonry made up of massive limestone blocks incorporated into the thirteenth-century structures, which appeared to be part of an 'enceinte' or enclosing wall belonging to an earlier fortification.[320]

An argument has also been made for the Record Tower being that begun by Meiler fitz Henry and his immediate successors.[321] Admittedly, it is not quite fully circular in that its north-western quadrant is stepped in externally to interlock with adjoining perimeter walls, as if never intended to be anything other than a purpose-built corner tower.[322] But since King John's initial instruction was that a single tower be built and then the rest of the castle added, one could imagine the builders making provision from the very beginning for the soon-to-be-connected curtain walls. John had ordered a tower for a specific purpose, for use as a treasury. Bearing this in mind, it may be worth noting that the Record Tower had extraordinary 5m-thick walls, substantially larger than those of the other towers, being, indeed, 'among the thickest walls of any castle in Ireland and Britain',[323] meaning that the interior space is of limited use but would make for a most fitting treasure-house.

The same 1228 account makes reference to some part of the castle – its nineteenth-century transcribers could not make it out because of damage to the parchment – which had been 'thrown down by the wind'. And it is interesting that financial accounts of the sheriff of Dublin, Hugh de Lega, covering the period 1234–5 also apparently referred to part of the castle falling down (although these records too were lost in 1922). Thankfully, J.T. Gilbert transcribed some of the text before that, and, although he does not supply the precise reference to the collapse of part of the castle, his notes make it clear that these years also saw substantial new building works in progress.[324] Now that four corner towers and their connecting walls were in place, it is interesting that all these subsequent interventions appear to be additions to the quadrangle's interior, presumably lining the walls on the inside. Hence, we are informed of the expenditure of £12 10s. 5d. on what was evidently a new kitchen building ('in *construccione coquine Castri Dublinie*') and 65s. 8d. for a house used for dispensing food-allowances ('*unius domus infra castrum, ad liberacionem ciborum*'), along with 68s. 4d. on the construction of a 'house of the engines of the castle of Dublin (in *construccione domus ingeniorum Castri Dublinie*)' – a building for storing such military hardware as trebuchets.

There were also substantial repairs to parts of the fabric of the castle that were already quite run down and, given that these records date to 1234–5, they provide further proof of the castle's age by then. For instance, monies were spent on 'the ruinous windows of the hall (in *fenestris ruinosis aule*)' and on making benches for it ('*scamnis faciendis*') and on the repair of the chapel ('*emendacione capelle*') and of other houses of the castle ('*et aliorum domorum castri Dublin*') and on the '*replacio*' of the great well ('*magni putei*') which may mean something like its restoration or reinstatement, or perhaps the making of a new wooden or metal covering. Work was also carried out to repair the bridge ('*emendacione pontis*') over the fosse at the main entrance, which included (although the roll is damaged at this point) something to do with its paving ('*…pontis pavimento*').[325] It is not clear where the other features were. No trace of the medieval well has been recovered but, as noted earlier, a possible well is marked on the 1673 Dartmouth plan (Fig. 1.12). A castle chapel is also shown on this plan, abutting the south curtain wall just east of the Middle Tower and, west of it, between the Middle Tower and Bermingham Tower, a hall is depicted, also abutting the curtain wall.[326] If these are the hall and chapel mentioned in 1234–5, the fact that they were in need of refurbishment might mean that this south curtain wall was a generation or more old by that stage.

Building the great hall

In the autumn of 1237, King Henry III, in a letter to his Irish justiciar, spoke of his wish to go to Ireland, and said that he would soon send an agent to inspect the state of the country, who was to be given custody of the castle of Dublin and reside there, and who was to be provided with all necessities for the king's use.[327] It is not known if this individual ever arrived, but neither did the king, who again, in 1240, announced his intention to visit Ireland after Easter the following year, writing to the justiciar to tell him to stock up his manors and castles there with wine and corn and other provisions pending his arrival and to 'repair and improve his houses (*domos*) where necessary', and to ensure that 'our chamber in our said castle be panelled (*cameram nostrum in castro predicto lambruscari faciatis*)'.[328] This was presumably a residential chamber within the castle, which was to have wooden panels fixed to the walls. Its location is unknown. It is just possible that it was located within the Middle Tower on the south curtain wall since this, as noted above, was later called the 'Privee Toure' presumably because it had more elaborate toilet facilities than were available elsewhere in the castle; more likely, though, it abutted this tower being the 'chamber of the justiciar' referred to in the 1302 accounts (discussed below).

In any event, King Henry's hopes of an expedition to Ireland in 1241 were also thwarted but the objective certainly remained. In the following year, the king instructed his treasurer of Ireland to 'cause the glass windows for the chapel of the king's castle of Dublin to be made'.[329] This does not imply that the chapel had been unfinished or indeed windowless to this point. Henry III, a fastidious improver of royal palaces and castles,[330] devoted considerable attention to precisely this business of upgrading the windows of important buildings, as when, in 1240, he ordered glass to be made for the chapel and chamber of Dover Castle and, later that year, two glass windows to be inserted in the gable of the hall at Woodstock and, in the following month, three glass windows in the chapel at the Tower of London, even stipulating the biblical scenes to be depicted.[331] The probability is, therefore, that in 1242, the famously pious king had ordered the installation of glass (presumably stained glass) windows in the chapel of the castle of Dublin because, for the duration of his intended imminent sojourn in Ireland, the castle chapel would be the official Chapel Royal.

This same 1242 instruction also ordered the treasurer of Ireland to cause 'the work regarding the hall to be finished'.[332] This instruction presumably refers to the hall we have earlier seen whose 'ruinous windows' were undergoing repair in 1234–5.[333] It precedes by a full year the famous and extraordinary letter sent by the king to his ministers in Ireland in April 1243 – from Bordeaux, where he was mired in his disastrous Poitou campaign to recover his lost Continental lands – to build another grand hall:

> The justiciar of Ireland and Geoffrey de Turville, treasurer of Ireland, are commanded, out of the king's perquisites, to cause to be built in the castle of

Dublin, a hall (*unam aulam*), containing one hundred and twenty feet in length, and eighty feet in width, and with windows and glass (*cum fenestris et verinis*) in the style of the hall at Canterbury. They shall have made in the gable, above the dais, a round window thirty feet in diameter (*in gabulo ultra deisium unam fenestram rotundam xxx pedes in qualibet parte rotunditatis continentem*). They shall also cause to be painted, above the same dais, the King and Queen, sitting with their baronage (*Depingi eciam faciant, ultra idem deisium, Regem et Reginam sedentes cum barnagio suo*); and they shall also cause to be built, at the entrance of the hall, a great portal (*ad introitum ejusdem aule magnum portallum*), so that that hall shall be completed by the lord king's arrival.[334]

This magnificent hall was certainly built – small repairs of the 'great hall' were already being undertaken in 1251.[335] So persistent was King Henry regarding it that, in November 1245, he wrote to the justiciar urging him 'to let the hall of Dublin be perfected' but also to 'cause water to come by a pipe from the conduit of the city of Dublin, so that the king may find it perfect in all things next summer'. At the same time, he sent a request to the 'mayor and good men' of Dublin, asking them 'to permit water to be brought from the said conduit'.[336]

Henry's great hall was to remain one of the principal features of the castle for centuries to come. Indeed, it survived long enough for its ruins (after a fire a few years earlier) to be described by Sir James Ware's son Robert in 1678 as

an ancient structure built after the forme of a Church, raised upon severall stately pillars in the lower part whereof was kept his Maiesties store… [The fire] destroyed the said storehouse and upper loft of that famous building wherein was anciently kept his Maiesties Courts of Justice and also were held both houses of Parliament…

The roof and lofts of this building being burned as aforesaid the most part of the Walls with the Arches were demolished in the time of the Earl of Essex his Lieutenancy [1672–7] and the stones thereof disposed of by him towards the building of Saint Andrews Church.

This great structure though built in the forme of a Church was anciently called the Hall of the Castle and had Iles [aisles] thereunto belonging covered with lead, untill ye time of King Edward ye 4th who caused the same to be sold by the Treasurer of Ireland for repair of the said structure…[337]

Ware's account is useful in a number of respects. What he describes is an aisled structure, having a nave separated from side aisles by piers, the aisles having been roofed in lead until the reign of Edward IV. Evidently Ware had access to the statute rolls of the Irish parliament for we read there that, in 1461–2, the parliament ordered 'that all the leads of the aisles of the hall of the said castle be sold by the Treasurer of Ireland, to make and repair the said hall'.[338] As to the piers which supported the main roof and separated the aisles from the nave, they are mentioned within a generation of the hall's construction when, around 1285, one of the charges of corruption brought against the then justiciar, Stephen de Fulbourne, referred to 'the pillars of marble [which he had] taken from the king's hall in the castle of Dublin and carried to Dunbro', his own manor, near St Margarets.[339]

The hall evidently also had an undercroft or a lower chamber at ground or below-ground level which was later (if not always) used as the castle's storehouse. We hear, for example, in 1400, that King Richard II had left a vast quantity of weaponry behind him in Dublin following his hasty departure and overthrow the previous year,

which John Luffewyke, keeper of the late king's privy wardrobe in the Tower of London, left in the great hall within Dublin castle until further order of the late king, namely 141 coats of mail, one tun full of bows, one coffer containing 96 bows, 30 pipes and one small one full of arrows, one barrel full of bowstrings, 353 lances without heads, one small coffer containing 356 lance heads, 335 'pavisses', 16 single cannons, eight short barrels (*ollas*) of cannons, eight 'stokkes' of cannons, six barrels full of gun stones (*petris pro canonibus*), 'suffles, tampons, hamours, touches', and 'fyr pannes' for cannons, one small barrel of 'gonne poudre', one 'fraile' barrel for coats of mail.[340]

All this was stored in the undercroft, the 'great hall' being above. This is what Ware means by the 'upper loft of that famous building wherein was anciently kept his Maiesties Courts of Justice and…both houses of Parliament'. Sure enough, the oldest known plan of the castle sketched in 1606 by Wattson (Fig. 1.15) portrays the hall with, in its four corners, the four courts of chancery, exchequer, common pleas, and king's bench.[341] It may seem extraordinary to us that judges and lawyers and members of parliament should sit in a building with such explosive material beneath their feet but it seems to have been the case, although there were certainly fears about it. As late as 1591 Elizabeth I's privy council noted that the Storehowse in the castle of Dublin ys in a place moche decaied, over the which the Courtes of Justice are kept, beinge a thinge very inconvenient yf anie accydent (which God forbidd) should happen,

and recommended that the suppressed Cistercian abbey of St Mary be used as a storehouse instead.[342] In fact, however, the courts rather than the storehouse were moved out of the castle and, in 1606, the then chief governor of Ireland wrote to the Crown to warn against them returning, saying that 'to bring the courts of law again into this castle, were to draw them just over the store of munitions, which…may be fired, to the exceeding detriment of this state, and ruin of this castle…we know it to be so dangerous (and at no time more than now) as we cannot without almost inevitable hazard adventure upon it'.[343]

Between the fire which consumed the great hall in 1671 and Robert Ware's manuscript account dating from just seven years later, the Dartmouth plan of the castle (Fig. 1.12) mentioned above was made, dated 1673, which depicts the hall with the legend 'Old Parliament house, and Store, Burnt'.[344] The map situates the hall precisely for us; it, as befitted a church-like structure, is orientated roughly east–west, and is built against the west wall of the quadrangle between the Bermingham Tower and the north-west corner tower (by then called the Cork Tower), being slightly closer to the latter. In most respects, this is a highly accurate map, to scale. Henry III had demanded a hall 120 x 80 feet (36.5m x 24m) whereas the map depicts a hall approximately 130 x 70 feet (40m x 21m) – near enough to the prescribed dimensions to indicate how closely such mandates were followed.

Henry III had instructed that his Dublin hall was to be 'in the style of the hall at Canterbury', which was a tall order (unless he meant merely that its circular or rose window was to be modelled on Canterbury). The great hall at Canterbury was second only to Westminster Hall in its huge scale – measuring internally 165 x 61 feet (50m x 19m) – using the latest architectural style from France.[345] It may have been begun under Archbishop Hubert Walter (d. 1205), was probably interrupted during the papal interdict (1208–14), and was certainly completed in time for the great festival translating Thomas Becket's remains to a new shrine in 1220 under Archbishop Langton. Like the hall later built at the castle of Dublin, it was aisled, being divided into eight bays at ground-floor level, the pillars being made of Purbeck marble, and each bay was filled with double-transomed windows. In each end-gable was a rose window, and, as we saw, King Henry ordered that one of the end walls of the Dublin hall was to have such a window (presumably the east wall since the west was incorporated into the castle curtain wall). At the east end of the Canterbury great hall was a dais, and we saw that Henry had ordered one to be constructed within his Dublin hall, above which a mural was to be commissioned featuring him and his queen at court. The Canterbury hall had a large vaulted undercroft with a line of five central pillars and this undercroft too we see at Dublin, being described by Ware as 'the lower part whereof was kept his Maiesties store'.

Unfortunately, few traces of the great hall at Canterbury survive following its demolition in the mid seventeenth century, but we can get a sense of the appearance of the Dublin hall from another of Henry III's great halls. Between 1222 and 1235 Henry had built a similar hall in the grounds of Winchester Castle, likewise oriented east–west. Whereas he had set dimensions for the Dublin hall of 36.5m x 24m, the Winchester great hall is 34.8m x 17.2m (internally). Like the Dublin hall, Winchester has a nave (of five bays) and side aisles, and, as at Canterbury, the columns are of Purbeck marble (Fig. 1.13).[346] Just as at Dublin, where Henry had ordered the painting of a mural depicting himself and his queen above the dais, at Winchester in 1235–6 he ordered a mural of the Wheel of Fortune and, in 1238–9, a Mappa Mundi, along with stories from the Bible and images of St George and St Edward.[347] The Dublin Castle mural was unusual, and perhaps unique,[348] in that Henry sought to depict himself and his queen surrounded by their baronage. But whatever point he sought to make by this, there is no doubt that his great hall of Dublin truly was to be a hall fit for a king, and fit for a king who had a particular preoccupation with architectural and artistic grandeur.[349]

The great hall required little maintenance in the decades following its completion. In 1300–2, it 'was covered, [and] gutters mended' but the sums involved were sufficiently small to suggest minor repairs, perhaps to leaks in its roof.[350] It was only in the immediate aftermath of the Bruce invasion (1315–18) that a major programme of refurbishment got underway. We hear in 1319–20 of £64 11s. being spent on the hall and of sums of £47 3s. 3d. and £51 11s. 4d. in the following year,[351] and another source records the payment to the keeper of the works of the castle of '£500 for carrying out the said works and repairing the great hall in the said castle'.[352] This was an extraordinary amount by the standards of the day (its precise purpose to be discussed presently), bearing in mind that the average annual revenue of the Irish exchequer at this point was only £2,370.[353]

But not a penny seems to have been spent on the hall for the next three-quarters of a century. In 1397, following the death of the archbishop of Dublin, it was recommended to King Richard II that the revenues of the diocese be redeployed during the vacancy to 'be spent on repairing

Fig. 1.13 An interior view of the great hall at Winchester. (Alamy)

the great hall of the king's castle of Dublin'[354] and in the following year a very large sum amounting to about £260 was spent 'for repair of defects in the hall and buildings of Dublin Castle'.[355] But this did not greatly improve matters. On 21 October 1407 there had been a meeting of the Lord Lieutenant and council which discussed 'how the great hall within the castle was ruinous and greatly needs roofing with lead', but these were straitened times and the £20 granted for that purpose was hardly likely to prove adequate.[356] Hence our sense of déjà vu on reading of a discussion, fourteen years later, in the same location, between the same ministers, 'as to how the great hall within Dublin Castle stands in need of a lead roof (tectura plumbea) and repairs', the solution that was offered amounting to a mere 20 marks (£13 6s. 8d.) of expenditure.[357] Unsurprisingly, in 1430, it was now being reported that 'for lack of repair of the hall, towers and buildings, the books and records are greatly damaged

by rain and storms', and yet the full extent of the remedy offered was renewal of the grant of 20 marks per annum out of the revenues of Ireland.[358]

It was this plight that caused the parliament of 1461–2, as we have seen, to take the desperate measure of ordering that 'all the leads of the aisles of the hall of the said castle be sold by the treasurer of Ireland, to make and repair the said hall',[359] which hardly sounds like a solution. Deterioration therefore continued so that it was reported in 1538 that 'the great hall of Dublin Castle to be repaired or the justices will be compelled to sit upon hills, like Irishmen, and the majesty of the law suffer'.[360] The last expenditure of note on the building came amid a flurry of other payments for works on the castle in the mid 1560s, which included 'making "archebutrises" to the great hall'[361] – flying buttresses which presumably arched upwards from the roof of the aisles on either side of the hall.

The later thirteenth-century castle

The great hall was the last major infrastructural addition to the castle of Dublin in the thirteenth century. Apart from a short-lived renewal of investment in the 1280s, for most of the second half of the century we tend to hear only of the expenditure of small sums dealing with wear and tear of the fabric, though these occasionally cast light on certain features.

Hence, in 1251, five shillings was paid for work on what we might perhaps translate as the 'privy below the castle (*ad garderoba infra castrum*)', including its repair and its '*cinenanda*', which may have involved its roofing with shingles (if it derives from *cindulare*: DMLBS, *s.v.*).[362] Our sources are then entirely silent as regards expenditure on works at the castle for a full quarter of a century until, in 1276, fifty marks was spent by the constable 'in repairing the tower of the gate of that castle which was burned by Hubert de Burgh and his accomplices, confined in the prison there', and a further ten marks on repair of the drawbridge ('*pontis turn*').[363] Hubert de Burgh was a scion of the great de Burgh (later Burke) dynasty which at this point held the lordship of Connacht and earldom of Ulster and evidently he had been imprisoned in the castle of Dublin, probably for rebellion. The castle gate had two D-shaped towers protecting it on either side and as late as 1678 Robert Ware stated that, upon entering the gate 'you may be pleased to take notice that ye Constable of ye Castle holds ye Tower on each side of ye Castle gate for ye custody of his Ma[jes]ties prisoners',[364] proof of a remarkable continuance in use of this facility in this precise location for a period of over 400 years.

In the later years of Henry III's reign and early years of his son and successor, Edward I, accounts show that, typically, only sums in the region of £10 per annum were spent on castle works, and then in 1280 we hear of £97 and of £107 in the following year, and in 1285 the clerk of works at the castle accounted for expenditure of £452 on 'the king's works of Dublin'.[365] Even if there is some measure of overlap in these figures, they are very large amounts (compare, for example, the costs in wages and materials of building a wall around Roscommon Castle in 1284, which came to £66 5s. 2d.).[366] But we have very few details of the specifics of the expenditure. In 1284, we hear of the clerk paying 'for timber boards, nails, etc., to make and repair a bake-house, wages, materials, and cost of carriage of materials', amounting to £68 14s. 9d.[367] This is presumably the same bake-house on which repairs had been carried out in 1228.[368]

The 1302 account

Somewhat later accounts of expenditure at the castle in the period 1300–02 have interesting details as to the disposition of structures within the complex (though, sadly, we only have nineteenth-century translated extracts):

> Dublin Castle and the Exchequer: Account of John Bouwet assigned about the works there, from…[30 September 1300] to…[29 June 1302]…Expended in building materials, repairs, wages, &c., £21. 5s. 8½d…
>
> The premises repaired, &c., include the old stable, the exchange (*cambium*), the oriel between the chamber of the justiciar and the chapel, the great hall which was covered, gutters mended, walls of the chamber near the gate opposite the exchequer plastered; chapel, old stable, chamber of the constable, and marshalsea tower, covered various prisons, towers, &c., all in the castle.
>
> Repairs of the houses of the exchequer, glass for windows, repairs of kitchen, &c.[369]

The last item in this list, repairs to the houses of the exchequer, does not relate directly to the castle since, at this point, the exchequer met in a separate building about 200m east of the castle at the corner of South Great George's Street and Exchequer Street (hence the name). The earlier items in the list do, however, refer to works that took place within the castle. Yet it includes the plastering of 'walls of the chamber near the gate opposite the exchequer'. In other words, this chamber is inside the castle, and is near a gate that is 'opposite' the exchequer, evidently a postern gate leading to the latter. The 1673 Dartmouth (Fig. 1.12) plan depicts it, on the eastern curtain wall just south of the Powder Tower, and perhaps the building beside it on that map, marked 'Lodgings', is (or is on the site of) the 'chamber' mentioned in 1302. This postern is mentioned in a case from 1310 in which the castle watchman alleged of the constable 'that he knocked down a certain old house in that castle beside its eastern gate (*quod prostravit quamdam veterem domum in eodem castro existentem juxta orientalem portam eiusdem castri*)'.[370] Robert Ware, in 1678, mentions the postern and another one on the south perimeter wall:

> There were untill of late two sally ports or posterne Gates lying open; the one towards Sheep Street [on the south curtain wall], the other towards ye Castle-yard [east curtain], but that towards Sheep Street was closed up by order of the Duke of Ormond [c.1663]…the other Posterne Gate is still open, but secured by a constant Guard, which will permitt you to descend thence into the Stable yard…[371]

The former gate, towards Sheep Street (now Ship Street Great) is probably the 'gardin dore' referred to in Sir John Perrot's survey of 1585, in which the writer tells us that, above it, 'the wall is verie thinne and weke, by meanes ther hath bene, as I thinke, a murdringe hole and perculles, and nowe ther is none'.[372] Although it had been sealed up in the

1660s, when John Dunton visited the castle about thirty-five years later he reported that, at the rear of the castle 'a broad wall stretched the whole length of the building and from it a stone arch over a little river [the Poddle] gave access to the garden by two spacious pairs of stairs'.[373] This arch, incidentally, seems to be what is intended when Perrot's survey tells us that the middle spike (loophole) in the lower room of the Middle Tower on the south wall 'skoureth the arches sowthwarde'.[374]

The postern which Ware describes as heading towards the castle yard and stable yard is presumably the one that the 1302 account indicates was used for traffic between the castle and the exchequer. (Strangely, none of these accounts mention the postern gate at the east end of the north curtain wall, just west of the Powder Tower, the lower part of which, with steps descending into the moat, was found in the Cross Block excavations in the castle in the 1960s.)[375]

Those using the eastern postern mentioned by Robert Ware and depicted on the 1673 Dartmouth plan (Fig. 1.12) were presumably able to cross over the Poddle and head directly east by a laneway later blocked up. Sir Bernard de Gomme's map of Dublin (Fig. 2.12) compiled at the same time depicts two bridges on the Poddle immediately east of the castle, less than 50m apart from each other. That the Poddle in this location to the east of the medieval castle – Robert Ware's 'Stable yard' where the modern Lower Yard and Chapel Royal are – presented no hugely insurmountable obstacle to traffic is apparent from his casual remark that 'there passeth through the Stable yard a full stream of water, issueing out of the Castle gardens which plentifully serves to all uses belonging unto the horse there kept, and to the severall artificers, and persons who minister to publique uses in that place'.[376] Ware's son-in-law Walter Harris describes the moat elsewhere as being dry but 'that part which lay to the east was filled with water by the flowing of the tide, and a branch of the river Dodder, which runs in a channel under an arch by the edge of the castle garden, and supplies the stables and other out-offices of the palace'.[377]

The 1302 account also mentions works on an 'old stable' at the castle. The stables were outside the walls in the days of Ware and Harris, but were surely within in 1302, and the account implies that new ones had been constructed (presumably as part of the major thirteenth-century building project) but that there was still an old stable complex from the pre-1204 era. The reference to the 'exchange (*cambium*)' is important as this was linked to the mint, being the office to which one brought old money to exchange for new, or bullion to exchange for the king's coin. Although we can be certain that the mint was located in the castle[378] there are in fact few references to prove it that are earlier than this one mentioning repairs to the exchange.

Another important detail in the 1302 account is the reference to 'the oriel between the chamber of the justiciar and the chapel'. In this context, 'oriel' appears to mean a passage or corridor.[379] No medieval source indicates the location of the castle chapel but the 1673 Dartmouth plan (Fig. 1.12) has a chapel abutting the south curtain wall just east of the Middle Tower. Above it is a stairwell leading to a 'Withdrawing room' and, to its west, the 'Presence Chamber'. Writing no more than five years later, Robert Ware also records each of these premises. Hence, he describes in this location an 'ancient piece of building, wherein upon the ground is a Chappell'. A note on the manuscript at this point, in the hand of Ware's son-in-law Walter Harris, reads 'The Chappell built by Sir Henry Sidney anno 1567',[380] but it is clear from Ware's own account that Sidney merely built the withdrawing room above the chapel and that the latter was, as just mentioned, an 'ancient piece of building'. Just west of the chapel, Ware – who, throughout his account, carefully distinguishes between old and new – describes 'the chamber of presence, the Lobbies, and the chambers thereunto appertaining which, being an ancient structure, is thought to want reparation or rebuilding'.

In the royal household – and the castle of Dublin sought to replicate these arrangements – the great hall was where public and formal business was conducted and the king's chamber was for more personal matters. However, under the Tudors and their successors, the king's chamber was also a place of business, being divided into the less restricted outer (or 'presence') chamber and the influential privy chamber, leading to the king's withdrawing room and, ultimately, his bedchamber.[381] A slightly less hierarchical version of this system is what both the 1673 plan (Fig. 1.12) and Robert Ware depict, with a Presence Chamber leading to a withdrawing room from which stairs led to the chapel below. And although, by the 1670s, major redesign had been underway at the castle for over a century – these precise terms had not even been coined in 1300 – more than likely the 'chamber of the justiciar' referred to in the 1302 account was the precursor of, and in precisely the same location as, the later Presence Chamber and withdrawing room, the 'oriel' being a portico or corridor linking it to the castle chapel. It was presumably the case that the justiciar (and indeed the king in the case of Richard II in 1394–5 and 1399) lived here when resident in the castle, and hence the need for the corridor linking the chamber with the castle chapel and, of course, its proximity to the 'privy tower' (the Middle Tower on the south wall). Adequate architectural records of English royal chapels coeval with that at Dublin are scarce but it is worth noting that the chapel built at Westminster in 1237–8 by Henry III's queen, Eleanor, was also entered by way of an oriel from her chamber.[382]

This 1302 account also refers to works done to the 'chamber of the constable, and marshalsea tower'. Robert Ware's 1678 account refers to the 'Constables Lodgings, very much beautified and reduced to the better accommodation of modern contrivance in the time of the Duke of Ormond's first Government [1662] after his Maiesties happy restauration'. The building was located immediately on the right as one entered the castle gate past the two gate towers and is labelled as such on the 1673 plan (Fig. 1.12). This is presumably the 'chamber of the constable' repaired in 1302. Ware, as we saw above, also stated that in his day the constable maintained both entrance towers as a prison. Although he was speaking of the gatehouse as at least partly rebuilt in 1617,[383] the old gate towers had evidently been used for this same purpose since, during the reconstruction, prisoners from the castle had to be housed in the city gaol.[384]

The 'marshalsea tower' recorded at the castle in 1302 is perhaps one of the two gate towers, as the marshalsea was certainly a prison. Besides judges, one of the most important officials of the courts was the marshal. In 1424, for example, one man held the office of marshal of the court of the chief place (king's bench), the court of common bench, and the court of the exchequer,[385] all of which by then sat in Dublin Castle, and the marshalsea was the prison to which his charges were committed, being closely linked to the office of constable of Dublin Castle. Hence, for example, in 1394, when John Laundey of Clane, Co. Kildare, was 'committed to the prison of the marshalsea' over a debt of £27, the justiciar and council of Ireland wrote to both the marshal and the constable of Dublin Castle, to the effect that John was alleged to be 'plotting to escape [and] intends to make various crafty prosecutions for his release'. They were ordered that 'if the said John is in their custody for that debt, they are to cause him to be kept duly and safely in the same prison until he satisfies' his creditor for the debt.[386] We may perhaps assume that since both the marshal and the constable had him in custody, his place of imprisonment was one of the two towers used by the constable as the castle gaol.

The castle could, of course, occasionally overflow with prisoners and it is interesting that the 1302 account also records that the clerk of works at the castle had 'covered various prisons', meaning that he had repaired the roofs of various buildings within the castle used for this purpose. Unsurprisingly perhaps, therefore, the earliest surviving plan of the castle, that by Wattson in 1606, depicts a 'prison' and a 'former prison' occupying most of the north-west quadrant of the castle interior abutting the north wall of the great hall.[387]

Rebuilding the king's mills

These repairs to the roofs of buildings may have been necessitated by a storm since we know that monies were spent in 1302 for the 'portage of millstones and timber from the king's mill under the castle of Dublin levelled by the flood, from the water to land'.[388] The water in question is the Poddle, the mill being located just east of the castle somewhere in the vicinity of the modern Lower Yard.

Mills had been located here for generations. A jury of 1331 found that a certain Richard de Feipo formerly had two mills beside the castle, between the castle and St George's church, 'on the other side of the water flowing below said castle, towards the said church (ex altera parte aque versus ecclesiam predictam currentis sub eodem castro)'. In order words, his mills were situated on the east bank of the Poddle. He, however, had given these mills to St Mary's abbey in 1235–6. Indeed, the charter still survives whereby Richard gave the abbey

my two mills along with their site and all my adjacent lands in the suburb of Dublin, which are situated between the castle on one side and St George's church on the other, as well as the mills' overflow of water (una cum refluctu aque ipsorum molendinorum).[389]

This latter feature is presumably that which is clearly illustrated on Speed's 1610 map of Dublin as a body of water lying alongside and immediately east of the Poddle, both converging on a millhouse. The 1331 jury found, however, that when John fitz Geoffrey was justiciar of Ireland (1245–56), he 'had a new mill belonging to the lord king built beside the said castle, on the other side of the same water towards the castle'. In other words, the king's mill was built on the west bank of the Poddle, even though St Mary's had held its mills nearby for twelve years or more by that stage.[390] The 1331 jury was entirely correct because we have a record of an inquisition having been held as far back as 1248 to determine whether the monks had suffered losses of up to ten marks per annum 'by the king's mills lately erected near the castle of Dublin', the outcome of which was a royal grant of lands elsewhere in compensation.[391]

These new king's mills continued to function at the castle, and perhaps supplied flour for its kitchen, until the flood, noted above, that required them to be rebuilt. Hence, in 1302 we hear of a certain John Mathew or Macheu having been assigned by the treasurer and barons of the Irish exchequer, 'to superintend the works of the king's mills to be constructed below Dublin Castle', for which he received £79 15s. 5d. 'expended in wages and building materials'.[392] Another account mentions £30 'to be spent on the two mills there to be constructed for the king's use'.[393] And for the period 1311–14, there is a record of the keeper of the king's mills spending monies

…for timber, planks, boards, nails, bolts and other necessary things bought for the newly-built wheels of the said mills and repair of other defects in the mills…[and for] wages of various carpenters for making the said wheels and repairing the defects… for iron and steel bought for making mill-spindles (*fusill'*) and other large and small instruments for the mill, and wages of a smith making the instruments and maintaining and sharpening them as often as necessary; 28s. 9d. for the purchase of a Welsh grindstone for the mill, and carriage and repair of the same before it was put in place; 4s. 9d. for tallow and grease for the maintenance of the mills; 60s. 7½d. for the maintenance of a horse serving the mills and for shoeing it.[394]

Further sums were accounted for in 1325–7, including timber, boards and nails bought to repair the mills, and millstones, during which time the individual who held the mill at farm could 'receive no profit by reason of the building of a new stone wall near the pool of the mills'.[395] Thereafter, there is no further record of the mills' maintenance or refurbishment although we regularly hear of individuals being given custody of the mills. Hence, in 1333, Thomas Smoth (of Smoth's Court, i.e., Simmonscourt near Ballsbridge), a clerk of the exchequer and keeper of the stores of the castle, submitted his accounts for the first two years of a ten-year tenancy as farmer of the mills. Among the expenses he was allowed was £1 6s. 8d. for

the multure of 40 crannocks of wheat which Anthony de Lucy when justiciar of Ireland [June 1331–December 1332] caused to be ground at the mill for the supplies (*expensis*) of his hospice in the summer [of 1331] whence Thomas should have received two crannocks toll, the price of each being one mark…

allowed £4 for multure of 200 crannocks of wheat similarly ground after summer, to serve until his [the justiciar's] departure from Ireland, from whence Thomas should have received 10 crannocks toll, the price of each crannock being 8s.[396]

From this we see that the mills attached to the castle were farmed out to well-connected individuals who paid a certain fee in return but kept the rest of the income the mills produced. The latter included a multure, a toll consisting of a proportion – in this case, one-twentieth – of the grain brought to the mill. And, even though these were royal mills attached to the castle, the king's justiciar was not exempt.

Works during and after the Bruce invasion
In the early fourteenth century there are annual costs in connection with maintenance works at the castle, though rarely amounting to much, as, for example, in 1307, when the keeper of works spent ten marks 'to repair the bridge

of Dublin Castle and other things in the castle'.[397] It was only the crisis caused by the invasion of Ireland by the Scots under Edward and Robert Bruce that secured enhanced expenditure. In 1315–16 the keeper of the works at the castle spent £92 11s. 8d.[398] which, though hardly excessive, was more than had been spent in a single year for a generation. And it was followed the next year by a grant to the keeper of £100 for

preparing and carrying out works there to avoid and suppress the malice of the Scots and their Irish allies, threatening the king's faithful people of the land of Ireland and threatening to attack and besiege the castle.[399]

This fear that the castle might be attacked by the Scots and laid under a siege had caused the king's special envoy to Ireland, John de Hotham, to decide,

for the security and protection of our castle of Dublin against certain danger which gravely threatened it, to demolish and pull down the bell-tower of the church of St Mary del Dam, next to the said castle, and to transport its stones into our castle to repair and emend it.

When, by 1319, the danger had passed, the king ordered that the bell-tower be rebuilt.[400] De Hotham also ordered the mayor and citizens of Dublin to provide twelve fothers of lead (a fother/fodder was approximately a cartload, later being defined as 19½cwt or 990kg) for repairs to the towers and houses of the castle.[401]

Other improvement-works followed. A keeper of works at the castle, Thomas Faucoun, was paid £26 for 'repairs and new works there' in 1319–20 while another account for 1320 has him receiving £200 for 'repairs in the castle'.[402] His successor as keeper of works, Luke de Hynkeleye, began a major refurbishment of the great hall, on which he spent £64 in 1319–20[403] and, in 1320, the enormous figure of £500 'for carrying out the said works and repairing the great hall'.[404] He continued spending large amounts on 'construction and repair of the houses of the castle and other necessary works there' for several years, including £37 in 1323, £103 in 1325, £47 in 1325–6, and an extraordinary total of £342 in 1326.[405] And in the period 1327–31 his successors spent £224 on 'constructing and repairing the buildings of the castle and other necessary works there'.[406]

At the completion of his term of office in 1327, Luke de Hynkeleye submitted accounts for his entire term since 1320, in which he accounted for receipt of a total of £692 17s. 6d. Indeed, others have estimated the total expenditure by de Hynkeleye as amounting to £922 19s. 6d.[407] This represents by far the greatest investment in the infrastructure of the castle since its construction a century earlier. These accounts reveal something of what was done to the great hall under Luke's stewardship. He states that a contract had been entered into to pay £80 – a very hefty sum – to two named 'master masons', John Corfe and John Titchmarsh,

> for breaking down and re-building the walls of the great hall of the castle…for clearing the said hall and making benches of stone as by like agreement; £9 6s. for free stones to be broken in the quarry of Coueneche, and their carriage to Dublin for said works [and] £6 13s. 9d. for free stones to be broken in the quarry of Carrykbrenan, and their carriage to Dublin for said works…£35 7s. 11d. for timber bought by said treasurer in gross at Ros, and for its carriage to Dublin…£113 15s. for iron and lead bought from divers persons at various prices, for said works, forging the iron, casting the lead, and for wood bought for the casting; £262 17s. 1d. for timber, boards, shingles and nails bought for said works; sand and clay; wages of carpenters, masons and other workmen; and other small necessaries for said works.[408]

The term 'master mason', in the Middle Ages, encompassed a range of activity far wider than the name suggests and applied to individuals who were architects of the building, the administrative officials of the building fabric, the building contractors, or technical supervisors of construction.[409] The 'free stones' referred to are not free in the sense of costing nothing; on the contrary, 'freestone' is a much-prized building material, such as fine-grained sandstone or limestone, 'free' only in the sense that it can be cut in any direction and readily shaped with a chisel for moulding and tracery (OED, s.v.). In this instance, it was evidently intended for the decorative elements of the new hall. It came from quarries named as Coueneche – which is unidentified unless it is near Drogheda, since in 1322 monies were given to de Hynkeleye 'for the carriage of free stone from Drogheda to Dublin for said works'[410] – and Carrykbrenan, which is Monkstown, Co. Dublin. Large amounts of timber were also sourced, apparently from Old Ross, Co. Wexford.

That this massive programme of works was needed indicates that there had been something radically wrong with the great hall as originally built, which required its dismantling and reconstruction at very great cost. It might suggest the possibility that its location within the castle was an area where the ground was unstable; perhaps it had been built up artificially as part of the project to construct the quadrangle or, indeed, it might be the case that there were in situ Viking deposits here which were not dug through for the foundations of the hall, contributing

to the ground's later instability. It is worth noting that problems remained, certainly in terms of leakages from the roof in later generations, and indeed in the mid 1560s large sums were spent 'making "archebutrises" to the great hall', that is, flying buttresses to stabilise the walls.[411] It is probably also significant that the hall was no more than 7m from the north-west corner tower which was so unstable that it eventually collapsed in 1624 being replaced by the Cork Tower.[412]

One imagines the castle was all the better for the brief period of careful attention during Luke de Hynkeleye's tenure as clerk of works in the 1320s, whereas the period from about 1330 to 1360 was by comparison a leaner one. Expenditure remained buoyant initially. King Edward III had announced in September 1331 that he would lead a major expedition to Ireland, at which point preparations went into full swing, before it was eventually cancelled a full year later.[413] It was because of the anticipated royal expedition that the keeper of works accounted for expenses of £97 12s. 7½d. over a period of 31 weeks from late July 1332, which included

> £34 2s. 1d. expended in the wages of a mason, carpenter and workman employed at these works on various occasions…£1 17s. 9d. similarly paid for the wages of an armourer; £22 14s. 3½d. expended in the purchase of iron to make divers things in said castle and the making of them, also for boards, wood, nails, timber, lead, tin, and small necessaries; £10 4s. 7½d. expended in the purchase of stone and bringing it to the castle, also of lime and sand: £4 paid to divers glaziers as well for glass as for fitting it for windows in the hall of the said castle.

After the cancellation of the royal visit, the same keeper's account for 35 weeks from late February 1333 saw negligible expenditure, including

> £2 15s. 1d. for boards, nails, iron and the forging thereof, lime, sand, and other necessaries; £1 3s. 4d. for iron to make 40 pole-hatchets (*polhachetes*), and the making thereof…£3 3s. 10d. wages of a carpenter, mason and workman employed at the castle on divers occasions during the period of the account; 4s. 1d. wages of an armourer in like manner; £5 13s. 6d. wages of a glazier working on divers occasions, and for divers colours bought for making the glass windows in said castle.[414]

These accounts do at least show us that work on the great hall was nearing completion as its new windows were being installed – complete with stained glass elements. But the purchase of stone suggests that other building work was ongoing. In 1334, works to 'repairs of walls, houses and other necessary things in the castle' were undertaken,[415] which included 'timber, carriage of the same, boards, nails, lime, clay, sand, tiles and iron, and the making of the same…wages of carpenters working in the castle and in the repair of the mill',[416] though it was reported in the following year that further funds were spent on 'repair of certain buildings there which were threatened with ruin because of their age'.[417]

This small-scale patch-up of 'houses, towers, and walls' continued in 1336 and for the next twenty-five years or so[418] during which time the accounts regularly refer to the purchase of boards (*assera, bordys*), shingles (*cindules*), stone, iron, lead, and so on and their carriage to the castle, and wages of masons, carpenters, tilers, and the like,[419] and we occasionally hear of the specific buildings under repair, such as in 1350–52, when defects in 'walls and towers and the chapel and other buildings within the castle' were addressed.[420] Typically, in this period, about £40 per annum was spent, the amount, however, declining as the years passed.[421]

The south-west tower and the de Berminghams

It was probably during this period that the south-west corner tower became known as the Bermingham Tower. The first mention of it under that name ('Bermyngehamestour') occurs in an official document dating from 1412 issued by the deputy lieutenant,[422] and we may take it therefore that the name had become common currency by that stage. We do not know how it acquired the name. Even the sixteenth-century Dublin writer, Richard Stanihurst, did not know, saying of the castle that it

hath beside the gate house foure goodlie and substantiall towers, of which one of them is named Bermingham his tower, whether it were that one of the Berminghams did inlarge the building thereof, or else that he was long in duresse in that tower.[423]

In other words, Stanihurst suggests two possible origins for the name: that somebody called Bermingham improved the tower or was imprisoned in it. If the latter, the obvious occasion – as Walter Harris seems to have been the first to speculate[424] – is in 1332 when the lord of Carbury, William de Bermingham, and his son Walter, were incarcerated in an unnamed tower of Dublin Castle, then accused of attempting to escape and, in William's case, hanged.[425] The execution caused quite a furore, the Dominican annals of Dublin – which admittedly have a strong de Bermingham bias[426] – containing a remarkable lament for the dead lord, 'a noble knight, among a thousand thousand knights the most noble in knightly works and the best. Oh! Oh! For shame he who, hearing of his death, could hold back tears'.[427]

Still, it would seem less likely that official sources would perpetuate the memory of a hanged rebel than one of their own and, on balance therefore, Stanihurst's other suggestion is perhaps preferable: that the Bermingham Tower acquired its name because of an association with a minister of the Crown (in the same way that the seventeenth-century Cork Tower received its name from the earl of Cork who oversaw its construction in his capacity as Lord Justice). If so, there are only two possibilities. The William de Bermingham executed in 1332 had, as noted above, been imprisoned in the castle of Dublin along with his son Walter. Walter managed to avoid sentence of death on a technicality, was subsequently restored to favour, and ended up serving as the king's justiciar for most of the period from May 1346 until October 1349. Perhaps it was he who refurbished the south-west tower – or, for example, moved his living quarters into it – so that the new-look tower became associated with him in some way (all the more so if he had earlier been a prisoner in that very location). The difficulty with this suggestion is that surviving accounts of expenditure on the castle indicate no great outlay for construction work around the time of his justiciarship.

On the other hand, Walter had an uncle, John de Bermingham (d. 1329) – the man who defeated and killed Edward Bruce at the battle of Faughart in 1318, being created earl of Louth in its aftermath – who was justiciar of Ireland from 1321 to 1324. Perhaps it was he who authorised (or got the credit for authorising) the rebuilding or re-edification of the south-west tower, if such occurred. Between the major expenditure on the castle in 1285 and a renewed programme of investment beginning in the early 1360s, by far the greatest amounts spent on the castle of Dublin were disbursed in the 1320s. John de Bermingham was appointed justiciar on 21 May 1321 and had taken up office before the end of the summer. The previous autumn, separate payments were authorised amounting to £700 for 'repairs in the castle' and 'for carrying out the said works and repairing the great hall': this was almost a third of the entire annual revenue of the Irish exchequer for that year.[428] And, as we have seen, substantial sums continued to be spent, tailing off after the expenditure of £342 in 1326.[429]

Since John de Bermingham was the man in charge for much of this period of largesse, one could well imagine his name becoming linked in popular memory to the improvements introduced. If that is the case, de Bermingham is a considerable figure in the history of the medieval castle of Dublin. It was to be a full quarter of a millennium before any one named individual would again become so closely associated with an infrastructural development there, that man being the great Elizabethan lord deputy, Sir Henry Sidney.

Chapter 1.3
The Late-medieval Castle: Decline and Rebirth

The plague-ridden and war-torn English colony in Ireland in the 1350s did not present an auspicious environment for investment in the castle of Dublin. It was only with the appointment as lieutenant in 1361 of King Edward III's younger son, Lionel of Antwerp (who was earl of Ulster in right of his wife and later duke of Clarence (Fig. 1.14)), that the outlook changed, temporarily.

The lieutenancy of Lionel

In 1362–4, the clerk of works at the castle received 'for building and repairing of houses and other works in the castle and exchequer', £267; in 1364–5, £185; and in 1365–6, £74.[430] Some interesting details of the expenditure survive. In May 1361 the clerk of works was reimbursed for £42 0s. 10d. spent on, among other things,

wages for masons (*cementariorum*) and carpenters (*carpentariorum*) and other workers and also on timber, boards, shingles, gutters and nails (*in maeremio, bordis, cindulis, gotteris et clavis*) purchased for divers works done there and in stock; and for the transport of the said timber, boards, gutters and nails; and for iron bought for twists, bars, hooks, hinges, spikings, large nails (*twystes, barres, hokes, genell, spykynges, magnos clavos*) and various other items needed; and for the wages of the smiths who worked the iron; and for two iron pickaxes (*pro duobus pykis de ferro*) newly made, and for tin bought to solder divers gutters there mended (*in stangno empto pro soudeare ad diversa gottera ibidem emendenda*); and for the wages of a plumber for making and repairing said gutters with lead from the stores (*in stipendis unius plumbarii pro eisdem gotteris faciendis et reparandis de plumbo de stauro*); and for lime, sand and clay (*in calce, sabalono et argillo*) bought for making and repairing various things from 1 April [1358]…to 10 March [1361]…[431]

Fig. 1.14 Duke of Clarence, Westminster Abbey. (Bridgeman)

These repairs were no doubt done in anticipation of Lionel's arrival and – although we have no proof one way or the other – we must assume that he lived in the castle while resident in Dublin. The most detailed account of expenditure at the castle during his lieutenancy – indeed the most detailed to date – comes from 9 March 1364 and records payments made to John Scrope, the keeper of works there, including

£118 8s. 8d. for wages of masons, carpenters, roofers and tilers (*pannatorum et tegulatorum*) for the repairing of the great hall, little and great chamber, little chapel, kitchen, scullery, bake-house, and of divers towers of houses within said castle (*ad diversa opera tam magne aule quam parve ac magne camere, parve capelle, coquine, scutillarii, pistrine ac diversarum turrium domorum infra dictum castrum reparanda*) and for a certain new chamber and a closet attached to it and a cellar under this (*nova camera et closetta dicte camere annexa et celario sub eisdem*) and for a certain house beside the bake-house, newly built (*quadam domo iuxta pistrinam de novo edificata*), and also for a certain closet attached to the little chapel (*quadam closetta parve capelle annexa*) by order of Lionel, earl of Ulster, our lieutenant in Ireland and...for other houses of said castle along with the common latrine of the said castle (*communi latrina*)...

And £133 12s. 3½d. which said clerk spent for timber, boards, nails, ropes, and one cable for said works, and their portage, and for purchase of iron for various bars, twists, hooks, great spikings, hinges, hasps, staples...and for great locks and other locks for various doors...and for stone, lime, sand, slates, slate-pins (*sclatpinnis*) and tin...and for carriage of sand and clay for those works and for burning a certain limekiln (*in combustione cuiusdam toralis calcis*) for those works...

And 118s. 9d. which said clerk spent in wages of glaziers (*vitriatorum*) and other workers and for other necessities bought and provided for the glass of the gable of the great hall and for the windows of the little hall, great chamber, and little chapel (*ad opera vitri gabule magne aule et pro fenestris parve aule, magne camere et parve capelle*) and also for windows in the new chamber and closet being newly made with glass from the castle stores (*pro fenestris in nova camera et closetta de vitro stauri castri predicti de novo faciendis*)...

And £6 15s. by our precept for timber, boards, nails, slates, and slate-pins for repair of a certain hospice of the earl of March nearby the castle of Dublin beside the Dam Gate (*pro reparacione cuiusdam hospicii quod fuit comitis Marchie prope castrum Dublinie iuxta portam del Dam*)...

And 5s. 10d. which said clerk spent on buying eleven ash-trees (*fraxinis*) from Nicholas de Bekenesfeld, escheator of Ireland, from a certain garden in the suburb of Dublin beside the church of St Michael del Polle which was William Alisaundre's, for hewing-stocks (*hewyngstockes*, i.e. chopping-blocks) for various works both in the castle of Dublin and the exchequer...

And £30 14s. ½d. spent by said clerk on wages of carpenters and other workers for making a certain wooden castle and wooden paling and a barge (*pro quodam castro ligneo et quodam pale ligneo et pro quadam bargia*) by order of our lieutenant, and for timber, boards, nails, spikings, roofnails, hatch-nails (*rofnaillis, hachnaillis*) for iron for twists and hooks for the rudder of said barge (*le rothr' dicte bargie*) and for buying other necessities for said works, and for iron and steel (*in ferro et calibe*) for axes and bills (*pro securibus et billis*)...

And for wages of various other workers for knocking down a certain house in the middle of the castle of Dublin called the Leaden-hutch (*pro quadam domo in medio castri Dublinie que vocabatur le Ledenhuche prostrinenda*)...and for various other supplies for the garden of said castle (*pro aliis diversis necessariis in gardino eiusdem castri*) and for making and repairing divers lawns there (*diversis herbariis ibidem faciendis et reparandis*)...[432]

This 1364 account reveals details to works done to a number of buildings and rooms in the castle of whose existence we were previously aware – the great hall, kitchen, scullery, and bake-house – but there are new premises mentioned and some interesting insights into others.

The *Ledenhuche* demolished in the middle of the castle seems to have been a hutch or hut made of lead, or perhaps a facility used for leadwork – for instance, when preparing lead for use in glassmaking or for guttering.

Instead of referring to the castle chapel, the 1364 account mentions on three separate occasions a 'little chapel' which surely presupposes the existence of a 'great' chapel. The earliest reference to a chapel in the castle seems to be that of 1225 wherein King Henry III appointed William de Radeclive as his chaplain there, receiving a yearly allowance of 50s. for his maintenance, along with a benefice of the value of 100s.; William was still ministering in the chapel thirteen years later (though he was yet to receive his benefice).[433] Minor repairs to the chapel were undertaken in 1234–5[434] and, in 1242, at a time when Henry was still contemplating an Irish expedition and urging completion of his great hall at Dublin, the king instructed his treasurer of Ireland to 'cause the glass windows for the chapel of the king's castle of Dublin to be made'.[435]

Two years earlier, King Henry had ordered that

the feast of St Edward [the Confessor, i.e., 5 January],
on the eve of the Lord's Epiphany, be celebrated with
800 lighted tapers made for that purpose, as well in
our chapel of the same saint in our castle of Dublin
as in the church of St Thomas the Martyr and the
church of the Holy Trinity [at Christ Church].[436]

It is clear from this that the castle chapel was dedicated
to St Edward, and in 1242 the king ordered that 'divine
service of St Edward and of the Blessed Virgin shall be daily
celebrated in the chapel, and on all Sabbath days mass shall
be solemnised there with fifteen, and on other days, with
four wax tapers'.[437] Yet in 1361 the clerk of works at the castle
was reimbursed for

£22 8s. 6d. which he spent on 600lbs of glass for
glazing (vitri…vitriandis) the windows of the chapel
in the castle; and on buckram, cloth, and linen of
various colours, and thread (in bokerame, pannis, lineis,
diversi coloris, et filo), bought for two new chasubles,
a cope, two tunicles with stoles, maniples, amices,
albs and one surplice (pro duobus robis chesible, una
capa, duabus tunykes cum stolis, fauonys, amytis, aubes, ac
uno supellicio); and for repairing one old chasuble and
making and repairing divers other ornaments in
the chapel; and also for repairing one chalice with
gold plate (unius calicis cum patena deauranda) and for
the making and painting a small crucifix for the
chapel and for painting the large crucifix and the
images of Mary and John and the image of Blessed
Mary with its tabernacle, and for making a stand to
carry the tabernacle of St Thomas the Martyr, patron
of the chapel; and for buying a tabernacle for same
and making and repairing and painting pillars and
keys for it; and in payment for one small bell and
one brass pyx (in uno pixide de laton) to hold the Body
of Christ…[438]

These expenses were in connection with a chapel dedicated,
not to St Edward the Confessor, but to Thomas Becket. There
are no earlier references to this chapel of St Thomas at the
castle but there is at least one later one in 1388.[439] It has been
suggested that the chapel's original dedication had been
changed.[440] However, the references in the 1364 accounts to
repairs of the 'little chapel' suggest that it was the original St
Edward's chapel, that it was small and considered unworthy
for use during the lieutenancy (and residence in the castle)
of the king's son, Lionel of Antwerp, and that in preparation
for the latter a new chapel dedicated to St Thomas was
constructed. The presence of two contemporary chapels
at the castle is in fact confirmed by accounts dating from

Lionel's lieutenancy which specifically refer to les deux
chapelles du dit chastel.[441]

This much is suggested by the extraordinary amount of
glass purchased for St Thomas's chapel. Dean Lawlor, in his
excellent essay on the chapel, calculated that 600lbs (272kg)
of glass would have covered a surface of about 200 ft (70m),
enough to glaze nine lancets each measuring 9ft (2.7m) x
2½ft (0.76m). He argues that this amount of glass 'could
hardly have been needed for ordinary repairs in a small
chapel',[442] and – although it is not a conclusion he reached
– it does rather suggest we are talking about the glazing of
a newly built chapel, presumably therefore a superior one
intended largely to supersede the original chapel of St
Edward, the 'little chapel', repairs to which were recorded in
the 1364 accounts.

In this regard we may note the curious fact that accounts
for the period 1364–6 record the payment of wages of three
men employed in the houses elsewhere in the city where
the exchequer met, in 'dismantling divers great cases for
our books and putting them in the chapel of the castle of
Dublin and likewise repairing and assembling said cases in
the aforesaid chapel (pro diversis magnis hustengis disjungendis
pro libris nostris in capella Castri Dublin imponendis, necnon ad
predicta hustenga in capella predicta reparanda et jungenda)'; others
were paid for carriage of the books and bookcases from the
exchequer to the castle.[443] For a time, therefore, in the 1360s,
a chapel in the castle of Dublin was fitted out to store the
books of the Irish exchequer. This is hardly in keeping with
the heavy investment at that very point in the ecclesiastical
fittings of St Thomas's chapel there. The conclusion seems
to be that, now that the castle was graced with this fine place
of worship, its perhaps dilapidated predecessor, the chapel
of St Edward, could be spared for more profane purposes.

The accounts for 1364–6 also refer to both a great hall
and a little hall. The location of the great hall is beyond
doubt, as previously discussed. The little hall may be the
'south hall' repaired, along with the great hall, in 1566,[444]
which another contemporary account appears to refer to as
the 'old hall'.[445] And if it lay at the south end of the castle it
is probably that depicted on the 1673 plan (Fig. 1.12), on the
south curtain wall midway between the Bermingham Tower
and the Middle Tower. This much seems to be confirmed by
the survey of the castle towers and walls commissioned by
Perrot in 1585, which states that 'the castle wall is weakest in
the south side, by the means of the hall windowes'.[446] Robert
Ware's 1678 account also records two halls, and states that (if
one were inside the castle facing the south curtain) 'on the
right hand are the [little] Hall, on the ground, the kitchen
and other places belonging to the offices below staires,
reaching as farre as Berminghams Tower'.[447]

The 1364 account also refers to repairs to 'the great
chamber (ac magne camera)' and glass-work 'for the windows
of the…great chamber (pro fenestris…magne camera)', and it

is clear from the way it is listed separately from the great hall that this chamber stood distinct from the hall. But in addition to an existing great chamber, the account refers to the construction of 'a certain new chamber and a closet attached to it and a cellar under this (*pro quadam nova camera et closetta dicte camere annexa et celario sub eisdem*)' and glass 'for windows in the new chamber and closet being newly made (*pro fenestris in nova camera et closetta…de novo faciendis*)'. Where these chambers were is a matter of speculation. The great chamber was not new – it was, after all, undergoing repair – and it may in fact always have been a feature of the post-1204 castle; back in 1240 King Henry III had ordered that 'our chamber in our said castle be panelled (*cameram nostrum in castro predicto lambruscari faciatis*)'.[448] And we have earlier seen reference to 'the oriel between the chamber of the justiciar and the chapel'[449] which, it was suggested above, is the forerunner to the 'chamber of presence, the Lobbies,

and the chambers thereunto appertaining' mentioned by Robert Ware in 1678, part of what he describes as 'an ancient structure…thought to want reparation or rebuilding'.[450] If so, the 'great chamber' mentioned in 1364 was located on the south curtain wall of the castle abutting its Middle Tower.

If that is the case, the 'new chamber and a closet attached to it and a cellar under this' mentioned in 1364 is perhaps that building which appears regularly from this point onwards under the name 'council chamber'. In 1421, for instance (after the exchequer had been relocated to the castle), we read that

in the chamber of the council near the exchequer called *le counsel chaumbre*, a discussion took place between the lieutenant and council as to how the great hall within Dublin Castle stands in need of a lead roof (*tectura plumbea*) and repairs.[451]

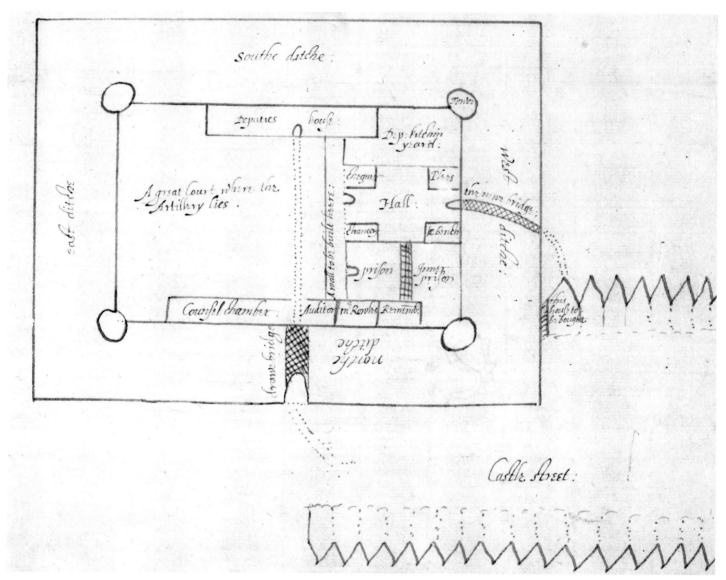

Fig. 1.15 Wattson's plan of Dublin Castle 1606. (NLI, MS 2656 (18))

The Council Chamber is indicated on Wattson's 1606 plan of the castle (Fig. 1.15) as being immediately on one's left as one entered the main gate, of which Robert Ware remarked in 1678 that a visitor to the castle

> may behold, on the right hand as hee goes out of ye Pallace, the place of the Council chamber, and what other roomes belonged thereunto, of late converted into an appartment for the Lodging of such persons of the Chief Governours household as are consigned thereunto.[452]

The 1673 plan therefore, in depicting the chamber, calls it the 'Lord Lieutenants Lodgins' and has immediately west of it, directly behind the right gate tower of the castle, a 'closet' (Fig. 1.12) and presumably this is the 'closet attached to said chamber (*closetta dicte camere annexa*)' mentioned in the 1364 account.

The latter is also one of the first accounts to refer to the castle gardens. There is a reference in 1248 to

> 40 librates of land beside Dublin which is not built upon (*juxta Dublin' in terra plana*), which the justiciar prefers to retain in the king's hand as well situated regarding the castle of Dublin (*bene sedentem castro regis Dublin'*)…[to be kept] as demesne of the king henceforth belonging to the king's castle of Dublin (*sicut dominico regis quod decetero pertineat ad predictum castrum regis Dublin'*),[453]

which may explain the origin of the later gardens. We hear of them again in 1308 in a deed of a certain Walter de Rypun granting

> a messuage with buildings and a garden in the suburbs of Dublin in Schepes-strete [Ship Street Great]…the garden extends…in width between the meadow of Dublin Castle (*pratum castri Dublin*) to the north and the land of Roger de Assheburne to the south.[454]

We also find that in 1434, at a time when Hugh Corryngham was clerk of works at the castle, his relative John Corryngham who had earlier held the role – along with the grand-sounding 'office of keeper of the king's palace within Dublin Castle (*officium custodis palacii regis infra castro Dubl'*)'[455] – was granted

> custody of a garden lying on the southern part of Dublin Castle (*ex parte australi castri Dubl'*), between the said castle and the orchard (*pomarium*) that previously belonged to John Passavaunt…and also custody of another garden, lying between the castle

> and the said garden, blocked off (*clausi*) in the last year past by the same John Corryngham for the safety of the foundations of the towers (*pro salvacione fundamentorum turrium*) of that castle.[456]

Another source refers to this or a connected grant to the same John as being of 'a parcel of land near Dublin Castle lying between Bermingham Tower and the South Tower, alias *le Privee Toure*'.[457] The latter may be the Middle Tower on the south curtain wall, and presumably therefore these gardens assigned to John Corryngham lay immediately south of this – though it is a mystery why none of these accounts refer to the Poddle in this location – being part of a collection of gardens here attached to the castle. Presumably he had walled off one of them to prevent erosion – or deliberate undermining – of the foundations of the Bermingham Tower and Middle Tower.

Corryngham had been acquiring lands around the castle for many years (and perhaps lived in the house known as Corryngham's Inns on Castle Street).[458] In 1421, he received from the deputy lieutenant a grant for life of lands described as

> a certain parcel (*parcellam*) of land, at present of no value and waste, below (*subtus*) Dublin Castle, called le Casteldyche, which in width extends between the castle to the east to a certain parcel of land to the west called la Shepeslane [now, Castle Steps], which John [Corryngham] and one John Bernard occupy; and in length between the same castle to the south up to the highway called la Castelstrete [Castle Street] to the north; and from the bridge of that castle up to the city wall (*ad murum civitatis*) adjacent to a certain tower of that castle called Bermyngehamestour.[459]

This grant of the ditch outside the castle's west curtain wall, and north curtain wall as far as the gate, makes no mention of the ditch being water-filled and hence we can assume that the arches in the city wall just west of the Bermingham Tower and north of the Powder Tower – which allowed for the diversion of the Poddle to provide a moat – had been blocked up at this stage, as excavation revealed.[460] The probability is that it was at least partly grassed over and encroached upon (perhaps only the inner part remaining as a much narrower and shallower channel) by individuals like Corryngham who wanted it for rough grazing to add to his other gardens to the south.

Perrot's survey of 1585 mentions a 'gardin dore'[461] which is probably the southern postern to Ship Street discussed by Robert Ware in 1678. If so, we can probably assume that the gardens granted to John Corryngham were in the same location as the castle gardens mentioned in the 1364 accounts as having had 'divers lawns made and repaired (*diversis herbariis ibidem faciendis et reparandis*)'.[462] King Edward III said of his son Lionel that he 'had caused to be made divers works agreeable to him, for sports and his other pleasures, as well within that castle of Dublin as elsewhere'[463] and perhaps it was in connection with, for instance, a tournament held in the castle gardens skirting the Poddle in this location that he ordered the construction of the 'wooden castle and wooden paling and a barge (*pro quodam castro ligneo et quodam pale ligneo et pro quadam bargia*)' we hear about in the accounts.

The Carlow hiatus
Before Lionel left Ireland he authorised one further set of payments in relation to Dublin Castle which included

divers works of the little hall and great chamber, the little closet beside the chapel, divers chambers, doors and windows, and of the drawbridge of said castle, and new building works of the cellar of the bake-house, the house of the goldsmith, and the covering of the great tower (*ad diversa opera tam parve aule et magne camere, parve closette, juxta capellam, diversarum camerarum, hostiorum, et fenestrarum ac pontis jactabilis dicti Castri; de novo construendo operarum, selarum pistrine, domus aurifabri et magne turris cooperiendo*).[464]

Apart from the goldsmith's house (whose location is unknown), we have come across these structures before, although it is rare indeed for any one tower to be singled out as the 'great tower'. Rather, in the way that it dwarfs everything else in, say, Charles Brooking's 1728 illustration of the castle (Fig. 1.20), we might perhaps conclude that the Bermingham Tower was what was intended. The latter's exceptional status is suggested by a letter of 1552 which mentions that 'there is no place certain or convenient for the safe guard of the king's majesty's records and muniments of his highness's chancery of this his grace's realm of Ireland, other than the tower within his majesty's castle of Dublin'.[465] It would seem therefore that Lionel reroofed the Bermingham Tower in 1366.

In general, Lionel's lieutenancy can be said to have secured vital new expenditure on the infrastructure after a period of neglect in the depressed decades that preceded his arrival. But he made one crucial decision that profoundly affected the status of the castle of Dublin. Before he left Ireland it was decided to transfer the seat of government to Carlow.[466] The view was that since the government's great preoccupation had become the assertion of royal control over the Irish of south Leinster, a government headquartered in Carlow would be better placed to control the vital Barrow valley. Hence, by the early 1360s, expenditure on Carlow Castle was beginning to take precedence over that on Dublin Castle.[467]

Neglect of Dublin Castle continued for as long as government officials and institutions remained at Carlow, including the exchequer and some of the courts of justice. Thus we hear in 1380 that

Dublin castle is ruined and devastated and in many places greatly undermined because of the negligence of the king's ministers who ought to attend to repairs, so that the king's cousin, Edmund Mortimer, earl of March and Ulster, the lieutenant, cannot hold a great council intended for the eve of SS Simon and Jude [27 October 1380] in that castle, nor can a parliament be held on the morrow of All Souls [2 November 1380] at Dublin, nor can the rolls and records be safely kept there for their protection, as is customary, to the king's great disgrace and detriment.[468]

This pessimistic portrayal of the status of the castle indicates that the Council Chamber – where the great council of ministers, presided over by the lieutenant, would have met – was in a state of disrepair and presumably too the great hall if that is where parliament would have been held, and also one or more of the towers, if that is where the rolls and records of government were being stored. But the response was negligible. The clerk of works was authorised to spend £20 for 'speedy and suitable repairs to the said castle', and similar sums followed: in 1386–8, £36 4s. 9d. was spent and, in 1391–3, £27 19s. 6d. was sanctioned for 'the repair of buildings and houses of Dublin Castle and for making various necessary items within the castle'.[469] These are hardly likely to have had much impact.

Richard II in Dublin
Only after King Richard II (Fig. 1.16) had been to Ireland himself in 1394–5 and seen the state of the castle at first hand did matters improve, all the more so once he had determined upon returning to the country, as happened in 1399. In the meantime, the king had abandoned the experiment of moving some central government institutions to Carlow, and this too refocused minds on the state of Dublin Castle. It is noticeable that when in 1395 Alexander Balscot was appointed chancellor – an office second only to chief governor in rank – the terms of his patent required him to be resident in Dublin, whereas hitherto this had been an itinerant office: evidently, Richard's policy was to reassert Dublin's importance, and hence the castle's importance.[470]

In April 1396, John Inglewood and John Blythe were commissioned to buy

for the repair of Dublin Castle and the hall and the buildings therein, stone, timber, tiles, lead and nails, and to arrest carpenters, masons, plumbers and other workmen thereof, and carriage for the

Fig. 1.16 Richard II. (Bridgeman)

same, in England, Wales and Ireland, at the king's charges. They are to take two each of the better sort of carpenters, masons and plumbers to Ireland, and set them to work at the king's wages, and to arrest ships and mariners for the purpose, and have power to imprison contrariants,[471]

which rather suggests a lack of faith in the capacity of Irish workmen to carry out the necessary tasks. A document sent to the king from Ireland in 1397 had a long list of proposals to improve the state of the country, but topping the list

was the recommendation that, since the archbishopric of Dublin was vacant, King Richard should divert its income for the time being to 'the repair of the great hall within the king's castle of Dublin'.[472] So, the king sent the deputy treasurer John Melton to Ireland 'for the hall and other things in his castle of Dublin (*pur la sale et autres coses en soun chastel de Divelyn*)' and wrote to the lieutenant, the earl of Kildare, the mayor of Dublin and the clerk of works at the castle asking them to help Melton 'in the repair of the said hall (*a la faisance de la dite sale*)'.[473]

In February 1398, the king sent another of his favourite clerks, Master Richard Maudeleyn, to Ireland and issued £100 to him 'for the reparation and amendment of the defects of the houses and other buildings within the castle of Dublin, in Ireland, against the arrival of the lord the king in the land aforesaid'.[474] Around the same time, another source records £280 being sent from England to be spent on the works in the castle.[475] This English subsidization of the castle works was a new departure, but the account spells out the purpose: it was to be spent specifically on the repair of those premises in the castle that would be needed during the king's forthcoming residence there.[476] Evidently, Richard liked his comforts – there is considerable evidence of other building projects and work on royal residences which he commissioned[477] – and these had to be put in place.

The fifteenth-century castle

Unfortunately for Richard, his arrival in Ireland in May 1399 was followed within weeks by the invasion of England by his cousin Henry Bolingbroke, a coup which saw Richard abandon his plans for Ireland and return home to face deposition and death. Even after Richard's shambolic departure from Ireland there was some commitment to maintain the progress of the works programme at Dublin Castle: it was ordered that 150 marks of the king's gold be delivered by one John Warre to the constable of Dublin, for the works of the castle.[478] But things dried up again then. One fleeting intervention, in 1407, occurred following a meeting in the Council Chamber of the lieutenant and council, which heard how the great hall of the castle 'was ruinous and greatly needs roofing with lead and repairing', £20 being granted for that purpose.[479]

The exchequer, following its relocation to Dublin from Carlow, was now housed within the castle. It had always had its own chapel and therefore such a premises was now required within Dublin Castle. The castle may, therefore, have had three distinct chapels at one stage – the early chapel dedicated to St Edward the Confessor (though this may ultimately have become defunct), Lionel of Antwerp's chapel of St Thomas the Martyr, and now the relocated chantry chapel of the Irish exchequer. Dean Lawlor argued against this (and in favour of the idea that only one chapel served both the castle and the exchequer) on the basis of a mention *c.* 1339 that

The custos of the stores [in the castle] owes an account of £2 received from the mayor and bailiffs for silken stuff, cendal, linen cloth and other necessaries for making two standards with the king's arms and two pairs of vestments for the chapel of the king in the castle and of the exchequer there,

but he concedes that another record of this same item refers to 'the *chapels* of the king in the castle and the exchequer there',[480] and, in any event, the gift by the mayor and bailiffs of two royal standards, and two pairs of vestments does rather compel us to think in terms of two separate chapels. Hence we find that, in 1413, repairs of the chantry and court of the exchequer were sanctioned along with payment of 44s. 4d. to the Carmelites, 'for celebrating service in the chantry of the exchequer, in part payment of their fee of 100s.', plus supplies for its altar.[481] This chantry chapel within the exchequer must surely be distinguishable from the king's chapel of St Thomas the Martyr. The latter in turn (as we have seen) was not the same as the 'small' chapel of St Edward the Confessor; but the fact that in 1339 the mayor and bailiffs gifted only one royal standard and one set of vestments for the king's chapel at the castle would seem to indicate that one of the two royal chapels was now out of use.

These same 1413 accounts also note funds spent on 'rebuilding and covering a ruinous tower of the castle of Dublin'[482] and it was in connection with these works that, in the following year, John Liverpool, the constable of Wicklow Castle, was appointed to

take and arrest...all planks [etc.] for covering and repairing buildings within Dublin castle, and also fuel, wherever these can be found within the town of Wicklow or elsewhere...and also ships and boats within the port of that town for carrying the planks and fuel to that castle, paying reasonably for the same by the king's money',[483]

while the clerks of works were instructed

to arrest all masons, carpenters, roofers and other necessary and sufficient workers for the repair and construction of buildings within the castle of Dublin, and also to take, purvey and arrest timber, planks and wood necessary for those repairs, wherever they can be found, both inside and outside liberties, paying reasonably for this by the king's money.[484]

This pressganging of workers and purveyance of supplies was a kind of buy-now-pay-later approach because the funds available for these tasks were derisory. Eight pounds were delivered to the clerk in 1420 for repair of buildings, and

a further £1 19s. 2d. later that year.[485] Even work required 'for roofing and repair of the great hall in Dublin Castle' in 1421–2 had a budget of £8 and the lieutenant himself stood over a payment of £10 for 'repair of the castle and chambers of the castle' in 1424–6.[486] How pathetic to read that, in December 1428,

a discussion took place between Sir John Grey, lieutenant of Ireland, and the council as to how the hall within Dublin Castle, and its windows, were ruined; and that there is in the treasury a certain ancient silver seal, which has been cancelled. It was ordained that the seal should be broken and placed on sale, and the money arising from this should be paid to John Corryngham, to be expended upon the repair of the said hall and windows.[487]

It appears one cannot underestimate the piteous state of the castle at this point. We read that, in the autumn of 1430,

a discussion took place between Richard [Talbot], the lord king's justiciar of Ireland, archbishop of Dublin, and the council of the lord king in that land as to how the king's castle of Dublin, the great hall and other buildings (*ac magna aula et alia edificia*) of the same, in which the books and records of the chancery, both benches and the exchequer are kept, are ruinous and stand in great need of repair; and that for lack of repair of the halls, towers and other buildings (*pro defectu reparacionis aulas, turrium, et edificiorum predictorum*), the books and records will be much damaged by rain and storms and thereby greater detriment would ensue to the king and his subjects unless a remedy is immediately provided. It was agreed that twenty marks a year out of the rents in Ireland should be expended upon those repairs by the advice of the treasurer of Ireland for the time being; and that John Corryngham should have twenty marks for the next ensuing year, paid at the exchequer, for the repairs, rendering an account thereof to the barons of the exchequer.[488]

Twenty marks amounts to a little over £13. If it really was the case that the buildings of the castle were ruinous (*ruinosa*), and so open to the effects of the rain and wind that the very records of government were in danger of being destroyed, the response to the crisis was deplorable. Corryngham received his 20 marks in 1431 and 1432, though this rose to £20 for 1433 and 1434 while, in 1435, the largest sum in a generation was spent: Corryngham was given £79 2s., although the account states that 'the tower at the entrance to the castle has not been repaired or built'.[489]

This would seem to indicate that the 'ruinous tower' mentioned back in 1413 was one of the gate towers, though it was to remain in need of work more than twenty years later. Giles Thorndon was appointed constable in 1435, and in 1442 he wrote to the king and council in England to the effect that

Item, lyke it you to understonde that the grete frostes and weders that han been thise iij. yere han so empeyred and hurte the walles of the castels of Develyn and Wygelowe [Wicklow] which woll drawen to ryght grete and notable sommes lesse than they been the souner reperailled and amended,[490]

that is to say that bad weather over the previous three years had adversely affected the state of the castle walls which were in urgent need of maintenance. Thorndon had become treasurer of Ireland himself in 1437 and hence there may have been a more favourable ear turned to requests for increased spending, as, in each of 1438 and 1439, £40 was authorised to be spent on the castle's repair.[491] But we hear nothing of the precise detail and, in any event, it was of little lasting effect.

Eventually, in 1462, parliament considered the issue

…at the request of the Commons of the land of Ireland. [Namely,] that whereas the castle of the king, our sovereign lord, of his city of Dublin, in which the courts of the said sovereign are held, is ruinous and like to fall, to the great dishonour of our said sovereign lord.

Whereupon the premises considered: It is ordained by authority of the said Parliament, that 40s. yearly be taken and received of the issues and profits of the Hanaper of our said lord, of his chancery of Ireland; and 40s. yearly be received of the issues and profits of the Chief Place [court of king's bench], and 40s. yearly to be received of the issues and profits of his Common Place [court of common pleas]; and £3 yearly to be received of the issues and profits of his exchequer in the said land; and 20s. yearly to be received of the issues and profits of the master of the mint for the time being, and the same to be delivered yearly to the clerk of the works of the said castle for the time being. And that he account yearly before the barons of the exchequer of the king in Ireland according to the ancient form, and that all the leads of the aisles of the hall of the said castle be sold by the treasurer of Ireland, to make and repair the said hall.[492]

This decree of parliament (which has been previously noted) indicates the depth to which the affairs of the castle had sunk by this stage. The sum total of parliament's solution to the problem of this, the most prestigious royal castle in Ireland – now 'ruinous and like to fall' – was an annual grant of £10 in total out of the issues of the four courts of chancery, exchequer, king's bench and common pleas, and of the mint which was, like them, based in that very castle. And as to its solution for the deficiencies of the great hall – the very building in which parliament was intended to meet when it sat in Dublin – that was to strip the lead from its side aisles, sell it off, and, presumably, patch up the main roof with the proceeds.

It would seem extraordinary that such modest provision would itself go unspent, but parliament was to return to the matter in 1475, at which point it was reported that the monies intended

for the maintenance and repair of his [the king's] castle of Dublin…are not made accordingly by reason of divers assignments made to divers persons to the great dishonour of the king and debasement of the land,[493]

meaning that the annual £10 allocation had been repeatedly spent elsewhere. We have occasional evidence of this. In early 1473, the clerks of the works of the castle – three of them are mentioned, although it is difficult to know how they passed their time given the budget available – received the princely sum of £5 13s. 4d.

in part payment of £10 per annum out of the issues and profits of the hanaper of the Irish chancery, the chief place, the common place, the exchequer and the mint, granted from 15 October 1462, according to the tenor of an act or ordinance made for the repair of Dublin Castle.[494]

Consequently, the 1475 parliament decreed that henceforth sheriffs should hand over the annual allocation to the clerk of works at the castle within three months of it coming into their hands.

The castle and the Geraldines

The government's failure to invest in the castle in this period was all the more remarkable since it was a time of relative prosperity and stability – despite the turmoil in England we call the Wars of the Roses.[495] It had to do with the fact that the administration's limited revenues were spent on putting armies into the field to protect the boundaries of the 'Four Obedient Shires' of the English Pale from Irish attack, so that little was left for infrastructural investment. Disregard for the upkeep of the castle would be a hallmark of Irish life throughout the period of governmental ascendancy exercised by the two great Geraldine earls of Kildare,

Gearóid Mór (1478–1513) and Gearóid Óg (1513–34) (Fig. 1.17). Their exploitation of the castle for their own political purposes was apparent from the start when, in 1478, a Kildare supporter who had been installed as constable of the castle (the prior of Kilmainham, James Keating) refused to hand the castle over to the king's deputy, Lord Grey of Ruthin, and

> fortified the said castle with armed men against the most noble lord Henry lord Grey, deputy lieutenant of Ireland and would not suffer his steward or officers to come into the said castle for his lodging or refreshment of the same, and also broke down the bridge of the said castle for his defence against the said deputy, contrary to his allegiance,

parliament subsequently ordering Keating to 'cause the said bridge to be made and repaired substantially and sufficiently'.[496]

At least Grey had *attempted* to use the castle for his lodging. It is surely significant that when a successor, Sir Richard Edgecombe, came to Dublin in 1488 in the aftermath of the Lambert Simnel crisis, he resided for the whole time he was in Dublin in St Saviour's Dominican priory; and all of the many gatherings of the lords spiritual and temporal of Ireland, and of the mayor and citizens, over which he presided in Dublin – and all of the many feasts at which he 'had right good cheer' – took place in St Thomas's abbey, St Mary's abbey, the priory of All Hallows, the guildhall, Christ Church cathedral and even the church of St Mary del Dam. Not one took place in the castle. In fact, Sir Richard seems only to have entered the castle once, towards the end of his visit, when he

> went into the Castle of Dublyn, and there put in Possession Richard Archiboll, the King's Servaunt, into the Office of the Constable of the seyd Castle, which the Kings Grace had given unto him by his Lettres Patent; from the which Office the said Prior of Kilmainham [James Keating] had wrongfully kept the said Richard by the space of two Yeres and more.[497]

GERALDVS·FILIVS·GERALDI· COMES·
KILDARIE·ÆTATIS·43·A° DNI·1530·

Fig. 1.17 Gearóid Óg Fitzgerald, 9th earl of Kildare. (Courtesy of the duke of Leinster)

It is not in the least surprising, therefore, to find that when, in 1495, Richard Nangle, 'supervisor of the lord king's works within the castle of Dublin (*supervisori operum domini regis infra castrum Dublin*)' was paid 31s. 7d. for these works, in the same year one John Norton received twice that amount, 61s. 2d., 'for certain repairs done by him by mandate of the lord deputy within the castle of Maynooth', the principal residence of the earl of Kildare.[498] Evidently, Kildare was siphoning off funds to improve the living conditions of his own castle while allowing the castle of Dublin to continue on its path of decline. After 1485, we do not hear of expenditure of the annual £10 parliamentary grant towards the castle[499] though this may be only for want of evidence in a period for which financial records are shockingly lacking.

It was not until the famous expedition by Henry VIII's lieutenant in Ireland, Thomas Howard, earl of Surrey (later duke of Norfolk) (Fig. 1.18), that gradual improvement began. Surrey arrived in Ireland in May 1520 and remained for slightly under two years. Most of his letters to King Henry or to Cardinal Wolsey were sent from Dublin, quite a few of which are specifically described as having been 'Scrybbled at Your Graces castell of Dublyn', in which he obviously resided[500] and Stanihurst's contribution to Holinshed's *Chronicles* records an irruption into the Pale by O'More of Laois, news of which came to Surrey while he was 'sate at dynner in the Castle of Dublin'.[501] But the castle was virtually in ruins, it would appear.[502] Surrey's chief administrator, Sir John Stile, was appalled by the state of the records in the castle, writing to Wolsey that the 'Kingis Courtes and recordes [are] ferr oute of order', and requesting that an expert clerk of the exchequer be sent from England 'to overse the Kingis recourdes, and to sorte thaym, and put

Fig. 1.18 Thomas Howard, 3rd duke of Norfolk, earl of Surrey by Hans Holbein. (Royal Collection Windsor Castle)

thaym in order'; he also reported that he had agreed with Surrey at the time of the latter's departure from Ireland in March 1522 that he would undertake 'the reparacions of the Castill of Dublyn'.[503]

When the earl of Kildare was restored as lord deputy, the indenture of agreement between him and Henry VIII, dated 4 August 1524, committed Gearóid Óg – among many other things – to spending

> about the reparacyons of the Kinges castels and manours of Dublyn and Tryme, and other the Kynges castels within this his lande of Irelande, of the rentes and revenues of the Kinges possession of the same lande, the first yere fourty poundes, and yerely fourty markes, durying the tyme of hys Deputacyon.[504]

This initial £40 and 40 marks per annum thereafter – only part of which, after all, was to be spent on Dublin – certainly would not be sufficient to arrest the decay (even if we assume that Kildare was true to his word). Indeed, it is instructive to read in a Dublin chronicle that, Kildare having been sworn in as lord deputy some 200m away from the castle in Christ Church – as appears to have been normal practice – this ceremony was then followed by a great banquet in St Thomas's abbey.[505] Again, the latter may have been normal

practice, but there is no mention of the other conventional stage of the investiture, the presentation of the sword of state[506] in the Council Chamber of the castle, presumably because, at this point, the castle was no fit place for such ceremonies and celebrations.

The result of Geraldine neglect of the castle was laid bare in 1533 when a minor member of the O'Byrne dynasty, Edmund Óg of the Downs, accomplished a feat that no-one since 1170 had managed and that had been beyond even the great Robert the Bruce: he overran the castle. An agent reported back to Thomas Cromwell in London that O'Byrne had gone to war with the Englishry, committing infinite burnings, preys, spoils, and manslaughter, and,

> within these 5 wikes, entrid with force, in the night tyme, in the Kingis Castell of Dublin, whiche is the strongest holde in Irlande, and led with him prisoners, at his pleasur, and cattail; which enterprise hath more discouraged the Kingis subjects there then the lostes of 2000£ of their goodes, insomoche as, nightly sethens [since], great watche is in the Citie of Dublin, fearing that the same shulde be pylferid, prostrate, and distroyde, wherof they never dredid somuche.[507]

It is astonishing to think that Edmund Óg had been able to enter the castle by force – albeit during the night – and almost effortlessly liberate prisoners from the castle gaol and make off with cattle which had presumably been intended to feed the garrison. It was an extraordinary indictment of those charged with the castle's management.

Geraldine contempt for the castle was pushed to its ultimate limit in the following year when Earl Gerald's son, 'Silken' Thomas, famously broke out in rebellion against the Crown. The Dubliner Richard Stanihurst, writing some forty years later, tells us that Thomas's forces were initially permitted by the citizens to enter the city to lay the castle under siege, and his men

> planted néere Preston his innes, right ouer against the castell gate two or three falcons, hauing with such strong rampiers intrenched their companie, as they litle weighed the shot of the castle.[508]

We do not know the precise location of the important building known as Preston's Inns[509] but when it had been acquired by the Preston family in 1359 it was described as being 'a stone messuage with two curtilages [i.e., a stone house with two property plots] in the lane leading from Fishamble Street (*vicus piscatorum*) towards the church of St Mary del Dam'.[510] This is probably the laneway called Copper Alley on de Gomme's 1673 map (Fig. 2.12) running parallel to Castle Street, in which case Preston's Inns may have been just about directly opposite the castle gate (perhaps stretching northwards from the current Dublin City Council Rates Office in Castle Street, across the line of the modern Lord Edward Street). Here, the Geraldine forces placed a few falcons (light cannon) and dug trenches in which their men could stand without being hit by fire from the castle. But nothing of consequence occurred and Thomas's men

> did not all this while batter aught of the castell, but onelie one hole that was bored through the gate with a pellet, which lighted in the mouth of a demie canon, planted within the castell.

It was only when the citizens ceased cooperating with the rebels and forced them outside the walls that a full-scale siege of the city began. The Geraldine army 'indeuored to stop all the springs that flowed vnto the towne, and to cut the pipes of the conduits, whereby they should be destitute of fresh water'. It was at this point that

> they laid siege to the castell in the Shipstreet, from whense they were hastilie by the ordinance feazed, and all the thatcht houses of the street were burnt with wild fire, which maister White deuised, because the enimie should not be there rescued.[511]

It is not quite clear how Dublin Castle could be successfully besieged from Ship Street – since the forces within would continue to enjoy free movement in and out of the main gate to the rest of the intramural town – and it seems that Thomas's intention was rather to bombard the castle walls from his extramural position to the south. In any event, he was the one who ended up being bombarded, the constable, John White, both turning his guns on them and casting inflammable wildfire (or Greek-fire) over the walls at the thatched houses in Ship Street in which the Geraldine army was sheltering, forcing them to beat a retreat.[512]

Although £177 14s. 9d. was spent on repairs to the castle in 1535–6,[513] it is unclear whether this was necessitated by the siege and there is in fact no evidence that Silken Thomas's canon did any damage to the castle walls or towers. In this regard it may be worth mentioning that the woodcut illustration that accompanies the earliest published version of Stanihurst's account, which appeared in Holinshed's *Chronicles* in 1577 – and which has been taken as a sincere attempt to depict it, showing a curtain wall fully breached and a tower near fatally undermined – is worthless for this purpose as precisely the same illustration is reused throughout the volume for sieges of other castles, in other eras and even in other countries.

The beginnings of Tudor reconstruction

The ill-fated siege of Dublin accelerated – if it did not make inevitable – the failure of the Kildare rebellion, which in turn accelerated the pace of new English intervention in Ireland. Part and parcel of the increasing centralization of Tudor policy was a demand for greater scrutiny of government finances and more careful preservation of government records, and these in turn were intended to add to royal revenues. All of these required the restoration of Dublin Castle out of which many of the organs of government operated, where its records were conserved and royal treasure stored. Hence, in 1537, John Alen, the master of the rolls, advised the lord deputy that

> because there is no place so meet to keep the king's treasure as is his grace's castle of Dublin, in the tower called Brymmyniame's Tower, it is convenient that not only the said castle be substantially repaired and fortified, but…where, in times past, the negligent keeping of the king's records hath grown to great losses to His Highness, as well concerning his lands as his laws…it is therefore necessary, that from henceforth all the rolls and muniments to be had be put in good order in the aforesaid tower, and the door thereof to have two locks, and the keys thereof the one to be with the constable, and the other be with the under-treasurer…and that no man be suffered to have loan of any of the said muniments from the said place, nor to search, view, or read any of them there but in the presence of one of the keepers.[514]

What Alen was calling for was nothing short of a public record office, which he envisaged as being located in the Bermingham Tower, which would also be used to store the king's revenues. Development of the Record Office and Treasury would, however, form part of a general investment whereby the entire castle would be, as he put it, 'substantially repaired and fortified'.

It is possible that the Bermingham Tower was indeed refurbished at this point: a document sent to Henry VIII in May 1543 described as 'An estimate of the king's revenues in His Majesty's realm of Ireland', included among the royal expenses, not just the fees and wages of the constable and garrison of Dublin Castle, but a total of £300 spent on repairs of various unnamed castles, much of which no doubt was spent on Dublin.[515] And that the Bermingham Tower was among the recipients of these funds can perhaps be deduced from a letter sent to England by the lord deputy, Sir Anthony St Leger, in May 1545 in which he notes that as Dublin Castle was so long suffered to run to ruin, although for two or three years past great cost has been done upon it, there are yet two or three of the chief towers uncovered for lack of lead, of which there is none here.[516]

Perhaps the Bermingham Tower was one of the *other* 'chief towers' and had recently been reroofed. It seems that St Leger's priority was the roofing of the towers with lead, 'for lack whereof', he had written earlier in 1545, 'a great piece of Dublin Castle may fall'.[517] He had identified a source of lead, namely, the roof of the recently dissolved Cistercian abbey of Basingwerk in Flintshire, and repeatedly wrote to England reminding officials there that the king had issued

a warrant for twenty or thirty fodder [cartloads] of lead, that lieth in the late abbey of Basynwerke in Wales, to be transported hither, as well for the covering of His Highness' castle of Dublin, which is like to be in great peril for lack thereof, as I have divers times written, as also others of His Majesty's castles and houses which are in like peril if brief remedy be not had.[518]

Yet the Bermingham Tower remained vulnerable. In 1552, the then lord deputy, Sir James Croft, wrote that he had been

informed by the lord chancellor and master of the rolls that there is no place certain or convenient for the safe guard of the king's records and muniments of his highness's chancery of this his grace's realm of Ireland, other than the tower within his majesty's castle of Dublin, which is both ruinous and…not a place meet for the daily resort of His Majesty's officers…through which the losses of the said records and muniments, besides other inconveniences, have and may well ensue.[519]

And soon afterwards funds were made available for the improvement of the tower: in the period 1557–8, the substantial sum of £124 5s. 5d. was spent specifically on 'Brymyngham's Tower'.[520]

These same accounts record the payment to the master of the works at the castle of £9 10s. 4d. spent on the construction of 'the master of the ordnance's lodgings'.[521] The office of Master of the Ordnance – with overall responsibility for the provision of military stores, artillery, and small arms, and for the maintenance of fortifications – had developed in England in the fifteenth century. The first recorded Master of the Ordnance in Ireland was Sir John Travers, who appears bearing the title in 1539,[522] shortly after which he was given possession of the now dissolved

St Mary's abbey – about 300m from the castle, directly to the north, across the ford at the modern Grattan (or Capel St) Bridge – which he converted into a storehouse for 'the safe custody there of the lord king's artillery and other munitions of war (*pro artillario et aliis abiliamentis guerre Domini Regis ibidem salvo custodiensis*)'.[523] This suggests that it was not safe to store these items in the castle.

But by 1550 Travers had rectified this deficiency and hence we hear of the payment of funds to

Sir John Travers [who]…hath disbursed certaine somes of money, as well about the edyfyeing of an ordynance howse, situate within the King's Majesty's castell of Dublin, as also for iron and other stuffe requyryd for the furniture of ordnance and munitions for the warres in his charge there,

and in the following year is recorded the appointment of Peter Fourde to 'the office of comptroller and surveyor of the ordnance artificers and workmen, for constructing, maintenance, and reparation of the ordnance, artillery, and stores, within the castle of Dublin'.[524] In this same year, 1551, a smith named John Morgan was given the task of 'working, repayring and mending' the king's ordnance in Ireland, and given a life grant of the office of 'smith of the ordnance', with wages of 12d. a day out of the revenues of Ireland, along with the house built 'for that purpose' within the castle of Dublin.[525] It was probably also Travers who ordered the construction of 'the master of the ordnance's lodgings',[526] though by the time of its completion he had been succeeded by Jacques Wingfield, who by 1560 was also constable of the castle and therefore had his choice of accommodation there.

We do not know the location of the ordnance house or, for that matter, of either the lodgings of the Master of the Ordnance or of the smith of the ordnance. However, we can roughly estimate where the latter house was as, sixteen years later, when Lord Deputy Sidney built a new chief governor's house inside the castle, abutting the central stretch of the south curtain, the smith John Morgan was given £29 13s. 4d. 'in recompense of his house anixed to the L[ord] Deputies lodging in the castell'.[527] Neither do we know the precise location of the mint within the castle although it too received attention in this period. Upon his accession in 1547, Edward VI resumed the coinage of money at Dublin, and ordered

the under-treasurer, controller, surveyor, assay-master, and other principal officers of the mint within the castle of Dublin, to take and retain…as many goldsmiths, [re]finers, parters, smiths, [en]gravers, moneyers, labourers, or any other artificer of what[ever] faculty or service they might be…

…also as many charcoals, colliers, coalmakers, or wood to make coal withal, with all manner of other wood necessary and requisite; and also to take all manner of copper, lead, argol [potassium tartrate], alum [aluminium potassium sulphate], saltpetre [potassium nitrate], tanners' ashes, copperas [iron sulphate], borax [sodium borate], mercury, potearth [potters' clay] ashes, and all other things requisite for making of our monies within our said mint…

The craftsmen and other workers were to be set to work in the castle and the metals and minerals and fuels were to be paid for at the going rate. As to the actual mint building itself, 'timber, tiles, brick, lime, and all manner of other stuff requisite of and for the new building, repairing or amending of the same mint' was to be similarly purchased.[528] This may be the earliest surviving mention of the use of brick in the castle works, if not in Dublin (Perrot's 1585 survey records one of the windows on the fourth floor of the Bermingham Tower being 'stopt up with breke').[529]

Partial abandonment

Despite these developments, other matters had not improved to any great extent. It was reported to the king's commissioners in Ireland in 1538 that the great hall of the castle needed to be rebuilt:

…some ordre to be taken immedyatly for the buildeing of the castell hall, where the lawe is kept; for yf the same be not buyldeid, the magestie and estimation of the lawe shalle perryshe, the justices being then enforceid to minister the lawes upon hylles, as it were Brehons, or wylde Irishemen, in ther Eriottes. Orayles fyne of the 1000 kyne wolde buylde it, and amende the gaylle of Trym.[530]

This is the same hall that had virtually been rebuilt from the foundations up in the 1320s within eighty years of its original construction. Evidently, it was still being used in 1537 to house the courts of law but was so inadequate that it was suggested the judges might as well have taken to the open air to dispense justice, like a brehon in a chieftain's *oireacht* (assembly). The view of the writer, Master John Alen, was that the expenses of rebuilding it and the gaol of Trim Castle might be defrayed from a fine of one thousand cattle recently levied from the Irish lord, O'Reilly. Alen was not heeded. Less than a decade later, when King Edward VI sought to suppress St Patrick's cathedral, he indicated that it would become the new home of the courts[531] and in 1549 the courts' sessions began there[532] though this experiment had lapsed by 1555 following the succession of Queen Mary.

Because the courts were meeting in St Patrick's, the lord deputy ordered in 1552 that the old library attached to the cathedral, rather than the Bermingham Tower, should be where records necessary for court purposes were kept:

…the Tower within His Majesty's castle of Dublin, which is…far distant from the late cathedral church of St Patrick's, where His Highness' courtes be now kept…and for that the late library of the said late Cathedral church is a meet and sure place for the safe guard and custody of said records and muniments near unto said courts…we order and appoint that the said late library be the place for the safe keeping of such of the said records and muniments as shall be kept out of the said tower of His Highness's said castle of Dublin; and all such of the said records and muniments as shall be out of the said tower shall be put and safely kept in the said library; and that you, the clerk of the hanaper of his majesty's chancery for the time being, shall provide and foresee that presses, or stages, chests, windows, doors, locks, and all other necessaries shall be provided, furnished, and made, as well in and for said library as the said tower of the castle, for the safe guard, sure keeping, and good ordering of the said records and muniments from time to time.[533]

Presumably, though, this use of the library of St Patrick's for the storage of government records expired following its restoration to cathedral status.

But the dissolution of the monasteries had thrown open the possibility of utilising other properties for government purposes. Dublin's only nunnery, the convent of St Mary de Hogges, was demolished and timber and roof-tiles from its church and conventual buildings were taken for the repair of the castle.[534] In 1547, at the same time that Edward VI was proposing a new use for St Patrick's cathedral, he recommended that the adjacent archbishop's palace of St Sepulchre would provide suitable lodgings for the chief governors of Ireland; and various holders of this office did use it for this purpose in the decades that followed.[535]

Likewise, when the splendid if rather rundown premises occupied by the Knights Hospitaller at Kilmainham came up for grabs – perhaps the richest of the dissolved houses of the Pale – it was reported in the extent conducted in 1541 that

the house, mansions and buildings on the site of the manor, which was the principal hospice of the prior and brethren, are very necessary and very well suited to be a mansion and habitation for the king's deputy in Ireland.[536]

In fact, even before this, the lord deputy had taken up residence there, Sir Anthony St Leger addressing letters from Kilmainham from the moment of his arrival in Ireland as deputy in the late summer of 1540.[537] Intermittent if not full-time use of the former priory for this purpose continued for many years. Ware's annals for 1557 report that

> August the tenth, the Lord Lieutenant having mustered his Forces…marched from the Hall of Kilmainam (being the Lord Lieutenants place of Retire) towards the North.[538]

Sir Henry Sidney recalled how, coming up to Christmas 1566, he 'dyned and sate under his cloth of estate in the Hall of Kilmaynham'.[539] And we can see Kilmainham as the place of issue of letters of the chief governors all the way to the 1580s[540] though, by then, Kilmainham too was very decayed.[541] Large amounts had been spent on it and as late as 1605 Sir Arthur Chichester applied for £750 sterling for its repair, as a residence for the lord deputy in the summer months,

> when the castle is somewhat noysome by reason of the prison, and especially when it pleaseth God to visit the citie of Dublin with sickness, as of late yeeres it hath been very greevously.[542]

This record illustrates, of course, that the development of one residence for the chief governor did not preclude the restoration of another. In 1566, for example, at a time (as we shall see) when large sums were being spent on Dublin Castle for the first time in many years, the clerk of works reported expenditure of £680 10s. 2d. on 'the house' of Kilmainham and a further £87 13s. on its chapel and stable.[543] And the chief governor's use of one residence did not preclude his use of another, and did not necessarily mean that Dublin Castle was no longer habitable or inhabited: he might use one residence in winter and another in summer, one in times when all was prosperous and another in a time of plague. But the implication of such references is that, when times were propitious, the chief governor could and did frequently choose to make Dublin Castle both his home and the headquarters of his government.

Sidney's great restoration

It was no great surprise therefore that efforts to restore the castle itself persisted throughout this period. Dudley Loftus's annals record under the year 1560 that

> this yeare the Castle of Killmanham being decayed the Queen gave order for to repayre and enlarge the buyldings within the Castle of Dublin, that it might be a fitt place for the residence of the cheife Governour of Ireland.[544]

In June 1562, a memorandum was addressed to the queen's commissioners in Ireland, relative to 'reparations within the Castle of Dublin', and ordering that the master gunner was to have 'his dwelling appointed [i.e. put in order] within the said castle'.[545] We do not, however, have a record of extensive expenditure on the castle in 1560 or for several years thereafter until, that is, the arrival in Ireland of the man most closely associated with the redevelopment at this juncture, Sir Henry Sidney (Fig. 1.19).

Sidney had served in Ireland in 1556–9, occupying a range of offices including vice-treasurer, treasurer at war for Ireland, and Lord Justice, deputizing for the then chief governor, the earl of Sussex.[546] Even in this period he showed himself concerned with the upkeep of the castle, writing from Dublin to the privy council in England in April 1559 requesting 4,000lb (1814kg) of lead,

> a great Part therof to be ment for and towards the Covering of a certein Tower within the Castle of Dublin, whose Rowf was taken down by my Lord of Sussex, and a Platfourme thereon made; and thereupon a Cannon planted…So as, if the same be not in Tyme couered agayn, it wilbe the fynall Decaye of that Tower; beside the Losse we haue in the meane, of the neither Rowmes there, for the Bestowing of Poweder, and other Munycions wherof (being as it is) we can lay there nothing.[547]

As we shall see presently, the tower in question – on which an artillery platform had been erected in place of its roof, so that its lower rooms could no longer be used for the storage of gunpowder and munitions – may be either the north-east or the south-east corner tower, but Sidney had left Ireland before he had any time to repair it.

It was only upon his own appointment as viceroy in 1565, a post he occupied for most of the next five years (another term of office followed in 1575–8) that Sidney could take charge of the castle works. Writing some few years afterwards, Richard Stanihurst proclaimed his contribution thus:

> When he had doone all such things as are before recited, for and concerning the due course of gouernment by order of law: then also he bethought himselfe vpon such other things as were necessarie in sundrie respects to be doone, as the castell and house of Dublin, which before his comming was ruinous, foule, filthie, and greatlie decaied. This he repared, and reedified, and made a verie faire house for the lord deputie or the chiefe gouernor to reside & dwell in.[548]

Fig. 1.19 Sir Henry Sidney. (NGI)

In fact, given Sidney's earlier interest in the castle's infrastructure, it is no surprise to find that he had intended to rebuild this 'ruinous, foul, filthy, and greatly decayed' castle from the moment of his arrival and indeed before: the various drafts of Queen Elizabeth's instructions upon his appointment in October 1565 – a plan to transform the political and administrative framework of Ireland – had had extensive input from Sidney himself,[549] including a directive to rebuild Dublin Castle.[550]

Sidney seems to have begun straightaway. We see his personal involvement from his 'remembrances' sent to Queen Elizabeth in April 1566 urging action on certain matters, including his request for 'lead to be sent for repairing the castles of Dublin and Carrickfergus'.[551] His magnificent stone bridge over the Shannon at Athlone was built at an astonishing pace being completed in eight months by July 1567,[552] and has a typically ostentatious and self-aggrandising inscription on a sculptured plaque:

This Bryge of Athlone from the maine earth vnder the water was erected and made the ninth yeare [1566–7] of the raign of ovr most dere soveraigne Ladie Elizabeth by the Grace of God Qvene of England Fravnce & Irland Defnder of the Faith et[c], & by the device and order of Sir Henry Sidney Knight of the Moste Nobil Order, the 2° daie of Ivlie [2 July]

then beinge of the ayge of 38 vyre, L[ord] President of the Covnsel in Walis and Marchis of the same and L[ord] Depvtie General of this Her Maiestis realm [of] Irland, finished in les then one year bi the good indvstri and diligens of Sir Petir Lewys clerke chantor cathedral chvrch of Christ Chvrch in Dvblin and steward to the said L[ord] Depvtie, in w[hi]c[h] yeare was begone and fineshed the faire newe wovrke in the Casthel of Dvblin besidis many other notable workis done in sordi other placis in this realme, also the arche rebel Shane O Neyl over throwen, his head set on the gate of the said Castel, coyne and livry aboleshid and the hole realme brovght into svche obedience to Hir Maiestie as the like tranqvilitie, peace and whiche in the memory of mane hath not bene sene.[553]

Here, Sidney's audacious boast that he had brought peace to Ireland, and reduced the country to unprecedented obedience to England, is preceded by a list of what he evidently (and, indeed, later generations) considered his most notable achievements, including the abolition of coyne and livery, the defeat and death of Shane O'Neill and the impaling of his head over the gate of Dublin Castle, and, in pride of place, the fact that he had 'begun and finished the fair new work in the castle of Dublin'.

In 1567, the constable of Dublin Castle, Jacques Wingfield, sought payment of £1,668 14s. 5½d., which included arrears of £105 of his fee for the constableship but also £150 for 'furnishing certain buildings at Dublin Castle' and a further £45 for 'furnishing of buildings at Dublin Castle bargained with the lord deputy'.[554] There is no specific detail and these latter are, in any event, rather inconsequential amounts. However, accounts for Michaelmas Term 1566 record that Constable Wingfield spent a total of £486 13s. 4d. on castle projects, including £333 6s. 8d. 'for reedifying the south hall, the Gale, with platform and divers floors in the southeast tower in the said Castle, removing certain earth, and making archebutrises to the great hall', plus £93 6s. 8d. on 'altering the roof of the lodging and office appertaining to the Treasurer of the Mint', plus £60 'flooring and roofing the south-east tower and one other tower'.[555]

Though not terribly detailed, these accounts do at least tell us that the constable of the castle had embarked on a refurbishment of six different buildings. This included work to the great hall, which had what are described as 'archebutrises', or flying buttresses, applied to its walls, no doubt indicating that it was as unstable – and perhaps prone to subsidence – as it had been at its original construction in the 1240s. (The reference to removal of earth may have been to facilitate the embedding of the buttresses on either side of the hall.) The castle also had another hall which the constable had now re-edified. His accounts refer to it as the 'south hall', another set of accounts for 1564 presumably mean it when they record expenditure of £133 6s. 8d. on repairs to the 'old hall',[556] and undoubtedly it is the 'little hall' mentioned in the 1364 accounts discussed above: it is clearly marked on the 1673 Dartmouth plan (Fig. 1.12), called simply 'Hall', abutting the south wall just east of Bermingham Tower. A third building re-edified is called the 'Gale' which is presumably the castle gaol: we know that the constable maintained prisoners in one or both of the gate-towers, in addition to which Wattson's 1606 plan (Fig. 1.15) records a 'prison' and a 'former prison' occupying much of the north-west quadrant of the castle. A fourth building that had work done to it was the lodgings and office of the treasurer of the mint, though we do not know where in the castle it was located.

Works were also undertaken to add a roof and flooring to an unnamed tower of the castle and the south-east tower also had floors redone and a roof added. The reference to the 'platform and divers floors in the southeast tower' suggests that it may be what Sidney was referring to in 1559 as a 'certein Tower within the Castle of Dublin, whose Rowf was taken down by my Lord of Sussex, and a Platfourme thereon made; and thereupon a Cannon planted'. Sure enough, the south-east tower is indeed called Gunners Tower on the 1673 plan (Fig. 1.12). This plan also depicts a curious square building abutting Bermingham Tower to the west, the earliest reference to which seems to be the Perrot

survey of the castle's towers and walls in 1585, which says of Bermingham Tower that 'adjoyning to the same, ther is a little square toure',[557] and on the 1673 plan this square corner tower has the word 'Platforme' written against it. It would appear, therefore, that there was an artillery platform on both the south-west and south-east corners of the castle.

There may indeed have been more: Robert Ware, writing in 1678, stated that the castle 'is furnished with great ordnances planted on the platformes of the *severall* Towers thereof'.[558] Hence, when the north-west tower collapsed in 1624, the then lord deputy wrote that 'one of the greatest towers of the castle fell down to the ground with the ordnance mounted upon it'.[559] Such arrangements do not of course stand still. When John Dunton visited the castle in the 1690s, he wrote to the effect that the castle 'was encompassed with a wall and dry ditch, over which was a drawbridge and within that an iron gate within which two brass cannon were planted and there are others on top of *one* [present author's emphasis] of the towers'.[560] These two cannon are presumably what Walter Harris, writing in the 1750s, meant in saying that 'since the invention of artillery, two pieces of great ordnance were planted on a plat-form opposite to the gate, to defend it, if the draw-bridge and portcullis should happen to be forced';[561] and they are perhaps the two cannon depicted facing the gate at ground level in front of the buildings on the south range in Charles Brooking's famous view (*c.* 1728) (Fig. 1.20).

Fig. 1.20 Bird's-eye view of Dublin Castle looking south, from Brooking's map of Dublin. (1728)

Elsewhere in his account Harris speculated that the tower which Sidney was concerned about might have been the north-east corner tower (on the grounds that Sir Henry mentioned it being used for storing gunpowder and this north-east tower was subsequently known as the Powder Tower).[562] But it is curious that the survey done for Lord Deputy Perrot (Fig. 1.21), in telling us that the north-east tower had five rooms, mentions 'the fifte roume, which is your lordships chamber'; this probably means that in 1585 the uppermost room of the north-east tower was where the lord deputy was then residing, which – assuming he would not choose to live over a gunpowder hoard – would suggest that the tower was not used for storing munitions at that point.

In any event, the works carried out on the castle in 1565 by Jacques Wingfield were not works on a grand scale. However, these same accounts for Michaelmas 1566 also note expenditure by a certain William Foster, 'having charge of the building of Dublin Castle', of a total of £1,352 8s. 5d.[563] This is expenditure capable of yielding substantial and lasting change to the castle superstructure.

Fig.1.21 Sir John Perrot. (National Library of Wales)

What Sidney achieved

The sad thing is that we simply are not told what this very large sum was spent on. But perhaps we should leave it to Sir Henry himself to describe his legacy at Dublin. When, in 1570, he decided that these new buildings and rooms he had constructed needed a full-time housekeeper resident in the castle, he begins:

> Whereas ther haith ben erected of late within hir majesie's castell of Dublyn, certen lodging and outher fair and necessarie roulmes, boeth for a convenient plaice for the lord deputie's howse, and a fit seate for the placing and receiving of any gouvernour heraftir, as for the bettir and more commodious resorte and assembly of the counsaill, and for the gretter ease of all sutors boeth riche and poore, whiche hertofore were accusomed to travaill to and from plaices boeth farder distant and lesse commodious for the dispatche of ther causes; whiche lodgings and buildings yf they shoulde not from time to time be well mayntained, loked into, ayred, clened, and dressed up in the absense of the gouvernour, they shoulde in short tyme come to grette decay and ruyne.
>
> We have therfor thought fytt, that as well for the keaping of the said howse, and roulmes newely erected, as for the clensing of all the gutters within the said castell, sweping and keeping clene of the walkes upon the walls and platform, as for the tending and keaping of the clocke within the said castell, whiche requireth daily attendance to be tempred and kept in frame, to appoint sume honest, carefull, and diligent person to take that chardge in hand, who should from tyme to tyme undertake the doinges of thos services, and in the gouvernour's absence to loke to the preservation of thinges appertaining to the howse...[564]

Here, from the horse's mouth, we discover Sidney's contribution. He had built a lord deputy's house and new lodgings for the chief governor, he had built rooms to provide a 'fit seat for the placing and receiving' of future chief governors (presumably rooms of state for such ceremonies as the chief governor's installation), he had had the Council Chamber revamped, or a new one built, 'for the better and more commodious resort and assembly of the counsel', and he had returned the courts to the castle (hence the reference to 'suitors, both rich and poor, which heretofore were accustomed to travel to and from places both farther distant and less...commodious for the despatch of their causes').

Incidentally, Sidney's mention that one of the duties of the new housekeeper would involve 'the tending and keeping of the clock within the said castle, which requires daily attendance to be tempered [i.e., regulated] and kept in frame' bears out a statement in the annals of Dudley Loftus that, in the year 1560,

> wer sett up 3 publique clocks, the one in the Castle, another in the Citie and a third at St Patricks church, which wer at there first setting up a very great pleasure to the people.[565]

The castle clock house is recorded on the 1673 Dartmouth plan (a D-shaped building attached to the north wall of the Presence Chamber (Fig. 1.12)).

Another responsibility of the new housekeeper would be the 'cleansing of all the gutters within the said castle' and the 'sweeping and keeping clean of the walks upon the walls and platform'. That the singular noun is used for the latter would suggest there was only one artillery platform at that point, while the 'walks upon the walls' are referred to by Sidney himself in his later memoir, recounting an episode that had occurred in the castle just some months prior to the housekeeper appointment: the escape of Sir Edmund fitzJames Butler of Cloghgrenan in November 1569, which he describes thus:

> Thus lying at Dublin, Sir Edmund Butler, being prisoner in the castle…having too much liberty, wearing no irons, nor locked up in any chamber, but had leave to use the walk on the wall, only guarded with two of my men, whom I thought to have been more vigilant than I found them; practised, by a small boy whom they allowed him, to have a small cord, I am sure not so big as my little finger…slipped by the same cord over the castle wall of Dublin, a wall I am sure as high or higher than any about the Tower of London; yet ere he came to the ground by three fathom [i.e., 3 x 6ft], the cord broke, and he with the fall sore bruised, leaving behind one of his mittens which he had prepared to slip down the cord, and much blood…[566]

It has been repeatedly written that Sir Edmund fell from the rope into the castle moat but Sidney says no such thing but rather goes on to state that, after fleeing as far as 'the bridge of the water of the Dodder [i.e., Ballsbridge], a mile and a half distant from the castle of Dublin', for some reason Sir Edmund waded into the Dodder at that stage. Obviously, this matters only as negative evidence: Sidney's memoir cannot be used to prove a wet moat around the castle in 1569.

What Sidney's memoir and the job-description he penned in 1570 for a castle housekeeper do show is that the castle had alures or parapet-walks – and walkways extensive enough for low-security prisoners to use them as a form of exercise – but we cannot say whether these were a recent embellishment. We do know of others of Sidney's embellishments. We have seen that Constable Wingfield had been entrusted by Sidney with 'reedifying the south hall', which abutted the south curtain. Perrot's 1585 survey concluded with a number of recommendations, among them that, since

> the castle wall is weakest in the south side, by the means of the hall windowes and other windowes, with prives and such other workes as hath bene of late yeares, that you would cause to be stronglie dichte on that side from Brimejam [h]is toure rounde about the gardin to the north este toure.[567]

Windows, therefore, had been broken through the south curtain wall to provide light for the south hall and other buildings erected by Sidney: indeed, earlier in Perrot's survey it is stated that

> betwene that same midle towre and the sowth weste [Bermingham] towre in the castle wall ther are ix. or x. spick holes and small windowes.[568]

Also, more than one privy had been added to rooms backing onto this wall, further weakening its defensive aspect. It was therefore recommended that the ditch outside the south and east walls (along the line of the Poddle) from the Bermingham Tower to the north-east tower should be strengthened and presumably re-dug.

One other small but significant Sidney improvement was to the Bermingham Tower itself. This tower housed the castle kitchen at this point. Perrot's 1585 survey tells us as much, and that it was located one storey up from the lowest level. Also, the area in front of the Bermingham Tower is called the 'Dep[uty's] kitchin yeard' on Wattson's 1606 plan (Fig. 1.15) and the tower itself the 'Kitchin Tower' on the Dartmouth plan of 1673 (Fig. 1.12), by which point buildings called 'Offices belonging to ye Kitchin' had been erected in front of it (one wall of which abutted the west curtain and another the great hall). Perhaps it was thought that the heat from the kitchen below would help keep the records dry and hence the recommendation in 1531 that they be stored there.[569] But evidently when Sidney took over as lord deputy the tower still lacked a roof, and so Stanihurst records that the records which were verie evill kept, not housed or defended from raine and foule weather, but laie all in a chaos and a confused heape, without anie regard; he [Sidney] caused to be viewed and sorted, and then prepared meete roomes, presses, and places for the keeping of them in safetie, and did appoint a speciall officer with a yearlie fee for the keeping of them,[570]

which is confirmed by one of Sidney's own letters to the privy council, sent in April 1566, to the effect that Henry Draycott, master of the rolls, 'hath had the perusing, sorting and kalendaringe of Her Majesty's recordes', which are 'well layd upp in a stronge chamber of one of the towers'.[571]

But the biggest innovation at the castle during Sidney's first deputyship was certainly the construction of the complex he himself called the lord deputy's house and which is marked and labelled as such on Wattson's 1606 plan (Fig. 1.15). Although only a rudimentary sketch, Wattson marks Sidney's house on the interior of the south curtain wall, occupying about half the entire stretch between the south-west and south-east towers, being precisely in the middle. In reality, however, the lord deputy's house comprised a number of buildings and rooms, the public ones of which are described in Sir William Brereton's *Travels in Ireland*, written in 1635 (in order, from west to east), as

the dining-room, wherein is placed the cloth of estate over my Lord Deputy's head, when he is at meat. Beyond this is the chamber of presence, a room indeed of state; and next onto this there is a withdrawing chamber.[572]

Despite alterations to Sidney's legacy throughout the seventeenth century, the 1673 Dartmouth plan is an excellent illustration of the full range of Sidney buildings and of their precise sequence. There, the dining room is shown attached to the east gable wall of the south hall. Incidentally, we can almost envisage the scene described by Brereton of the lord deputy sitting below the canopy of state because we have a contemporary illustration of it (albeit not in the castle but when on itinerary): John Derricke's famous woodcut of the supposed submission of Turlough Luineach O'Neill in 1567 shows Sidney seated beneath an ornate *baldequin*, with the sword of state resting beside him.[573]

The 1673 plan then shows a door linking the dining room with the 'Presence Chamber', the latter separated from the Middle Tower on the south curtain by a large room called a 'Closet', presumably a private chamber for the lord deputy's use. The Presence Chamber is then shown leading to a very large 'Withdrawing Roome' at first-floor level (which also has a closet between it and the curtain wall) connected by stairs to the chapel at ground-floor level. Robert Ware

noted this complex in 1678, describing it as an 'ancient piece of building, wherein upon the ground is a Chappell, over which is a stately drawing room built in the time of Sir Henry Sydney his government whose armes are placed thereon'. As Ware clearly implies that Sidney built the withdrawing room rather than the chapel, it would seem that Sidney erected his house around, and partly above, the traditional chapel building.

It is noticeable that, in his 1570 description of the castle improvements, Sidney referred several times to 'certen lodging *and* outher fair and necessarie roulmes', or to the new 'lodgings *and* buildings', or to 'the said howse, *and* roulmes newly erected' (present author's emphasis). This suggests that the actual lord deputy lodgings, the sleeping quarters constructed by Sidney, were a distinct structure. Now, writing in 1678 in reference to a building to the east of the withdrawing room, Robert Ware states that there

was lately raised a stately and convenient structure, contained within these walls by the Earl of Essex… in this appartment are the Lord Lieutenants private lodgings and the rooms thereunto appertaining.[574]

One could be forgiven therefore for concluding that this chief governor's private lodgings was unrelated to Sidney's complex and had been constructed *ab initio* during Essex's lieutenancy (1672 to 1677). But this may not be the case. This building, called 'Lodgings', is marked in this precise location (about midway between the Middle Tower on the south curtain wall and the south-east tower) on the 1673 plan (Fig. 1.12). Since Essex had only arrived in Ireland the previous August, it is hard to see how the 'stately and convenient structure' which so impressed Ware in 1678 could have been completed in time for the 1673 map. More tellingly still, Ware goes on to point out that Essex's residence was 'on the place of an old decayed building', the new lodgings being 'much more noble and convenient than formerly they have bene'. It would seem, therefore, that the 'Lodgings' building marked on the 1673 plan was this older, now dilapidated, premises, and that it was quite probably the residence Sidney had built for himself a century earlier.

Sidney's commemorative plaques
Vainglorious as ever, Sir Henry erected a plaque containing his coat of arms in memory of his handiwork at the castle, which was still visible on the exterior wall of the withdrawing room when Robert Ware visited a century later ('a stately drawing room built in the time of Sir Henry Sydney his government whose armes are placed thereon'). Sidney also seems to have erected another plaque, with a verse inscription on it, on another location within the castle. We know of this stone because one of his successors

as lord deputy, Thomas Wentworth (later earl of Strafford), dismantled and re-erected it in 1633, at which point he wrote to Sidney's grandson, the earl of Leicester, as follows:

I confess I made a Fault against your noble Grandfather, by pulling down an old Gate within this Castle, wherein was set an inscription of his in Verses, but I did so far contemplate him again in his Grandchild as to give him the best Reparation I could, by setting up the very same Stone, carefully taken down, over the new one, which one Day your Lordship may chance to read, and remember both him and me by that token.[575]

It is not very clear what had happened here. Strafford speaks of a gate *wherein* the stone had been located, which perhaps suggests it was the keystone (or directly above the keystone) of an archway surrounding the gate. When, therefore, he says that he set up 'the very same Stone, carefully taken down, *over* [present author's emphasis] the new one', he possibly means that he had built a new gateway and reinstated the plaque above it.

We do not know where this gateway was. It was not the front gate since Wentworth refers to it as 'an old Gate *within* [present author's emphasis] this Castle'. The 1673 Dartmouth plan (Fig. 1.12) of the castle was drawn exactly forty years after Wentworth had pulled down the old gate and re-erected a new one. It employs the device of a thick black line (by far the thickest on what is a very careful plan) to illustrate what seems to be a very grand wall connecting the east gable wall of the great hall with the clock house. Since the clock was only installed in 1560, this wall presumably postdates it and may have been a Sidney intervention. There is an opening at the midway point of the wall where there was evidently a gate (the plan does not show an actual gate here but then neither does it show the front gate of the castle, merely the walls on either side). The gap in this internal wall is located at precisely the entrance point to Sidney's dining hall and perhaps therefore it was on an arch above this gateway that Sidney had erected the plaque taken down and reinstated by Wentworth.

This plaque does not appear to survive. But, as we have seen, Robert Ware speaks of another plaque on the withdrawing room wall illustrating Sidney's heraldic arms and quite a number of such Sidney plaques still survive from Ireland, including from the Cork Gate at Kinsale, from Johnstown, Co. Kildare, and a number from both Christ Church cathedral, Dublin, and, most famously, the bridge of Athlone.[576] In 1844, the *Proceedings* of the Royal Irish Academy record the receipt of a 'letter from the Secretary of the Lord Lieutenant, presenting to the Academy the stones containing the inscription from the old bridge of Athlone', undoubtedly the lengthy inscription quoted earlier eulogizing Sidney's purported achievements in Ireland.[577] Almost twenty years later, in 1863, Sir William Wilde reported on a later receipt by the Academy from the commissioners of public works of a large number of inscribed stones from

a richly-ornamented limestone entablature containing a long inscription, in relief, descriptive of the erection of the bridge…Above and around this inscription were several well-executed bas reliefs of figures and coats of arms, all of which are now in the Academy.

Prior to the bridge being taken down by the Shannon Commissioners, in 1843–44, drawings of the monument and the bridge were made, and sent to Dublin Castle; but they cannot now be discovered. All the sculptured or inscribed stones were, however, forwarded to Dublin, and were by the Treasury placed at the disposal of the Lord Lieutenant (at that time Earl de Grey), who presented the stones containing the inscriptions to the Academy in April, 1844…but the effigies and coats of arms, &c., the most interesting portion of the monument, remained in the Custom-house until now, when I have been commissioned by the Board of Public Works to present them also to the Academy…[578]

Wilde therefore believed that all these surviving Sidney heraldic plaques were erected by him at Athlone, but the fact that they made their way to the Academy (and subsequently the National Museum of Ireland) in two separate batches nineteen years apart leaves some slight room for doubt. There are also some repetitions of subject matter and some obvious stylistic differences among the plaques, which caused Conleth Manning to remark: 'The two largest armorial plaques in this collection, with decorative surrounds, are out of keeping with the remainder of the material from the entablature and may not be from the bridge at all. They repeat arms already found on the other stones and are more like plaques from a building.'[579] One of the plaques has the quartered arms of England but the other is a Sidney plaque, quite exquisite and by far the most intricate and delicately carved in a collection some items of which are rather naïve. It is just conceivable, therefore, that this elaborate plaque originated in the castle of Dublin.

If so, it was possibly the plaque Robert Ware saw on the exterior of the withdrawing room 'built in the time of Sir Henry Sydney his government whose armes are placed thereon'. But about two years after Ware penned his account, another famous antiquarian, Thomas Dineley, visited Ireland, and in 1681 wrote an important account of his travels, in which he remarked that

Dublin Castle was first founded by John Comyn Archbishop of Dublin and since beautified by s[i]r Henry Sydney then Lord Lieutenant Anno 1575 under Queen Eliz. as appeares by Inscripc[i]on.[580]

This appears to mean that he saw a plaque on the castle commemorating work done by Sidney in 1575. Since Dineley was fascinated by such objects – indeed he wrote a book on the subject called *History from marble*[581] – his observation is likely to be accurate and it is a fact that Sidney did indeed return to Ireland for his final term as chief governor in the summer of 1575 (staying three years). The Sidney plaque from Kinsale contains the date 1576[582] and his mural tablet in Christ Church has the date 1577.[583] So the addition of dates to his plaques was very much a feature of this final term, and we can assume that it was such a plaque, with the date 1575, that Dineley saw a century later.

It was presumably not the plaque that had been moved by Wentworth in 1633 since that one contained, as Wentworth himself put it, 'an inscription of his in Verses'. We cannot be entirely certain what was stated in this inscription since, as already noted, it does not appear to have survived. However, it is a curious coincidence that Richard Stanihurst, an admirer of Sidney and member of his circle, penned fourteen lines of Latin verse in honour of Sidney's works on the castle:

Gesta libri referunt multorum clara virorum,
Laudis & in chartis stigmata fixa manent.
Verum Sidnaei laudes haec saxa loquuntur,
Nee iacet in solis gloria tanta libris.
Si libri pereant, homines remanere valebunt,
Si pereant homines, ligna manere queunt.
Lignaque si pereant, non ergo saxa peribunt,
Saxaque si pereant tempore, tempus erit.
Si pereat tempus, minimè consumitur aevum,
Quod cum principio, sed sine fine manet.
Dum libri florent; homines dum vivere possunt,
Dum quoque cum lignis saxa manere valent,
Dum remanet tempus, dum denique permanet aevum,
Laus tua Sidnaei, digna perire nequit.[584]

[Books record the famous deeds of many men /And marks of glory are stamped on their pages; /But these stones speak the praises of Sidney: /So great a glory lies not in books alone. /If books should perish, men can still remain. /If men should perish, yet stone shall not; /And if stones should perish with time, yet time will last; /If time should end, eternity is not finished: /It has beginning but no end. /While books flourish, while men exist, /While stone, along with timber can survive; /While time remains, while in the end eternity endures, /Your deserved glory, Sidney, cannot die.][585]

This epigram first appeared in the 1577 edition of Holinshed's *Chronicles*, where Stanihurst himself prefaces it with the remark:

The castle of Dublyne was buylded by Henry Loundres (sometyme archebishop of Dublyne, and L. Justice of Irelande) aboute the yeare of our Lord 1220….This castle hath béene of late [the date 1566 appears here in the margin] much beautified wyth sundrye and gorgious buildinges in the tyme of Sir Henry Sydney, as nowe, so then, L. deputie of Irelande. In the commendacion of which buyldings an especiall welwiller of his Lordshippe penned these verses ensuing.[586]

If, when he arrived back in Ireland in 1675, Sir Henry Sidney set about commemorating his restoration of the castle of Dublin by the erection of a mural tablet inscribed in verse, he did so at precisely the point at which Stanihurst was preparing his materials for Holinshed. It is, therefore, very possible that the lines Stanihurst published in the latter – though he nowhere says such – incorporate the inscription erected on the castle. This is no doubt the meaning of the line in the poem proclaiming that 'these stones (*haec saxa*) speak the praises of Sidney'.

Perrot's survey (1585)
In the aftermath of Sidney's restoration – in the prelude to the Spanish Armada and Ireland's bloody Nine Years War (1594–1603) – a detailed survey of the castle walls and towers was commissioned, by the then chief governor of Ireland, Sir John Perrot (Fig. 1.21), in 1585. Although a full third of a millennium had passed since King John's famous 1204 instruction that a new castle be built at Dublin, in its essentials, Perrot's survey remains an excellent guide to the castle that had taken shape in the early thirteenth century.

Perrot's survey of the castle walls and towers[587] is distinct from, but was undertaken at the same time as, a very similar survey of the town walls and towers.[588] Simultaneously, a brief inventory of ordnance belonging to the city was also made.[589] The town survey is told clockwise from the Bermingham Tower to the Dam Gate, as is the castle survey, from the right-hand (eastern) gate-tower full circle to the left-hand (western) gate-tower.

Incidentally, it is a curious fact that neither survey refers to the stretch of city wall from the Dam Gate to the castle's north-east tower (all the more so since the lower courses of this stretch of wall survive, having been exposed during excavation).[590] The town walls survey ends at the Dam Gate as if there is nothing between it and the castle. As for the castle survey, it says of a loophole on the north-east tower, which should have in its sight the stretch of town wall from it to the Dam Gate, that it 'skoureth the gardens northwarde', i.e., one does not see a wall but rather gardens lying west of the modern Palace Street. These omissions might seem mere oversight were it not for the fact that John Speed's map of Dublin – published some twenty-five years later (Fig. 2.13) – depicts a complete circuit of town walls around Dublin, with a single exception: the stretch from Dam Gate to the castle's north-east tower.[591]

It is possible that the wall here had survived for as long as the church of St Mary del Dam which backed onto it. This church was still in existence in 1533 (when some residents of the castle – possibly inmates of its gaol – used it as their place of worship) but had been merged with St Werburgh's by 1559 and no doubt became rapidly dilapidated thereafter. All properties on the site were leased to Sir George Carew in 1589 who in turn passed them to Sir Richard Boyle who, in or after 1604, was building the mansion that, after his elevation to the earldom of Cork in 1620, became known as Cork House on Cork Hill.[592] It is quite likely that the surveying for Speed's map was done around the time that Boyle began to build his house,[593] which perhaps explains why it has no trace of either the house, which had yet to appear, or of the extinct church of St Mary, which had perhaps been swept away along with an adjacent decaying stretch of the city wall. It is, however, possible that the wall was rebuilt in 1610,[594] in which year the city assembly roll records:

Whear[as] the commons made humble suyte unto this assemblye, praieing that some speedy course mighte be taken for building of the newe wall in Castelstreet, which is daily required to be sett forward by the right honorable the lord deputye [Sir Arthur Chichester], and very requisit it should be fynyshed: it is therfore ordered and agreed, by thaucthority of this assembly, that the masters of the woorkos shall presently goe in hand with the making of the said wall, and that the thresurer and Sheryfes shall deliver monny to the masters of the woorkes uppon Mr. Maiors warrant for the effecting of the said worke.[595]

Since Speed had done his work before this ordinance was passed, the wall in question cannot be that which he depicts running in a zigzag from Dam Gate to the castle gate: perhaps the latter is the surviving precinct wall of St Mary's. The most likely explanation therefore is that the city wall between Dam Gate and the north-east tower of the castle was rebuilt in 1610. It is referred to in a lease of 1660[596] and is shown as extant on de Gomme's 1673 map of Dublin (Fig. 2.12).

Be that as it may, Perrot's survey is a most useful guide to the other elements of the castle's defensive infrastructure. Perrot depicts a castle with four corner towers, a middle tower on the south curtain wall, and another two towers on

either side of the gate. He makes only passing reference to the castle drawbridge, recording that the ground-floor room in the eastern gate tower had three loopholes, 'the firste flanking [westwards] into the gate, the seconde northwarde ower the ende of the bridge, the thirde flanketh the [north] wall betwexte it and the north este towre'. Besides the main gate, he also records a 'gardin dore' which seems to be on the east wall: it is interesting that we tend to think of the castle gardens as lying exclusively to the south of the castle but the Perrot survey repeatedly refers to the east wall as being the garden wall. Hence, speaking of a room in the north-east corner tower, the survey says:

In the seconde rowme, ther be twoe spickes [i.e., spikes or loopholes] and towe windowes, wherof the firste flanketh the wall towards the gate [the north wall], the seconde skoureth the gardens northward [as discussed above, gardens east of Palace St, around the modern Bernardo Square], the thirde being a spicke skoureth the gardens estwarde [the Lower Yard], the fourth flanketh the este wall, being the gardin wall.[597]

As described by Perrot, the castle's two gate towers seem dissimilar. The east one has three rooms with 'spikes' or loopholes in all three, facing westwards, northwards and eastwards. In the west gate tower, however, only two rooms are noted, and each has only one loophole, which is blocked up. The probability is that it was used for maintenance of prisoners. Gilbert's edition has a slight error at this point. Speaking of the west gate-tower, he prints 'In the lower rowme ther is one spicke, that is stopte upe, which flanketh the north wall towardes the norweste toure'. This is fine, and means that the room had one blocked-up loophole facing west. He then prints: 'In the seconde roume, one spicke standing in lick sorte betwene both toures righte over the gate, one windowe and a spick'. This makes little sense, but the manuscript, in fact, reads: 'In the seconde roume, one spicke standing in lick [i.e., like] sorte. Betwene both toures righte over the gate, one windowe and a spick'.[598] In other words, the spike in the second room was similar to that in the first (blocked-up, facing west) but between both towers, directly above the castle gate, there stood a window and a loophole.

Perrot records the corner towers as being similarly mismatched. The north-east tower was unique in having five storeys. It had a total of eight windows and only three gun-loops, and it is the only tower recorded as having a staircase. This tower, he tells us, housed Sir John Perrot's chamber on the top storey. How different this feels from the north-west tower which one might have expected to replicate: instead the latter has four storeys, only one window but seven gun-loops and, at its lowest level, the only dungeon recorded in the survey. The rear towers are likewise lop-sided, the south-east being three storeys and the south-west four. And into the south-east tower's three storeys a total of eight gun-loops were inserted but only three windows, whereas the south-west (the Bermingham) tower had only five gun-loops but four windows (one of which was bricked up).

Perrot also records details of the Middle Tower on the south wall: it was three storeys high and had three loopholes at its lowest level, a window in the top room and three windows in the second-storey room, which no doubt meant it was a high-status chamber. The nine or ten loopholes and small windows he records as being in the stretch of wall between this tower and the Bermingham Tower no doubt also attest to the recent refurbishment in the area undertaken primarily by Sir Henry Sidney. And finally, in its discussion of the Bermingham Tower, the survey notes the existence of what the author calls 'a litle square toure' adjoining it, three storeys high having a total of seven loopholes on its upper two storeys.

The author tells us that there were a total of eighty loopholes and windows on the castle's exterior. Assuming the author had power to recommend improvements to the castle's security, we may conclude from the minor nature of the enhancements he advised that he was reasonably content with its current state. He recommended the addition of a murder-hole (or machicolation) and a portcullis over the front gate. He was concerned that the east wall over the 'gardin dore' was thin and weak: he speculated that the explanation was that there had previously been a machicolation and portcullis here which were subsequently removed. He observed that the battlements of the north-east, south-east, and Middle Tower on the south wall had no loopholes and neither had the parapet walls connecting them. And he considered the south wall the weakest, because of the 'hall windowes and other windowes, with prives and such other workes as hath bene of late yeares', and therefore advised that it be protected by being 'stronglie dichte [ditched] on that side from Brimejam [h]is toure rounde about the gardin to the north este toure':[599] in other words, that the ditch be dug or re-dug along the course of the Poddle (about which defensive feature he is, like so many of our sources, strangely silent) outside the castle's south and east curtains. We know from other sources that at least one artillery platform had been installed on top of one of the castle towers, and the surveyor makes reference to plans for more: 'As conserning the plate formes, I think your lordship hath taken order for them alredie'.

The aftermath of Sidney's restoration

Such concern with the castle's defensive capabilities sits ill alongside the preoccupation of Sir Henry Sidney and some of his successors with creating a thing of beauty there. In this new environment, it seems the castle's military men

lost out. Throughout Sir Henry's time as lord deputy, the constable of the castle of Dublin was Jacques Wingfield. Wingfield had come to Ireland in 1558 as Master of the Ordnance – an office based in the castle – and acquired the constableship soon afterwards since he was already resident there, which he tells us in his own words, penned in 1573:

> ...by the advice of the earl of Sussex then lord deputy of Ireland, I bought the constableship of the castle of Dublin. Sussex thought the office most fit for the master of the ordnance because his whole charge was within the castle.[600]

As earlier discussed, Wingfield had been preceded as Master of the Ordnance by Sir John Travers of whom he adds:

> I enjoyed on the south side a lodging in the castle of Dublin as Sir John Travers, late master of the ordnance, long before had done.
>
> From which being, by the late lord deputy Sir Henry Sidney, in consideration of his building there, removed to the north side of the castle, I bestowed of my own charge over and above the £60 given to me as well in consideration of the reparations done in my first lodging and towards the finishing of my later lodging, £100 of which I was promised by the late lord deputy...
>
> And in case I may not enjoy the same lodging, my proved charge would be allowed and I to have by concordatum a yearly allowance for a house in the city as Morgan, the queen's smith, has the sum of £5 sterling per year.[601]

It seems therefore that, prior to Sidney's building works commencing in 1565–6, the house of the Master of the Ordnance had stood against the south curtain wall, as had the house of the smith of the ordnance, John Morgan. The latter lost his house, evidently being ejected from the castle by Sidney, and in 1567 (as earlier noted) was given £29 13s. 4d. 'in recompense of his house anixed to the L[ord] Deputies lodging in the castell',[602] after which he rented a house in the city. Wingfield, for his part, remained in the castle, but moved to a premises on the north wall and claimed to have spent £160 refurbishing both houses and only to have obtained £60 in compensation. (We know that in 1567 he received £45 for 'furnishing of buildings at Dublin Castle bargained with the lord deputy' which no doubt refers to this arrangement).[603]

Now, however, following Sidney's replacement as lord deputy by Sir William Fitzwilliam, in April 1571, it was proposed that Constable Wingfield lose his home in the castle entirely. Wingfield complained of this to the queen's chief advisor, William Cecil, Lord Burghley, and in one of several surviving letters states:

I delivered your letters on my behalf to the lord deputy…They aroused the lord deputy's anger…He said that the lord treasurer [Burghley] had written to him of…my lodging in the castle which the lord deputy meant to use for his children…The lord deputy said he would not grant [it] to me.

The lodging has been costly to me and I have lived there during several changes of government. I have no other dwelling so that, to put me out of the castle, I would not only be thrust from my charge of the ordnance and munitions but also from the charge of the prisoners, being constable…

My cottage in the castle stands on the north wall joined to the constable's prison. The deputy's palace is on the other side of the court on the south side of the wall. After so many years' service in this realm in office of charge, to be thrown forth of doors in these my latter days is hard dealing.

The self same rooms and fewer by the auditor's and chief remembrancer's lodgings served a lord deputy who lived here sumptuously, and chargeably kept his children with sundry kinds of schoolmasters, finding room sufficient both for himself and them, nor any officer of countenance or charge lodged out of the castle.[604]

Wingfield's letter tells us much. To make way for Sidney's new house, he had vacated the Master of the Ordnance's lodging on the south wall and now occupied what he calls a cottage on the north wall. This too he was about to lose because the new lord deputy, Fitzwilliam, intended installing his children there (which suggests it was rather smarter than a run-of-the-mill 'cottage'). Wingfield objects to this on the grounds that the lord deputy's residence had more than enough room for Fitzwilliam's children since a previous lord deputy had lived there 'sumptuously' and had housed 'sundry kinds of schoolmasters' in the deputy's house. This is undoubtedly a reference to Sidney whose wife Mary came to Dublin with him when he was appointed deputy in 1565, bringing six children, the oldest of whom – the future writer and poet, Philip – was aged eleven: even though Mary returned to England on grounds of ill-health in 1567 (the year in which one of their daughters died in Dublin, being buried in Christ Church,[605] the children were in Dublin with Sidney, and certainly by this stage living in the restored castle, for his second term as deputy, only returning to England in 1571.[606]

Wingfield adds that Sidney had had even less space than Fitzwilliam now had because he shared his lodgings not only with his children and their schoolmasters but with the auditor and chief remembrancer. Evidently, however, both the latter had been given quarters elsewhere in the castle by the time of Wingfield's complaint in 1573 (thus making the

lord deputy's lodgings even more commodious). Wattson's 1606 plan (Fig. 1.15) – surprisingly, perhaps, given how little detail it records – does confirm this point. It shows that, immediately on the right as one entered the castle, there were three terraced premises occupied respectively (from east to west) by the 'Auditor', by 'Mr Rowles', and by the 'Rememb.'. The first of these was the auditor-general of Ireland and the third the principal officer of the Court of Exchequer, the remembrancer; the second was presumably the 'master of the rolls', the keeper of the records of chancery, though it is just possible that it refers to William Rolles (or Rowles) who, in 1601, was appointed collector and receiver of fines at the commission for ecclesiastical causes established in 1594 and at the court of castle chamber set up by Sidney.[607] Since Wingfield states that, at the time of writing, 1573, he was occupying lodgings 'on the north wall joined to the constable's prison', it is quite possible that he was living in the rooms between the auditor's and remembrancer's lodgings which Rowles was using in 1606, which are indeed next to the prison marked on Wattson's plan.

But Wingfield's protests were of no avail. Later in 1573 he writes to Lord Burghley to inform him

of the loss of my lodging within the castle of Dublin which had been the only assured place of my dwelling within this realm…I am thereby not only shaken out of doors but also shut from my charge, the only arsenal and storehouse of Ireland.[608]

Wingfield was undoubtedly, in the end, a victim of the changes wrought by Sidney. These had as their goal the transformation of the castle of Dublin from a ramshackle medieval fortress to a seat of government fit for the most narcissistic of Elizabethan courtiers. Individuals and offices associated with its castellated past were being downgraded – indeed, literally evicted – to make way for a new order of prized occupant. And, as the Tudor reconquest of Ireland ushered in the modern age, the aristocratic viceroys who followed in Sidney's wake embellished and beautified and made ever grander the Renaissance palace he bequeathed to Dublin.

Endnotes

1   Duffy 2014.

2   Swan 1983; 1985.

3   Ronan 1940, 483–4.

4   Clarke 1977, 39; idem 2004, 148; Bradley 1992, 52.

5   Buckley and Hayden 2002; Coughlan 2003; Ó Néill 2004.

6   O'Donovan 2008.

7   Gowen 2001, 43–4, 48.

8   McMahon 2002.

9   McCullough and Crawford 2007, 2, fig. 1; Ó Carragáin 2010, 61–6.

10 Simpson 2002, 70; 2004, 16–17.

11 Gilbert 1884, i, 216, no. 190; cf. McEnery and Refaussé 2001, no. 4.

12 St John Brooks 1936, nos 143–4; McNeill 1950, 68–9.

13 McEnery and Refaussé 2001, no. 498.

14 Clarke 2002, 17.

15 McEnery and Refaussé 2001, nos 88, 498, 575, 662.

16 Clarke 2002, s.nn.; Simpson 2004, 14–18.

17 McEnery and Refaussé 2001, no. 575; cf. 615, 617.

18 Ibid., no. 662.

19 ASC

20 Dolley 1973.

21 Whaley 2009, 257–8.

22 Simpson 2005.

23 Carroll 1953.

24 McEnery and Refaussé 2001, no. 88.

25 ASC; Allott 1974.

26 ASC.

27 AU, AFM 795; Downham 2000.

28 AU 798; AFM 793=798.

29 Purcell 2015.

30 Simpson 2005.

31 O'Donovan 2008.

32 AU 821.

33 AU 836; Bhreathnach 1998.

34 AU 827.

35 MacShamhráin 2016, 47.

36 Etchingham 1996, 67–8.

37 AU.

38 CS.

39 AU 837.

40 Meyer 1906, §48.

41 Kelly and O'Donovan 1998.

42 AU 837.

43 Bhreathnach 1998; Maas 2008; Gibbons and Gibbons 2008; Downham 2010; Kelly 2015.

44 AU 841, 842.

45 Simpson 2005, 36–7.

46 AU 841.

47 AU 842, 845.

48 AFM 845=847.

49 AU 848.

50 CS 849.

51 Simpson 1999.

52 AU 851.

53 Dumville 2005; Etchingham 2010; Downham 2011.

54 Downham 2007; chapter 2 this volume.

55 Downham 2007, 17–23.

56 AU 867; AFM 865=867; FAI 867.

57 AU 871.

58 AU 893.

59 AI 893.

60 AU 894.

61 AU 902.

62 AFM 897=902.

63 Simpson 1999.

64 AU.

65 CS; Etchingham 2010b.

66 AFM.

67 AFM 918=920; Jaski 1995; Downham 2003–4.

68 AU 920.

69 AFM 919=921.

70 AU 927.

71 CS 935=936.

72 AU 937.

73 AFM 936=938.

74 AFM 937=939.

75 AFM 941=943.

76 AU 943.

77 AFM 942=944.

78 CS 943=944.

79 AFM 935=937.

80 Boyle and Breatnach 2015, 42, 46.

81 See, e.g., Wallace 1992; Simpson 2000, 29–34; Simpson 2011, 34–42.

82 AFM 945=946.

83 AFM 946=948.

84 AU 951; AFM 949=951.

85 AT 979=980; CS 978=980; cf. AFM 979=980.

86 AFM 988=989; AT 988=989; CS 987=989.

87 Sweetman 1875–86, i, no. 1227.

88 Berry 1890–91; Jackson 1958–9.

89 Cleasby and Vigfusson 1874, s.v.

90 Holm 2015, 77; cf. Wallace 2000.

91 AU 1029.

92 AFM 1151.

93 AFM 1162.

94 Simpson 1999, 30–1.

95 Etchingham 2017, 133.

96 AI 993, 995; AU 994; AT 995

97 CS 993=995; AFM 994=995.

98 AU 1029.

99 Dolley 1966.

100 AFM 994=995.

101 AFM 995=996.

102 AU.

103 AT 999=1000.

104 AI 1000.

105 Marstrander 1915, 167.

106 Todd 1867, 112–13.

107 Woods 2013.

108 AFM 1004=1005.

109 Todd 1867, 150–1.

110 Duffy 2013, 174.

111 Todd 1867, 180–1, 190–1.

112 Joyce 1869, i, 291–2.

113 AFM 1014=1015.

114 Walsh 2012; Phelan 2010.

115 AI 1026.

116 AFM; AT; CS 1052.

117 AI 1111.

118 As we shall see; see also, Duffy 1992.

119 Clover and Gibson 1979, 67–9.

120 Clover and Gibson 1979, 67–9.

121 AU 1070.

122 AFM 1070.

123 AI 1072.

124 McNeill 1950, 28.

125 Duffy 1992, 104.

126 AI.

127 CS 1072.

128 AI 1089.

129 AT.

130 Duffy and Mytum 2015.

131 AFM; AU; AT; AI.

132 Power 1986, 2005.

133 AFM; AU 1102.

134 AI 1108.

135 AI.

136 MIA 1114=1115.

137 AFM; AT; AU; AI 1115.

138 Scott and Martin 1978, 66–7.

139 Duffy 1998, 81–5.

140 Ogilvie 2011.

141 AFM 1117; AT 1117; CS 1113=1117.

142 AI 1117.

143 AT 1118.

144 MIA 1119=1118.

145 Flanagan 1989, 30, n. 67.

146 Etchingham 2000, 25–6; Perros-Walton 2013, 291–2.

147 Leclerq 1962–92, ii, 313–8.

148 Rule 1884, 297–8.

149 Hemmeon 1914.

150 AU 1124.

151 AT 1125.

152 AT; AFM; AU; MIA; AT; AI 1126; CS 1122=1126.

153 MIA 1126=1127.

154 Ó Corráin 1974, 68–71; O'Conor et al. 2010; O'Conor and Naessens 2012; Flanagan 2017, 230–2.

155 AFM; AT 1166.

156 AT 1134; AFM 1137, 1138.

157 AFM 1141.

158 AFM 1142.

159 MIA; AT; CS; cf. AFM.

160 AT; CS.

161 AFM; MIA 1149.

162 AFM 1150.

163 Flanagan 1989, 174–99; Charles-Edwards 2013.

164 AFM 1154.

165 AFM 1156.

166 AU; AT; AFM.

167 AFM 1162.

168 AT 1162.

169 AFM 1162.

170 AU 1162.

171 AU; AT.

172 AU 1165.

173 AT; AFM 1166.

174 AT 1166.

175 Orpen 1892.

176 Scott and Martin 1978, 66–7.

177 AU.

178 AT 1170.

179 AFM 1170.

180 Walsh and Kennedy 2007, 112–13.

181 Mullally 2002, ll 1714–23.

182 Scott and Martin 1978, 68–9, 76–7.

183 Mullally 2002, l. 1601; Stubbs 1868–71, i, 269.

184 Mullally 2002, ll 2285–8.

185 Scott and Martin 1978, 76–7.

186 Clarke 2002, 28, s.v. 'Dam'.

187 Mullally 2002, ll 2330–1, 2343–54.

188 McNeill 1921.

189 Scott and Martin 1978, 76–9.

190 Mullally 2002, ll 1752–9; Scott and Martin 1978, 79.

191 AT 1171.

192 Mullally 2002, ll 1959–62 .

193 MIA 1171; Scott and Martin 1978, 90–1.

194 Scott and Martin 1978, 89.

195 Stubbs 1867, i, 28–9; Stubbs 1868–71, ii, 32.

196 Eyton 1878, 162.

197 Stubbs 1867, i, 28–9; Stubbs 1868–71, ii, 254.

198 Scott and Martin 1978, 97.

199 Duffy 1998, 2005.

200 MIA 1172; see also, Flanagan 1989, 174–207; Sims-Williams 1991; Charles-Edwards 2013, 27–30.

201 Stubbs 1867, i, 30.

202 Mullally 2002, ll 2711–14.

203 Hayden 2011.

204 Veach 2014a, 34–41.

205 Orpen 1907b, 233; Hayden 2011.

206 Scott and Martin 1978, 190–1, 194–5; Flanagan 1989, 300.

207 Stubbs 1867, i, 270.

208 Scott and Martin 1978, 194–5.

209 Gilbert 1884, ii, 305.

210 Gilbert 1897, 47; McNeill 1950, 2.

211 Nicholls 1972, 107.

212 Sayles 1979, no. 46.

213 St John Brooks 1933.

214 Gilbert 1865, 505.

215 Cole 1844, 81.

216 Gilbert 1889, 369–70.

217 AU 1172.

218 Gilbert 1884, i, 205–6.

219 Gilbert 1889, 388.

220 St John Brooks 1936, no. 175.

221 35th DKR, 46.

222 McEnery and Refaussé 2001, no. 48.

223 Lawlor 1908, 41.

224 Twiss 1920, 39.

225 Chartae, 8.

226 Close rolls, 1231–4, 552.

227 Gilbert 1870, 50.

228 Palgrave 1835, ii, 172; CDI 1171–1251, no. 116.

229 Duffus Hardy 1833–44, i, p. 6; Gilbert 1870, 61–2; CDI 1171–1251, no. 226.

230 Sweetman 1875–86, i, no. 973.

231 Stewart 1989.

232 Duffus Hardy 1833–44, i, 34.

233 Dolley and O'Sullivan 1967.

234 Duffus Hardy 1837, 176.

235 Veach 2014b.

236 CDI 1171–1251, 287.

237 Duffus Hardy 1835; CDI 1171–1251, no. 315.

238 Duffus Hardy 1837, 172; CDI 1171–1251, nos 319, 345.

239 CDI 1171–1251, no. 346.

240 St John Brooks 1935–7, 361–3; Orpen 1911–20, i, 392.

241 Gilbert 1865, 504.

242 Orpen 1911–20, ii, 242–65.

243 Harris 1747–50, i, 73.

244 White 1943, 26.

245 Berry 1907, 395.

246 Gilbert 1889, 147.

247 CDI 1171–1251, nos 404, 406, 407.

248 CDI 1171–1251, 409, p. 67; Robinson 1994, 8–9; Gravett 2013, 17.

249 Coxe 1841–4, iv, 233–4.

250 ALC 1210.

251 AClon 1210=1211.

252 Orpen 1907a; 1911–20, iv, 283.

253 ALC 1212.

254 Orpen 1907a, 266.

255 Orpen 1907b, 461.

256 Davies and Quinn 1941, 14.

257 CDI 1171–1251, no. 529.

258 Gilbert 1884, ii, 279, 312; McNeill 1950, 299.

259 Barry and Morgan 2014, 98–9.

260 Ware 1705, 45.

261 Wilson 1917, 85.

262 Cal. misc. inq., i, no. 26; CDI 1171–1251, no. 2760; AFM 1212=1213; Manning 2003a.

263 CDI 1171–1251, nos 843, 999.

264 CDI 1171–1251, nos 612, 840, 891, 955, 1037, 1142.

265 Duffus Hardy 1835, 105; White 1957, 4.

266 Pat. rolls, 1225–32, 338.

267 CDI 1171–1251, no. 1790.

268 Pat. rolls, 1216–25, 100.

269 Duffus Hardy 1833–44, i, 369.

270 CDI 1171-1251, nos 1353, 1384, 1672.

271 McEnery and Refaussé 2001, nos 18, 41, 48.

272 Lynch and Manning 2001, 194.

273 Murphy 1995, 55.

274 White 1941a, 182.

275 McEnery and Refaussé 2001, nos 44, 106.

276 McNeill 1950, 42; Clarke 2009, 43.

277 Twiss 1920, 286.

278 White 1941a, 182–3.

279 Morrin 1861, 331.

280 Duffus Hardy 1833–44, ii, 48.

281 Pat. rolls, 1216–25, 100.

282 Pat. rolls, 1216–25, 57.

283 Duffus Hardy 1833–44, i, 298.

284 Round 1920, 193–5.

285 Duffus Hardy 1833–44, i, 228; CDI 1171–1251, no. 656.

286 Pat. rolls, 1216–25, 264–6; CDI 1171–1251, no. 949.

287 CDI 1171–1251, nos 1015, 1018, 1020.

288 Brown 2016, 254.

289 CDI 1171–1251, no. 1227.

290 Sweetman 1875–86, ii, no. 1294, p. 241.

291 Maguire 1974, 7.

292 Gilbert 1889–1944, ii, 560.

293 Gilbert 1865, 515.

294 Gilbert 1889–1944, ii, 559.

295 Maguire 1974, 8, 10.

296 35th DKR, 29.

297 Gilbert 1865, 514.

298 Loeber 1980, 58.

299 Maguire 1974, fig. 3.

300 CDI 1171–1251, nos 2692, 3058; ii, 1535.

301 35th DKR, 45.

302 CDI 1171–1251, nos 404, 409.

303 CSPI, 1509–[1603], iv, 164.

304 CSPI, 1588–92, 154.

305 Stanihurst 1979, 53.

306 35th DKR, 29.

307 Sweetman 1875–86, i, no. 1227.

308 Duffus Hardy 1833–44, ii, 52.

309 Moss 2015, 29.

310 35th DKR, 34.

311 Ware 1705, 45.

312 35th DKR, 30.

313 Manning 2017–18.

314 Gilbert 1889–1944, ii, 559.

315 CoA, MS PH 15174, 57.

316 Harris 1766, 22.

317 Gilbert 1889–1944, ii, 560.

318 Manning 1998; Manning 2017–18.

319 L. & P. Hen. VIII, 1537, pt 2, 261.

320 Lynch and Manning 2001, 183 and pl. 3.

321 O'Keeffe 2009.

322 Manning 2017–18.

323 Manning 2003b, 93.

324 Gilbert 1865, 514.

325 35th DKR, 34; Lydon 1966–7, 12.

326 Maguire 1974, fig. 3.

327 Close rolls, 1234–7, 571.

328　Close rolls, 1237–42, 225, 227.

329　CDI 1171–1251, 2581.

330　Colvin et al. 1963, i, 93–159.

331　Hudson Turner 1851, 196–8.

332　CDI 1171–1251, 2581.

333　35th DKR, 34.

334　Close rolls, 1242–7, 23; CDI 1171–1251, no. 2612.

335　Lydon 1966–7, 20.

336　Cal. Pat rolls, 1232–47, 467.

337　Maguire 1974, 10–11.

338　Berry 1914, 19.

339　CDI 1285–1292, no. 2, p. 15.

340　Cal. pat. rolls, 1399–1402, 79.

341　Maguire 1974, fig. 2; see Appendix 4.

342　APC, xxi, 325.

343　Harris 1766, 45–6.

344　Maguire 1974, fig. 3.

345　Rady et al. 1991.

346　Biddle et al. 2000.

347　Smirke 1845, 54–6; Hudson Turner 1851, 264–74; Borenius 1943, 49.

348　Watts 2002, 251–2.

349　See Borenius 1943.

350　39th DKR, 25.

351　Connolly 1998, 267–8, 272, 277.

352　CIRCLE CR 14 Edw II, §24.

353　Richardson and Sayles 1961, 94.

354　Sayles 1979, no. 284.

355　Connolly 1998, 548.

356　CoA, MS PH 15174, 43.

357　CIRCLE, CR 9 Hen. V, §40.

358　Connolly 1998, 568–9.

359　Berry 1914, 19.

360　L. & P. Hen. VIII, 1538, pt 1, 238, 641.

361　HMC De L'Isle MSS, i, 398–9.

362　Lydon 1966–7, 20.

363　CDI 1252–1284, no. 1294, p. 241; Connolly 1998, 13.

364　Maguire 1974, 9; see Appendix 4.

365　CDI 1252–1284, nos 1650 (p. 339), 1739, 1890; CDI 1285–1292, no. 169 (p. 75).

366　36th DKR, 75.

367　Ibid.

368　36th DKR, 29.

369　39th DKR, 25.

370　Craig 1984, no. A658.

371　Maguire 1974, 11; see Appendix 4.

372　Gilbert 1889–1944, ii, 560.

373　McNeill 1931, 53.

374　Gilbert's edition of the text has 'archers' but the manuscript appears to delete the letter 'r' to read instead 'arches': CARD, ii, 558; TNA, SP 63/121 f. 226.

375　Lynch and Manning 2001, 194.

376　Maguire 1974, 11; see Appendix 4.

377　Harris 1766, 23.

378　See, e.g., CDI 1285–92, no. 169, p. 70.

379　OED, s.v.; Lawlor 1923, 53.

380　Hughes 1940, 87; see Appendix 4.

381　Girouard 1978, 1–118; Thurley 2003, 52–3.

382　Colvin et al. 1963, i, 125; Robinson 1994, 110.

383　CSPI, 1615–25, 196, 202.

384　CSPI, 1615–25, 245.

385　CIRCLE, CR 2 Hen. VI, §22.

386　CIRCLE, CR 17 Ric. II, §31.

387　Maguire 1974, fig. 2.

388　CDI 1302-1307, no. 3, p. 4.

389　Gilbert 1884, i,100–01.

390　Gilbert 1884, i, 14–15.

391　CDI 1171–1251, nos 2941; 3007; Gilbert 1884, i, pp 194, 304; Gilbert 1870, 439–40; CIRCLE, CR 4 Edw. III, §10.

392　38th DKR, 65.

393　Mills et al. 1905–56, i, 411.

394　Gilbert 1870, 471–2; 39th DKR, 51.

395　42nd DKR,78.

396　43rd DKR, 48–9.

397　TNA, E101/233/23, §37; CIRCLE, CR 1 Edw. II, §1.

398　Connolly 1998, 234.

399　Connolly 1998, 240.

400　Gilbert 1870, 405–6.

401　Lydon 2016, 284.

402　Connolly 1998, 267–8; CIRCLE, CR 14 Edw. II, §10.

403　Connolly 1998, 267–8, 272.

404　CIRCLE, CR 14 Edw. II, §24.

405　Connolly 1998, 288, 291, 297, 303, 306, 311, 316; CIRCLE, CR 20 Edw. II, §49; CR 20 Edw. II, §34.

406　CIRCLE, CR 20 Edw. II, §96; Connolly 1998, 325, 329, 334.

407　Lawlor 1923, 37.

408　43rd DKR, 27–8.

409　Shelby 1964.

410　42nd DKR, 47.

411　HMC De L'Isle MSS, i, 398–9.

412　CSPI, 1615–25, 489.

413　Frame 1982, 197–202.

414　43rd DKR, 57.

415　Connolly 1998, 364.

416　CIRCLE, CR 8 Edw. III, §175.

417　CIRCLE, CR 10 Edw. III, §12.

418　Connolly 1998, 391, 403, 413, 416, 441, 447.

419　CIRCLE, CR 18 Edw. III, §§12, 98; 20 Edw. III, §§12, 79; CR 22 Edw. III, §26; CR 28 Edw. III. §5; CR 29 Edw. III, §174.

420　Connolly 1998, 441, 447, 453, 459, 468, 497.

421　Connolly 1998, 339, 342, 345, 350–01, 391, 403, 413, 416.

422　CIRCLE, PR 13 Hen. IV, §68.

423　Stanihurst 1979, 49.

424　Harris 1766, 19–20.

425　Connolly 1994; Connolly 1995.

426　Williams 2001, 159.

427　Gilbert 1884, ii, 377.

428　Richardson and Sayles 1961, 100.

429　e.g., CIRCLE, CR 14 Edw. II, §§10, 14; CR 20 Edw. II, §§34, 49.

430　Connolly 1998, 512, 516, 519.

431　Gilbert 1865, 544–6; CIRCLE, CR 35 Edw. III, §2.

432　NAI, RC 8/28, 346–50; Connolly 1978, 330–1.

433　Sweetman 1875–86, i, nos 1309, 1701–2, 1967, 2047, 2403.

434　35th DKR, 34.

435　Sweetman 1875–86, i, no. 2581.

436　Close rolls, Hen. III, 1237–42, 227.

437　Sweetman 1875–86, i, no. 2581.

438　CIRCLE, CR 35 Edw. III, §2.

439　Cal. pat. rolls, 1385–9, 424.

440　Lawlor 1923, 40, 43; Moss 2015, 32–3.

441　NAI, RC 8/28, 341–5; Robinson 1994, 114.

442　Lawlor 1923, 40; Ronan 1923.

443　Gilbert 1865, 546–8.

444　HMC De L'Isle MSS, i, 398–9.

445 Longfield 1960, 121.

446 Gilbert 1889–1944, ii, 561; see Appendix 1.

447 Maguire 1974, 10; see Appendix 4.

448 Close rolls, Hen. III, 1237–42, 227.

449 39th DKR, 25.

450 Maguire 1974, 9–10.

451 CIRCLE, CR 9 Hen. V, §40.

452 Maguire 1974, 11; see Appendix 4.

453 Close rolls, Hen. III, 1247–51, 74.

454 Smyly 1945, 32–3.

455 CIRCLE, PR 3 Hen. V, §86.

456 CIRCLE, PR 13 Hen. VI, §9.

457 CoA, MS PH 15174, 57.

458 For which, see Clarke 2002, 29.

459 CIRCLE PR 13 Hen. IV, §68; cf. PR 25 Hen. VI, §15.

460 Lynch and Manning 2001, 194, 197.

461 Gilbert 1889–1944, ii, 560.

462 NAI, RC 8/28, 346–50; Connolly 1978, 330–1.

463 Gilbert 1865, 219–20.

464 Gilbert 1865, 546–8.

465 Morrin 1861, 287.

466 Connolly 2008.

467 Connolly 1978, 198.

468 CIRCLE, CR 4 Ric. II, §9.

469 Connolly 1998, 545, 546.

470 Johnston 1977, 248.

471 Cal. pat. rolls, 1391–6, 693.

472 Sayles 1979, no. 284.

473 Sayles 1979, no. 285.

474 Devon 1837, 266.

475 Connolly 1998, 548.

476 TNA, E364/34/I; E403/561; Johnston 1977, 273, 297.

477 See, e.g., Colvin et al. 1963, i, 529–33, ii, 968, 998, 1008, etc.

478 TNA, E159/184; Johnston 1977, 496.

479 CoA, MS PH 15174, 43.

480 Lawlor 1923, 38, 46.

481 Gilbert 1865, 570; Lawlor 1923, 47.

482 Gilbert 1865, 570.

483 CIRCLE, PR 2 Hen. V, §192.

484 CIRCLE, PR 2 Hen. V, §191.

485 Connolly 1998, 549, 552.

486 Connolly 1998, 552, 554.

487 CIRCLE, CR 6 Hen. VI, §29.

488 Gilbert 1865, 578–9; CIRCLE, PR 9 Hen. VI, §44.

489 Connolly 1998, 574.

490 Nicolas 1834–7, v, 323; Gilbert 1865, 581.

491 Connolly 1998, 577.

492 Berry 1914, 19.

493 Gilbert 1865, 589; Morrissey 1939, 252–5.

494 Connolly 1998, 626.

495 Ellis 1998, 38.

496 Morrissey 1939, 665–7.

497 Harris 1747–50, i, 74.

498 L. & P. Ric. III–Hen. VII, ii, 300.

499 Quinn 1941, 27.

500 See, e.g., S.P. Hen. VIII, ii, 47, 77, 83, 84.

501 Holinshed 1577, ii, 80.

502 Quinn 1993, 664–5.

503 S.P. Hen. VIII, ii, 95–6.

504 S.P. Hen. VIII, ii, 117.

505 TCD, MS 543/2/14.

506 Gilbert 1865, 34, 450, 485–6.

507 S.P. Hen. VIII, ii, 169.

508 Holinshed 1577, ii, 90.

509 Clarke 2002, 29.

510 Mills and McEnery 1916, 85.

511 Holinshed 1577, ii, 91.

512 Holinshed 1577, ii, 91; Gilbert 1889–1944, i, 411–12.

513 Ellis 2019, 718.

514 Gilbert 1857–8, 305–6.

515 L. & P. Hen. VIII, xviii, pt 1, 322.

516 L. & P. Hen. VIII, xx, pt 1, 365–6.

517 L. & P. Hen. VIII, xx, pt 1, 273.

518 L. & P. Hen. VIII, xx, pt 2, 46–7, 55; Gilbert 1857–8, 611.

519 Morrin 1861, 287.

520 HMC De L'Isle MSS, i, p. 377.

521 Ibid.

522 Ball 1900, 111–13.

523 Gilbert 1884, ii, 42.

524 Morrin 1861, 225, 235.

525 Cal. pat. rolls, 1549–51, 290.

526 HMC De L'Isle MSS, i, p. 377.

527 CSPI, 1566–7, rev. ed., 214.

528 Gilbert 1857–8, 611.

529 Gilbert 1889–1944, ii, 559.

530 S.P. Hen. VIII, ii, 501.

531 Monck Mason 1819, 153.

532 Gillespie 2009, 162.

533 Morrin 1861, 287.

534 Ronan 1926, 493.

535 Monck Mason 1819, 153; Holland 2011, 51–2.

536 White 1941a, 82.

537 L. & P. Hen. VIII, xvi, 42, 552, 926, 1097, 1284.

538 Ware 1705, 142.

539 Brady 2002, 49.

540 For example, CSPI, 1574–85, 67, 68, 70, 72–4, 76, 96, 114, 115, 117, 168–70, 388–90.

541 Falkiner 1904, 44–51; Kenny 1995, 37.

542 CSPI, 1603–6, 381.

543 HMC De l'Isle MSS, i, 398.

544 White 1941b, 236.

545 CSPI, 1509–1603, i, 1509–73, 196.

546 Brady 1994, 113–58.

547 Collins 1746, i, 5–6.

548 Holinshed 1586, ii, 152.

549 Brady 1994, 117–19.

550 CSPI, 1509–73, 274–5; CPSI, 1566–7, rev. ed., 48.

551 CSPI, 1566–7, rev. ed., 41.

552 Berry 1902; Bradley 2007; Manning 2010.

553 FitzGerald 1915, 118–19; Bradley 2007, 184.

554 CPSI, 1566–7, rev. ed., 202.

555 HMC De L'Isle MSS, I, 398–9; CSPI, 1566–7, rev. ed., 213.

556 Longfield 1960, 121.

557 Gilbert 1889–1944, ii, 560; see Appendix 1.

558 Maguire 1974, 9; see Appendix 4.

559 CSPI, 1615–25, 489.

560 Hughes 1940, 86.

561 Harris 1766, 18.

562 Harris 1766, 22–3.

563 HMC De L'Isle MSS, i, 398–9; CSPI, 1566–7, rev. ed., 214.

564 Harris 1766, 37–40; McNeill 1934, 364–5.

565 White 1941b, 236.

566   Brady 2002, 77.

567   Gilbert 1889–1944, ii, 561.

568   ibid.

569   L. & P. Hen. VIII, v, 197–8.

570   Holinshed 1586, ii, 152.

571   CSPI, 1509–1573, 294.

572   Hughes 1940, 86; see Appendix 3.

573   Derricke 1581.

574   Maguire 1974, 198; see Appendix 4.

575   Knowler 1739, i, 168, 224; Kinsella 2011, 129.

576   Manning 2010; Kinsella 2011.

577   PRIA, 2 (1840–4), 576.

578   Wilde 1861–4, 324–7.

579   Manning 2010, 10.

580   Ball 1913, 299.

581   Nichols 1867.

582   Manning 2010, 8.

583   Kinsella 2011, 114.

584   Holinshed 1577, ii, 12.

585   Barry and Morgan 2014; Barry 2009, 46–7.

586   Holinshed 1577, ii, 12.

587   Gilbert 1889–1944, ii, 558–61; see Appendix 1.

588   Ibid., 551–7; Clarke 2002, 32–3.

589   Gilbert 1889–1944, ii, 557–8.

590   Lynch and Manning 2001, 197.

591   Andrews 1983; Simpson 2006.

592   Gilbert 1854–9, ii, 1–6; Clarke 2002, 17.

593   Andrews 1983, 210.

594   Clarke 2002, 20.

595   Gilbert 1889–1944, ii, 528–9.

596   Gilbert 1854–9, ii, 8.

597   Gilbert 1889–1944, ii, 558; see Appendix 1.

598   TNA, SP 63/121, f. 226.

599   Gilbert 1889–1944, ii, 561; see Appendix 1.

600   CSPI, 1571–5, rev. ed., 383.

601   Ibid.

602   CSPI, 1566–7, rev. ed., 214.

603   CPSI, 1566–7, rev. ed., 202.

604   CSPI, 1571–5, rev. ed., 222.

605   Kinsella 2011, 115.

606   Holland 2011, 63.

607   Morrin 1861, 290–5, 595; Crawford 2005.

608   CSPI, 1571–5, rev. ed., 335.

Frontispiece 2 Thomas, Viscount Wentworth, later 1ˢᵗ earl of Strafford by Sir Anthony van Dyck c. 1635–6.
He was Lord Lieutenant of Ireland 1632–40. (© Lady Juliet Tadgell)

Part 2: Dublin Castle 1560–1684
by John Montague

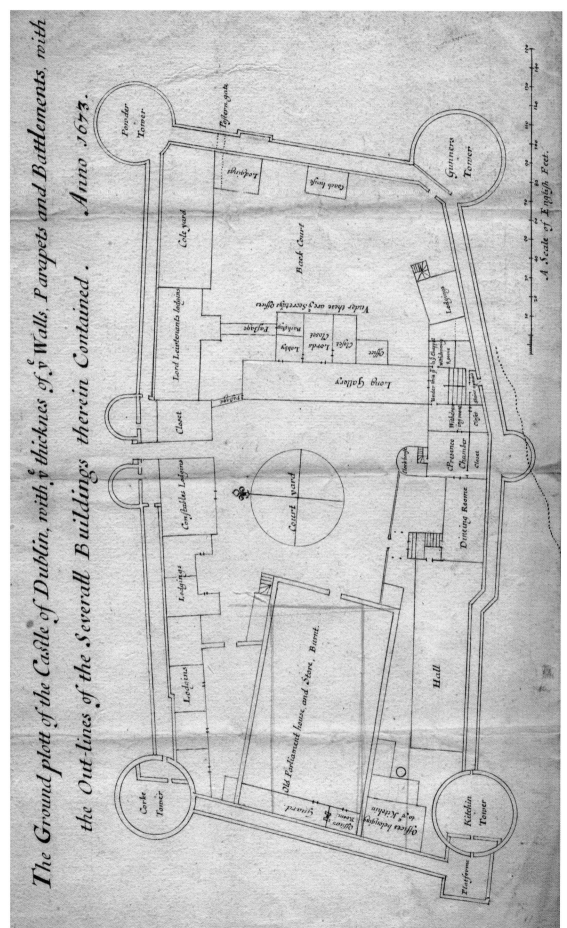

The Ground plott of the Castle of Dublin, with the thickness of the Walls, Parapets and Battlements, with the Out-lines of the Severall Buildings therein Contained. Anno 1673.

Powder Tower

Postern gate

Lodgings

Coach house

Coleyard

Back Court

Gunners Tower

Lord Leiutenants lodgins

Under these are the Secretarys offices

Closet

Passage

Lobby

Lord's Closet

Back stayer Closet

Passage

Office

Long Gallery

Lodgings

Court yard

Under this the Chappel

Withdrawing Roome

Constables Lodgins

Wthdraw ing roome

Chy stayer opens

Lodgings

Presence Chamber

Closet

Lodgins

Back house

Dining Roome

Offices belonging to the Kitchin

Hall

Corke Tower

Guard

Officers belonging to the Guard Roome

Platforme

Kitchin Tower

A Scale of English Feet.

Chapter 2.1
Introduction

Throughout the period under review, the castle of Dublin retained its late thirteenth-century appearance. This can be seen clearly on the 1673 Dartmouth plan (Fig. 2.1)[1] and on the two plans made by Thomas Phillips in 1685 (Figs 2.2, 2.3).[2] This was a rectangular castle with great circular corner towers. Excavations in the 1980s delineated the circuit and confirm the reliability of the 1673 plan in nearly all its details. The circular towers resembled the great keeps of that age, such as Pembroke Tower in Wales, or the round tower at Nenagh, Co. Tipperary.[3] By the late seventeenth century, the castle incorporated within this thirteenth-century enceinte a number of later structures including the fourteenth-century great hall, the residential complex built by Sir Henry Sidney in the 1570s, the arcaded gallery built by Viscount Falkland in the 1620s, as well as other ranges and extensions to these, such as the great stables built by Wentworth in the 1630s. Almost none of this survives, and therefore what follows is based on contemporary records, including the crucial plan evidence already noted, and what we know of its archaeology, as well as the very sparse elements of surviving built form.

The castle at that time, as it continues to be, was deeply immersed within the city itself. Thus, none of the opportunities of the Renaissance-style Portumna Castle – where disparate functions were integrated within a single house, and the gardens were a series of stately courts – was possible. It was for this reason, among others, that Wentworth would build the great folly at Jigginstown in the 1630s. Such a new build allowed for the most up-to-date types of internal layout, not possible within the crammed site at the centre of the city, which by necessity demanded an agglomerative approach to design.[4] We might also contrast the situation of Dublin Castle, directly in the centre of its city, with the position of Whitehall withdrawn from London, or even Versailles in its remove from Paris. In Dublin, this led to a continued conversation on whether to leave the site and begin afresh elsewhere, or indeed to demolish in situ and start anew.[5] However, as Toby Barnard has so aptly put it, the administration was as short of cash as it was of space, particularly when so much of the money was 'creamed' to the English administration, as when it was directed to Charles II and Hugh May's rebuilding of Windsor Castle during the 1670s.[6] Also, in contrast to the fifteenth century when chief governors were usually from native families such as the Kildares and Fitzgeralds, in the seventeenth century, with the exception of the duke of Ormond, the English court usually sent English governors to Ireland, on what must have appeared to many of them as some kind of gruelling trial, if not a form of cultural and personal exile.[7] Thus, it seemed to most of the chief governors, when newly arrived from the luxuries of the English court, as it did to Wentworth, that Dublin Castle was like 'a very prison'.[8] It was against this backdrop of decayed lodgings and medieval detritus that some of these governors, including Wentworth, sought to effect some improvements, as we shall see.

In 1560, Elizabeth I, having noted that 'the castle of Kilmainham [was] decayed…gave order for to repayre and enlarge the buyldings within the castle of Dublin, that it might be a fitt place for the residence of the cheife Governour of Ireland'.[9] Among the most active builders in the country – having constructed bridges at Athlone and Ballinasloe in Co. Galway, in Carlow town, and in Johnstown, Co. Kildare, and instigated works on Christ Church cathedral, and on the castles of Carrickfergus and Dublin – was Sir Henry Sidney (Fig. 1.19), governor from 1565 to 1571 and from 1575 to 1578.[10] Sidney modernised the interior of the castle and did much to consolidate the medieval curtain wall, its

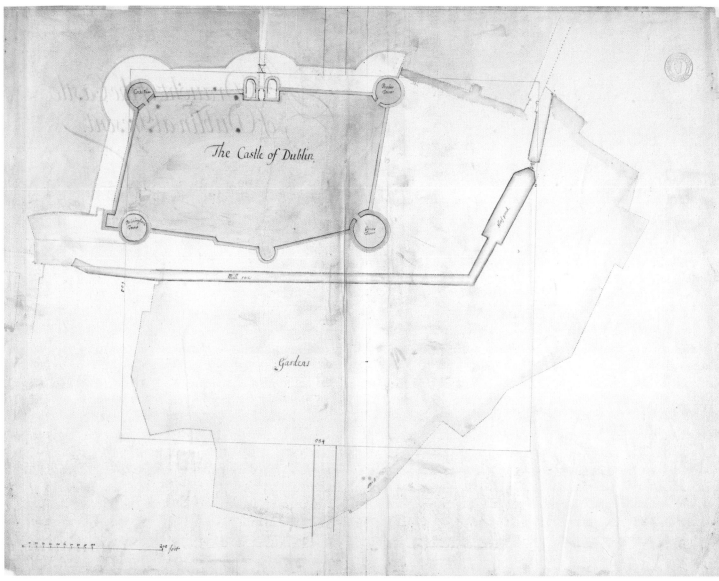

Fig. 2.2 Plan of Dublin Castle by Thomas Phillips, 1685. (NLI, MS 3137/3)

corner towers and entrance gate. He built a new governor's residence along the south wall of the castle, which included a Presence Chamber, ante-rooms for withdrawing, and a number of private closets, as well as a chapel and a clock tower. Sidney also built a Council Chamber just inside the gatehouse on the opposite side of the castle yard. He was praised in Holinshed's *Chronicles* for having found the castle 'ruinous, foule, filthie, and greatlie decaied' and for having 'repared, and reedified, and made a verie faire house for the lord deputie or the chiefe gouernor to reside and dwell in.'[11]

Over the following 120 years, the residential and administrative buildings were further augmented, while the medieval enceinte was kept in adequate repair. In 1585, Lord Deputy Sir John Perrot (Fig. 1.21) commissioned a survey of the city and castle walls, in which were recorded the numbers of floors and 'spickes' (window loops) on towers, their general state of repair, and their topographical positioning

in relation to each other.[12] However, no programme of works is known to have taken place as a result.

The late sixteenth century was a volatile period. At least two plots to take the castle were recorded for 1598, including one by the friar, Peter Nangle. Whether or not such a figure could have mounted a real threat, reprisals in the following years against recusants were severe. Sir Arthur Chichester, lord deputy (Fig. 2.4), was responsible for executions that resulted in the perceived martyrdom of his victims. Chichester also had difficulties convincing the Catholic members of parliament to attend the 1613 session, afraid as they were of the gunpowder stored under the chamber in the old hall in which the parliament was to be held. Unsatisfied with the residential quarters within the castle, Chichester built his own house on Hoggen Green, a house that would later be used as a parliament. Estimates to repair the castle were made, and rejected, and only smaller-

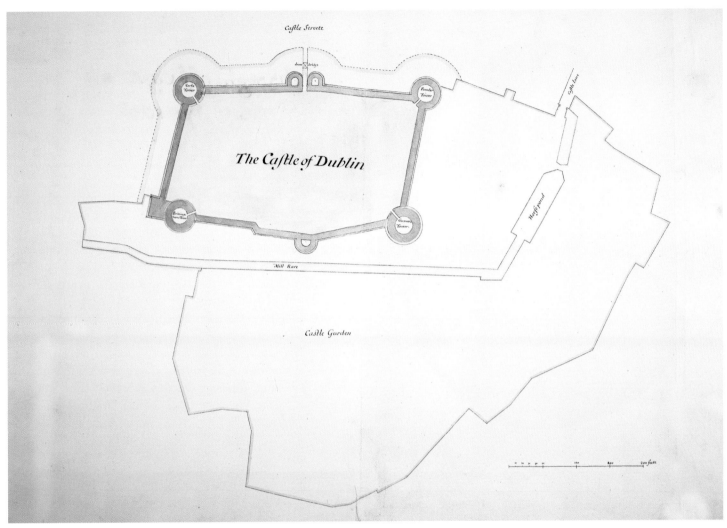

Fig. 2.3 A second plan of Dublin Castle by Thomas Phillips, 1685. (NLI, MS 2557(1))

scale works were carried out, including on the great hall in 1610 and 1613, and the building of a summer house in the castle garden in anticipation of the arrival of George Carew in 1611.

In 1614, Chichester was instructed to make repairs to the house and rooms (the governor's residence) which were 'much decayed', and to repair the gatehouse, 'being the prison for persons of quality'.[13] This work was eventually carried out by his successor, Oliver St John, in 1616–17. It was during his period of office (1612–22) that the Council Chambers collapsed – perhaps in 1620, after a fire of late 1618 or early 1619 – one of a series of building disasters which befell the castle during the century.[14]

While Henry Cary, Viscount Falkland (Fig. 2.11) was lord deputy in Ireland (1622–9), a detailed estimate of works needed to be carried out to the castle was made by Nicholas Pynnar, co-director general and overseer with Sir Thomas Rotherham of fortifications and buildings in Ireland. In a report dated 5 April, 1624, Pynnar identified works to be done on the walls and towers. Major defects were found in the

north-west tower – Pynnar noted the 'Rubbish and mud... in great aboundance' in the moat – and in the western and southern curtain walls and a number of unnamed towers.[15] Pynnar's survey was precise in one particular, the parlous state of the north-west tower, which collapsed less than a month later, on 1 May. Much hand-wringing followed without any action taken for its repair, or the upkeep of the rest of the walls. Nevertheless, Falkland managed to find money for the building of a significant ceremonial gallery linking the residential range on the south wall to the Council Chamber on the north, as we shall see.

During the interregnum between Falkland and his successor Thomas Wentworth – later the earl of Strafford (Fig. 2.5) – the country, and the castle, were managed by the Lords Justice, Richard Boyle, the earl of Cork, and archbishop of Dublin, Adam Loftus, later Viscount Ely. Neither invested in the residences in the castle, as both had houses in the city. But the castle continued as a meeting place of the council and as the seat of the administration. The birth of the future Charles II in 1631 was celebrated in the castle,

Fig. 2.4 Arthur Chichester.

the earl of Cork recording that the 'daie was generally comaunded to be kept a holly daie thoroughowt the Kingdom' and that he and the lord chancellor 'kept a Joinct ffeast in the great Hall', the celebrations costing £136 8s.[16] Before his arrival, both Cork and Ely wrote to Wentworth warning against expecting a residence fitting to his station, stating that it was 'much decayed, and very ruinous'.[17] In 1631, the earl of Cork rebuilt the north-west tower and placed his coat of arms high upon it. The tower was from then named in his honour.

Wentworth (Fig. 2.5), who considered himself the 'type' of the king,[18] that is an exemplar of royal ceremonial and political presence, sought to effect his own style of monarchical impact on the castle, and on other buildings in the country – his great trophy house at Jigginstown, Co. Kildare, being the most lasting example.[19] Charles yielded money to Wentworth for the aggrandisement of the castle. Indeed, an order was given in February 1632, before his arrival, that George Hull 'was to make all the preparations for the reception of the new Deputy Lord Wentworth' including making a full survey of the castle to 'see how much money would be necessary in order to repair it, and to give money for it at once'.[20] Wentworth arrived in July 1633 and, breaking with tradition, received the sword of state in the castle rather than in the nearby Christ Church cathedral.

This was carried from Cork's house, directly north of the castle, as far as the gallery, and from there processed to the Presence Chamber, where it is said that Wentworth made a great show of bowing to the king's and queen's pictures there.[21] Despite the preparations for his arrival, Wentworth, as we have noted, saw the castle as 'little better than a very Prison' and he began to make plans to make it 'as easeful and pleasant, as the Place will afford'.[22] As a result, he demolished one of the towers, perhaps the north-east one.[23] Most significantly, possibly, Wentworth had grand stables built in the Lower Yard, fit to house eighty horses. William Brereton, who visited the castle in 1635, was impressed by the stables, but his account also lends considerable insight into the state and appearance of the rest of the buildings, as will be noted below. Wentworth was known to some of his contemporaries as the 'Visier Basha', a name derived from the chief minister of the Sultan of Turkey, and had a reputation for 'oriental magnificence'.[24] His pretentions at times were imperious, as suggested by the full-length portrait (Frontispiece 2) Wentworth had van Dyck paint of him just before he left for Ireland. Based on a Titian painting of the Habsburg emperor Charles V, which then hung at Whitehall Palace, Wentworth was portrayed holding a baton of command in one hand with the other resting on an Irish

Fig. 2.5 Thomas Wentworth, earl of Strafford. (OPW Kilkenny Castle)

wolfhound.[25] Wentworth's hubristic career ended in ignoble disaster; his impeachment in November 1640, and his attainder and execution in London in May 1641, anticipated the demise of his former patron, Charles I.

The year 1641 was one of rebellion in Ireland. In response to plans by the rebels to take the castle in October that year, the governor of the fort in Galway, Sir Francis Willoughby, came to the capital and took control of Dublin Castle. In 1642, forty-six Catholic members accused of being rebels were expelled from parliament. Several Old English, who submitted to Ormond (Fig. 2.6), were brought to the castle and imprisoned including 'Lord Dunsany, Sir John Netterville, Sir Andrew, Gerald and George Aylmer, Edward Lawrence, Nicholas and Stephen Dowdall, Sir Nicholas White and his son, John Talbot, Gerald FitzGerald, Patrick Barnewall and W. Malone' all from the Pale.[26] The period was marked by Ormond's resistance to the English parliamentary takeover of the administration, and his efforts to manage and conciliate between Old English rebels and royalist forces. In April 1646, Corporal Robert Lloyd, one of Sir John Borlase's men, tried and failed to take the castle. He managed to enter it with seventeen associates and was armed with a loaded musket, which he misfired. Lloyd was executed for his troubles on a specially erected gibbet in the castle yard.[27] In June 1647, Michael Jones, a colonel in Cromwell's army, arrived as the new governor of the castle. Ormond was forced to send hostages to England, including his son Richard.[28] Ormond later surrendered the city to them by agreement, although he retained the sword of state until late July and remained resident in the castle with his family until then.

In August 1649, part of Ormond's army was routed at Baggotrath Castle, Dublin, and he was defeated at Rathmines. Two weeks later, Oliver Cromwell arrived at Dublin, greeted by the firing of the great guns in the castle as a welcome to him.[29] Cromwell is traditionally said to have resided in the cagework house that was situated at the end of Castle Street, at the junction with Werburgh Street, although some proclamations were made in the castle, including one against Dubliners' 'profane cursing'.[30] In 1655, the Irish were forbidden to enter the castle after sunset.[31] No parliament was held in Dublin during the 1650s as members attended at Westminster instead. During his four years in Ireland (1655–9), Cromwell's son, Henry Cromwell, rather than residing in the city stronghold, stayed at Phoenix House, which he extended to accommodate his family and retinue.[32]

On 13 December 1659, the castle was seized in a *coup d'etat* by Sir Theophilus Jones and Major Edward Warren among others.[33] The coup began with the casual entry into the fortress by soldiers who were former members of the castle guard. After walking around for a while, they asked to be let out by the back gate, and in doing so let in their comrades who, 'without striking a blow…seized the main guard, and

Fig. 2.6 Duke of Ormond. (OPW Kilkenny Castle)

possessed themselves of the Castle. Immediately they shot of[f] 3 great Guns, and in several parts of the Town came in 3 Troops with Swords drawn, crying unanimously for the Parliament'.[34] Although pro-parliament, they were the harbingers of the Restoration of the monarchy,[35] and this was proclaimed in the castle on 14 May only six days after Charles II's formal entry into London. Members of the Irish privy council processed from the Custom House on the river, to the gate of Dublin Castle, where the clerk made the proclamation, and the king was acclaimed to trumpets and drum rolls.[36]

In 1662, Ormond (Fig. 2.6) was once again returned as viceroy, remaining in this position until 1669, although he would resume office for a last time from 1677 to 1685. Although much influenced by Wentworth,[37] Ormond was the most active in creating a successful and splendid viceregal court. The early post-Restoration phase was marked by a degree of consolidation and there are some records of structural repair and renewal. It was most likely during this period in office that he installed a grand staircase and entrance portal (discussed below), which led to the dining room and the old hall on the south wall. In 1666, an account by the earl of Anglesey shows that moneys received out of England, from which payments were made for repairs and buildings in Dublin Castle, 'being for several years allowed to go to decay', amounted to £4,627 19s. 8d.[38] Two attempts were made in 1663 to take control of the castle and to assassinate Ormond, resulting, as discussed below, in the closing up of the postern gate to Ship Street in 1663.

In between Ormond's two post-Restoration periods in office, were the lord lieutenancies of Lord Robartes in 1669, Berkeley in 1670–2, and the earl of Essex in 1672–7 (Fig. 2.7). Robartes took the incisive decision – later reversed by Ormond – to remove the powder then stored in the great hall to a new purpose-built store in the castle garden. Berkeley, although an active supporter of building in the city, including the Wooden Bridge, which was the first new bridge across the Liffey since the Middle Ages, was less active as a builder at the castle. He did move the powder to a new store in Merrion, from which it was later moved to Crumlin, before Ormond returned it to the castle, and the north-east tower. Although not well liked in the city, Berkeley held a twice-weekly court for his mistress, Lady Clanbrassil, at which there was music and dancing.[39] The most important event in the castle during his period

in office was the fire of 1671 (see below), which destroyed the thirteenth-century great hall that had been used both as a court of law, and from 1613 until then, as the location of parliament.

His successor, Arthur Capel, the earl of Essex (1672–7), was unimpressed by the castle, and in an effort to secure the residence in the Phoenix Park, against the king's granting that demesne to the duchess of Cleveland, Essex referred to the castle as 'one of the most incommodious dwellings that I ever came in'. But he noted:

> I am confident if his Majestie knew the inconvenience every chief governor must live with here, if he be deprived of this Parke, he would not pass the Grant…there is no Place of pleasure belonging to it [the castle], nor any House to retire for a little Aire on occasion of sickness, but only those within the Parke.[40]

Like Berkeley, Essex was also a sponsor of improvements to the city, particularly the works of Sir Humphrey Jervis, who honoured him by naming the new bridge to his northside suburb, Essex Bridge, and by calling the principal thoroughfare through the estate, Capel Street. Essex also added a new wing to the lord deputy's lodgings and made improvements to the dining room (discussed below). Damages to the castle were recorded as a result of a storm in April 1677.[41] Despite his deep-seated aversion to 'popery',[42] Essex entertained Catholics at the castle including Oliver Plunket whom he believed to be 'one of the best men of his persuasion I have met with…more conformable to the government than any other titular bishops in this country'.[43]

During Ormond's final period as viceroy, records suggest that he lived in considerable style. Enormous sums were spent on provisions, evident for example in the £3,539 5s. 7d. held in storage of beef (bullocks), mutton, wine (Canary, French, Rhenish, Burgundy and Sherry), seacoal, charcoal, stonecoal, hay, straw, oats and beans.[44] In architectural terms, both as a monument in its own right and for its influence on discourse about the castle, the building of the Royal Hospital Kilmainham by Surveyor General, Sir William Robinson (Fig. 2.8), under the orders of Ormond (1680–7), was of considerable significance. In European terms, Robinson's military hospital was the most up-to-date, largest and most magnificent, public building to appear in the country in this period. Its grandeur was an embarrassment to the confused and cramped quarters at the castle and suggested the necessity for a new building altogether, or for demolishing the fortress and rebuilding a palace instead.

The complex and sometimes conflicting roles of the castle as viceregal court, palace and fortress, as location of the four courts and of the parliament, as the place of the principal

Fig. 2.7 Arthur Capel earl of Essex and Elizabeth countess of Essex. (National Portrait Gallery, London)

Fig. 2.8 William Robinson.
(Courtesy of the Huntingdon Art Museum. Gift of Beatrix Farrand)

Fig. 2.9 Earl of Arran.
(Image: Bridgeman. ©National Trust at Chatsworth)

state prison, and at the same time the chief armoury and powder keg of the country, was a point of often rehearsed, but never resolved, contention within the administration, and one played out in correspondence with London. The large numbers of people, of Irish or English extraction, who came to the castle on legal or administrative business were being allowed, not only access to, but also a kind of surveillance over, the central bolthole of the government in Ireland. The fact, as we shall see in greater detail below, that for many years the store of gunpowder was held in the vaults of the great hall, which was used as the courts of law and later the parliament house, was an inherently unviable situation, and yet it continued unabated. Ormond, for one, was reluctant to allow the powder to be stored anywhere outside the castle for security reasons. From 1669 as we have seen, the powder was briefly kept in a purpose-built store in the garden, where it remained vulnerable to capture or attack, and was returned to the north-east tower, the so-called, Powder Tower, shortly afterwards.

Finally, it was in an effort to protect the Powder Tower, that a great part of the internal residential and administrative buildings, developed since the time of Sidney, was destroyed. On 7 April 1684, between one and two in the early hours of the morning, the earl of Arran (Fig. 2.9), son to the duke of Ormond, and the lord deputy of Ireland in his absence, was awoken to the sound of crackling in the room next to his. Opening the door to his chamber he was beaten back by flames and smoke. For the following two hours, Arran and a young man called Cuffe, among others, bravely fought back the flames. By using gunpowder to create controlled explosions, Arran destroyed enough of the residential buildings to save the great powder store in the north-east tower to the castle, and in turn, perhaps, a great deal of the city itself.[45]

Ormond was understood to have lost effects to the value of £10,000, by a fire 'which hath burnt the best rooms, but the castle and magazine all safe'.[46] Sir William Petty, among others, appears to have drafted a plan for a new palace estimating its cost at £20,000,[47] and it was reported by Falkiner that a king's letter was drafted authorising the sale of the site and materials of the castle,[48] although no such document has been found.[49] The wholly new citadel proposed for Ringsend in 1685–6, by Thomas Phillips, which would have cost as much as £126,750 10s., also came to nothing.[50] Instead, the debris was cleared and a new castle was developed on the same site over the course of the following century.

By so doing, the medieval castle and all that was built in the late sixteenth and early seventeenth century were replaced almost completely.

Chapter 2.2
Walls and Towers

The medieval walled enclosure of the castle survived for most of the seventeenth century. It was only demolished or built over when the castle came to be rebuilt after the destruction of the 1684 fire. This enclosure was clearly delineated in a number of contemporary surveys. The best of these includes the 1673 Dartmouth plan (Fig. 2.1) and the pair of surviving plan surveys carried out by Thomas Phillips in 1685 (Figs 2.2, 2.3). These show a broadly rectangular enclosure with circular-plan towers on each of the four corners, a double D-shaped towered gatehouse as entrance in the centre of the north wall, and a smaller rounded turret projection towards the centre of the south wall. The wall between the south-west tower and the turret in the middle of the south wall is staggered southwards slightly about halfway between the main tower and the turret. There is also a squared projection to the west of the south-west tower. It is possible that this was added to give flanking protection to the western wall of the enceinte. The latter does not line up to the position of the south-west tower, which may predate the large enclosure by approximately a decade.[51] We know from written sources that there were at least two postern gates, one into Ship Street, and a second into the castle's Lower Yard. The latter is shown on the 1673 plan (Fig. 2.1) to have been on the eastern curtain wall, south of the north-east tower, between the 'Cole yard' and some lodgings in that north-eastern corner.

The walls were surrounded by a wide ditch or moat which, in medieval times at least, was sometimes filled by water from the Poddle, but by the seventeenth century had become backfilled with refuse, and in places built upon. A wide moat is indicated on both of the Phillips plans (Figs 2.2, 2.3). However, other markings on those plans make it difficult to discern what was projection and what was survey. The trajectory of the walls as represented on these late seventeenth-century plans has been confirmed to a greater or lesser degree by excavation, although the wall on the east side in reality appears to follow a much more clearly north–south direction than the north–north-east line it takes on these earlier images.[52]

Walls

In 1635 William Brereton referred to the 'very high walls… of great strength, and a drawbridge which is pulled up every night'.[53] The walls were wide enough to afford a platform for walking, as is shown on the Dartmouth plan (Fig. 2.1). While explaining the escape over the wall by Sir Edmund Butler, the Lord Lieutenant Henry Sidney noted that Butler 'had leave to use the walk on the wall, only guarded with two of my men, whom I thought to have been more vigilant than I found them'.[54] It is possible, as Hughes argues, that the walls were damaged by a very significant explosion of gunpowder in 1596. Up to 144 barrels were being delivered to the castle, but the explosion took place somewhere north of it, between the castle and the Liffey at Wood Quay, where the powder was landed.[55] It may be that some superficial repairs were carried out by Lord Deputy Chichester (from 1604–15) and others in the 1630s by Wentworth.[56] Nicholas Pynnar's survey of the castle in 1624 noted defects in the north-west tower, the walls to the south and west being 'weather beaten' and in the 'West end…a crack from one tower to the other [which] must be pynned, both in that place and som[e] others'.[57] The more substantial damage to the western walls seems consistent with what may have happened as a result of the 1596 incident, as the explosion took place to the north-west of the castle. Brooking's 1728 castle image (Fig. 1.20) shows some remaining portions of its wall still extant following the large-scale rebuilding that took place after the 1684 fire. Brooking's illustration suggests that a very tall wall, approximately three storeys high, survived on the north side between the gates and the location of the former north-west (Cork) tower, which had been demolished by then. However, a portion of wall survives still beneath the present St Patrick's Hall on the western section of the south wall. Hughes also speculates about the possibility that the terrace in front of the eighteenth-century state apartments was partly formed by the collapse of the wall there when the powder store (discussed below) was exploded in 1689.[58]

Unnamed towers

Sometimes the towers are referred to in general, or without specifying any tower in particular. For example, Sir Roger Jones' petition to the privy council in *c.* 1627–8 urges 'that the towers of Dublin Castle be built up, "that the place where the Houses of Parliament sit may not lie open to the attempt of ill-affected multitudes"'.[59] Sometime after 1633, Wentworth demolished one of the towers stating that the others were 'so crasy, as we are still in fear Part of it might drop down upon our Heads'.[60] Towers were often used to house prisoners or hostages. In a letter to Secretary Williamson in 1663, Col. Vernon stated that 'You will hear how that most notorious villain Alden broke prison… so subtle was the knave that 'tis not imagined how he broke loose, for the window bar that he broke was upon the top of all the castle in the highest turret'.[61] We might suspect in this description more defensive hyperbole than topographical accuracy.

More often, references are to specific towers, and these will be treated individually starting with that on the north-west, later called the Cork Tower, and moving clockwise as far as the tower on the south-west, usually known as Bermingham Tower.

North-west tower – later known as the Cork Tower

According to Perrot's 1585 survey of the castle and city walls, the north-west tower was of four storeys including a 'dongeon [where] ther is never a spicke' – a spicke being a window loop.[62] Thus is suggested a basement or dungeon storey without light. Perhaps this was the tower where Archbishop Creagh was imprisoned in 1567. He says he was put

first in a hole, where without candle there was no light in the world, and with candle (when I had it) it was so filled with the smoke thereof (chiefly in summer), that, had there not been a little hole in the next door to draw in breath with my mouth set upon it, I had been soon undone.[63]

Notwithstanding the absence of lights into the basement dungeon, the 1585 report lists flanking loops on all levels and in multiple directions, which, along with other details from this Perrot report, casts some doubt on the accuracy of the closely contemporary woodcut plate, Derricke's *Image of Irelande* (1581), in which only one large window (not a spicke)

is shown (Fig. 2.10).[64] Pynnar's 1624 survey found the north-west tower in perilous condition. Costs for repair, estimated at some £891, were mostly to do with mortar, timber-work, and lead, as all stone was to be reused. It was noted, however, that the foundations were on clay rather than on limestone, and the building was subject to subsidence. Timber needed replacement, particularly for the roof trusses, which were to hold the weight of artillery.[65] The top of the tower may have been open, as it appears to have been when Henry Fitzsimon, the Jesuit priest, was held there from 1599–1604, and described himself as entering into disputations with passers-by in Castle Street: 'from the Castle or the cell I challenged them in a stentorian voice'.[66] According to Pynnar, the north-west tower was 63ft (19.2m) high, with a circumference of 124ft (37.8m), taken from the middle of the wall, and a wall thickness of 10ft (3m).[67]

Pynnar's and others' misgivings about the tower were shown to be well-founded soon after the survey, when the tower collapsed on 2 May the same year, nearly killing the Lord Chancellor Archbishop Loftus and some of his grandchildren who were nearby.[68] The tower 'fell down to the ground with the ordnance mounted upon it. The fall has shaken a great part of the wall, and it will cost much to replace, which had better be done at once, but money must be sent to do it with'.[69] Falkland stated that £1,000 would complete it, despite the fact that 'the surveyors' certificates exceed that amount by £300'.[70] However, the money was not forthcoming, and eventually, according to the antiquary James Ware, Richard Boyle, 'the opulent first Earl [of Cork] of that name anno 1629 undertook the finishing thereof at his own proper cost and charge' of £408.[71] Boyle's arms were placed on what from now on would be called in his honour, the Cork Tower:

This daie (god be ever praised) the worck I vndertook, which was to reedifie the Tower of his Ma'ts castle of dublin that was fallen down, was fynished at my own chardge, without Costing his Ma'ty one penney, eyther for the rebwylding therof, or platforming it with lead and three inche plancks; the whole chardge of which bwylding coste me in ready moneys owt of my purse £441 3s 8d. The God of Heaven bless me, and enable me by his grace to doe many more such lyke, and other good worcks.[72]

The only certain visual evidence we have for the tower are the plans made in 1673 and 1685. Labelled as the 'Corke Tower' on the earliest of these (Fig. 2.1), the tower is shown as fully circular in plan with the curtain abutting rather than breaking into or being integrated with the tower. An indication is given of some sub-rectangular chamber on its eastern side with a doorway giving onto the wall walk of the north curtain wall. The two plans produced in 1685 by

Phillips present apparently contradictory evidence. On MS 2557 (Fig. 2.3) the tower is shown more or less as depicted in the Dartmouth 1673 plan, i.e., as being circular in plan; while on MS 3137 (Fig. 2.2) the north-west tower is shown as being merely rounded on the exterior, but integrated into the walls, and presenting a straight wall to the courtyard of the castle. This plan may, however, represent the upper parapet level – the walls are thinner for example – and so suggests that the upper level of the tower may have been lopped off in its construction at this height, and by these means gave access to the parapet.[73] The tower did not survive the reworking of the castle carried out in the eighteenth century: it does not appear on Brooking's 1728 image of the castle (Fig. 1.20), which suggests that it had been demolished to make way for the eastern range of buildings in the newly configured Upper Yard.

Gatehouse

Following the two-storey interpretation of the 1685 Phillips plans as outlined in the preceding section, the second-storey plan on manuscript NLI, 3137(3) (Fig. 2.2) yields to us a fairly explicit indication of the nature of the gatehouse. It is formed by two D-shaped towers, joined in the centre at this level by a small square chamber, which no doubt stood over the archway of the gate itself.

John Derricke's much earlier depiction of 'Sir Henry Sidney leaving Dublin Castle' in his *Image of Irelande* (1581) (Fig. 2.10)[74] appears to match the Phillips plans for the most part. Here we have two towers, the one on the east being round, while the western turret is presented as octagonal. Once again, we should not depend on Derricke regarding the issue of arrow loops,[75] although it is interesting that the artist has suggested putlog holes below and above the windows, at the second stage of what appears to be a

Fig. 2.10 Henry Sidney riding out of Dublin Castle from Derricke's *Image of Irelande* (1581).

three-stage tower.[76] Sidney is shown in procession out of the gatehouse across an arched permanent bridge, rather than a drawbridge, a structure sometimes mentioned in the sources. Perhaps this was licence on the part of the artist, although the existence of a wall to the front of the moat, a perhaps unusual feature, is confirmed as we will see below, by other sources. There is also a portcullis behind the lord deputy, and the heads of Irish rebels are stuck on pikes above the main portal:

> These trunckles heddes do playnly showe, eache rebeles fatall end,
> And what a haynous crime it is, the Queene for to offend.[77]

There is an alternative interpretation of the Derricke image which may better fit the references to a drawbridge, as well as the archaeological evidence.[78] Derricke's view may instead represent a barbican, i.e., a defensive outwork which reached away from the main gate by way of a causeway which could have crossed the moat twice. The first time was over the drawbridge – located within the barbican and consequently behind the portcullis depicted in Derricke – and the second by way of the bridge as shown. Excavations revealed such a causeway, with a secondary smaller ditch closer to the exterior. Thick walls found on either side of the causeway were consistent with the possibility of a superstructure, of the type found for example at the barbican at the Dublin Gate of Trim Castle.[79] This suggestion would fit nicely with Hugh O'Donnell being confined 'to the castle bridge',[80] which perhaps alludes to this type of barbican, which would have had a small chamber above the outer gate. That there were no such barbican towers shown on the Phillips or Dartmouth plans may be explained by the possibility that the barbican was demolished during works on the gatehouse, carried out in 1614–18, and which cost £929.[81] Alternatively, work on the gate at this period may have been to provide useful accommodation at the rear of the gate. The Phillips and Dartmouth plans may simply have omitted features partly obscured by private dwellings, shops and other buildings at this time. In this regard also, Wattson's more roughly rendered plan of 1606 (Fig. 1.15), while referring to the 'drawe bridge', gives no hint at such a projecting structure – unless we are to take the round arch at the end of the drawbridge as some kind of portal. Indeed, the X-shape contained within straight lines, some way along the path north of the gateway on de Gomme's 1673 map of Dublin (Fig. 2.12), could also be suggestive of such a structure in front of the gate. The strongest evidence against the proposition that there was a projection to the front of the gatehouse, however, must be Perrot's seemingly exhaustive 1585 survey, which does not mention a barbican or any other structure in this location.[82]

Fig. 2.11 Henry Cary, 1st viscount Falkland. (National Portrait Gallery, London)

Whatever of the vital questions to do with the architectural form of the gatehouse, Derricke's image (Fig. 2.10) remains deeply significant as a rare insight into the social and sometimes ceremonial splendour of life in Dublin Castle which, while its colour and details continued to change over the years, nevertheless represents an aspect of continuous military if not courtly display up until the early twentieth century. Derricke shows the lord deputy sitting high upon his charger, in civilian clothes with a breastplate over them, wearing a tall felt hat. He is flanked to the rear and front by an armoured guard in procession along Castle Street towards Christ Church cathedral. To his front the guard of seventeen horsemen hold spears erect and another blows an annunciatory trumpet. At least four guards, armed with spears, emerge beneath the portcullis to the rear of the lord deputy. At the head of, and guiding Sidney's horse, is a boy with a staff.[83] It is interesting to note, as Dougal Shaw has, that images such as this, and of Sidney being ceremonially received into the city by the mayor and aldermen of Dublin, may have given some embarrassing substance to the Butler claim that their rebellion of 1569

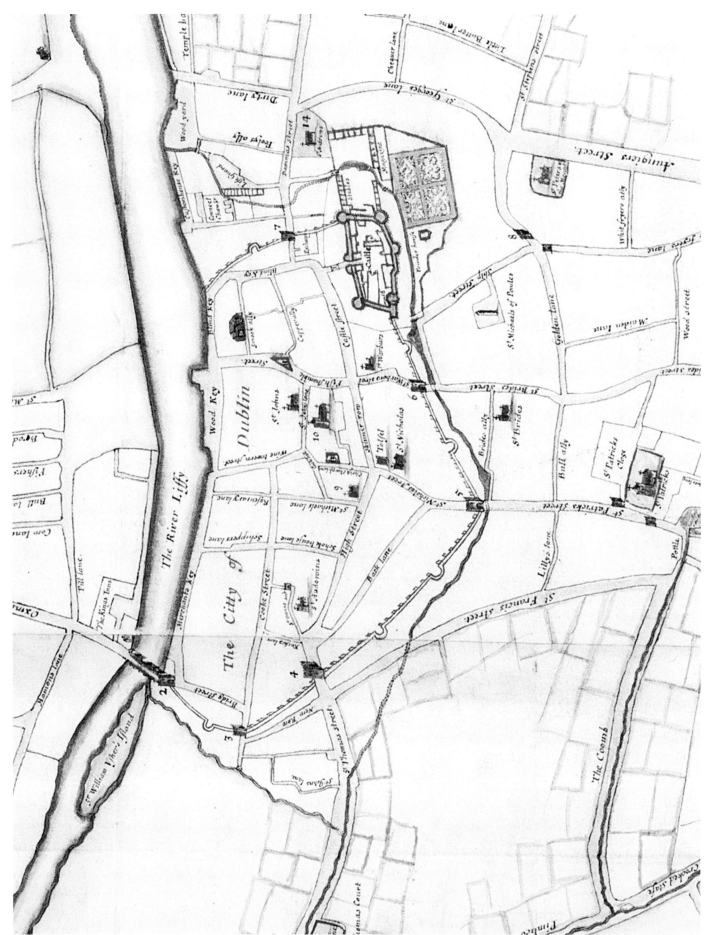

Fig. 2.12 Detail from the map of Dublin 1673 by Bernard de Gomme. (National Maritime Museum, Greenwich)

was merely in defence of Elizabeth, and against Sidney who was 'conspiring to be king of Ireland'.[84] A perhaps related image of a procession out of Dublin Castle, this time to St Patrick's cathedral, may be conjured up from the account of Lord Deputy Wentworth setting out for his first Irish parliament in 1634. From his own contemporary description, we know that he was flanked on either side by footmen and yeomen of the horse, his train supported by Lord Brabazon, Sir Robert Loftus, and Mr. Arthur Jones. Behind him were the Gentleman of the Horse, leading 'an Horse of Estate, The Colonel, The guard, Two trumpets and a troop of Horse'. He was proceeded by one foot company, two trumpets, one troop of horse, and two messengers, who were followed by all present officials of state, members of parliament, in order of precedent, and in pairs, gentlemen, knights, baronets, barons, earls, the bishops of the Church of Ireland, and by the earl of Ormond carrying the sword, and the earl of Kildare, the cap of estate.[85]

There are other references to the bridge and to the drawbridge. A 1590 account by Sir George Carew of a mutiny among the castle guard stated that in the resulting standoff, there was enough room on the bridge for seventy-seven protesting soldiers and the Lord Deputy Fitzwilliam on horseback.[86] Sir William Brereton's 1635 description refers to 'a drawbridge which is pulled up every night'.[87] In 1698, John Dunton noted the 'wall and drye ditch over which is a drawbridge and within that an iron gate'.[88] By 1728, Brooking depicted a gatehouse similar to the one shown on the Phillips plan, with rounded towers on either side of a flat-fronted portal (Fig. 1.20). Brooking's gatehouse turrets are also shown with typically Irish crow-step crenellations, a modification which may have replaced the more regular type shown by Derricke. Finally, the possibility that some portion of the western gatehouse tower survived within the body of the eighteenth-century Bedford Tower, as Hughes suggested, may be discounted following recent archaeological examination.[89]

In 1614, some reconstruction works were proposed by Lord Deputy Chichester for the gatehouse, it 'being the prison for persons of quality'.[90] This work was not carried out until 1617, under Lord Deputy Sir Oliver St John. It is not clear what was undertaken, other than perhaps some timber and stone repairs or, as suggested above, the possible demolition of a barbican. During the reconstruction works prisoners were transferred to Newgate, and Edward Horton, the keeper of Newgate, was paid 'for his charge'.[91] A concordatum of '£929 11s English' was granted to Humphry Farname Esq. for this and other works.[92] In 1618, it was recorded that 'the new gatehouse' was 'nearly finished'.[93]

In 1590, in one of two dramatic escapes carried out by Hugh O'Donnell, he was said to have escaped from the gatehouse when he was confined 'to the castle bridge'.[94]

Another prisoner 'condemned in the Castle broke his fetters, and by the help of other prisoners got over the wall at the grate [sic], and escaped'.[95] In 1632, the king gave instructions to the Lords Justice for removing prisoners from the castle, ordering that they be kept 'in some other part of the city, and not in the gate where they are on the Deputy's road to church, and may be a danger in case of an infection'.[96]

North-east tower (Powder Tower)

Like the other three corner towers, the one on the north-east was also circular in plan, and according to the 1673 Dartmouth image (Fig. 2.1) communicated directly with the wall walks. It is described as a five-storey tower in Perrot's 1585 survey, and it was on the fifth floor of this tower, in fact, that Perrot stayed while at the castle. Perrot's survey also noted the many 'spickes' (arrow loops) and windows in this tower. These included the windows on the third floor 'the firste skouring northweste, the seconde northeste, the thirde flanketh the gardine wall'.[97] The base of this tower was uncovered during excavations by Con Manning in 1986, which showed that there was a floor below ground level.[98] A report of a sighting of Spanish ships in Dublin Bay in 1627, 'from the top of the Castle Tower here',[99] was possibly from this tower. Hughes suggests that this was the tower to which Wentworth referred when he claimed in a letter of 1633 to have been 'enforced to take down one of the great Towers, which was ready to fall' citing the previous collapse of the north-west (later Cork) tower, and the 'crasy'-ness of the others.[100] Wentworth may have been referring instead to demolishing the fifth floor of the Powder Tower, which may have been erected just before, or during, Perrot's time at the castle.[101] Alternatively, he may have been referring to some reduction to the 'small square tower' (as it was described by Perrot in 1585,[102] and which was the platform projection to the south-west tower as shown on the Dartmouth and Phillips plans), as works were carried out some time in the seventeenth century to convert that to a platform for artillery.[103] In 1663 Captain John Paine, 'director-general and overseer of the king's fortifications',[104] put in an estimate of £62 8s. for works 'besides the Powder Tower and two stores', which expression suggests that the stores and the Powder Tower were among the £1,478.09.04 worth of works billed for the previous October.[105] Sometime in 1669, Lord Lieutenant Robartes, removed the powder store to a new one in the castle garden, although the foundations of this later building failed and necessitated the transfer of the store back to the north-east tower of the castle temporarily, before being moved again to Merrion and then to Crumlin, in the southern outskirts of Dublin. Unlike Robartes, Ormond was less confident in the powder being stored away from the castle – where it could be better safeguarded – so that at some date after 1678, perhaps 1682, when a payment of £600 was made to William Robinson for works done, Ormond had the powder returned to what was for some time referred to as the Powder Tower.[106] This of course was what forced Lord Arran, his son, and deputy, to destroy Falkland's gallery by explosion, in order to prevent the fire that broke out in 1684 from reaching the powder store in the same north-east tower, and the almost inevitable destruction of the castle and a considerable portion of the city. Although the tower survived that event, it was no longer there by the time Brooking depicted the castle in 1728 (Fig. 1.20). The location was being used as another store, perhaps for the office of the Ordnance, from some time in the early eighteenth century.

South-east tower (Record Tower, Wardrobe Tower, Gunners Tower)

The south-east tower was also circular in plan, and according to the 1673 Dartmouth image (Fig. 2.1) it communicated with the wall walks through a door in a flat wall on the side facing the castle yard. It is labelled as 'Gunners Tower' on this and on the Phillips 1685 plans (Figs 2.2, 2.3), although it was also referred to as the Wardrobe Tower and the Record Tower as its function changed.[107] It was possibly referred to as the Black Tower in a newspaper report of 1689,[108] probably because of the use of black Dublin Calp limestone in its construction, despite this being the material used for all of the walls and towers. According to Hughes, this tower measured approximately 50ft (15.2m) in diameter, with walls 16ft (4.9m) thick.[109] Manning has noted that this is the most 'massively built of all of the corner towers', being the most exposed, at the furthest reaches from the rest of the medieval city and its defences.[110] On Brooking's 1728 image (Fig. 1.20), the tower appears to be slightly lower than the two-storeys-plus-dormer range built by William Molyneux and William Robinson in the later 1680s (see Chapter 3.2). Seeing as this was described in the 1585 report as being only a three-storey tower rather than, say, the five storeys of the north-eastern tower, this relative height as represented by Brooking seems about right.[111]

The suggestion that Hugh O'Donnell made the second of his two dramatic escapes, at Christmas 1591, via the garderobe of this tower, may be discounted.[112] The most detailed account of his life, the *Beatha Aodha Ruaidh Uí Dhomhnaill*,[113] simply notes that O'Donnell and his comrades descended through a privy with a rope and went off through the crowded streets 'in front of the castle' and then out through the gates of the city. Had he escaped from a tower on the south side of the castle he would already have been free of the city, as the enceinte of the castle on its south forms part of the city walls in this south-eastern corner of the city.[114] Even if his movement through the gates of the city is an embellishment by the author of O'Donnell's life, there is no specification given regarding from which tower he departed.

In 1628, Robert Cottrell was appointed as housekeeper and keeper of the king's wardrobe in Dublin Castle and was granted the south-east tower as a residence. His office involved the 'keeping, cleaning, airing, and dressing up of all the houses, rooms, and buildings erected, or to be erected in his Majesty's Castle of Dublin, and of the charge of keeping, cleaning, and airing of all robes, hangings, cloaks of state, chairs, stools, and other utensils…and likewise to the office of keeping and setting of the clock; also a grant of the south-east tower within the castle, for the residence of the said Cottrell'.[115] In 1678, Ware stated that 'the King's royal Robe, the Capp of maintenance, and other furniture are kept' in what Ware called the Garderobe Tower, and these would be 'preserved by a Patent officer who had a competent salary for that imployment'.[116] As noted, however, this tower was also later called Gunners Tower, and when Dunton in 1698 described the 'two brass field pieces…on top of one of the towers', he may therefore have been referring to this one.[117] It was only in 1813, following its conversion, that it became the Record Tower, and so replaced the Bermingham Tower as the repository of state and other official archives.[118]

South (Middle) Tower

A small tower in the middle of the south wall appears on a number of the later seventeenth-century maps of the castle. It does not appear on Wattson's rough sketch of 1606 (Fig. 1.15). It is rendered as a circular swelling along the exterior of the wall on the 1673 and 1685 plans (Figs 2.1, 2.2, 2.3). The ground-floor Phillips plan, NLI, MS 2557(1) (Fig. 2.3), seems to confirm this impression of an adjunct or non-integrated exterior construction. However, the nine or ten smaller windows or loops listed in the 1585 survey, between this tower and Bermingham's Tower, suggests the likelihood that this was connected to some of the internal courtyard buildings we know stood here, such as the smaller hall, and other residential buildings.[119] Pynnar's 1624 survey states that at this time, this smaller tower 'hath no platforme and is very needefull to have a peece of Artillery'.[120]

South-west tower – Kitchen Tower, Bermingham Tower

The Bermingham Tower was probably the most substantial of all of the circular towers on the four corners, and plausibly may have been the first to have been built, thus predating the medieval enceinte that survived to the seventeenth century.[121] According to Ware in 1678, this was 'the statelyest, highest, and strongest Tower in this ffortress'.[122] Perrot's 1585 survey noted that this tower was of four storeys.[123] In 1624, echoing his assessment of the South (Middle) Tower, as just noted, Pynnar suggested that 'Bremagems Tower wanteth no stonework but it hath no platforme, w'ch is a place fitt for a peece of Artillery'.[124] This would suggest that the south-west tower was not substantially affected by the 1596 explosion to the north-west of the castle which appeared to have damaged the west curtain wall and the north-west tower. However, Hughes suggests that the walls of the Bermingham Tower were only about 8ft (2.4m) compared to the 16ft (4.9m) of the Record Tower, and that the tower was only 44 ft (13.4m) in diameter compared to the 50ft (15.2m) of the Record Tower.[125] In contrast to this, Brooking's 1728 map shows the south-west tower – arguably under reconstruction at the time it was recorded, rather than being in a state of ruin as it appears[126] – to be much larger in girth and in height than the south-east tower. Both the 1673 Dartmouth plan (Fig. 2.1) and the 1685 Phillips plans (Figs 2.2, 2.3) show what on the 1673 map is labelled as a platform to the west of this tower. This is described as the 'little square toure' in the survey made of the castle for Sir John Perrot in 1585.[127] This was probably built to give flanking protection to the western wall of the enclosure, which does not align itself properly with the round south-west tower. Arguably, this was the tower first ordered by King John in 1204, and was possibly associated with an earlier, smaller enclosure.[128] Based on excavations, this square tower appeared to have had an extra face added to it, probably in the seventeenth century, and was converted to a platform for artillery.[129]

The Bermingham Tower appeared to have had at times a double function, both as repository of records – until the early nineteenth century – and as the kitchen. Records of state were brought there as early as 1537.[130] In a communication from the lord deputy to the privy council in 1566, it was noted that 'Henry Draycott, Chancellor and Remembrancer of the Exchequer, now Master of the Rolls, "hath had the perusing, sorting and kalendaringe of Her Majesty's recordes" which are "well layd upp in a stronge chamber of one of the towers of Dublin Castle"'.[131] In 1578, fees of £13 8s. 6d. were recorded as due to 'Thomas Cotton, gentleman…as Keeper of the Records in the Bermingham Tower'.[132] It is possible that this Thomas Cotton (c. 1544–92) was the father of Sir Robert Bruce Cotton, antiquary and politician, from part of whose collections their descendent Sir John Cotton, created the Cotton Library, purchased for the British nation by an Act of Parliament in 1701.[133] The existence of the records in this tower created the necessity for the second of Arran's two controlled explosions carried out on the night of the castle fire in 1684, this time to the western part of the southern residential range. That this was kept as a record repository seems hard to square with its also known function as a kitchen. According to Perrot's 1585 survey of the castle, the kitchen was in the second storey of the Bermingham Tower. It is possible of course that the repository was held elsewhere in the tower, but such a risk of destruction by accidental fire damage seems difficult to reconcile. According to Ware, the servants' quarters ('the

offices below stairs') and the kitchen were nearby,[134] and the Wattson 1606 plan shows the 'Dep[uty's]: Kitchin Yeard' connecting this tower, the great hall and the deputy's houses.

Sidney's gate with inscription

One feature of which there is evidence, but whose location is unknown, was a gate with an inscription over it, built by Sir Henry Sidney in 1576. Our knowledge of it is confined to notes by Wentworth, who demolished the gate, but preserved its inscription, and by Thomas Dineley who viewed the inscription in the 1680s. Wentworth's information comes by way of a confession, to the earl of Leicester, who was a descendent of Sidney:

> I confess I made a Fault against your noble Grandfather, by pulling down an Old Gate within this Castle, wherein was set an Inscription of his Verses, but I did so far contemplate him again in his Grandchild as to give him the best Reparation I could, by setting up the very same Stone, carefully taken down, over the new one, which one Day your Lordship may chance to read, and remember both him and me by that Token.[135]

It was Dineley who noted the date of 1575, stating that Dublin Castle was 'beautified by S'r Henry Sydney then Lord Lieutenant [in] Anno 1575 under Queen Eliz. as appears by inscripc'on'.[136] The Latin inscription spoke of the great deeds of men which after books decay will be preserved in stone. Maguire, who provides a translation of it, noted the irony that it was by way of a book – Stanihurst in Holinshed's *Chronicles* – that the inscription came down to us.[137]

Postern to Ship Street

We are aware of two known postern gates, one to Ship Street in the south-west of the castle, and one to the Lower Yard, close to the north-east tower. We also have a record of another proposed sally port which was to be built to allow access to Castle Street, which is discussed below. The postern to Ship Street is only known by way of documentary evidence, and no indication is given on any of the seventeenth-century plans as to where it had been located. The gate existed as early as 1641, when Sir Francis Willoughby ordered that the steps from Ship Street to the castle be demolished.[138] The gate must nevertheless have remained open, as two unsuccessful conspiracies to take the castle and to assassinate the duke of Ormond, Lord Lieutenant, took place in 1663. The first was to have taken place on 4 March, and was scuppered by Jenkin Hopkins, a spy in the rebel camp.[139] The second, the more famous, was the Warren, Jephson and Blood conspiracy of 21 May, when confusion was to be caused during the expected morning delivery of bread through this gate, with eighty rebels to be posted here, and more at the main gate and the postern to the Lower Yard.[140] The closing of this gate may have been among the works carried out from 1661–3 by, among others, 'Mr. [John] Mills, the Master Carpenter' to the Royal Works in Ireland.[141]

Postern to the Lower Yard

The second known gate was the postern gate to the Lower Yard. This gate is shown on the 1673 Dartmouth plan (Fig. 2.1) as being directly south of the Powder (north-east) Tower, not below the Record Tower as Hughes, who had not seen the 1673 map, had postulated.[142] On the 1673 map it is labelled as 'Postern gate', and is represented by a pair of dotted lines cutting through the wall which continue between the 'Cole yard' along the north wall, and some 'Lodging' directly south. According to Ware in 1678, this 'other Posterne gate is still open, but secured by a constant Guard, which will permit you to descend thence into the Stable yard, where you may take delight in seeing the great horse ridden, …the office for the Ordnance is now kept at the issuing out of the said last mentioned Gate'.[143]

Proposed postern on the west wall to Castle Street

This gate was proposed by Sir Edward Brabazon in a letter sent to the earl of Salisbury in 1606. The Wattson plan (Fig. 1.15) already referred to was drafted in order to make the topography of the castle and these proposed changes, clearer to the recipient.[144]

A major flaw in the internal and defensive arrangements of the castle was the public access to the law courts – which took place in the great hall (see below). To this end, Brabazon proposed that a new wall be built on the east end of the great hall, blocking the courts from the rest of the castle, and that access to them, and this western part of the castle be channelled through a new postern gate to Castle Street.[145] This is shown on the Wattson plan as an arched portal leading to 'the new bridge' across the western moat or ditch, which in turn led to Castle Street. The houses on the latter are shown in saw-tooth profile, with the first, most eastern, labelled as 'this house to be bought' suggesting that the gate was set to the rear or south of the street, and access from gate to street would need to be made by demolishing the first house. The postern gate to Castle Street does not seem to have been built. Some of its functions may have been taken up by the Ship Street postern, which may have been built between this proposal and the 1640s when it is first noted (see above).

Moat or ditch

The medieval castle was surrounded by a moat which contained varying levels of water from the Poddle river which passed close to it. The area of the moat at least, if not filled by flowing water, survived into the seventeenth century. In the sixteenth century, there is a record of augmenting the medieval fosse, when some house and garden plots were shortened in order to enlarge the ditch, and when some fruit trees were pulled up. Robinson notes that this might have been 'associated with the building of a wall on the outer edge of the ditch at the expense of the city, in 1577', but that the wall was demolished before 1612.[146] A wall was depicted on the outer lip of the moat on Derricke's *Image of Irelande* (1581) picture of Sir Henry Sidney processing out of the main gate, as already noted above (Fig. 2.10). In his description of Derricke's image of the castle, D.B. Quinn suggested that men depicted in the same image as working, it appears, up to their waste before an extended curtain wall, may have been working on extending the moat of the castle.[147] However, this points to either a misunderstanding of Derricke's image, or alternatively a misconstruing of the castle by Derricke in the first place. This extended wall goes beyond what is clearly Cork Tower (mislabelled by Quinn as Cook Tower), and therefore is either Derricke's fantasy of a larger extended castle, or his hint at what might have been the extended city walls – albeit ones whose sighting from this angle would have been impossible through the houses of Castle Street and Werburgh Street. Nevertheless, if they indeed represent to Derricke the extended city walls, then digging out a moat on the inside of these walls, makes no sense. In 1584, a Dublin Corporation deed to Edward Peppard (former sheriff of Dublin), mentions a site set 'from the wall of the castle ditch of Dublin'.[148] Pynnar's survey of 1624, mentions the £60 it will cost to clear the 'Rubbish and the Mudd…in greate aboundance' from the moat.[149] An undated document (although possibly dating to 1663 or early 1664), perhaps in Captain John Paine's hand, contains an estimate of £14 in order to 'open & cleere ye water courses and to make 2 new water courses from ye Castle wall to the River'.[150] That the water was gone by the later century seems also to be confirmed by Ware's note that the castle had been stronger 'when it was encompassed and fortifyed by the flowing of ye sea around about it'.[151] As already noted, Dunton in 1698 stated that the castle was 'encompasst with a wall and drye ditch over which is a drawbridge'.[152]

In terms of its outline, Wattson's 1606 plan is merely schematic, and refers to the 'southe ditche', 'west ditche', 'north ditche', and 'east ditche' which are rectangular and hardly convincing in terms of their dimensions or topographical appearance (Fig. 1.15). The ditch is not included on the 1673 Dartmouth plan. However, both of the Phillips 1685 plans give detailed delineation of the nature of the moat, particularly on the ground-floor plan NLI, MS 2557(1), (Fig. 2.3). By this date, if not by many years before, the moat only survived on the north and west sides, and is shown with large curving lines to take in the shapes of the towers, and to maintain a suspiciously even 30ft (9m)-width measure across all of its indicated surviving extent.[153] According to Thomas Burgh, writing in 1710, the ditch was uniformly 24ft (7.3m) wide.[154] All of the rest of the castle to the east and to the south are within a very large extended castle precinct, or what is known as the Lower Yard, which is discussed below.

Finally, although we have no idea of how they may have been related to the moat or ditch, according to a report of 1644, defensive outworks were built in preparation for a feared siege in 1641,[155] and others in 1646,[156] when Ormond's wife personally got involved. We do not know the location or the nature of either of these works or their impact.

Chapter 2.3
Residential, Administrative and Other Buildings Inside the Walls

Introduction

Our most accurate conception of the range of administrative and domestic buildings within the castle towards the end of the seventeenth century must be based on the 1673 Dartmouth plan (Fig. 2.1). Our knowledge is further augmented by Robert Ware's written description of the castle made in 1678.[157] What follows is an assemblage of what we can tell of the original construction and function of the castle, and its maintenance and use during the seventeenth century, based on Ware's account and on the 1673 plan.

Throughout the seventeenth century, many general estimates for planned work, or requests for payment for works carried out on the castle were made. Often, neither the nature of the works, nor whether they were made to the defensive structure of the walls and towers, or to the buildings enclosed within them, was specified. For example, in 1663, a petition for expenditure for works carried out in the previous two years listed costs for works done by carpenters, joiners, sawyers, bricklayers, masons, plasterers, a nailer, a slater, a glazier, pavers and a plumber as well as fees for the supply of timber, bricks, tiles and flagstones.[158] The nature of the professions involved suggests that this was for work on buildings in the domestic ranges rather than, or as well as, on defensive or merely administrative structures. However, we do not know specifically on which buildings they worked. Suffice then to say that a great deal of work must have been carried out on the domestic and administrative ranges of buildings shown within the enclosure of the curtain walls, without our being able to say exactly on which. What follows is based on what can be gleaned about individual buildings and building ranges, and the many references and costings of general works will not be listed here.

We can say, that as a group, the domestic and administrative buildings within the castle were listed in the hearth tax returns as the most significant building (strictly a collection of buildings) in the country, with 125 chimneys, in 1672.[159]

Great hall

Both the 1606 Wattson plan (Fig. 1.15) and the 1673 Dartmouth plan (Fig. 2.1) show that the medieval great hall had survived into the seventeenth century and was located running in an east–west direction with its western end against the west curtain wall of the castle. Based on the Dartmouth plan, the hall's external measurements were approximately 120ft by 70ft (36m by 21m). Access to an upper level may have been gained by way of an external stair shown in this plan on the north-east corner. On the former plan, the building is labelled as 'Hall' and contains in four clumsily delineated chambers the courts of 'Exchequer', 'Pleas', 'Chancery' and 'King's Bench', and in the latter the same building is named as the 'Old Parliament house, and Store, Burnt.' Thus, the three major early modern functions of the hall are suggested: a place for the four courts, the location of the parliament and theatre, as we shall see, and the store house for munitions and powder.

The hall was built according to a mandate of Henry III in 1245. This stated that the hall at Dublin Castle was to be like the hall of the archbishop of Canterbury, with its rose window and wall paintings. However, it seems to have been rebuilt in the 1320s, perhaps because the foundation of the original building had failed.[160] Like many halls of its status in the Middle Ages in England, this was an aisled hall. The great hall was an important component, with the lord's chamber and a chapel, of any medieval castle, the hall often being aisled like a church. Some constructed of stone, such as that at Oakham Castle (Rutland), survive, but many other aisled halls built of timber, such as those depicted on the Bayeux Tapestry, or William Rufus' great hall at Westminster, tended to perish much more readily than the keeps or dungeons that were built generally of masonry.[161] The remains of the thirteenth-century stone halls at Trim, Co. Meath, or Adare Castle, Co. Limerick, may serve as a comparison to the hall at Dublin Castle.[162] According to Ware, the Dublin Castle hall was 'built after the forme of a Church, raised upon severall stately pillars in the lower part'.[163] Thus, the ground-floor chamber was likely to have been divided into three aisles separated by arcades supported on columns. According to Ware, there was a loft above, and it was there that the courts of law and later the parliament, as discussed below, were held, 'untill the wisedome of the State thought fitt to free the Castle from so great a Catastrophe for Concourse of people as usually frequented that great assembly, and to hold the last Parliament att Chichester house'.[164] The external stairs on the north-west corner, as shown on the Dartmouth plan, may have given access to this chamber (Fig. 2.1). In the 1560s, Jacques Wingfield, Constable of Dublin Castle,[165] is described as constructing 'archebutrises' in the great hall, thus perhaps buttressing or consolidating the arcade in some way.[166]

The courts were held in the castle at least from the 1570s, when Sir Henry Sidney returned them there 'for the greater ease of all suitors, both rich and poor, which heretofore were accustomed to travel to and from places both farther distant and less commodious for the despatch of their causes'.[167] However, as noted in the discussion above of the proposed postern gate into Castle Street, the holding of courts in the castle and the consequent access by the public was a concern:

> The keeping of her Majesty's storehouse so nigh onto her Highness' courts, or keeping the courts so near the storehouse, where all men may view and overlook her Majesty's munition, provision and store of all sorts for defence of this her Highness' realm, is not convenient; for in the term time the greatest rebels within this land may boldly come thither in some civil order, and, by their villainous devices, treasons, and conspiracies, in short time destroy all her Majesty's offices and loving subjects as they sit in her Highness' affairs.[168]

In 1599, it was decided that 'terms' should be 'kept in some other convenient place in town' because of the dangers of the gunpowder being stored directly under the courts of law.[169] The courts were moved in 1605 to Sir George Carew's

house on Hoggen Green, and in 1608 were established in the precincts of Christ Church cathedral where they remained until the late eighteenth century.[170] The suggestion that they be returned to the castle in 1606 was rejected by Chichester on the grounds that it would 'draw them just over the store of the munition, which not only by practice (as formerly hath been attempted), but by using fire for burning prisoners in the hand, is exposed to be fired and this Castle ruined'.[171]

In 1610 the great hall was repaired in anticipation of a 'marriage feast', and in 1613 the same hall was again 'fitted up' for the meeting of parliament,[172] for which it was used until it moved in the 1660s to Chichester House on College Green,[173] where a purpose-built parliament house was erected in the 1730s.[174] Before the seventeenth century, the Commons seems to have met in the Common House at Christ Church, in an area which Falkiner identifies as the 'sumptous fabric'; in the seventeenth century it met on the site of the Four Courts; but in the Middle Ages the Commons met in the zone of the claustral ranges, while the lords met in the castle, probably in the great hall.[175] At the first session of the new parliament of 1613, the Catholics objected to its being held in the medieval hall because of the presence of the gunpowder, fearing that it and the great mass of troops would be used against them.[176] Referring ironically to the recent gunpowder plot in England, Chichester stated that:

> Concerning powder being under the room, it is merely imagined for it was lately removed to places of more safety. Let it be remembered of what religion they were of, that placed the powder in England, and gave allowance to that damnable plot, and thought the act meritorious, if it had taken effect, and would have canonized the actors.[177]

According to the earl of Cork, the great hall was set up for theatricals by Wentworth. Having attended a tragedy in the parliament house in January 1636, he quipped that it 'was tragicall, for we had no suppers'.[178] It is likely that theatrical performances, amateur and professional, took place at the castle, although direct evidence of this has not survived. However, Wentworth was certainly interested in these, bringing in his company to Dublin the actor James Shirley, and the sometime mapmaker and theatre director John Ogilby, who in 1635 or 1636 established the first theatre house in Ireland at Werburgh Street, directly west of the castle.[179] However, both Shirley and Ogilby seem to have been with Wentworth in Dublin for the two to three years before the establishment of the theatre building, which suggests an outlet for such performances among the court circle in the castle, just as described by the earl of Cork. Based on his correspondence with the earl of Arundel, Wentworth was also keenly interested in the masques designed by Inigo Jones for Charles I then taking place in London, sometimes in the Banqueting House, and sometimes on the street, where even the king was known to have on occasion taken part.[180] We have no record of such performances at Dublin Castle during this period, but Wentworth engaged in the similar practice of architecture and processional pageantry combined, in his triumphs into Kilkenny, Clonmel and Limerick, and his emulation of all things of the English court suggests that the occurrence of masques at the castle cannot be ruled out.[181]

Sir William Brereton, who visited the castle in 1635, was less than complimentary about the parliament house in the castle, stating that it was

> much less and meaner than ours. The Lords' house is now furnished with about sixty or seventy armours for horse, which are my Lord Deputy's: this is a room of no great state nor receipt. Herein there sat the first session about eighty lords; not so many the latter. The Commons House is but a mean and ordinary place; a plain and no very convenient seat for the Speaker, nor officers. The Parliament men that sat in this house were about 248.[182]

The great hall was eventually destroyed by fire on the night of 20 May 1671. The powder had been fortuitously removed by Robartes to the powder store in the garden two years earlier, although Ormond's son, Sir John Butler, still had to retrieve a couple of barrels of it from the burning building.[183] Somehow it was not completely razed to the ground – this may have been partly to do with the 'height and thickness of [its] stone walls'[184] – as the shell of the building remained until Essex had it demolished, and reputedly ordered that its stones be used in the rebuilding of St Andrew's church in Suffolk Street.[185] As Essex was Lord Lieutenant in 1672–7, and the church was built 1670–74,[186] this suggests that the hall was demolished c. 1672–4.

Kitchen and related buildings

As noted above, the south-west tower, or Bermingham Tower served the double function of a repository of records and as the location for the kitchen, which according to Perrot's 1585 survey, was located on the second floor. The 1673 plan confirms this function almost a century later when it labels the south-west tower as the 'Kitchin Tower' (Fig. 2.1). It, and the earlier 1606 plan (Fig. 1.15), indicate that the area between the deputy's house and the hall on the south wall, and the great hall on the west wall, was dedicated to kitchen and related service functions: Ware referred to 'the Kitchen and other places belonging to the offices below stairs [servants' quarters], reaching as farre as Berminghams Tower'.[187] The 1606 plan refers to the 'Dep. Kitchin yard'.

The 1673 plan shows three rectangular buildings set into the south-western angle between the great hall and the west curtain wall, with the chamber to the south labelled as 'Offices belonging to ye kitchin'. A small circle is also shown, which might be a well. Alternatively, it could represent the chimney to a scalding house (a place for skinning poultry or preparing the carcasses of other animals) recorded as having been built, probably by John Paine, and possibly close to December 1663. The same document also records repairs to 'a Shead in the Bakers yard'.[188] On the other hand, Wentworth had complained of the bake-house in his view 'just under the Room where I now write' in 1633.[189] In 1664, it was ordered that 'the clerk of his majesty's store [was] to deliver to Charles Conway four elm planks to be employed for dresser boards in the kitchen of Dublin Castle'.[190] Other 'below-stairs' functions included in a 1679 inventory of the duke of Ormond's goods at the castle, included a wash-house, laundry, bake-house, room for sick people, kitchens, pastry [house], great kitchen, scullery and larder.[191] A slightly later inventory lists 'the Scullery mans Chamber' and the room of 'Negallty, Fourth Cook', a room for the 'Firemakers', a room for the 'Pantlers Assistant', and the 'Confectioners Office', 'the Yeoman of the Wine Cellars office' and the 'Buttery', which then held 'two old glass Presses [and] one Forme'.[192]

Hall on the south wall

The 1673 Dartmouth plan (Fig. 2.1) shows a second 'Hall' at the western end of the residential range on the south wall of the castle. This must have been the 'south hall' which Jacques Wingfield repaired in the 1560s.[193] Perrot's report of 1585 suggested that 'the castle wall is weakeste in the south side, by the means of the hall windowes and other windowes, with prives [privies] and such other workes as hath bene of late yeares…'.[194] In 1678, Ware also referred to this hall 'on the right hand' as he looked towards the residential range. In terms of area, it is approximately halfway between the great hall and the dining room. Its location close to the Bermingham Tower, which arguably predates the thirteenth-century enceinte,[195] suggests the possibility that this too may have been related to the earlier castle, and possibly predated the great hall built after 1245. It seems probable, based on a comparison to the 1673 map, that this possibly very early building had still survived into the early eighteenth century, as a long low building behind the arcade under construction by Thomas Burgh is shown almost abutting the Kitchen Tower on Brooking's 1728 image (Fig. 1.20). This relationship of hall to kitchen is consistent with the medieval type of cross-passage halls where the kitchen was located at the west end – in this case to the west of the hall in the tower, but not in the hall itself – while the dais where those of the highest status sat, was placed at the east end.

Residential range

The most architecturally significant range of buildings within the curtilage of the perimeter wall of the castle during the seventeenth century was the residential range in the south-eastern quadrant of the castle yard understood to have been substantially built by Sir Henry Sidney in the 1560s, although augmented by his successors. It was in this range that the fire started in 1684, causing the destruction of most of these residences and some other connected buildings, such as Falkland's gallery (discussed below), and which led to the eventual complete redevelopment of the castle. Descriptions of the course of the fire, as we shall see, give us our best opportunity to understand how these buildings worked and were connected in sequence, particularly when this description is combined with the detailed 1673 Dartmouth plan (Fig. 2.1). The latter lists a 'Dining Roome', a 'Clock house', a 'Presence Chamber', a 'Withdrawing roome', two 'Closets', a 'Stairs upward', which was over 'ye Chapel', the 'Long Gallery', a second 'withdrawing Roome', some 'Lodgings', and a number of unnamed stairs. Patrick Dun's contemporary description of the 1684 fire also notes the lord deputy's bed chamber, his dressing room (where the fire started), his closet and 'my Ladys drawing room in which she receaved the ladys [which] was in fire'.[196] All of these seemed to have been located in a residential range built by the earl of Essex in the 1670s, and are likely to have been the range labelled as 'Lodgings' on the eastern end of the residential range. The most comprehensive list of rooms can be had from an inventory of the duke of Ormond's possessions taken in 1679, in which the following set of rooms may be extracted: dining room, king's presence room, king's withdrawing-room, old supping-room, his grace's dressing room, his grace's bed-chamber, drawing room, her grace's bed-chamber, her grace's closet, farther closet, room over the drawing-room, long gallery, his grace's closet, his grace's inward closet, lobby, chapel, earl of Arran's lobby, chamber that was the earl of Arran's, his dressing room, his closet, Lady Gowran's lodgings, Lord Arran's new bed-chamber, and another closet.[197] Ware's 1678 description of the castle (cited in the various subsections below) also adds to this picture of the residential ranges, while the whole range appears on Wattson's 1606 plan (Fig. 1.15) as the 'Deputies House'.

Such a large variety of rooms may be better understood if divided in terms of their function into the rooms of state, the private quarters of the Lord Lieutenant's family, and the service quarters, including kitchen, wash houses and such like. Wentworth's Jigginstown, built in the 1630s as a viceregal, and as he claimed, royal, country retreat from the castle, was built with two sets of formal rooms, those for the family and those for purposes of important business of state, the latter closed off when not in use.[198] As we shall see below, Wentworth put great emphasis on the protocol associated with these rooms in Dublin Castle, particularly who should

or should not have access to the great chamber (the dining room), the drawing room (or Presence Chamber), gallery and most exclusively, the Council Chamber.[199] Thus the division was outer rooms for public ceremonies, and private or inner accommodation for the Lord Lieutenant's family. This represented a late Renaissance and early modern move away from the kind of castle accommodation centred on the great hall, where public ceremonies, and private accommodation and entertainments had been more closely integrated architecturally and in terms of their ceremonials.[200] The development of separate suites of apartments for the lord and his lady, and for each of their sons and their wives, in Ormond's time, reflected the adoption of French custom by the English court at this time.[201] The architect Hugh May, who designed the state apartments for Charles II in the 1670s and 80s, is known to have advised the duke of Ormond on similar refurbishments at Kilkenny Castle.[202]

Details of fixtures and fittings emerge infrequently. Some of those which cannot be assigned to known spaces are included in this section. While we have no record of the goods held by Lord Deputy Sidney (1565–71, 1575–8), the detailed record of his accounts from his years as Lord Treasurer in Ireland (1556–9), while he lived at Thomas Court in Dublin, may suffice to at least hint at some of the types of goods he was in possession of, less than a decade later, when he was viceroy. At Thomas Court, Sidney had ten Arras (coloured tapestries with scenes) costing £51, he had six Flanders chairs, at £3, and '2 little chairs for the Lady Mary Sidney, 5s.', 'a bathing tun' which cost £1.7.6, a 'pair of Virginals' costing £3, and a further £1 was spent on mending and tuning, and another 13s. was paid out, for 'making of a lute and mending another'. '[S]undry necessaries' included 'gloves, squirrel bells, 2s., [and] a French book, 5s.'. During these three years at Thomas Court, Sidney also spent £225 on horses, and £14.6.5 on hawks: 'two falcons, an odd hawk, two casts of merlions, hawks-meat, leashes, hoods and bells'.[203] In a similar historical leap of faith, an 'Inventory of the King's Goods in the Castle of Dublin' of 1693, which, while post-dating the fire of 1684 and the closing date for this chapter, also suggests, in its spare paucity and in the fact that much of these pieces are recorded in servants' rooms, that most of the furnishings that were listed were left over from the pre-fire period. These include the 'Turkey worke Chayres' in Owen the Footman's room; the 'Turkey work'd Chaise' in the footman Francis Baynes's room; 'Four pieces of Tapestry hangings of Marcus Aurelius, one in Guilt [*sic*] Frame, One painted Screene, One Mapp' in the Steward's room; 'One Inlaid Table, one Cane Chayse, one Leather Chayse' and 'Two Pieces of Tapestry Hangings' in the Pantler's Office; 'One large square table with falling leaves, [and] One large Ovall Table with falling Leaves' in the office of the 'Clerke of the Kitchen'; and numerous cane or Turkey worked chairs and tables in the rooms of the 'Yeoman Ushers', in Mr Rebaud and Mr Weston, Gents of the Bed Chamber's rooms, in the butler's and the master cook's rooms.[204]

In 1636, it was stated that James Hornecastle was to have the office of 'keeping cleaning, ayring and dressing up all of the houses, rooms and buildings…within our Castle of Dublin, and of the charge of keeping cleaning and airing of all robes, hangings, cloths of state, chairs, stools and all other utensils usually kept and remaining within the Castle, and likewise the office of keeping and setting of the clock within the same'.[205] In 1660, Richard Wilson petitioned for a quarter of a year's salary for keeping in repair the windows of the castle and of Phoenix House.[206] The following year, Richard Booker of Newcastle in Staffordshire, after spending five months in Dublin trying in vain to recover his money from Captain Paine, petitioned Ormond for payment of £80 for 'ironmongers ware' which he had delivered to Dublin Castle a year earlier.[207] Perhaps, the most salubrious court was kept by Ormond and his family, although Ormond also had a base in Kilkenny Castle among other locations in the country, giving him an advantage over other chief governors.[208] When the king announced his intention to remove Ormond the first time, in 1669, for example, Ormond's wife wondered whether the 'persons employed by the new Governor' might be prepared to buy the ironwork she had previously purchased and installed there, including locks, keys and iron chimney 'racks'.[209] Ormond lived in considerable luxury in the castle as can be detected from his house inventory of 21 March 1679, which lists the rooms, the furniture, the Turkish carpets, Dutch tapestries, paintings, his silver plate etc.[210]

A 1570 report, quoted by Harris in the late eighteenth century, stated that

> …ther haith ben erected of late within hir majestie's castell of Dublyn, certen lodging and outher fair and necessarie roulmes, boeth for a convenient plaice for the lord deputie's howse, and a fit seate for the placing and receiving of any gouvernour heraftir, as for the bettir and more commodious resorte and assembly of the counsaill…[211]

The accounts for the years 1560–7 show a bill from William Foster, clerk of works, for £1,352 8s. 5d., from John Whitney, for unspecified works at the castle £51 6s. 8½d., and other works by Jacque Wingfield [Jaques Wingfelde], already noted, for £486 13s. 4d., although this probably does not cover the total expenditure by Sidney (lord deputy, 1565–71, 1575–8) on his house.[212] Richard Stanihurst stated that 'This Castle hath béene of late much beautified wyth sundrye & gorgious buildinges in the tyme of Sir Henry Sydney'.[213] We know nothing of the appearance of these works by Sidney, which formed the frame onto which all later extensions were added. However, the style was likely to have been

in that sub-classical mongrel style which characterised Elizabethan architecture at this time. Only the decorative or articulating components of a building – its doorways, chimneypieces, some balustrades and windows – were given a classical dress, often based on images found in architectural treatises such as Sebastiano Serlio's, while the overall composition often lacked the integrated cohesion one expected in Italian Renaissance buildings of this time.[214] Although stone was shipped by Sidney from Ireland to his residence at Penshurst, Kent,[215] his contribution to that ancestral home, and to Ludlow Castle, Shropshire – from the fifteenth to the seventeenth century, the location of the Council of Wales and the Marches – when Sidney was Lord President of the Council, appears to have been 'modest',[216] and we are unlikely to find clues from either place as to the appearance of Sidney's residential range in Dublin.

In the 1630s, Wentworth repaired the range and added rooms including some for his wife, children and entourage. His third wife Elizabeth Rhodes gave birth to a son there in September 1634, although the child died some eighteen months later.[217]

After the Restoration, windows were kept in repair, and the clock was fixed.[218] In October 1662, John Paine signed for payments due to 'Carpenters, Joyners, Sawyers &c.' for £112.07.04, 'to the Masons that built ye Staire-case', £33.4, 'to several other Masons', £10.16, 'to the Plaisterer', £186.19.6½, 'to the Smith', £106.03.08½ , 'to the Naylor', £91.18.04, 'to the Lyme-burner', £54.01.10, 'to the Paviers', £9.10, 'to the Glazier', £104.14.01, 'to Harvy the Scavenger', £57.0.05, and to 'other Scavengers & Sand-men', £12.18, to 'Mr Tho. Digby', £8.10.06, 'to the Turner', £7.08.05, 'to the Carver', £4.10, 'to Mr Cross for Tymber Deales &c', £265.14.09, 'to Mr. Westenra for Deale Boards', £67.04, 'to Mr. Groffstem for Deales & Baulkes', £25.11.08, 'to Mr. Dan. Wỹbrant, for Deales and Baulkes', £14.13, 'to Mr. Crow for Brickes', £27.09.02, 'to Mr Boyde for blocke Tymber', £1.02, 'for 110 foote of Flagg Stone & Laying', £2.15, 'to Mr Harrison ye Slater', £76.17.03, 'to Mr Sanderton ye Plummer', £196.11.04, and to 'Mr Pooley for Latts', 9s., all coming to a total of £1,478.09.04. It is most likely that these works encompassed the residential buildings in the castle; they were undertaken at the beginning of the duke of Ormond's third period as viceroy.[219]

Lord Arran's letter to Ormond, his father,[220] and Patrick Dun's to William King,[221] both describing the course of the fire of 1684, allow us some insight into the layout of the rooms as noted.[222] The fire first began in Arran's chamber, which was most likely in the 'Lodgings' built by Essex (see below) on the east end of the range. A 'Crakling noise & smoake' came from the room next to his, formerly his mother's closet – 'my Ladys drawing room in which she receaved the Ladys', as Dun refers to it.[223] After opening and closing the door on the closet that was on fire, Arran went through the chamber door that led (westwards) towards the rooms of state, opening as he went all the doors as far as Falkland's gallery. At this point he emerged into the court and mustered the alarm. The Surveyor General, Sir William Robinson was not in Dublin, so Arran got the help of a young man named Cuffe, who retrieved barrels of powder from 'the private store'. Next, in anticipation of setting an explosion to limit the damage on the rest of the castle, particularly the Powder Tower on the north-east corner, Arran rescued what papers he could from Ormond's closet – these likely to have been the group of closets and offices built onto the eastern side of the gallery. Arran then blew up the gallery:

> I was afraid that if the gallery took fire it would scarce have been possible to have saved the magazine of powder…there being no very close place to put the powder in, the first trial did not blow up so much of the building as I expected, but with the next, which was placed nearer the end of the gallery, we put the magazine out of danger of being fired…and then finding that, though the wind was full west, yet the fire gained much towards Bermingham's Tower where the records are kept, I ordered the blowing up that part of the building that joined to the chapel's, which had so good effect that we then mastered the fire.[224]

This suggests that the block containing the Presence Chamber was destroyed by that second explosion. The progress of the fire – which Arran believed was caused by 'a piece of timber that lay under part of the hearth of the closet' – was stopped about 4 am. Arran did not get dressed until 6 am, when Mr Kingdon [sic] and the earl of Longford gave him some 'linning and a suite of clothes'. 'The city of Dublin had a great deliverance, by the powders being saved from which we are all bound to bless God'.[225]

Although we know very little about the appearance of any of these buildings, information about individual portions of the residential range can be picked up from the sources nevertheless.

Chapel

According to Ware, Sidney was responsible for building the chapel, thus either in 1565–71 or 1575–8, the two periods of his governorship.[226] Although its location is not known, there had been a chapel in the castle from the 1220s, if not earlier.[227] There is a possibility that Sidney's chapel was damaged in a fire in 1638, according to the memories of Alice Thornton, a cousin of Wentworth's, who had lived in the castle as a child. She claimed that there had been a fire at that date which destroyed 'the stately chapel built by my lord [Wentworth]', although her report also implied, as we may note, that the chapel had been built by her relation,

sometime since taking office five years earlier. Indeed she also noted the destruction of 'the chapell chamber above the chapell, which was most richly furnished with blacke velvett, imbroidered with flowrs of silke worke in ten stich; all fruit trees and flowers, and slips embroidered with gold twist'.[228] In August 1661, Sir John Stephens, knight, was ordered to issue on account £10 'towards providing a pulpit cloth and other necessaries for the Chapel in His Majesty's Castle of Dublin'.[229] In 1673, the earl of Essex (Fig. 2.7) ordered that copies of the Book of Common Prayer were to be purchased for the castle chapel.[230] The 1673 Dartmouth plan (Fig. 2.1) shows a grand ceremonial staircase in between two withdrawing rooms, on which it is labelled that 'Under this p[ar]t is ye Chappell'. Ware confirms this stating 'wherein upon the ground is a Chappell, over which is a stately drawing room built in the time of S'r Henry Sydney his government whose armes are placed thereon'.[231] The colour scheme of black velvets recorded by Wentworth's niece had changed by 1679, according to a detailed inventory, which records an 'altar-cloth and carpet of crimson taffety and purple mohair,…[t]wo crimson taffety curtains' around 'his Grace's seat' which was an 'elbow-chair of crimson velvet with silver and gold fringe' and had a 'serge foot-stool' with 'a serge cushion; a figured velvet cushion and a Persia carpet'. The duchess's seat of red serge also contained 'four cane-bottom chairs; one elbow-chair of crimson figured velvet; six damask cushions; one long damask cushion; one Persia carpet; [and] two curtains of crimson taffety'. There were also '[f]our sconces [candle holders] in the chapel'.[232] If not destroyed during the alleged fire of 1638, the chapel must have been destroyed by the 1684 fire, although it is notable that it was not mentioned by those who described the consequences of that conflagration.

Drawing room

Records from May 1590, mention the lord deputy – Sir William Fitzwilliam – reading a letter in the withdrawing chamber in the castle, and how 'the Lord Deputy and Council assembled together about eight of the clock in the morning and sat in Council' also in a withdrawing chamber.[233] The former was probably the room shown on the 1673 Dartmouth plan over the chapel, and closest to the lodgings; the latter, a more formal chamber, is more likely to have been the withdrawing room on the plan, beside the Presence Chamber. The order by which William Brereton describes the castle suggests one possible reading of prioritisation, from Council Chamber (on the north side of the castle yard), to the hall (perhaps in this case the hall on the south wall, as shown on the Dartmouth plan), to the dining room, the Presence Chamber, and finally the 'withdrawing chamber'.[234] An inventory of 1679 illustrates some of the contents of the drawing room during Ormond's last viceroyalty:

Five pieces of Lambeth hangings, ten foot and a half deep; sixteen elbow-chairs of crimson velvet with a fringe cased with crimson colour serge; one large silver looking glass; eight silver sconces; a silver table and stands; a pair of large silver andirons; four silver dogs; a silver fireshovel and tongs; a looking-glass table and stands, varnished with gold and silver; a picture over the chimney, two yards long and a yard and a half deep; a Portugal mat, four yards and a half long, three yards and a half deep; two window rods.[235]

Sidney's arms

These arms, referred to by Ware as just noted in the section above on the chapel,[236] are not to be confused with the inscription over an unidentified gate discussed above, but refer to Sidney's coat of arms placed over the building housing the dining room and chapel. These have not survived. However, other Sidney coats of arms, particularly a set said to be from a bridge at Athlone built by Sidney, and which are understood to have been retrieved when the bridge was replaced in the mid nineteenth century, have survived. At that time donated to the Royal Irish Academy and later to the National Museum of Ireland, these at least give us some indication of how the arms must have appeared.[237] It is also possible that not all of these Sidney arms now in the National Museum are from the Athlone Bridge, and that those within frames were in fact the arms from Dublin Castle.[238]

Presence Chamber

A Presence Chamber is noted on the 1673 Dartmouth plan (Fig. 2.1) and is listed by Ware: 'The next part of the Pallace contiguous hereunto is the chamber of presence, the Lobbies, and the chambers thereunto appertaineing which, being an ancient structure, is thought to want reparation or rebuilding…'.[239] This is likely to have been part of the 'howse, and roulmes newely erected' by Sidney in 1570.[240] The Presence Chamber was a room in which one was brought into the most public presence of the king or, in this case, the lord deputy, and may be contrasted to the more private spaces in which one gained more exclusive access, such as in the lord's or king's chamber, or his closet, and at Dublin Castle, the long gallery. The Presence Chamber had a canopied chair raised on a dais, for the viceroy, and tapestries on the wall to indicate its importance. Indeed, we know that a consignment of tapestries from Brussels, costing £411.11.03, 'for furnishing the presence drawing Chamber and Councell Chamber in the said Kingdom of Ireland' was organised through the Spanish ambassador in 1636 for Lord Deputy Wentworth.[241] A certain modicum of respect and behaviour was seen as necessary in such rooms, although the fact that Wentworth deemed it necessary to remind the Irish that all

who appeared here, and indeed in the great chamber (the dining room), 'are to be bare',[242] that is bare-headed, suggests that this sense of ceremonial decorum was not always adhered to. Wentworth used the Presence Chamber for the second part of his grand investment ceremony of 1633; his actual inauguration as lord deputy, as we shall see, took place in the more exclusive Council Chamber. Afterwards they processed from there to the Presence Chamber where Wentworth would go on to create a number of knights – just one of what would turn out to be many dangerously monarchical gestures associated with his tenure.[243] In related theatrical fashion, Wentworth 'coming before the cloth of state…made two lowe and humble courtesies to the king and queen's pictures which hang on each side the state, and fixing his eyes with much seriousness, showed a kind of devotion'.[244] It is almost certain, as Dougal Shaw has shown, that these paintings were gifts given by Charles I to Wentworth on his departure to Ireland, the king in Garter robes by Daniel Mytens, and the queen, a portrait from the studio of the English royal court painter, Anthony van Dyck.[245] Although we don't know what it looked like, the cloth of state for the Presence Chamber was also brought to Dublin Castle from England by Wentworth.[246] Later, Ormond, whose taste for monarchical splendour picked up where Wentworth's left off, introduced two new chairs of state to the Presence Chamber, made up of 56 yards (51m) of 'branched velvet and 525 oz of gold and silver fringe'. These were paid for by the state, while Ormond himself paid the significant sum of £447 for the 'gilded sconces which glittered on the walls, the tables, upholstered chairs and woven hangings'.[247] The Ormonds, who were the only dukes in Ireland, and enormously wealthy, emulated the courtly manners and accoutrements they had witnessed when in exile on the continent with Charles II during the 1650s.[248]

According to Maguire's post-fire reconstruction map, this building was among those destroyed in 1684.[249] There are two pieces of evidence that suggest that some portion of the range containing this chamber might have survived. In his description of the fire, the physician Patrick Dun stated that 'there was burnt & blown up, the new buildings built by the Earle of Essex [his lodgings, discussed below], my Lords closet [appended to the eastern side of Falkland's gallery, see below] and the long gallerie *and all betwixt the new buildings & the tower on which the Clock stood* [the present author's italics]'.[250] This might suggest that this tower, and the buildings directly south of it were saved – the text being ambiguous. The second piece of tentative evidence is on Brooking's 1728 map (Fig. 1.20). This shows, as we shall see, that the dining room had survived, it being the shaded two-storey building which is recessed behind the rusticated portal with the coat of arms. But in front of the dining hall and to its east (to its left on Brooking) is what remains of a building (i.e., the two-storey building with the cannons in front), which steps out into the yard almost as far as the portal, just as this part of the building does in the 1673 Dartmouth plan (Fig. 2.1). Notice on Brooking how the ground floor projects further to the right (west) than the first floor, suggesting a building which has been partially destroyed, or is in a state of partial deconstruction. This building, with its two chimneys, is certainly in the position of the range of buildings which included the Presence Chamber and may well suggest that part of the Sidney complex had survived into the early eighteenth century.

Clock house

A bow-fronted 'Clock house' that communicated with the Presence Chamber by way of a winding staircase is shown on the 1673 Dartmouth plan. An order was made by Sidney for the 'tending and keaping of the clocke within the said castell, whiche requireth daily attendance to be tempred and kept in frame, [and] to appoint sume honest, carefull, and diligent person to take that chardge in hand'.[251] Perhaps the clock was erected by Sidney, as some have concluded,[252] but a previous clause in the same sentence made claim by him to the 'roulmes newely erected' while this was simply the 'clocke within the said castell', thus suggesting the possibility that the clock was already there upon his arrival. The man with the suggestively appropriate name who got the job for its upkeep was 'our well biloved George Arglass of Dublin, gentilman, servant unto us the sayd lord deputy' who was paid 16d. a day with his lodging in the castle.[253] In the 1630s, the same responsibility was in the hands of James Hornecastle, whose other works of maintenance and upkeep throughout the castle have already been noted.[254] In October 1661, Jeoffrey Malbone was paid £22 11s. for his fee as Keeper of the Clock at Dublin Castle, which included '15s. by him laid out for repairing the said clock'.[255] In the fire of 1684, the physician Patrick Dun reported that all was burnt 'betwixt the new buildings & the tower on which the Clock stood', which might suggest that it survived that conflagration.[256]

Clock towers were a common feature of royal palaces in England at this time, often being placed at a good height to be seen from afar. Sometimes these were raised on turrets over gatehouses, such as the octagonal clock turret introduced to the royal palace at Oatlands in 1593–4, or the clock surmounted on the inner gatehouse at Nonsuch for Henry VIII, perhaps in 1544, or the hexagonal lantern with a clock case and dials at the king's lodgings at Royston, which was added in 1613–14.[257] Inigo Jones seems to have designed a clock-house structure of some kind for Whitehall Palace in 1626–7.[258] In 1638, David Ramsey, the king's clockmaker, provided a clock and dial for the gatehouse of the upper ward at Windsor.[259]

Dining room

The 'Dineing Roome' on the 1673 plan (Fig. 2.1) is shown between the hall and the Presence Chamber, and communicates also with a set of stairs and an entrance portal (discussed below). Based on this image, its dimensions were approximately 40ft by 20ft (12m by 6m). According to Ware in 1678, this had been 'lately re-edifyed and raised to a stately height, together with all ye upper parts of ye building proportionably thereunto by the Earl of Essex', who was lord deputy in 1672–7 (Fig. 2.7).[260] It is likely that this work was carried out by the Surveyor General, William Robinson, who billed in 1676 for an amount of £1,029 3s. 4d. 'for several buildings Erected and Repaires made' in Dublin Castle, Chapelizod House and Phoenix House.[261] Alternatively, as Loeber has argued, Essex's kinsman, the architect Hugh May, who was employed by Essex at his English home of Cassiobury (Hertfordshire), may have played a part in its design. Essex rewarded May with £300 worth of table silver for, he stated, his 'many kindnesses…since my being here [in Ireland]'.[262] Comparing the 1673 plan to Brooking's 1728 image of the castle (Fig. 1.20), it seems clear that what may have been Essex's dining room had survived until the early eighteenth century, recessed and depicted in the shadows as it is.[263] Here we see a building of two storeys, with three first-floor windows shown over a rusticated ground floor without windows. This is a Renaissance treatment, with banded masonry on the ground floor, distinct from the *piano nobile* or grander first floor, in which the receptions and meals must have taken place. It is possible that the building had been at ground-floor level before it was 'raised' to this 'stately height'.

The 1679 inventory of the duke of Ormond's goods noted the following contents in the dining room:

A Turkey-work carpet, six yards long, three yards three quarters broad; two other Turkey-work carpets for sideboards and two leather carpets for them; twenty-four Turkey-work chairs of festoon pattern; two elbow-chairs of Paris Turkey-work; seven gilt sconces; a long red cloth carpet, nine yards, and a green one, four yards and a half; three green carpets to play at cards off; a large landscape over the chimney; three paragon curtains.[264]

A post-fire inventory of the castle records 'Five pieces of fine Tapestry Hangings of the history of the Sunn' in the dining room, and 'Five pieces of Fine Tapestry Hangings Landskip' in the 'Old Dineing roome'.[265]

The dining hall, so-called, was the equivalent in function and status to what is sometimes named the great chamber in the suite of rooms of state. It was a place for great feasts and public ceremonies involving large attendances and also a gathering place where all who sought an audience with the viceroy or his officials waited. More important and exclusive business took place in the Presence Chamber and withdrawing or drawing rooms and the long gallery, or closets of the lord deputy or the government administration. Despite the slightly less privileged status of the dining room, Wentworth, as we have already seen, insisted that all remained 'bare' here as well as in the Presence Chamber.[266]

Lodgings built by Essex

On April 1, 1674, Charles II responded to complaints by Essex regarding the general condition of the castle – 'straightened for want of convenient lodgings in ye Castle for many of your family' – and his request for £500 for 'some small building' as lodging for them, allowing him to draw down that amount.[267] Essex (Fig. 2.7), who arrived in Dublin as the Lord Lieutenant in August 1672, may already have begun these new lodgings, as such a building is marked on the eastern end of the general residential range on the south wall in the 1673 Dartmouth plan (Fig. 2.1).[268] We know, for example, that in December 1673, Essex examined a chimney piece, which he got from the Dutch marble dresser Francis Cavenburge, and he even sent some Irish marble to his English country seat at Cassiobury.[269] Ware states that 'Hereunto on the place of an old decayed building was lately raised a stately and convenient structure, contained within these walls by the Earl of Essex, whereon are fixed the Kings armes, and underneath his own coat of armes, in memory of his name[;] in this apartment are the Lord Lieutenants private lodgings and the rooms thereunto appertaineing, much more noble and convenient than formerly they have bene'.[270] The Dartmouth plan shows the 'Lodgings' as a small square-planned building with a winding stair on the north-east corner, implying that the lodgings were at least two storeys high, as we might expect. This was built by the Surveyor General, William Robinson, who received a warrant of £500,[271] and whom Essex considered to be a 'very ingenious man and well skilled in some parts of ye Mathematicks'.[272] As with the dining room, as noted, there may have been some influence from Hugh May, then the Comptroller of the Royal Works at Windsor, but also, after Essex retired as Lord Lieutenant, the architect of his reconstructed mansion at Cassiobury Park, Hertfordshire.[273] The latter, according to John Evelyn who visited in 1680, was 'a plain fabric…[with] divers fair and good rooms, and excellent carving by [Grinling] Gibbons, especially the chimney-piece of the library'. As already alluded to above,

Evelyn also commented that 'Some of the chimney mantels are of Irish marble, brought by my Lord from Ireland, when he was Lord Lieutenant, and not much inferior to Italian'.[274] Essex's Cassiobury house included a great carved staircase also attributed to Gibbons,[275] although more recently to Edward Pearce, which survives in the Metropolitan Museum, New York.[276] The house, which was demolished in the early twentieth century, was recorded on its Kip & Knyff engraving of 1720 as having an H-shaped ground plan.[277] There is little that we can conclude about the appearance of the Dublin Castle lodgings from this, other than to remark on Essex's taste for fine Irish marble chimneypieces, and to once again ponder the slim possibility that Essex's kinsman, the architect Hugh May, had some limited part in its design – whatever that was.

If this was the location of the main private lodgings of the household, it is likely that this was where the bedroom, and 'his Grace's dressing room' were situated when the inventory of the duke of Ormond's goods was made in 1679. Of the bedroom, it had the following to record:

A four pillar bedstead with mat and cord, a yard three-quarters wide; a feather-bed and bolster with a Flanders tick, a yard three-quarters and three inches wide; two blankets, one two yards and a half, the other a yard and three-quarters; a green rug, two yards and half-quarter wide; four case curtains of gray serge containing six breadths, head-cloth of the same and a case tester; the hangings of the room of gray baize; a table and three chairs; a chamber-pot and basin.

In the duke's dressing room were the following:

Four pieces of new gilt leather hangings, nine foot deep; two window curtains of yellow paragon containing six breadths; a window rod; seven elbow-chairs with cane bottoms; seven cushions of yellow damask, with yellow tassels and paragon covers; a walnut-tree table, and stands; a table, bedstead and a yellow paragon carpet, two yards and a half; a quilted flock bed and bolster, three-quarters and a half wide; a pair of blankets, one two yards, and the other two yards and a quarter; a coverlet, one yard three-quarters; a pillow; nine gilt leather chairs and one elbow one suitable; a new table and stands covered with Spanish leather; a serge carpet.[278]

As already noted, the 1684 fire started in these chambers on the night of 7 April, and this and much of the rest of the residential range were destroyed as a result.

Battle-Axe Chamber

In 1663, John Mills, Master Carpenter to the Royal Works in Ireland, and a large number of other tradesmen and building suppliers, were paid for a number of works in the castle, which may possibly have included the erection of a hall for the Battle-Axe Guard.[279] A flight of stairs (discussed below) from the courtyard to the dining room and hall seems to have been part of these works too. On 8 December, 1662, a warrant for quartering the Battle Axes near Dublin Castle was issued.[280] These were a corps of about sixty halberdiers, modelled on the Yeomen of the Guard in London, although with more modest costumes than the colourful Tudor-style clothes worn by their comrades in the English capital.[281] Theirs were mainly ceremonial duties, accompanying the Lord Lieutenant on state occasions, as when he processed to the cathedral or the parliament in Chichester House on College Green.[282] They were billeted on the city close to the castle.[283] We do not know the exact location of the Battle-Axe Chamber in this range, as it is not listed among the rooms of the 1673 plan.

Staircase

As Ware entered into the castle yard, that is, according to his description of his perambulation of the castle in 1678, he noted 'the beautifull forme of a fair building, unto which you ascend by a noble stayrcase [sic] lately erected in the time of the Duke of Ormond's government under our Royall soveraigne Charles the second since his most happy restauration'.[284] This must have been built in Ormond's first post-Restoration phase as governor, i.e. from 1662–9, as the second phase, 1677–85, was after the 1673 plan on which the stairs are already illustrated.[285] Thus the stairs predate Essex's raising of the dining room. Remarkably, the 1673 plan and Brooking's 1728 image (Fig. 1.20) may be matched up quite closely, and consequently, the latter gives us a clear depiction of the portal to the front of this projecting staircase block. On the plan, the staircase projects out slightly from the hall on its west, and more so from the dining room on its east, which is set back further than the wider hall. This is exactly repeated by the portal building as shown on Brooking. The four dots on the 1673 plan (Fig. 2.1) to the front of that portal, may be an attempt to represent the short obelisks shown there on the Brooking image. Hence, Ormond's 1660s two-storey portal with great rusticated opening on the ground floor, surmounted by an intermediate balustrade and topped by the royal coat of arms, with a pediment above, survived to 1728 at least.

An alternative reading is that Ware was referring simply to the staircase being built by Ormond, rather than to the building itself. This would allow us to compare the coat of arms on its portal as shown by Brooking, to a quite similar set of arms set within a classical frame which was erected by Wentworth at King's Manor, Yorkshire, after 1628, when he was appointed the Lord President of the Council of the North.[286] Although Wentworth was responsible for instating two new doors at King's Manor, York (one with his own coat of arms, and the second with the royal arms of Charles I),[287] there can be little doubt that it is to the royal arms at King's Manor, that we should compare Brooking's image at Dublin Castle. In both there is a play of double pediments and a rectangular field containing the king's arms. At Dublin, the actual doorway is rusticated in a monumental fashion, while both doors at King's Manor are flanked by classical terms.

Long gallery and the lower/back court

According to the 1673 plan (Fig. 2.1), a second 'Stairs upward' was located towards the centre of the southern residential range. On either side were withdrawing rooms, and beneath the one on the east was the chapel. The stairway, which was on a ceremonial scale, also gave access directly onto what is labelled as the 'Long Gallery', which bisected the yard north to south, just to the east of the main gate. Based on the 1673 plan, it measured 100ft by 20ft (30m by 6m).[288] The gallery originally linked this residential range to the Council Chamber (see below) on the north wall, just east of the gate. On this map it is shown to stop slightly short of the 'Lord Leiutenants [sic] lodgins [sic]' which were built in the location of, or were a new use for, the former Council Chamber. The fact that the gallery stops short of the Lord Lieutenant's lodgings suggests the probability that the latter was reduced in its north–south extent from that of the former Council Chamber, and consequently was a new building. By 1673, the short distance further north from the original gallery is covered by what is labelled simply as 'Passage'.

The area thus enclosed to the east was referred to as the 'Back Court'. This in turn incorporated a range of court offices which were attached to the eastern wall of the gallery and included the 'Lords Closet' an 'Office' a further 'Closet' a 'Lobby' and a 'Back stayre' which was connected to a second 'Passage' which brought one to the Lord Lieutenant's lodgings on the north wall, as already noted. Underneath this cluster of buildings, there were 'ye secretary's offices'. Arran, who was not the Lord Lieutenant, seemed more likely to have resided in the lodgings built by Essex that were located on the eastern end of the southern residential range, as described above, rather than in the Lord Lieutenant's lodgings on the north wall. The cluster of buildings around the 'Lord's Closet' seem to have been the principal administrative heart of the castle. There is no evidence regarding when these were built, but it was perhaps to these 'closets' that Arran referred when he talked of clearing 'my lord's closet' before he demolished the gallery in 1684.

According to an annotation on Ware's 1678 description of the castle, the gallery was built around 1624, which was during the viceroyalty of Lord Deputy Falkland (1622–9) (Fig. 2.11).[289] Falkland also boasted of it to Wentworth, his successor: '…you found how much less a Prison the Castle was, through the Benefit of the Gallery I built, nor more for the King's Honour than for your Ease and Delight.'[290] One must wonder where the funds were secured for such a ceremonial and aspirational building, considering the collapse of the north-west tower at this time (see above), and the desperate search for funds to rebuild it. Falkland had informed the English privy council 'of the ruins of other parts of the Castle, which increased daily, so that it was unsafe for him to continue in it, except present order were taken for money to repair and strengthen it'.[291]

Much is revealed regarding its function as a ceremonial conduit between the courtly chambers of the main south-range residence and the august chamber of the council on the north side of the castle in an order from Charles II to his English privy council which he extended to the privy council in Ireland:

When the body of the Council assemble they are always to pass through the Presence Chamber [on the south side of the castle] and not to come the private way, except on special secret Committees… Upon days of meeting none but noblemen shall come further than the drawing chamber, the gallery shall be free for only those that shall be of the Council. All their servants shall stay in the Great Chamber, where they and others are to be bare as well as in the presence, there being a State in both alike. The Gentlemen Ushers of the Lord Chancellor and Lord Treasurer shall leave the Lords at the presence door, where the Chancellor is to take the purse and carry it himself when he comes into the more inward rooms.[292]

In 1635, Sir William Brereton described it as a

pretty, neat short gallery, which leads to the council chamber…the lower part of it is built arch-wise and very gracefully, so as it is a great ornament to the castle,[293]

while Ware in 1678 stated:

From this building towards the Gate, extends itself a statelie structure on your left hand as you pass from the Gate to the Pallace door, erected in the time of the Lord Deputy Falkland, borne upon Pillars in the nature of a Piazza [an arcade or colonnade], a stately long Gallerie…[294]

A further detail of a balcony on the gallery emerges in a short tale told at a time of great volatility in Dublin and the country. An emissary between Ormond and the confederates, Lord Taaffe, was described as 'being then in the Castle Gallery, [when he] stepped into the balcony looking into the court, and with a loud voice cried out, "Where are these roundheads? Bring hither all the roundheads, here is news for them"'.[295]

Built in the early seventeenth century, it might be compared to the kind of galleries found in Elizabethan or Jacobean trophy houses, where paintings were displayed, such as the gallery in Ormond's Kilkenny Castle built by Thomas, 10th earl of Ormond in the 1580s,[296] or the Long Gallery in Carrick-on-Suir Castle, Co. Tipperary (also an Ormond castle) of the 1560s.[297] This Elizabethan and Jacobean type was usually integrated within the body of the building, as it was at Kilkenny and Carrick-on-Suir.

However, the gallery built by Deputy Falkland in Dublin Castle was free-standing, designed as a linking passage between a collection of disparate buildings spread across the yard of the castle and constructed at different times. This was more consistent with the type of covered-in and glazed gallery, raised on an arcade or colonnade, built by Henry VII at Richmond, which overlooked the privy court garden on one side and the river on the other, or the galleries built by Wolsey at Hampton Court and Windsor, and those at Nonsuch built by Henry VIII. A type that evolved in France during the fifteenth century, the glazed gallery – a contrast to the open loggia found in Renaissance Italy – spread from France back to Italy, and to Scotland and England.[298] Those in England, nevertheless, may also be compared to an older tradition of single-storey pentices or alleys, found at a number of medieval royal and ecclesiastical English palaces, such as the arcaded covered galleries built by Henry III at Clarendon Palace,[299] or the still partially surviving twelfth-century arcaded walk at the archbishop's palace at York.[300]

At the royal palaces in England this kind of free-standing linking gallery was, according to Howard Colvin, 'used for exercise in wet weather, for dancing, and no doubt for a good deal of social and political intercourse'.[301] As well as in the key royal palaces, such galleries began to appear in courtiers' houses too, such as in Sir William Fitzwilliam's house at Cowdray, Sussex.[302] George Cavendish described Wolsey's 'golleries' at Whitehall as 'fayer, both large and long, to walk in them when that it lyked [him] best'. When Wolsey came to establish his Cardinal's College at Ipswich, he carried out the formal ceremony in his gallery at Hampton Court.[303] R.W. Berger, in his review of Wolfram Prinz's book on the development of the early modern gallery in Europe, stated that 'The long gallery was a most important part of the house due to its size and decoration, and was often treated as the climax of interior room progression'.[304] This sense of exclusivity is of course confirmed in the instructions on courtly protocol proclaimed by Wentworth in the 1630s, and reiterated by Charles II, as noted above. In this case the gallery also provided a threshold zone between the rooms of state (on the south side of the palace) and the Council Chamber on the north side. Wentworth insisted that the latter be accessed by the members of the privy council by way of the rooms of state, through the gallery, and only then to the Council Chamber itself, thus providing a processional route of very rarefied privilege and honour.[305] These efforts to create an exclusive honorific zone, founded on an English architectural iconography, with French, and ultimately Italian origins, continued to be a source of irritation for Wentworth, as is shown by his complaint that there was a 'Woodreek just full before the Gallery Windows; which I take not to be so courtly, nor to suit so well with the Dignity of the King's Deputy'.[306]

Unfortunately, this piece of Renaissance courtly architectural display did not survive, nor was it visually recorded, other than in plan. As noted, Arran was forced to destroy the gallery using explosives during the fire of 1684.

Council Chamber – afterwards the Lord Lieutenant's lodgings

According to the 1570 report already quoted, among the 'fair and necessarie roulmes' introduced to the castle by the chief governor, Sir Henry Sidney, was 'a fit seate for the placing and receiving of any governour heraftir [i.e., for his investiture], as for the bettir and more commodious resorte and assembly of the counsaill'.[307] The council referred to was the privy council to the Lord Lieutenant. A 'Counsel chamber' appears on the 1606 Wattson plan (Fig. 1.15) just inside the gatehouse on the north wall of the castle on its eastern side. Other than the rectangular building shown on this plan, we know little else of its form. In 1635, Sir William Brereton described 'the council-chamber, wherein stands a very long table, furnished with stools at both sides and ends. Here sometimes sit in council about 60 or 64 privy councillors'.[308] In 1619, payment was made to Sir William Usher, clerk of the council, for money paid out to purchase 'a carpet and other necessaries for the Council chamber after the fire lately happened there'.[309] Further, possibly related, difficulties arose the following year, when 'the roof of the Council Chamber and several lodgings over it' fell to the ground, and an order for their repair was made in August 1620.[310] In December that year, Lord Deputy Oliver St John thanked the lords of the council for the sum of £200 for rebuilding the Council Chamber, although he noted that the expense would be almost £300.[311] We have already mentioned above, the Brussels tapestries bought on Lord Deputy Wentworth's behalf by the Spanish ambassador in 1636, for the Presence Chamber, withdrawing chamber and Council Chamber.[312]

Regarding protocols for meetings of the council, Wentworth stated 'that no Man speak covered save the Deputy; and that their speech may not be directed one to another, but only to the Deputy'.[313] Indeed this injunction about speaking protocols was part of a much longer complaint by Wentworth regarding irreverent practices throughout the chambers of state in the castle, not matching, in his view, the correct protocols as observed in the London court:

> The Rooms of this House are almost become common, every ordinary Gentleman thinking it a Disparagement to stay any where but in the Drawing-Chamber, which indeed is occasioned in part, by suffering the Presence [Chamber] to be so familiar, that for the most Part it is filled with their Servants, whilst their Masters are within.[314]

From the very start, Wentworth set out to establish more exclusive ceremonial and procedural protocols than were customary. Investiture as viceroy had heretofore taken place at Christ Church Cathedral, but Wentworth moved the moment of inauguration itself – much to the disappointment of potential local spectators – to the most exclusive public zone of all in the castle – the Council Chamber. Here the oath took place and the sword of state was handed over to him, before a select group which included the council, the Lords Justice, Lord Ely and Lord Cork, and the master of rolls, Mr Wandesford.[315] Only after this was enacted did the party proceed to the Presence Chamber to sit before a wider audience, make speeches, and invest a number of knights – as already noted. Indeed, after this again, the main party withdrew to the 'privy chamber' where the ladies had waited, including Wentworth's wife Elizabeth Rhodes, who was saluted 'by the justices with a kiss one by one as she stood next to the countess of Tyreconnell'.[316]

In 1656, the council removed from the castle to new chambers close to the Custom House.[317] A number of years later, in accounts for 1661 to 1663, payment was made to a very large number of tradesmen, and building suppliers, including to John Mills, master carpenter, for works which may have included converting the Council Chamber into the Lord Lieutenant's lodgings, for the duke of Ormond.[318] In March 1663, Mathew Harrison was paid £65 for slating the roof of the Council Chamber.[319] As noted above, the 'Lord Leiutenants lodgins' were by then recorded in the location of the former Council Chamber on the 1673 Dartmouth plan (Fig. 2.1). These lodgings, as recorded on the 1673 plan, were approximately 57ft by 25ft (17m by 7.5m), with a portal or portico projecting southwards to the front. As already noted in the discussion of the gallery above, this appears to have been a shallower building than the former

Council Chamber, which must have extended as far as the gallery, which on this plan is some 20ft (6m) away from it. Thus, the Council Chamber would appear originally to have been approximately 77ft (23m) or so in depth. In 1678, Ware recorded that 'the place of the Council chamber, and what other roomes belonged thereunto, of late converted into an appartment for the Lodging of such persons of the Chief Governours household as are consigned [sic] thereunto',[320] suggesting that perhaps the lodging was more for the entourage of the Lord Lieutenant than for the governor himself, and that he remained when present, as Arran did, in the lodgings in the great residential range on the south wall of the castle.

Constable's lodgings

Sometime in the 1560s, Jacques Wingfield talked of building a residence for himself at his own expense: with 'my cottage in the castle that standeth on the north wall of the castle joined to the constable's prison'. Wingfield successfully resisted the justiciar Sir William Fitzwilliam's attempts to have him removed from his lodgings.[321] The constable's lodgings built by Wingfield were not depicted on Wattson's plan (Fig. 1.15), but as he described them on the north wall beside the constable's prison, we can assume that the offices of 'Auditor', 'Remembrancer' and 'Master of the Rolls', which are in this location on that map, represent Wingfield's house put to alternative use. This seems to be confirmed by the fact that a house called the 'Constables Lodgins' appears on the 1673 Dartmouth plan (Fig. 2.1) in that location, i.e., just inside the main gate on the north wall, on the west side. Ware also corroborates this when he states: 'And on the other side of the Gate [to the Council Chamber] hee may place his eye on the Constables Lodgings, very much beautified and reduced to the better accommodation of modern contrivance in the time of the Duke of Ormond's first Government after his Maiesties happy restauration [i.e. 1662–9]…'[322] The sum of £275 18s. was paid to Captain John Paine in May 1664 for these works.[323] In the light of such repair works, it is possible that the constable's residence may have been used by the Lord Lieutenant as his own after the fire of 1684.

Lodgings or apartment built of brick

After describing the constable's lodgings, Ware, in his 1678 perambulation of the castle, goes on to state that the visitor may see 'also the appartment built of brick in the time of the Earl of Strafford, for the accommodation of S'r George Radcliff, Bart…', which Maguire plausibly identifies as the next building to the west labelled as 'Lodgings' on the 1673 Dartmouth plan (Fig. 2.1).[324] Ware goes on to say that 'Next to this appartment are other more ancient brick buildings in

the same range under the Castle wall which were built in the time of King James, and are now within a Portall adioyneing to Cork Tower'. As Maguire has suggested, these in turn can be plausibly identified as the next set of 'Lodgins' further to the west, in the direction of the north-west or Cork Tower. The existence of a brick range built by Wentworth brings to mind his building of the vast brick Jigginstown in Naas, Co. Kildare, c. 1637.[325] But, as noted by Ware, and quoted above, this was predated by an earlier 'more ancient' range at Dublin Castle, which he stated was built during the reign of James I (1603–25).[326]

In 1606, according to the Wattson plan, and as already noted, these buildings, including the former constable's house, were being used, east to west respectively as offices for the auditor, master of rolls, and the remembrancer, with the last adjoining the north-west tower. It is possible for example that the auditor's brick building described by Ware predated the reign of James. There was at least a residence for the auditor in the castle from the late sixteenth century. In 1596, Sir Geoffrey Fenton, Secretary of State in Ireland, petitioned the council 'to have rooms in Dublin Castle which have lain vacant since Mr. Auditor Jennyson died' in order to store the 'records of the surveyorship' which had been kept in a private house until then.[327] The following year, the queen granted the former auditor's quarters to Fenton for that purpose.[328]

Prisons identified on the 1606 Wattson plan

Numerous reports, particularly in reference to their escape, refer to the holding of prisoners in various of the towers, as already alluded to in Chapter 2.2. However, the 1606 Wattson plan also shows two buildings in the north-west quadrant of the castle, which he refers to as a 'Prison' and as the 'Former prison'. In the 1560s there is a reference to Jacques Wingfield repairing or rebuilding the jail.[329] In 1585, instructions from the government secretary Geoffrey Fenton, sent to the lord deputy in Ireland, refer to a 'Grate' prison, 'where malefactors lie' which was 'adjoining' to the powder house under the great hall, all of which is consistent with their depiction in the Wattson plan.[330] In 1609 there was an estimate of money to be expended on inter alia 'enlarging of the gaol there…to the constable of Dublin Castle, for dieting of prisoners…[and] for money disbursed by the late constable of Dublin Castle in repairing the gaol there'.[331] The jail(s) seemed to serve both the city and the Crown, so that in 1609, in a letter from the king to the lord deputy and chancellor, the king directed that 'In consideration of divers inconveniences attendant on the keeping of the common gaol within the Castle of Dublin…they shall consider of some other suitable place in the city to which it may be removed', although 'certain prisoners of state should still continue to be confined within the precincts of the castle' and 'that a wall shall be built, separating such persons from the part reserved for the lodging of the Lord Deputy'.[332] This was reiterated in 1611, when it was directed that 'the gaol… is to be built by the country, and for that which is to be done within the castle the estimate seems very high; so there is now no purpose to do anything but what is necessary, especially the castle being freed of the ordinary prisoners and of the courts of justice'.[333] These prison buildings appear to have been dismantled by 1673, as they do not appear on the Dartmouth plan (Fig. 2.1). Indeed, as noted above, at least some of the buildings in the range of lodgings along the north-western wall dated to the reign of James I, if not before, suggesting that the prisons did not survive much later than the creation of the 1606 plan. After the jails were dismantled, prisoners of state who were being held in the castle were then most likely to have been held in the towers.

Chapter 2.4
The Lower Castle Yard

General position and location

In the seventeenth century, the Lower Yard consisted of a complex of secondary buildings and open spaces associated with the castle but not protected by its medieval walls and towers. A number of contemporary plans, including de Gomme's city map of 1673 (Fig. 2.12), show us that these buildings and yards were located – as they are today – to the east and south of the medieval enceinte.

The portion directly to the east, in the position of the present Lower Yard, and steeply sloping downwards from the medieval enclosure, was 'the Stable yard, where you may take delight in seeing the great horse ridden, and managed by the rules of the best horsemanship, and of martiall skill'.[334] This Lower Yard was approximately as wide, east to west, as the medieval enclosure, and was bisected by the River Poddle, part of which was used as a horse pond. The two Thomas Phillips plans of 1685 (Figs 2.2, 2.3) extend the view southwards to show the area which enclosed the garden, albeit without including any details of it. The only visual evidence for the garden, where it is shown as a large, enclosed rectangle divided in four, is in de Gomme's city map. Although shaped differently, it is in the same position, more or less, as the present castle gardens. Speed's 1610 Dublin map (Fig. 2.13) shows a watermill just below the city walls, to the south-west of the castle enclosure, although this was likely not to have been part of the so-called Lower Yard. On the other hand, Phillips' 1685 plan of the castle (Fig. 2.2) describes a portion of the Poddle directly south of the castle walls as the 'Mill race'.

Stables and stable yard

The 'Stable yard' is delineated in some detail in a manuscript map prepared by Sir William Robinson in February 1684 (Fig. 2.14),[335] as part of a response to a petition submitted by Sir Robert Reading.[336] Reading, who was the supplier of water

to the castle and an entrepreneur of diverse ambitions,[337] sought permission to build a mill on a section of the Poddle on the northern end of the yard downstream from that part used for the horses. The horse pond is depicted by Robinson, and in Phillips' plans, as a rectangular swelling of the river. Directly to the south, the river seems to have been culverted, as it is shown by means of dotted lines on the Robinson diagram. Other buildings shown here include a number of stables on the eastern range, the 'Grand Stables' on the north range on the west side of the river, and a 'Coach House' also on the north range, on the east side of the river. Between these is a gate – which it was proposed to move a little bit to the south – which gave access to 'Castle Lane', in the general location of the present Palace Street. There is also a dunghill close by, and an area called the 'Wash ground', which was 'desired by the petitioner'. Finally, while nothing of the main castle is shown on the Robinson drawing, the outline of its western side matches exactly the lines of the exterior of the eastern boundary as depicted in the very reliable 1673 Dartmouth plan (Fig. 2.1). Thus, Robinson's outline includes a quadrant of the south-east (Record) tower, and an extent of the eastern castle wall up to and including a small rectangular projection, shown on both maps. This projection might conceivably have contained garderobes. The Robinson map also suggests that there was a further unidentified, but significant, building, or walled enclosure, which was not labelled, located to the east and south-east of the north-east (Powder) tower. This may have been the office of the Ordnance, which Ware tells us was 'at the issuing out of the said last mentioned postern Gate'.[338] The location of this eastern postern gate is identified on the 1673 Dartmouth plan directly north of the rectangular projection discussed, and consequently would have led into this rectangular enclosure suggested by the Robinson map.

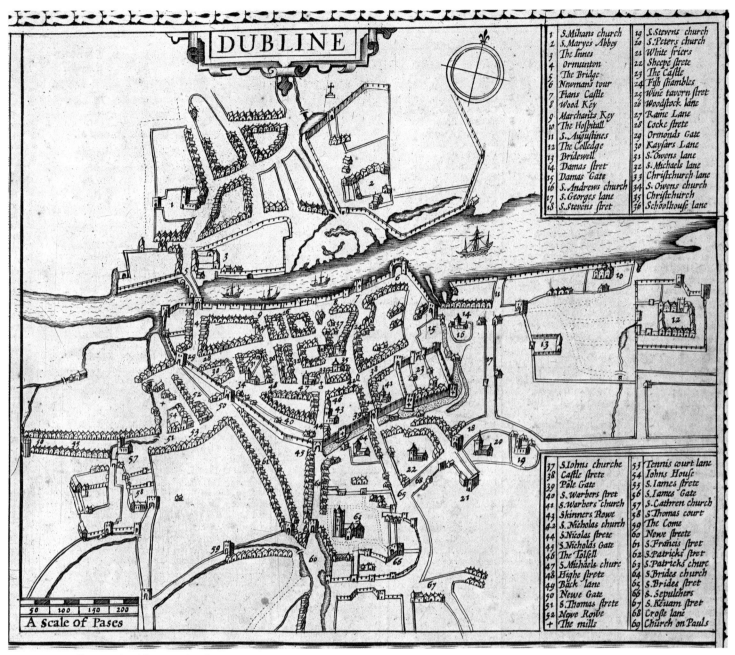

Fig. 2.13 Speed's map of Dublin 1610. (RIA)

Wentworth's stables

The 'Grand Stables' on the north-west of the Robinson plan (Fig. 2.14), which according to it measure approximately 110ft by 40ft (33m by 24m), most likely refer to the stables built by Thomas Wentworth within three months of his arrival in Dublin as lord deputy in July 1633. Land to build these and other outhouses, as well as for the enlargement of the gardens, was purchased for £150.[339] Some of the land was got from Sir Henry Talbot, in exchange for lands in an intended plantation of Connacht.[340] In a letter from Charles II to Wentworth, the king was recorded as stating that the castle 'is become so ruinous as in a short time it will

not be habitable either in point of decency or safety' and that Wentworth was to be allowed to put 'not more than £2,000 in addition to the sum allowed by concordatum for repairing the castle, and in addition of stables and gardens thereunto'.[341] More details regarding the circumstances of its construction can be gleaned from Wentworth's letter to Secretary Coke in October 1633:

> There is not any Stable but a poor mean one, and that made of a decayed Church, which is such a Prophanation as I am sure his Majesty would not allow of; besides there is a Decree in the Exchequer

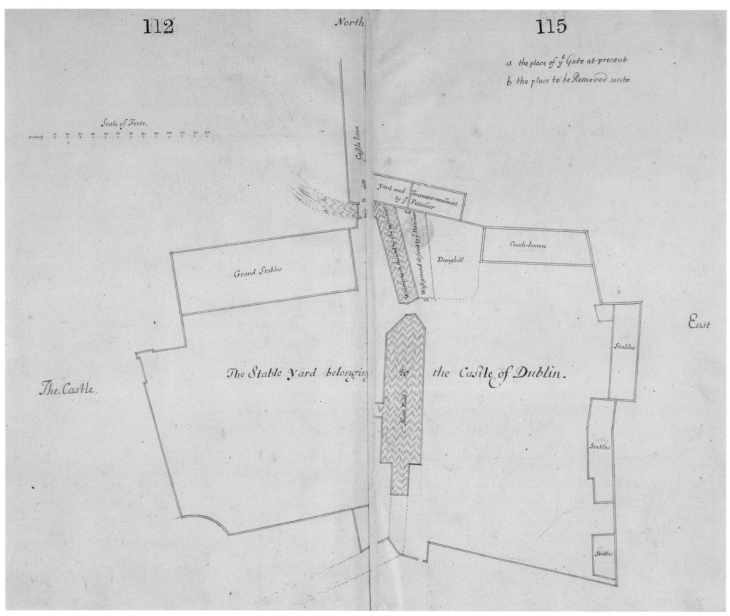

Fig. 2.14 Plan of Lower Yard by William Robinson, 1684. (NLI, Ormond MS 2436)

for restoring it to the parish whence it was taken: I have therefore got a Piece of Ground whereon to build a new one, the most convenient for the Castle in the World: the Foundation is already two Yards high, and shall be finished by the end of June next, with Granaries and all other Conveniences. There will be room for threescore Horses, and so many good ones I have in this Town already, to fill it and make up such a Troop of Horse, I dare say, as Ireland hath not been acquainted with; I am the more careful to compleat my own Troop, that so I may freely call upon other Captains to perform their Duties. And I trust his Majesty will allow of the Charge, being so necessary, and for so good a Purpose.[342]

The church profanely used as a stable was likely to have been St Andrew's parish church, which can be located on the John Speed *Dubline* map of 1610 (No. 16 on Fig. 2.13), on the south side of Dame Street, between George's Lane and the present Palace Street. In their own grounds, extending to the south, the church and churchyard were just to the north-east of the castle enclosure. Indeed, not only did Wentworth build a new stable, but he also restored the church to its proper use. In Secretary Coke's reply to the lord deputy in November 1633, echoing Wentworth's own sentiments, the restoration of the church is noted, as was the importance of the example that a great stable would give to other local lords in whom an interest in breeding great horses for the service of state, it is imputed in the letter, had waned considerably at this time:

...[the king] is well pleased with your pious Restitution to the Parish of that decayed Church, which was so decreed in the Exchequer. He is also well satisfied with the new Building of a Stable to contain your whole Troop of Horse, and commendeth your noble Resolution to make your own Troop so compleat with brave and serviceable Horses, that you may, with Confidence, press others to do the like: Where, by the Way, let me tell you, that Ireland, in my Memory, was so replenished with fair Hobbies, that they furnish'd England and other Countries, and were every where much esteemed. Now we hear so little of them that it seemeth the Honour of Breeding for Service hath no more Esteem. If your Lorship can renew it, you shall do a worthy Act, for which his Majesty shall have Cause to give you Thanks.[343]

Not long after they were completed, the stables were described by Sir William Brereton, who visited the castle in 1635:

Here my Lord Deputy hath lately erected a gallant, stately stable as any I have seen in the king's dominions; it is a double stable, there being a strong wall in the middle, to either side whereof stand the horses' heads. Thirty horses may stand at ease on either side, the stalls being very large; these are exceeding high, at least five or six yards, and very near the same breadth; no planks [were] made use of, but Holland bricks placed upon the edges, whereon the horses lie and you walk; these as easy to walk upon as to lie upon, and these are made of Holland earth, which is harder and more durable much than our clay: with these the streets are paved in Holland.[344]

Wentworth also used so-called Holland (or Dutch) bricks in the construction of his great house at Jigginstown, Co. Kildare,[345] and brick was used in a pair of buildings along the north wall of the castle, as already noted. Wentworth, as president of the Council of the North, had made a number of Renaissance-style modifications to his otherwise medieval brick house at King's Manor, Yorkshire.[346] Although innovative, and indicative of high luxury, Dutch-style brick had been in use in England from at least the fifteenth century at, for example, Herstmonceux in Sussex and Tattershall in Lincolnshire, and in the sixteenth century in Hampton Court, London.[347] Giles Worsley suggested that bricks laid on their side in this way was unusual, although such an approach was noticed in the later seventeenth century by Sir Roger Pratt at stables at Horseheath, Cambridgeshire,

and that such 'clinkers' – as Worsley believes these bricks to have been – can also be seen in the stables at Powis Castle.[348]

Wentworth's competitive pride in this work is demonstrated by the self-regarding and overblown comparisons he sought to make between his own work and that of the great architect of the age, Inigo Jones. In a letter to the earl of Arundel, he stated that he had built 'a better stable for ye King here in Ireland than ever [Jones] did in England'.[349] Indeed, a little earlier he had stated that 'without Offence to Mr. Jones, or Pride in myself be it spoken, I take myself to be a very pretty Architect too'.[350] Although the stables in question do not survive, we have Wentworth's curious, but hardly exemplary, work at Jigginstown to compare to the work of the celebrated Jones.[351] When Edward Lovett Pearce, the pre-eminent architect of early eighteenth-century Ireland, recorded the plans of that house he found the suggestion that it may have even been designed by Jones difficult to swallow, stating that he 'could not observe any particulars in it worthy of so great a master' unless, he suggested, Jones 'was oblieg'd to accommodate him self to the humour of those times or the particular inclination of the Lord'.[352] And on the subject of stables themselves, despite Wentworth's remarks to Arundel, Jones was responsible for a fine set of stables – albeit three years later than Wentworth's Dublin stables – in 1638–40 at Holland House, London. At Jones's London stables, there were Palladian arcaded entrances, with Tuscan pilasters between arches leading into double horse boxes. A better comparison, with the nevertheless very impressive stables at Dublin Castle, might be those built by Robert Hooke at Somerset House, London, where a wall also divides the stalls down the centre, there being places for only ten more horses at these later London stables than the sixty provided for at Dublin.[353]

Other stables

There were of course stables associated with the castle before and after Wentworth's time. There are references to their repair in 1619.[354] In 1673, Dame Fridiswid Stephens, the widow of John Stephens, petitioned for £200 spent by her husband in the construction of stables while Ormond was Lord Lieutenant.[355] These are likely to have been those shown on the eastern side in the Robinson map. Around 1667, the Athlone herald, Richard Carney claimed to have 'made and erected one dyal over the Castle stables and another brasse dyal for the Castle' for which he charged £5.[356]

Armoury

Ware's 1678 description of the stable yard lists, besides the 'statelie stables of an elegant contrivance' built by Wentworth, 'a place designed for a mint, and other offices for the forgeing of Armes and other uses appertaineing to the stores'.[357] He also lists 'a great store house for keeping of all furniture belonging to Warre', which according to the de Gomme map (Fig. 2.12) may be identified as the 'magazine' on the exterior of the south wall of the stable enclosure. Ware's text suggests that this armoury was built also 'in the time of that vast minded Governour', Wentworth.[358] An inventory made by Lord Mountjoy of the ordnance, arms and ammunition in Ireland in 1684 lists in the stores of Dublin, brass ordnance including cannon of seven (10ft (3m) long), demi cannons, culverins, sakers, falcons, 'falconets', 'rabonets', 'mynions', three pounders (referring to the weight of the shot they fired), sling pieces and brass petards. The inventory also included precise quantities of round shot, 'granado shells', 'Birr shot', stone shot, and other ammunition, as well as full lists of the necessaries for the train, iron and iron-work, timber and timber-work, carriages, 'spare carriages and wheels, gynns etc.', and other arms and instruments.[359]

Powder store

Separate to the armoury was a powder store built in the garden by Lord Lieutenant Robartes in 1669.[360] This may be identified with the 'Powder house' illustrated to the west of the rectangular garden, which is shown on the de Gomme map of 1673 (Fig. 2.12). The danger of storing gunpowder within the castle enclosure should have been an obvious one and was often discussed; this did not prevent its being kept throughout much of the seventeenth century on the ground floor of the great hall, despite its use as parliament house and the courts of law at various times, as we have seen. That the powder had been cleared out of there by Robartes just two years before the same building was burnt to the ground, was fortuitous. Nevertheless, some kegs had still to be rescued from the hall during the fire. The removal back to the castle was because of the failure of the foundations of the garden storehouse.[361] This old building was blown up in 1689.[362]

Castle gardens

Little is known about the garden itself, other than the rectangular grid illustrated on the de Gomme map (Fig. 2.12). We know that some landscape of retreat existed from as early as 1602, when Lord Delvin, who was imprisoned in the castle, and 'convalescent', sought 'leave to "walk in the garden within the Castle"'.[363] In 1610, a summer house was built in the castle garden by Lord Lieutenant Chichester,[364] and in 1634, as we have seen, Charles I granted funds for repairing the castle, 'and in addition of stables and gardens thereunto' suggesting that new gardens were laid out at that date.[365] Indeed Wentworth, who was lord deputy at that

time, stated in a 1633 letter to Secretary [Sir John] Coke, that he had 'bought as much more Ground about the Castle as costs one hundred and fifty Pounds, out of which I will provide the House of a Garden, and Out Courts, for Fuel and such other Necessaries belonging to a Family, whereof I am here altogether unprovided'.[366]

Interest in gardens was widespread among the New English in Ireland throughout the Elizabethan and Jacobean eras, when Renaissance ideas imported from Italy suggested gardens of rectilinear compartments, subdivided into geometrical shapes of diamonds or more elaborate 'knots' or patterns, bordered by parterres of bedding plants, hedges and raised terraces, with stairways, statuary and water features.[367] With the unrest during the middle years of the seventeenth century, no new gardens were likely to have been made, and we have no record of any garden work by any of the viceroys at the castle after the Restoration, until works carried out in the 1690s by Henry Sidney. Thus, the tightly controlled geometrically laid-out gardens depicted on de Gomme's map, suggest that what was being represented were the gardens more or less as they had been laid out in the early decades of the seventeenth century by Chichester and Wentworth, as suggested by the sparse historical record outlined above.

There are a number of gardens with which we might compare what we see on the de Gomme plan. The grounds at Dunluce Castle, Co. Antrim, a site abandoned soon after it was laid out, and therefore still preserving in the surviving earthworks its early seventeenth-century form, shows in aerial photography as a simple rectangular layout with raised terraces and rectangular flower beds. This is not much different from what we may otherwise have been tempted to see as an overly simplified depiction of the castle gardens by de Gomme.[368] Terraces, used either as long walks for views, or as a series of compartments set at different levels, were also favoured around this time. At one of his houses, Richard Boyle, the earl of Cork, laid out a terrace of 160 yards (146m) overlooking the town of Youghal, c. 1612–14, which was combined with his own series of knot gardens, with stairways, balustrades and statues. At his house at Lismore, the terrace built in 1624 and the castle also survive.[369] Wentworth laid out a raised walk and a rectangular garden to the front of his house built c. 1635 at Jigginstown.[370] Closer to hand, at Chichester House, in Dublin, purchased by Lord Deputy Chichester in the first decade of the seventeenth century, there was an L-shaped 'Terrace Walk' of 20ft (6m) width, which was 67ft (20.4m) along its shorter axis, and 261ft (79.6m) along the longer one.[371] Also in Dublin, and slightly earlier, were the master's gardens at Trinity College, dating to the 1590s, and recorded in a drawing of c. 1600.[372]

These show the kinds of simple geometric patterns, or knots, made up of diamonds and rectangles, created with flower beds and different coloured sands, that were favoured at the time, and that are suggestive of the patterns on the de Gomme plan of the gardens at Dublin Castle. What is seen on de Gomme was no doubt replaced towards the end of the century, when a garden was created by Henry Sidney, who had accompanied William of Orange to Ireland in 1690, and was a Lord Justice in 1691–2 and Lord Lieutenant in 1692–3. According to one visitor, Sidney's gardens were dominated by 'a broad terras walk the length of the building, the walls coverd with greens and flower potts. From hence, on a stone arch over a little river, you descend by two spacious paire of stone staires into the garden'.[373] Although changes, including the 'stone bridge over a little river', may be noted, the terrace continued to dominate the new scheme, and nothing radical in this hemmed-in urban garden was attempted.

Chapter 2.5
Conclusion

The 1684 fire wreaked havoc upon the fabric of the medieval and Renaissance castle, and in this way cleared the ground for its own redevelopment in the centuries that followed. In order to understand the site inherited by its future developers, it is worthwhile in conclusion to compile a brief inventory of the parts of the castle that seem to have survived the conflagration. Our major sources for this are the contemporary written descriptions of the fire itself, William Robinson's 1684 plan of the Lower Castle Yard, Thomas Phillips' 1685 plans of the castle walls, and Brooking's 1728 view of the Upper Castle Yard, as we've interpreted these documents in various passages above, and taking into account that Brooking's map was made some forty-four years after the event, and already shows *inter alia* the nascent arcaded southern ranges constructed in the meantime.

We may begin, as we did above, with the medieval enceinte, or castle walls and their towers and gates. Phillips' plans (Figs 2.2, 2.3) show that these were intact in 1685, and therefore had withstood the worst effects of the fire. Lord Arran's two controlled explosions were executed in order to prevent fire spreading to the Powder Tower on the north-east corner and the Bermingham Tower on the south-west corner, both of which were saved. Hughes suggests that the remains of the wall in the south-east quadrant may have formed the foundations for the eighteenth-century state apartments,[374] while some portion of the south wall is still intact and upstanding running eastwards from the Bermingham Tower and forming part of the south wall of the present St Patrick's Hall. Both of the southern corner towers have survived in one form or another, although heavily restored and altered since 1684. Neither of the northern towers is extant, and indeed both were gone

even by 1728 (Fig. 1.20). Cork Tower (on the north-west) was removed no doubt to provide room for the new early eighteenth-century western range, and the Powder Tower (on the north-east) was replaced by what might have been the office of the Ordnance store, as suggested above.

Otherwise, the great majority of the buildings that filled the central ground must have been lost to the fire, and were no doubt quickly cleared away afterwards to make way for rebuilding. Therefore, the residential range built by Sir Henry Sidney in the 1560s, the place indeed where the fire started, was almost entirely destroyed. Arran himself 'blew up' Falkland's gallery in order to protect the Powder Tower on the north-east, and with this arcaded building went the residential quarters attached to it on its eastern side in the area known as the back court (the eastern half of the Upper Castle Yard). Sidney's chapel, if not destroyed during an alleged fire of 1638 (discussed above), must surely have gone up in flames in 1684. There is no record of it afterwards.

However, despite the recorded loss of the greatest part of the chief residential structures that ran along the south wall of the castle, Brooking's image shows an uneven row of buildings set behind the arcaded two-storey range with dormers on the south-east, continuing behind the partially built, ground-floor-only arcade on the south-western side. These must belong to the pre-fire period. Based on comparison with the 1673 Dartmouth plan (Fig. 2.1), and as reviewed in detail above, we can identify the two-storey dining room block, with its double-storey entrance portal. Its upper-level coat of arms, topped by a pediment, is set above a balustrade and rusticated door. Even the two obelisk-like pillars set in front of the portal in the Brooking image are suggested in plan form by dots to the front of the portal in the 1673 Dartmouth image. The partially ruined remains of what appears to be the Presence Chamber are depicted by Brooking behind a pair of cannons whose muzzles point to the ground. Most extraordinary of all is the possibility that what is labelled as 'Hall' against the south wall on the Dartmouth plan (Fig. 2.1) (also known as the south hall), survived to this time. As pointed out above, this may be among the earliest buildings at the castle, predating the great hall built in 1245. The same building appears to be represented on Brooking's image as a low building with four dormers and two chimneys, behind the ground-floor arcade on the south-western quadrant of the castle. Other than the castle walls and towers, this would have been the longest-standing structure in the interior of the castle, here surviving, if we are correct, from the early thirteenth century until the first decades of the eighteenth century – some five hundred years.

Finally, there is no suggestion in any of the contemporary descriptions that the Lower Yard was affected in any substantial way by the April 1684 fire. Therefore, the buildings recorded in William Robinson's map of this area, made some three months earlier (Fig. 2.14),[375] were likely to have been intact when plans for the restoration of the post-fire complex began. As noted already, these buildings included among others the 'Grand Stables' built by Wentworth in 1633. Sometime soon after this map was made, no doubt, the horse pond shown on Robinson's map was covered over, and one of the last open runs of the River Poddle, the source indeed of the former castle moat, was sealed up for good.

Endnotes

1 Staffordshire Record Office, 1673; Maguire 1974, fig. 3, p. 8; Lennon 2008, Map 7.

2 NLI, MS 3137(3) & MS 2557(1).

3 Manning 2003b.

4 Fenlon 2011b, 155–60.

5 Barnard 2000a, 256.

6 Barnard 2000a, 257.

7 Brady 2012; Barnard 2000a.

8 Wentworth to Coke, Oct 14, 1633, in Knowler 1739, i, 132.

9 Annals of Dudley Loftus, Marsh's Library MS 211 (Z4.2.7), f. 436, 1560, as reproduced in White 1941b, 236.

10 Moss 2014c.

11 Holinshed 1808, vi, 403.

12 Gilbert 1889–1922, ii, 558–61; see Appendix 1.

13 5 June 1614, CSPI 1611–14, 482.

14 Feb 6, 1619, claim made by Sir William Usher, Clerk of the Council, 'for monies disbursed, to buy a carpet and other necessaries for the Council Chamber after the fire lately happened there', and Aug 13, 1620, a note from the lord deputy and council of Ireland to the privy council to 'Apprise them that of late part of this castle, and the roof of the Council Chamber and several lodgings over it, have fallen to the ground', CSPI 1615–25, 246, 294; Robinson 1994, 268.

15 Falkiner 1904, 38–40; see Appendix 2.

16 Grosart 1886–88, iii, 43.

17 Knowler 1739, i, 68; Robinson 1994, 278–9.

18 Fenlon 2011a, 210.

19 See Fenlon, op. cit.; and Craig 1970.

20 21 Feb 1632, CSPI 1625–32, 648.

21 Bagwell 1909–16, i, 200–01.

22 Knowler 1739, i, 132.

23 Ibid., 131.

24 Howarth 1997, 192.

25 Shaw 2006, 340.

26 Carte 1735–36, ii, 422; Robinson 1994, 298–9.

27 HMC Egmont, i, 285; Robinson 1994, 304.

28 Robinson 1994, 309.

29 Ball 1902; Corish 1976a; Robinson 1994, 314.

30 Cromwell 1820, 43; Robinson 1994, 314–15.

31 Dunlop 1913, ii, 544.

32 Loeber 1981, 20, 72; Robinson 1994, 319.

33 Clarke 1999, 108–11.

34 Mercurius Politicus, 29 Dec 1659–5 Jan 1659 [1660], 989–90.

35 McCormick 2018, 96; Corish 1976b, 356.

36 Gilbert 1889–1922, iv, 572–3.

37 Barnard 2000b, 4.

38 1666, CSPI 1666–69, 258; see also Bodl. Carte MS 52, f. 288, record of £2,600 'that was payd for repaires of Dublin Castle and other repaires abt it by 4 severall warr[an]ts', during his first year as viceroy after the Restoration, i.e., 'for that yeare of his Graces landing twixt the 27th of July 1662 and to the 20th of March following'.

39 Robinson 1994, 348.

40 Airy 1890, 59.

41 Letter from William Ellis to Sir Cyril Wyche, Chief Secretary to the duke of Ormond, 1676–82, 'I was with the stewards when the comptrollers chamber of ye same building and next adjoyning fell, if he had bin there he may have bin killed, severall other parts of ye Castle have suffered particularly ye Exchange such though very low, shielded as ye wind by the Castle wall was laid flatt, it is look'd upon to have bin a kind of a Hurricane, …', NAI, Wyche MSS 1/1/14.

42 Gibney 2009.

43 British Library, Stowe 213, f. 308, October 13, 1673, letter from the earl of Essex to his brother, 'There is one Oliver Plunkitt, ye Romish Titular Primate of this Kingdome who seems to be one of ye best men of his Persuasion I have mett with and tho I doubt not but he is industrious enough in promoting his owne relgion yet I could never finde but he was of a more peaceable temper & more conformable to ye Government then [sic] any of their Titular B'ps in this Country…I should be glad for ye reasons above mentioned [if] you would yr selfe & some of our ffriends secure this Gentleman from any such severitie which should be singly & personally inflicted on him'.

44 HMC Ormonde ns, vii, 133–4.

45 A more complete descriptions of these events is given below in the section on the residential range in the castle.

46 17 Apr 1684, HMC 7th Report, 1879, 499; Lawlor 1923, 50.

47 'Building a new Palace for the Governour', William Petty in his Political Anatomy, published posthumously in 1691, as reproduced in Hull 1899, i, 147.

48 Falkiner 1904, 25, who cites 'The viceregal court historically vindicated, a pamphlet by J.P. Prendergast, the well informed author of the Cromwellian settlement, but he does not give his authority'.

49 Loeber 1980, 62.

50 HMC Ormonde, ii, 320–2, 333; British Library, Maps K.Top.53.3.2., reproduced in Lennon 2008, Map 10.

51 Con Manning has argued that the south-west or Bermingham Tower is likely to have been the original tower ordered to be built by King John in 1204, and that the larger enclosure did not come about until the second phase of building associated with Henry of London, from 1213 to the 1220s. Part of an older curtain wall, north of the tower, was found during excavations, and this was likely to have been part of an earlier enclosure associated with this first tower. See Manning 2017–18.

52 Manning, pers. comm.; Lynch & Manning 2001.

53 Hawkins 1844, 141; see Appendix 3.

54 Brady 2002, 77.

55 Hughes 1940, 88.

56 Robinson 1994, 266–7, 281, 283; Knowler 1739, i, 131; Falkiner 1904, 21–2.

57 Falkiner 1904, 39–40; see Appendix 2.

58 Hughes 1940, 90.

59 c. 1627–8, CSPI 1647–60, 111.

60 Knowler 1739, i, 131.

61 19 June 1663, CSPI 1663–65, 139

62 Gilbert 1889–1922, ii, 560; see Appendix 1.

63 Hogan 1894, 11.

64 Manning 2003b, 90.

65 Falkiner 1904, 39.

66 Hogan 1881, 223–4; Robinson 1994, 246–8.

67 Falkiner 1904, 39; see Appendix 2.

68 CSPI 1615–25, 489; Knowler 1739, i, 131

69 CSPI 1615–25, 489.

70 CSPI 1615–25, 526.

71 DCLA Gilbert Coll. MSS 74–6, ff. 23–4.

72 6 March 1631, Grosart 1886–8, iii, 75.

73 It is also possible that one plan represented Phillips' record of the castle, the other proposed alterations.

74 Derricke 1985.

75 Perrot 1585, in Gilbert 1889–1922, ii, 558, 560; see Appendix 1. Manning (pers. comm.) notes from Perrot that the 'survey describes only two storeys in the western tower of the gatehouse, with only a blocked loop flanking the north wall westwards in the lower of these. The second storey had a window and two loops, one of which commanded the area in front of the gate. The east tower of the gateway is described as having three storeys all with three loops.' Unsurprisingly, given the constraints of such a woodcut image, none of this detail is provided by Derricke.

76 Derricke was Sidney's war artist in Ireland. The images in this collection are generally taken to be made on location, partly on the basis of the accuracy of the dress of the Irish soldiers, and for some of the topographical content of this image, including the nature of his depiction of the houses on Castle Street (Morgan 2007).

77 Derricke 1985, plate vi.

78 Manning 2003b, 91.

79 Hayden 2011, 177–81.

80 Robinson 1994, 221.

81 See discussion of these works below.

82 Manning 2003b, 91.

83 Derricke 1985, opp. plate vi.

84 Shaw 2006, 336.

85 Knowler 1739, i, 282–5; Shaw 2006, 350.

86 28 May 1590, Carew MSS 1589–1600, 31–3.

87 Hawkins 1844, 141; see Appendix 3.

88 Dunton 2003, 139; see Appendix 7.

89 Hughes, 1940, 96; Con Manning pers. comm.

90 5 June 1614, CSPI 1611–14, 482.

91 CSPI 1615–25, 245.

92 23 Feb 1617, CSPI 1615–25, 196: 'A concordatum of £929 11s. English, granted to Humphry Farname, Esq.,…for the new building of the gate house of the Castle of Dublin and other reparations within the same'.

93 CSPI 1615–25, 202: June 29, 1618, 'The new gatehouse of the castle of Dublin nearly finished'.

94 Robinson 1994, 221.

95 Feb 27, 1597, Carew MSS 1589–1600, 227.

96 26 May 1632, CSPI 1625–32, 665.

97 Gilbert 1889–1922, ii, 558; see Appendix 1; Robinson 1994, 403.

98 Manning 2003b, 91.

99 31 July 1627, CSPI 1625–32, 258.

100 Knowler 1739, i, 131; Hughes 1940, 89.

101 The 1585 survey refers to Perrot having his accommodation at the top of this tower; Gilbert 1889–1922, ii, 558–9; see Appendix 1.

102 Gilbert 1889–1922, ii, 560; see Appendix 1.

103 See discussion of the square tower in section on the south-west or Bermingham Tower below.

104 Loeber 1981, 82–3.

105 NLI, MS 2487, f. 125, 'An Estimate of what is at present very needfull to bee Repaired in & about his Ma'ies Castle of Dublin besides the Powdar Tower, and the 2 stores &c.' NLI, MS 2327, f. 111, 'Remaining due to workemen and for Materialls used in the Repaireing his Ma'ies Castle of Dublin &c the 18th of October 1662'; Gilbert 1899–1922 iv, 277; Loeber 1980, 55.

106 Ormond in a letter to the earl of Anglesey 29 Nov 1678, stated 'That the powder house is at the distance mentioned is (to my great trouble) too true. There I found it, and cannot tell whither to remove it till I am able to build a fitter place for it. Your Lordship knows in my time it was kept [in] one of the towers in the Castle, but the next succeeding Governor thought it no good neighbour, and so it was removed into the Castle garden, to a house built by my Lord Roberts, but the foundation failing, it was sent by my Lord Berkeley, I think first to Merrion and then to Crumlin, and at last brought to where it now is; from whence I would remove it to the tower wherein I left it, but that it rains in, and is like to fall. But it is not true that the whole store [of powder] of the kingdom is there (though, to my great grief, a small house will contain it), for there is ammunition at Duncannon, Waterford, Cork, Limerick, Kinsale and Galway'; HMC Ormonde ns, iv, 253; Robinson 1994, 371.

107 Manning 2003b.

108 Hughes 1940, 90.

109 Hughes 1940, 93; Manning 2003b, 81, based on an analysis of an 1813 plan and elevation by Francis Johnston (Lawlor 1923), broadly corroborates these measurements.

110 Manning 2003b, 92.

111 Manning 2003b, 91.

112 Robinson 1994, 221–3; Hughes 1940, 93–4.

113 Walsh 1948–1957, ii, 19–21.

114 See also Manning 2003b, 74.

115 Morrin 1863, 395.

116 DCLA Gilbert Coll. MSS 74–6, f. 24; see Appendix 4.

117 Dunton 2003, 139; see Appendix 7.

118 Hughes 1940, 91.

119 Manning 2003b, 90.

120 Falkiner 1904, 40; see Appendix 2.

121 While the Bermingham Tower may be counted to have been the most substantial of all of the towers in its overall dimensions, the tower with the thickest walls was the south-east or Record Tower, as noted above.

122 DCLA Gilbert Coll. MSS 74–6, f. 24; see Appendix 4; Hughes 1940, 92.

123 Gilbert 1889–1922, ii, 559–60; see Appendix 1.

124 Falkiner 1904, 40; see Appendix 2.

125 Hughes 1940, 93. However, Manning 2014, 347, states that 'Between 1775 and 1777 the Bermingham Tower was rebuilt with thinner walls on its original base'; this base survives and is visible on the south side, while it was partly exposed during excavations by Ann Lynch in 1985 (Manning 2003b, 90; Manning 2017–18).

126 Con Manning, pers. comm.

127 Gilbert 1889–1922, ii, 560; see Appendix 1.

128 See footnote 51 above.

129 Lynch & Manning 2001, 183–7.

130 The archives were stored here from 1537 until the establishment of the Record Commissioners in 1810, CSPI 1603–6, lxxiii–lxxiv; Hughes 1940, 93.

131 13 Apr. 1566, CSPI 1509–73, 295.

132 CSPI 1574–85, 150.

133 Handley 2004.

134 DCLA Gilbert Coll. MSS 74–6, f. 26; see Appendix 4.

135 Knowler 1739, i, 168, 224; Robinson 1994, 187–8.

136 NLI, MS 392. Thomas Dineley, 'Observations in a voyage through the kingdom of ireland', f. 58.

137 Maguire 1974, 12–13.

138 Bagwell 1909–16, I, 322.

139 Carte 1735–36, ii, 262; Robinson 1994, 339.

140 c. 21 May 1663, CSPI 1669–70, 454–5.

141 HMC 8th Report 1881, 526; Loeber 1980, 54.

142 Hughes 1940, 91.

143 DCLA Gilbert Coll. MSS 74–6, f. 32; see Appendix 4; Hughes 1940, 91.

144 HMC Salisbury, xviii, 381–2; Robinson 1994, 189–90; Maguire 1974, 5–7.

145 'The hall now in use in the Castle of Dublin is very fit but it is suggested to be inconvenient for greater respects. The same stands convenient from the Deputy's house without impediment, where there may be one gate broken down in the wall at the west end and a bridge framed to pass over the Castle ditch, by which plot may be avoided all inconveniences, for if the door at the east end of the same hall leading into the Castle be shut up, it makes a safety from any sudden surprisal of the rest of the Castle.
Or if there shall be a wall made at the east end to sever the hall from the rest of the Castle and thereby to include the several offices belonging to the courts adjoining to the hall, the same wall will divide his Majesty's house and the rest of the Castle from the hall, so as thereby no inconvenience in the kind of treason can ensue to impeach the State. But if one house lately built upon the entry of the passage now intending towards the new bridge does not hinder this proceeding, then this plot may be allowed whereby his Majesty may save the sum of £1,200 now demanded. For I can direct how these works may be finished for £400 so as the passage at the entry may be procured', HMC Salisbury, xviii, 381–2.

146 TCD, MS 772, f. 18r; NAI, SPO OP 165:12, described in an enclosed note from John Warburton who donated the document in August 1803 'to Government' as 'an Inquisition taken the 20th of June, in the 20th year of the Reign of Queen Elizabeth, 1579 for finding the Boundaries of the Castle of Dublin', and which states 'quod Fossat castri … Regine nunc de Dublin se extendit ex boriale pate usque ad novum murumjam aedificat per Inhabitantes Civitatis Dublin' [that the ditch of the Queen's castle now extends on the northern side to the new wall built by the residents of the city of Dublin]'; Robinson 1994, 193.

147 Derricke 1985, introductory notes before plate vi.

148 NAI, PROI D19722.

149 Falkiner 1904, 39; see Appendix 2.

150 NLI, MS 2487, f. 125. Although this manuscript is undated, it seems to be related to the Dublin Assembly Rolls document, Gilbert 1889–1922, iv, 277, of 10 December 1663, which states that 'the duke of Ormonde, takeing [sic] notice of the want of water for the supply of his majesties castle of Dublin, had severall times by his lettres sent unto the citty, that a speedy course might be taken therein, whereby the water might be brought to the said castle, as was usuall in former times'; Loeber 1980, 55.

151 DCLA Gilbert Coll. MSS 74–6, f. 25; see Appendix 4.

152 Dunton, 2003, 139; see Appendix 7.

153 The plan is provided with a scale, which is one inch to forty feet, 1:480.

154 Gilbert Coll. MS. 195; as interpreted by Hughes 1940, 96–7.

155 CSPI, 1633–47, 764–5, 770: '16 Dec. 1641, £100 to Capt. Thos Stutvil, towards making outworks for the defence of Dublin Castle.'; Robinson 1994, 296.

156 Robinson 1994, 306, although without reference to any source.

157 DCLA Gilbert Coll. MSS 74–6, ff. 23–33; see Appendix 4.

158 HMC 8th Report 1881, 526.

159 Hull 1899, i, 143.

160 24 April 1243, CDI 1171–1251, 389: 'Mandates to the justiciary and treasurer of Ireland, that they…cause to be constructed, in the castle of Dublin, a hall 120 feet in length and 80 feet in breadth, with glazed windows after the manner of the hall of Canterbury; and that they cause to be made in the gable beyond the dais a round window 30 feet in diameter. They shall also cause to be painted beyond the dais the King and Queen sitting with their baronage; and a great portal shall be made at the entrance of the hall. The whole shall be completed by the King's arrival.'; 43rd. DKR, App. II, 27–8: 'Dublin Castle, &c. – Account of Luke de Hynkeleye, custos of the works at the Castle, Exchequer, and the King's mills, Dublin, from 30 Nov. a.r. xiv., Ed II [1321/22] to 3 Mar. a.r. i., Ed. III [1327/28]…Allowed £68.6.9 paid to John de Corf' and John de Tychemerch', master masons, in part payment of £80 for breaking down and re-building the walls of the great hall of the Castle, as by their agreement with master Walter the then treasurer; £5 for clearing the said hall and making benches of stone as by like agreement; £9.6 for free stones to be broken in the quarry of Coueneche, and their carriage to Dublin, for said works; £6.13.9 for free stones to be broken in the quarry of Carrykbrenan, and their carriage to Dublin, for said works;…', 57 [1332–33], '£4 paid to divers glaziers as well for glass as for fitting it for windows in the hall of the said castle'; see also O'Keeffe 2015, 220–1, n.112–13, for a speculative reconstruction of the appearance of this Canterbury-like early Dublin Castle hall.

161 For a discussion of the early appearance of aisled halls in England see Montague 2006, 57–60; Blair 1993, 1–21.

162 Hayden 2011, 196–01; O'Keeffe 2015, 221–2; McNeill 1997, 20, 115–16.

163 DCLA Gilbert Coll. MSS 74–6, ff. 26–7; see Appendix 4; see also the thirteenth-century description of 'the pillars of marble' in the king's hall, CDI, 1285–92, 13.

164 DCLA Gilbert Coll. MSS 74–6, f. 27; see Appendix 4.

165 Hughes 1960, 140.

166 HMC De L'Isle, i, 399; recorded here as Jaques Wingfelde.

167 'Concordatum for the housekeeper of the Castle. By the Lord Deputy and Council. Henry Sydney', Nov. 15, 1570, Dublin Castle, in McNeill 1934, 364–5.

168 Robert Legge to Sir John Perrotte 21 Jan 1585, Carew MSS 1575–88, 401–02.

169 3 Feb 1599, CSPI 1598–99, 472.

170 J.T. Gilbert 1861 i, 133; Gilbert 1889–1922 ii, 501; McParland 1985b, 144–74.

171   CSPI 1603–06, 460.

172   Falkiner 1904, 21–2.

173   Usher 2012, 32.

174   The present building, now the Bank of Ireland, was built to the designs of Edward Lovett Pearce in 1729–39. See McParland 1989.

175   Falkiner 1904/1905, 520–1.

176   CSPI 1611–14, 342–3.

177   CSPI 1611–14, 344–5; a full account of the parliament, and the objection by the recusants to its location in the castle, in found in Barnaby Brian et al., 'A brief relation of the passages in the parliament summoned in Ireland anno 1613', Lodge 1772, i, 415–30.

178   Grosart 1886–8, iv, 147; Townshend 1904, 238.

179   Clark 1955, 27–39; Montague 2014b, 486; Montague 2012.

180   Howarth 1997, 205.

181   Howarth 1997, 212–13.

182   Hawkins 1844, 140; see Appendix 3.

183   CSPD 1671, 256; Robinson 1994, 350–2.

184   CSPD 1671, 256.

185   DCLA Gilbert Coll. MSS 74–6, f. 27; see Appendix 4.

186   Vestry Minutes, St Andrews Church, TCD, MS 2062, ff. 1–2; Loeber 1981, 51; Usher 2008, 119–32.

187   DCLA Gilbert Coll. MSS 74–6, f. 26; see Appendix 4.

188   'A large new bricke Chimney to bee made in ye Scalding house', which cost £5, NLI, MS 2487, f. 125. A scalding house was for processes related to the butchery of animals, the preparation of their carcasses etc. See e.g. Woolgar 1999, 144; Sabine 1933; Tighe 1988, 118.

189   Knowler 1739, i, 132.

190   1 June 1664, HMC Ormonde, i, 307.

191   HMC Ormonde ns, vii, 497.

192   NAI, Wyche MSS, 2/142, f. 1 & 4.

193   HMC De L'Isle, i, 399.

194   Gilbert 1889–1922, ii, 561; see Appendix 1; Hughes 1940, 85.

195   Manning 2017–18.

196   King 1906, 62.

197   Robinson 1994, 409 based on HMC, Ormonde ns vii, pp. 497–508.

198   Fenlon 2011a, 218.

199   Knowler 1739, i, 200–01.

200   Fenlon 2011b, 141–2, 145.

201   See for example, the 1679 inventory of Ormond's goods at Dublin Castle for 1679, to be found at HMC Ormonde ns, vii, 497–508, which lists separate suites of rooms for Ormond, his wife, the earl of Arran (the duke's son Richard), and for Lady Gowran (the widow of the duke's son, John).

202   Fenlon 2011b, 168.

203   HMC De L'Isle, i, 381.

204   NAI, Wyche MSS 2/142, 'Inventory of the King's Goods in the Castle of Dublin', May 1693, f. 2.

205   18 July 1636, CSPI 1633–47, 137.

206   10 Aug 1660, HMC Ormonde ns, iii, 384.

207   HMC 8th Report 1881, 544–5.

208   For a discussion of the viceregal court, and Ormond's advantages in his creation of one, see Barnard 2000a.

209   16 February, 1669, HMC Ormonde ns, iii, 441.

210   HMC Ormonde ns, vii, 497–508, 509–12; some of the details from this inventory are included under the relevant descriptions of separate spaces below: the chapel, the drawing room, the dining room, and a bed-room and 'his Grace's dressing-room', under the section 'Lodgings built by Essex'.

211   Harris 1766, 37.

212   HMC De L'Isle, i, 398–9.

213   Stanihurst 1577, 584; Colm Lennon, pers. comm.; Robinson 1994, 185.

214   Girouard 2009, 147.

215   'Payd for fraught and carriage of my lord's great marble stones, and Mr. Packenham's from Yreland to Towerswharf, £16 13s 4d.; and more for there [sic] cariadge thence, 5s.', HMC De L'Isle, i, 250; Moss 2014a, 22.

216   Girouard 2009, 9.

217   Grosart 1886–8. iv, 46, 52, 173.

218   HMC Ormonde ns, iii, 384, 397.

219   NLI, MS 2327, f. 111 'Remaining due to workemen, and for Materialls used in the Repaireing his Ma'ies Castle of Dublin &c the 18th of October 1662'; Loeber 1980, 54.

220   Earl of Arran to Ormond, 1684, April 4, HMC Ormonde ns, vii, 218–19.

221   King 1906, 62–3.

222   The following is also enhanced by Maguire (1974, 9–12), which is in turn a close reading of the 1673 Dartmouth plan with Ware's 1678 description.

223   King 1906, 62.

224   Arran to Ormond, HMC Ormonde ns, vii, 219.

225   King, 1906, 62–3.

226   DCLA Gilbert Coll. MSS 74–6, f. 26; see Appendix 4.

227   In 1225, Henry III approved that his chaplain William de Radeclive, was 'to minister in the chapel of the King's castle of Dublin, receiving yearly of the King's gift, during pleasure, 50s. for his maintenance'. A mandate to the king's justiciary also stated that he was to be provided with 'a benefice of the value of 100s'.; CDI, 1171–1251, 198, no. 1309, 24 July 1225; Hardy 1833–44, ii, 52.

228   Thornton 1875, 11–12; Lawlor 1928, 50–2.

229   17 Aug 1661, HMC Ormonde ns. iii, 385.

230   CSPD 1673–75, 198.

231   DCLA Gilbert Coll. MSS 74–6, f. 26; see Appendix 4.

232   HMC Ormonde ns, vii, 499.

233   18 & 28 May 1590, Carew MSS, 1589–1600, 30, 31.

234   Hawkins 1844, 140; see Appendix 3.

235   HMC Ormonde ns, vii, 499.

236   DCLA Gilbert Coll. MSS 74–6, f. 26: see Appendix 4.

237   Bradley 2007, figs 10.9 & 10.10.

238   I am grateful to Con Manning for this suggestion.

239   DCLA Gilbert Coll. MSS 74–6, f. 25; see Appendix 4.

240   Harris 1766, 38.

241   Howarth 1997, 209, based on PRO, E 403/2751, f. 60.

242   Knowler 1739, i, 201.

243   For this and what follows see, Shaw 2006.

244   Shaw 2006, 347, quoting from British Library Add. MS 72414 Add. II.(e), f. 106r-v.

245   Shaw 2006, 342–3, and figs 5 & 6.

246   Shaw 2006, 347, n. 51.

247   Barnard 2000a, 258, n. 25, referring to Bodl. Lib. Carte MS 53, f. 134; NLI, MS 2554.

248   Barnard 2000a, 258–60.

249   Maguire 1985, 14, fig. 1(b).

250   King 1906, 62–3.

251   Harris 1766, 38.

252   Falkiner 1904, 17, who also notes public clocks in Dublin 'over the Ostman's gate and at St. Patrick's Cathedral'. Regarding other Dublin clocks in Dublin at this time, see Moss 2014b, 159 and Moss 2014d, 538.

253   Harris 1766, 39.

254   18 July 1636, CSPI 1633–47, 137.

255 HMC Ormonde ns iii, 397.

256 King 1906, 63.

257 Colvin 1982, 196, 212, 239.

258 Colvin 1982, 335.

259 Colvin 1975, 331.

260 DCLA Gilbert Coll. MSS 74–6, f. 25; see Appendix 4.

261 Loeber 1980, 60 quoting British Library, Stowe 214, f. 343v; Stowe 216, f. 10, by February 1676, Robinson had 'yet received no monys for ye building at Dublin Castle'; Stowe 209, f. 46, by which Robinson on 5 February, 1675, also petitioned for his money, 48, petition from William Robinson to the Lords Justice and Council of Ireland, c. 1675, for £881.03.04, for 'severall buildings Erected, and Repaires made in his Ma'ties Castle of Dublin, Chappleizod and Phoenix', and another £148 on account.

262 British Library, Stowe MS 214, f. 209: 'I should be glad you would bespeak some plate for Mr Hugh May, such as you think most convenient, but I conceive same for his Table will be best, of about ye value of £300…'; Essex, earl of 1770, 1; Loeber 1980, 60.

263 Patrick Dun's contemporary description of the 1684 states that the dining room survived the fire; King 1906, 62.

264 HMC Ormonde, ns, vii, 498.

265 NAI, Wyche MSS, 2/142, ff. 4–5.

266 Knowler 1739, i, 201.

267 British Library Stowe MS 205 f. 49; MS 204 f. 169; 214, f. 164v; Loeber 1980, 58.

268 When describing the fire of 1684, Patrick Dun stated that 'the fire began in my Lord Deputys [Lord Arran's] dressing room, in the new buildings built by the E. of Essex'. That Arran had to then blow up the long gallery in order to prevent the fire from spreading to the range of buildings to the north, particularly the Powder Tower, implies that this building had to be on the south of the castle yard. Dun also suggests that these lodgings were to the east of that range, against the castle wall; King 1906, 62.

269 CSPD 1673–75, 42, 52; Loeber 1980, 58, quoting from de Beer 1955, iv, 199.

270 DCLA Gilbert Coll. MSS 74–6, f. 26; see Appendix 4.

271 British Library, Add. MS 4760, f. 108v: 'to cause to be erected in this his Ma'is. Castle such a building as we shall thinke most convenient for the accommodation of our family, & to cause this charge thereof to be borne, satisfied and paid out of the moneys alloted by the present Establishm't…provided the sum does not exceed the sum of five hundred pounds…to pay unto William Robinson Esq'r…in Erecting of such a building within this Castle as wee shall finde most convenient, and direct, for the better accommodation of our family…24ᵗʰ of Aprill 1674'.

272 25 August 1674, British Library, Stowe MS 214, f. 260, 'Mr Robinson, who now attends you is a very ingenious man & well skilled in some parts of ye Mathematicks, & indeed by as much as I can finde very just & honest, I doe not know a better servant ye King has for what he has undertaken than himself; what share of business you shall think fitt to employ him in I know not, but I am confident He will not in any thing faile yr. expectation'; see also Loeber 1980, 58.

273 Loeber 1980, 48.

274 Bray 1850, ii, 140.

275 Parker 1957.

276 http://www.metmuseum.org/art/collection/search/197338 (accessed 21 July, 2021).

277 L. Knyff & J. Kip, Cashiobury the Seat of the Rt Honble the Earle of Essex in Hartfordshire (London, 1720).

278 HMC Ormonde ns, vii, 498 and 499.

279 As noted above. HMC 8ᵗʰ Report 1881, 525; Loeber 1980, 54; Hughes 1940, 86.

280 1662, HMC 4ᵗʰ Report, App. (Ormonde) 1874, 563.

281 Robinson 1994, 334.

282 6 Aug 1666, CSPI 1666–69, 175.

283 HMC Ormonde, i, 260, 318.

284 DCLA Gilbert Coll. MSS 74–6, f. 25; see Appendix 4.

285 Therefore, these stairs were most likely completed by the many tradesmen whose bills are listed above, dating to 1663.

286 Fenlon 2011a, 210–12; Howarth 1997, 194.

287 HMSO 1975, 30–43.

288 Compare this for example to the long gallery at Henry VIII's Bridewell Palace, which was 200 ft (61m) by 30 ft (9m) in length. Although the Dublin gallery is only half as long, and only two thirds as wide, it was still of considerable size, and was at least in the order of scale, of such royal premises; see Colvin 1982, 19.

289 DCLA Gilbert Coll. MSS 74–6, f. 25r; see Appendix 4.

290 Knowler 1739, i, 102.

291 30 Sept 1624, CSPI 1615–25, 526.

292 CSPI 1647–1660, 315–6; Hughes 1940, 87. This order, which simply extends the same protocols to Ireland as were already established in England, echoes very closely, by using some of the exact same language, the orders made on this same subject by Wentworth some thirty years earlier, for which see Knowler 1739, i, 200–01.

293 Hawkins 1844, 140–1; see Appendix 3.

294 DCLA Gilbert Coll. MSS 74–6, f. 26; see Appendix 4; piazza in this instance does not refer to a large open space or square, but instead to a colonnade or arcade, here supporting the first floor, see Montague 2007.

295 8 Oct 1644, HMC Egmont, i, 240.

296 Fenlon 2001, 26.

297 Fenlon 2011b, 145–52; Fenlon 1996.

298 Coope 1986, 43–72, 74–84; Colvin 1982, 17–20; Berger 1973.

299 Turner 1851, 184.

300 Montague 2000, 36–7; see also Colvin 1963, i, 124; and Coope 1986, 44.

301 Colvin 1982, 17.

302 Colvin 1982, 19. Although Fitzwilliam was to be the viceroy in Ireland 1588–94, there is no direct connection between his construction and that of his successor at Dublin Castle.

303 Colvin 1982, 19.

304 Berger 1973, 459.

305 Knowler 1739, i, 200–01.

306 Knowler 1739, i, 132.

307 Harris 1766, 37.

308 Hawkins 1844, 140; see Appendix 3.

309 6 Feb 1619, CSPI 1615–25, 246.

310 13 Aug 1620, CSPI 1615–25, 294.

311 31 Dec 1620, CSPI 1615–25, 311.

312 Howarth 1997, 209, based on PRO, E 403/2751, f. 60.

313 Knowler 1739, i, 200.

314 Knowler 1739, i, 200–01. As already noted, Wentworth's injunction very closely echoes, and therefore anticipates, a very similar ruling from Charles II some thirty years later, and as quoted above.

315 Shaw 2006, 345–6, referring to British Library Add. MS 72414.

316 Shaw 2006, 347, n. 50, referring to British Library Add. MS 72414.

317 MacLysaght 1944, 284; Usher 2012, 30–1.

318 HMC 8ᵗʰ Report 1881, 526; Loeber 1980, 54.

319 Bodl., Carte MS 52, f. 261; Loeber 1980, 54.

320 DCLA Gilbert Coll. MSS 74–6, f. 31; see Appendix 4.

321 Jacques Wingfield's petitions to Burghley for his lodging in the castle, 25 Sep 1572–12 Jul 1573, O'Dowd 2000, 217, 326, 327, 372; Falkiner 1904, 36.

322 DCLA Gilbert Coll. MSS 74–6, f. 31; see Appendix 4.

323 12 May 1664, 'To Captain John Paine for repaire of the Constables Lodgings in the Castle', Bodl. Carte MS 52, f. 266; Loeber 1980, 55.

324 DCLA Gilbert Coll. MSS 74–6, f. 31; see Appendix 4; Maguire 1974, 11.

325 This date is based on the letter sent by Wentworth to archbishop Laud in December 1637, describing how he had told the king the last time he was in England that he planned to build this house, and that he had gone on since to complete it. See Knowler 1739, ii, 105; transcribed and discussed in Craig 1970, 109; see also Fenlon 2011a, 212.

326 DCLA Gilbert Coll. MSS 74–6, ff. 31–2; see Appendix 4.

327 December 1596, HMC Salisbury, vi, 555.

328 Greenwich 1597, May 23 and 18 July, CSPI 1596–97, 295–6.

329 Robinson 1994, 183.

330 'Instructions, to be sent to the lord deputy, and council in Ireland, by Geoffrey Fenton, esq; her majesty's secretary in that realm, Dec. 1585', in Lodge 1772, i, p. 49, 54.

331 1609, CSPI 1608–10, 234–5.

332 29 March 1609, CSPI 1608–10, 175.

333 May 1611, CSPI 1611–14, 63.

334 DCLA Gilbert Coll. MSS 74–6, f. 32; see Appendix 4.

335 NLI, MS 2436, f. 112/115.

336 ibid., f. 99–101, which includes Reading's original letter, and Robinson's response to it, in which he states 'that the place by him desired for Erecting a Mill being over ye shoar or waterway that Runns thro the Stable yarrd belonging to the Castle, has not hitherto been used by any person, nor is it of any use at present to the Castle Stables'.

337 For example, Reading was granted a royal patent in 1665 to build six lighthouses around the coast of Ireland. See Montague 2014a, 157.

338 DCLA Gilbert Coll. MSS 74–6, f. 32; see Appendix 4.

339 Knowler 1739, i, 131–2.

340 CSPI 1660–62, 139.

341 22 Oct 1634, CSPI, 1633–47, 81.

342 23 Oct 1633, Knowler 1739, i, 131.

343 Knowler 1739, i, 158; Wentworth's purchase of ground in the area between the old Liffey waterline and the castle, previously reclaimed by Jacob Newman, is referenced in the 1674 vestry minutes of St Andrew's, TCD, MS 2062, f. 4.

344 Hawkins 1844, 141; see Appendix 3.

345 Fenlon 2011a; Craig 1970, 107, in which a letter quotation from Edward Lovett Pearce refers to 'Dutch brick'.

346 Howarth 1997, 194.

347 Goodall 2004; Foyle 2002.

348 Worsley 2004, 44–5.

349 Howarth 1997, 207, quoting from Sheffield City libraries, Wentworth Woodhouse Muniments, 16 March 1635, 8/205–7.

350 Knowler 1739, i, 348; Fenlon 2011a, 209.

351 Howarth 1997, 209–10, suggests that, as an act of gross political folly, the building of Jigginstown by Wentworth 'was as disastrous for Strafford as Ceausescu's palace in Romania'.

352 Craig 1970, 107, quoting a letter of October 1726, sent from Edward Lovett Pearce to Lord Burlington, that was found 'among the muniments at Chatsworth'.

353 Illustrated in Worsley 2004, 91, after British Library, Add. MS 5238, f. 89.

354 12 Feb 1619, CSPI 1615–25, 246.

355 7 Oct 1673, CSPD 1673, 571–2; also in Loeber 1980, 57.

356 c. 1667, HMC 10th Report, App. pt.5, 1885, 54.

357 DCLA Gilbert Coll. MSS 74–6, f. 32; see Appendix 4; there are references to an exchange and mint in Dublin Castle in the medieval period, but this appeared to have been closed in 1549, and perhaps re-established in 1601, but its location is unknown; Clarke 2002, 23.

358 DCLA Gilbert Coll. MSS 74–6, f. 32; see Appendix 4.

359 HMC Ormonde, i, 358–63.

360 HMC Ormonde ns, iv, 253.

361 HMC Ormonde, ns, iv, 253.

362 Hughes 1940, 90.

363 9 Jun 1602, CSPI 1601–03, 411.

364 Falkiner 1904, 21.

365 22 Oct 1634, CSPI 1633–47, 81.

366 23 October 1633, Knowler 1739, i, 131–2.

367 Reeves-Smyth 2004.

368 Reeves-Smyth 2004, 104.

369 Reeves-Smyth 2004, 124.

370 Reeves-Smyth 2004, 125.

371 1734 survey plan, by Thomas Cave and Gabriel Stokes, reproduced in Haliday 1969, plan facing p. 239; Curran 1977, 3; Reeves-Smyth 2004, 125.

372 Hatfield House, MS plan, c. 1600, as discussed and reproduced in Nelson 1991, 185–6, 212; see also McParland 2001, 144.

373 Dunton 2003, 139; see Appendix 7.

374 Hughes 1940, 90.

375 NLI, MS 2436, f. 112/115.

Frontispiece 3 Detail from Malton's view of the Upper Yard 1794. (NLI)

Part 3: Dublin Castle 1684–1850
by Kevin V. Mulligan and
Michael O'Neill

Chapter 3.1
Introduction

The palace of the Viceroy, Monsieur the Duke of Ormont…who has a fine court, and a suite altogether royal… is at one of the ends of the town, and within its ancient walls, which at present do not contain one third of its extent. The Castle is strong, enclosed by thick walls, and by many round towers, that command the whole town, on them are mounted a good number of cannon. The court is small, but the lodgings although very ancient are very handsome and worthy of being the dwelling of the Viceroy. The principal gate is in a great street, called Casselstrit [Castle Street], that runs from one end to the other of the town…

Albert Jouvin, *c.* 1667.[1]

On 8 April 1684, the day after the devastating castle fire, the primate Michael Boyle in a letter to the duke of Ormond (Fig. 2.6) wrote of its being 'so terrible in its appearance, and wrought such an amazement and consternation upon the generality of the inhabitants in this City, that they rather prepared themselves for a sudden ruin and destruction'.[2] There was certain consensus that the conflagration had destroyed the best rooms, including the most recent, housed in the brick building erected by the earl of Essex, and with them many possessions introduced by the Ormonds, whose losses were valued at '10,000 at least'.[3] Some sense of the kinds of chattels destroyed may be imagined from the detailed inventory of 'all the Goodes belonging to his Grace' prepared in 1678/9 which lists Turkey-work carpets and chairs (24 of 'ffestune pattern') in the dining room, new gilt leather hangings in the duchess's dressing room and, in the drawing room, five pieces of Lambeth horse tapestry, sixteen crimson-velvet chairs and numerous silver furnishings.[4] Afterwards, the duke, perhaps a little

sourly, limited the sense of damage to the fact that 'the King has lost the most habitable part of the worst house any Governor of a Kingdom & Province in Europe lives in'; this was a sentiment already plainly expressed by his son, the earl of Arran, when reporting his efforts to save 'the worst Castle in the worst situation in Christendom'[5] (Fig. 2.12). Despite the destruction, the fire seemed timely. Notwithstanding the sense of the castle's courtliness and its apparent worthiness as a viceregal residence, as described in the late 1660s by Jouvin – which admittedly must have been partly attributable to Ormond's possessions and their presentation – the deficiencies of the buildings had become a recurring theme in the correspondence of successive Lords Lieutenant and while Essex and Ormond had initiated considerable works, these achieved little more other than to perpetuate the sense of a varied assemblage of ad hoc buildings within the medieval walls.[6]

Just two years before the fire, serious consideration had already been given to rebuilding the castle entirely, in part necessitated by the destruction of the great hall in 1671 whose loss – having formerly served as the four courts and seat of parliament – had greatly reduced the functioning apparatus of state within the castle walls;[7] and further damage was caused when several parts of the castle collapsed during a storm in 1677.[8] Overseeing repairs and improvements at the castle was the Yorkshire-born William Robinson (Fig. 2.8), Engineer and Surveyor General since 1672, appointed to the position during Lord Berkeley's term as Lord Lieutenant.[9] In 1679 Robinson was associated with the erection of a Presence Chamber at the castle, located beside the lodgings he had overseen in 1674 for Lord Essex who had adjudged him a 'very ingenious Man, & well skilled in some parts of ye Mathematicks, & indeed…very just, & honest…'.[10] The same high opinion was expressed by the earl of Orrery who thought Robinson 'a very ingenious and diligent

Fig. 3.1 Internal courtyard of Royal Hospital Kilmainham. (NMS)

person' and in respect of his achievements at the Royal Hospital in Kilmainham, 'Men of Value and Experience in Building' acknowledged that Robinson 'shewed the parts of an excellent Artist in the Contrivance' having introduced with this building a wholly new standard of classicism (Fig. 3.1). With this building he would establish the accent of new public architecture in the city that would endure well into the eighteenth century.[11] As Surveyor General, and in view of his success at Kilmainham, it was inevitable that Robinson should attempt the transformation of the castle from a tattered citadel to a more fitting and unified complex with an underlying classical formality. His ability to do so, however, was frustrated by local indecision, amounting at times to apathy and an overall lack of official response to the idea, which invariably was reduced to the question of resources.

Ireland's dependency on England, and the difficulties in obtaining resources for Crown buildings in Ireland was apparent during the 1670s when the Irish customs were directed by Charles II towards his own building ambitions, including for Windsor, funds which otherwise might have been utilised for Dublin projects.[12] The evolving political uncertainties in the closing decades of the seventeeth century make it easy to understand why there was little success amongst those pressing for a new castle; in any case

with the Four Courts, Council Chamber and Parliament House re-established outside the castle precincts, the sense of urgency about rebuilding was somewhat undermined.[13] Thus was any serious building initiative thwarted, except with the building of the Royal Hospital (Fig. 3.2), which was commenced by the duke of Ormond in 1680.

In normal circumstances, the achievement of the Royal Hospital, its architecture partly inspired by L'Hotel des Invalides in Paris, and which was ready for occupation in 1684, should have strongly influenced any considerations being given before the fire to rebuilding the castle on a new site. As the 'city's first large scale exercise in the classical style' and contrasting with the still largely medieval city, it must to some extent have served to show up the inadequacies, indeed the embarrassments, of the castle while its scale and prominence on an unrestricted site over the Liffey can only have positively encouraged those who desired a more fitting complex, more suitably located, to accommodate what still amounted to the most important building of government.[14]

With Robinson at the helm after the fire, having recently demonstrated the great potential of new public architecture at Kilmainham, the unique opportunity to rebuild the castle in something of the same spirit might reasonably have been seized more enthusiastically, and for a time there was evidently considerable support as many interested parties made proposals for it. Ultimately, however, the matter seems to have been already worn out in earlier discussion and the impetus appears to have been lost in the hesitation so that little progress was made, except for repairs and partial rebuilding. Meanwhile greater attention continued to be given to completing the Royal Hospital, where Ormond naturally showed a close interest and concern, even to the extent of his willingness to reside there temporarily, in the master's lodgings, while the castle was being repaired.[15] Indeed the fire at the castle possibly even allowed greater emphasis to be given to the hospital decoration.[16] At the end of a long lord lieutenancy, perhaps the completion of the hospital represented a more satisfying and lasting achievement for Ormond. In 1684 it was still without its chapel and tower and some of these works could certainly be more easily progressed, funded as they were by a tax on soldiers' pay, whereas any works at the castle normally depended on funds from the civil list – though there were proposals that a new palace might be funded differently, or

even in the same manner as the hospital.[17] Besides, Ormond was amply catered for when in Ireland, his own impressive country seats were available for 'sport, entertaining and official duties', leaving the need for a Dublin palace a much lower priority, and of course these could also be made available to others while the castle was being rebuilt, as when Lord Rochester was offered Kilkenny Castle as an alternative residence while in Ireland.[18]

It was likely then that only complete destruction – a catastrophic event such as experienced in the fire of London – could ever have stimulated the urgency, if not interest and effort, to rebuild the castle with greater enthusiasm.[19] The result was that even when two-thirds of the castle had been built by the 1720s, and although there were certain consonances between the two buildings, the Royal Hospital remained the grandest building in the city, and a unique example of Carolean classicism, while the rebuilding of Dublin Castle 'was fitful, undistinguished and protracted', its completion drawn out over many decades.[20]

OLD SOLDIERS HOSPITAL, KILMAINHAM, DUBLIN.

London Pub.d by Js.t Malton & O.Gowen Dublin Feb.y 1794.

Fig. 3.2 View of the Royal Hospital Kilmainham, 1794 by James Malton. (NLI, PD 3181 TX97)

Chapter 3.2
Rebuilding the Castle 1684–1700

Necessary improvements to the country's fortifications and the idea of building a proper citadel for the capital had been ongoing issues that are likely to have impacted on considerations about dealing with the damaged castle. In the months after the fire, though not necessarily directly related to it, the engineer Thomas Phillips and Mr. Francis Povey, former store keeper of the garrison at Tangier, together with William Robinson, were commissioned to make 'an exact survey' of 'all the ordnance, ammunition, arms and other habiliments of war' throughout the country (Fig. 2.2). Phillips was given 'particular instructions' to take an 'exact view of the several forts, castles, and garrisons' with a view to establishing their existing condition and needs, as well as the cost of necessary repairs and/or the cost of 'fortifying each place in such manner as he should conceive most advantageous for putting them in a good posture of defence for his Majesty's service'. The findings were presented to the king by Lord Dartmouth, Master General of the Ordnance, almost two years after the fire (and discussed in further detail below).[21] Whatever inadequacies existed on the castle site before the fire – and there were many including its restricted location and design, various structural challenges and a need to maintain some defensive characteristics – the situation was greatly exacerbated by it, and clearly needed to be adequately addressed. The only known scheme for the castle that can be placed in this period, by Robinson or his office and perhaps even resulting from this process, include an ambitious (even if only sketched in outline), somewhat novel scheme for rebuilding at the same location.[22] It shows a great square citadel, overlaid on the existing castle and extending to the east and south so that it encompasses more than twice the area while adopting a formalised, moated arrangement which is likely to have been determined by the existing rectilinear castle form and the site constraints.[23] Supporting documentary evidence that might help to elucidate the context of this particular idea – whether it predates the fire or was conceived afterwards – is not known to exist, although the same idea, on a larger scale (584ft x 509ft (178m x 155m)), is (faintly) present on one of Thomas Phillips' surveys of the castle (Fig. 2.2). It is possible, therefore, that such a proposal was conceived as part of the ongoing (since 1674) discussions about building an improved 'citadel' for the capital as part of broader efforts to improve the 'habiliments of war'; or it may even have prompted the exploration in 1682 of the possibility, if not the expediency, of establishing a new 'palace' elsewhere, or indeed it might actually have come about as a response to the rejection of the idea of moving the seat of government from the castle site.[24]

Some of the indecision about rebuilding immediately after the fire seems likely to have been partly based on the 1682 discussions about whether the castle should be sold and an entirely new site chosen where, if funds permitted, a 'magnificent palace and court house' could be built.[25] A keen advocate for rebuilding was Sir Francis Brewster, a merchant and city politician and former lord mayor, who in May 1682 introduced the possibility that the farmers of revenue might be induced to advance £10,000 'for the Palace'.[26] Brewster had become sufficiently involved to present proposals in July that were submitted to Primate Boyle, as one of the Lords Justices, although Ormond's son and deputy at the castle, the earl of Arran was sufficiently unimpressed, enough to report to his father 'so far as I understand it I do not like it' adding to this his concerns about the suitability of the other 'projectors' involved.[27] Brewster appears to have carried two proposals to the primate in this period, 'one for 9,000l. and his own' and on 11 July he wrote directly to Ormond, explaining that 'the former put the Primate in a passion' while his own was considered 'not enough to do the work'. As the primate also objected to the idea of taking the necessary monies from the civil list, Brewster suggested diverting some £28,000 in funds associated with the Royal Hospital, which he deemed enough 'to build a magnificent palace and court house, all materials and building being very low'.[28]

Whatever Ormond thought of this proposal is unknown, though he seems to have given serious attention to both possibilities – either rebuilding the castle on its existing site or else selling it and starting afresh elsewhere – and he appears to have even gone so far as to instruct Brewster to assess in some way where 'the Castle falls short of the sum designed for the palace'.[29] Brewster's correspondence does suggest that no single firm idea was at all well advanced or favoured, but, however, hints that serious consideration was being given to improving the existing site. There was also the suggestion that, if progressed, the plans could be ambitious (as indeed the enlarged moated design suggests). This was evident when, in writing to Ormond, he advised that 'if your Grace continues your thoughts relating to the Castle it imports the contractors before it be known, to secure St George's Lane, Sheep Street, Castle Street and Damaske [Dame] Street so many houses as may make four fair streets into the Castle, which may be too late easily to procure it once the design be known'.[30] By early December, however, Ormond had declared a more decided position in favour of a completely new start elsewhere:

> I am still of the opinion that by the sale of ground, housing and materials belonging to Dublin Castle, a chief Governor may be better seated than he is, and the King put to no considerable charge in the exchange, if to any, the rather that much less money than 30,000l. will make a better residence than the Castle. There has been so much building about Dublin, and Mr. Robinson is so well acquainted with the rates of work and materials and the value of ground, that methinks a probable estimate and calculation may be made, at the worst it will be but a little time lost to discourse it and try what the Castle will yield.[31]

However, there seems to have been considerable resistance to the idea in Dublin, shared by the primate and Lord Arran who, despite stating his knowledge that 'it can come to nothing', still undertook to seek 'bidders for the Castle and ground in order to build better for the Government'.[32] When, in January, Ormond queried the basis of his son's unequivocal assertion, wishing to know 'whether the project about the sale of the Castle will come to nothing because money will not be given for it, or not enough, or for what other reason', the response was clear – Brewster who had been the chief proposer 'about the pulling down this castle, and building another place for the Chief Governor' was

now no longer willing 'to meddle in it'.[33] While the reasons are not given, it is possible that the idea was becoming controversial amongst the city merchants, who had much to lose by relocation. That some building work – unspecified – was carried out in this period, though probably no more than repairs, is indicated by the Surveyor General's claim in March 1682 for £600 in respect of works carried on at the castle.[34]

As a consequence of the fire, Lord Arran, rather understandably, now appeared to look more favourably upon the proposals for selling the site that had been put forward two years earlier, suggesting to Ormond that 'for the value of the ground it stood upon, and the land belonging to it, his Majesty may have a noble palace built' and even gave some sense of a wider enthusiasm for it by adding, 'I believe there are a hundred projectors at work already about framing proposals'.[35] Among those who joined the 'great talke' of rebuilding and 'where ye same shall be' was Sir William Petty, the only person known to have given serious consideration to the idea in the immediate aftermath of the fire, suggesting as part of his approach that the 'chief Governors dwelling be never more within those walls…'.[36] The larger economic implications were perhaps simply too great, however, and Arran quickly reverted to his earlier position, expressing the view that 'removing it far from the place it stood in will undo the City' and further justified his position with a personal expression of gratitude to its inhabitants because 'they have been so kind to me, that I am obliged to stand their friend'.[37]

The experience of the fire had clearly shaken Lord Arran despite his evident heroism, and having made temporary arrangements for himself at Lord Longford's house at Whitefriars on Aungier Street, and for Ormond at the viceregal lodge at Chapelizod, he was understandably reluctant to return immediately to the castle while the powder remained there.[38] Arran somewhat optimistically believed that the castle could be 'fitted up for doing public business as well as it ever was' without significant expense, and indicated that once the powder was removed, offices for 'servants and their lodging' – presumably the buildings on the north side, including the constable's lodgings (Fig. 2.1) – could be speedily repaired for little expense, allowing him to return 'within a fortnight, to keep his table there'.[39] To this end, Robinson, as Surveyor General, was instructed to prepare plans for moving the powder to 'within the square of the Hospital' and to clear the rubbish and carry out all the necessary works to facilitate the lord deputy's return.[40] This proved a necessary expedient as discussion around rebuilding the castle continued to be affected by the competing financial demands required to increase the army, even though Ormond admitted that the fire now created a perfect opportunity to revisit the plans for rebuilding, and that revenue surplus could adequately support the cost.[41]

Confirming that proposals for rebuilding were unlikely to be dealt with expeditiously, however, at least not until it had 'been well considered and referred over', Ormond expressed a concern that if Arran resumed residence in the castle soon it might 'retard the provision of a more cheerful house than could possibly be formed within the Castle, unless the whole wall from the powder-magazine to Birmingham's Tower be taken down at least below the second story, that there may be some prospect and a freer passage of air'. He also made it clear that the Treasury was not 'startled' at the likely costs of restoration although, as he indicated, the Treasury and the king realised it would defer the raising of a new regiment; consequently, Ormond ceased to push for it for the time being, adding his own resistance to the idea that vital funds should be needlessly used in the short term 'to patch up a pitiful new building'.[42]

Lord Arran was satisfied that for now what had survived the fire was sufficient 'to keep up the necessary formality of state' (though it would still be inadequate for Ormond's visit that summer) and that rebuilding could wait.[43] He had also become firmly of the mind that, when the time came, 'if part of the castle wall was pulled down, and the graft filled up, it would be as wholesome living there as any part of this city'.[44]

The reference to the graft, meaning the castle ditch, and the concern for a freer passage of air suggests that the castle environs were at this time rather unsavoury, even squalid, and that the west and south sides associated with the castle ditch added greatly to the deficiencies of the site and even likely motivated earlier desires to move to a new location.[45] Although 'the ground in the circuit of the ditch' had clearly been shown to have been part and parcel of the castle in 1579, it seems to have begun to suffer encroachment – Thomas Phillips certainly confirmed this after the fire when he described the castle as being 'pestered up with houses and other offices both within and without' – which will have greatly detracted from its salubrity.[46] Indeed, its entire function as a citadel was denuded by such developments, 'shut in on all sides' but especially to the east so that it no longer could claim unbroken views to the sea.[47] Having been closed off, probably in the fourteenth century, the moat had long ceased to have any defensive function and from its original size – 22m wide and up to 10m deep – it eventually became filled up, and along the west side deliberately inundated with rubbish and spoil so as to reclaim the area for building in the eighteenth century, the evidence for this especially clear by the excavation of the house sites associated with Cole Alley.[48] Pollution, however, was likely to have presented the most pressing problem for the castle inhabitants through the late seventeenth century. It had been evident, for example, in 1624 when clearing the 'great aboundance' of rubbish and mud from the moat was a factor in building works, and it is likely that the situation

was becoming more exacerbated at this time by the steady expansion of the city to the west where the most intense industrialised activities were concentrated along the course of the Poddle, which of course still flowed openly directly below the state apartments.[49]

By the end of April 1684, Robinson had produced his plans for moving up to 1,500 barrels of powder (an interesting figure when compared to the six barrels lost in the castle fire) to Kilmainham, and in a manner that would not 'take off of the beauty of the Hospital'.[50] In early May work had commenced to fit up temporary accommodation in the castle, Arran confirming again that he did 'not intend that that place should be a seat of government unless the walls may be pulled down to the height of thirty foot' and was willing to wait, retaining his opinion 'that a new regiment is better than a new house'.[51] However, Ormond believed that first, before works commenced, careful consideration was needed, referring to 'a model and a computation of the charge' that would be necessary to assess 'how much of the Castle wall should be pulled down, and of the towers, and how much of the graft filled where a new house is built so as to make the remaining offices and buildings useful to it'.[52] Arran's response indicated that schemes for rebuilding the castle would take some time but that Robinson would 'have time enough this next long vacation'.[53] It is possible that Ormond's resolve to visit Dublin in the summer was in some way related to formalising these proposals.[54] At the end of June and in advance of his arrival, Ormond had clearly given some direction to Arran 'about the model for a new seat for the Chief Governor'. Instructions were obviously communicated to Robinson, who began working up the scheme which Arran had hoped would be ready to send some days later, but which was still not finished by 16 July despite Robinson having 'been at work day and night upon it'.[55]

The only drawings that may be associated with this period – a series of closely related proposals unfortunately neither signed nor dated but usually attributed to Robinson (Figs 3.3–8) – are most likely to have emanated from the Surveyor General's office. While there is no evidence that they can be directly connected with Robinson's industrious efforts of July 1684 – on the contrary it has been argued that the scheme is perhaps much too ordinary and unambitious to have resulted from such a time-consuming process – it is certain that they provided the key starting point for the redevelopment, and indeed remained a guiding influence over successive phases in the following century.[56] Among these drawings is a ground plan (Fig. 3.3) showing the existing castle walls on which a group of strictly rectilinear ranges have been transposed on three sides with the 'chief apartments' in the south-east corner forming the eastern wing of a symmetrical south range, the symmetry enforced by a central entrance block, labelled with 'great hall' and

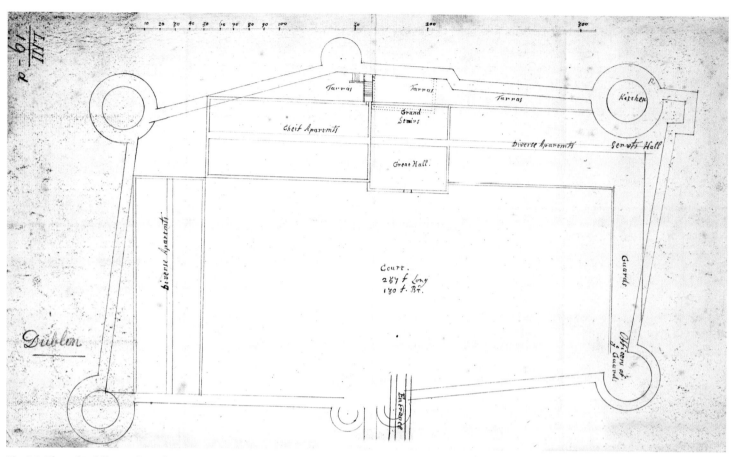

Fig. 3.3 Plan of Dublin Castle with proposed new ranges c. 1684, office of William Robinson (south at top). (BL, Map K Top 53/19d)

'grand staires' and probably related to the design for one of the elevations included in these plans (Fig. 3.8). The west range, planned to incorporate the 'kitchen' (Bermingham) tower, is labelled 'diverse apartments' and 'servts' Hall'. The intervening space between the south range and the existing castle walls is labelled as 'terras', with a flight of stairs descending from the south-west corner of the 'chief apartments' – a dotted outline, projected from the castle wall behind the proposed entrance block, appears to correspond to the walls of the old dining room as shown on the 1673 plan (Fig. 2.1). Along the west side a narrow 'Guards' range extends north to the Cork Tower (labelled 'officers of ye guard') while the east range is comparable in scale to the south ranges, and is merely labelled 'diverse apartments'.

The arrangement in the south-east corner, which created a sizeable open area adjoining the Record Tower (on its west side), was clearly the result of the challenge posed by the desire to set a formal rectilinear design within the obtuse angle presented by the existing castle walls. This seems to imply a clear intention to retain the Record Tower even if the outcome was an awkward and unsatisfactory space and, more generally, confirms a desire to keep development strictly within the confines of the original walls (even if these might be reduced in height as both Arran and Ormond

had intimated).[57] The plan, however, is not in any sense a fully developed design; the ranges are clearly only intended as indicative while the idea of creating a new entrance into the court is simply represented as an unresolved passageway drawn over one of the existing gatehouse towers. The thought given to imposing this uncompromisingly rectilinear design within the existing boundaries highlights the challenges of finding agreement on site between the obvious desire for a uniform and appropriately formal building and the realities of its irregularly defined perimeter and the significant changes in levels across the site. These constraints are likely to have been exacerbated by certain structural difficulties (many of which would become more apparent later, especially along the east side of the court) and the desire to retain some aspect of the castle's defensive character, even if the castle ditch no longer functioned in the way it had been originally intended. A more perfect understanding of this early phase of redevelopment is somewhat frustrated by possible disagreements between the archaeological and documentary evidence. This centres on the difference between the angle of the east curtain wall first shown in the 1673 plan (Fig. 2.1) and repeated in subsequent surveys (Figs 2.2, 2.3), and what may be contradictory evidence from the 1960s' excavations of the site.[58] However, the disparity may be explained by the possible rebuilding of the curtain wall soon after the fire, due perhaps to structural necessity. In doing so, a more regular alignment was chosen to facilitate the more formal layout being envisaged within the walls, as hinted at in one of the 1680s proposals for rebuilding (Fig. 3.3), and the approval that was granted for partial demolition of the castle in July 1684.[59] Ultimately, the approach adopted in these plans limited the scale and architectural potential of redeveloping the existing site, and some recognition of this perhaps contributed to the decision, eventually, to commence work only on the south-east portion affected by the fire.

When approval for the demolition of the ruinous and decayed walls of the castle was sanctioned by the king in July 1684, the warrant reiterated the negative contribution its high walls had on the air quality.[60] The recently widowed duke of Ormond had arrived in Ireland the following month and therefore would have been in a position to witness, if not directly oversee, the beginning of the works.[61] In early September, Ormond wrote to Lord Coventry that 'the present unpleasant shift for a lodging in the Castle here will be insufferable, when the new houses shall be building' and a week later it was reported that the 'walls of the Castle are pulling down in order to repair and make the Castle more beautiful and larger'.[62]

Just as the works commenced, William Robinson had surrendered his patent in favour of a new one in which he resumed the position jointly with William Molyneux (Fig. 3.9), a figure who was highly recommended to Ormond, both as one who enjoyed a 'reputation for parts and learning', and as qualified 'an engineer as any in this kingdom, or perhaps in any other'.[63] The reasons are not clear, but there is evidence that at this time the office of the Surveyor General was involved in much broader activities besides the castle project and its other building responsibilities.[64] Ultimately, however, Ormond did not remain long enough to witness any real progress in the building, having been recalled by the king before the end of the year, ostensibly to spare him the embarrassment of putting into effect controversial reforms in favour of Roman Catholics.[65] The death of Charles II in 1685 cannot have helped the pace of progress, bringing a sense of uncertainty amongst those who did not support his Catholic successor, his brother, James II. To appease the Protestant interest, the new king gave temporary control of the country to the Lords Justices, Primate Boyle and the earl of Granard until the carefully chosen Lord Clarendon, the king's Protestant brother-in-law, assumed the post of Lord Lieutenant in January 1686.[66] The fire-damaged ruins had been swept away in the initial campaign of works with possibly some ongoing repairs and rebuilding of the walls, and by March it was reported that the new Lord Lieutenant 'hopes that it is more than p[ro]bable that he will soon procure money proportionable to his designs of rebuilding, reforming and enlarging the Castle'.[67]

At the same time Thomas Phillips had completed his report, which was presented to the king and the privy council at Whitehall on 24 March, almost two years after the fire in the castle.[68] It seemed that even after all this time, no decisive action would be taken in dealing with the castle. Believing there was 'no want of ill-minded people', Phillips considered the city vulnerable, where any successful attack and loss of control would expose 'the whole kingdom' to danger. The severity of the situation was obviously compounded by the condition and inconvenience of the castle, 'being all in rubbish by the late fire' and the belief that even 'when in perfection' it was 'not capable of securing his Majesty's stores of war, without great hazard of their being destroyed by fire, it being so pestered up with houses, and other offices, both within and without'. Phillips further regarded that even 'if it were capable of being made strong, it would not be convenient to have the residence of the Chief Governor near the general stores, by reason that all people covet to have their offices, as near to the Court as possible, so that in time the place becomes so blocked up, that the stores become more exposed to danger, than in an open place'.

Although the transfer of the powder and 'train of artillery' to the hospital had already taken place, this arrangement did not provide a long-term solution, the location being 'of an indifferent strength' incapable of being made so 'for the several hills that command it' and being 'too far from the seaside, so that it can in no way be supplied, or relieved'. Nor was the castle or hospital considered suitable to secure 'the records of the kingdom'. The only solution, according to Phillips, was for a citadel, a great star fort, 'as hath already been proposed' at Ringsend by Bernard de Gomme in 1674 (Figs 2.2, 2.3, 2.12); however, in this instance a more preferred location 'between the city and the seaside' was suggested, close to St Stephen's Green. While it may be that some serious consideration was being given at this time to providing a separate citadel, perhaps limiting the castle site to administration, it was unlikely ever to represent a realistic proposal, the scale of the proposed star fort overwhelming in scale (as de Gomme's had been, and disproportionate to any real threat), and its cost equally so, estimated at over £126,000.[69]

In reality, the restriction on funds remained the principal obstacle so that even after all that had been considered about rebuilding in Ormond's time (including extending the lodge at Chapelizod), there was still no definitive decision about how best to proceed, other than adopting an ad hoc approach. The initial focus concentrated instead only on essential repairs and then on some limited new work, but even then these were slow to effect any real improvement in the living conditions at the castle. Work had commenced in April, now exactly two years after the fire, when Clarendon could claim that 'reparations of this no-castle are very great' while at the same time repeating the old denigration of it as the 'worst and most inconvenient lodging in the world'.[70] A few months later, in August, the issue of obtaining adequate funds from the Exchequer was problematic, and such that Clarendon knew 'not how to move the laying out any money' despite what he considered (and, it seems, rather unselfishly) the pressing need of a suitable 'habitation' for the chief governor:

> I do not think it necessary he should have a royal palace fit to hold the King, Queen, and the whole court; but a good house he ought to have, and the country deserves it. Such a one, fit for him to be decently accommodated in, I am sure might be built for 5,000l. or 6,000l.; and it should be a better house than any is now in London.

Clarendon offered to send over a 'model, and an estimate' and, anticipating at best an unenthusiastic response, suggested a cautious approach whereby 'if that were once done, more might be added to it hereafter, whenever the King pleased', and stressed again his own inconvenience, and frustrations:

> ...as it is now, I have no necessary convenient room. In a word no gentleman in the Pall-Mall is so ill lodged in all respects. I hope I am not immodest in what I propose, especially considering that I have put the King to no expense since my being here...I might add, that in keeping up, that is, the keeping dry this pitiful bit of a Castle, costs an incredible deal...'.[71]

Progress was eventually as much limited by Clarendon himself who, always aware of his own tenuous position and the attempts of Lord Tyrconnell to undermine him, and presumably keen to demonstrate his own fiduciary responsibilities, became increasingly reluctant to engage in anything other than essential repairs to the castle and modest building work at the viceregal lodge: 'how short soever my stay be here I will value myself (though Lord Tyrconnel laughs at me for it) for having never proposed anything of expense to the king, which may look like a conveniency to myself'.[72] How Clarendon's 'model' of the proposed building (possibly the drawings attributed to Robinson, Figs 3.3–8) was received in London is unknown, but there were obviously still no substantive improvements made in the conditions at the castle that year. But, by the end of November, Clarendon could do little else but renew his criticism of it as the 'worst lodging a gentleman can lay in' with a need for 'perpetual tiling and glazing'.[73]

Lord Clarendon was recalled in January 1687, obliged to surrender control to Tyrconnell who was made lord deputy in his place. It is difficult to gauge whether, or how far, any work on the new buildings had been advanced by this time. To visitors to the city then, the castle, though 'not larg, nor beautifull', could still appear impressive, especially from the south, appearing 'on high, strongly fe[nced] with dithces, towers' and it was obvious that having been burnt, it had recently been rebuilt.[74] Like many of the city's Protestants, Robinson took flight, travelling to England with Tyrconnell's arrival, leaving any ongoing works at the castle in the hands of his colleague. Eventually Molyneux too was forced to leave Ireland due to 'the severities of Tyrconnell's government'.[75] However, it appears that by the time he left, before the end of 1688, work on the new state apartments had been completed, with Molyneux ultimately claiming personal credit for 'that part of the Castle of Dublin which stands upon the Piazza, with the turrets to the South'.[76] The completion of works at this time is further evinced by the claim that Tyrconnell had removed himself to the new buildings from Chapelizod 'for that house was so disturbed with spirits they could not rest'.[77]

Even if he was forced to move by restless spirits, it is unclear whether Tyrconnell himself in any way directly helped to expedite the building work, though with James having been deposed and bound for Ireland in 1689 there was certainly greater incentive, if not an urgent requirement, for the building to be completed if the king was to be fittingly received in his castle.[78] With news of the king's arrival in Kinsale on 12 March, 'great preparations were made for his reception, of plate and furniture for the Castle'.[79] On his arrival in Dublin on horseback twelve days later, James was triumphantly welcomed 'as if he had been an angel from heaven', and is said to have wept as he entered the castle. He remained in the capital long enough to summon and address a new parliament in May and must have dwelled there for certain periods until his final departure in 1690.[80] Any peaceful occupation, however, will have been greatly disrupted in August, when 'whether by treachery or chance we know not' the 'little store house' in the castle garden exploded, an event likely to have caused that same night the collapse of 'the mid Rampire of the Black Tower of the Castle, with the fane, on which was displayed the Crown and Regal Arms'.[81] At the beginning of the following year, before William of Orange made his fateful landing in June at Belfast Lough with a fleet of some 300 ships, it had been reported that Tyrconnell was 'as much as the thing will bear it, fortifying the Castle'.[82] It was hardly necessary. With the decisive battle of the war fought at the Boyne in July, and the flight of James to France a month later, Dublin and its castle were easily delivered into Williamite hands.[83]

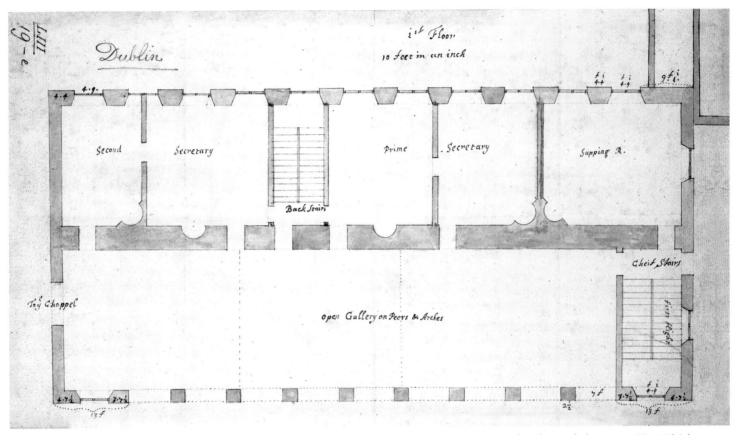

Fig. 3.4 First-floor [ground] plan of south-east range of state apartments *c.* 1684, office of William Robinson (south at top). (BL, Map K Top 53/19e)

One of the members of the new regime who occupied the castle in the immediate aftermath was William's Secretary at War, Dr George Clarke. In a personal account of the recent events, he offers a fleeting glimpse of the newly completed apartments in 1691, when after assuming the post of Chief Secretary ('which I said belonged to me') he was given lodgings there, describing them as being among 'the cloisters… under the rooms of State, looking out upon the terrace walk' and where he had 'fitted up a room for the Lords Justices to meet in and despatch their business'.[84] It is a description that agrees with the contemporary plan (Fig. 3.4), which shows the offices of the 'Prime' and 'Second' secretaries disposed either side of the back stairs. The room 'fitted up' for the Lords Justices may well have related to the 'supping room' shown in the south-west corner of the plan, beside the 'Prime Secretary's' offices behind the 'chief' stairs closed in at the west end of the arcade.

Based on the surviving drawings (Figs 3.4–6), the block was given windows in its end walls and hipped ends to the roof, indicating that it was, if only for the time being, intended as a free-standing block, and perhaps until the rest of the buildings could be commenced; this of course follows Clarendon's suggestion that if the building were 'once done, more might be added to it hereafter, whenever the King pleased'.[85] The fast changing political situation is likely to have favoured this approach, and with a degree of continuing uncertainty, and indeed more immediate priorities for the new government, the detached character of the state apartment implies that there was no expectation that the rebuilding of the entrance block or the remainder of the south side would proceed in the short term.[86]

A further impression of the castle in this period is given by John Dunton, visiting in 1697, who found it 'encompassed with a wall and drye ditch' still with its drawbridge and 'within that an iron gate', while its defensive bearing was made more fully complete with the two cannons supported on one of the towers. He refers to the new apartments – that 'part of the house' which rises 'over a large stone gallery supported by severall pillars of stone'; his overall impression of this building was that it was 'handsome' but 'without much magnificence on the outside'.[87] Entering 'up a noble stairs' he found 'several stately rooms one of which is called the Presence chamber and has a chaire of state with a canopy over it'. To the rear of the state apartments was 'a broad terras walk the length of the building the walls covered with greens and flower pots' and Dunton also described how

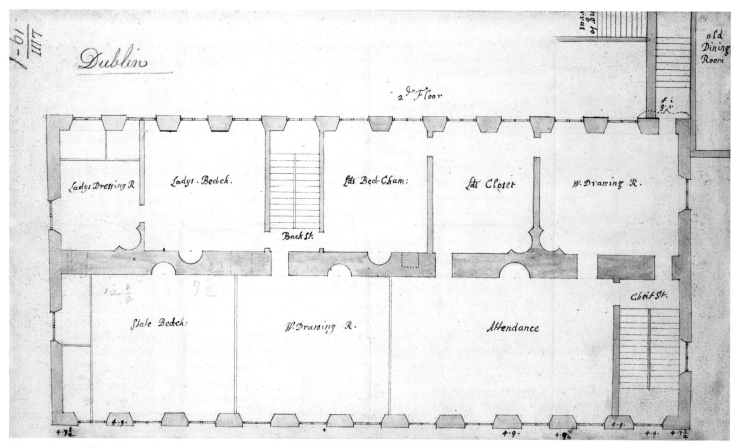

Fig. 3.5 Second- [first-] floor plan of south-east range of state apartments *c.* 1684, office of William Robinson (south at top). (BL, Map K Top 53/19f)

'from hence on a stone arch over a little river you descend by two spacious pair of stone stairs into the garden'.[88] He also noted the chapel, though mistakenly he says it lay on the north side while going on to refer to some of the other features in the Lower Yard, including the ordnance office, the coach houses and the Poddle that separated them.

The location of the chapel on the east side is confirmed in plans (Fig. 3.10) to extend the state apartments in 1698. These were devised ostensibly to provide improved 'accommodation for the Governour's households', as well as improving access to the chapel. The plans had been forwarded to the Treasury in March by the two acting Lords Justices, Winchester and Gallway, who appear to have shared the apartments of the chief governor.[89] As the arrangement was proving inadequate for 'two families', the lords had these additions devised, perhaps by Robinson, which they claimed 'will add much to the ornament & convenience thereof', and sent with them their hope that they would 'receive the necessary direction and authority' to proceed, indicating that 'for putting the work in hand the season will now very soon be proper'.[90]

The plans show the first and second storeys (a difference in height of '12 ½ clere' and '14 ¼ clere' respectively) with the new work highlighted, representing a sizeable addition (extending more than 40ft (12.2m) to the south), and intended to fill most of the intervening space between the 'Gunners' Tower and the 'Old Building', leaving just a small open 'Airey' [area] to light the two staircases proposed.[91] The arrangement of a staircase on the lower storey to access the tower suggests some of the possible challenges in matching the levels between the new and the old. In fact the relationship between the staircases and the layout is not clearly understood from the plans, and remains so in the absence of any sectional elevations of the buildings from this period. Of some interest is the proposed end wall where it projects north from the tower on the 'First Story' plan, shown here to abut a more substantial solid wall to the north that seems to represent a portion of the eastern curtain wall, its perpendicular alignment disagreeing with earlier plans of the castle (Figs 2.1–3, 3.3).[92]

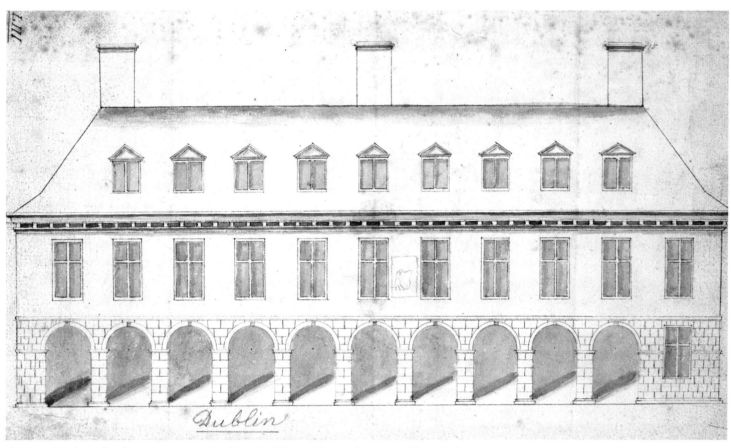

Fig. 3.6 Elevation of south-east range c. 1684, office of William Robinson. (BL, Map K Top 53/19g)

This easterly extension to the state apartments involved extending the eleven bays of the existing building by a further five bays which, if carried out, would (with the exception of one bay) have been subsumed later into the new eastern Cross Block. The evidence from Rocque's map (Fig. 3.11), along with Thomas Eyre's later scheme c. 1758 to enlarge this block to the south (Fig. 3.49), and Euclid Alfray's plans (Figs 3.18–9) made a decade later, would all seem to suggest that either the 1690s extension as proposed was never carried out, or alternatively, if built, was altered soon after to accommodate the erection of the Cross Block (see following section).[93] Mention in 1706 of building a 'bagnio' between the Lord Lieutenant's bedchamber and the chapel, and the evidence from Rocque's map does indicate that the apartments were ultimately extended eastwards, but in the latter source a passage to the terrace is shown separating a structure that was appended to the west side of the tower. The original character of this extension is likely to have been completely erased with Eyre's enlargement of the entire block even though the staggered plan at the eastern termination of the block (to accommodate a larger, open-well stairs) does accord to some extent with the outline depicted on Rocque's map.[94] The only surviving correlation between the 1698 proposals and later plans (Fig. 3.18) is the

retention of the open space, the 'Airey' on the west side of the tower, which in the later surveys (Figs 3.24, 3.61) is differentiated as a larger L-plan space.

By the time these additions to the state apartments were proposed, Robinson, who may well be their author, had returned to Ireland and resumed his post, retaining it until he resigned due to infirmity in 1700.[95] With the completion of the new state apartments in the south-east corner of the Upper Yard by 1688, and their possible extension a decade or so later, the sedate astylar façade with its arcuated ground floor (Fig. 3.6) may appear to have represented little if any progress from the architecture of Falkland's long gallery; however, its careful positioning and simple modular formula established a new and sedate classical accent within the castle precincts which, if applied with aesthetic rigour, could (and would) be easily replicated to replace a legacy of chaos and visual discordance. Thus the medieval complexion of the castle was gradually overtaken, its former existence as an ancient citadel soon confined to the surviving towers and gatehouse, with only a single prominent portion of the curtain wall remaining by the time that Charles Brooking published a view of the still evolving castle some thirty years later.

Chapter 3.3
The Lower Castle Yard 1684–1700

The impacts of the 1684 fire seem to have been entirely concentrated within the confines of the Upper Yard. Knowledge of the arrangement of the buildings that occupied the Lower Castle Yard from 1684 may largely be gleaned from de Gomme's map of 1673 (Fig. 2.12) and Thomas Phillips' more contemporary plans (Figs 2.2–3), and in greater detail from a survey of the yard by William Robinson in 1683 (Fig. 2.14).[96] The horse stables, dunghill and coach houses were accommodated along the north and east sides and prominently watered by the Poddle, its course formally expanded here with straight sides to create a sizeable horse pond bisecting the Lower Yard which Robert Ware in 1678 had observed 'plentifully serves to all uses belonging unto the horse kept there, and to the several artificers'.[97]

De Gomme's 1673 survey 'exactly described' the extent of the grounds to the east and south of the castle. Although based on its overall delineations, which include graphic representations of most of the key buildings, its details are largely generalised, which is perhaps understandable given the scale to which it was drawn. It portrays the Lower Yard to the east as an essentially rectilinear enclosure with its principal access provided by means of a gate opening off Castle Lane (Palace Street) more or less centred on the northern boundary of the yard, and almost straddling the outflowing Poddle, a detail confirmed in the 1683 plan (Fig. 2.14) where the gate stands over the watercourse which presumably provided some defensive advantage. Extending west inside the northern boundary, Thomas Wentworth's stables are clearly indicated, with an intervening building shown adjoining the Powder Tower. This western ancillary structure closely corresponds to the one indicated by Robinson in 1683, and possibly is the office of ordnance mentioned by Robert Ware.[98] There are other (unidentified) structures suggested against the east curtain wall on de Gomme's survey (though not indicated on the Dartmouth

plan (Fig. 2.1) which in any case excludes structures outside the Upper Yard), but these do not appear in later surveys, including Robinson's. This would therefore seem to rule out the possibility that these were lost in the fire and explosions of April 1684, having already (according to Robinson's plan) disappeared by then.[99]

The Poddle river is clearly delineated in the 1673 survey, flowing through the stable yard as a natural waterway, coursing along the southern edge of the castle ditch, and meandering between the chapel range and the prominently labelled 'Magazine' opposite, a range which extends from the Poddle across to the eastern boundary with a longer, narrow rectangular yard directly behind it. A further range, most likely stables, is shown extending to the north along the eastern boundary and probably closely relates to the buildings shown here in 1683. However, the strict uniformity of all the buildings in the Lower Yard implied by de Gomme, suggesting a rather formal rectilinear layout, seems entirely contrary to the later surveys, perhaps therefore limiting the extent to which one can rely on this survey as an exact representation of what actually existed on the ground in 1673. This is especially evident along the north-east portion of the Lower Yard where the shared boundary between the castle and the graveyard surrounding St Andrew's church is drawn on a straight alignment, with no buildings shown inside the castle walls and thereby disagreeing considerably with Robinson's and Phillips' 1680s surveys which show a more irregular boundary and suggest more long-established buildings in this area (notwithstanding Robinson's references in his written report about the area next to the watercourse 'not made use of but remains waste').[100]

The existence of an armoury at the castle can be confirmed by various references to it between 1673 and 1684 with its location most likely to be consistent with the 'Magazine' labelled on de Gomme's survey, which perhaps in some

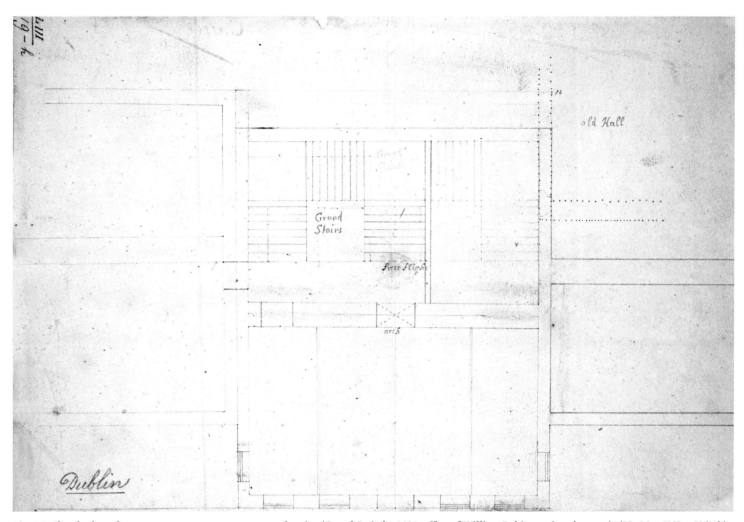

Fig. 3.7 Sketch plan of new entrance to state apartments showing 'Grand Stairs' *c.* 1684, office of William Robinson (south at top). (BL, Map K Top 53/19h)

way incorporated workshops for 'artificers'.[101] This southern range may represent the store house built in 1670–2 during the lord lieutenancy of Lord Berkeley, although Robert Ware mentions it as having been erected in the time of the earl of Strafford.[102] While improvements, such as formalising the course of the Poddle to make the horse ponds, may have occurred in the intervening period, essentially any disagreements between de Gomme's 1673 representation and Phillips' and Robinson's more detailed surveys a decade later, are probably best explained by differences in scale.[103]

In 1684 Thomas Wentworth's 'Grand Stables' of 1634, built partly to address 'a poor mean one' and to accommodate some sixty horses (including the thirty-six associated with his bodyguard and part of his intention that horses would give greater prominence to the passage of the lord deputy through the streets) is likely (as indeed Ware implies) to have still dominated the north-west portion of the yard ('the most convenient for ye Castle in ye world') on the site now associated with the Treasury block.[104] Wentworth's own assessment of the 'Grand Stables' was expressed boastfully to Lord Arundel, revealing both an inflated sense of his

own abilities in architecture and an established personal (somewhat childish) rivalry with Inigo Jones, by declaring his willingness to tell Jones he had 'built a better stable for ye King here in Ireland than ever he did in England'.[105] Sir William Brereton seems to have endorsed this claim when, soon after its completion, he described the building as 'a gallant, stately stable, as any I have seen in the King's dominions'.[106] Despite such boasts, Wentworth's stable block survived less than a century, its details largely known from Brereton's description of the internal arrangements and in the outline of the building as captured on de Gomme's 1673 map (Fig. 2.12) – shown divided into six compartments – and on the survey of the Lower Yard of 1683 by William Robinson (Fig. 2.14). In the same period Robert Ware confirms their imposing character, describing them as 'large statelie stables of an elegant contrivance'.[107]

By the end of the century the stables were perhaps overshadowed architecturally by the development of the state apartments in the Upper Yard. While there are indications that new stabling was built in 1689 'round the yard next to the Bowling Green, and round the Artillery

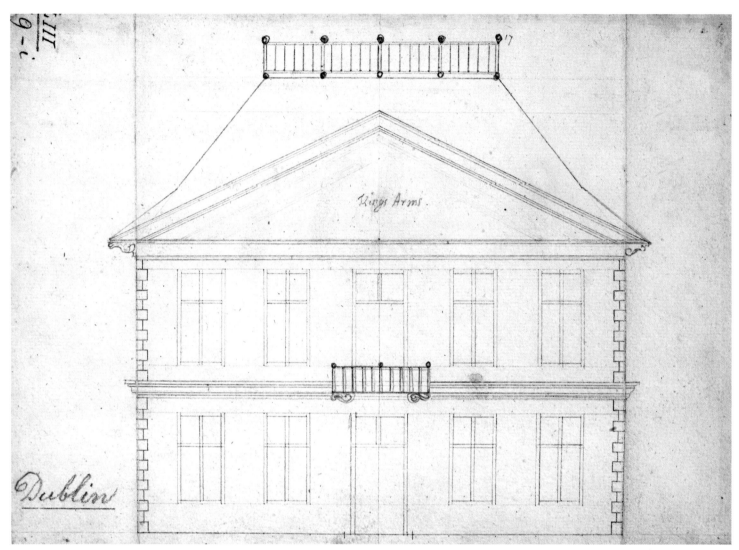

Fig. 3.8 Elevation of proposed new entrance to state apartments *c*. 1684, office of William Robinson. (BL, Map K Top 53/19i)

Yard', when John Dunton visited in 1697, he referred simply to the stable yard as 'a large peice of ground' and singled out only the 'King's stables', though he seems to have been underwhelmed by them, interested enough only to say, 'as they are not extraordinary so they are no way despicable, but convenient and big enough'.[108]

In 1683 there was also a sizeable coach house opposite the stables – located just east of the castle gate and the Poddle – which appears with a curious and suggestive skewed east end. Its outline can also be detected in Phillips' survey, although significantly it is shown here outside the castle boundary (and further appears to be concomitant with the parish boundary given in Charles Brooking's 1728 map (Fig. 3.15)), which on this evidence would appear to locate the building within the property of St Andrew's church. Given its location here, and in view of Wentworth's 1630s description of the castle's 'poor mean' stable 'made out of a decayed Church', there is the (perhaps remote) possibility that the coach house of 1684 actually represents, or incorporated fabric

from, the old parish church of St Andrew's.[109] The distinctive skewed, or diagonal line of the end wall of the coach house extends beyond the building to connect with a straggling group of stables, set as three disparate ranges along the east side and perhaps, at least partly, to be identified with stables built by the castle governor Sir John Stephens (before 1668) at a cost of £200, and perhaps even among these was the stable that had been adorned with a brass sundial made by the Athlone herald Richard Carney, who also provided one for the castle itself.[110] Both the coach house and part of these stables appear to have survived into the nineteenth century, and indeed the area defined as the dungstead in 1683 also remained discernible on later surveys (Figs 3.37, 3.62).[111]

A major development in the Lower Castle Yard before the end of the seventeenth century was the relocation of the castle chapel. On the castle plan of 1673 (Fig. 2.1), an inscription, 'Under this part is ye Chappel', places the castle chapel at ground level, beneath the staircase at the south of the long gallery, presumably extending perpendicular to the gallery, inside the south curtain wall. Earlier, in Speed's map of 1610 (while accepting the limitations of its accuracy) there is one double-height building depicted within the castle precinct in approximately the same position (Fig. 2.13), though perhaps too individually distinct to be easily reconciled with the integrated building suggested by the 1673 plan. It still remains entirely plausible, however, that this was the site of the medieval chapel within the castle, first mentioned in *c.* 1225 and believed to have been substantially rebuilt on at least two occasions after the fifteenth century, and most substantially perhaps as part of Sir Henry Sidney's 're-edification' of the castle.[112] The chapel was known to have been repaired by the earl of Essex in the decade before the fire which ultimately destroyed it.[113] Whether entirely consumed by the fire or largely blown up in the attempt to stop its spread to the Powder Tower, nothing further is known of this older chapel structure.[114]

After the fire, a new chapel was established to the east of the Gunners (Record) Tower though it remains unclear whether it was simply accommodated here, within an existing building – a structure being evident here in 1673 and 1683 – or was built entirely anew on the site.[115] One plan (Fig. 3.4) dated to about 1684 may indicate the existence of the

chapel here, while the outline of buildings at this location appears to be represented again on Thomas Phillips' survey of 1685 (Fig. 2.2) and if its treatment in outline suggests a ruin, it may well be the chapel which the duke of Tyrconnell refurnished for Roman Catholic service in 1687.[116] One brief description of about 1688 locates it on the 'south side' of the yard, and refers to it more intriguingly as 'a new Popish chapel & small priory for Dominican-fryers'.[117] Confirmation that a new chapel had been established at this time is the existence of silver-gilt Royal Plate (now in the collection of Christ Church cathedral) which was presented by William III to the Chapel Royal. The silver marks date the collection to the 1690s, the king providing suitably decorated alms dishes, patens, chalice, flagons, candlesticks, and cups for his Dublin chapel, thereby suggesting that the building was completed and furnished during this decade.[118]

Ultimately, the 1698 plans (Fig. 3.10) for the extension to the state apartments confirm the new chapel's location abutting the 'Gunners' Tower' which at the very least continued the very long-established tradition of having the chapel closely connected to the viceregal lodgings, and Dunton certainly locates it in the Lower Yard in 1697 ('to which Lord Galway goes constantly every morning to prayers'), though somewhat confusingly places it on 'the north side' and next to the 'Office of the Ordnance'.[119] However, in placing the stable yard 'before these buildings' it seems clear that he is referring to the ranges (the chapel range and the magazine range) shown by de Gomme on the south side of the yard. Provision for enlarging the chapel range was made before 1714, as shall be discussed below, and by 1756 the eastern extension of the range was used by the Arsenal Guard, and later as accommodation for the town major (Fig. 3.12).[120]

While a castle garden can be understood to have already existed before the early seventeenth century, nothing of its character, extent or indeed precise location is known.[121] An inventory of windows and loops in the castle, looking in different directions from the walls and towers in 1585 mentioned gardens to the south and east, with those to the south almost certainly related, in part at least, to the existing garden area. A reference to 'a parcel of land within the precinct of the castle of Dublin containing half an acre lying against the east and south side of the castle in which it appears there have been fish ponds or weirs' may also accord with the idea of established gardens in the area, utilising the waters of the Poddle.[122] Nothing of a garden adjacent to the castle is even suggested on Speed's 1610 map, although one may well have been accommodated at this time in the vacant area immediately to the south and east, between the castle and 'Sheeps St.' and George's Lane. It is known that in addition to purchasing a piece of ground on which to build his stables, Wentworth as lord deputy had bought additional land surrounding the castle in 1634 ('as costs

Fig. 3.9 Portrait of William Molyneux by Godfrey Kneller. (National Portrait Gallery, London)

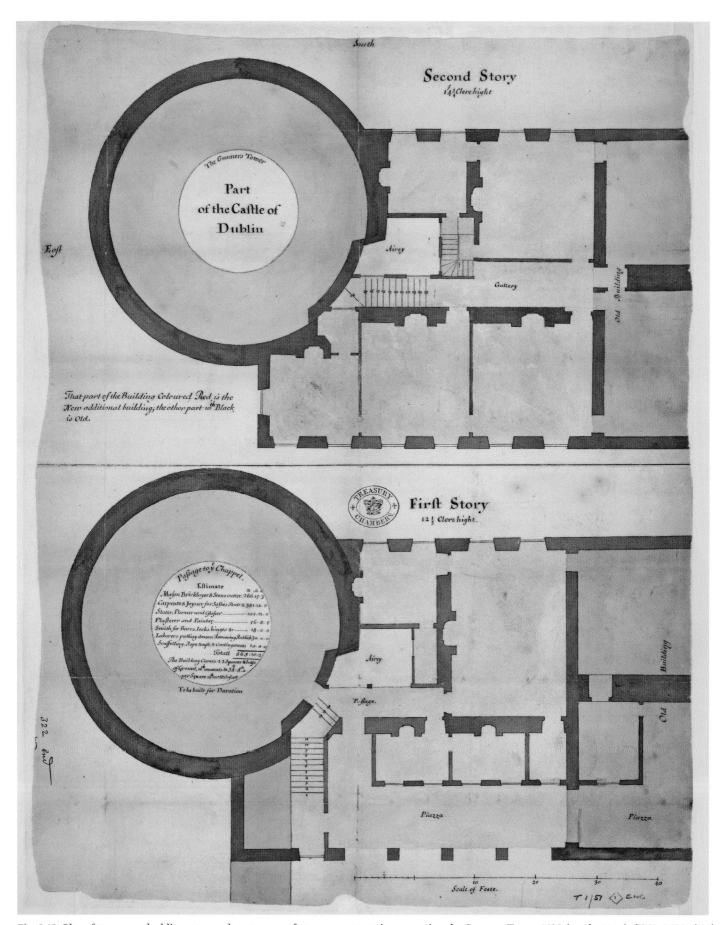

Fig. 3.10 Plans for proposed additons to south-east range of state apartments, incorporating the Gunners Tower, 1698 (south at top). (TNA, MPD1/188)

one hundred and fifty Pounds') on which he intended to establish a 'House of a Garden and out-courts for fuel and such other necessaries belonging to a family (whereof I am now altogether unprovided)'.[123] The sense of a constrained environment – ill-disposed to upholding the 'dignity of the king's deputy' – was made apparent in his complaint about 'the Bake-house, in present, being just under ye room where I now write and ye Woodreek just full below of ye gallery windows'. The enlargement and more formal arrangement of the garden within the castle precincts was clearly part of Wentworth's endeavours 'to make this habitation easeful and pleasant…whereas now upon my faith it is little better than a very prison'.[124]

The extent to which any gardens endured to the east of the castle is not known, but certainly by 1673, when Bernard de Gomme produced his survey, the principal castle garden lay to the south, depicted as a sizeable rectilinear area accommodated within the irregular castle precincts, partly bounded by the Poddle and formally laid out with cross paths and the suggestion of extensive planting. In the same period (1678) Robert Ware described leaving the Upper Castle Yard via the east postern gate and descending into the stable yard where he passed Wentworth's 'large statelie stables' and 'a full stream of water, issuing out of the Castle gardens'. While de Gomme's 1673 survey provides the clearest indication for the existence of a formalised

garden, its location is suggested as much further east than it is at present (or indeed as indicated by Brooking in 1728, and Rocque in 1756); however, the triangular plot of ground shown to the east would appear to be consistent with the area that later became used for the artillery ground, as confirmed by the eighteenth-century maps. The free-standing 'Powder House' is clearly shown in 1673, located to the west of the formal garden, in the centre of a plot of ground with an irregular and jagged western plot boundary; this area was perhaps also part of the gardens given that in 1689, when it was reported that 'the little store house' was blown up, it is described has having been 'built in the garden remote from the Castle'.[125]

In December 1689 it was stated that stables were being built 'round the yard next to the Bowling Green, and round the Artillery Yard', indicating that the gardens by then were perhaps more simply laid out with lawns and paths, rather than with the extensive planting suggested by de Gomme.[126] When John Dunton visited the castle in 1697 there had clearly been significant alterations since de Gomme's survey, though in substance perhaps only minor. The Poddle was then still evident coursing through the Lower Yard, with the 'coach houses and hay stacks' on the opposite side of it. To the rear of the state apartments Dunton described 'a broad terrace walk the length of the building the walls covered with greens and flower pots' and how 'from hence on a

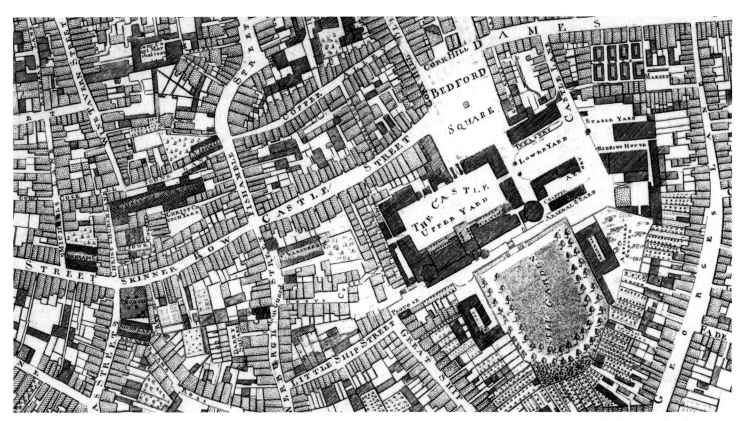

Fig. 3.11 Detail from John Rocque's Plan of the city of Dublin (revised edition 1762) showing Dublin Castle and the short-lived Bedford Square. (TCD)

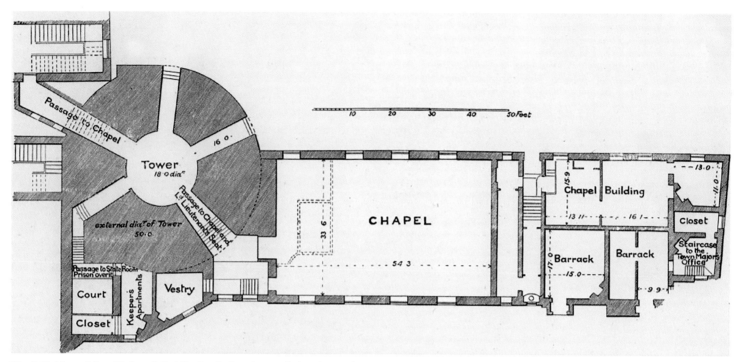

Fig. 3.12 Plan of the old chapel, Dublin Castle (north at top). (Lawlor 1923)

stone arch over a little river you descend by two spacious pair of stone stairs into the garden, which is handsomely laid out into grass plots with green and gravel walks, and at the north side there are two rows of flourishing lime-trees, beneath which lies another grass walk'.[127] His description of the garden, which had been laid out during Lord Sydney's lord lieutenancy (1692–5), correlates to the formal garden depicted on Brooking's map (Fig. 3.15) three decades later, while the twin rows of trees remain evident decades later on Rocque's map (Fig. 3.11).[128]

Chapter 3.4
Rebuilding the Castle 1700–30

John Dunton's impression of the castle in the late 1690s, that 'ye Grandeur they live in here is not much inferior to what you see in London', was at least evident in the state apartments in the opening decade of the new century during the 2nd duke of Ormond's first lord lieutenancy, which commenced in 1703.[129] Inventories of the castle reveal that in the state bedchamber, besides the bed (which like the walls was covered with crimson damask 'trimed with: gould Lace & fringe' with a 'Case Curtin of Crimson Taphety'), there were silver-gilt candlesticks on carved gilt stands, two gilt mirrors and a suite of seat furniture: 'Easey Chair, six Ellbow chayres, four square stooles, two round stooles trimed with: gould'.[130] However, despite the princeliness of the duke's court (in 1711 it included bringing the Italian soprano 'Nicolini' (Nicola Grimaldi 1673–1732) to Dublin[131]) which equalled that of his grandfather, building efforts around the castle following his arrival were limited: in July 1706 (adding somewhat to the sense of princely luxuriance) there is mention of Ormond's 'order to build a bagnio between the closet at the end of his Grace's bedchamber and the chapel'.[132] The reality was that without the Ormonds' personal contributions to the castle and its interiors, there was little to impress in architectural terms, so that even with the newly built south-east range, the state apartments still constituted a haphazard collection across the south range and it is difficult to identify any improvements at the castle in the early years of the eighteenth century as anything more than a continuation of the earlier programme of modest additions and routine repairs.[133]

Ormond was replaced by the earl of Pembroke in 1707, who in turn was succeeded briefly by the duke of Wharton in 1710 before Ormond returned for a second term in 1711. Only Wharton seems to have contemplated undertaking any major work, having examined the possibility of opening up a new entrance to the castle. By then responsibility had passed to Thomas Burgh, an experienced military engineer promoted from his position of third engineer on the Irish Establishment to the post of Surveyor General in 1700 to succeed Robinson.[134] The apparent lull in activity in the Upper Yard, however, was matched by certain works within the precincts from 1703, recorded in payments to Burgh.

After assuming this role in 1700, Burgh was also given responsibility for buildings to the newly constituted Overseers of Barracks (Barrack Board), appointed its chief engineer, director general of fortifications and architect of barracks.[135] The existence of this new post followed the financial provisions implemented in 1697 to accommodate soldiers in barracks throughout the country, and amongst the first to be undertaken at this time were the Royal Barracks, initiated in 1703 for a site across the Liffey on Oxmantown Green that had previously been considered as a site for a new palace to replace the castle.[136] A further consequence of the institution of a Barrack Board was that the funding of building works at the castle was no longer independent of parliament.[137] Given the events of the previous decade (and the earlier warnings that had been sounded by Phillips) it was perhaps inevitable then that the government would devote its chief building efforts in these years to preserving the security of the kingdom. With the Royal Barracks – 'the largest public building constructed in the entire realm' – it naturally claimed a sizeable portion of the available resources and was progressed at the expense of the castle.[138]

In 1705 Burgh's activities were also devoted to the provision of stables for the Horse Guard, which included removing the Horse Guard to the barrack ground, and the building of a riding house at the castle.[139] Two years later some attention was given to the need for an appropriate

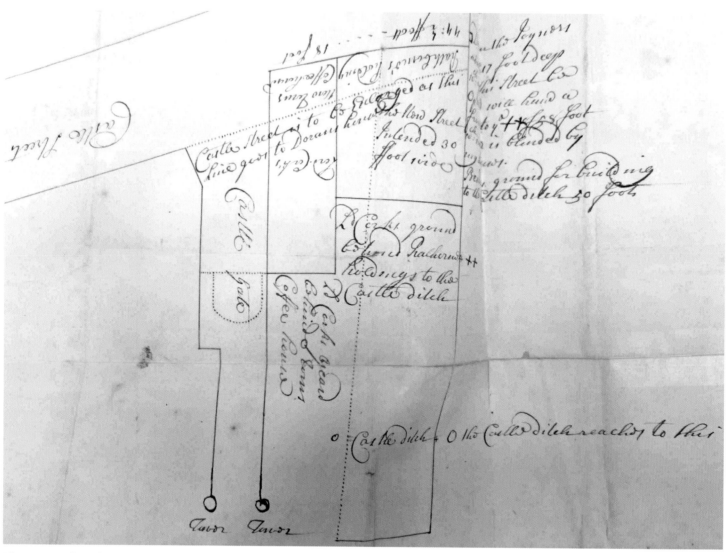

Fig. 3.13a Outline plan of the area around the entrance to the castle *c.* 1710 with instructions regarding properties (north at top). (DCA, Gilbert MS 195)

magazine as the powder was still being stored at Kilmainham and with 'no other security than the bare walls of the house it is lodged in'.[140] A solution could not immediately be found, though by the end of the decade some work was started on a new arsenal in the Phoenix Park. Meanwhile, some renewed interest in the Upper Yard at the castle occurred in 1710, in response to Lord Wharton's plans for a new entrance, initiated partly to address the 'narrow and incommodious' passage to the castle from Blind Quay and Cork Hill.[141]

Concern about the propriety of the location of the castle within the city in the late seventeenth century would continue over the course of the eighteenth century, and in fact was never satisfactorily resolved, despite the ambitious schemes and activities of the Wide Streets Commissioners. As early as 1682, before the fire, the issue had been raised by Lord Arran with his father, suggesting that 'if your Grace continues your thoughts relating to [rebuilding] the Castle it imports the contractors before it be known, to secure

St George's Lane, Sheep Street, Castle Street and Damaske [Dame] Street so many houses as may make four fair streets into the Castle, which may be too late easily to procure it once the design be known'.[142] The castle's continued role as the administrative and political heart of a rapidly expanding city ensured that it remained both relevant and symbolic, with a part to play in how the city was to be reimagined. Gradually, as the castle began to cast off its medieval character, so too did the cityscape which enclosed it, with efforts to reshape the city often focused on providing a fitting approach and entry into the castle. This in part explains Lord Wharton's motives in seeking to widen Cork Hill, the proposal approved in 1710 and a grant of £3,000 sought by the House of Commons in order to purchase the ground necessary to effect the plans.[143] The funds were to be applied specifically towards purchasing 'ye ground on ye street and ye severall buildings thereon leading up Cork Hill to ye Castle of Dublin, and of enlarging & levelling of said

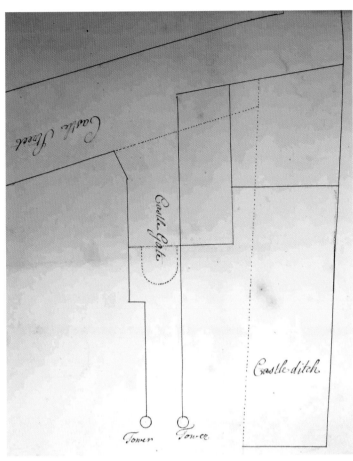

Fig. 3.13b Outline plan of the area around the entrance to the castle (north at top). (DCA, Gilbert MS 195)

street and making a new way into the Castle'.[144] A committee was established to examine specifically 'how to enlarge and level' the street leading from Cork Hill to the castle and to assess implications, including compensations for existing property owners. After its deliberations, having resolved that it was 'necessary to open a new way into the castle of Dublin thirty foot broad or more in a direct line from the Blind key into the said Castle', the committee determined that to achieve this would require taking 'thirteen feet off the two houses next Crane Lane and sixteen feet from the Swan Tavern and that the houses from the Swan Tavern to the Pillars leading into the Chief Baron's yard be pulled down and taken away'.[145] The 'Pillars' were perhaps the 'two toms' and probably refer to towers on the outer gateway leading up (what had formerly been the drawbridge or causeway over the ditch) to the castellated entrance to the Upper Yard (see below).

Some further detail is contained in the surveys (Figs 3.13–4) of Cork Hill accompanying the committee's report, and an agreement made with John Rathborne, owner of houses on the site of the proposed route.[146] The outline survey (Fig. 3.13) of Cork Hill and part of Castle Street that

relates to this scheme shows clearly the location of the new passage, just east of the existing one, and reveals that it was intended to align it with Cork Hill.[147] As part of the same scheme it was also proposed to widen Dame Street and Cork Hill by setting back various properties (including the Swan Tavern and a large site associated with Robert Molesworth) on the north side from Crane Lane to Cork Hill.[148] A further survey (Fig. 3.14) shows greater detail about the nature of the proposals affecting Castle Street and the existing passage to the castle. The intention to widen a portion of Castle Street involved the loss of the front of the 'Two Toms Coffee House' and Rathborne's houses, which adjoined the existing passage to the castle on the east side.[149] As the new 30ft (9m) passage east of the existing one cut through most of Rathborne's holding he was offered the site of the coffee house and the vaults under the new passage (built for his benefit) as well as the materials of the coffee house and 'of the two old Towers now standing on the said old passage'.[150] The survey (and another related one) is of further interest as it shows the existing passage leading to the 'Castle Gate' – an archway rendered as a dotted outline on the plan without towers, located some 50ft (15m) north of the main entrance (also twin-towered and shown in outline).[151] The towers are not shown in the drawing, but are described in 1721 as being 'twenty feet in front and fifty feet in depth' and perhaps similar to the main gate, as represented in Brooking's vignette of the castle.[152]

John Rathborne appears to have initiated part of the work by opening about 24ft (7.3m) of the intended 30ft-(9m-) wide passage before the plans were changed in about 1712, evidently because of a scheme to enlarge the castle to the north towards Castle Street ('to be brought about twenty five feet nearer to the street that it now is'), thereby requiring some of the ground that had been promised to Rathborne.[153] A new agreement allowed Rathborne £600 for his loss of a strip (25ft x 50ft (7.6m x 15m)), the materials of the coffee house and half of the vaults.[154] The proposal, at least from the evidence of Brooking's maps (Figs 1.20, 3.15), can be seen not to have been completely carried out, except for the clearance of the site, while another entrance into the Upper Yard is evident, further east of that proposed in 1710. The creation of a new passage in this area 'for the conveniency of carrying on the new buildings' is referred to by 1721, but the old entrance remained in use and the towers survived until at least 1738 when plans for a new passage were revisited. Brooking's map, which although not showing the old gateway in any distinct way, clearly reveals the awkward, indirect passage into the castle.[155] By then the difficulty of the off-centre position of the entrance could also be more satisfactorily resolved with the planning and completion of the new buildings in the north range over the following decade.

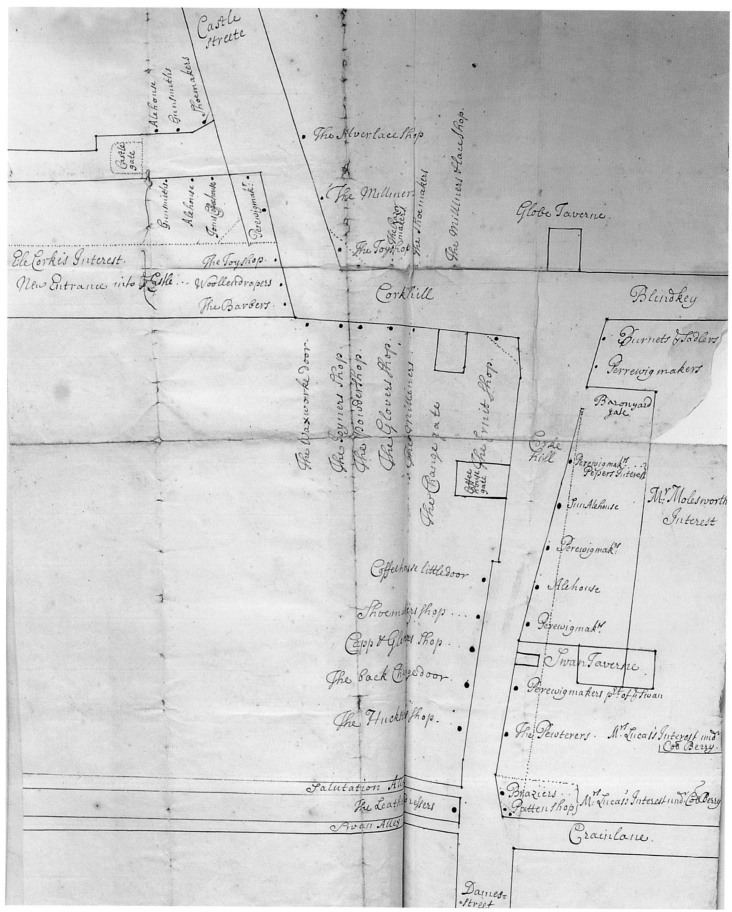

Fig. 3.14a Outline plan of Cork Hill and Dame Street showing various properties (west at top). (DCA, Gilbert MS 195)

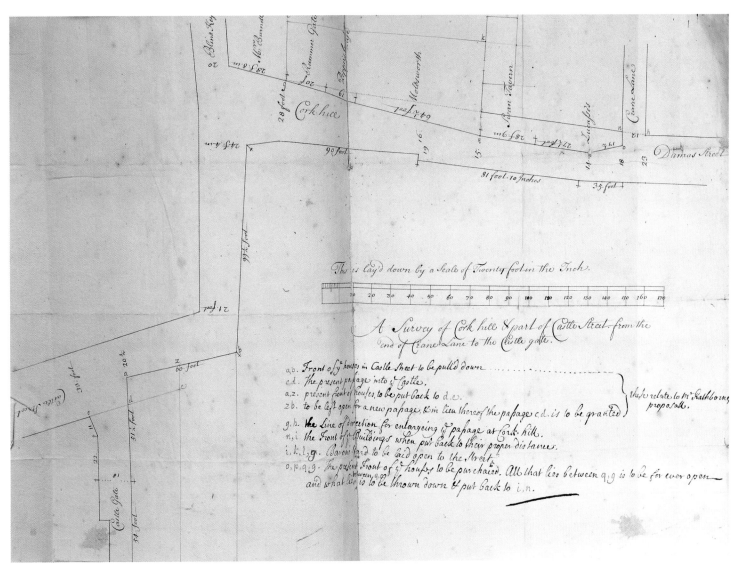

Fig. 3.14b Outline plan of Cork Hill and Dame Street *c.* 1710 with instructions on widening streets (north at top). (DCA, Gilbert MS 195)

While these efforts took their course, there were no immediate changes made to the Upper Yard, and other priorities dominated for the time being. Soon after the duke of Ormond's reappointment at the end of 1710 (whose return to Dublin was met 'with abundance of joy'), Thomas Burgh's brother-in-law, James Smyth, reported that 'all thoughts' of building an arsenal were 'laid aside' on grounds of expense, and added that consideration was instead now being given to 'two little redoubts for the security of the stores'.[156] The reason was not simply a matter of expense, however, and instead it seems that serious abuses in the accounting had been exposed during the building work leading Ormond to suggest, as a remedy, the possibility of accommodating some of the requisite stores within the castle, explaining, 'all that was wanted in Dublin was an arsenal or magazine to hold the arms…which might more properly be built in

the Castle, and a place for securing the powder, to be built a little out of the town, and both there at far less expense and in half the time…'.[157] There was some initial resistance to retaining an armoury in the castle, the existing site deemed 'too scanty by much for such buildings' and 'so very low and moist…small arms cannot be preserved from rust'.[158] But Ormond insisted, and after viewing 'the ground in the Upper Castle Yard' with Burgh, the Lord Justice and Master General of the Ordnance, Sir Richard Ingoldsby, eventually agreed that 'a proper magazine may be built there for 12,000 small arms with several other stores, and at a very easy rate'. In sending Ormond a plan, presumably by Burgh, Ingoldsby also suggested 'that the place we now keep our arms in, with a very little expense, may be made into very convenient work houses for our fire masters, smith, carpenters and collar makers as well as a timber yard'.[159] Although Ingoldsby mentions examining a site for the magazine in the Upper Yard (and the precise location cannot be identified) an armoury was eventually commenced in the Lower Yard, erected opposite the new Treasury offices.[160]

Ultimately the duke of Ormond's second term coincided with resumption of a more concerted programme of building in the Upper Yard. That the efforts to progress Wharton's scheme for a new approach into the castle signalled the beginning of a more ambitious scheme for the Upper Yard is suggested in correspondence by Burgh's brother-in-law, who in June 1711 wrote that in conjunction with pulling down the houses on Cork Hill, consideration was now being given to 'rebuilding the Castle to fit it for the reception of our chief governor'.[161] Certainly, an added sense of urgency will have been created as a consequence of the fire in April 1711 that affected the Council Chamber and associated offices. Breaking out in the early hours of the morning 'in one of the clerk rooms at the farthest end, next to Essex Street', it destroyed 'all the upper part of that large building' including the muster master general's and Surveyor General's office and all their papers along with most of the council papers.[162] While this event will naturally have encouraged a reassessment and revision of any existing plans from Wharton's time, it appears that this had in fact already been done at Ormond's instigation. He is known to have procured designs 'ffrom England' before the fire, which, although otherwise unidentified, were sent to Sir Richard Ingoldsby. His (unofficial) response to the designs, expressed to Ormond's Chief Secretary Edward Southwell, was rather scathing:

> I have by this post sent you a draft of Capt. Burgh's, and another sent me by his Grace from England, which I pray you will be so kind as to look over with his Grace, for I think I never saw so defective a thing (as that sent out of England) in all its parts, as for example look in to our own office, how scanty it is, and ill contrived, how the windows and doors, then view the Council chamber, the size and shape with the other conveniences, and that it has but one window if I do not mistake, nor must I forget the way of entrance into it, as to the arsenal, the very figure, with the design at each end must sufficiently disgust you; without saying how useless they have made it, but of all things I pray remark the order and placing of the clock house, and the entry of that side of the Castle when you have examined the dimensions of each room, and the conveniency of each apartment, pray let me know if you can find any one regular inch in the whole design.

> I had almost forgot the constable's lodgings, and the prison or the place for state prisoners, and the hall near the arsenal, for the Vice Roy's servants, which I believe is not above 18 foot square, but all this to yourself, I am sure the design when you bring the operation to reason upon it must make you laugh.

> Perhaps you will now expect some encomiums upon Burgh's draft, you know I have no reason to do it, not do I think it wants it but this I will venture to say, that Mr. Burgh assures me, it will not cost 2000 pounds more than the other, and by his draft you will enlarge the Castle, by the whole ditch, as you will see by the pricked lines, and will be cheaper to pull down the old walls, than pare them; everything is brought in to an exact square straight line, more noble and convenient, and the Castle yard larger than at present.[163]

While offering little more than a tantalising glimpse (and presumably the design showed the existing accommodation as well as what was proposed), it is easy to understand Ingoldsby's disdain for the imported plan, his description of their being not 'one regular inch in the whole design' is enough in itself to suggest that the underlying intention of this scheme was merely to continue the existing ad hoc approach to the castle's development. This was in contrast to Burgh's evidently more formal approach which, expanding on Robinson's and Molyneux's early ideas (Fig. 3.3), envisaged bringing everything into 'an exact square' while essentially ignoring the delimiting effect of the surviving curtain walls, pushing the proposed new buildings beyond these confines so as to erect them, in part at least, over the moat.[164] Ingoldsby inevitably (and as someone connected by marriage to Burgh, perhaps, naturally, despite implying disinterest) favoured this approach, which would not only result in a larger upper court, but also facilitate a more uniform, coherent design.[165] The decision to adopt Burgh's 'draught', with its resultant expansion of the Upper Yard certainly agrees with later changes to the government's 1710 agreement with John Rathborne, discussed above, but unfortunately the precise nature or extent of the scheme are not known as no drawings for it survive.

The concerns of Ingoldsby's letter were quickly overtaken by events, and within a few months the more pressing objectives seem to have shifted on the need 'to rebuild in proper places a Council Chamber and Treasury, and provide for the other offices which were all consumed by the late fire in Essex Street'.[166] Before the end of May 1711 'convenient rooms in the Castle for a council office' had been made available pending the building of a new one.[167] However, by February 1712, it was reported that there was 'no manner of work going on as yet about the Castle'.[168] But work did commence on the demolition of the Powder Tower a month later (29 March), possibly as preparation for the erection of the eastern Cross Block, and if so will also have required the demolition of the curtain wall to foundation level.[169] A few months later the decision was made to erect accommodation for the Treasury and other related offices in a new building in the Lower Yard.[170]

Although the precise location of the initial site for the Treasury is not clear, Thomas Burgh was not entirely in favour of it despite having already begun to prepare the foundations. The reasons given were the unsuitability of the 'narrow passage' through Castle Lane (Palace Street) that offered the only access to the proposed building, and the proximity of the site to the 'rampe' leading into the Upper Yard, which would, in effect, turn this into a 'public thoroughfare'.[171] In response to Burgh's concerns, two alternative locations were suggested by the Under Secretary, Joshua Dawson – the site of the former Council Chamber on Essex Street, and that 'part of the yard attached to Lucas's coffee house, which adjoins the Castle wall', that is if 'Lord Cork's Commissioners might be induced to sell'.[172] The challenging difference in levels (as implied by the use of the term 'rampe') between the Upper and Lower Yards was a likely factor in choosing a suitable site, although not necessarily an insurmountable problem, and while Dawson's second option was obviously to be preferred, with the added attraction that it offered an opportunity to progress plans for the desired new entrance, the density of development around the castle precincts was just as challenging with its issues of ownership, often complex, and which had already frustrated the efforts to form the new passage on the north side initiated by Lord Wharton in 1710.[173]

The original site for the Treasury may even in some way have been related more closely to the site of the Powder Tower, the structure having been taken down at much the same time as Burgh's objections arose.[174] The fact that the tower site (the space between the east block and the Treasury) was for so long unbuilt strongly suggests it presented certain difficulties that endured into the following century.[175] In reality, it seems the present location of the Treasury block, being still close to the 'rampe' and served by the entrance from Palace Street, was likely not all that far removed from Burgh's original, objectionable site, and ultimately he believed this was the 'place where the said offices might stand to greatest advantage, beauty and public convenience'; unfortunately (but without any sense of regret on Burgh's part), it necessitated the demolition of Wentworth's 'old' but once magnificent stables.[176]

The full scope of the building works undertaken at the castle from 1712, and the priorities, can be gleaned from a memorial dated 1714 prepared for parliament by Thomas Burgh which offered a detailed account of what buildings 'were provided for by the parliament, what progress is made in such buildings [and] which of them are finished'.[177] He included in this his opinion of which 'publick buildings are of absolute necessity to be perfected, and what sum of money will be necessary to finish the same'. The memorial explains that funds for the castle (besides some provision for the powder magazine and gun sheds elsewhere) were first approved by parliament (in 1712) for the Council Chamber and its associated offices, the armoury and the wide range of offices that would ultimately be accommodated in the Treasury building, namely those required for 'the Receiver General, Chamberlains of the Exchequer and the Clerk of the Pells, for the Auditor General, Surveyor General of the lands and Commissary General of the Musters; for the Board of Generall Officers Overseers of the Barracks and for Court Martials; for the Register of Deeds'.[178] All of these elements together were costed at just over £11,000. Burgh then proceeded to provide estimates for the 'further expense for carrying on the building designed for the accommodation of her Majesties chief governor', the works to include – in the Upper Yard – the west range, the front to Castle Street and a 'terrace walk to the garden front'. Also included, but without referring to their locations, were 'new kitchens & other offices, coal yards & sheds' as well as – in the Lower Yard – 'two large ranges of stables, covering the watercourse and lenghtning the building where the chappel is'; there was also provision for certain 'demolitions' and the removal of earth. While acknowledging that these additional estimates had not been previously placed before parliament for approval, it was noted that 'the works they refer to were laid down in the plan which was considered there and were approved by the Government'. These additional works increased the overall costs significantly, computed at almost £18,000, and by May 1714 more than half that amount had already been spent.

It is clear from this document that the accommodation that was prioritised in the earliest phases were primarily those affected by the fire in Essex Street, though in reality, besides the armoury (which was roofed by May, 'but not floored, nor the windows put in' and £1,500 required to complete it) several elements of the additional works were completed first, including the new kitchens, its offices and the coal yards and sheds, as well as one range of stables and culverting the Poddle.[179] The reasons for expediting these elements are not given, though some did constitute less expensive works, and presumably, therefore, were more straighforward and achievable in the short term.

While works on the Treasury offices had obviously been progressed in 1714, elsewhere Burgh merely reported that a 'great part of the other works at the castle are raised to a considerable heigth [sic]'. This presumably included the entire east range of the Upper Yard, designated for the Council Chamber and associated offices (estimated at some £400 less than the Treasury). However, it remains unclear how far this range had been progressed because some of the work still outstanding in 1714 seems to include the demolition of 'several of the present conveniences' that was necessary 'to make way for the council chamber and the other new works'.[180]

Although there was an obvious need to complete all the buildings in the plan, the 'Treasury and offices of public record' alone were singled out as priorities for completion by Burgh, who argued in May 1714 that these should not be delayed, largely because of the high rents being paid for some of the temporary accommodation, some of which was also unsuitably located in narrow streets, poorly equipped for their purposes, exposed to the risk of fire and too close to 'tipling houses and in the neighbourhood of the dwellings of the most ordinary people'. Burgh rather optimistically projected that all the work could be done in three years if £10,000 a year was allowed. However, perhaps fully conscious of the difficulties involved in securing the funds at once (or at all), he suggested that if £6,000 a year were allowed, the programme could be achieved in five years and be applied to buildings 'as the service may mostly require'. Before the end of June a warrant provided a further £6,000 towards the works.[181]

The Treasury building and the east range were essentially completed the following year, though it seems that fitting out the buildings was delayed for some time.[182] Raised to three storeys over basement with an eighteen-bay façade, the Treasury building has a monumental scale, all symmetrically arranged with four separate entrances in three discrete six-bay blocks, the centre block slightly advanced with a doorcase in each of the end bays.[183] The articulation and massing of the design, and especially its scale, makes the building rather analogous to Burgh's Old Library, as suggested by McParland, so that with its (by now) established 'Castle livery' of red, Flemish-bonded brick and granite dressings – rusticated quoins, sills, platbands, cornice and blocking course – its effect justifiably 'resembles a domestic version' of its contemporary counterpart.[184]

With work on the Treasury and the armoury progressed more or less together as early priorities, they were also positioned as opposing blocks creating the strong impression that together they formed part of a more developed purposive idea, possibly in line with Ingoldsby's comments as to regularity in 1711 and to satisfy Burgh's objection about access, and reflecting perhaps the earliest conscious effort to formalise the easterly approach to the castle (which would not be properly addressed again until decades later). Unfortunately, without certain evidence (including plans or elevations) for the scale or elevational treatment of Burgh's armoury it is difficult to fully assert this as a deliberate intention or ambition at this time, though the difficulties and delay in progressing works on the north ranges of the Upper Yard (Fig. 1.20) do support the impression that the efforts to improve access to the castle were, for now, and for a time, concentrated here instead.[185] The sense of a formal idea having determined the disposition of these two ranges – the Treasury and armoury – is certainly implied by their appearance on Charles Brooking's map of Dublin of 1728 (Fig. 3.15) though the south range is noticeably narrower, its scale no doubt determined by the existing chapel range. When the castle is eventually represented with a little more accuracy in 1756 (Fig. 3.11), the southern (armoury) range is shown clearly as the end section of two discrete buildings (a prominent but unidentified L-plan to the west with the 'armory' – slightly deeper in plan to the south – named at the east end) though without any suggestion that any disruption occurred across the main (north) façade. However, by 1801 (Fig. 3.62) this entire range had already been reduced by about half its length with the complete disappearance of the end section identified as the armoury in 1756.

Thomas Burgh's report in May 1714 that a 'great part of the other works' were raised to a considerable height, with a good deal of the timber work also executed, might indicate that the west Cross Blocks and a portion of the north range on the east side (as implied by Brooking's map) had all been started in unison with the east range.[186] Although Burgh could not firmly determine, beyond the Treasury, 'which of those buildings is of absolute necessity to be perfected, nor which ought to be proceeded on with greatest dispatch' the growing requirements for more diverse accommodation at this time can be demonstrated by what we know about the size of the Lord Lieutenant's establishment in 1713, comprising as it did 106 officers and servants, of which about thirty were upper servants including steward, comptroller, chaplain and ushers, some of whom would be given sizeable quarters in the west Cross Block.[187]

It is also not entirely certain whether the kitchens completed as a priority in 1714 were related in any way to those serving the state apartments, which certainly had been long established in the south-west range, and had occupied part of the Bermingham Tower since at least 1585 (then indicated as being in the 'second room', i.e. in the second stage, above the lower or basement level) and consequently referred to sometimes as the 'Kitchen Tower'.[188] If extensive rebuilding was required, the location of new kitchens at basement level in 1712 would have proved difficult without impacting on the existing buildings above, and so perhaps it simply involved remodelling; of course the critical necessity of these facilities, to make the castle fully serviceable, would likely have expedited their completion in this early phase of works.[189] Significantly perhaps, there was no specific mention of any works involving the completion of the south range other than allowing £350 for the 'Terrace walk to the garden front'.[190]

A valuable visual impression of the castle is offered by the vignette reproduced on Charles Brooking's map (Fig. 1.20). This shows the Bermingham Tower with its upper stage in a ruinous state, which, it has been suggested, may reflect the possibility that the upper stages of the tower were deliberately demolished during Burgh's building campaign in order to make the stucture less prominent in the midst of the new buildings, by then still unfinished.[191] In 1678 Robert Ware had considered it the 'stateliest, highest and strongest' and this impression is certainly still evident in Brooking's view, despite the obvious ruinous condition shown. In considering this theory, one might even go further and suggest there was perhaps an intention (as with the others) to remove the tower in its entirety, which ultimately, when works resumed in their fitful way, simply gave way to pragmatism with its consolidation and remodelling, which later views (Figs 3.16, 3.41, 3.54) would seem to confirm. Whatever the original intention, the derelict view of the tower in 1728 and the partially constructed colonnade

screening the old hall seems to confirm the impression that all work on the south-west range had been halted for some time, rather than suggesting any work was underway at this time. Some of the difficulty must have related to the ongoing use of the building – the rusticated seventeenth-century entrance bearing aloft the king's arms still dominated in its slightly off-centred, westerly position amid the new works. As the new buildings were progressed over these years, and the place obviously full of disruption (even when works were halted), the ceremonies of state were still being upheld by the castle authorities, demonstrated for example in July 1715, when the substantial sum of £705 was issued for two new canopies of state 'with proper chairs & stools', it having been 18 years since the last ones were supplied.[192]

Burgh's three–five-year timescale given in 1714 was certainly overly ambitious, and beyond the additional £6,000 granted towards the works that year, there were further stoppages, and in fact estimates were even being submitted for works to many of the completed buildings well into the 1720s.[193] While a fuller appreciation is frustrated by the lack of drawings and plans, some, more detailed insights into the progress of the work in this period are revealed much later in a document of 1738, which explains that the stonecutter, John Whinnery (a mason favoured by Burgh, used for example at the Royal Barracks and in his Dublin churches, including St Mary's and St Werburgh's) had in 1712 been

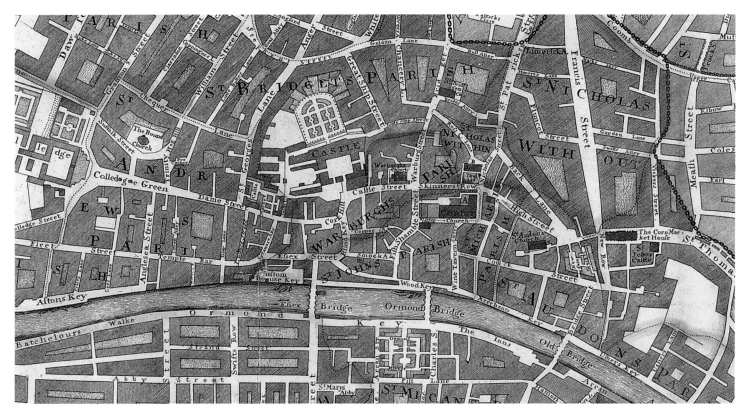

Fig. 3.15 Detail from Charles Brooking, *A Map of the city and suburbs of Dublin*, 1728 showing Dublin Castle (south at top). (RIA)

Fig. 3.16 Sketch view of 'Round Tower at Michael a Pools church near Ship Street', by William Betham after J. Grogan, 1751. (NLI, 1959TX, 54)

instructed by the Surveyor General to supply stones and men for the castle rebuild. Despite bringing and preparing 'a large quantity of stones' on site (with some imported from England) and obviously having made some progress with the buildings, 'a sudden stop was in the year 1716 put to the works' – and this in spite of a report from another source made in 1716 that the castle was being 'augmented' with new buildings, with others 'proposed'.[194]

By the time construction had been halted, the sum of just over £3,200 had already been paid to Whinnery for quite a wide range of works, listed as 'ye east building where ye council chamber and offices lye, the west building and Piaza where ye stewards and other officers apartments are [the colonnade of the south-west range] & ye building in ye lower Castle yard where ye Treasury & other offices are kept'.[195] Direction for work to resume was given in 1717 and this was completed in 1724 leaving just a modest sum due to Whinnery.[196] While this evidence would seem to imply that the remaining works – the resumption of the south-west range, and the building of a front to Castle Street – were

carried out over these seven years, there is further evidence, not least from Brooking (Fig. 1.20), to show that the south-west range actually remained unfinished for another twenty years. The north-west block, where the Under Secretary's accommodation was located, may have been established here before 1727 (although this is by no means certain) while works to complete the last phase of the north range would not be carried out until the 1750s (the medieval gatehouse actually surviving till at least 1738).[197]

Overall, Brooking's vignette does seem to offer an accurate portrayal of the castle in 1728 (assuming of course that it was taken contemporaneously with the production of the map, and not based on an earlier view), confirming that by then only half of the Upper Yard had been completed, and that the most recent of the ongoing and uncompleted works were concentrated on the façade of the south-west range (including, possibly, works to the Bermingham Tower) and the demolition of the north-east section of the curtain wall. In its incomplete state, the south-west arcade partly screened the low-lying old hall behind, with the seventeenth-century entrance, its rusticated arch supporting the royal arms, still prominent on one side; set back further behind it and the south-east range are a collection of disparate buildings representing the old dining room (in shadow) and Presence Chamber (with gun carriages in front). The northern portion of the castle still retained its medieval character with the partly dismantled curtain wall and the battlemented gate house. In the north-east corner, some detail has been excluded from the view, failing to represent for example the site of the Powder Tower, though a portion of the north-east range does extend into the frame (though implied at a much higher level than the east Cross Block), aligned more or less with the base of the demolished curtain wall. At the west end, the north curtain wall terminates abruptly, as does the gable end of the west Cross Block, the space between most likely representing the site of the Cork Tower. As rebuilt in 1624–9, this tower and the adjoining curtain walls were demolished to a height of about five metres, and thus utilised as a foundation for the new buildings.[198] As with the Powder Tower, nothing is known of the tower's seventeenth-century appearance, although from the surviving base the limestone masonry was markedly of better construction than the rest, using fine courses, in contrast to the wide joints associated with the thirteenth-century work.[199]

The adoption by Robinson and Molyneux of a modular formula in the south-east corner of the Upper Yard meant that the medieval appearance of the castle would gradually be subsumed by an orderly design of classical simplicity (Fig. 3.17). The intention stated in 1712 that the new buildings of the east range were 'to be of the same Form and Make' as the adjoining south-east range confirms this approach to the design, although it need not necessarily be understood as imposing a stylistic straitjacket on Thomas Burgh – even if much of his other work points to the Royal Hospital as a common ancestor.[200] In fact he simplified the architecture for the east and west ranges (perhaps largely as an expeditious economy). Although there are many obvious shared affinities with the architecture of both Robinson and Burgh what we see in the castle buildings merely reflects at best the stylistic expressions of the era, and at worst what might be interpreted as the accepted forms of a cheap and wholesome brand of civil service architecture. Ultimately, while circumstance may have prevented Robinson from having the opportunity to oversee much of the progress and the completion of his designs in the Upper Yard, his stylistic influence seems to have passed relatively undiluted to his successor, who naturally must have striven to complete as far as possible what can be considered Robinson's original vision for the castle, and in the most up-to-date style.

Essentially Burgh's building campaign in the Upper Yard helped shift the more ancillary, defensive aspects of the castle away from the functional and ceremonial, while consolidating and extending (and in fact even restoring in part) provision for the administrative apparatus. This can be detected in the provisions to move the powder store permanently outside the walls (while retaining a limited armoury close by), and the steps taken to begin building over the moat – an indication that the castle need no longer present an overtly defensive stance as the political outlook gradually improved, especially after 1715, with the decisive defeat of the Jacobite rising and the affirmation of the Hanoverian succession. Thus, through Charles Brooking's depiction of the castle we glimpse how the core buildings in the Upper Yard were transformed, shedding the rebarbative qualities of a citadel for an orderly array of administrative suites for the chief offices of government, supporting and effectively enclosing the ceremonial rooms of state spread out across the south ranges. With these new buildings, including the new Treasury block in the Lower Yard, there was nothing restless or overly emphatic just a constancy in proportion and rhythm, asserting a placid spirit not unsuited to the attitude of the governing apparatus.

Fig. 3.17 Photograph of south-east corner of the Upper Yard about 1960. (NMS)

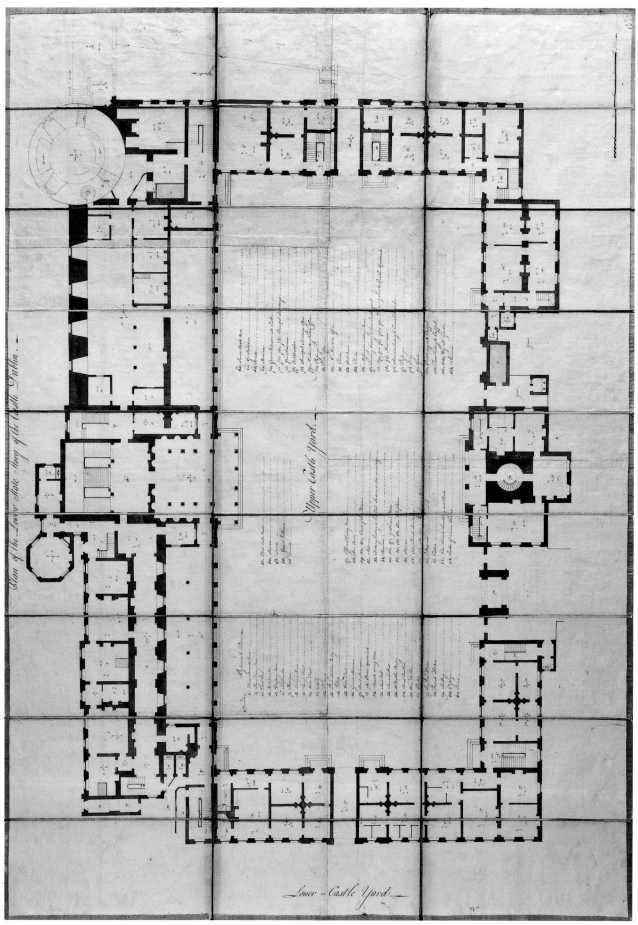

Fig. 3.18 Ground-floor plan of Dublin Castle taken in the year 1767 by Euclid Alfray (south at top). (NAI, OPW 5HC/1/61)

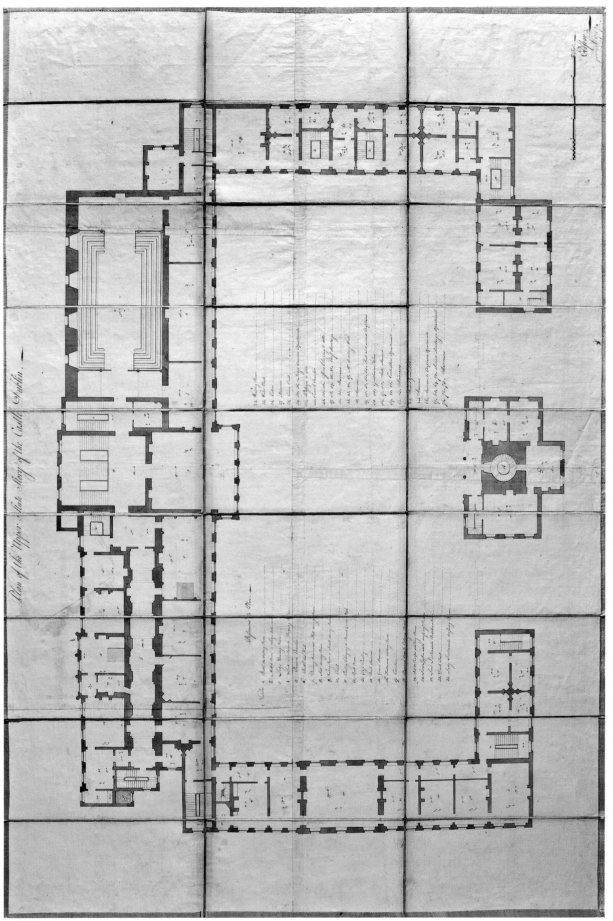

Fig. 3.19 First-floor plan of Dublin Castle taken in the year 1767 by Euclid Alfray (south at top). (NAI, OPW 5HC/1/61)

Inside, well-serviced by various staircases, these new administrative ranges were largely functional, all the rooms possessing good wholesome Georgian fittings, none of these surviving now. However, some sense of the original plan and architectural character survives in the west Cross Block, where wholesale modern renewal of the fabric in the 1990s sought to replicate aspects of the original detailing. The earliest surviving floor plans (and of first and second floors only) of the east and west Cross Blocks date to 1767 (Figs 3.18–9), many years after the buildings were completed, by which time both are likely to have undergone many successive repairs and perhaps considerable remodelling, such as the north-east corner (if not also most of the east Cross Block), for example, which was substantially rebuilt in the 1740s.[201] In 1673 (Fig. 2.1), a building labelled 'Officers' Room' and 'Guard' was set inside the west curtain wall, and across the west end of the ruined Parliament House. In one of the late seventeenth-century schemes for rebuilding the Upper Yard after the fire (Fig. 3.8) a narrow 'Guards' range was proposed along the entire west side, labelled as for 'officers of ye guard', indicating some continuity with older arrangements was intended and presumably a reference to accommodation for Ormond's Battle-Axe Guard; in contrast the east range was rather vaguely labelled as 'diverse apartments'.[202] By 1767 the ground-floor rooms south of the central arch in the west range were essentially utilised as part of the kitchen services, where besides the 'Officers' Dining Room' (apparently then shared with a store room) there were the clerk of the kitchen's apartments, with the central archway leading to the 'Coal Hole, Sheds and other conveniencys'.[203] On the upper floor, three rooms represented the 'Controllers' Apartment' (the person who 'checked accounts and paid bills, kept viceregal residences in order and saw to the comforts of the viceroy's guests'), with the largest room, at the north end, reserved for the Board of Green Cloth (the body that oversaw the management of the household and accounts).[204]

At the northern end, the majority of the rooms on both levels were given over to the gentleman usher (three rooms on the ground floor and two above – up to 1764 there were usually two gentlemen ushers whose role was to regulate levees, including determining 'who could properly be introduced to the Lord Lieutenant') and the chaplains (given five rooms on each floor) with three rooms on the first floor, including the two over the central arch, reserved for the state steward ('a person of rank' who 'was responsible for the viceroy's domestic arrangements, house and table').[205]

From the outset the east Cross Block was primarily the focus of new accommodation for the Council Chamber. In 1767 the ground floor presented an almost symmetrical plan with the staircase to the Council Chamber on the first floor terminating the south end of the block, accessed through a passage off the south-east colonnade (two further staircases, set back-to-back adjoined it to the north). The room sizes did not vary substantially across the range, the majority of those on the ground floor being the same near-square size with most to the south labelled as having been formerly 'Lord Walkworth's' apartments.[206] With the apartments on each side of the arch similarly disposed, those to the north were used as either ante chambers or offices for various secretaries and clerks, with the largest reserved for the Under Secretary.[207] It is not clear where the Chief Secretary was accommodated in the early years of the century, as his apartments in the north range are entirely attributable to the later works of 1742. These were loosely symmetrical – four rooms grouped around a central stack with a staircase at either end. On the upper floor, the Council Chamber dominated the east range, occupying the central three bays, flanked to the south by a suite of 'Ladys Womans' Apartments' and to the north by offices serving the Council Chamber.

As much as we may wish to know about the furnishings of Burgh's new buildings at the castle may be gleaned largely from the accounts of Robert Baillie who was appointed Upholsterer to the Government by the earl of Sunderland when Lord Lieutenant, and who, as well as carrying out repairs, supplied goods and furniture relating to the east and west Cross Blocks between 1714 and 1720 when accounts were furnished for fitting up an office for the Trustees of the Linen Manufacture in the east range.[208] A certain degree of fitting architectural decoration must have been applied to the treatment of the Council Chamber, where in 1724 a ball for the prince's birthday was held, a use that underlines the continuing deficiencies of the state rooms for ceremonial events.[209] A further hint of the improvements here were the new canopies of state, proper chairs and stools, already mentioned, that were supplied in 1715.[210]

Burgh's adherence to the architectural accents set decades earlier might easily be considered to have squandered an opportunity and retarded greater architectural ambitions in the capital. The events surrounding the rebuilding of St Werburgh's at this time – when Burgh's design was favoured over those of Alessandro Galilei – seem to confirm as much (and indeed the arrival of a competing design, sent by Ormond from England, might be seen as an attempt to wrestle the castle from a moribund tradition – notwithstanding Ingoldsby's wholehearted dismissal of it).[211] Certainly the use of brick with spare stone trim and the preference for simple arcades became fixed, representing a straightforward classical vocabulary that must have appealed perfectly to Burgh's ability and sensibility as first and foremost a military engineer, and so was deemed satisfactory for all of the most important public commissions that emanated from the office of the Surveyor General over suceeding decades – from the Royal Barracks to the College Library. Its influence can be detected in the neighbourhood, as the façade of the Presbyterian Meeting House on Eustace Street shows; it was built as late as 1728 – though of course the castle buildings were still being completed at this time so that builders in the capital might well have still regarded its enduring style as perfectly up to date. While to the architectural historian of today, the completion of two-thirds of the Upper Yard reveals no indication of architectural progress in almost half a century since the 1684 fire, the pace of progress would change dramatically within a few years with Edward Lovett Pearce, whose design for the Parliament House greatly disrupted the static tradition; and although Pearce claimed the surveyor generalship in succession to Burgh in 1730, his tenure was all too brief and his opportunities at Dublin Castle limited to minor works.[212] However, the new potentials of public architecture had been firmly set by Pearce's extraordinary classical precedent given centre stage on College Green, and the completion of the castle over the succeeding decades, and the work of several Surveyor Generals, would ultimately reflect that fact.

Chapter 3.5
Towards Completion – Buildings 1730–1800

Succeeding to the post of Surveyor General in January 1731, following the death of Burgh the previous December, Edward Lovett Pearce fulfilled the position for so short a period that his direct contribution to the castle seems, on the evidence at least, to have been almost negligible. However, his abilities and achievements as 'one of the pioneers of European neo-classicism' did directly influence the stylistic development of the castle in the 1740s and 50s.[213] Having bypassed Burgh to win the design of the Parliament House (Fig. 3.20), this remained his principal commission at the time of his death in 1733, earning him a knighthood for his efforts and introducing a design so radical and influential, it made Dublin a stage for the contemporary cause of Palladian neo-classicism, serving in effect as 'a great architectural school for later architects'.[214] While it is understandable that in the recent past Pearce's name was usually invoked when efforts were made to establish the identities of the probable designers for the Bedford Tower that completed the north range of the Upper Yard, and the extension of the south-east range of the state apartments, further research has lessened that likelihood, not least because these works occur too late in the chronology to accord with his period as Surveyor General. However, it should be borne in mind that the slow progression of building campaigns at the castle generally need not rule out the possibility that designs by Pearce were carried over, perhaps even adapted – after all Burgh's work demonstrates stylistic continuity with Robinson and Molyneux, and this in turn was rather faithfully adhered to over many decades.[215] At the very least it would seem reasonable to ascribe the Pearcean attributes of these later castle buildings to the more mediocre talents of his successors (and their deputies) who, in seeking to finally achieve a satisfactory completion of the Upper Yard after an extremely fitful pattern of rebuilding over the course of some seventy years, would naturally turn to their 'greatest

predecessor' for inspiration to conform to the new wave of architectural taste.[216] The actual recorded work at the castle by Pearce amounts to little more than an undated design for a 'new office' adjoining the ordnance stores in the Lower Yard, and to the decoration of the old hall or ballroom (the predecessor of the present St Patrick's Hall) in 1731, as briefly mentioned by the duke of Dorset (for whom it was carried out) and Mary Delany who had explained to her sister that the room had been 'ordered by Capt. Pierce, finely adorned with paintings and obelisks'.[217] There is, however, some likelihood that Pearce was also concerned with other alterations in the Upper Yard that have yet to be identified.[218]

While none of the spark of brilliance that characterised Pearce's originality may be found in his successor, Arthur Dobbs (Fig. 3.21) was an intellectual and active man with an enquiring mind, a founder of the Dublin Society, and so may be assumed to have naturally held a serious interest in architecture and been knowledgeable enough to carry out the job, or at the very least to give competent guidance and oversight to his subordinates.[219] After all, his first responsibility was to act as overseer for the completion of Pearce's Parliament House, work which occupied him until about 1739.[220] While he undertook some major works at the castle, though mostly concerned with repairs and the resolution of the long-running issue of a new approach, he gradually became sufficiently distracted elsewhere to resign the post in 1743 in order to pursue other interests. Dobbs' successor was Arthur Jones Nevill who paid £3,000 to secure the surveyor generalship. Holding the post for the same short duration, he had, on the face of it at least, a much more formative influence on the architecture of the castle than his predecessor.[221] By the time that Nevill was dismissed in 1752 (because of issues of administration relating to barrack building), the castle's south range was finally completed,

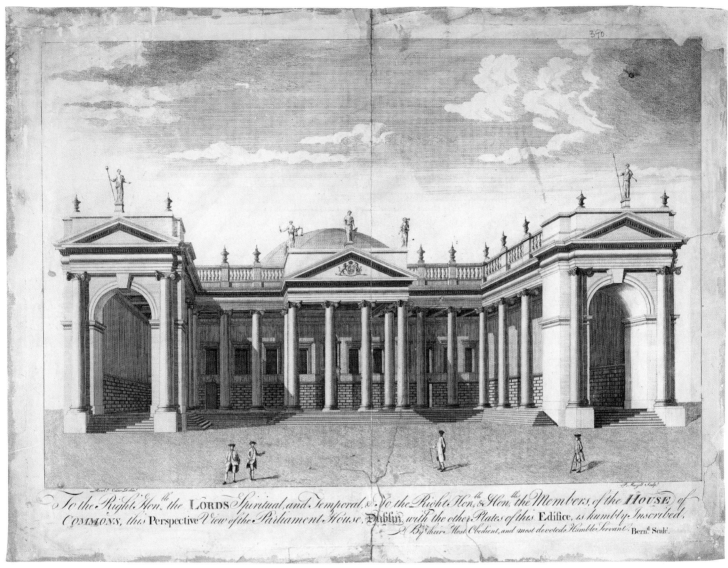

390.

To the Right Hon.ble the LORDS *Spiritual, and Temporal, & To the Right Hon.ble & Hon.ble the Members, of the* HOUSE *of* COMMONS, *this* Perspective *View of the* Parliament House, Dublin, *with the other Plates of this* Edifice, *is humbly Inscribed, By their Most Obedient, and most devoted Humble Servant.* Bern.d Scalé.

Fig. 3.20 Front elevation of the Parliament House on College Green, Dublin, engraved by Peter Mazell after Roland Omer, 1767. (NLI, ET C 463)

including the addition of an impressive new entrance block and a rebuilt ballroom, while the design for the completion of the north range had been settled and work begun on its erection. Despite being known as 'jobbing Jones', Nevill, like Dobbs, was not necessarily a mere sinecurist and outside of his official career could demonstrate a suitable level of interest in architecture, and clearly possessed both discernment and confidence in the subject.[222] For example, in the 1740s, when he was busy with works in the castle, he had built for himself No. 40 Stephen's Green, for which he commissioned the Apollo Ceiling in 1746, a tour de force of the stuccodore's craft that, following the demolition of the house, was rather appropriately relocated (1964–8) to the state apartments where it now adorns the Apollo Room – a compensation of sorts for the loss of the Presence Chamber which was one of Nevill's chief contributions to the castle interior.[223]

Arthur Jones Nevill was succeeded as Surveyor General by Thomas Eyre (Fig. 3.22), son of an established gentry family from Galway, who, like his father, had pursued a military career, serving as an engineer in North America through much of the 1740s. He held the position of sub-engineer for Georgia and South Carolina before (having for a time returned to England) moving on to Jamaica where he obtained the rank of captain again. There he served as an engineer until he retired in 1752, about the time he purchased Nevill's patent, assuming the post on 31 August. Eyre made Joseph Jarratt his deputy, and it is largely through Jarratt's surviving drawings (Figs 3.48–9) that the Surveyor General's activity at the castle is measured, although the extent to which he can claim credit for the actual designs (over Jarratt) remains difficult to establish.

Fig. 3.21 Mezzotint portrait of Arthur Dobbs by William Hoare, engraved by James McArdell. (NGI)

Fig. 3.22 Portrait of Thomas Eyre. (Photograph by Davison & Associates. Courtesy of the Office of Public Works)

Among the earliest works at the castle during Eyre's tenure were some new buildings, including the house he designed and built for himself in the Lower Yard in 1756 (Fig. 3.23), and a new laboratory built near the castle garden a year later. From 1758 much of Eyre's (and Jarratt's) work involved repairs or additions to existing buildings as well as the completion of the Upper Yard. The most substantial of these was the guard house, built as a northerly extension of the Bedford Tower, and the completion of the unfinished tower itself, apparently in accordance with Nevill's original scheme. There were also repairs carried out to the Record Office and the completion of the north-west corner block to accommodate the Under Secretary and the offices of the Linen Board. The culmination of Eyre's career as Surveyor General was the extension of the south-east range of the state apartments, creating in the process a new octagonal library at one end of the terrace, and, more substantially, the application of an imposing ashlared façade of silver granite, overlooking the castle garden.

After just over a decade in office, Eyre was to be the last Surveyor General, as the position was abolished in 1763 in favour of the creation of two architectural posts connected with the Barrack Board. According to the new division, the Architect to the Board assumed responsibility for barracks, essentially military buildings, while the Clerk and Inspector of Civil Buildings in Dublin (from 1788 the title became 'Architect and Inspector') in effect took charge of the administrative buildings in the capital, such as the castle, the Parliament House and Four Courts. Distinguishing the responsibilities of the two principals in respect of the castle, however, becomes a little confused when Henry Keene, appointed architect to the Barrack Board in 1762, had survey plans (Figs 3.18–9) prepared of the Upper Yard, drawn by Euclid Alfray, his assistant from 1760. The purpose of the survey is not known, though it is perhaps significant that its date coincides with the lord lieutenancy of Lord Townshend, whose term marked a shift in approach towards the sustained residency by the Lords Lieutenant during

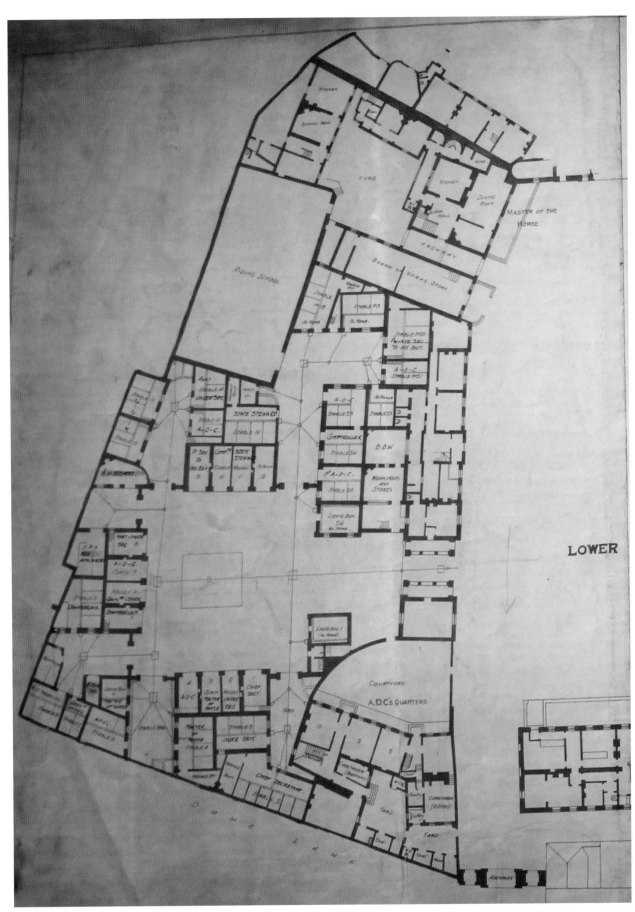

Fig. 3.23 Detail from plan showing former Surveyor General's house (marked Master of Horse) in the Lower Yard (south at top). (OPWT, E000486. U16-3 – early twentieth century initialled H. G. Leask)

their term in Ireland – Townshend's residency from 1767–72 establishing a pattern that was more or less maintained by each of his successors.[224] After Keene's retirement in 1766, Christopher Myers assumed the post, and it is possible that he too took some interest in works at the castle, where his influence has been detected in the rebuilding of the Bermingham Tower in 1775–7.[225]

The first Clerk and Inspector, in effect succeeding Thomas Eyre, was his deputy Joseph Jarratt, who served from 1763 until his death in 1774 with little or no opportunity to carry out any substantial works in the castle, or to in any way demonstrate the development of architectural tastes in favour of European neo-classicism, as had so outstandingly been demonstrated within the castle's own precincts in 1769 with Thomas Cooley's design for the Royal Exchange. It was perhaps inevitable then that Cooley would succeed Jarratt in 1775. However, until his death in 1784 (most of which time he served as subordinate to Myers and his son Graham), Cooley equally had little or no opportunity to display his talents in the castle, except possibly in his first years, if given some part in rebuilding of the Bermingham

Tower with Christopher Myers.[226] Regretably, much the same may be said of his successor Thomas Penrose, another neo-classicist who followed Cooley, serving from 1784 until 1792, during which time the title was simplified to architect. Penrose did, however, leave a valuable survey of the upper floor of the castle (Fig. 3.24), drawn in 1789, which allows some of the alterations since 1767 to be noted. These included the conversion of the Battle-Axe Hall into a new Presence Chamber (the Throne Room), though it seems probable that this had little impact on the architecture of the room, and so largely involved a change in name only. With Penrose's death, the Roman-born artist Vincenzo Waldré, a protégé of the marquess of Buckingham who had employed him as an architect and decorator at Stowe, was appointed architect having, after Buckingham's second appointment as Lord Lieutenant in 1787, been occupied with the decoration of the ceiling of St Patrick's Hall. This great artistic endeavour still survives and indeed represents Waldré's main contribution to the castle even though he was forced to abandon it upon taking up the official post, a role which ended with the passing of the Act of Union in 1801.[227]

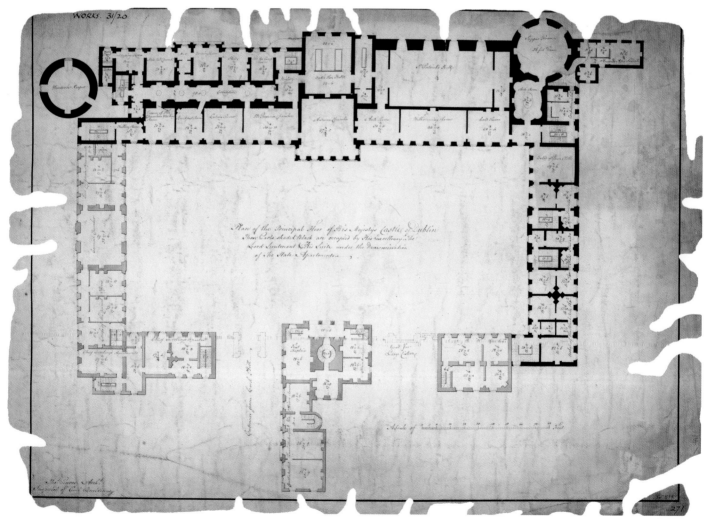

Fig. 3.24 Principal floor of His Majesty's castle of Dublin, by Thomas Penrose, Nov. 1789 (south at top). (TNA, Works 31/20)

Chapter 3.6
The Upper Castle Yard 1730–1800

By October 1727 the first fully-staged performance of musical entertainment was held in the castle, giving the sense that it was now becoming a more fitting place for the pageantry of the viceregal court.[228] However, it is a little later, during Edward Lovett Pearce's occupancy of the surveyor generalship, that we gain some impression of the state apartments, obtained in the company of Mary Delany, (then Mrs Pendarves, but from 1743 married to Dr. Patrick Delany, chancellor of St Patrick's cathedral and eventually Dean of Down), who visited for the first time in September 1731. She makes passing reference to the apartments, which she says 'consist of three rooms, not altogether so large as those at St James's, but of a very tolerable size'. Weeks later she returned for a ball and describes the room (not specifically identified) as having been 'ordered by Capt. Pierce' and 'finely adorned with paintings and obelisks, and made as light as a summer's day'.[229]

Referring to the same event, the Lord Lieutenant, the duke of Dorset, explained how he had resolved to make 'use of the old hall, which had been much disused and very much out of repair'.[230] He used Pearce to 'fit it up', the walls covered in extraordinary fictive canvasses, painted in distemper and attributed to the scene painter William Van der Hagen, 'the space…so contrived as to make it look as big again'. The ball itself was captured in a view that is usually also attributed to Van der Hagen (Fig. 3.25).[231] A similar scene is again evoked by Mrs Delany when a few months later she attended another ball in what she then called 'the old beef-eaters Hall' explaining how it held seven hundred people seated, where the assembled guests were 'all placed in rows one above another, so much raised that the last row almost touched the ceiling'.[232] Remarkably, some of the distinctive hangings from this time still survive (fourteen in all, the largest measuring approximately 14ft by 12ft (4m by 3.6m)),

having been rediscovered during the 1990s in the attics of Knole in Kent, the seat of the Sackvilles, formerly dukes of Dorset.[233]

Alas this was the only notable and verified contribution made to the castle during Pearce's short career, besides plans for a building attached to the arsenal in the Lower Yard (see Chapter 3.7).[234] Therefore many of the old deficiencies of the buildings in the Upper Yard remained at this time and there were insufficient repairs carried out, leaving it still somewhat inferior to the object of accommodating a more dignified viceregal court. The continuing poor arrangement of the south-west range is evident where the Council Chamber, some distance away, was used as the supper room during this time, a situation also demonstrated in the way it was also being used for theatricals (presumably based on its newness and respectability). Although Lady Anne Conolly could regard the ballroom in 1733 – then hung with gilt leather – as 'the prettiest thing I ever saw', Pearce's replacement, Arthur Dobbs, was considering proposals in 1737 for rebuilding the neighbouring state dining room and other apartments, though this seems not to have been progressed immediately.[235] Instead Dobbs seems to have focused his attention on the north range and providing a new entrance into the castle.

Whereas the work begun in 1710 to create the passage was frustrated, resolving the matter continued to be discussed over the succeeding years and real progress was only achieved after Arthur Dobbs initiated the erection of a new gateway into the Upper Yard in 1738.[236] In March that year Dobbs had produced an estimate of the expense involved in building the 'new Passage with side walls, peers, gate and doors…and to pulling down the two old towers on the Old Passage' – though whether these related to the towers at the outer gate (the 'two toms') or at the entrance

Fig. 3.25 William Van der Hagen, *The State Ball at Dublin Castle 1731*. (Photograph: OPW; © Drayton House)

proper (as many have accepted) is not perfectly clear.[237] If the surviving medieval gate (as represented in Brooking's vignette (Figs 3.15, 1.20) and where eventually the Bedford Tower was built from 1750 onwards) was taken down as part of the 1730s works, the nature and extent of the intentions for the site at this time remain elusive.[238] The requisition of the strip of ground adjacent to the new entrance and 'the new passage' leading to it had been part of the earlier efforts under Burgh, and in this instance appears to have been revived in 1735.[239] As Lord Cork's successor, the site (which was formerly associated with Cork House) had passed to the earl of Burlington and it now belonged to Joseph Gascoyne who was offered compensation for the area required.[240] The reason for appropriating the site now, as stated in the agreement, was that it provided a 'means

to prevent annoyance, which otherwise might attend the entrance into the passage, by letting it to tradesmen, to build upon in which case the Castle would be deprived of air and proper lights, and if any accident should occur it would be very dangerous'.[241]

Gascoyne's site, 'with the whole range of vaults', lay immediately east of the passage, and just outside the Chief Secretary's apartment in the north-east range (and extending further eastwards as far as the 'city wall') separated from it by a strip, approximately 18ft (5.5m) wide, belonging to the castle and presumably consistent with the castle ditch. Adjoining the plot to the north was 'the brick wall at the lower end of Lucas coffee house yard', while to the west were 'Mr Gascoyne's vaults under the new passage into the Castle' – proof again of how far the castle precincts had suffered encroachment.[242] Interestingly, the small area of ground immediately south of these, at the new entrance, contained part of 'the Castle vaults'. The agreements with Gascoyne eventually became more complicated and the detail provided in various sources is still somewhat unclear. What may be deduced from the two maps (Figs 3.26–7) associated with the legal agreements – dated 1741 and 1745 respectively – is that he retained an interest in the Lucas Coffee House, and that after 1742 a substantial portion of this site was added to the requisitoned property to form a larger site which, as the 1741 agreement suggested, was perhaps necessitated by the intention to create a much enhanced approach while also removing 'annoyances'. These likely included the boisterous emanations from Lucas's notorious coffee house and the risk of potential dangers.[243]

In April 1738 Dobbs sought a warrant to enable him to proceed with the new passage.[244] And although it was 'delayed by difficulties arising', works on the new entrance were eventually completed by 1741.[245] More difficult now, is an understanding of the difference in the treatment of the new passage and gateway suggested by the two 1740s maps. Although it may be explained simply by a more generalised approach on the part of one surveyor, in 1741 the gateway is shown perfectly aligned (and sharing the same thickness) with the south wall of the Chief Secretary's block, its plan a straightforward tripartite opening – implying a central arch flanked by pedestrian gateways, in the manner of the Palace Street Gate – whereas in 1745 the entrance is suggested as part of a much more interesting and sophisticated arrangement, set slightly forward (south) of the castle buildings, narrower in its proportions and extending between the walls aligning the passage that opens off Castle Street. The central passage is also lined with what appear to be square-plan piers, perhaps simply intended to represent linked bollards designed to separate the pedestrian passages on each side, although the proportions could equally imply piers as part of a covered passage, of a form then common in Dublin, and it seems that a similar architectural idea was later proposed in the putative square to be formed before the castle (Fig. 3.28).[246]

With Dobbs' new entrance closely following the original 1710s arrangement, and placed off-centre on the eastern side of the north range, it remains unclear whether any alternative solutions at this time had (besides issues of land ownership) been constrained by the survival of the old towered gateway or some aspect of it that was still in use, and not yet sanctioned for removal. It is, however, also likely that the new entrance simply represented part of a more developed, long-standing scheme for the north ranges, and was perhaps progressed at this time because of the necessity to extend and rebuild the north-eastern corner of the castle on which work commenced the following year. How far the entrance might have been conceived as part of any greater plan – whether originating with Burgh, or even inherited

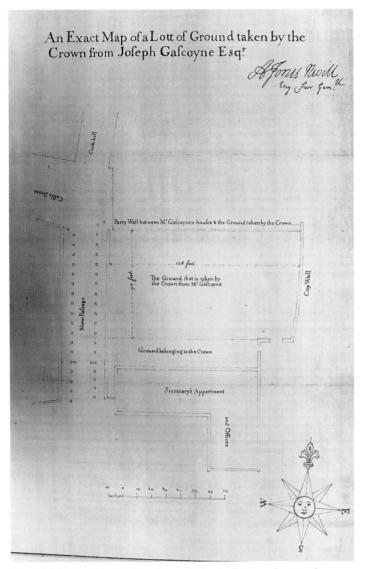

Fig. 3.26 An Exact Map of a Lott of Ground taken by the Crown from Joseph Gascoyne Esq, 21 September 1745. (Copy of tracing in NMS)

from a newer scheme devised by Lovett Pearce – is not known, however, nor is it clear whether this work in any way anticipated the eventual solution of flanking entrances each side of a pivotal block as was ultimately achieved with the erection of the Bedford Tower. There is the possibility that at this time consideration was already being given to opening up the ground on Cork Hill, especially as Dobbs' new entrance was to be retained as a core feature in later 1750s schemes of the Wide Streets Commissioners (Figs 3.28–9); here it represented one of two entrances to the castle set at the ends of a 'piazza' proposed for the south side of a new Parliament Square on Cork Hill, and with the intention that the newly extended north-eastern block would consequently form a sort of public frontispiece for the castle. The possibility that this had been part of a long-established idea might even explain why the space between the east block and the Treasury was for so long unbuilt (although it may be too much to suggest that the early demolition of the Powder Tower by Burgh was based on such an intention).[247] As a solution to opening up the castle, Dobb's entrance was not entirely satisfactory in the short term, not least because of the difference in ground levels between the Treasury and the east range, and problems with subsidence, which may even provide one of the reasons why the completion of the north range was not fully resolved at this time.

Progress in completing the Upper Yard to achieve anything close to a more unified design was, for the time being, affected by the need to rebuild the north-east corner due to structural problems. In June 1742 Dobbs submitted estimates for 'pulling down' and rebuilding 'that part of the... Castle... that is now Prop'd with Timber, where the Linnen Office and Council Office, Chief Secretaries Apartmt & his Offices were formally', and 'for Continuing the building from the Linnen Office Stair Case to the New passage...'.[248] This addition essentially involved extending the north range to provide the offices for the Chief Secretary (which previously had been incorporated in the south-east range associated with Robinson and Molyneux).[249] Salvaged entablatures, quoins and window sashes were to be reused in the new building, which involved 'taking down with great care 1200 feet of Architrave frieze & cornice', all

evidence that the works were, in part at least, concerned with resolving structural issues.[250] Therefore, what is seen in Brooking's vignette in the north-east corner was entirely rebuilt and extended at this time with the resulting six-bay range integrated with the new entrance thereby (if not already decided) limiting, or perhaps helping to define, the possibilities for the design to complete the north side, which as a starting point required the replication of Dobbs' rebuilt eastern block on the west side.

This issue of 'annoyances' at the castle entrance in 1741 was undoubtedly resolved by the provisions to move the Horse Guards to here from Essex Street in 1746. Prior to this, the Horse Guards were located off Dame Street, at a site next to the Council Chamber on Essex Street, established in buildings erected by John Paine in the 1660s.[251] In 1745, however, these buildings, or their successors, were inadequate, and a year later the site that had been appropriated from Joseph Gascoyne largely on grounds of propriety was proposed by the new Lord Lieutenant, Lord Chesterfield, for the relocated establishment. There is no sense that moving them here was in anyway designed in concert with the new entrance to enhance the approach, with Chesterfield writing to the Lords Commissioners of the Treasury in April 1746, stating that the stables and buildings used by the Horse Guards on Dame Street were in

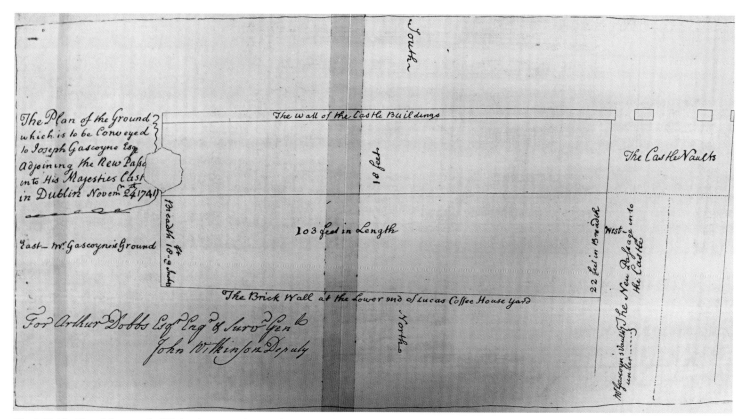

Fig. 3.27 *The Plan of the Ground which is to be Conveyed to Joseph Gascoyne adjoining the new passage into his Majesties Castle in Dublin November 24th, 1741* by John Wilkinson. (Copy of tracing in NMS)

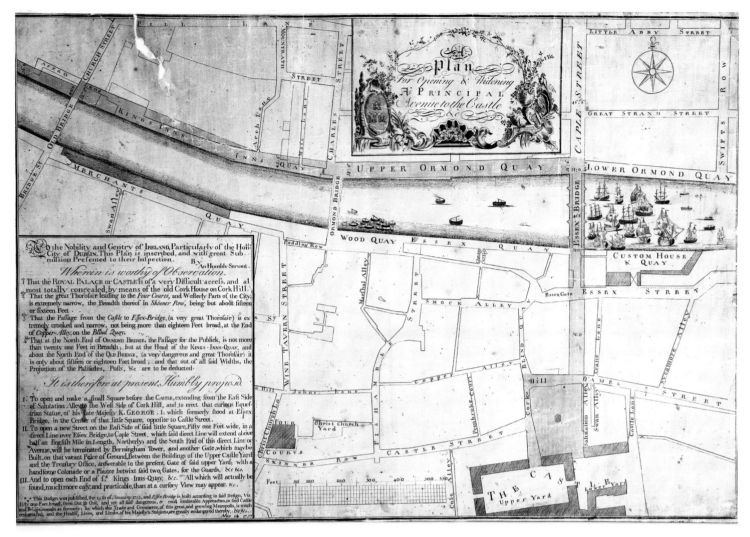

Fig. 3.28 *Plan for Opening & Widening a Principal Avenue to the Castle, 1757. (DCA, WSC 329)*

a ruinous condition. Furthermore, since the lease there was up for renewal, he suggested that moving the Horse Guards to the site adjoining the north-west range would allow, rather appropriately, room for the town major 'and the foot officers and soldiers that maintain guard upon the Castle'.[252]

Nothing of the appearance of the buildings is known other than their outline on maps (Figs 3.30–1) which simply suggests two straightforward rectangular blocks, set at right angles to one another enclosing a sizeable yard in front of the Chief Secretary's block (bordering its basement area) – the stables appearing as a narrow range on the north side and the office projecting onto the castle approach along the east side. While certainly given prominence at the new entrance, it is difficult to ascertain whether these buildings were ever conceived or utilised with the erection of the Main Guard opposite a decade later, to satisfy the idea of an impressive architectural display on the approach up to the Upper Yard. When plans for a new piazza on Cork Hill first began to be considered, the retention of the Horse Guards buildings was

contemplated in at least one scheme, even if in a modified way (Fig. 3.29); otherwise they were to be sacrificed to achieve a more imposing piazza. In the early 1760s they were again to be retained in two proposals (Fig. 3.31), one suggesting a reduced piazza, and another that envisaged the entire Horse Guards complex concealed behind houses that would instead frame the approach by closing the vista from the newly made Parliament Street.[253] Ultimately with the building of the Royal Exchange here after 1769, it required the rebuilding of the east range of offices, set back on a new alignment.[254] This resulted in a wider passage into the castle, though how this was presented, or indeed contrasted with the new guard house (or Main Guard) (Figs 3.32–3) built opposite the approach in 1758 (its architecture clearly intended to bring dignity to the castle) is unknown. Later in the 1770s a scheme (Fig. 3.34) for the Lower Yard made a new Horse Guards building the impressive centrepiece at the point of entry from the east, conceived as part of a grand approach to the castle in a manner that seems to have

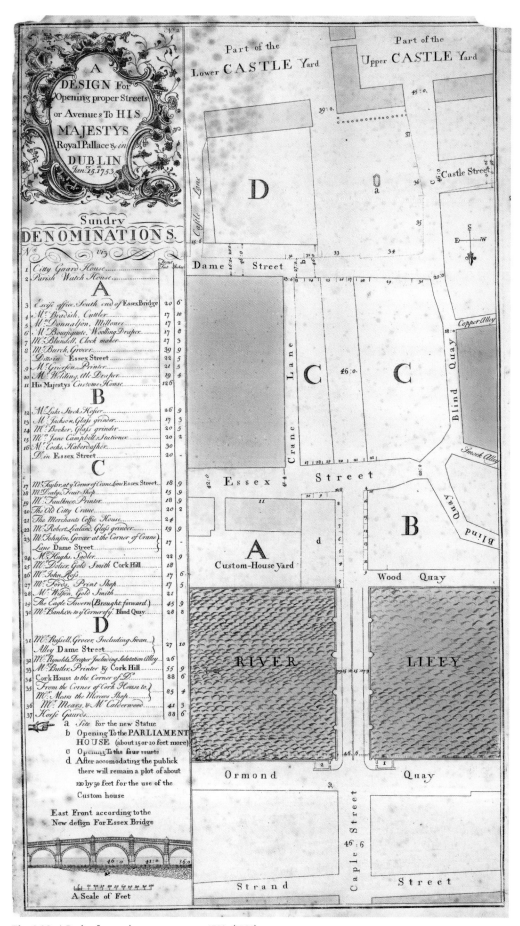

Fig. 3.29 A Design for opening proper streets…1753. (NGI)

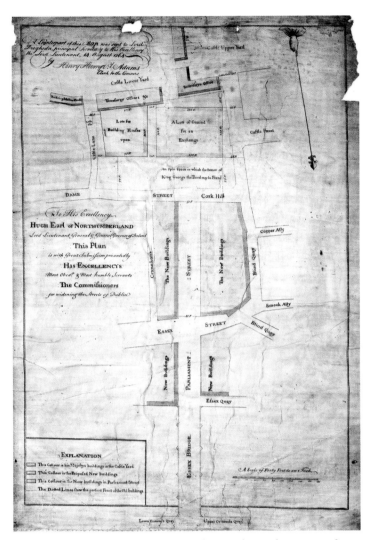

Fig. 3.30 Plan of part of Dublin Castle, showing former 'Horse Guard Yard' adjoining Cork Hill, *c.* 1764. (DCA, WSC 537/1)

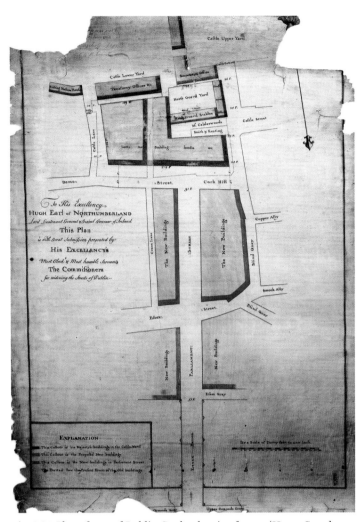

Fig. 3.31 Plan of part of Dublin Castle, showing former 'Horse Guard Yard' adjoining Cork Hill, *c.* 1764. (DCA, WSC 537/2)

been intended to evoke something of the arrangement of its counterpart at Whitehall. Before the end of the century, however, the Horse Guards complex on Cork Hill was eventually swept away to accommodate the extension of the Chief Secretary's offices.

It was Dobbs' successor, Arthur Jones Nevill, who finally addressed the unfinished and deteriorating state apartments in the south range, facilitated in 1745 by the appointment of Lord Chesterfield (Fig. 3.35). Reluctant at first to do anything 'either within or without but what is really necessary in order to make those Apartments habitable', the new Lord Lieutenant found, however, on his arrival in Dublin that 'more than one half of the chief side of the Court… now lyeth in one great ruin' – a description that might have as easily applied to Brooking's depiction of it and therefore as much a reflection of the unfinished works as of its decrepit condition.[255] Essentially encompassing everything from the main entrance to the Bermingham Tower (the great stair, state dining room, the

Battle-Axe Hall, chaplain's apartments and the servants' hall – though the ballroom is not specifically mentioned) it was claimed that the buildings were 'continually propped at considerable expense' and in 'immediate danger of falling to the ground', which even after considerable repairs left much to be desired in their continued use, undermining Chesterfield's efforts to uphold what he called 'the dignity and convenience' of His Majesty's Government.[256] By early 1746, fully ensconced in his role as Lord Lieutenant, Lord Chesterfield now seemed better disposed towards 'useless decorations and Ornaments', writing to the Treasury in London with estimates for taking down and rebuilding the apartments, arguing that 'great sums of money were already being expended to very little purpose to repair and support these buildings'.[257]

As a result of Chesterfield's interest in the work, the south-west range was finally completed in 1747, more or less to the original design, retaining many, by now, old-fashioned features such as the camber-headed windows

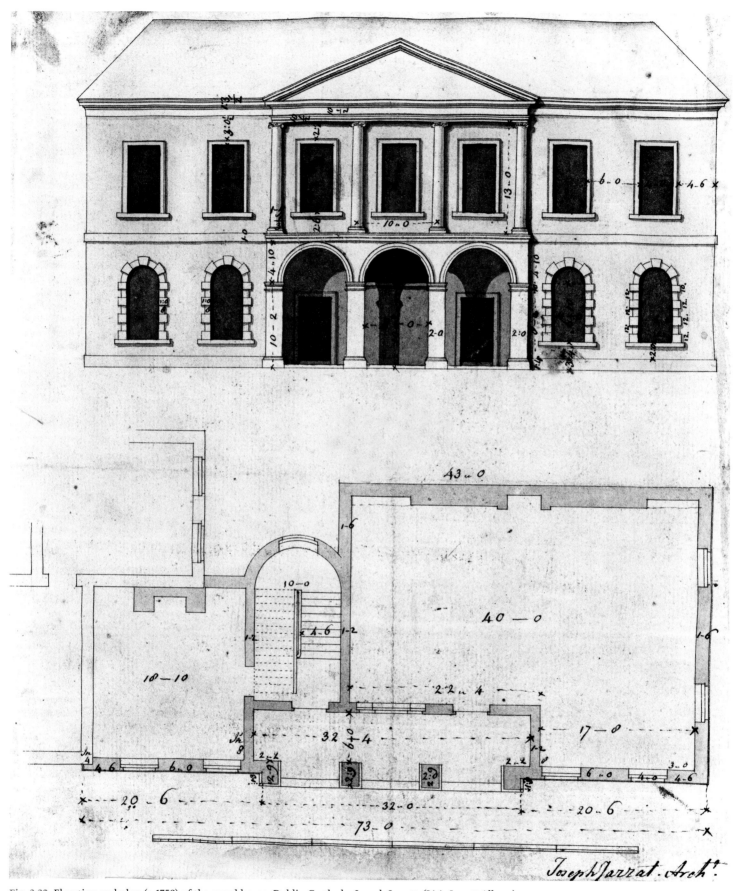

Fig. 3.32 Elevation and plan (*c.* 1758) of the guard house, Dublin Castle, by Joseph Jarratt. (IAA, Jarratt Album)

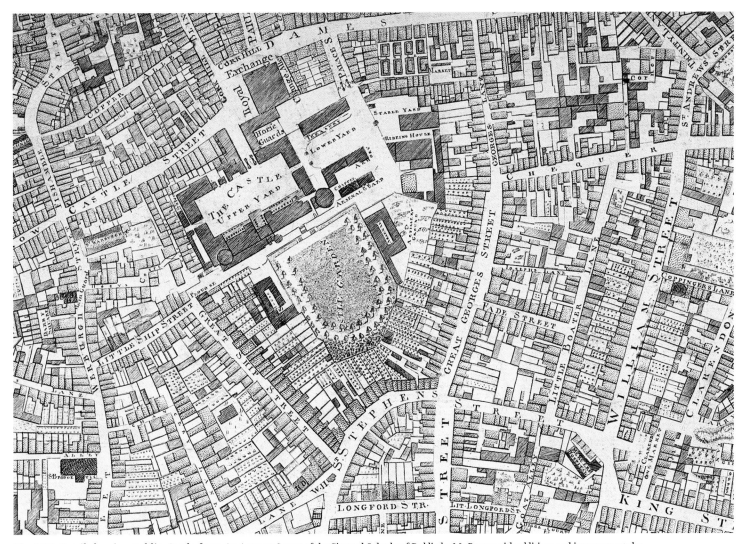

Fig. 3.33 Detail showing Dublin Castle from An Accurate Survey of the City and Suburbs of Dublin by Mr Rocque with additions and improvements by Mr Bernard Scalé to 1773. (NLI)

with their scrolled keystones.[258] Similarly, the works largely upheld the old arrangement of the rooms and followed the established planning protocols found in English palaces. The usual sequence of stairs, great chamber (Yeomen Guard), Presence Chamber, drawing room, state bedchamber and closet (study) was maintained in Dublin (Fig. 3.19) with the arrangement of the Battle-Axe stairs, Battle-Axe Hall, Presence Chamber, Lord Lieutenant's drawing room, lady's drawing room, with the state bedchamber and study set together in adjoining rooms to the rear.[259]

The greater result of this phase, however, was the creation of a more formal, unified sequence of state rooms, evident for example in the new building on the west side where an orderly suite of rooms was created above the colonnade, and in the way that the state dining or supper room was flanked by a drawing room and small dining room without disrupting the hierarchies of the established sequence. The stately formality of the south range as a unified composition

was at last realised with the creation of the new entrance, a rather clean, discrete block in ashlar work, its design effecting in mass, if not in detail, the original seventeenth-century proposal. In replacing the free-standing rusticated portal attributed to works undertaken by Captain John Paine in the 1660s, it provided a more fitting entrance, executed in Portland stone as a novel material against the otherwise prevailing use of red brick.[260] The material suggests a conscious emulation of the Parliament House; certainly its Palladian identity – the use of the orders over two storeys in a manner reminiscent of the Palazzo Chiericati – seems a conscious attempt to generate some idiomatic consonance with Pearce's innovative expression of public architecture and a desire to conform to the most modern taste. Projecting from the centre of the south range, the structure realises at last an idea first proposed in the 1680s, but claims greater authority by introducing for the first time on the castle exterior an overt reference to the orders, chosen as Roman

Doric, with round columns forming an open portico on the ground floor and carrying the projection of the Battle-Axe Hall above. Here, at first-floor level, Ionic pilasters assert the correct classical orthodoxy which becomes complete with the formation of the raking pediment and balustraded parapets (although this observance of the rule would in effect be abandoned with the use of Doric for the Presence Chamber (Fig. 3.36), which was located on the first floor beside the Battle-Axe Hall). The sense of stately decorum was enhanced by the use of the internal colonnade (originally open entirely to the entrance), mitigating the low proportions of the hall, and providing a fitting prelude to the imperial staircase (since rebuilt), an idea which Nevill also seems to have taken from the seventeenth-century plans, though making these a broader and more commanding feature than seems to have been originally envisaged (Figs 3.3, 3.7) by absorbing some of the space previously occupied by the old dining room, which was perhaps a constraint on the original proposals. Ultimately this new arrangement allowed for the creation of the Battle-Axe Hall or guard room

(the present Throne Room, as adopted by the marquess of Buckingham in 1788) as a fitting and courtly antechamber, though later remodelling has made its original appearance unknown (Fig. 3.37).[261] With its relationship to the Presence Chamber, and the private apartments beyond, the creation of this antechamber helped to effect a greater integration with the rooms on the opposite side, including the state drawing room and ballroom, and accepting that these two rooms were of central significance in every sense, they could certainly justify their rich treatments.

Also significant in these works was the remodelling of the ballroom, the present St Patrick's Hall, raised up on the old walls to the level of the piano nobile (Fig. 3.38).[262] It is impossible now to perfectly recreate its original appearance, or decoration, though Mrs Delany some years later referred to it as 'very fine, much better than at St. James's'.[263] Its grandeur will certainly have been improved by the scale and creation of a coved ceiling, for which glass lustres were provided in the same period, though generally, in architectural terms, it seemed to reflect Lord Chesterfield's

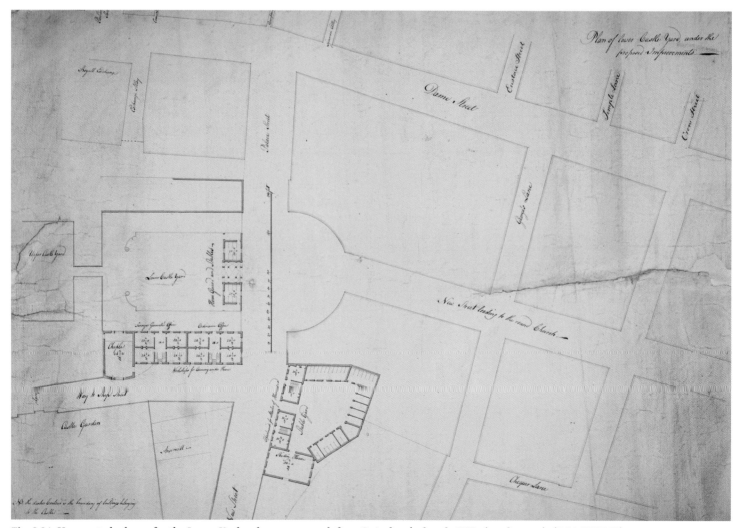

Fig. 3.34 Unexecuted scheme for the Lower Yard and a new approach from St Andrew's church, 1770s (north at top). (DCA, WSC 90)

Fig. 3.35 Portrait of the earl of Chesterfield by Stephen Slaughter 1746. (Courtesy of OPW Dublin Castle)

initial attitude, expressed in 1745, when he demurred from any unnecessary expense towards useless decoration and ornaments at the castle; that much is certainly evident in the room's rather ponderous external south elevation.[264]

On the ground floor, behind the open arcade, the site of the old hall was utilised as a servants' quarters. The back wall of the arcade appears to date from the abandoned work of 1712–16, and to have been later buttressed at basement level to take the superimposed load of the 3ft- (0.9m-) thick brick wall that separates St Patrick's Hall from the supper room (now the Picture Gallery) and the storey above. Apart from the panelling in the Picture Gallery, no significant internal decoration now survives from the 1740s.[265]

After Chesterfield's departure and towards the end of the earl of Harrington's second term as viceroy (March 1750), further monies were issued to Nevill to extend his work in order to repair the Presence Chamber and the adjoining apartments in the east (Robinson–Molyneux) range. Other than the additions proposed in 1698, no major works were recorded to the rooms here since the structure was built, which perhaps accounts for the assessment that 'the Cielings and Floors belonging thereunto are worn out and the Furniture entirely decay'd'.[266] The major element

of these works involved enlarging and remodelling the old 'Attendance' chamber as the Presence Chamber, which was complete by 1751, at the beginning of the duke of Dorset's second term as Lord Lieutenant. The room (Fig. 3.39) was enlarged by dispensing with the old stairs that gave direct access to it, their purpose made obsolete by Nevill's new entrance as part of the works to complete the west range. The new room was given a strong architectural treatment including a fine Doric chimney piece with a carved timber overmantel attributed to the Dublin carver, John Houghton (Fig. 3.40), and engaged Roman Doric columns round the walls, though the effect was curtailed on the window elevation as the location of the openings meant that to correspond with the use of a complete order on the opposite wall, only the capitals could be used here, set on enriched brackets instead of the column shafts. This awkward necessity was in part determined by the use of a full and emphatic Doric entablature supporting a high coved ceiling. The coves were enriched with a flourish of heavy stucco grotesques, including oversized birds and garlands bearing nereid-like figures supporting imperial cartouches (crown and septres); the ceiling was, in contrast, filled with a geometric design, elaborated with foliated decorations, which despite its impressive boldness must have seemed entirely frumpish when compared with the light and fanciful treatment of the ceiling of the Battle-Axe Hall.[267]

An early impression of how the newly completed apartments were put to use was provided by Benjamin Victor, deputy manager of the Smock Alley Theatre, in a letter to Colley Cibber in London (Poet Laureate, actor, and playwright who had collaborated with Sir John Vanbrugh), in which he attributes the design of the ballroom to Chesterfield himself:

I was at the Castle on the Birth-Day, as an Officer of Importance, though with less satisfaction than you enjoy that Hour at St James's Palace…Since I have accidently fallen on this courtly subject, I cannot quit it, in Justice to the present Lord Lieutenant, without informing you, that nothing within the Memory of the oldest Courtier living, ever equalled the Taste and Splendor of the Supper-Room at the Castle on Birth-Night. The Ball was in the new Room design'd by Lord Chesterfield, which is allowed to be very magnificent. After the Dancing was over, the Company retired to an Apartment form'd like a long Gallery, where, as you pass'd slowly through, you stopp'd by the Way at Shops elegantly form'd, where was cold Eating, and all Sorts of Wines and Sweetmeats; and the whole most beautifully disposed by transparent Paintings, through which a Shade was cast like Moonlight. Flutes, and other soft

Fig. 3.36 Interior of the old Presence Chamber, state apartments. (IAA)

Instruments were playing all the while, but like the Candles, unseen. At each End of the long Building were placed Fountains of Lavender Water constantly playing, that diffused a most grateful Odour through this amazing Fairy Scene, which certainly surpass'd every Thing of the Kind in Spencer, as it proved not only a fine Feast for the Imagination, but after the Dream, for our Senses also, by the excellent Substantials at the Sideboards.[268]

A further glimpse of the splendours that could be achieved within the new accommodation is gained in November 1753 when, for the celebration of the king's birthday, the castle was 'decorated and illuminated in the most grand and superb manner', the design emanating from Nevill's office and executed by the artist Joseph Tudor. *Faulkner's*

Dublin Journal described 'the extraordinary, magnificent and elegant decorations of the Supper-room...adorned in imitation of an Egyptian Saloon...at the far end the Temple of Comus...Round the three sides of the Temple ran an arcade of azure pillars, gilt, in imitation of lapis lazuli, and exquisite enchantment'.[269]

If, as seems likely if not certain, the old twin-towered entrance survived up to this time, possibly even continuing in use after the new passage and entrance were created, then the question of how to deal with it and the off-centred position of the new entrance presented a significant challenge to the intention of completing the Upper Yard to a unified plan. There is no way of knowing precisely when the solution was conceived, but its execution was certainly commenced under Nevill, when in February 1750 he had drawn a plan for the 'rebuilding and finishing that part of

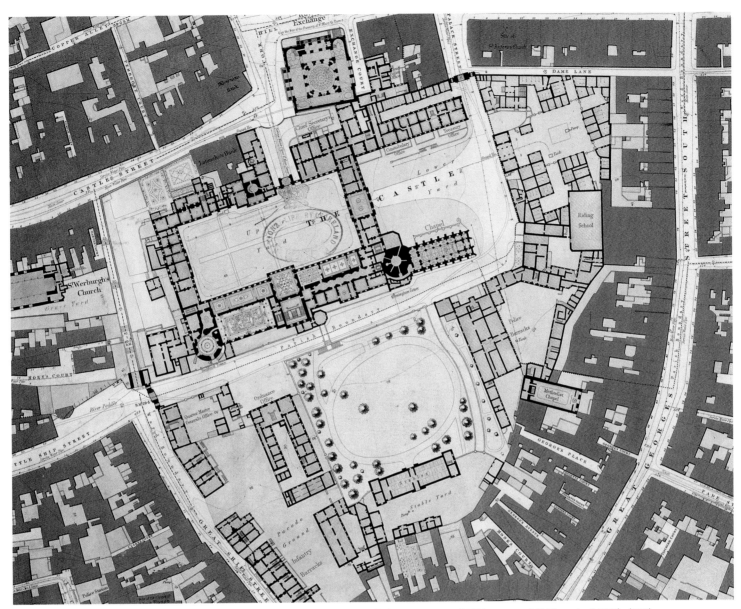

Fig. 3.37 Detail from Ordnance Survey, 'The Castle Sheet', Five feet to one mile (1:1056, surveyed 1838, engraved 1840, revised 1843). (NLI)

the Castle joyning Castle Street', which was presented to the Lord Lieutenant along with an estimate for almost £6,700.[270] The proposals were passed on to the Treasury, explaining further 'the great necessity that there is of rebuilding one half of the square part of our Castle at Dublin', and including a representation about other necessary works concerning the state apartments.[271] In May 1750 it was reported that Nevill was 'pulling down the old buildings in the Castle as fast as he can' which must relate to the surviving old buildings along the north side of the Upper Yard.[272] There is, however, no clear agreement between what was shown in Brooking's map of the castle and the vignette (Figs 1.20, 3.15), where a section of the original, short, north-east range, the medieval gate towers and the western portion of the curtain wall are shown. No firm evidence exists to reveal the extent of survival of any of these up to 1750, or indeed

to show whether any of the older buildings remained inside the curtain wall – where various lodgings existed in 1673 – but, if they still existed, these, with any other surviving elements of the castellated gateway and curtain walls, were among ruinous buildings finally cleared by Nevill.[273]

The construction of the new central building – named for the duke of Bedford, Lord Lieutenant from 1757 – and its flanking gateways, was largely overseen after 1752 by the new Surveyor General Thomas Eyre and his deputy Joseph Jarratt and was not complete until 1761. Whether or not the design can be attributed in its entirety to Nevill, the entire scheme was represented in Joseph Tudor's view of the Upper Yard of 1753 (Fig. 3.41), many years before it was completed, confirming that a contemporary plan and elevation existed and were consulted, though these are not otherwise known and seem not to have survived. However, the main block

Fig. 3.38 Sherwin oil sketch painting of the Knights of St. Patrick in St. Patrick's Hall in 1783. (NGI)

was closely based on Colen Campbell's design for Lord Herbert's house in Whitehall of 1723 (Fig. 3.42) while, more appositely, the cupola derives from one in a design (Fig. 3.43) by Inigo Jones proposed for Whitehall Palace, and known from William Kent's *Designs of Inigo Jones*, published in 1727. These earlier neo-Palladian references help, in part, to explain the Pearcean character sometimes ascribed to the composition of the tower and its flanking gateways, which (unless the theory of a surviving plan has merit) might be taken as evidence for relative stasis in Irish architecture where relatively unambitious architects like Nevill and Eyre were blithely derivative in their approaches, and happy to rely on dependable sources like Campbell and Kent so as to conform to the prevailing (and enduring) tastes for

neo-Palladian architecture, while at the same time using these models to honour and uphold the architectural brio first introduced by their most accomplished predecessor. Ultimately, however, with this design they more effectively (whether consciously or otherwise) demonstrated that Dublin was capable of keeping in step with the Burlingtonian influences in London, building in Dublin a structure that could be seen as being in perfect consonance with (and in proportion to) Whitehall. Used as offices for various clerks, the Bedford Tower (Fig. 3.44) is far more imposing, impressive and handsome than its uses warranted, and thus its role was to provide an authority and dignity to the Upper Yard in a way that compared with the presence and stature then being given to the erection of William Kent's Horse

Guards building at Whitehall, designed from 1745, but only commenced in 1750 two years after the architect's death, and completed in the same years as the castle building.[274] Here in Dublin, however, the real success and interest of the Bedford Tower as a design relates more to its ingenuity in asserting a symmetrical composition for the north range, achieving a fitting edifice directly opposite the state apartments despite the fact that the main entrance into the Upper Yard remained off-centre; the anomaly was overcome by using flanking gateways – the main gateway to the east, balanced by another to the west, a false one, which adjoined the north-west block housing the existing apartments of the Under Secretary.[275] Powerful rusticated archways on a monumental scale with open segmental pediments reflect the scale of the design, which is enhanced by the flanking, pedimented pedestrian doorways set into the side walls, and the overall effect is altogether made more imposing by the statues of *Fortitude* and *Justice* by John Van Nost, the

Younger, which were raised onto the receiving pedestals in 1753 (even though the cupola on the main block would not be completed until the end of the decade).[276]

With so much rebuilding finally achieved, and being planned, in the Upper Yard by 1750 it was inevitable perhaps that improving the formal relationship between the castle and the city would again be attempted in earnest. The challenges – at times insurmountable – that attended the creation of a new entrance to the castle, and the delayed completion of the northern side of the Upper Yard, reflected the realities of the castle's place in the city, a centrality that proved problematic yet vital (as the resolute commitment to the site in the seventeenth century had demonstrated). As rebuilding in the Upper Yard at the castle began exchanging the last prominent vestiges of the old, tattered citadel for a distinguished and well-ordered classical court, its position within the old cityscape needed to be reassessed more urgently perhaps than at any other time in the past.

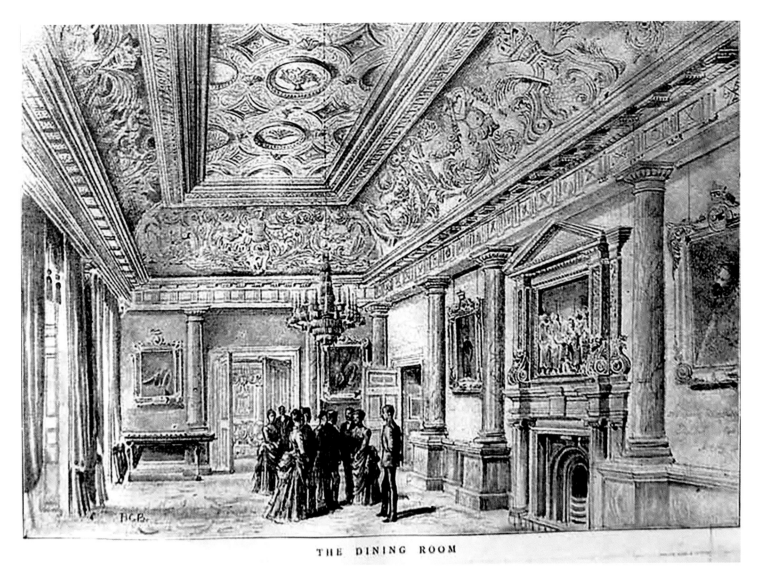

THE DINING ROOM

Fig. 3.39 View of the Presence Chamber. (*The Graphic*, 14 Apr. 1888)

Fig. 3.40 Marcus Aurelius overmantel. (Photograph Davison & Associates; courtesy of OPW Dublin Castle)

Consequently, as the city expanded and its layout began to be reimagined by the improving spirit of a cohort of some of the most powerful political figures in the capital, the idea of restoring the castle's centrality with dignity became more of an unresolved imperative.[277] The very earliest initiative to reflect this involved the opening of the passage between Essex Bridge and the castle, the impetus having been generated by the building of Essex Bridge by George Semple in 1753. This key development culminated in the setting up of the Wide Streets Commissioners in 1757, which, given adequate powers and resources by 1759, became the greatest force in shaping the modern city, achieving results effectively and relatively quickly.[278] The completion of Parliament Street within five years demonstrated the commissioners' desire for the castle to be given a fitting prominence and dignity (making it also a better counterpoint to the Parliament House) in a reordered city, beginning with this new axial relationship to the River Liffey.

With the completion of Essex Bridge, Semple had expectantly drawn up a scheme anonymously, proposing a new street leading up from the bridge to a new square or piazza, opening before the castle (Fig. 3.28). Although this

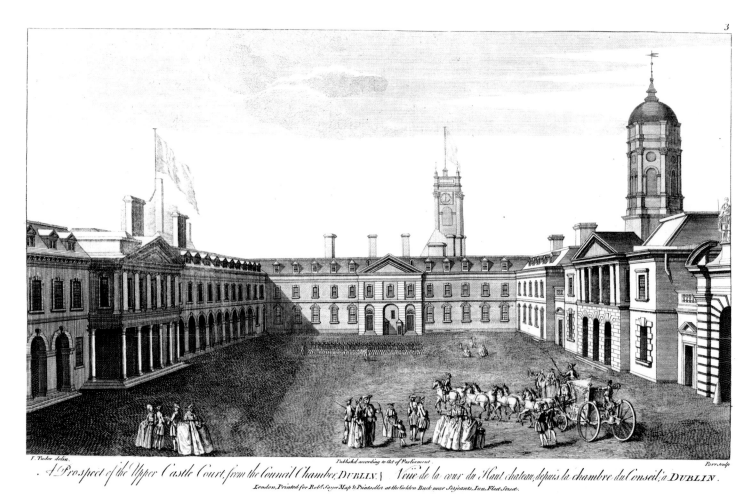

Fig. 3.41 A Prospect of the Upper Castle Court from the Council Chamber by Joseph Tudor 1753. (RIA)

was actually only reviving an existing design 'for opening proper streets or avenues to his majesty's Royal Pallace' – drawn up in 1753 (Figs 3.29, 3.45) and clearly conceived as a natural progression on completion of the new Essex Bridge – it was altogether more grandly conceived so as 'to open and make a small Square before the Castle' as the termination for a new street 'fifty one feet wide'.[279] In providing the basis for the commissioners' earliest project, Semple set his proposal in the context of the perceived inappropriateness of the city's 'great' thoroughfares, noting for example that the major east–west 'thoroughfare' which wound its way from the Parliament House on College Green, past the castle and to the old Four Courts at Christ Church, was excessively narrow, obtaining at Skinner's Row a width of no more than 16ft (4.9m). More significantly, he asserted that the 'Royal Palace' was 'of a very Difficult access' and pointed out the prominent obstacle of 'the old Cork House on Cork Hill' which not only 'almost totally concealed' any view of the castle but stood as a major obstruction on the line of a direct route from the newly built Essex Bridge to the castle. The existing passage from the bridge, along Blind Key, was of course considered utterly inadequate being 'extremely crooked and narrow'.[280]

The castle itself was to be utilised as far as possible so as to visually terminate the new street which was to be formed in a direct line from Capel Street, continued over the new bridge creating an imposing 'avenue…above half an English mile in length' and entering the new square on the eastern side so as to allow the Record Tower (incorrectly named as the Bermingham Tower) to form a visual termination. To address the off-centre position of the castle gate and the proposed new route, a new gateway was suggested 'answerable to the present Gate', to be built on the vacant site between the Chief Secretary's office and the Treasury, formerly occupied by the Powder Tower and in line with the new street. The symmetry was to be reinforced by the creation of a 'handsome Colonade or a Piazze' extending across the Chief Secretary's range between the gates.[281] Although Semple's involvement ended after quarrels with the commissioners and his scheme was rejected, the fundamental objective for a new street and piazza continued to be pursued. In early January 1758 grants were sought in the House of Commons and before the end of the month £7,000 had been committed towards making 'a new way' from Essex Bridge.[282] Although the new Parliament Street opened in 1762, the piazza was never fully realised; while further plans were considered and properties compulsorily acquired, by 1765 the parliament had yielded to the petitions of the city merchants, obliging the commissioners to grant the greater portion of the site to the Guild of Merchants for the proposed Royal Exchange, essentially putting an end to the matter.[283] Maps, including Rocque's (Fig. 3.11), do imply, however, that the open space at least was actually formed

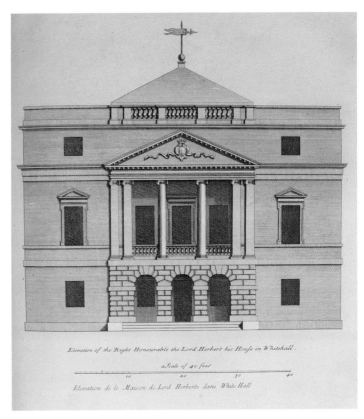

Fig. 3.42 Elevation of Lord Herbert's House, Whitehall, engraved by H. Hulsbery after Colin Campbell, 1725. (Campbell 1715–25)

but once the area for the Royal Exchange was finally agreed, what remained after road widening was then divided into lots and sold off to private developers.[284]

The Wide Streets Commissioners' second major initiative affecting the castle was conceived some years later and involved the realignment of Dame Street between Cork Hill and College Green, proposed by setting back the building line on the southern side.[285] It also envisaged creating a new parallel street to the south, aligned with St Andrew's church (the Round Church), incorporating three new north–south intersections, the westerly one opening as a circus (with a central monument) on a greatly widened Georges Street, from where a new approach veering south-west was aligned with the hexagonal guard house in the Lower Yard of the castle. Significantly, and as if also in response to the failure to create the piazza on Cork Hill, an alternative route (Fig. 3.34), more resolved and detailed and much more ambitious with even greater potential to enhance the approach to the castle, was also mooted. Again, this involved creating a new parallel street, fully aligned with St Andrew's, but terminating instead in a semi-circular space that involved rebuilding much of the Lower Yard with a new symmetrical rigour. Essentially this envisaged extending the Upper Yard into two parallel ranges (using the existing Treasury block and building another opposite to incorporate a new

Fig. 3.43 William Kent, engraved detail of cupola proposed for Whitehall Palace. (Jones 1727)

a proposal put forward by two influential commissioners, Col. William Burton Conyngham and David LaTouche, in 1772.[286] The designers are unknown, and neither scheme – most likely too ambitious and costly anyway – was carried out, thus depriving the castle of an opportunity to more fully partake in the neo-classical revolution in the city, and once again preventing it being properly integrated with its surroundings; likewise, the failure to pursue either scheme missed a unique opportunity to fully exploit the promising 'scenography' of the sloping site of the Lower Yard.[287] This idea of setting the castle more formally on an east–west axis has been rather naively described as like 'a miniature Versailles' whereas in reality the effect suggests greater affinity with ideas likely to have been inspired by the architecture and street planning of London, in particular the treatment of the Horse Guards in Whitehall (see Chapter 3.7).[288] Following these abortive schemes, the widening of Dame Street was initiated in 1777 when £5,000 was granted for the purposes, with efforts to be concentrated in the vicinity of the castle. Work began in 1782, by which time the commissioners were given greater scope 'to make or widen other ways thro' said city, or to widen the several roads to it within 2 miles to not less than 100 feet'.[289] Thereafter, much of the later work of the commissioners was concentrated to the east of the castle, their greatest achievement the creation of a major new north–south axis with the bridging of the Liffey at Sackville Street and the laying out of new streets in the vicinity.

Contemporary with the castle schemes, Bernard Scalé's 1773 revision of Rocque's map (Fig. 3.33) shows the degree to which the work of the Wide Streets Commissioners was effecting change in how the castle was approached, though it also makes clear how the entrance to the Upper Yard remained rather unsatisfactory. This was partly because of the way the castle itself had continued to evolve: as well as revealing the new Royal Exchange for the first time (which in architectural terms now entirely upstaged the castle) and the widened Cork Hill, the map shows the new Main Guard building and the deep passage it formed by the rebuilding of the short-lived Horse Guards buildings opposite.[290] Scalé also shows the empty space behind the Treasury, once considered for the Royal Exchange but where the sites of some of the demolished buildings had been purchased by the Commissioners of the Barracks.[291] By 1801, and presumably partly in compensation for the loss of the Horse Guards yard, a narrow and disparate range of single-storey buildings, principally associated with the stables of the Cavalry Guard, had been built here, at the rear of the Treasury, separated by a passage known as 'the Cavalry Picket Yard'.[292] With the Horse Guards yard removed, and the extension of the Chief Secretary's block onto part of the site, the offices of the 'Head Police Office' (now demolished) were built on the remainder of the site (Figs 3.46–7).

chapel set at right angles to the existing one – shown with a shallow, bowed end projected to the south). This would have resulted in an extended symmetrical entrance front, centred on a new Horse Guards block in which the entrance was located. Although clearly these are related schemes, neither are dated but may directly concern such

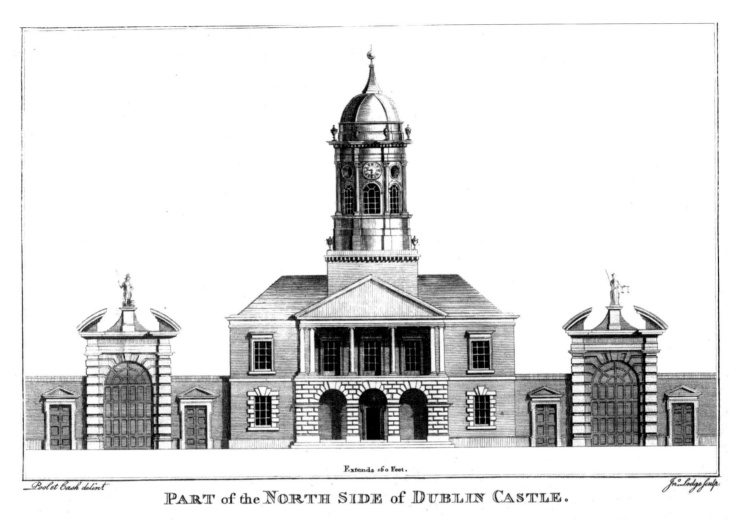

Extends 160 Feet.

Pool et Cash delint   _Jno Lodge sculp_

PART of the NORTH SIDE of DUBLIN CASTLE.

Published according to Act of Parliament March 1st 1779.

Fig. 3.44 _Part of the North Side of Dublin Castle_, from Pool and Cash 1780. (Courtesy of Andrew Bonar Law)

Meanwhile, within the Upper Yard in the late 1750s attention was turned to the earlier south-east range which Eyre and Jarratt doubled in size in order to enlarge the private apartments of the Lord Lieutenant, building a new front to the south overlooking the garden, with a formal classical façade composed of granite and Portland stone, with a pedimented frontispiece created for the slightly projecting central bays (Fig. 3.48). The new building was wedded to the old by the opening of a ceremonial (originally top-lit) state corridor running along the spine of the building (Figs 3.49, 3.50), intended almost certainly, with its emboldened, by now somewhat old-fashioned Palladian design inspired by Pearce's Parliament House corridor, to dignify the route to the Council Chamber though, given its proximity to the private apartments, it could never have been either entirely appropriate or practical.[293]

For the first time in the castle's history rare insight into the processes of building can be traced through Eyre's correspondence, which reveals some of the 'archaeological'

difficulties affecting its initial progress. In August 1758 the Surveyor General wrote to Richard Digby, Lord Bedford's secretary, explaining about 'the Difficultys and Obstructions we met in clearing the Foundations; wich was attended with much labour, perplexity and expence from the looseness of the ground, and the great number of old sewers, and walls that we found buried in the terrass, runing in all directions, some across, other parallel to, and others in the line of our foundations, and which must all necessarily be taken up and removed in order to come at a foundation that could be depended on'.[294] This required sinking 'from ten to twelve feet under the surface' and once achieved the building was expected to rise quickly so that from a height of 'eight feet above ground' it was intended to have it raised to the first storey within a week. There had been good progress by the end of November – the roof on and the plumbers at work to cover it, most of 'the floors, doors, windows and wainscot work…for the most part prepared' along with Eyre's promise to 'omit nothing in my power to have the apartments

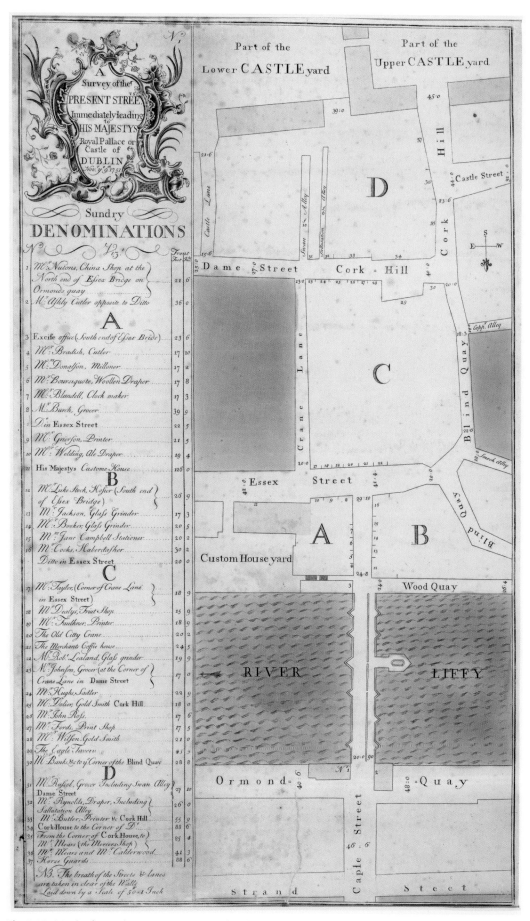

Fig. 3.45 A Design for opening proper streets…1751. (NGI)

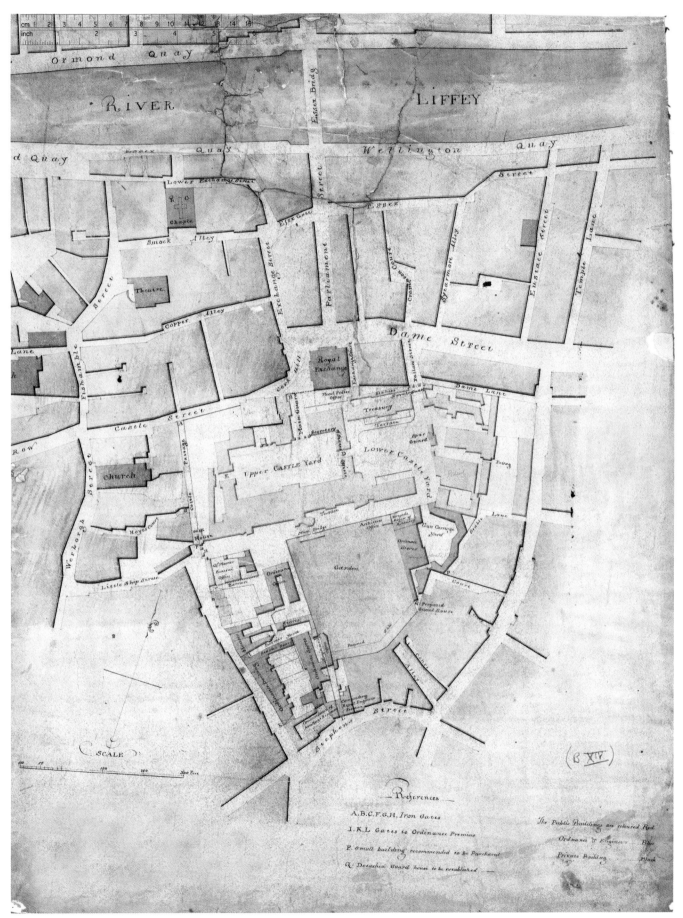

Fig. 3.46 Map of Dublin Castle site *c.* 1810–20. (OPWT, E000480 U16-1)

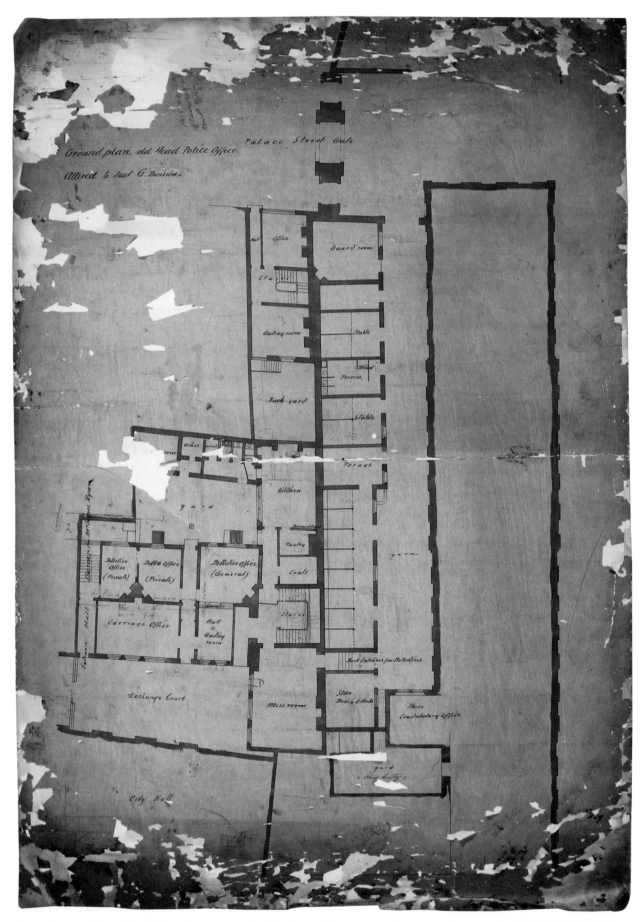

Fig. 3.47 Ground Plan old Head Police Office altered to suit G Division (mid-late nineteenth century) (east at top). (OPWT, E000505 U16-7)

Fig. 3.48 Elevation of new garden front to state apartments by Joseph Jarratt (late 1750s). (IAA, Jarratt Album)

thoroughly air'd and season'd against my Lord Lieutenant's arrival…'. While 'constant fires' were maintained 'both day & night' in all but the attic rooms, to assist the drying out, the carpenter's work and decoration was scheduled for completion the following March; by early June the rooms were 'so near being finisht that they will be ready to receive the furniture' once the 'Lord Lieutenant and the Dutchess' had made their decision about how they wished their bed chamber and dressing rooms decorated, 'whether with silk, or paper or with any other covering'.[295] Further impressions of how the decoration of these apartments was decided, and how they might have been presented (Fig. 3.51) is revealed when Eyre asks if 'the Dutchess chuses to have any of her rooms hung with paper I request to know whether flock paper or a Chintz pattern would be most agreeable: The Colour must suit with that of the curtains; and in regard to Lady Caroline's apartments I beg to be informed whether they are to be hung with any thing but paper'.[296] A decade after they were completed, the apartments were visited by the intrepid preacher John Wesley who, while admiring Bedford's 'noble addition to the lodgings, which are now both grand and convenient' found that 'the furniture suprised me not a little; is by no means equal to the building. In England many gentlemen of 500 a year would be utterly ashamed of it'.[297]

Other works by Eyre at the castle had included, in 1753, the demolition and rebuilding of the 'Round, Square & Water Closets' at the junction of the Robinson–Molyneux range and Nevill's 'main staircase'. An octagonal library took their place (Fig. 3.18) and a plan and elevation showing such a simple octagonal tower survives.[298] In 1756, Eyre built in the Lower Yard a new gateway from Palace Street, and a house 'to serve as an office and apartment for himself and successor's in Employment'; a year later he was granted £405 to build a 'laboratory' for the ordnance in the Lower Yard, located 'between the Lower Arsenal Gate and the Garden' belonging to the Provost Marshall. Although built, it was apparently destroyed by an explosion in 1764.[299] Much more prominent, though relatively straightforward, was the erection of a new guard house, for which he was granted £2,495 in 1758.[300] Drawings for it (Fig. 3.32), signed by Joseph Jarratt, correspond closely to the red brick structure as built.[301] It stands as a northerly extension to the Bedford Tower, expressing a more simplified Palladian form, complete with a pedimented Ionic frontispiece to complement the tower. This represents the main elevation, extending along the western side of the eastern passage into the castle, across from the 1740s Horse Guards offices that formerly stood opposite in a separate building (but whose appearance is unknown).[302]

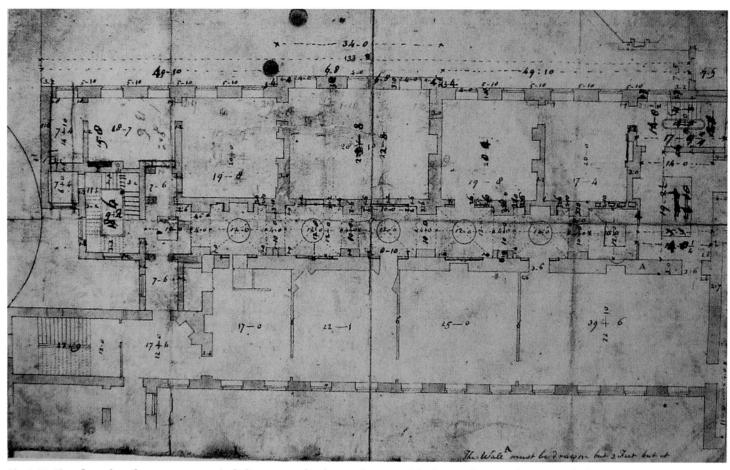

Fig. 3.49 First-floor plan of state apartments including new garden front and state corridor by Joseph Jarratt (south at top). (IAA, Jarratt Album)

From then on, the history of the Upper Yard in the eighteenth century is largely one of repair and minor alteration. The roof of the ballroom, for example, required complete replacement in 1769 while periods of disuse were having an impact on the conditions of the interior, as in 1775, when during the queen's birthday ball, it was found 'that the rooms were so cold & damp by disuse or so long without fire and other warming things in them, that the ladies were afraid to venture themselves in such bleak enclosures'.[303] It seems then that only limited opportunities became available to present the architectural and decorative advances of the neo-classical age.[304] Most substantially, the Bermingham Tower was taken down and rebuilt in 1775, the erection of a lighter structure facilitating the creation of a handsome Gothic interior; the forms and decoration of both the supper room and an adjoining antechamber (Wedgwood Room) are a reflection perhaps of the architectural discernment of the then Lord Lieutenant, Lord Harcourt.

Having remained the most formidable medieval component of the complex, the Bermingham Tower was most likely the first part of the original castle constructed in response to King John's mandate of 1204 (Fig. 3.16). The

structure was then subsumed into the much larger walled enclosure built between 1213 and the late 1220s. Set to the east on the south-east corner of the castle, a square tower had been built adjoining it to the west to provide flanking cover for the west curtain wall. The plan of one floor of the medieval tower is given in the castle survey of 1767 (Fig. 3.52), indicating walls some 10 ½ ft (3.2m) in thickness with an external diameter of 49ft (15m) and an internal one of 28ft (8.6m). Service buildings are shown running westwards from the tower and accessed through it. Steps in the entrances to the tower indicate that its floor levels did not coincide with those of the eighteenth-century south-west ranges, though it has been argued that the tower as depicted on Brooking's map of 1728 had not necessarily been abandoned and derelict, but may in fact have been included in the building campaign that was suspended in 1716.[305] Instead, given its survival, what Brooking appears to have captured was the removal of the upper storey of the tower, perhaps to reduce its excessive dominance over the Upper Castle Yard and to try and integrate it more successfully, ensuring it did not disrupt the orderly approach being adopted in the new ranges.

The tower, or some part of it, had served as a record store since the lord deputyship of Henry Sidney, and an official return of 1723 (by Arthur Hill, keeper of the records) described the records as stored in presses all round the office (Fig. 3.53).[306] The lower portions of the structure had, in part, continued to serve the kitchens (a use that is documented as early as 1585 and confirmed by its description as the Kitchen Tower in 1673).[307] It was clearly a hazardous arrangement: in 1758 a fire in the tower destroyed five out of the ten presses in which records were stored but fortunately the keeper had removed documents from two of these to preserve them from rain which came in through the roof, suggesting that perhaps rehabilitation of the ruined structure shown by Brooking was not as thorough as it might, or indeed should, have been.[308]

After Brooking, three views depict the Bermingham Tower in the middle decades of the eighteenth century: a 1751 sketch view by James Grogan known from copy by Sir William Betham, Joseph Tudor's engraved view (1753), and an anonymous painting of the Lower Yard preserved in the collection of the Royal Society of Antiquaries of Ireland (c. 1767–75 – the date of demolition, which provides a reliable *terminus ante quem*) (Figs 3.16, 3.41, 3.54). Both Betham and the anonymous artist depict battlements on the reduced height tower, the latter more explicitly depicting stepped battlements in the late-medieval Irish manner. This suggests an early example of Gothic Revivalism or perhaps an example of Survivalism, with a later medieval stepped battlement suggesting that in lowering and repairing the tower in the 1720s the architect elaborated the tower parapet by forming a late-medieval detail – either introducing it for the first time or repeating a detail that had previously existed.[309]

With the superstructure removed in 1775, the tower was rebuilt with thinner walls, essentially halved and consequently gaining some 10ft (3m) so as to achieve rooms of 36ft (11m) diameter over the retained medieval base. The structure now rises in three stages over the medieval base whose stonework, with its pronounced batter, remains exposed. Above it, the ground floor is now partly in an unrendered state (with the exception of some rather crude, and inexplicable twentieth-century cement-render detailing) with five tall lancets together bringing generous light into the south wall of the enlarged state kitchen within. A deep stringcourse runs immediately over the window heads, serving as a plinth to the main floor above, and distinguished as such by being given three wide and tall lancets, generous windows filled with nine-over-nine sashes with Y-traceried tympana under hood moulds. In contrast, the three upper-floor windows are small and plain segmental-headed openings. With the walls of these upper stages coated in late twentieth-century cement render with

Fig. 3.50 Section and detail of soffit of new state corridor by Joseph Jarratt. (IAA, Jarratt Album)

a thin dressed stone cap to the parapet, the entire effect now is that of a rather flat, basic solid. Dissolving into the unprepossessing elevation of St Patrick's Hall, the tower has lost every sense of its former medieval prominence, yielding to Francis Johnston's masterful treatment of the Record Tower, and it is only with the windows of the supper room that there is any lingering hint of its late eighteenth-century sophistication.

Inside, the large circular Gothic room was appropriately (given its accessible location directly above the kitchen) conceived as a supper room. The walls are handsomely divided by the three tall lancet windows on the south side and corresponding blind arches opposite – these framing doorcases; the repetition of the effect is enhanced by mirrored and switch-line traceried tympana reflecting the natural light. A carved marble fireplace is set between the arches on the west side, with another opposite, both decorated with traceried Gothic panels, echoing those of the doors. The flat ceiling expresses a delicate radial design of Perpendicular tracery, corresponding perfectly with the

Fig. 3.51 'Private study of the Lord Lieutenant' (The Graphic, 18 April 1888)

restrained approach to decoration typical of the neo-classical period, with outer diamond panels enclosing quatrefoils between four larger polygonal panels filled with rosettes, and supported by a cornice formed with a continuous series of cusped pointed arches.

Although the architect for the rebuilding has not been identified in documentary evidence to date, its execution during the viceroyalty of Lord Harcourt means Thomas Cooley, appointed Clerk and Inspector of Civil Buildings in Dublin in 1774, is a strong possibility, the design easily conforming stylistically with his work, though perhaps with some input from his superior, Christopher Myers.[310] As part of the tower rebuilding, a new antechamber (used as a billiard room in the nineteenth century and known since 1952 as the Wedgwood Room) was formed to the north, essentially by extending the room that in 1767 had served

as a pantry for the Board of Green Cloth, and remodelled as an oval space with wide corner niches flanking the doorways, and decorated in an elegant neo-classical style with shallow fan reliefs.[311] The provision of a new supper room reflects certain changes in room use across the state apartments after 1767, perhaps directly in consequence of these additions – therefore the sequence of drawing room, state dining room and small dining room in the south-west range (Figs 3.18–9, 3.24) was altered to ante room, dining room and card room. Meanwhile, in the south-east range the changes, some attributable to the eager pomposity of the marquess of Buckingham in 1788, including the relocation of the Presence Chamber to a redecorated Battle-Axe Hall (Fig. 3.55), reflected a greater consolidation of the private rooms of the Lord and Lady Lieutenant.[312]

Despite criticisms of the castle in the 1770s as 'not very elegant' and reference to the 'bleak inclosures' of a 'mill-dewed Palace', the resulting spatial complexity introduced by these new rooms represents rather refined improvements, their subtlety and elegance now underappreciated against Buckingham's more gilded extravagances of a decade later.[313] The quality of the neo-classical decoration introduced in the 1770s naturally affirms an attribution to Thomas Cooley, who of course enjoyed the official capacity to undertake the work; however, given the distinctly Wyattesque quality of the decoration of the Wedgwood Room, there may be an argument for Thomas Penrose as architect, having acted as a representative for Wyatt's Irish clients, though there is no evidence for his employment on the castle before his succession to Cooley.[314] Regardless of authorship, these rooms reflect the marked advance in architectural tastes that otherwise found limited expression anywhere else in the castle buildings; stylistic progress failed to show even in Buckingham's remodelled Battle-Axe Hall and ballroom, so that as the century closed the castle gained nothing that could compare with the architecture of Cooley's Royal Exchange,

Sir William Chambers' works for Lord Charlemont, or at Trinity College; indeed not until after the arrival of James Gandon would the architecture of government be placed to the fore in the display of neo-classical taste.

In 1783 the ballroom was renamed St Patrick's Hall in honour of the newly instituted Knights of St Patrick (Fig. 3.38), founded during the marquess of Buckingham's first term as Lord Lieutenant (then Earl Temple) in 1782.[315] In the last works to be carried out on the interior of the castle in the period, he certainly aggrandised the room commensurate with his pompous vanity. Returning as Lord Lieutenant in 1787 and elevated to the marquessate, he employed the Italian artist Vincenzo Waldré, whom he brought from his seat at Stowe, to ornament the three ceiling panels with painted canvasses, which had smaller grisaille panels to the coves (since removed) and it seems (based on Penrose's 1789 plan) to add a giant order of columns and pilasters.[316] The effect was a greatly embellished hall, the combination of its new grandeur and scale upstaging every other state room, in what seems to us now a fulfilment of Buckingham's declaration to his wife that the magnificence of his entertainments

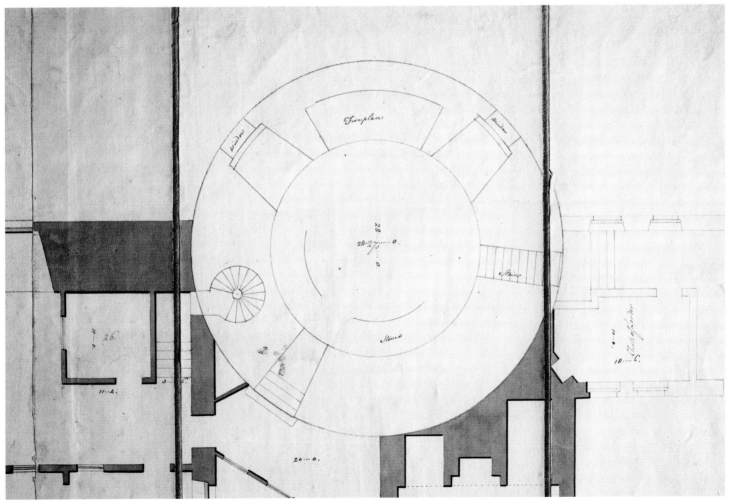

Fig. 3.52 Detail from Euclid Alfray's ground-floor plan, showing plan of Bermingham Tower 1767. (NAI, OPW 5HC/1/61)

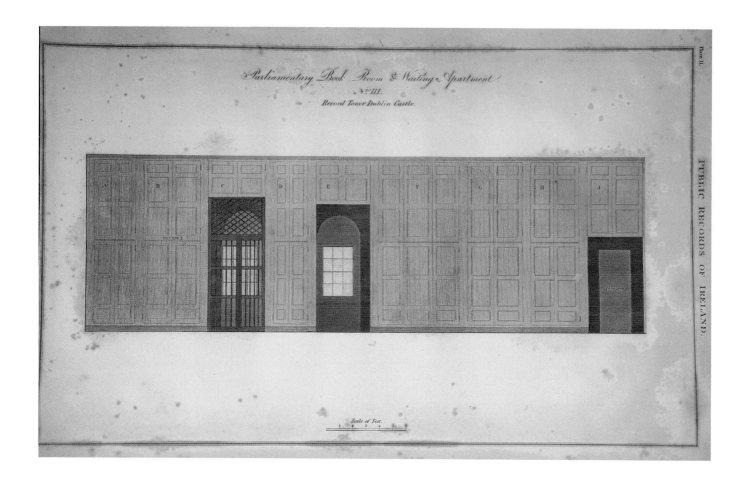

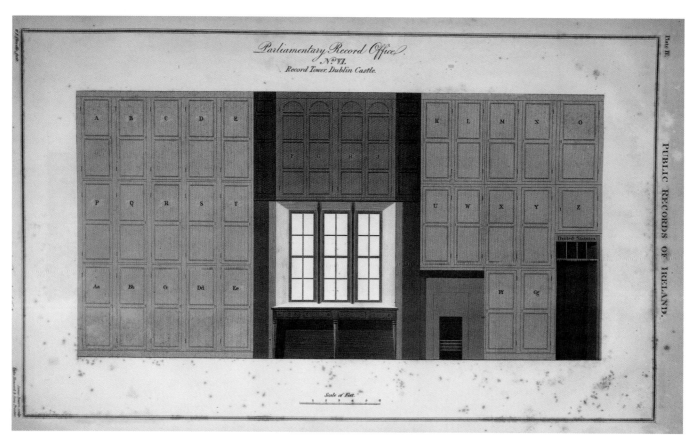

Fig. 3.53 Plates of Record Room from Supplement to 8th Report RCPRI, 1816–20.

Fig. 3.54 Anonymous view of Lower Yard showing the Bermingham Tower, the garden front of the state apartments, the Wardrobe Tower (later called Record Tower) and the seventeenth-century chapel, post 1760 and ante 1775. (© Royal Society of Antiquaries of Ireland)

would be beyond everything ever seen in Ireland, and part of the intention expressed in 1788 to make the castle 'the seat of hospitality and mirth, the rendezvous and meridian of the bon ton'.[317] Some sense of the achievements of these intentions is gained in the description of the room from this period:

> The decorations of St Patrick's Hall on Monday night at the Castle were extremely splendid. A table extended the whole length of the Hall and over an arcade of considerable height, supported by transparent pedestals elevated on the best fancied scroll-work, appeared a regal Coronet; on either side illuminated suns were superadded, which, with stars

that accompanied them, seemed to float in the air. The stars had the words 'Vive le Roy', Pater Patriae", &c. in golden characters. At both ends of the Hall, in the centre of each gallery, were capitally executed transparencies. Besides the great banqueting table in the centre, two elevated ones ran parallel on upper seats. The whole formed a splendid coup d'oeil, much to Mr Waldrea's taste and contrivance.[318]

Although the ceiling was further remodelled in the nineteenth century, Waldré's heroic canvasses still remain (Fig. 3.56); in the centre, *The beneficence of George III attended by Liberty and Justice*, at the west end, *St Patrick lighting the Paschal fire and east, the Submission of the Irish Chiefs to Henry*

II.[319] The room's significance was further enhanced by the introduction of an imposing canopy of state, gilded with draperies, set at the west end, which survived until 1922 (Fig. 3.57).

Besides the works associated with the Bermingham Tower, an important initiative of the 1770s, completed only in the 1820s, involved the decision to replace the old-fashioned dormered attics (Fig. 3.58) with a solid attic storey, beginning on the east range and extending into the Chief Secretary's offices in the north range (Fig. 3.59).[320] However, before this could be advanced to the rest of the ranges, major structural repairs on the east range of the Upper Yard were required in the early 1790s, work that appears to have been undertaken by the builder George Darley, as part of the substantial enlargement of the Chief Secretary's accommodation.[321] It is unclear whether this rebuilding and extension was initiated because of the poor structural condition of the building, or if the condition and any associated problems were only revealed during the course of the works, as Darley's later reports seem to suggest. The fact that Burgh's buildings at this location previously needed propping and rebuilding in 1742, so soon after completion, reinforces the impression that persistent subsidence problems on the east side were due to the existence of the moat.[322] This was certainly the impression of the antiquarian, Austin Cooper, who had witnessed the demolition of the northern half of the block which had cracked some years earlier owing, he thought, to inadequate filling in the castle ditch.[323]

Work on the rebuilding here had commenced by the beginning of September 1793, when it was reported in the *Dublin Evening Post* that the 'east wing of the terrace front of Dublin castle is taken down to its base', with reference to the fact that 'a better foundation for the new masonry is effecting by the means of a number of beams or piles pointed with iron, which are to be driven into the ground to a considerable depth by Vanlue's celebrated pile engine, one of which, with its apparatus, being constructed there for that purpose'.[324] This refers to the watchmaker James

Fig. 3.55 View of 1780s Presence Chamber from *Walker's Hibernian Magazine*, 14 Jan. 1795. (NLI)

Fig. 3.56a, b Ceiling canvases at either end of St. Patrick's Hall. (NMS)

Fig. 3.56c Central ceiling canvas in St. Patrick's Hall. (NMS)

Valoué, who in 1737 designed a horse-powered pile driver used in the construction of Westminster Bridge, and for which he received the Copley medal in 1738 from the Royal Society.[325] However, it does seem that for the time being only partial rebuilding was required here, the newspaper report going on to say that 'it was at first, as we are told, in contemplation to take down the entire front; but the stability of the remaining part being now ascertained, that part only which is now taken down next the garden will be rebuilt'.[326]

Problems soon emerged with Darley's extension of the north range, the preparatory work failing to find a suitable surface even after sinking the foundations to a depth of 36ft (11m), which necessitated a solution that seems rather different to Valoué's system, using instead of piles, a series of granite blocks bolted to timber beams.[327] Darley subsequently found that the 'west front and other parts of the old building' would now need to be demolished, and in December 1797 he was given sanction to 'Excavate the Basement Story of said Building and build a Basement Story'. Issues again arose

Fig. 3.57 Early twentieth-century photograph of thrones in St Patrick's Hall. (NLI Lawrence Collection)

over the foundations, but sufficient progress was made to allow the roof to be finished by November the following year. However, in June 1799 Darley was advising that 'the Front flank and Staircase walls' needed to be rebuilt, the staircase walls having collapsed, being only a mere nine inches (22.7cm) in thickness (the length of a brick). As part of the rebuilding of these, Darley was ordered to take down 'the Chimneys which were built on the front cross walls two Stories high' and rebuild them 'in the middle Wall'.[328]

In dealing with the problems of the east range in the early 1790s, it had also been reported that 'the old black tower to the westward of the chappel is to be demolished as a useless fabric that gives a disgraceful gloominess to the Viceregal residence, little according with the style and elegance of the other parts'.[329] It was, however, a more stable dependable structure than those now placed around it and deserved its reprieve. No other insight into the tower is offered during the eighteenth century. On Alfray's 1767 plan it appears as a faint outline, while in 1789 only an upper stage room is shown, labelled 'Wardrobe Keeper' and lit by two windows – one due east and the other due south (Fig. 3.82). To the north-west, a doorway to the state apartments is suggested, though no connection is obvious. While the 1793 comments reveal less about the condition of this surviving tower and more about contemporary attitudes towards the castle's medieval past, the structure was quite successfully retained. It is noteworthy that in the early years of the next century the approach of the architect Francis Johnston in keeping it was to enhance it, mindful perhaps of the advantage that retention of an authentic and prominent antiquated component might contribute to the authority of the castle and to the validity of his own designs for the new Chapel Royal.

GREAT COURT YARD, DUBLIN CASTLE.

Fig. 3.58 View of Upper Yard 1792, from James Malton, *A picturesque and descriptive view of the city of Dublin...* . (NLI)

Chapter 3.7
The Lower Castle Yard 1700–1800

As well as facilitating the care of horses for the household and cavalry, and where the 'rules of the best horsemanship, and of martiall skill' could be seen and enjoyed, the Lower Castle Yard also served as a parade ground, where in 1697 'two companies of foot parade every morning, one of which mounts the town guard and the other that of the Castle'.[330] Over the course of the eighteenth century the Lower Yard seems to have been gradually more formally organised to support the ceremonial functions of the viceregal court as, for example, when 'On Toasting the King's, the Queen's and the Royal Family's Health, the Lord Lieutenant's and Prosperity to Ireland, the great Guns fire, which is seconded by a volley from the Foot Guards, drawn up to that purpose in the lower Yard of the Castle…'.[331] With the destruction of the Council Chamber on Essex Street by fire in 1711 affording an opportunity to reconsider rebuilding plans within the castle complex, the building of the armoury and the Treasury between 1712 and 1715, set together as opposing ranges, offers the impression, on plan at least, that the same formal approach guiding the developments in the Upper Yard, was being adopted here; even if it never came fully to fruition, with expediencies inclined to get in the way, the idea seems to have remained an aspiration for the rest of the century, and even into the next.

With the building of the Treasury effecting the loss of Wentworth's 'Grand Stables', the main stable yard was thereafter largely contained within the east side of the Lower Yard, inside the castle gate. Shown on both Rocque's and Brooking's maps (Figs 3.11, 3.15), it extended along much of the eastern boundary and was entirely enclosed, separated from the Lower Yard by a screen wall with two entrances each side of a polygonal guard house. Among the earliest works following Thomas Burgh's appointment to the role of Surveyor General in 1700 was erection of a riding house here in 1705.[332] The following year a payment of £25 (on a

quarterly basis) was made to 'Lieut. Noah Regnaut Mas[te]r of the Rideing House', suggesting that the building was by then ready for use.[333] This building type, which in its simplest terms can be defined as 'a covered, barn-like structure', is considered an English innovation associated with the evolving practice of horsemanship.[334] In this context it is significant that the riding house at Dublin Castle was one of only a few built anywhere in the British Isles between 1660 and 1740.[335] It is not known whether in building the castle riding house Burgh had replaced an older building, although Ware's description of the stable yard in 1673, 'where you may take delight in seeing the great horse ridden and managed by the rules of the best horsemanship, and of martiall skill…' certainly implies there was some form of equitation school already established here.[336] Of course, demonstrations of horsemanship may well have always taken place without any purpose-built building, simply organised in the open air rather as in the open ménages used in the French tradition of haute école.[337]

Whereas the 2nd duke of Ormond's promotion of the riding house in this period obviously accorded with interest in the tradition of haute école – essentially the practice of horsemanship as a 'courtly art' – the use of riding schools did eventually become essential for cavalry training, as the obedience and agility of horses were vital to success on the battlefield, explaining perhaps why such a structure remained at the castle into the nineteenth century.[338] The 1705 riding house in the Lower Yard is clearly evident on Brooking's survey (Fig. 3.15), having only first been identified on Rocque's later 1756 survey (Fig. 3.11), represented as a substantial structure that dominates at the south end of the stable yard, implying it conformed perfectly with the usual straightforward typology.[339] The building required unspecified repairs in 1749, perhaps of a routine nature, and essentially it seems that Burgh's core structure survived

197

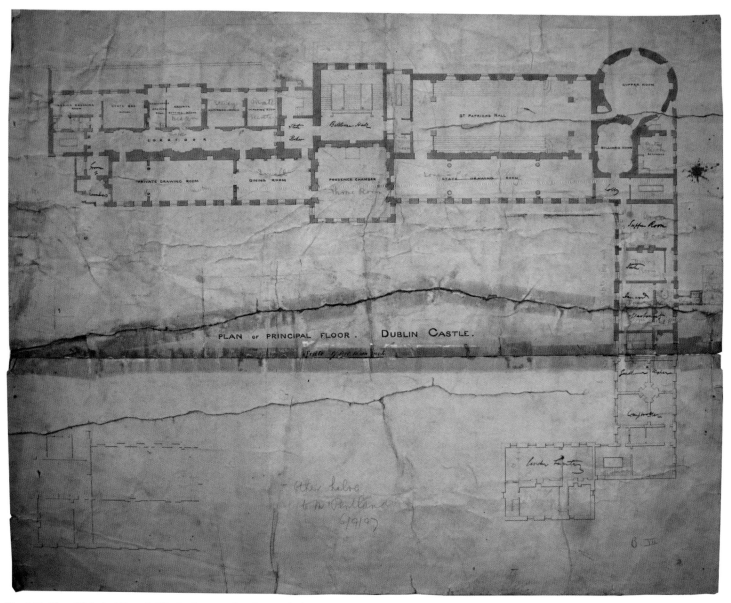

Fig. 3.59 *Plan of Principal Floor, Dublin Castle c. 1821 (south at top). (OPWT, E000505 U16-7)*

largely intact into the nineteenth century.[340] While little understanding of its architectural design may be gleaned from the various eighteenth-century surveys, it is usual for the design and decoration of riding houses to be determined strictly by their function, and so typically they comprised 'a rectangular building about 40ft wide and about three times as long, with plenty of indirect light, easy access and a viewing gallery'.[341] Most eighteenth-century riding houses conformed to these characteristics and because of their size and use, the buildings were architecturally unambitious, the only architectural emphasis usually provided by the windows which were often lunettes, set high to avoid direct light and to ensure the horses were not dazzled by sunlight.

A survey of the Lower Yard in 1769 by Thomas Reading, known from a copy of 1804 (Fig. 3.60), offers a little more detail about the building and its setting.[342] It shows the

entrance to the riding house on the north-west corner, and adjoining the building on the south side is a range of stables and a small square yard. An irregular, enclosed yard is represented against the west gable (a feature that was perhaps already present on Rocque's survey (Fig 3.11) though the area is rendered as a solid building and is implied as a strictly triangular form). The riding house also had an open area on the north side, and a wedge-shaped 'stable lane' to the east.[343]

It is difficult to establish precisely the nature or extent of any stables developed in the Lower Yard in conjunction with the building of the riding house; Thomas Burgh certainly received funds to build stables for the Horse Guard in 1706 though the precise location of these cannot now be determined.[344] Burgh's memorial of 1714, detailing the

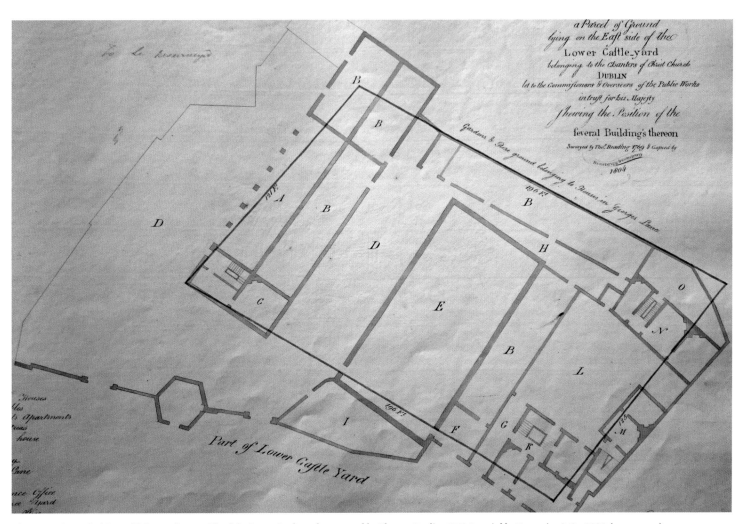

Fig. 3.60 *A Parcel of Ground lying on the east side of the Lower Castle yard…surveyed by Thomas Reading 1769 & copied by Brownrigg & Co. 1804 (east at top).* (NLI, MS 2789 f46)

progress of the buildings 'provided for by the Parliament', indicated that approval had already been given for £4,000 worth of works in the castle, including 'two large ranges of stables' and 'covering the watercourse'.[345] By the end of May the works to the watercourse and just one range of stables had been completed.[346] Where precisely this early stable range was located is not entirely clear except that its erection on a new site may well have been expedited when Wentworth's stables were sacrificed to facilitate the erection of the Treasury.[347] It seems most likely that Burgh's new stables were represented by the large central block, immediately north of the riding house and in the stable yard by 1728 (Fig. 3.15), though this structure was possibly in turn either replaced or added to in 1746, when 'new stables, hay lofts and granaries' for the Horse Guards were to be built to designs by Arthur Jones Nevill near the riding house, as requested by Chesterfield.[348] Based on Reading's survey, the main stables and coach houses at this location were set back-to-back in a single block, with two further

ranges of stables similarly set together at the east end, and across the west end the servant's apartments, and a staircase.

Other stable-type buildings were also depicted at the north-east and eastern perimeters of the stable yard as early as de Gomme's map (Fig. 2.12). As already indicated, it appears that part of the old coach house building, as shown in Robinson's 1683 survey (Fig. 2.14) with its skewed east gable wall, survived into the nineteenth century. Rocque (Fig. 3.11) represented this range as a staggered group of buildings (which when compared with later surveys (Fig. 3.61) seems reasonably accurate) set cheek by jowl with other buildings to the north (these later impacted upon by the creation of Dame Lane, which resulted in the making of a small yard area behind the castle buildings); the block eventually was identified as stables.[349] Between 1756 and 1773 (Fig. 3.33), a house with an angled façade was built at the west end of this block, identified in 1801 (Fig. 3.62) as the 'Riding Master's House', and it is possible this relates to the proposal to build two houses in the Lower Yard in 1762.[350]

Another range of stabling can be identified with the narrow range set along the eastern boundary, directly behind the riding house and taking the place of the straggling building shown here in 1683, and perhaps this building represented the stables and lofts intended for the Horse Guards initiated in 1746.[351] Located in the middle of the screen wall that separated the stable yard from the Lower Yard stood the eighteenth-century hexagonal guard house built directly over the course of the Poddle, presumably following, and perhaps even part of, Burgh's 1714 'covering of the water course'. It was certainly existing on Brooking's map (though here it is suggested with a square plan) (Fig. 3.15) and on Rocque's surveys (Fig. 3.11); pictorially, it is also clearly shown in Sautelle-Robert's early nineteenth-century view of the Lower Yard (Fig. 3.63). Short wings were added to it on the eastern side of the screen wall, c. 1800 (Figs 3.62–5) by which time it was known as the Spur Guard.[352]

While the establishment of the chapel in the Lower Yard is evident from seventeenth-century sources, the earliest known allusion to it in the eighteenth century, and confirming its existence on the present site is found in Swift's satirical poem, written at the beginning of Lord Carteret's term as Lord Lieutenant (1724–30), entitled *A poem on the erecting a Groom-Porter's-house adjoining to the Chapple, in the Castle of Dublin*.[353] While concerned only with the morality and propriety of creating such a 'Luciferian dark confine' in close proximity to the chapel, it confirms the close integration between it and the state apartments (where 'a wall only hinders union/ Between the dice and the Communion/ And but a thin partition guards/ The Common-Prayer Book from the cards').[354] That proximity is first evident on Brooking's 1728 map (Fig. 3.15) and more accurately confirmed by Rocque's 1756 survey (Fig. 3.11), although curiously in this instance a connection to the tower is not represented.

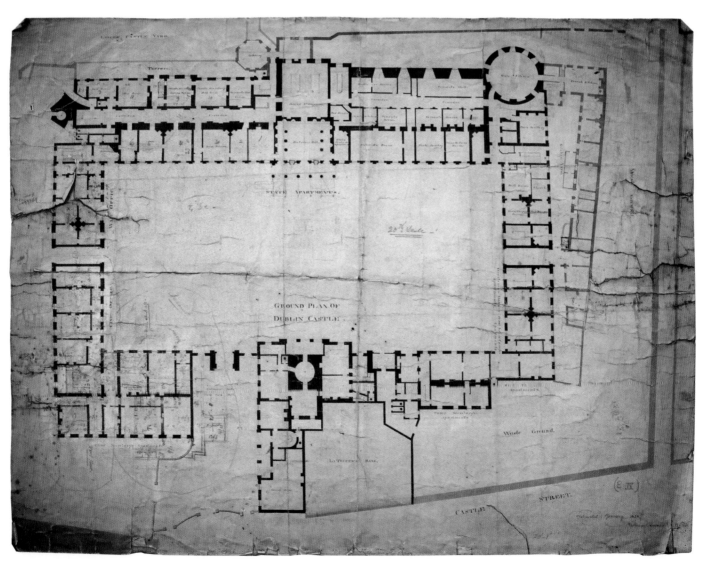

Fig. 3.61 Ground plan of Dublin Castle by William Murray, January 1828 (south at top). (OPWT, E000505 U16-7)

Impressions of the chapel, such as may be gleaned from the limited published sources, are unfavourable, suggesting a 'mean structure, built of brick' that in both its external and internal appearance was deemed 'but little consistent with its attachment to a Royal Palace'.[355] However, a topographical view of the Lower Yard (Fig. 3.54) and a ground-floor survey (Fig. 3.12) of the chapel range give a fairer indication of the building and its character. Importantly, both sources agree in their details. The engraved plan, which is attributed to a survey by James Gandon, shows the chapel integrated with the south-east corner of the surviving medieval Wardrobe Tower, with an irregular shaped vestry extending to the west along the south side of the tower (with rooms for the keeper abutting it to the west), which on the exterior presented a skewed two-storied façade with just a single bay.[356] The chapel had four bays (on each elevation, and only the western bays not aligned), and was some 23ft (7m) wide and 54ft (16m) long. There was no window in the east gable as

further buildings adjoined it to the east, two rather curious, narrow spaces separating them. The main element of this easterly appendage was divided between barrack rooms to the south and three rooms to the north labelled 'chapel building'. The plan does not depict the internal arrangement in the chapel, except to show in outline the position of the Lord Lieutenant's pew, accessed (along with the vestry) from the south-west, and very possibly located at an upper, gallery level. The painting, which offers a view westwards showing the south elevation of the castle in perspective, reveals the brick chapel, its windows tall, narrow and round-headed, the eastern one of a reduced height, with an open sash window, west of these, lighting the narrow room at the west end. The outline of a steep east gable is also evident, its apex carrying a simple cross; its steepness is distinct from the adjoining roofs, adding to the sense that the building was discrete. The simple character of the building represented here largely endorses the impression offered

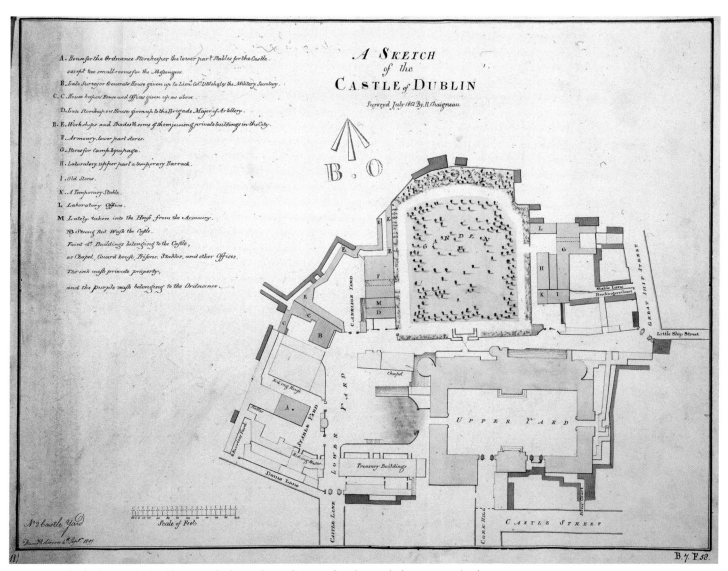

Fig. 3.62 A Sketch of the Castle of Dublin surveyed July 1801 by H. Chaigneau (south at top). (TNA, MPH1/202)

several decades later that the 'former Chapel of the castle was a small and incommodious building of brick, evincing no great antiquity'.[357] Towards the end of the century, the structure had begun to fall into decay, said in 1790 'to be in a very tottering state, and, is in every respect unbecoming the dignity of the representative of Majesty'.[358] There is a suggestion that for a time up to 1802 the chapel had been used as a barracks, though the reference may simply relate to the rooms adjoining it, which were labelled as barracks on a contemporary plan (Fig. 3.12).[359] As previously indicated, the idea of a new chapel is present on one of the Wide Streets Commissioners' proposals (Fig. 3.34), and in 1790, perhaps because of its condition, a firmer decision seems to have been taken to replace it – possibly with its poor condition and unsuitability having been highlighted by the works planned for the east Cross Block.[360] It is possible that its condition contributed in the same period to the assessment of 'the old black tower…as a useless fabric that gives disgraceful gloominess to the Viceregal residence, little according with the style and elegance of the other parts'.[361] It was perhaps

at this time then that the chapel was given over to use as barracks, while the provision of a new chapel was certainly delayed until after the passage of the Act of Union.[362]

In the second half of the eighteenth century, the chief additions in this area of the Lower Yard included a house for the Surveyor General, built in 1756 by Thomas Eyre who contributed substantially towards its cost.[363] It was located immediately south of the riding house and set at an angle facing the chapel, with the carriage yard adjoining it to the south, giving access to a large yard behind (Fig. 3.63).[364] In the south-east corner, behind the Surveyor General's house (where a small stable building was shown in 1683), another house stood forward of the narrow eastern stable range. It may be the same building shown here by Rocque in 1756, but is first clearly detailed only in 1769 (Fig. 3.60) and ultimately can be identified as the housekeeper's apartments.[365] It represented a two-storied house, three rooms with corner fireplaces on the ground floor, with an enclosed yard set directly behind.

Fig. 3.63 Thomas Sautelle-Roberts, *View of Lower Yard*, aquatint by R Havell & Sons, published by James Del Vecchio 1816. (Courtesy of OPW Dublin Castle)

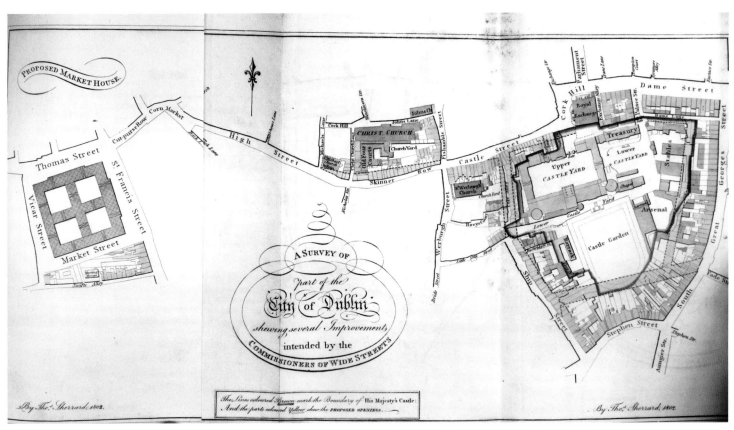

Fig. 3.64 Thomas Sherrard, *A Survey of part of the City of Dublin showing several improvements intended by the Commissioners of Wide Streets* (1802). (DCA)

In 1673 Bernard de Gomme's survey of Dublin (Fig. 2.12) clearly showed the magazine at the castle as a long range set forward of the gardens, with an equally narrow yard behind. In 1697 John Dunton referred to the 'Office of the Ordnance', located 'next the Chapel' which possibly refers to the same building, though perhaps more likely this was a building incorporated within the chapel range, and that the building nearby where 'the King's gunsmiths and armourers work' represented the magazine proper, somewhat affirming this impression by adding, that 'before these buildings lies a large piece of ground called the stable-yard'.[366] By the eighteenth century the magazine or armoury can be more accurately located in the triangular plot of ground to the east of the formal garden. As all the older structures represented by de Gomme were evidently rebuilt, and there exists some limitations as to the precision of his survey, it remains difficult to establish whether there was any close relationship between these older buildings ('the Magazine') and the site which became firmly associated with the 'Arsenal' from at least the mid eighteenth century.[367]

Certainly by 1707 the need for a proper magazine 'for storing up arms and all other materials and necessary instruments and habiliments of war' was a matter for some concern, and it was clear that both the storage of arms and the powder were considered completely deficient 'for the better security and defence of the nation or to answer any occasion the Crown may have for furnishing troops to be sent on any expedition'.[368] The powder stored at Kilmainham, for example, was deemed to possess 'no other security than the bare walls of the house it is lodged in'. In assessing an appropriate site for 'a proper magazine', Thomas Burgh had examined what had been the 'Ordnance grounds' lying adjacent to the gardens 'at the back of the Castle'. These he found 'confined and strangely irregular' and 'so low and moist that we can never keep arms free from rust'. The proximity of neighbouring houses and their backyards and gardens also raised concerns about security, being 'so much higher that in the night time any number of people may easily get into it, and either steal or destroy what they please'.[369] Although Burgh provided a 'rough draft' of what the site could accommodate in terms of the need for an armoury for up to 30,000 arms, various store-houses and 'work-houses for artificers' and all costed at £5,000, he recommended it would be 'more advisable to choose a spot of ground somewhere else to make a complete arsenal'.[370] While a fortified arsenal was commenced in the Phoenix Park in 1710 under the instruction of the earl of Wharton, it failed to progress and with the succession of the 2nd duke of Ormond attentions turned instead towards a less ambitious proposal, making some new provision in the castle, and 'two

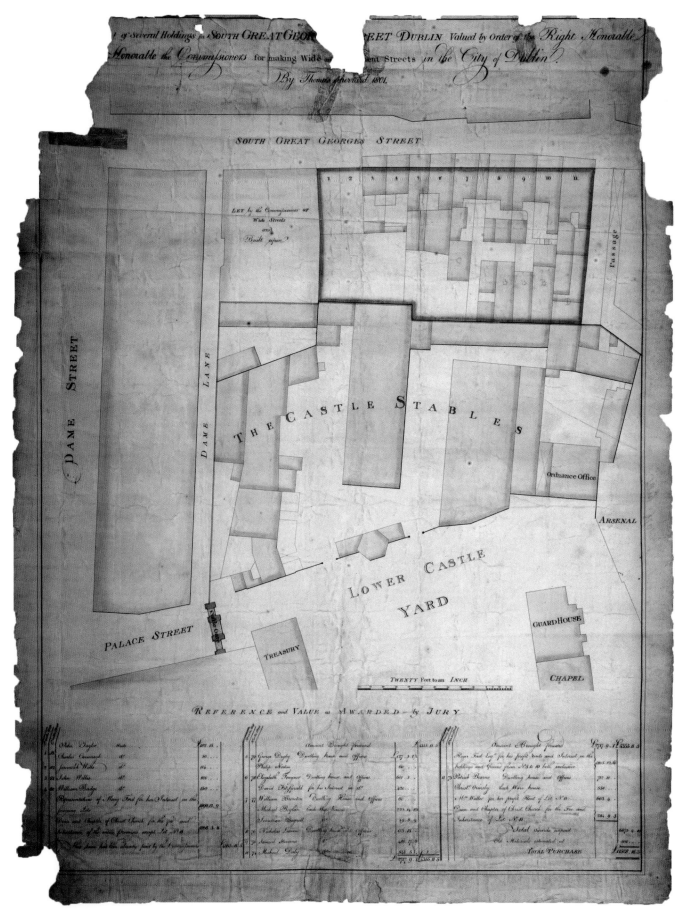

Fig. 3.65 Thomas Sherrard, map of properties adjoining 'The Castle Stables', 1801 (east at top). (DCA, WSC 187)

little redoubts' in the park for the powder.[371] While little progress was made even on these elements, the armoury in the castle was progressed enough to be substantially built by 1714, and there are indications that it was subsequently extended at least twice in the eighteenth century, in the 1730s and 1740s.[372] It is difficult, however, to tie any of these references down to a specific building as none of the castle structures are named on the earliest known Georgian map (Fig. 3.15), while on Rocque's survey (Fig. 3.11) the situation only becomes confused because both an armoury and arsenal are shown separately, and even then long after various phases of rebuilding were carried out in the 1730s and 1740s. In 1756, the armoury is clearly implied as a relatively short building, occupying only the eastern end of the L-plan range lying immediately north of the chapel, though given the gradient of the site it must have risen to at least two, perhaps three storeys. This range is shown in existence in 1728 and on other eighteenth century surveys but survived only in part into the early nineteenth century, before the rebuilding of the chapel.[373] This is most likely to represent Burgh's building of the 1710s, built in concert with the Treasury block opposite as part of a formal concept for the arrangement of the Lower Yard (see discussion of this scheme above), an impression reinforced by the quadrant screen walls formed at the western ends of the buildings.[374]

The arsenal ('armoury') to the south of the chapel may have been begun by Burgh in the same period to provide some other element of the ordnance department, perhaps even intended as a residence for the overseer of the armoury, and certainly such a dwelling is known to have existed in 1725; indeed the front portion of the arsenal is consistently shown as a dwelling house on various surveys, and even today its architectural character is essentially domestic in appearance.[375] The existence of an armoury and arsenal as separate buildings, certainly by 1756, and the 'old fashioned' appearance of the surviving building, further makes it difficult to understand precisely to which of these buildings recorded works in the eighteenth century actually refer. The southerly building located on the east side of the garden certainly became the chief arsenal, and the structure here is usually attributed to works undertaken by Edward Lovett Pearce in the 1730s, and Arthur Dobbs a decade later, though there are problems with this interpretation, partly based on its surviving architectural character.[376]

This two-storied building, now adjoining the carriage house, is certainly the result of various works, although it is difficult to isolate its different phases. It has a deep rectangular plan, ten bays by five bays, which essentially evolved from a hollow or courtyard plan. The main front with its boldly moulded cornice, steep roof and general proportions together with the evidence for an internal arcade (not seen) all support an early Georgian building that would naturally fall within Burgh's tenure. However,

in 1728, Brooking's plan (Fig. 3.15) suggests only a modest single range of building, slightly forward of this location, set flush with the adjoining garden wall and fronting the large triangular 'Artillery Yard'. By 1756, Rocque (Fig. 3.11) indicates a much larger structure corresponding more closely to the site of the present building (including the long narrow projection from the south-west corner), but with its façade set well back – and formerly behind a tall screen wall – so as to suggest the earlier building was demolished entirely. Perhaps its fabric was reused by Pearce or Dobbs – a practice that was common – which may explain its enduring old-fashioned appearance. Later surveys (Figs 3.37, 3.62, 3.64, 3.67) all confirm the relative accuracy of Rocque's plan. However, they also offer a clearer indication of the layout, treating the front block as a discrete building, evidently a dwelling house, occupied by the store keeper before being given up to the Brigade Major of Artillery in about 1800, for whom it was enlarged with the ordnance stores extended behind in the main two-storied block.[377] This, therefore, could have been the building indicated on Brooking's map although inaccurately represented as too far forward of its actual location.

John Dunton's account of the castle in 1697 mentioned the existence of workshops in the Lower Yard, and in 1724 estimates were produced concerning the cost of building shops, evidently of brick, in the Lower Yard 'for the gunsmiths to work in'.[378] These are perhaps to be identified with the narrow, southerly extension to the arsenal which was first shown on Rocque's survey (Fig. 3.11), and certainly by 1801 (Fig. 3.62) it can be identified as 'workshops and sheds' along with the more extensive buildings by then ranged around the triangular carriage yard. On Brooking's survey (Fig. 3.15) two small projections are shown within the yard on the east wall, which could indicate the workshops of 1724 that perhaps by 1756 had been replaced by the narrow range shown on the arsenal; at this time there were no buildings at all suggested around the carriage yard, then named as the 'Artillery Ground' and shown with wheeled cannon and stores of cannon balls.

A painted view (Fig. 3.54) of the Lower Yard, looking west along the old castle chapel and state apartments, shows the high wall that screened the carriage yard, including a pedestrian gateway and tall entrance with cannon balls set atop its plain, square piers, and beyond it the lower brick wall that screened the armoury. A similar view with the new chapel is shown by Sautelle-Roberts (Fig. 3.63), which also includes a glimpse of a portion of the former Surveyor General's house to the east, eventually to be incorporated into the carriage house built by Jacob Owen in the 1830s. The façade of the arsenal and its screen wall is also shown in the background of George Petrie's 1830s view of the chapel (Fig. 3.66). Other buildings in the Lower Yard, the location of which are not clear, include 'the Provost Marshal's at the

Fig. 3.66 George Petrie, *The Castle Chapel and Record Tower.* (RIA)

back of the Castle' which required repairs in 1721, though it is likely perhaps to have been in some way related to the old chapel range, and the town major's accommodation, because in 1727 an estimate was produced for repairing the marshalsea at the back of the castle of Dublin, and arching over the watercourse adjoining.[379]

West of the castle garden, the plots of the houses running back from Great Ship Street seem, in 1728 (Fig. 3.15), to confirm the late seventeenth-century impression, that the castle was being 'pestered up with houses'. In Brooking's survey, Little Ship Street is effectively shown as a narrow passage off Werburgh Street implying restrictive access into the castle precincts at the north end of Great Ship Street, but that sense of restriction is much less a few decades later when Rocque set down an overall more detailed and reliable record. Brooking's survey does, however, suggest that the even narrower passage, identified in later surveys as Buckridge's Court, extended directly up to the garden wall (and with a stable lane shown further south). On Rocque's survey (Fig. 3.11), the court, entered through one of the houses on Ship Street, now terminated at what is shown as a large store house (its identification barely legible) – a

structure almost entirely enclosed with a central court that to some extent mirrored the armoury on the opposite side. Part of this complex eventually incorporated the 'Laboratory' built by Thomas Eyre the year after Rocque's survey.[380] Its precise location, however, is not known for certain, but in July 1764 the structure was destroyed by an explosion, an event recorded by the Under Secretary, Thomas Waite, to the Chief Secretary, the earl of Drogheda:

60'c in the morning of 3rd July, fire and explosion in the Laboratory in the Lower Castle Yard. The timber of the roof and the slates of the building were by explosion driven over the Ballroom, into the Upper Yard and upon some of the houses in Castle Street. The Windows of the Ballroom and also Birmingham Tower were forced in, and many of the branches of the lustres in the Ballroom were broken to pieces. Several of the houses in Ship Street nearest to the Laboratory were very considerably damaged, but the Arsenals in the Lower Castle Yard and every other part of the Castle have escaped.[381]

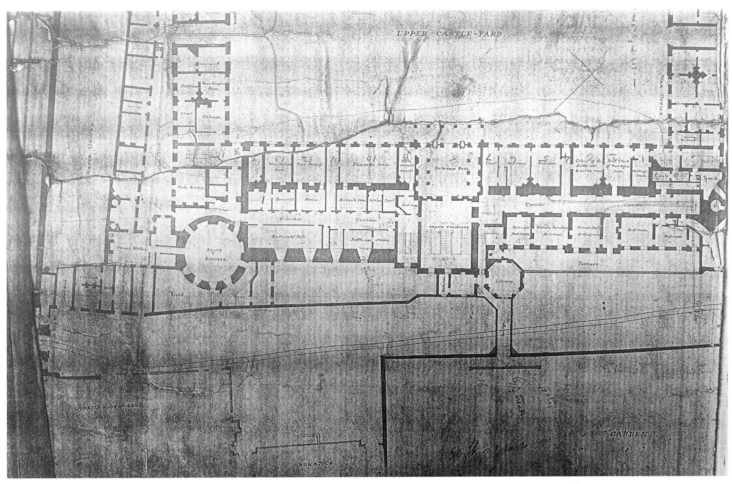

Fig. 3.67 A general plan of Dublin Castle by William Murray, August 1829, showing relocated bridge. (Photostat copy NMS)

It is unclear what caused this explosion (the obvious risks associated with the laboratory's use notwithstanding), or the extent of damage to the adjacent stores, but even if much of the force appears to have been directed towards the north it is likely that there was some serious impact on other adjacent buildings.[382] However, the essential form of the store house building did not change fundamentally and in 1801 (Fig. 3.62) the front, northern portion of it was still referred to as 'Old Stores', with a temporary stable on the eastern angle, and with the eastern return of the building accommodating the 'new' laboratory on the ground floor with a temporary barrack above – presumably its occupants unaware of the fate of the old lab! The western return extended into a more sizeable block, used as stores for tents or 'camp equipage' with a 'Laboratory Office' projected on the east side, closing off the yard extending along the side of the entire complex.

Of the castle garden in the eighteenth century, there is little impression beyond its appearance on maps. It was depicted by Brooking (Fig. 3.15) as formally laid out, perhaps fancifully, as a series of parterres, with cross paths and a

row of perimeter trees, suggesting that little had changed since Dunton's visit. Rocque, however, shows a simpler arrangement with a double row of perimeter trees around what seems like a uniform lawn, and suggests that the area had been extended to the south-west, densely planted, and the overall result a more irregular outline (Fig. 3.11). In 1714 Thomas Burgh proposed works which allowed provision for a 'terrace walk to the garden front' at a cost of £350-0-0. Though evidently related in some way to the narrow terrace outside the state apartments, it is difficult to know the precise nature of the work, how it related to the main garden and to what extent this may have been carried out.[383] It is possible that it included the bridge and steps that allowed direct access down to the gardens from the terrace. This feature is first evident on Brooking's survey, and again in greater detail on Rocque in 1756 and by Chaigneau in 1801, as well as pictorially in a late eighteenth-century view (Fig. 3.54) but the bridge was later relocated to its present position adjoining Eyre's library, sometime before 1829 (Fig. 3.67).

Whatever about the certainty of Burgh's intention to set the Treasury within part of a grander scheme in 1712, later efforts to integrate the castle more prominently and formally within the city, including consideration of the approaches from the east, resulted in plans for a reconfiguration of the buildings in the Lower Yard – but retaining the Treasury – so as to invest it with a greater sense of order and fitting courtliness. An undated scheme associated with the Wide Streets Commissioners, prepared in advance of the building of the Royal Exchange in 1769 and proposing the widening of Castle Lane, shows the old gateway terminating the lane and leading into the Lower Yard.[384] As part of the works to widen Castle Lane, and its more appropriate renaming as Palace Street, the present gateway was built, thus ensuring that the castle could 'be properly enclosed as it always used to be'. Forming a solid, no-nonsense tripartite entrance, built of granite with a pedimented central arch, the design is attributed to Thomas Eyre though it was built some years after his term of office ended.[385] These early efforts by the commissioners may well have provided the impetus to consider further, more ambitious, schemes to improve access to the Lower Castle Yard, leading to the two proposals already introduced in the discussions above, that would make the stable yards the unlikely focus of a rather stately point of entry into the castle. This new emphasis given to an approach from the east, created in tandem with proposed new accommodation for the Horse Guards, seems likely to have taken its inspiration from Whitehall, where even to 'this day the Horse Guards building serves as the official point of entry to the royal palaces'.[386]

As noted previously, the background to these schemes and indeed the dates of their conception are not precisely known, though both were clearly conceived as part of proposals to widen Dame Street, which was begun in the late 1770s.[387] The more ambitious scheme for the eastern approach (Fig. 3.34) proposing a new street parallel to Dame Street, leading from the Round Church, and set at a skewed angle to the castle, was intended to terminate in a semi-circular piazza at the intersection of Palace Street, while a new street to the south extended alongside the arsenal. The scheme also envisaged an entire remodelling of the Lower Yard, displacing the existing stables (to be replaced by a new stable yard to the south, accessed off the new street) so as to achieve an extended symmetrical entrance façade to the castle and Lower Yard (of which the Treasury was part) with a grand gateway as the centrepiece, modelled it seems on a triumphal arch and incorporating new Horse Guards offices. Although only known in plan, it certainly shared something of the pretensions of its Whitehall counterpart by Kent which was completed in the late 1750s as 'a monument to George II's passion for military order and display'.[388] In a manner not dissimilar to the London building, the Dublin design brought together a number of core functions, providing accommodation for the ordnance magazine or armoury, gunsmiths workshops and administrative offices which in Dublin set the apartments of the Surveyor General and the ordnance office side by side, next to the chapel. Although the plan would seem not to have been pursued any further, it first introduced the Horse Guards block that was eventually erected by Jacob Owen decades later. The design, as built, accorded both axially and in plan to the 1770s design, though its precise position did not correspond, leaving some uncertainty as to whether hopes still remained in the nineteenth century of integrating the castle more formally with the city to the east.

Chapter 3.8
The Castle 1800–50

Two surveys (Figs 3.62, 3.64) of the castle and its surroundings in 1801–02 very usefully present the layout of the castle as it appeared in the aftermath of the Act of Union. Seven months after the Irish parliament voted itself out of existence, the architect Henry Chaigneau made a detailed survey of the entire castle and its immediate environs.[389] The purpose of the survey appears to have been to distinguish the properties within the precincts associated with military functions from those occupied by the civil administration, and perhaps indirectly to show the line upon which architectural responsibilities had become divided.[390] Among the changes wrought by the Union was the abolition of the Board of Ordnance and the role of the chief engineer of the ordnance was now assumed by the commanding Royal Engineer of Ireland, a position appointed by the British Board of Ordnance.

It is unclear how far some of the responsibilites for the castle buildings were shared, but it seems that overlap must have been inevitable, while undoubtedly problematic. There certainly were two forces at work in how the castle developed in the first decade of the nineteenth century, determined on one hand by political threats and a need to improve security for which the chief engineer would undoubtedly assume some responsibility, and a need to consolidate and expand the civic adminstration and perhaps in some ways to enhance the viceregal court as part of the compensation for the loss of the national legislature: within twenty years of the Union the castle would host George IV, the first king to visit Ireland since the time of James and William, and some significant works in the Upper Yard can be ascribed to this event.[391]

In 1800 responsibility for civil aspects of the castle accommodation certainly lay with the Barrack Board and Board of Works whose architect, Lord Buckingham's former protégé Vincenzo Waldré, was entirely independent of the Royal Engineers. However, by December the new Lord Lieutenant, Lord Hardwicke, was clearly determined that the military and civil divisions of the Board be formally separated and so the Board of Works, responsible for civil buildings, came into being as a distinct entity in January 1802.[392] Ironically, as part of this reform, Waldré was transferred to the Barrack Department, and his place was taken by Robert Woodgate, a former apprentice and assistant of the London architect, Sir John Soane.[393] However, for a time during this period of transition, it had seemed as if the chief architect of the moment, James Gandon, who in the preceeding twenty years had so dramatically transformed civic architecture in the capital, would be persuaded to extend his influence over the castle.

As Hardwicke prepared to introduce his reforms, he approached Gandon through the Chief Secretary, Charles Abbott, requesting plans for a new chapel and other works at the castle, reviving, it seems, an idea that had first been considered at least a decade earlier.[394] This approach to Gandon was perhaps made in anticipation of Waldré's move, but it is significant for the fact that it was not made by the Commissioners and Overseers of the Barrack and Public Works. Gandon was understandably wary, and in his response expressed reluctance to trespass in an area that was clearly Waldré's responsibility. In reply to this, Abbott reassured him, indicating that the proposed reforms of the Board would remove this difficulty – evidently anticipating

Waldré's move to the Barrack Department. Convinced, Gandon produced as many as 'seven different designs for the intended Chapel' yet despite his efforts, and their approval, Robert Woodgate had been appointed in the meantime (in January 1802) to replace Waldré, and so Gandon resumed his reluctance to remain involved having been given no official mandate to carry out the task.[395]

Gandon, 'Architect Generalissimo' of the capital, had in effect already usurped Cooley (having been placed second to Cooley in the Royal Exchange competition) and his successors by completing the Four Courts and earning the commissions to design the Custom House and House of Lords extension to the Parliament House, and later the King's Inns.[396] It seems then that he belatedly became a reluctant promoter of his own interests, at least as far as these works to the castle were concerned. Excusing himself from direct involvement in the project, he offered to 'explain many particulars to Mr Woodgate for better understanding of my Ideas in Order to make my Design more perfect, presuming that in some future establishment I may not be undeserving of Notice'.[397]

This may not have been the end of the matter, however, as on 30 March 1804 Gandon wrote to the Board of Works, responding to a letter from Robert Woodgate, explaining that his appointment as architect to the Four Courts 'was from his Grace the Duke of Rutland when Chief Governor'. He certainly had still not been paid for his efforts three years earlier, which had evidently extended beyond simply designing a new chapel, because in April that year he responded to a question about his remuneration 'for all the plans of the Treasury & Site of the Old Chapel together with a very large Elevation of the Castle all of which being from Actual measurements, exclusive of the Various Designs of Plans, Elevations, Sections for the Intended Chapel', somewhat plaintively stating 'that considering the length of time they required & Estimates in order to value them within the Compass of his Excellencies Wishes, I hoped my charge would have been deemed so very moderate as to have induced your Lordship to have taken notice of it'.[398]

Woodgate seems neither to have had the opportunity to avail of Gandon's advice nor, presumably, to devise a scheme for the chapel himself and he died in 1805. No details of Gandon's chapel schemes are known to survive and Woodgate was suceeded by Francis Johnston, a former pupil of Thomas Cooley who by then had earned an acknowledged primacy in the profession in Dublin, and so the task passed to him, with work finally proceeding in 1807, but only after certain efforts to improve the castle security had been addressed.[399]

Despite the wide demands of the post (and a busy private practice), which would include the Houses of Parliament conversion (1803–08) and design of the General Post Office (1814–18), Johnston was involved in overseeing works at the castle, though apart from the chapel, the extent to which he had a direct hand is unclear; at least some of the works on the chapel there were undertaken by Thomas Hart, his clerk of works, who continued to be employed at the castle, with responsibility in 1821 for improvements in preparation for the visit of George IV and whose signed drawings represent the first comprehensive survey of the Upper Yard.[400] Johnston was succeeded by his cousin, William Murray, who had entered the architect's office in 1807. Established in private practice in 1819, he became Johnston's official assistant in 1822 until 1826 when Johnston retired. Although Murray was recommended to replace him, he was not confirmed in the appointment until 1827, and retired in 1832, a year after the reorganisation of the Board.[401] Although actively employed by the Board, knowledge of his work at the castle is limited to relatively minor additions. There were greater opportunities for his successor Jacob Owen, who before his retirement in 1856 designed a number of key new buildings within the castle complex.

The documentary evidence for the architectural development of the castle in the nineteenth century is much greater than for any previous period. This is due to a combination of the effects of the reorganisation of the Barrack Board and the establishment of the Board of Works, the change demonstrating greater accountability, diligence and record keeping; and of course the survival of records, as always, is down to no more than a fair degree of chance and luck. The opportunity to examine all the relevant material in the voluminous minutes, accounts and letter books of the Board of Works, which would offer a more detailed and comprehensive account of the historic development of the castle in this era, is beyond the scope of this study. Given the extent and complexity of the works, especially the degree of minor changes recorded, any attempt to describe it in sequence and intelligible detail would prove too perplexing to the reader, and therefore here is limited to the most significant works and aspects of the castle and its setting that are of greatest relevance to the purpose of this study. Besides the rebuilding of the chapel, there was no major building work undertaken in the first decade of the nineteenth century, limiting the scope of architectural development, though the efforts to improve the castle security, which dominated the work in the early years, did extend the site of the castle significantly. This coincided with the expanding population within the complex, the late eighteenth and nineteenth century witnessing increases in the number of people employed there in administrative and military capacities.[402] This expansion – relating both to accommodation for personnel and services – influenced many of the works over the succeeding decades, which, besides various reordering and remodelling in the state apartments, included the conversion of the Wardrobe Tower to receive the public records, the completion, in the 1820s, of the conversion of dormers to attics in the Upper Yard, the closing of the ground-floor arcades of the south range, as well as many other ancillary works in the Lower Yard, including additions by William Murray at the base of the entire south range; Jacob Owen built a new stable block in the castle garden in the 1830s, and in the 1840s made a further extension to the Chief Secretary's office. Over the same period, military expansion was primarily focused to the west and south of the existing ordnance office to include the new Quarter Master General's office by Johnston, infantry barracks, parade ground and Royal Engineers office, while the old armoury and artillery ground to the east of the castle gardens was eventually converted into a police barracks by Owen.

Chapter 3.9
Consolidation and Expansion 1800–50

The lingering threats of conspiracy and insurrection after the events of 1798 were a cause of great anxiety to the government and in the years immediately after the successful passage of the Union it began to focus a good deal of its attention on improving the security of the castle. The reorganisation of the United Irishmen under Robert Emmet and his formulation of plans in 1803 to take Dublin Castle would ultimately justify those fears. Bereft of its core medieval defences – its battlemented walls and surrounding moat – and with its precincts crowded about in an array of habitations and shops set in narrow alleyways and courts, there was undoubtedly an increased sense of vulnerability amongst its occupants which led to a concerted campaign of activity to remedy this in the opening decades of the century.

On Henry Chaigneau's survey (Fig. 3.62), some recent changes of use among the various castle buildings are noted, the new temporary arrangements suggesting some of the contingencies made necessary by a changing or expanding military presence, and presumably intended to improve castle security. The former Surveyor General's house in the south-east corner of the Lower Castle Yard and the adjoining housekeeper's house and offices have been 'given up' to Lieutenant Littlehales, Military Secretary, while the store keeper's house, part of the armoury on the east side of the garden, has been given up to the 'Brigade Major of Artillery'. In the same year Thomas Sherrard's survey, prepared in his capacity as secretary to the Wide Streets Commissioners (Fig. 3.64), perfectly captures the integration of ideas between the castle authorities – both civil and military – and the commissioners in their approach to rationalising the streets and thoroughfares which surrounded it, and in the process demonstrating just how far the body had evolved its role in relation to the castle and the city since 1757.[403] From the 'several improvements' proposed on the map, the jagged

outline of the castle precincts, highlighted in red, is ignored and curtailed in order to provide a rectangular interlocking network of streets that would help to further redefine the castle within the city by reasserting its presence more fittingly. However, more than is suggested by Chaigneau's survey, the context for this scheme would appear to lie principally in the security concerns of the administration. The proposal here was essentially to isolate the castle, surrounding it with broad thoroughfares and open lines of sight, replacing houses and gardens and open courts, partly developed over its ancient defences and now lapping up, as it were, against the castle precincts to become an ongoing threat to its security.

On the south side, a straight passage was envisaged, just north of the curved layout of Stephen Street, which would cut through the southern end of the castle garden, and disrupt, on the east side, many of the properties along South Great George's Street – with at least four buildings on the street front likely to have been lost entirely. Entering onto George's Street opposite its junction with Fade Street, this thoroughfare intersected with a widened Ship Street on the west side – the widening here resulting in the loss of most of the existing buildings on Ship Street which would, in effect, have greatly reduced the accommodation available within the castle precincts. Another new street, parallel to South Great George's Street and west of it (and staying outside most of its existing property boundaries here), was projected across the rear of the castle stables and the arsenal yard, connecting to a widened Dame Lane at the northern end, and at the south end, with the new street.[404] North of the castle, west of the Royal Exchange, part of Castle Street was also to be widened, the proposal entailing the demolition of almost half of Eyre's guard house at the Cork Hill (Fig. 3.68) entrance into the Upper Castle Yard. In addition, the front of the La Touche Bank (Figs 3.69–70) and

Fig. 3.68 Henry Brocas, *View of Cork Hill* (NLI, PD 1963 TX (30))

houses on the north side of Castle Street would also have been lost. However, Silver Court, a tiny, enclosed precinct comprising three substantial properties hard against the north-west corner of the castle and accessed by a narrow passage between nos 18 and 19 Castle Street, would have been largely spared in this scheme. Cole Alley, a long narrow passage parallel to the west side of the castle, lined on both sides with small premises (twenty-five in all, also entered by a narrow, arched passage located between nos 14 and 15 Castle Street) would be eradicated in order to provide a thoroughfare on the west side of the castle, linking Castle Street to Great Ship Street, and essentially extending the latter (Fig. 3.71). Although Great Ship Street – west of the castle garden, the barracks and stores – was to be widened by demolishing most of the houses on the east side, it seems that it was not the intention to continue this widening as far as Stephen Street, implying that the plan was more concerned with the exigencies of securing the castle rather than creating something grander in concept. However, also shown as part of this scheme is the proposed widening of Skinner's Row – between St Michael's Lane and Fishamble

Street – the area immediately south of Christ Church and the old Four Courts, the result creating a straighter alignment and more impressive approach to the castle between High Street and the Royal Exchange.

Ultimately the commissioners' scheme was not proceeded with as proposed, its design perhaps too confining, limiting any future expansion of the castle which, since the late eighteenth century, supported a rapidly growing administration. The new thoroughfares to the south and south-east, therefore, never materialised, though the treatment outlined for Castle Street, Cole Alley and Ship Street did perhaps provide the genesis for a later scheme which focused on the north-west corner and was extended further along Great Ship Street in the following decade. As a result, the developments in the castle precincts moved away from an idea that would have imposed constraints, to a plan that allowed the castle to expand, if modestly, over the next half century, and in a way that benefitted both its security and to some degree its ambiance. As part of this, some additional ground was acquired to the east of Exchange Alley north of the Treasury block, and while

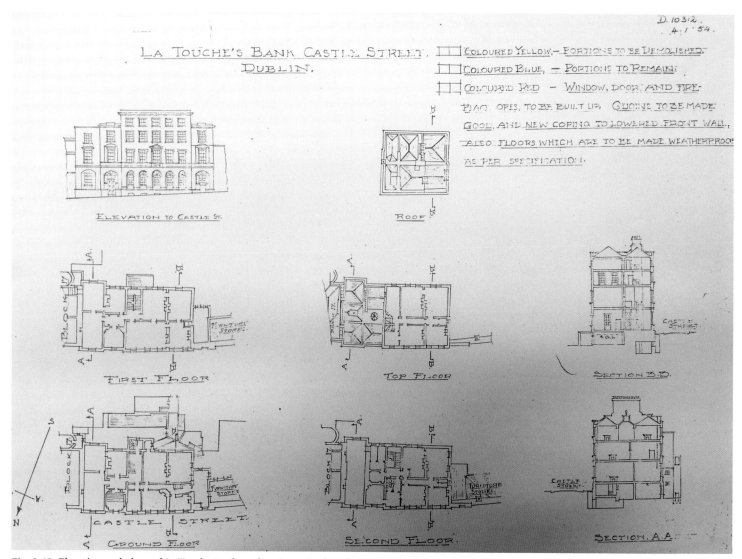

Fig. 3.69 Elevation and plans of La Touche Bank made prior to its demolition in 1945. (Photostat copy NMS)

the guard house and the La Touche Bank were untouched, the houses to the west of the bank, up to the junction of Cole Alley, were removed and replaced by a curtain wall. The houses on both sides of Cole Alley were demolished and the space effectively subsumed into the castle behind a curtain wall with a narrow pedestrian passage, the surviving castle steps being newly created immediately outside this wall. An even more radical extension was made along Ship Street where the castle authorities acquired all the ground up to, and including, all the buildings on the east side of Ship Street as well as those in the western half of Stephen Street, on the north side. Meanwhile, the boundaries further south and to the east remained unchanged, and a comparison of Sherrard's 1801 survey and the castle outline half a century later confirms the fossilised nature of this boundary. The deep plots on Stephen Street, and those on the west side of South Great George's Street had, in 1756

(Fig. 3.11), gardens to the rear bounding the castle garden. A century later (Fig. 3.37) many of these garden plots had been built over, creating internal courts accessed through arched passageways leading off the respective streets.[405]

In examining more closely the efforts to improve the castle's security in the early years of the century, the earliest action is connected with the initiatives of the Dublin silversmith, Jeremiah D'Olier, a member of the Wide Streets Commissioners who had been consulted by the government 'as to the means & expense of purchasing the grounds and houses in Cole's Alley'.[406] The initiative seems to have been taken in response to a Court of Exchequer decree directing the sale of the majority of houses there in February 1802, properties which were owned by the Thwaite family.[407] In May 1802, D'Olier claimed that 'a very favourable opportunity now offers to accomplish that object at a very reasonable & fair price', though it is not clear how this was related to the February sale. D'Olier indicated that the 'small sum' necessary to purchase the properties and the guarantee of a good rental income, meant no loss 'can possibly arise' should the project be abandoned in the future.[408] The government's immediate response is not known, but Emmet's failed attempt on the castle over a year later, on 23 July 1803, and the murder of the Lord Chief Justice, Viscount Kilwarden and his nephew, introduced a new sense of urgency to its intentions 'to insulate and secure the Castle', which was clearly stated that August.[409] A number of houses were purchased by September, D'Olier presumably having been permitted to effect the sales.[410] By November some of the houses had been demolished, their materials sold by public auction and, despite ongoing difficulties about title and compensation for adjoining owners, the chief engineer, Lt. Col. Fisher, reported in mid December that 'most of the houses in Cole Alley, as also several in Castle Street and in Silver Court are now taken down and the rubbish in part removed'. [411]

Unlike the scheme published by Thomas Sherrard (Fig. 3.64), there is no clear sense that any subsequent overall plan for the castle environment had been devised and agreed, as a more piecemeal approach seems to have been adopted for the works that were progressed over the following years. However, a map detailing the existing properties in Cole Alley and Silver Court was prepared by Robinson and Green in 1803 (Fig. 3.71).[412] It reveals that more than thirty house plots (mostly within Cole Alley) occupied the ground to be subsumed into expanding the castle precincts to the west, and which was to include the area required for the creation of the castle steps.[413] Both Cole Alley and the enclave of Silver Court were accessed from Castle Street through arched and vaulted passages, with Cole Alley terminating at the medieval wall overlooking Ship Street.[414] On the Robinson and Green survey roughly sketched parallel lines, added later, indicate the intended passage now associated with the castle steps – its alignment, closely paralleled with Cole Alley, running through the rear of the plots on the west side, starting slightly to the west of the arched passageway, skirting St Werburgh's graveyard and emerging into Ship Street beside the lower castle gate. As already noted, in August 1803 the government had communicated to the vestry of St Werburgh's its intentions 'to take down several houses in Cole Alley and Castle St. in order to insulate and secure the Castle' and as part of its measures expressed 'their desire that the several parties and persons likely to suffer in their properties by that measure should forthwith give in an estimate of the several losses so likely to be sustained'.[415] The vestry, whose interest included vacant ground intended for a school house, and an alms house with twelve widows apartments, prepared its response with the assistance of 'Mr. Arthur Battersby an experienced builder' (and the carpenter

Fig. 3.70 Elevation of La Touche Bank by Joseph Jarratt. (IAA, Jarratt Album)

who was to work on the new Chapel Royal).[416] Among the other premises located here was one formerly called the 'Chop House' and there were also jewellers, cutlers, gold and silver smiths and watchmakers operating in Cole Alley, their concentration here a basis perhaps for D'Olier's involvement in the negotiations.[417]

Approximately twelve houses on the south side of Castle Street were also incorporated into the newly defined castle enclosure at this time. The majority of plot widths here were narrow, between 11ft and 13ft (3.3m and 4m), with the exception of one (no. 18) to the west of the arched entrance to Silver Court which was more than 22ft (6.7m) wide. This plot was more than 100ft (30.5m) deep, possibly the full width of the medieval moat, perhaps the site of a cagework house.[418] The houses to the east had relatively shorter plots, the three immediately east of the passageway were shallow enough to accommodate the three houses of Silver Court behind them. These shorter plots continued further east with other property divisions accommodated behind them, all backing onto the castle. A narrow glimpse of the street is afforded in a view of 1788 (Fig. 3.72), which suggests narrow tall Dutch-type gabled houses to the west of the La Touche Bank.[419]

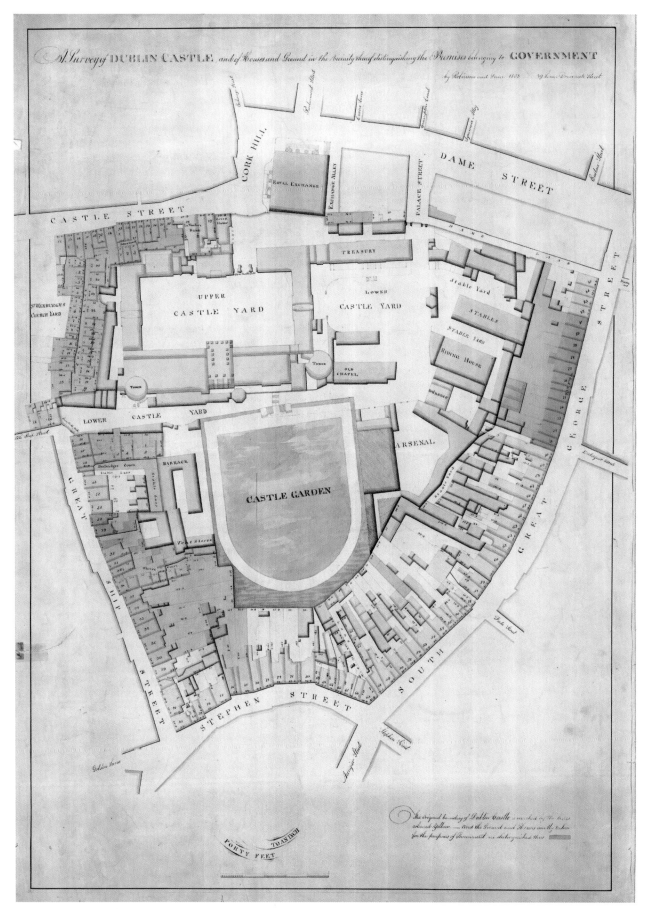

Fig. 3.71 Map of Dublin Castle by Robinson and Green, 1803, showing the original boundary in yellow and the properties recently acquired in blue. Copy drawn by P. Coyle in 1953. (OPWT, E000486 U16-3)

Fig. 3.72 View of Castle Street, Dublin with the La Touche Bank and Newcomen Bank from *Gentleman's Magazine*, Vol. LVIII, December 1788. (NLI)

Proposals for the castle steps appear to have been well underway by 1806.[420] A surviving plan (Fig. 3.73) from this period shows the curtain wall and steps as built, its straight passage and sequence of steps and the articulation of the wall surface all matching exactly.[421] Unfortunately it is unsigned and undated, and with Woodgate having assumed the post in January 1802 (following the death of Vincenzo Waldré) which he retained up to his own unexpected death in 1805 when he was succeeded by Francis Johnston, it is possible that either architect could have initiated the proposals, perhaps in consultation with the chief engineer, Lt. Col. Fisher, who oversaw the clearance of houses in Cole Alley and Silver Court. It seems more likely, however, that Johnston was largely responsible and oversaw the new works, construction commencing in November 1806 with the closure of the pavement on Castle Street in order to accommodate the laying of the foundation 'of the flank wall of the new works'.[422] A 'Guard House' adjoining the new Ship Street entrance gate is shown on the plan, and the provision of this building appears to have been first indicated to Johnston by the Commissioners of the Board of Works in December after the works began, with plans for the new gate, guard house and curtain wall submitted the following March.[423] The wall was completed that year and the 'Cole Alley Passage' certainly in use and being maintained by the paving authorities in the early months of 1808.[424]

The wall itself comprises a tall and imposing edifice enclosing the castle on the west end of Castle Street and running south at the castle steps and stepped in correspondence with them. Impressively formidable, it towers over the street and passageway, its surfaces largely rendered in a dark roughcast with contrasting dressed granite trimmings and elaborated in stages with tall granite pilasters set at wide intervals with the space between expressed as a sequence of three large rectangular recessed panels, diminishing to a smaller and deeper panel in the centre, edged with thickly chamfered granite blocks. The careful consideration given to the design and materials produces a highly effective impression of great depth and absolute impenetrability, somewhat 'terroristic' in its attitude, while eschewing an otherwise monotonous stretch of curtain walling, not seen since the medieval walls were taken down.[425] Despite its defensive, militaristic bearing, the design of the curtain wall may fairly, and with reasonable confidence, be attributed to Johnston; indeed it has certain affinities with the boundary wall of King's Inns (there built in common limestone and calp) where Johnston was working *c.*1813 onwards. In contrast to its forbidding outward expression, the area now enclosed appears, before 1838, to have been transformed into a series of elaborate gardens, at least based on its representation on the Ordnance Survey published in 1843 (Fig. 3.37).

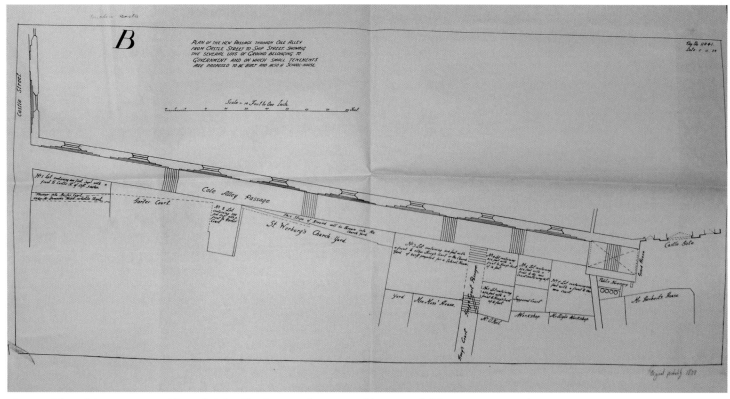

Fig. 3.73 'Plan of the New Passage Through Cole Alley from Castle Street to Ship Street...'. (Photostat copy NMS)

Where the steps descend into Ship Street, the passage passes through the guard house, its lower storey generously arched to accommodate it as the Ship Street façade is integrated with the main gateway, all handsomely expressed in granite ashlar with rustication, a Greek-key stringcourse and a thin cornice and deep blocking course. Over the passage arch, Johnston's guard house rises plainly with two storeys faced in brown Flemish-bonded brick and small tripartite windows in its two bays. The narrower eastern bay is slightly canted to align with the gateway below, and here on the lower storey an archway opens onto a wall walk that extends between the parapets of the gateway, obviously intended for defence while also providing a link to the former Quarter Master General's office, a building for which Johnston was also responsible in the same period and evidence that some of his work at the castle extended to military accommodation.

Strengthening the security of the castle not only impinged on the property and income of St Werburgh's parish it also had a direct effect on the external fabric of the church.[426] The spire of St Werburgh's was built in 1768 as a result of a specific bequest of Rev. Sir Henry Hoby, who left £1,000 in 1766. Joseph Tudor's view of the Upper Castle Yard of 1753 (Fig. 3.41) shows the church tower before the spire was added, its presence obvious yet somewhat picturesque rising off-centre between the still proud Bermingham Tower and the cupolaed Bedford Tower (though in reality

the latter building was as yet incomplete). The upper storey and tower, dating from the 1720s, and complete with the 1760s spire, are depicted in the Pool and Cash drawing of the west front, published in 1780, while James Malton's 1792 view of the Upper Castle Yard (Fig. 3.58) in effect updates Tudor's view, showing the east elevation of the tower and spire.

In 1788 the vestry had been concerned with the state of the 'steeple and bells' and the following year both steeple and spire were repaired by Alex Roche.[427] Twenty years later, in 1810, the state of the steeple was again a concern for the vestry, this time forced on them by the sessions of the Grand Jury which 'presented the steeple of Saint Werburgh's as a nuisance in danger of falling'.[428] Within days the vestry accepted a proposal from Edward Robbins, master of the bricklayers. However, efforts were made to retain the steeple and a meeting of the parishioners at the beginning of June examined proposals by Edward Carolan for propping up the spire, under the direction of Francis Johnston.[429] However, it resolved to adhere to its previous resolution and Robbins was contracted to take down the spire, the tower surviving until 1836 (Figs 3.74a, 3.74b, 3.74c). [430]

The proximity of St Werburgh's church to the castle had ensured royal patronage in the eighteenth century to support its erection in 1716, and rebuilding after a fire in 1754, the resulting architectural sophistication of the parish church likely to have served only to highlight the inferiority

Fig. 3.74a Samuel Brocas (d.1847), The Upper Castle Yard showing the spire of St Werburgh's Church in place (NLI, PD 1963 TX)

of the castle chapel. As previously discussed, proposals for rebuilding the chapel, which can be detected in 1770 and again in 1790, were revived in 1801 when the Chief Secretary, on behalf of the earl of Hardwicke, recently installed as Lord Lieutenant, requested James Gandon to submit designs. Although Gandon had designed all of Dublin's recent, major public buildings, he did not hold an official architectural post, and in this instance was aware of this and the potential conflict it might cause. While the project has the appearance of a personal one for Hardwicke, its initiation immediately after the Act of Union was undoubtedly of deeper, political significance. Catholic emancipation had been promised, or at least implied, in the lead up to the Union, but was vetoed by George III. The early decades of the nineteenth century saw a large-scale rebuilding of the stock of the Church of Ireland's church buildings. Hardwicke's initiative in the castle therefore may be seen as a harbinger of this process. However, it was stillborn. Robert Woodgate had been appointed Architect to the Board of Works in January

1802 to succeed Vincenzo Waldré and, despite this, Gandon proceeded to prepare 'Seven different designs for the intended chapel', expecting – with the Chief Secretary's reassurance – to have his involvement specially facilitated. However, although he received a favourable response to the designs from Hardwicke, his decision not to take on any further responsibility for the project came from a realisation that his involvement would in fact encroach on Woodgate's responsibilities.[431] Woodgate died in 1805, and it fell to his successor as Architect to the Board, Francis Johnston – and to Hardwicke's successor, the duke of Bedford – to revive the project.

Gandon's designs do not appear to have survived, but it seems certain that he was working with the old chapel site.[432] In March 1807 Johnston presented his estimate of £9,532 for building the new chapel (Fig. 3.75), the proposal also including an estimate for additions to the Treasury, costed at £1,373.[433] The Board responded with the suggestion that, as part of the works, the Wardrobe Tower should be remodelled

Fig. 3.74b Samuel Brocas (d.1847), The Upper Castle Yard. The pencil outlines suggest scaffolding and the recent removal of the spire. (NLI, PD 1963 TX)

to complement the new chapel.[434] Exactly a month after Johnston presented his estimate, the foundation stone was laid, though the 'apartments adjoining to the Castle Chapel' still stood on the site, and in fact it was only in the following month that their occupants were removed from the building 'in consequence of their being pulled down to clear the way for the new Chapel'.[435] Aside from the obvious restrictions of the site, the proximity of Poddle, which in Burgh's time had been culverted to flow around two sides, was somewhat problematic and the location also made finding a suitable foundation difficult, the exposure of an old limestone quarry meaning that piles were necessary.[436] It is not surprising therefore that Johnston's original estimate proved wildly optimistic, the final cost being in the region of £42,000, and the result of seven years' work.

Without question, the chapel is the single most important building erected in the castle since the eighteenth century, and the only one of major architectural significance among the nineteenth-century buildings, as well as being the principal survivor, retaining its interiors (with the exception of the pulpit and some pews). The building (Fig. 3.66) is more than twice the size of its predecessor, and whereas it was built cheaply of brick, Johnston's chapel was built of Dublin limestone in big ashlar blocks with finer Tullamore limestone used for the extensive carved detail. It has a large, boxy massing, enlivened with the full Gothic panoply of buttresses, battlements, pinnacles and a multiplicity of sculpture, with the medieval tower – dressed up as the Board requested with machicolated battlements – serving in effect as an imposing west tower. The challenges of the sloping site were rather successfully overcome; the building was raised over a brick-vaulted undercroft to achieve an essentially two-storied side elevation, the expression according with the galleried churches of the period. The result is an essentially rectangular plan of six bays, all vigorously defined with buttresses, the profile diminishing as they rise into crocketed pinnacles and finials, with a vestibule across the west end, the elevation stepped down to meet the tower and where the entrance opens on the north side. Between the buttresses, the parapets – a stringcourse giving them depth

Fig. 3.74c Samuel Brocas (d.1847), The Upper Castle Yard with the spire removed. (NLI, PD 1963 TX)

– are battlemented to reinforce the chapel's integration with the medieval tower. The tall clerestory-level windows, three lights under a heavy, pointed hoodmould on carved busts, contribute a great deal to the building's lightness and elegance; beneath these a row of squat four-centred arches to light below the galleries, and simpler single-lights to the undercroft nicely detailed with cusping under square heads. It is suggested convincingly that the side elevation of Magdalen College, viewed from the quad, was a source for the elevation here, while the upper windows may be based on the blind tracery of the cloisters of Gloucester cathedral which Johnston visited in 1796.[437]

The east end is handsomely composed, framed by shorter towers which contain vestries and stairs to the galleries, the height of the towers presented on the elevations in a way that balances the vestibule at the opposite end – a reminder of the principles of Georgian symmetry that essentially underlay Johnston's approach to Gothic design. Despite the diminutive scale of the towers, they are fully expressed with three storeys, each one rather like the tower of a rural

parish church complete with angle corner buttresses, so that against the higher form of the main gable with its raking line battlements, and the bold three dimensionality of the whole design, the sense of increased scale here is rather effective and the result quite imposing. The impression that this constitutes the 'west front' is reinforced by the battlemented vestibule at ground level, slightly recessed between the towers with an oversized entrance, leading not into the nave, as is suggested, but merely to give access to the tower stairs.

The large Perpendicular window, set over a projecting porch, embraced by a deeper pair of embattled towers of three storeys, certainly evokes the north end of old Westminster Hall (Fig. 3.76) in London which is frequently suggested as Johnston's source.[438] Westminster Hall was probably the best-known Gothic structure in Britain and Ireland and because of its legislative role it was particularly appropriate as a model for the church to serve this extension of national government, the viceregal court. The likely English sources for exterior features of the chapel do not exclude the

Fig. 3.75 Elevation of chapel, office of Francis Johnston. (OPW Dublin Castle)

Fig. 3.76 Entrance front of Westminster Hall. (John Goodall)

possibility that Johnston was also influenced by medieval Irish buildings he knew, which undoubtedly included the nearby St Patrick's and Christ Church cathedrals, and indeed those he had worked on like Armagh. The triple light windows of the ground floor, whatever their source, would become a design feature of many windows in the second stage of western towers of churches throughout the country. While the upper-floor windows are a very accomplished design, the individual elements, including cusped ogee lights under a square head, cusped ogee upper lights and supermullions, were not unknown in Irish medieval churches. Embattled towers on east and west gables and on transepts could be found at that date on Christ Church and St Patrick's cathedrals in Dublin and a number of parish churches within the Pale had quite similar features. The crocketed ogee arch over the east window terminating in a crocketed finial is a feature taken from later Irish medieval wall tombs.

There is an extraordinary profusion of figure sculpture on the chapel exterior, represented as busts with conventionalised dress to terminate the hood moulds, mark the apex of arches and as supports to the gables of the buttresses. They were carved by Edward Smyth, the most accomplished sculptor of the time, a pupil of Lord Charlemont's distinguished sculptor Simon Vierpyl, who worked here until his death in 1812 with his son, John, who was a worthy successor to his father's skills both as a carver and stuccodore. Figures include St Peter, Dean Swift (this rehabilitation of Drapier by the castle amusing enough in 1813 to warrant some fitting lines of poetry – *Can it be true – is this the head of peculations foe and dread?...*), Brian Boru and St Patrick, and busts of Charity and Hope to each side of the chancel window, and Faith (with a cross and chalice) above, under the ogee arch.[439]

Inside, Johnston adopted for the layout, the auditory church interior of Wren's city of London churches – a hall church with a U-shaped gallery intersected and supported by columns – and dressed it up in a curious mixture of almost fanciful, at times personal Gothic and some more established Georgian sculptural elements.[440] The deep, tall nave rises from an arcade of clustered colonettes into a delightful plaster rib vault, formed with a sexpartite arrangement, the ridge rib punctuated with large stiff-leaf bosses at the intersections and the vault ribs descending to large bust corbels set between the arches of the piers. Here the spandrels above the arches and the vault formeret are decorated with crocketed ogee arches given elaborate foliage finials. In 1825 it was claimed that the 'plans of the groined ceiling, and of various parts in the detail of this splendid pile, are derived from the most highly-ornamented divisions of York Cathedral', and the details suggest that Johnston was influenced by the relatively recent publication of Joseph Halfpenny's, *Gothic Ornaments in the Cathedral Church of York*.[441]

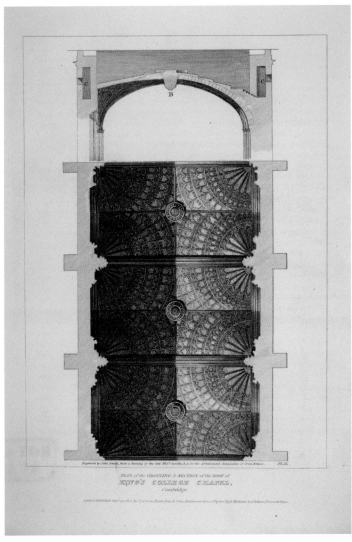

Fig. 3.77 Plan of the ceiling of King's College Chapel, Cambridge (Britton 1807–27, vol. I).

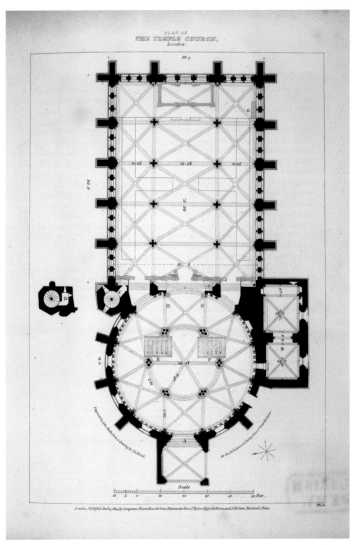

Fig. 3.78 Plan of the Temple Church, London (Britton 1807–27, vol. 1).

Contrasting with the clean and expressive Early-English form of the nave vault are the deep, exquisite conical fan vaults of mature Perpendicular Gothic that adorn narrow aisles over the galleries, and are repeated in a simpler form on the lower levels, but which in fact are first introduced with brio in the entrance vestibule. Richardson has argued convincingly that this may represent an elaboration of the initial design by Johnston, based on the growing availability of suitable pattern books. By 1807 John Britton had begun to publish his *Architectural Antiquities*, introducing illustrations that 'achieved an accuracy and detail never before attempted', and within two years Johnston could have availed of Britton's illustrations of the fan vaulting of the King's College Chapel, Cambridge (Fig. 3.77); he would also have gained insights into round churches, including the interesting plan of the Temple Church in London (Figs 3.78–9) which has more than a passing resemblance to the relationship between the Record Tower and the castle chapel.[442]

The sumptuous, virtuoso displays in the interior, both in the plaster work and the carving of the gallery frontal, naturally focus attention on the skills involved in executing the work. While 'all the sculptural figures and heads' were by John Smyth 'after the death of his father, who assisted him in the designs and models at the commencement of the work', the ceilings were carried out by George Stapleton, an outstanding Dublin stuccodore of the period, who like Smyth was the son of an accomplished artisan.[443] By 1813 Stapleton had been paid almost £2,800 for his work, which largely involved all the complicated mouldings and the traceries of the fan vaulting.[444] How far Stapleton may have contributed to the design is not known, though his surviving drawings do include a number relating to Gothic details, including corbel figures, and a sketch for a foliated ceiling boss comparable to those employed along the nave ridge: in 1812 he was paid £21 for '6 large Bosses of Gothic ornament foliages on intersections of crown arch ribs & centre main

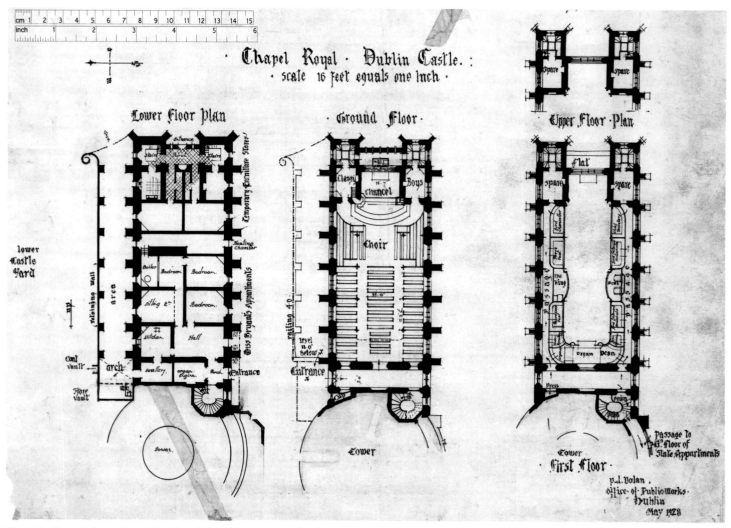

Fig. 3.79 Ground-floor plan of the Chapel Royal from a survey by P.J. Nolan, May 1928. (OPWT, E000519 U16-11)

rib' at a charge of £3/10 each.[445] The versatility of the Smyths in stone and plaster was matched by John Stewart and his son Richard Stewart who, as well as carving in stone, were highly skilled wood carvers; despite his disputatious character, it is to Richard that the best of the carved work – the extraordinary pulpit (now at St Werburgh's) and the coat of arms of the viceroys incorporated into the gallery frontals – is attributed.[446] More extensive by far than either Stewart's or Stapleton's contributions, was the work of the chapel carpenters. Less obvious, but vital for the entire structure and overall success of the interior including the rib and fan vaulting, this was mostly undertaken by Arthur Battersby, who besides being involved in regular timber work, making, reinforcing and installing the trusswork for the roof, the joists and flooring, was responsible for running all the mouldings, including for the columns and ribs as well as all the formwork and grounds for the plasterwork, his measured work listing, for example, 396ft (120.7m) 'for the circular grounds and studs…to take stucco moulding etc. of ceiling over main aisles'.[447] Perhaps the most impressive element of

Battersby's work was the passage to the chapel, for which he received £195 in 1812.[448] Most of those involved in the works at the chapel were employed regularly and extensively by the Board of Works, including elsewhere in the castle, with Stapleton, for example, involved in plastering works at the Record Tower in 1815, and later in the Upper Yard for works related to the visit of George IV in 1821.[449]

Still striking today, the appearance of the finished and furnished interior is presented in an early nineteenth-century view by the antiquarian, George Petrie (Fig. 3.80) in which the auditory arrangement is emphasised by the central authority of the double-decker pulpit, placed to the fore in the nave, comprising Stewart's goblet-like pulpit surrounded by the reading desk that has long since vanished. Suitably raised to address the elevated gallery pews of the viceroy, Lord Chancellor and the peers and peeresses, the visual focus of the pulpit and its decoration – the stem rising to the Bible-crowned heads of the Evangelists, with the equally symbolic arms of four monarchs who supported the Reformation displayed above – were all part of the fundamentally Protestant character of the building, and the insistent iconography of the Word that runs through the chapel.[450] Visible also in Petrie's view is the imposing canopied pew of the viceroy in the centre of the south gallery, and below, some of the original benches (which survive, used elsewhere), rather casually arrayed. However, by 1849 (Fig. 3.81) a series of Victorian high-backed pews had taken their place, most likely introduced with the choir stalls evident by then in the centre of the nave and shown more clearly in a view of the interior in 1854 by James Mahony.[451]

As the Gothic Revival gained currency in the nineteenth century, the Chapel Royal was subjected to greater academic scrutiny and changing attitudes to religious architecture that became increasingly doctrinaire; yet with all the structural dishonesty of its plaster vaulting, painted to imitate stone and its timber windows convincingly carved to imitate tooled stone mullions, it did not suffer the complete denigrations of the ecclesiological movement. In fact in

1852, at the height of the, at times frenzied, public discourse about architectural and liturgical reform, the building even earned the attention of the highly influential *Ecclesiologist*, its correspondent reporting that with its 'date and its locality both considered, there is perhaps hardly any more curious foreshadowing of the ecclesiological movement to be found in the kingdom'.[452] By 1860 the pulpit and reading desk were removed entirely (first to St John's beside Christ Church and later to St Werburgh's where the pulpit remains), replaced by – to our eyes – an incongruously heavy pulpit in Caen stone by the ecclesiastical artists and decorators Hardman & Co., set to one side with an equally bold iconography that reflected the spirit and aesthetic of the Gothic Revival in the wake of Pugin and the ecclesiological revolution of the 1840s.[453]

In its consideration of the chapel plans in 1807, the Commissioners of the Board had requested that the design also embrace 'ornamenting the old Tower immediately adjoining, so as to correspond with the elevation of the Chapel…'.[454] In 1793, just a couple of years after thoughts had first been given to rebuilding the chapel, the tower (Fig. 3.82) has been dismissed 'as a useless fabric' and accused of giving 'a disgraceful gloominess to the Viceregal residence, little according to the style and elegance of the other parts'.

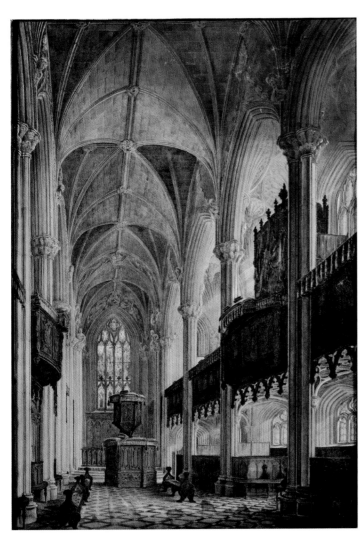

Fig. 3.80 George Petrie, early nineteenth-century view of the interior of the Chapel Royal. (Private collection, image courtesy of OPW Dublin Castle)

Fig. 3.81 Interior of the Chapel Royal from The Illustrated London News, 11 Aug. 1849. (Courtesy of OPW Dublin Castle)

WARD-ROBE TOWER of DUBLIN CASTLE.

Fig. 3.82 Woodcut view of the Wardrobe Tower from J.C. Walker 1788. (Cooper Walker 1788, 94).

Its survival was almost certainly due to its usefulness: as a result of 'the neglected condition of the public records' the tower soon 'attracted the serious attention of government [and] this ancient and massy pile was selected as the place of their future conservation'.[455]

Built in the early thirteenth century, its different names – Gunners Tower, Wardrobe Tower and Record Tower – reflected the variety of uses to which it was put over centuries, which also included a prison within its massive walls. In the late seventeenth century, entrance to the tower was from the Upper Yard beside the state apartments as shown in proposals in 1698 (Fig. 3.10). Thomas Penrose's plan of 1789 (Fig. 3.24) shows an entrance in the south-east corner (though not reflecting the true wall thicknesses), and this was evident again in the plan of the old chapel of c. 1800 (Fig. 3.12) with another shown to the south-east, passing through the tower wall to a passage that connected the state apartments to the old chapel. A later plan by Johnston implies this opening had, with the building of the new chapel, been filled in, a reflection most likely of the difference in levels between the tower and the old and new chapels respectively (Fig. 3.83).[456] Undertaking the works in tandem with the chapel, Johnston rebuilt the entire upper section of the tower walls (shown rather plainly in the late eighteenth-century topographical view Fig. 3.54), adding

rather emphatic machicolated battlements based on the Windsor Castle prototype. Inside the interior he sealed off the mural chambers formerly used as prison cells and inserted granite slab floors carried on radial brick walls to enhance the fireproofing. While exploiting the natural fire proofing of its thick walls and making the tower a completely independent building, as though essentially free standing, served its new role, this did in effect obstruct access to the chapel. Besides the difference in levels between the tower and the new chapel, accommodating new openings in the tower would have been difficult even if desired due to the thickness of its walls, which range from 9ft (2.7m) to 12ft (3.6m). This means the tower was never likely to be easily integrated with the new chapel. To overcome this, Johnston rather cleverly bypassed the tower by means of a castellated passage for the Lord Lieutenant and his retinue, which followed an elegant curve from the state apartments to end in a stair burrowed into the side of the tower, delivering the viceregal contingent into the south end of the chapel vestibule. Built outside the south tower wall, the passage is set back at first-floor level above the lower, canted building that skirted the tower base (Figs 3.83–4).[457] Erected by the carpenter Arthur Battersby, it is a lightweight structure in complete contrast to the ponderous masonry of the tower, built of timber – including its battlements – the framework filled with brick as a form of nogging, and coated in ruled and lined plaster, painted to blend with the masonry.

While these works were completed by 1813, it is uncertain whether any progress had been made to the additions to the Treasury that were envisaged in the same period. It is possible the idea was abandoned in response to concerns over costs, notwithstanding the recommendation that the board's own tradesmen should be employed to undertake the work in order to counteract 'the delay, bad workmanship, or other defects, so frequently attendant on Contracts for Public Works'.[458] The space between the original Treasury and the east range of the Upper Yard was already partly built up before 1801 (Fig. 3.62) and a plan of the ground floor in 1829 (Fig. 3.67) shows the space occupied by the Chief Secretary's kitchen, suggesting that this had been added as part of Darley's work from the 1790s.[459] This kitchen seems only to have been accommodated at the lower level with an access stair to one side, the entire screened from the Lower Yard, as Sautelle-Robert's view of the Lower Yard confirms (Fig. 3.63).[460] The interior of the Treasury was modernised under Jacob Owen, who in 1837 inserted a granite, double return stair, but otherwise the exterior retained its early Georgian character.[461] By 1843 (Fig. 3.37) the building had been extended substantially to the west, and two unsigned, undated plans of the Upper Yard, which can be ascribed to this period, show these additions in greater detail, and based on analysis appear to relate to Owen's additions to the Chief Secretary's office from 1840–1 (Figs 3.85–6). This essentially provided a series of offices, with a large library projected behind to the north. In filling the space between the Treasury and the Cross Block, Owen respected entirely the established architectural detail of the Upper Yard, the effect of its scale and detail, especially the extended attic storey, resulting in a rather jarring contrast with the Treasury block.[462]

In the years up to 1802, works at the castle had amounted to the rather significant sum of £70,000.[463] Much of this expenditure related to rebuilding the Chief Secretary's office from the foundations and associated works from the 1790s.[464] For the rest of the decade, as the building of the chapel got underway, works elsewhere were limited to essential repairs, which included the roof of St Patrick's

Hall, Johnston conducting repairs here in 1808.[465] After 1815 attention seems to have turned again to the Upper Yard, where a programme of comprehensive works was undertaken; the most significant and far reaching for the external appearance of the building involved the continuation of the attic storey above the cornice, first introduced here in the 1770s to replace the dormers which had characterised the other ranges, having been first introduced on the south-east range in the late seventeenth century.[466] Some associated works also related to the pending visit of George IV in 1821, though these most likely focused on the suitable presentation of the interiors of the state apartments.[467] Certainly the impression gained within the next few years suggests that any works carried out for the royal visit were largely superficial. In 1823,

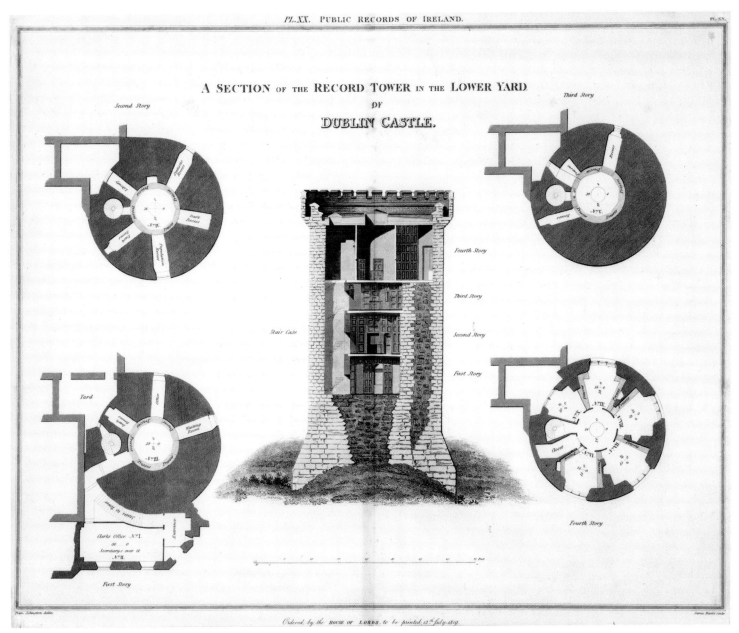

Fig. 3.83 Plans and section of the Record Tower by F. Johnston, 1813 engraved by James Basire. (RCPRI 1810–15)

SOUTH VIEW OF THE RECORD TOWER,
IN THE
LOWER YARD OF THE CASTLE OF DUBLIN.

Fig. 3.84 *South View of the Record Tower*, 1813 drawn by W. Flavelle, engraved by James Basire. (RCPRI 1810–15)

Francis Johnston produced an assessment of the buildings in the Upper Yard in advance of recommending a series of phased works.[468] He found the state apartments to be in poor condition generally, with repairs required throughout to windows and floors; the ceiling of the Presence Chamber (Throne Room) was said to be 'giving way' and the portico was beginning to lean forward 'three inches beyond its perpendicular position' – the result of 'an ill-constructed roof, lately replaced'. However, Johnston had specifically surveyed the rooms over the 'Public Drawing Rooms' of the state apartments as well as 'the upper floor and roof of the Western Range and of the return on the North side as far as the Bedford Tower' and found that 'these three divisions' were in a state of dilapidation, with 'the roofing, the slating, and the upper floors' especially found to be in a 'state of progressive decay', and altogether a source of 'continual expense' and a challenge to be kept 'in any degree habitable'.

Johnston also charted some of the recent history of the stilted progress, noting that 'parts of this Quadrangle, have at different periods been new roofed, and the attic stories improved by elevating the front wall, and substituting proper windows instead of the Dormant [*sic*] ones formerly placed in the roof, which has added to the convenience and comfort within, as well as to the appearance on the outside of those Buildings'. He also confirmed that Darley's complete rebuilding of the Chief Secretary's offices between 1798 and 1805 (works which straddled Waldré's and Woodgate's tenures as chief architect) included provision for the attic storey as a continuation of those on the east Cross Block begun more than a decade earlier. As a result, the attics were extended right across the east range as far as the state apartments, the work to extend it on the south range only resuming during the lord lieutenancy of Lord Talbot (1817–21). Completed in 1819, it was extended west from the Record Tower only as far as the entrance portico, terminating over the old Presence Chamber.

Given his assessment of the upper floors of the remaining parts of the Upper Yard in 1824, Johnston advocated that the completion of the attics was 'useful and necessary, for the preservation and Security of the Castle Buildings'. To achieve this, he proposed phasing the works over three years, the bulk of the work to be carried out in the first year at a total estimated cost of £5,247. This involved completing the attics over the south-west portion of the state apartments, including alterations to the roof of St Patrick's Hall, converting it 'from a deep valley into a raised platform covered with Copper', as well as new floors and windows in the 'Public Drawing Rooms' and structural 'alterations on front and interior of the Presence Chamber and for the permanent security of the portico and Ceiling'. The following year he proposed forming the attics over the west range, then occupied by the state steward, chamberlain and gentleman usher.[469] In the final year, 1826, he proposed extending the attic storey over the Under Secretary's office in the north-west corner, as far as the Bedford Tower.

An unsigned, undated plan of the attic storey (Fig. 3.87), very possibly by Johnston, relates directly to these proposals, showing clearly the extent of the works, highlighting even the alterations to the roof of St Patrick's Hall. The entire scheme was progressed over the ensuing years, and perhaps the most interesting element involved the introduction of free-standing columns in the Presence Chamber (Throne Room), designed to support the sagging beam across the northern projection of the room.[470] The works must have been largely complete by 1826 when an estimate of £3,399 was submitted for furnishing the state apartments.[471]

The results of Johnston's programme of works is evident from the visible differences between two views of the Upper Yard based on drawings by George Petrie (Fig. 3.88), published in 1821 and 1832 respectively.[472] In the earlier view the attics

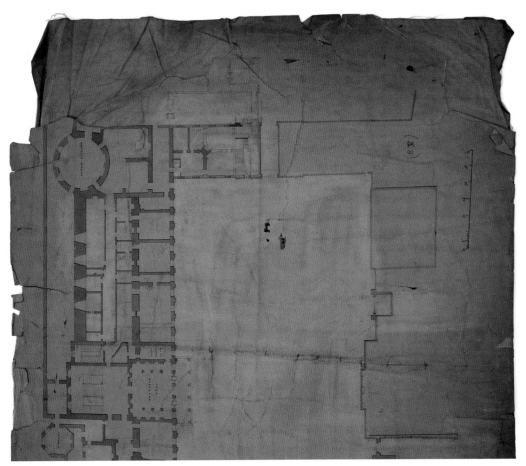

Fig. 3.85 Detail from a plan of the Upper Yard *c.* 1840 (west at top). (OPWT, E000508 U16-8)

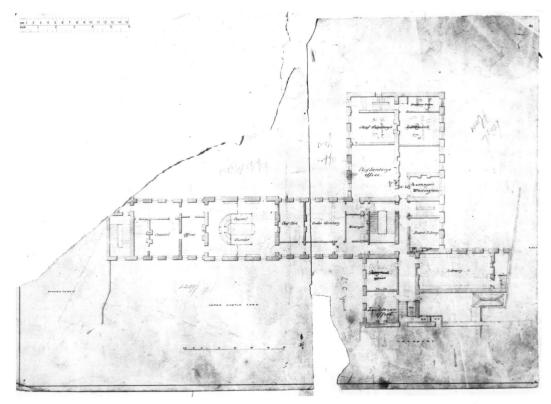

Fig. 3.86 Plan of additions to Chief Secretary's offices *c.* 1840 (west at top). (OPWT, E000508 U16-8)

between the south-east and north-east corners have been raised (that the attics on the east Cross Block are extant at this time is confirmed in Sautelle-Robert's 1816 view of the Lower Yard, Fig. 3.63) while the dormers remained across the western roofs, and in the later view only the Bedford Tower remains to be treated. Although the estimates do not refer to the attics of the Bedford Tower, these were completed later – obvious in the difference in the brick that was used – most likely by William Murray's successor Jacob Owen, and certainly were extant by 1844 when Michael Angelo Hayes (Fig. 3.89) showed them in a view of a *St Patrick's Day Military Parade at Dublin Castle* in the Upper Yard. However, there is evidence for a more dramatic treatment, in an unresolved design (Fig. 3.90) that can be attributed to Owen, most likely produced in the late 1830s. This envisaged the elaboration

of the end bays in the Bedford Tower, with the insertion of tripartite windows and the creation of a low attic, which is given a proportionably low tripartite window (similar to the example in Owen's carriage house) and shown with its own pyramidal roof rising over the parapet. As part of this, it was proposed to extend the screen walls flanking Nevill's pedimented gateways by raising them up above the level of the gates to create an upper floor, the main cornice extended across and a low attic expressed above. The effects were not entirely happy, upsetting the pleasing hierarchies and balance attained in Nevill's design; the fact that the drawing has not been fully worked up suggests that this realisation quickly became clear in a task perhaps forced by the pressures for increased accommodation, and (with the proposed enlargement of the windows) desires to modernise

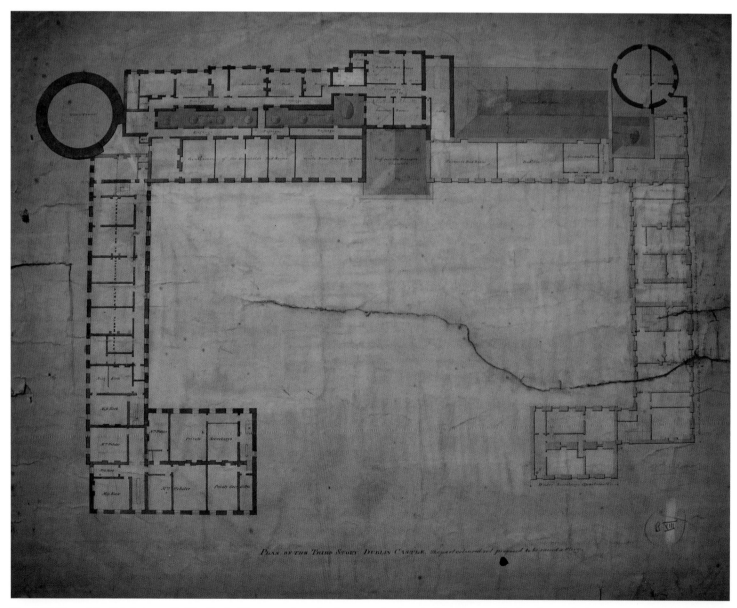

Fig. 3.87 Plan of the third-storey, Dublin Castle. The part coloured red proposed to be raised a storey, *c.* 1825 (south at top). (OPWT, E000505 U16-7)

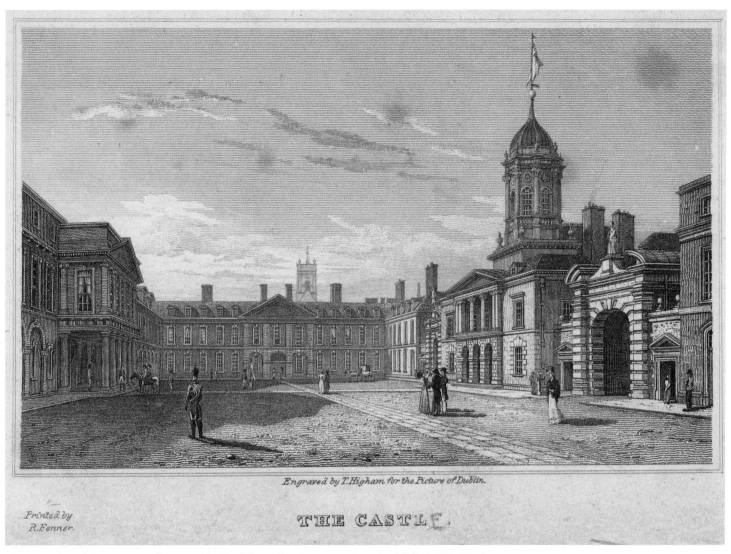

Printed by
R.Fenner.

Engraved by T.Higham for the Picture of Dublin.

THE CASTLE.

Fig. 3.88 View of the Upper Yard engraved by T. Higham after George Petrie and published 1839. (NGI)

conditions. More successful in design, but equally failed in realisation, is a design (Fig. 3.91) – perhaps related – for the addition of a porte cochère to the main entrance that is also attributable to Owen. The plan of the entrance hall and grand staircase behind remained unchanged, having been faithfully rebuilt 1825–6 by Johnston to address structural problems caused by the Presence Chamber above.[473] However, Neville's 1740s staircase was remodelled by Owen in the 1830s, given its present iron balustrade attributed to the ironmaster Richard Turner, and it is possible the extension of the portico was envisaged as part of these works.[474] The design proposed projecting the entire ground-floor order, repeating the hexastyle form but expressing it in an elaborated Italianate style, with two free-standing Roman Doric columns in a double row, set in antis, between piers given pilasters to the corners and framing a niche inset between. The entablature is crowned with a balustrade, with low recessed panel to the blocking course over the end bays.

While this was not executed, the previous open arrangement of the entrance was already by then enclosed, and while further thoughts were given to extending the entrance with canopies, these were only effected later and were of lighter, less permanent nature (Fig. 3.92).[475] Inside, Owen carried out further remodelling in the state apartments, extending over a number of years from 1838. This included opening up the three south-facing state rooms in the west wing, including the former state dining room, and inserting a screen of Greek Ionic columns in the opened-up walls (Fig. 3.59) to create a single, large state drawing room (now the Picture Gallery). On the opposite side, the rooms beyond the former Presence Chamber were united to form the private drawing room, a screen of Corinthian columns introduced at the east end. The increased scale and grandeur of these rooms is rather marked, reflecting the expanding social role of the viceregal court, the castle season becoming the highlight of the year for Victorian and Edwardian high society (Fig.

231

Fig. 3.89 Michael Angelo Hayes, *St Patrick's Day Military Parade at Dublin Castle* 1844.
(Photograph: Davison and Associates; courtesy of OPW Dublin Castle)

Fig. 3.90 Elevation showing unexecuted alterations to the Bedford Tower *c.* 1840. (OPWT, E000528 U16-14)

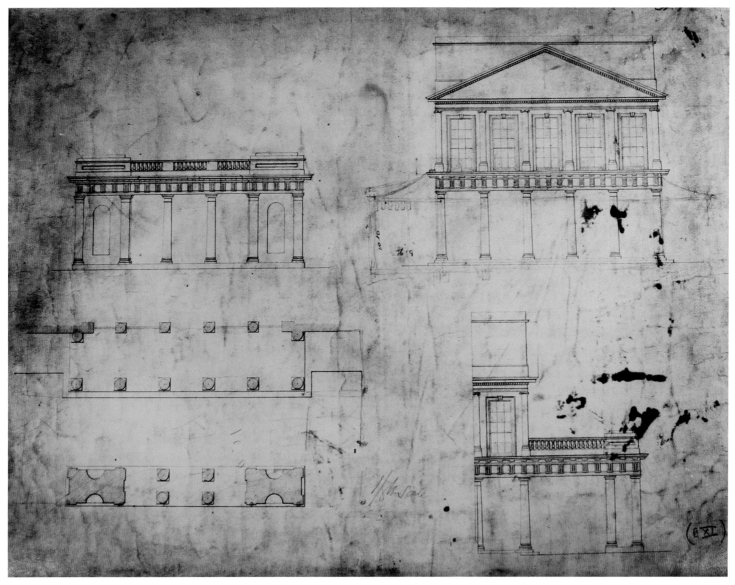

Fig. 3.91 Proposal for a porte cochère for the entrance to the state apartments *c.* 1840. (OPWT, E000528 U16-14)

3.93). Most interesting among Owen's works in this period was the raising of the ceiling of the Presence Chamber, completed by 1848 when he published a description of the process:

> For the purpose of affording additional means of ventilation, and for the improvement of the architectural character of the Presence Chamber... it was determined to give increased elevation to the room, and as the pilasters and surrounding entablature, which was continued round the walls, formed prominent features worthy of being preserved, it was deemed expedient that the design of the new ceiling, should be subservient to this end...[476]

Essentially having removed the slates and cut away the former flat ceiling, the framed queen post roof structure was raised using screw jacks and secured, with a new cove formed to allow the existing entablature to be successfully retained. The effect, while sacrificing the recent, highly decorated stucco ceiling (Fig. 3.37), was certainly more impressive, providing fitting ostentation for the pomp of the Victorian viceroys. Minor works involved remodelling of the vestibules under the galleries to St Patrick's Hall, the doorcases distinguished by their Greek Revival design.

Fig. 3.92 Late nineteenth-century view of the Upper Yard showing canopy at the entrance. (NLI, Lawrence Collection)

Fig. 3.93 FJ. Davis, view of *The State Ballroom Dublin Castle c.* 1850. (Private collection; image courtesy of Sotheby's)

Chapter 3.10
The Lower Castle Yard 1800–50

William Murray's plan of the castle stable yard in 1829 (Fig. 3.94) offers the most detailed survey of the buildings and their uses in the early decades of the nineteenth century. The main stable yard continued to be screened off at the eastern side of the yard. By then, the wings of the Spur Guard were extended on the west side, leaving only the western face of the hexagon as a shallow projection, with, on each side, a single, blind bay. Murray's survey shows that, by then at least, the main stables still occupied a large block in the centre of the yard while the riding house remained the largest and most dominant structure, set to the south, with nine bays on the north elevation and a single window opening in the centre of the east gable.[477] The boiler house and yard are shown against the north elevation, but there is also an external staircase shown beside the main entrance, while on the south side the yard has been enlarged, and the stables much reduced from their extent in 1817, the latter a modest two-bay block on the south-eastern corner, shown with five stalls and represented as the 'gentleman usher's stables'. The irregular plot across the unfenestrated west gable is still evident, and in 1829 was now labelled as 'Mr Keck's house' – a reference to Thomas Keck who was Keeper of the Civil Office.[478]

In 1817 (Fig. 3.95), without apparent alteration to the older plan, the main stable block seems also to have accommodated 'Ordnance Offices'. As delineated by Murray, major remodelling, perhaps even rebuilding, appears to have been undertaken here before 1829. The servants' apartments indicated here in 1769 had been reordered to become the gentleman porter's house. Ranged behind this house, and extending to the eastern perimeter wall, the stables and coach houses had also been completely reconfigured, still divided into two ranges by a spine wall, but each differently subdivided – the north range accommodating a series of coach houses (with six bays) and stables for the coach horses

(with ten stalls), while to the south there was a series of three discrete stables, the largest indicated for saddle horses (six stalls) and road horses (ten stalls). There was also a staircase, presumably to give access to hay lofts. By 1843 (Fig. 3.37), after the stable accommodation within the castle was reorganised by Jacob Owen, this entire block was reduced in scale when the gentleman porter's house, some of the coach houses and saddle horse stables were demolished and replaced instead by four new coach houses across the west end.

The former riding master's house in the north-west corner of the stable yard was labelled as the 'Aid-de-Camps' House' in 1829, and visible in an early twentieth-century aerial photograph of the yard (Fig. 3.96) where it appears as a substantial three-storied, stucco-fronted block with parapet, suggesting it was remodelled by Owen as part of the major reconfiguration of the yard after 1843 (Fig. 3.97).[479] The residence of the town major, Major Sirr (d. 1841) was attached at the east end of this block, his accommodation here presumably necessitated by the loss of the old town major's quarters during the rebuilding of the chapel. Adjoining Sirr's house, extending transverse-wise to a deep narrow plan and set parallel to one another, was a workshop and the Under Secretary's coach house. Next to these the Under Secretary's stable with eight boxes and the Chief Secretary's stable with nine boxes, were set side by side, the latter slightly deeper in plan with a triangular staircase set to one side, extending towards the skewed east wall which enclosed an adjoining triangular (perhaps open) space. Another coach house with two bays lay to the south of the triangular stair and the Chief Secretary's stable. In the north-east corner of the stable yard, set in its own enclosed space, was the farrier's yard including forge building and a stable with three boxes.[480] The eastern range, extending from the main stable block behind the riding house to the

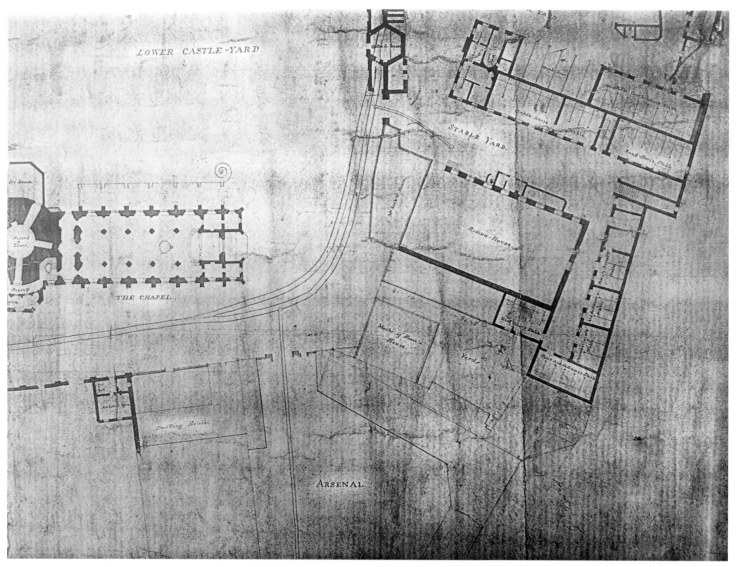

Fig. 3.94 Lower Castle Yard from a general plan of Dublin Castle by William Murray, August 1829. (NMS xerox copy)

housekeeper's apartments, provided further stables with no change evident since 1817 (Fig. 3.95) other than minor reconfiguration to extend the 'First Aide-de-Camp's Stable', the open flight of steps at the north end of the range presumably still leading to the coach men's apartments above the stables.[481] By 1800, Thomas Eyre's house at the south-east corner of the yard had been divided between the 'Ordnance Office' and 'Ingineers Office'; it was surrendered to the Military Secretary in the early nineteenth century and in 1817 it was shown divided between the 'Under Secretary of Wars' house' and the 'Secretary at Wars' Office'. By 1829 it was the residence of the 'Master of Horse'.[482] It survived until the 1960s. Outside of the confines of the eastern stable yard, there was additional stabling accommodated on the north side of the Lower Yard, on a site closely related to Wentworth's kingly stables but now directly behind the Treasury block (Fig. 3.98), separated from it by a passage

later named the 'Cavalry Picket Yard'.[483] In 1829 this narrow range accommodated stables for the Cavalry Guard, which dominated at the north end with a guard room between the two buildings, closing the north end of the passage. Adjoining the main Cavalry Guard stables to the south, in the same range but slightly deeper in plan, were a number of individual stables (including the town major's) and a coach house with the 'Cavalry Guard Room' at the end adjoining the Palace Street gate.[484]

Despite the failure of the ambitious schemes of the Wide Streets Commissioners to remodel the entire stable yard in the 1770s (Fig. 3.34), some elements of the scheme appear to have been revived in the 1830s when a new guard house was built, after the south side of the castle garden was given over in 1832 for a substantial new stable and coach house range, built in a formidable castellated style by Jacob Owen (Figs 3.99–100).[485] Built in 1837, Owen's new building replaced the

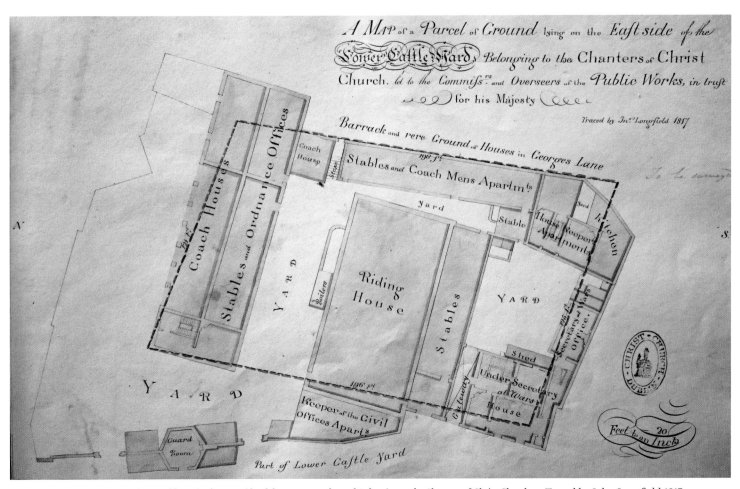

Fig. 3.95 *A Map of a Parcel of Ground lying in the East side of the Lower Castle Yard Belonging to the Chanters of Christ Church.... Traced by John Longfield 1817* (east at top). (NLI, MS 2790 f54)

old Spur Guard or Cavalry Guard house. The new building is shown on the first editions of the Ordnance Survey (Fig. 3.37), represented as a much more substantial five-bay block, replacing the more modest hexagonal eighteenth-century building with its various additions shown in Longfields's map of 1817 (Fig. 3.95). With two storeys and a raised parapet, the new guard house appears to have deliberately evoked the idea of a triumphal arch, evident particularly in the projection of the central bay and the creation of a tripartite archway that extended, rather grandly, with internal columns forming an arcade passing through the building (Fig. 3.101) from front to rear, and all purposely aligned with the central archways of the east range, leading into the Upper Castle Yard. The clear affinity this building has with earlier formal schemes of the Wide Streets Commissioners to open up the easterly approach to the castle suggests that either these plans were not entirely made redundant after 1800 (notwithstanding the discouragement likely to have been generated by valid security concerns), or at the very least that Owen may simply have been inspired by them. Owen's design accords axially and in plan, though is actually

positioned further east than the position indicated on the eighteenth-century plan (Fig. 3.34). The internal stable court was made square and rather formal in the following year, with corresponding gateways set symmetrically in each of the corners, and as part of this the aide-de-camp's house was retained to the north, remodelled with a stuccoed façade and given a new, enlarged enclosure to the front with a small yard behind (Fig. 3.96). As part of the ongoing rebuilding of the entire stable yard after 1843 Owen – who retired in 1856 – also seems to have rebuilt the riding house on a new site set against the east wall, and on a reduced scale to its predecessor; but clearly any lingering intention to open up this area of the castle as formerly envisaged was never advanced further. [486]

The classical stucco-fronted carriage house, with its rusticated ashlar ground floor, was erected as a western extension of the spur that projected from the former Surveyor General's house (Fig. 3.101). Designed by Owen in 1838, it formed part of the conversion of the arsenal into a barracks for the Dublin Metropolitan Police, and was erected over the former entrance to the old carriage yard

Fig. 3.96 Aerial photo of Lower Yard including stables with aide-de-camps' house visible lower right (late 1940s). (Air Corps photo, Military Archives)

(its tall solid square piers topped by a cluster of cannon balls is shown in the late eighteenth-century topographical view – Fig. 3.54), its central segmental arch overlooked by a pedimented tripartite window maintaining the access to the yard, which thereafter became the 'Police Commissioner's Yard' (Fig. 3.103). West of this, beside the eighteenth-century arsenal ('armoury') the architect's office is a neat two-storied building to a square plan with a shallow pyramid roof built between 1801 and 1829 inside the north-east angle of the garden wall, its design attributable to either Johnston or Murray, and later made part of a formal composition with an ashlared screen wall – probably by Owen (Figs 3.37, 3.101). On the opposite side, William Murray made proposals (Fig. 3.102) in 1828 to remodel the 'old wall' at the base of the state apartments that aligned the route from Ship Street

into the Lower Yard. He proposed a new castellated screen wall and indicated that by partly 'straightening the new line of wall' the passage could be widened by 5ft (1.5m). The wall was relieved by gently projecting square towers at each end and a central one intended as a meat larder, while the intervening walls on each side screened various stores and yards, including coal and charcoal stores (to the west) and a yard for the state kitchen and engine shed (to the east). By 1828 the bridge from the south terrace to the castle garden had been located further west (and heightened?) from its former position, and where it is now accessed through the tower surviving from Eyre's octagonal library. Both the tower and the terrace wall received stepped battlemented tops and battlements, possibly all done as part of Murray's work on the screen wall in 1828.

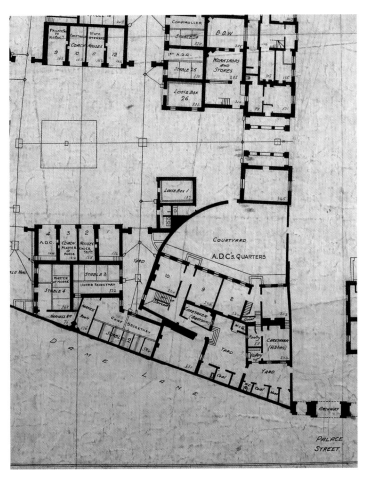

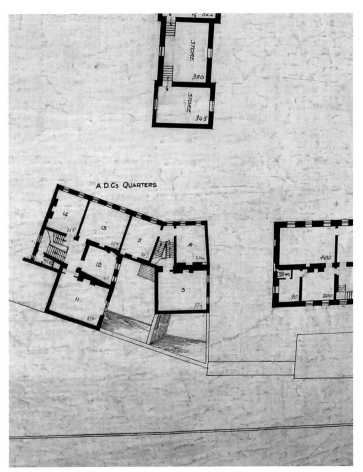

Fig. 3.97a Ground-floor plan of aide-de-camp's house from an early twentieth-century survey (south at top). (OPWT, E000486 U16-4)

Fig. 3.97b First-floor plan of aide-de-camp's house from an early twentieth-century survey (south at top). (OPWT, E000486 U16-4)

By 1801, the formality of the castle gardens seems to have been dispensed with, the perimeter path remaining but enclosing instead a more more naturalistic, random arrangement of tree clumps in the centre and with perimeter beds and shrubberies inside the walls, giving the overall impression that the gardens had been gradually adapted to reflect gardening fashions, including ideas of the picturesque to which the provision of new stables naturally contributed. What was intended as a 'State' stable and coach house in the castle gardens in 1832, soon after Jacob Owen succeeded Murray to the post of architect, reflected both the growing ceremonial splendour of the viceregal court, and the gradual agglomeration of additional government departments within the castle precincts, which necessitated extensive changes of use and rebuilding throughout the Lower Castle Yard, including alterations to the main stable yard, largely to maintain the stabling needs of the key members of the household.[487] Built in sombre calp limestone as a long, low battlemented range (Figs 3.99, 3.104) with a central gatehouse and narrow machicolated end towers, its design, deliberately perhaps, amplifies Murray's earlier screen wall opposite, and to greater picturesque effect. Inside, either side of the gatehouse was given over

to stalls, sixteen to the east, and twelve to the west where a deep coach house adjoined as a separate area, while the associated grooms' accommodation was provided in the two-storey towers at each end. More extensive provision, including the state coach house, harness rooms, carriage washing rooms and a manure yard, was eventually disposed around the large stable yard created behind the building, accessed directly through the gatehouse, and from the drive formed along the east side of the garden (Fig. 3.100). As a consequence of this new building, the garden layout was changed again, its reduced scale clearly represented in 1843 (Figs 3.37, 3.105). The design, however, still remained largely informal, dominated by a circular path and with only limited planting suggested, implying that emphasis was being given to selected specimens.

On the west side of the castle garden the old store house building seems to have been more fully adapted as a barrack after 1801 (Fig. 3.62) and it remained the principal barrack until remodelled in 1819 as the ordnance office (now The Chester Beatty Library and known as the Clock Tower Building) with a much enlarged front (though in Sautelle-Robert's 1816 view (Fig. 3.63), even without a clock tower it appears as a substantial block), most likely to designs by Francis Johnston.[488] With the transfer of the infantry barracks to the rebuilt houses along Great Ship Street, the southern portions, including most of the tent stores and the laboratory office, were demolished to make way for the parade ground and the Royal Engineer's office (Fig. 3.37).

By 1850 all buildings on the east side of Ship Street and the western half of Stephen Street had been fully incorporated into the castle precincts – in two stages from 1808–20 when the works were overseen by Francis Johnston assisted by William Murray, and the remainder after 1843.[489] In contrast to the works affecting Cole Alley and Castle Street, an entirely different approach was taken for enclosing the castle along Great Ship Street, which extends along the south-west flank of the castle gardens. Comparing the 1801 surveys (Figs 3.62, 3.65) and the 1843 Ordnance Survey (Fig. 3.37) reveals the extent to which Ship Street had been absorbed into the castle in these intervening years. The alignment of the street did not alter, and it even appears that some of the older houses on Ship Street were initially retained.

Already discussed in detail, Thomas Sherrard's map (Fig. 3.64) of the castle clearly showed its early-nineteenth-century extent, revealing its jagged or stepped property boundaries on the Ship Street side. Unlike on Castle Street and Cole Alley, the property boundaries behind the houses facing onto Ship Street were much deeper, indicating of course that these were altogether more substantial houses. Comparing Chaigneau's and Sherrard's surveys there are many anomalies between them, notably in how the buildings on Ship Street are depicted; the difference may be explained because Chaigneau's survey was concerned principally with buildings associated with the castle and so did not detail all adjoining properties outside of government ownership or occupation. If so, it underlines the rather incoherent collection of buildings around the castle periphery, which justified the efforts of the castle to consolidate its ownership and control of Ship Street.

After the initial phase of works on Ship Street c. 1807, involving Johnston's new west gate and guard house, the works progressed on the adjoining site at the north end of

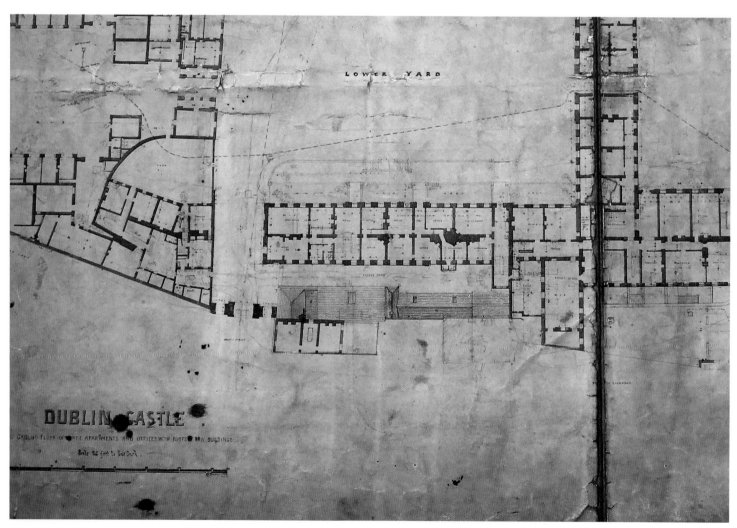

Fig. 3.98 Buildings to the rear of the Treasury, from a general survey c. 1850 (south at top). (OPWT, E000486 U16-3)

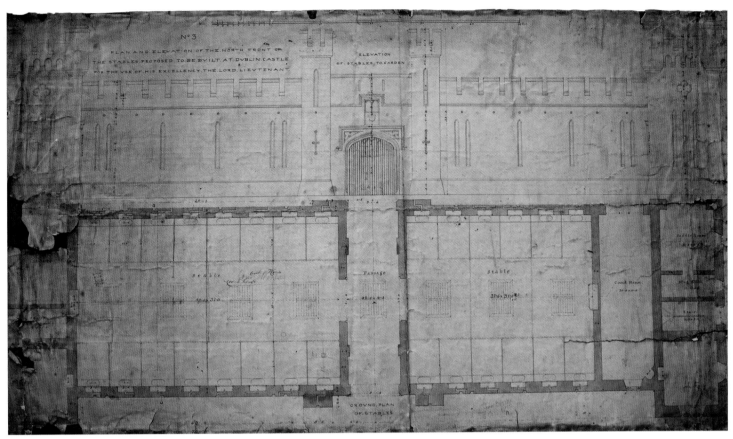

Fig. 3.99 Elevation and plan of new stables signed by John Butler 15 Oct. 1832. (OPWT, E000505 U16-7)

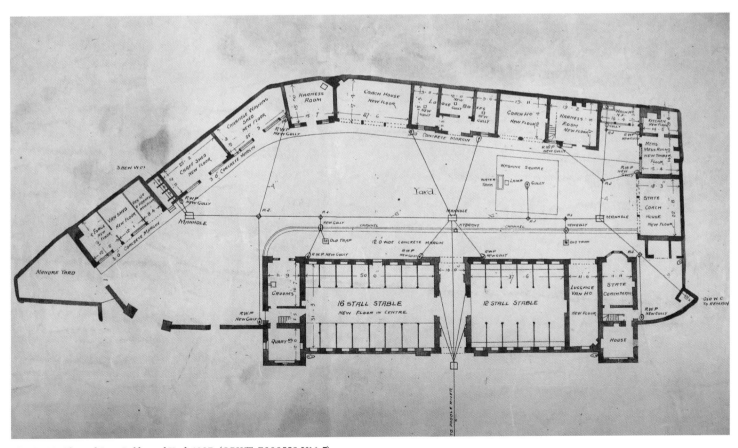

Fig. 3.100 Plan of *State Stables and Yard*, 1897. (OPWT, E000558 U16-7)

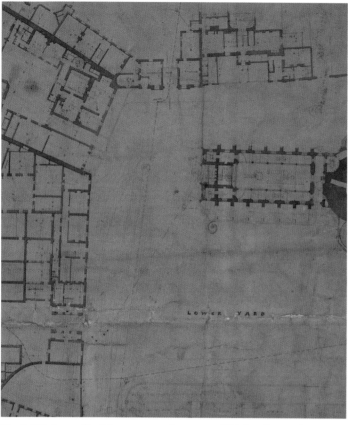

Fig. 3.101 Lower Yard from a general survey *c.* 1850 (south at top). (OPWT, E000486 U16-3)

the street, which involved the demolition of a large number of premises to accommodate the Quarter Master General's office.[490] On part of this site, after the first four houses, the narrow passage of Buckridge's Court (evident on Rocque's map in 1756 – Fig. 3.11) entered through one of the houses on Ship Street, and leading directly to the rear wall of the principal barrack, a large U-plan building on the west side of the castle garden which was later enlarged as the ordnance office (now The Chester Beatty Library).[491] It is clearly represented in 1756 and again in Sherrard's 1801 survey where a tightly compressed group of smaller buildings, aligned north–south, faced into the court along the north side, with a wall to the south dividing a separate passage servicing some of the mews buildings attached to the adjacent houses fronting Ship Street (both appear on Chaigneau's 1801 survey, labelled respectively 'Buckeridger's Court' and 'Stable Lane'). The court is mentioned in *Pigot's Directory* in 1824, however, it seems most likely that it survived in name only, the Ordnance Survey of 1843 (Fig. 3.37) confirming that the passage and the complex interlocking group of buildings on its north side, along with the three houses at the north end of Ship Street, were all entirely replaced by Johnston's new Quarter Master General's office. Although the precise date of its erection is not known, the Quarter Master's complex was certainly in existence by 1820.[492]

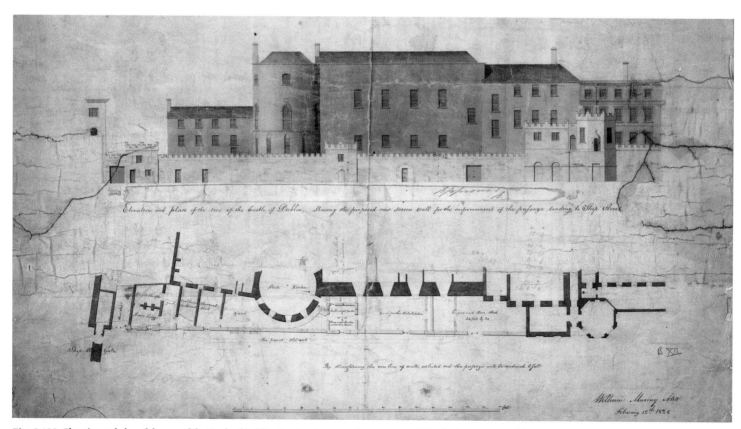

Fig. 3.102 *Elevation and plan of the rear of the Castle of Dublin, showing the proposed new screen wall for the improvement of the passage leading to Ship Street.* William Murray. February 12 1828. (OPWT, E000505 U16-7)

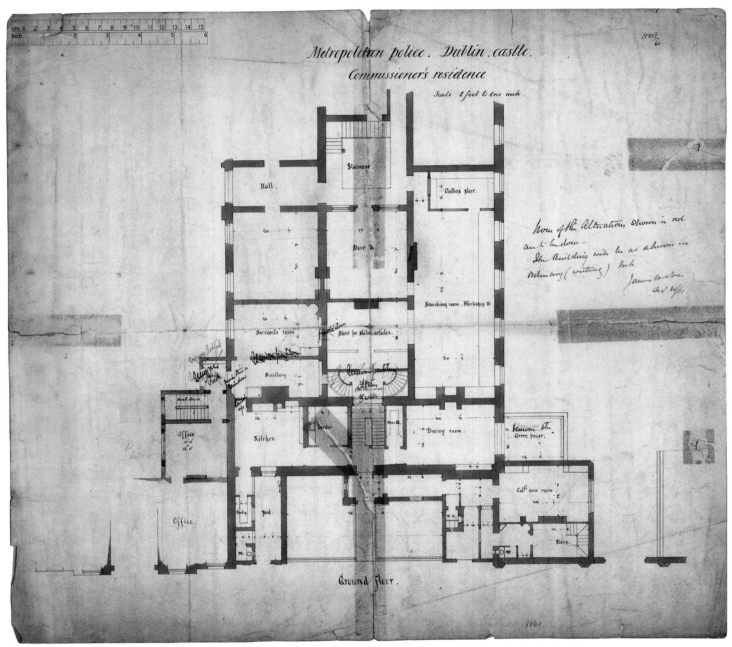

Fig. 3.103 Plan of Metropolitan Police Commissioner's residence, Lower Yard. 11 Oct. 1861 (south at top). (OPWT, E000505 U16-7)

However, as the building was set further back on Ship Street than its predecessors to align with the new gateway, with a yard and offices extending behind, it is likely that it was conceived as an integral part of the works of 1807–08.

By 1843 most of the houses at the southern end of Ship Street had become part of a discrete military complex, now incorporating the infantry barracks. An undated survey of the castle and its environs, possibly by Johnston and made after 1807, clearly shows the new Quarter Master complex (Fig. 3.46) and details a variety of proposals, mostly affecting Ship Street and Stephen Street. On Ship Street, the group of four houses immediately south of the Quarter Master block

are rendered differently, presumably indicating that they remained in private occupation, while the following three blocks are simply listed as 'houses'. South of the passage to the 'Barrack Yard' the first building, which extends along most of the passage, is identified as 'stables and stores' with the remaining seven houses on Ship Street labelled as 'Ordnance Dwellings'. The remaining section of the street and returning into Stephen's Street is represented by a large U-plan block for the 'Commandant of Artillery's Residence'. Beside it the 'Commanding Royal Engineer's Residence', which relates to Leitrim House, continued in use as officers' quarters, and is where the central passage, which is still such

Fig. 3.104 The state stables. (NLI Lawrence Collection)

a distinctive feature of the house, originally provided access to the Royal Engineer's office at the rear though this access seems no longer available by 1843.[493] The Royal Engineer's office had been enlarged before 1843, extended into the space where the ordnance stores stood, its place largely given over to a parade ground. After Buckridge's Court was demolished, it was replaced by an extended infantry barracks facing onto Ship Street and the parade ground was enlarged to the north in the area between the barracks and the ordnance office.

Although Ship Street had been regularised into a tall terrace of relatively uniform blocks, the untidy rear elevations and backyards of houses on Stephen Street and George's Street must have become more evident, meaning that Owen's stable and coach house now served an enhanced aesthetic function, to block, or at least distract from, this relatively unsightly ensemble, when viewed from the rarefied, gilded interiors of the state apartments.

Fig. 3.105 The castle gardens. (NLI Lawrence Collection)

Chapter 3.11
Conclusion

In considering the presence of the court at Dublin Castle in the seventeenth century, Toby Barnard has pointed out how it 'suffered the benefits and problems of centrality'; as long as it could accommodate the Lord Lieutenant for the brief periods when parliament was sitting and was able to administer the business of government through the core personnel based in it, there seemed no urgency to devote unnecessary expense or effort to its improvement. In any case the long-standing restraints of the city centre site, together with the continued use of, if not dependency on, older buildings meant that only a piecemeal improvement was possible without upsetting the ongoing occupation of the site.[494] Such were the circumstances that it is perhaps not too difficult to understand, and even accept, the view that the castle is not to be considered even a work of architecture, but essentially a 'piece of…make-do-and-mend'.[495]

However, as it gradually evolved over the eighteenth century, the entire complex successfully shed the characteristics of a medieval fortress and eventually the Upper Yard gained a more graceful, dignified group of buildings with an impressive and stately formality (Fig. 3.106). The castle always supported an impressive array of functions, but alongside its everyday role of upholding and accommodating the bureaucracy of the State, it was seasonally brought to life to serve and uphold the honour and dignity of the court. By 1850, the culmination of almost two centuries of rebuilding and remodelling had achieved a building that was perhaps more impressive, more coherent and more useable than at any other time in its long complex history; as a consequence, the castle successfully reclaimed its former dominance at the heart of the imperial city.[496] And so it remained relatively intact, until after 1922 when it was 'quietly handed over to eight gentlemen in three taxicabs'.[497] Since then most of the castle complex has been modernised, and on occasion to the detriment of the historic fabric, with a great deal of demolition carried out between the 1960s and the 1990s when, regrettably certain works were carried out throughout the complex that led to the removal of original interiors and fittings, with significant loss to the architectural heritage. The best sense of the historic building now is found in the surviving State Apartments, including the Chapel Royal and Record Tower.[498]

Sic Transit Gloria Mundi

Fig. 3.106 Interior of the Picture Gallery – state drawing room. (NLI Lawrence Collection)

Endnotes

1   Falkiner 1904, 413.

2   Bod. Lib., Carte MSS 232, 143–4 (IAA, EMcP).

3   Horwood 1879, 498 (17 April 1684): 'There hath been a fire in Dublin Castle, which hath burnt the best rooms, but the castle and magazine all safe. Your coz the Duke hath the greatest loss, 10,000 at least.' While many of the furnishings in the castle had originated from the time of the earl of Essex, having been bought by the duke of Ormond in 1677, the majority of these related to essential furniture in the staff lodgings throughout the complex, rather than the grander luxury furnishings which the Ormonds had introduced themselves, and recorded over a year later: NLI, MS 2528 'An Inventory of Goods bought at ye Castle of Dublin from ye Earle of Essex his Steward for ye use of his Grace James Duke of Ormond on ye 18th day of August 1677'; NLI, MS 2554: 'An Inventory of all the Goodes in Dublin Castle belonging to his Grace the Duke of Ormonde Lord Lieut of Ireland the 21st of March 1678'. A pamphlet dated the day after the fire (7 April 1684) reported 'it has consumed all the new brick-buildings, (viz) the Queen's Drawing-Room, my Lord's own Apartment, and the Ladies Appartments; wherein my Lady Duchess has received very considerable loss, to the value of several thousand pounds, in rich furniture, &c. it has likewise destroyed the Chappel, the King's drawing room, the Presence, and the great Dining Room so that that Row is quite burnt, from the Great Door and Stairs of the Castle Eastward, to the Closet, the Secretaries Office, and all the other offices below, with the lodgings over them, (viz. where the young lady lay) are all blown up'. B.R., *A True and Particular Relation of the Fire which happened in the Castle of Dublin in Ireland* (London 1684); the pamphlet is illustrated in Gibney 2006, 19; see Appendix 5. Bod. Lib., Aslim. G.12, 200 (IAA, EMcP). In a slighly varied account by Sir Patrick Dun he claimed 'there was burnt and blown up, the new buildings built by the Earle of Essex, my Lords closet and the long gallerie and all betwixt the new buildings and the tower on which the Clock stood' (Belcher 1866, 23–4). Another account is found at BL Add. Ms 21135 (IAA, EMcP).

4   HMC *Ormonde*, n.s., VII, 498–9. See also NLI, MS 2554 and for a comparison with the Ormond residences in Kilkenny, see Fenlon, 2003, 41–123. The tapestries probably refer to Francis Cleyn's (or Clein) highly treasured series, the *Horses*, designed for Mortlake and reproduced at Lambeth; it was represented in at least one other Irish collection, in a set commissioned by Sir Edward Brabazon of Kilruddery, 2nd earl of Meath. Where it was usual for furnishings to be moved between residences, the set may in fact no longer have been hanging at the castle in 1684, based on a letter of 1682, whereby instructions were given for three sets of tapestries, including *Horses* to be sent from Kilkenny to London (Fenlon 2010, 121–2; Campbell 2007, 195–201; Marillier 1927, 12–14).

5   Bod. Lib., Carte MSS 50, 335; HMC *Ormonde*, ns, Vol. VII, 218f.; BL Add. Ms 41803, 64 (Lord Arran's account of fire, 1684). Ormond did put the financial cost in context and was naturally relieved that his son had been spared, writing to him on 15 April 'your preservation after you had performed your duty outweighs all the loss we have sustained'. HMC *Ormonde*, ns, VII, 221.

6   Barnard 2000, 258.

7   This followed proposals mooted almost two decades earlier when in 1665 Ormond's Governor of the Castle, Sir John Stephens gave a detailed account of the 'insecurity' of the castle, referencing especially the towers used as powder magazines. To address the issue Stephens recommended building a citadel 'to oppose all Ireland for six months' if need be. Bod. Lib., Carte MSS 215, 172–3 (IAA, EMcP files).

8   NA, Wyche MSS 1/14; see also NA, 1A/41, 70a – Breen c), 29; NMS, DCCI. The 1671 fire was apparently started 'by a rat carrying a lighted candle'. Fire posed an even greater risk to government buildings than any ordinary security threat. Another fire which threatened a key apparatus of government was recorded in 1681, resulting in the, unlikely as it seems, death of an elephant and its child keeper along with their makeshift timber 'booth'. The extent of this conflagration, and its precise location is not perfectly clear but clearly had threatened the destruction of the Council Chamber, then located on the corner of Essex Street and Crane Lane, just north of the castle; after the fire (while still emitting 'very noisom steams') the elephant was apparently examined in a hastily erected shed 'very near the Council-Chamber, and the Custom House' (Mullen 1682, 4–5). In a letter from Dublin Castle, by W. Ellis to Sir Cyril Wyche (16 June 1681), it was stated that the 'elephant brought lately hither was together with a little boy consumed by a fire which happened in a building of deal boards erected on purpose for exposing that beast to view, it had like to have burnt the Council Chamber, one side of which is something damaged by it and some few papers burnt'. 57th DKR, 484. See also Barnard 2000, 257. The Council Chamber, along with the Treasury, would eventually be destroyed by fire in 1711.

9   Robinson may have come to Ireland earlier through the patronage of the duke of Ormond (Loeber 1981, 88).

10   Loeber (1981, 89, 93, n.7) identifies this Presence Chamber with Dublin rather than Kilkenny Castle. BL, Stowe Ms 214, 259, quoted in Loeber (1981, 88) and McParland (2001, 56). Loeber (1981, 70–1, 89), however, argues that Hugh May, Controller of the Royal Works in England and a kinsman of Essex, may have had a hand in the design of the castle lodgings although there is no documentary evidence to support this and ultimately the buildings themselves were destroyed.

11   Orrery's comments were made in January 1677/8. HMC *Ormonde*, ns, IV, 99. The reference to Robinson as an 'excellent artist' is quoted in McParland (2001, 56), citing RIA, MS MR/17/B/3, 135, 137–8: *The Secret Intreigues of the Romish party in Ireland*, licensed 14 Aug. 1689.

12   Barnard (2000, 257–8); BL Stowe Ms 209, 28: Essex Papers Vol X, 387ff., Jan–June 1676: relates to a warrant, ordering that £20,000 yearly from Ireland to be paid to William Chiffinch 'to be employed in our buildings at Windsor Castle, Whitehall'.

13 Barnard 2000, 257.

14 Casey 2005, 674; McParland 2001, 53–69; Olley, 1991, 65–72; McParland 1985a, 1260–3, 1320–4.

15 HMC *Ormonde*, ns, VII, 250.

16 It has been suggested that Ormond's 'plan to reside there temporarily, following the fire at Dublin Castle in 1684, may well account for the quality of the craftsmanship in the N range then in progress' (Casey 2005, 676).

17 Although Primate Boyle had estimated the cost of the hospital at £12,000, it cost almost twice that, £23,559, the figure given by Thomas Wilson (1713, 49–52), cited by McParland (2001, 53). The sumptuous decoration of the chapel was complete by 1687 just as building finally commenced at the castle. The chapel was consecrated in January 1687, which was also the month when the carver James Tarbary sought payment for his work (McParland 2001, 54).

18 Barnard 2000, 258; see also n.61 below.

19 As suggested by McParland 2001, 1.

20 *Ibid.*

21 HMC *Ormonde*, 14th Report, App. VII, 309–35. The commission, undertaken immediately, had formed one of the directions given to Lord Dartmouth as part of his responsibilities as Master General, as ordered by Charles II on 24 August 1684.

22 Loeber 1980, 51, plate 3

23 Loeber (1980, 51, 64) in suggesting William Robinson as its possible author, considers that he may have based it on contemporary French or Italian designs, though no comparative examples are given and most European forts adopt the star or tenaille form.

24 The proposal to build a new citadel at Ringsend originated with the earl of Essex in 1674 when a scheme was devised by Bernard de Gomme. The proposal was revisited by Thomas Phillips in 1685. HMC *Ormonde*, 14th Report, App. VII, 313. The degree of consideration given to a new location for the castle is suggested by the number of sites proposed, which included St Stephen's Green, Aungier Street, College Green, St Mary's Abbey, and at Oxmantown Green where Ormond had been granted seven acres (Irish Measure) in 1665; the site, shown enclosed on de Gomme's 1673 survey (Fig 2.12), was eventually acquired for the Royal Barracks in 1704 (McParland 2001, 92; McCullough 1989, 39–40; Dunlevy 2002, 8–10). See also BL, Add. MS 21135 (IAA, EMcP) concerning an alternative site for the Lord Lieutenant's residence.

25 HMC *Ormonde*, ns,VI, 400.

26 Bod. Lib. Carte MS 39, f. 539 (IAA, EMcP files); Johnston-Liik 2002, Vol III, 261–2.

27 HMC *Ormonde*, ns, VI, 398, 400.

28 HMC *Ormonde*, ns, VI, 400. The sum seems realistic when compared with the figure of some £23,500 associated with Kilmainham. See n.17 above.

29 HMC *Ormonde*, ns, VI, 421. Brewster's response to Ormond was made in August and was conducted despite Arran's plainly expressed dislike for any of the current proposals for the castle, one by Major Deane, and an earlier one sent to him by Ormond. HMC *Ormonde*, ns, VI, 408. For a later revenue farming proposal by Deane, submitted to Ormond in September 1683, and which included a sum of £20,000 'for the building of his Majesty's Royal Palace near Dublin', see HMC *Ormonde*, ns VII, 130–1.

30 HMC *Ormonde*, ns, VI, 421.

31 HMC *Ormonde*, ns, VI, 487. Presumably Robinson's good knowledge of the Dublin rates was based on the works at the Kilmainham Hospital.

32 HMC *Ormonde*, ns, VI, 502.

33 HMC *Ormonde*, ns, VI, 509; 514.

34 HMC *Ormonde*, ns, VI, 354. The primate wrote to Ormond: 'Mr Robinson is very earnest for the commissioners to take his accounts upon his disbursements for the King's Castle &c. upon which he pretends that there is £600 due to him.' Various unspecified payments to Robinson in the 1670s are found at Bod. Lib., Carte MSS 53 (IAA, EMcP files). There is the suggestion that the king had sanctioned the sale of the site and building materials. Falkiner gives the source for this reference as Prendergast (1886), while noting that the author 'does not give his authority' (Falkiner 1904, 25).

35 HMC *Ormonde*, ns, VII, 218ff.

36 The detail of Petty's scheme is not known, though he seems to have given the idea some consideration years earlier, probably after the 1671 fire, when in 1672 he had projected that the cost for 'Building a new Palace for the Chief Governour' would require an estimate of £20,000 (Hull 1899, Vol. I, 147). See Bod. Lib., Carte MSS 40, 341 [1684]: 'The humble opinion of Sir William Petty to the Lord Deputy concerning the repair & apportionment of the Castle of Dublin; and the erection of a palace for the Chief Governor of Ireland. Drawn up upon occasion of the partial destruction of the Castle, by an explosion of gunpowder.' Petty's description of the fire is at BL Add. Ms 72856, 232 and see also McParland 2001, 92 and Loeber 1980, 62.

37 HMC *Ormonde*, ns, VII, 220; McParland 2001, 92.

38 HMC *Ormonde*, ns, VII, 221; CSPD (James II), 1685, 154, 176. The costs for 'refitting' the constable's lodgings at the castle, and 'repairing the houses in White Friars and Chapel Izod for the Lord Deputy and Lord Lieutenant's reception' are recorded in early 1685, the report indicating that on the day after the fire (8 April), Lord Arran agreed terms with Lord Longford 'for the use of his house for one year'. In 1660 the Chapelizod house possessed just 13 hearths and in the 1730s it was described as a building 'that makes no figure at all, being a very plain single brick house'. John Loveday, quoted in Barnard 2000, 258.

39 HMC *Ormonde*, ns, VII, 220–1. CSPD, Vol. 27, 187, recording the Petition, 28 October 1684, of James Clarke, Constable whose 'lodgings he is now deprived, the same being used by the Lord lieutenant, the Chief Governor's lodgings being burnt down…'.

40 HMC *Ormonde*, ns, VII, 220–1.

41 HMC *Ormonde*, ns, VII, 224. This competition for resources already existed before the fire, with Sir John Temple writing to Ormond in January 1684: 'if there should be an overplus of money, a good part thereof might be reserved, to be yearly laid out on that which your Grace hath sometimes had in your thoughts, the building of a more convenient house for the Chief Governor's residence, if it should not all be thought fit to be applied towards increasing the Army here', HMC *Ormonde*, ns, VII, 178–9.

42 Bod. Lib., Carte MSS 220, 44, 50 (IAA, EMcP); HMC *Ormonde*, ns, VII, 225–6.

43 In advance of his arrival, Ormond wrote to this son: 'The greatest difficulty will be how to accommodate myself…with any kind of tolerable habitation while I stay at Dublin, which will be for as little time as I can, there being that I can call to mind no one commodious house for myself though my wife should live at Chapelizod, nor any two or three houses that can be put together. …I have thought that I might have some conveniency in the Master of the Hospital's lodgings for a short time especially if the Hospital be not completely filled, so that I might have some of the soldiers' rooms'. HMC *Ormonde*, ns, VII, 250.

44 Bod. Lib., Carte MS 169, 63–4 (IAA, EMcP files); HMC, *Ormonde*, ns, VII, 227.

45 In January 1683, the countess of Arran complained to Ormond that finding the 'air of the Castle soe close' she was compelled to move to Chapelizod. HMC *Ormonde*, 14th Report, App. VII, 56.

46   NLI, MS 3137/3; HMC *Ormonde*, 14th Report, App. VII, 313; NA/SPO OP 165,12 (NMS, DCCI); probable encroachments resulted after sections of the new wall outside the ditch were let in 1612 to owners of adjoining properties (DCEL, 168–172) and is implied in the reference, in a lease of 1614, to James Ware's house in Castle Street being 'situate within the precincts of the castle ditch' (CPRI Jas. I, 355) – all these citations are taken from Breen c), 22–3. Instances of leases concerning the moat are evident in the late sixteenth century, as for example in 1578 with grants of parcels of land adjoining the castle to George Ardglas, including one lying against the east and south sides of the castle 'in which it appears there have been fishponds & weirs' and another granted by the Crown to Christopher Huchenson concerning a parcel (100ft x 150ft (30m x 45.7m)) 'within the precinct of the castle of Dublin called the castell ditch'. Fiants Eliza 3416; 3377 (NMS, DCCI). In 1588 the Crown granted to Isabell Fallowes a house and shop 'with two little backsides, lying within the precinct of the Queen's castle ditch of Dublin and all land from the bridge of the castle westward to the city walls, and from the castle against the west and north side, the water and watercourse of the castle ditch 24 feet broad excepted…'. It also includes reference to an earlier lease of the property, mentioning 'the pulling up of certain fruit trees and the reducement of the backsides in enlarging and scouring the ditch' and the proviso that the lessee, 'must not erect any building without license, or do anything to the nuisance or stopping of the ditch'. Fiants Eliza 5175. See also CSP XIII, 62 referring to 'various tenements adjoining the Castle and Castle ditch' in 1606-7 (NMS, DCCI).

47   Falkiner 1904, 26.

48   Lynch and Manning 1990, 68.

49   Pynnar's 1624 estimate for Lord Falkland, relating to the rebuilding the Cork Tower, which included 'For Clensing the Moate from all Rubbish and the Mudd', is given in Falkiner 1904, 38–9; see Appendix 2. Industrial growth had become increasingly evident within the Liberty of St Thomas Court and Donore and the Coombe, which had expanded under the earls of Meath and where intensive, high-polluting activities encompassed everything from dyeing, to brickmaking and tanning. Excavation of the moat in the 1980s revealed that up to two metres of refuse and building rubble lay underneath the eighteenth-century houses that were built over the moat, though it is interpreted that this was dumped deliberately so as to raise the ground level for building. It is unclear whether the fabric of a sixteenth- or seventeenth-century timber frame house, found during the excavation, represented the reuse of a building that was previously erected on the site of the moat, or was brought here from elsewhere (Lynch and Manning 1990, 68; Lynch and Manning 2001, 194–5, 197). See TNA, T1/176/92 (IAA, EMcP), where Thomas Burgh, in a memorial to the Lord Lieutenant dated 22 May 1714, refers to covering the watercourse.

50   The suggestion of moving it here had been originally proposed soon after the fire by Ormond 'if the building a powder store will not to much incumber and disgrace the Hospital', and on 16 April he wrote to his son: 'I am absolutely of the opinion to have the powder in the middle of the square [central court]'. In response Arran stated that 'one of the flankers in the Hospital is thought the properest place for the magazine of powder, which if approved of on that side, I will out of hand have fitted for that use, and it will not spoil the beauty of that edifice'. HMC *Ormonde*, ns, VII, 222, 227–8.

51   HMC *Ormonde*, ns, VII, 231; Robinson's petitions for payment for work done after fire are at TNA, T14/4 p. 121 (IAA, EMcP). At the end of June, while arranging suitable accommodation for the duke's impending visit, Arran noted 'one apartment I have fitted up in the Castle which I believe your Grace will be pleased with, and with the help of the Constable's lodgings, my Lord and Lady Ossory [Ormond's grandson, who became 2nd duke of Ormond, and his first wife Anne, daughter of the earl of Rochester] may make a shift to lodge there also for the short time your Grace intends to stay in town'. Bod. Lib., Carte MS 169, 77–9 (IAA, EMcP); HMC *Ormonde*, ns. VII 252–3.

52   HMC *Ormonde*, ns, VII, 234.

53   HMC *Ormonde*, ns, VII, 235.

54   Ormond's imminent arrival was a concern to his son who seemed to enquire a little nervously (repeating some of the anxieties he had felt after the fire) about the cause: 'I long to know the reasons why your Grace comes so soon, for I am jealous that somebody has done me ill offices with the King, because I hear it is by his command your Grace comes before Spring. It will trouble me much if it proves so, for then I shall not know how to dispose of myself; but if, on the contrary, he is pleased with my administration for these two years past, I shall cheerfully endure any hardships and it will make me easier to bear any other misfortunes'. In response to Ormond's resolve 'to return hither this summer' Arran suggested that 'my Lord Longford's house [on Aungier Street], though bad' as the only place 'you can with any conveniency live in, the offices of the Castle lying so near'. Bod. Lib., Carte MSS 169, 77–9 (IAA, EMcP); HMC *Ormonde*, ns., VII, 222, 225, 252–3.

55   HMC *Ormonde*, ns, VII, 253, 257–8.

56   McParland 2001, 94.

57   However, McParland (2001, 93) argues that the apparent independence of these ranges, implies 'that the architect did not forsee the retention of any of the original towers'.

58   Limited material from the excavation was available for this study, including a 'General Plan of Areas Investigated' from an unpublished 'Account of the Archaeological Investigations carried out at the Cross Block, Dublin Castle November 1961 – February 1962' prepared by Marcus Ó hEochaidhe (Assistant Inspector, National Monuments Branch) which shows the alignment of the curtain wall as parallel with the east range based (it would appear from the map and the portions of the report made available) on the exposure following demolition of 'a course of yellow-mortared masonry' along the east side and the evidence contained in two excavation trenches. The 1980s excavations did not reveal any 'definite solid evidence' for the alignment of the curtain wall. (Information from Con Manning via email, 15 April 2015).

59   As an explanation for the disparity in the evidence relating to the eastern curtain wall, the correctness of the 1673 survey has been questioned, (notwithstanding the fact that in other respects it 'has been found to be quite accurate') with the possibililty that the 'overall plan is slightly more elongated than it should be in reality and the north ends of the east and west curtain walls are skewed more to the east than is truly the case' (Lynch and Manning 2001, 176; see also reconstructed plan in Manning 1998, 120.) However, a more cautious approach to this issue may be warranted given that, at best, the dispute is based only on partial archaeological evidence, weighed against a relatively detailed, and convincing seventeenth-century survey. This argument also relies on the notion that any errors in 1673 were unwittingly repeated in later surveys, despite the experience and competence of those involved (Figs 2.2, 3.3). It would seem from the evidence in Marcus Ó hEochaidhe's account of the 1961–2 excavations, that the upper layers (archaeological horizons from at least the fourteenth century, to the present day) had been destroyed by demolition and associated excavation prior to his investigations. Significantly, however, Ó hEochaidhe did note that in one of the trenches (Trench B), the curtain wall somewhat anomalously 'should be coursed and faced for a depth of 8ft below' the early thirteenth-century ground level; while a lack of information prevents a better understanding of this evidence, it could indicate a later rebuilding of the wall, perhaps in the seventeenth century (on a new alignment) and to a greater depth in order to achieve a better foundation. In trying to resolve this question, the evidence of the 1697/8 'First Story' plan of the Record Tower (Fig. 3.10) should also be considered, showing as it does (and discussed further on p.148-9, 150) the existence (at this time) of a substantial spur wall extending north from the tower, and at a perfect right angle to the state apartments. While arguably this could be used to support the idea that the 1673 survey is inaccurate, it is just as likely to indicate that the wall had actually been rebuilt by then, on a more perpendicular alignment. And whereas the evidence from the various excavations has been interpreted as providing the general impression that the 'towers and curtain wall appear to have been part of one coherent plan of work' (with the exception of the Bermingham Tower and a section of earlier walling close to it), it is significant

60 that a portion of walling still visible in the basement of the eastern Cross Block (inspected by the authors in October 2015), built of regular, coursed masonry, is not medieval in character, strongly supporting therefore the possibility that the eastern curtain wall was rebuilt on a new alignment after the fire. This is a reasonable proposition, as the curtain wall in this location is likely to have been seriously affected by fire and explosion damage in 1684 (and also bearing in mind that subsidence would prove to be an ongoing issue in this area). See note 62 below.

60 Loeber 1980, 64, citing NA M2549, 75. See also warrant concerning rebuilding, 1684 TNA, SO.1/11, 31 (IAA, EMcP).

61 Once established in the castle, Ormond, clearly uncomfortable with the temporary provision of accommodation ('where I make a very uneasy and unpleasant shift to lodge and eat'), was naturally conscious of the impact of pending works, believing that living there 'will not be sufferable or indeed possible'. He therefore suggested that the 'only expedient will be to put his Majesty to a charge of £1,000 for an addition to a little lodge about two miles from hence, whence the Chief Governor may come to Church & Council'. A few weeks later Ormond was informed that the 'draft' he had sent of the proposed addition to the lodge had been forwarded by the king to Lord Goldophin, Lord Rochester's successor as First Lord of the Treasury. However, the complete deficiency of any suitable accommodation remained apparent at the end of the year when Ormond made provision for Rochester (now Lord President of the Council. His daughter was married to Ormond's grandson, earl of Ossory, later 2nd duke of Ormond) to stay in Kilkenny if he 'will be in the country that season and whilst this place will be rubbish'. In March 1685, the cost of 'clearing the ruins at Dublin Castle…refitting the lodgings there and repairing the houses in White Friars and Chapel Izod for the Lord Deputy and Lord Lieutenant's reception' amounted to just under £350 (CSPD, 1684–5, Vol. 27, 136; HMC Ormonde, ns. VII, 270, 273, 303; CSPD (James II), 1685, 154, 176). William Robinson apparently undertook the additions to Chapelizod House (Loeber, 1981, 94).

62 CSPD, 1684–5, Vol. 27, 139, 'Newsletter to John Squire, Newcastle', 10 September 1684. The warrant allowed for the demolition of the ruinous and decayed walls of the castle and 'as many towers as should be thought fit' and if the result of this was a programme of works largely concerned with the curtain walls, this may well have included the realignment of the east wall as part of the castle's enlargement – or at the very least, its regularisation. Regardless of the extent of these works, they effected little improvement in the accommodation, so that for example in 1686 it was still regarded as 'rather like a prison of state than a palace'. Dudley Loftus to Abp. Sancroft, 6 March 1685/6 in McNeill 1943, 484.

63 Molyneux 1820, 30; Loeber 1981, 76.

64 Molyneux had paid Robinson £250 in 1684 to induce him to surrender his patent, in favour of a new one which allowed them to hold the position jointly, and agreeing to 'not intermeddle with the salary without his consent, and unless by his consent I acted in his place' – implying that he only acted with the consent of Robinson. It is clear that Molyneux's career was promoted by Ormond, and there is some significance in the fact that in May 1685 he travelled to the Low Countries, ostensibly to view fortifications, but in fact while there was intriguing with the House of Orange on behalf of Irish landowners, suggesting that there were certain ulterior motives for holding the post. Therefore, while Robinson busied himself with schemes for the castle, Molyneux was abroad – absent from May 1684 to September 1685 or 1686, but just in time to take over responsibility for the work at the castle when Robinson fled to England (Johnston-Liik 2002, Vol. V, 268; Loeber 1981, 76–7).

65 Simms 2009, 478.

66 Simms 2009, 479.

67 McNeill 1943, 484.

68 The report was then referred to Lord Clarendon, for consideration. HMC Ormonde, 14th Report, App. VII, 309–20, see esp. 313, 320. The following discussion is based on this published version and on Phillips' report and drawings at NLI, MS 2557 and MS 3137.

69 HMC Ormonde 14, App. VII, 309–13; 320–2; NLI, MS 2557/3; MS 3137/2. De Gomme's earlier proposal for a citadel was estimated at the even greater figure of £130,000 (McParland 2001, 140).

70 The exact quotation given in Singer's text refers to 'this no-castle…' corrected to 'non-castle' in Loeber 1980, 65. The constraints on expenditure had been spelt out at the beginning of Clarendon's term, where the 'seventh article' of his instructions from London included the direction 'that no additional charge be made to the present establishment for that…kingdom, but that the surplusage of our revenue be laid up in our Exchequer, there to be disposed of as we shall from time to time direct…' (Singer 1828, Vol. I, 354–5, 650).

71 Curiously Loeber erroneously interprets Clarendon's letter as if related to the accommodation needs of the earl of Tyrconnell, an interpretation that wrongly implies that, as the recently appointed Lieutenant General of the army in Ireland, he somehow had an entitlement to a house worthy of the country. He further states that Tyrconnell rebuilt Carton for himself, as if to suggest that this was to answer for the absence of any suitable government accommodation (Loeber 1980, 65–6). Clarendon, capturing something of the uncertainty of the time, and the desperation of his position, finishes his letter: 'God knows whether I am designed to be long-lived enough here to do anything of this work; that pleaseth God, and the King. I will think no more of it till you direct me…'. The shortage of funds for essential expenditure was made clear again in the same month, when Clarendon, reiterating a need expressed in April 'that money should be laid out upon the forts and buildings', explained to Lord Darmouth that 'if the King could contrive it so as to lay up 30,000' or 40,000l per annum of his revenue here, then he might be able in a few years to put all the fortifications and magazines in the condition they ought to be…' (Singer 1828, Vol. I, 354–5, 530–1, 546–8).

72 Singer 1828, Vol. I, 577.

73 Although Clarendon prepared an account in November 1686 'of the buildings at Chapel Izod, and the repairs about the Castle' conducted over the period between March 1685 and September 1686, the precise details and costs are not known, other than an outstanding balance of £626 'which is due to severall workmen, who are poor and will be clamorous'. With respect to Chapelizod, Clarendon claimed the building there 'is the cheapest that has been erected' that 'nothing had been laid out but what was of absolute necessity to make it habitable'. See n.61 above (relating to provisions at Chapelizod) (Singer 1828, Vol. I, 462; Vol. II, 87).

74 Lennon 2008, 37.

75 In his own words Molyneux stated: 'upon my Lord Clarendon's leaving our Government, in February, 1687, Mr Robinson though fit to retire to England, and left me in the execution of the Surveyor General's Office, wherein I continued about a year and a half, till Tyrconnell turned me out amongst all other protestants in place. During this time I built the Great New Building on piers and arches, that runs along the south wall of the castle with the terrace walk behind it' (Molyneux 1820, 30–1, 63).

76 See n. above. Although the term piazza originated as an open space surrounded by buildings, by the seventeenth century it was in common usage to describe an arcaded or colonnaded ground floor. See for example Dyche and Pardon (1750): 'Piache or Piazza, a walk that is arched or covered over by buildings; it properly signifies the open area of a market &c. whence it also became applied to the walks or porticoes around them'. Despite great intellectual ability (with Sir William Petty he was founder of the Dublin Philosophical Society), Molyneux's qualifications for the post are unclear, his only obvious connection that an uncle had been Clerk of the Royal Works in Ireland. No drawings by Molyneux are known and there is no evidence that he was involved in the office after 1688; he died ten years later at the age of 42. However, his level of interest in architecture, and seriousness about the subject, might reasonably be implied from the range of key architectural books owned by his son in 1730, and which may have originated in his library (Johnston-Liik 2002, Vol. V, 268; Loeber 1981, 76–7).

77   HMC *Ormonde*, ns, VIII, 354. 'A Diary of Events in Ireland from 1685 to 1690'. In an entry for 30 October 1688, it states 'About this time the new building in the Castle of Dublin was finished, and the Lord Deputy removed from Chapelizod…'.

78   Two later visitors, in 1699, attributed the new building (then occupied by Lord Galway and described as 'a convenient house') to Tyrconnell (Loeber, Dickson and Smyth 2012, 57).

79   HMC *Ormonde*, ns, VIII, 361

80   HMC *Ormonde*, ns, VIII, 362, 364. Simms 2009, 489. The Royal Hospital will also have provided fitting accommodation if necessary, however, see the inventory of 'Good furniture' left at the castle after the king's departure, RIA, MS 24 G 4, f.47 (IAA, EMcP); see also Inventory of Dublin Castle, May 1693, NAI, Wyche 2/142.

81   The collapse resulted in the death of a sentry 'found dead among the rubbish' (Hughes 1940, 90 – quoting a pamphlet which may be found at NLI, Thorpe Collection of pamphlets No. 644 (microfiche) – with thanks to Con Manning for a transcript).

82   HMC *Dartmouth*, 11, App. V, 249. The previous September the 'scholars were put out of the College to make it a garrison', and it was reported that soldiers were 'busy in fortifying the city, trenching the streets, and setting up gates and palisadoes', while 'the great brass gun that stood in the Castle' was melted down to make brass coinage. HMC *Ormonde*, ns, VIII, 371.

83   Simms 2009, 478–508, 497–9.

84   HMC, *Report on the Manuscripts of F.W. Leyborne-Popham* (1899), 278.

85   Singer 1828, Vol. I, 531.

86   The elevation (Fig. 3.8) usually associated with an unexecuted scheme for the entrance block has no corresponding plan, though it can in scale, if not entirely in detail, be reconciled with the elevation for the state apartments. Its balustraded roof platform is interesting, intended either for defence, the review of military parades, or perhaps simply to take in views of the castle gardens and according with the provision of roof top observatories in Carolean English houses such as Clarendon House, Piccadilly and Coleshill, Berkshire (O'Dwyer 1992, 158–160; McParland 2001, 93).

87   McNeill 1931, 53–4, but see also Carpenter 2003, 139, and Maguire 1985, 16.

88   See Appendix 7. It was suggested that the terrace had been formed as a result of the collapse of the 'Mid Rampier of the Black Tower' in August 1689, the debris having been levelled off to form 'a solid mass of masonry 15 to 20 feet thick'. A section of walling visible in the 1940s, in a then disused boiler room, had 'its stones in oblique and not level courses' and so was taken to support this interpretation (Hughes 1940, 90).

89   The marquess of Winchester (Charles Paulet 7th marquess, and later 2nd duke of Bolton), the earl of Galway (Henri Massue de Ruvigny, earl of Galway) and the earl of Jersey (Edward Villiers, formerly Viscount Villiers) had been appointed Lords Justices in 1697, though Lord Jersey appears not to have served. In March 1697/8 Winchester and Galway wrote to the duke of Shrewsbury (Charles Talbot, 1st duke of Shrewsbury, Secretary of State for the Southern Department, and later Lord Lieutenant of Ireland) from Dublin Castle complaining about the earl of Jersey's attempts to obtain 'a third of the salary of a lord lieutenant' indicating that 'he is not entitled as he never came to Dublin to be sworn as a Lord Justice'. See BL Add. Ms 35933. By 1699 Galway remained as Lord Justice and was the only resident at the castle '& indeed the onely acting one of the three Lord Justices…Lord Bolton & the Lord Barclay but seldome there & when there doe nothing' (Loeber, Dickson and Smyth 2012, 57).

90   TNA, T1/51, 319 (IAA, EMcP), Lords Justices Winchester and Galway to Treasury, 18 March 1697/8. The costs of the additions were indicated at £868.10.2. Small payments to William Robinson for work on buildings & magazine 'about ye castle of Dublin', *c.* 1690 are at PRONI, T689 referenced as 'Payment and receipt book for Revenue and Army, Ireland 1690–1691'. It seems unlikely, however, that these would relate to the plans of 1698.

91   As one of the reasons why this site had not already been built upon, Lawlor (1923, 51) suggests that it 'must have been here that Arran placed his first two charges of Powder, which saved the magazine'.

92   See p.148-9, 150 above and n.59

93   Brooking's 1728 map is too general an impression to offer any clarity as to how the buildings were related and does not easily correspond to the vignette.

94   Brooking's vignette gives the impression that there was an opening in the south-east corner of the Upper Yard, which perhaps led through to the garden terrace. Mention of the bagnio is found in HMC *Ormonde*, ns, VIII, 245, and is discussed further below. A water closet and cistern shown on Alfray's 1767 survey of the castle, are all part of the suite of rooms added along the south front *c.* 1758 during Thomas Eyre's period as Surveyor General, and which, with the stair at the end of the state corridor, contribute to the stepped outline of the plan.

95   Loeber 1981, 90.

96   This and other material related to the petition of Sir Robert Reading for a lease of 'a small piece of ground in the Castle Yard' – the site of the stable dung stead, for the purposes of establishing a mill ('which may be of good use to your said castle on occasion of service'), is located at NLI, MS 2436, 99–101, 112–15 (the plan illustrated by Loeber (1980, 67) is included). Loeber incorrectly dates the survey to 1684. The map is undated but Robinson's accompanying report bears the date 16 May 1683, with the decision on the matter made the following February 1683/4; see also HMC *Ormonde* Papers VII, 193–4. Reading's petition sought a ninety-nine year lease of the 'twenty foot front of the ground whereon the dung lieth, with liberty and use of the yard belonging to a smal tenement without the gate'. Robinson reported 'that the place by him desired for erecting a mill, being over the shore or watercourse that runs through the stable yard belonging to the Castle, hath not hitherto been used by any person, nor is it of any use at present to the Castle stables; and…[that the] watercourse is partly made use of for laying dung, but that part thereof next unto the said watercourse is not made use of but remains waste'. He suggested that if 'a partition wall or fence be made betwixt the dunghill and waste ground, there will be excluded such a piece of ground as is desired by the petitioner, and if the old gate of the stableyard be removed about nine foot backwards into the said yard, the petitioner may have a convenient passage into the said waste ground, without taking away or using the yard belonging to the tenement, without the gate in the petition mentioned, and without any predjudice or inconvenience to the stable-yard'. On 20 February 1683/4, having obtained Robinson's report, Sir John Temple wrote to the earl of Arran to express his view that the lands desired by Reading were 'not of any use at present to the Castle stables' and his belief that granting the lease would not present any inconvenience.

97   De Gomme's survey shows it widening here, but in a naturalised way suggesting perhaps that it was only formally treated after 1673 and before 1683, even if one can reasonably question the accuracy of the detail in the 1673 survey. Whereas in 1663, works overseen by the Surveyor General John Paine included 'opening and cleaning of the water courses and making two new water courses from the Castle wall to the river', there is no certainty that this might have involved works on the Poddle at this location (Loeber 1980, 55). See Appendix 4.

98   Comparison with the 1673 plan implies that the postern gate opened directly into this building, making it likely to correspond with the office of ordnance which Robert Ware mentions being at the postern gate (see p. 141). See Appendix 4.

99   There is insufficient detail in these surveys to locate the various workshops and the 'place designed for a mint' mentioned by Ware. See Loeber 1980, 67. Equally, the same difficulty exists with Dunton's later 1697 description in which he fails to locate the 'King's gunsmiths and armourers work' other than to say they are 'near' the office of the ordnance (which he says is 'next the chapel'). In eighteenth- and nineteenth-century surveys, the 'Castle forge' is clearly identified with a building just east of the Palace Street Gate, its place eventually taken by Dame Lane, but it is likely that this only served the adjoining stables. In Henry Chaigneau's 1801 survey (Fig. 3.62) various workshops and sheds are disposed around the carriage yard, and extending along the west side of the castle garden.

100   NLI, MS 2436, 99–101, 112, 115.

101   TNA, W.O. 55/1726, undated Survey of Stores in Ireland, probably prepared by William Robinson in 1673 (IAA, EMcP); HMC *Ormonde* 14, App. VII, 358–63. Lord Mountjoy's 'Account of Ordnance, Arms and Ammunition in Ireland' which for Dublin included the castle, listing extensive ordnance either 'in the Castle' or 'in the stores' as well as the culverins (long cannons) on the Gunners Tower and Cork Tower.

102   Maguire 1974, 11.

103   Thomas Philips' 1685 survey closely agrees with Robinson's plan (and is perhaps even based on it), showing exactly the same regular treatment of the Poddle to form the horse ponds; further west the river is shown completely canalised and labelled as a mill race. However, none of the internal buildings in the Lower Yard are depicted by Philips. NLI, MS 3137.

104   'I have therefore got a piece of ground whereon to build a new one, the most convenient for ye Castle in ye world. The Foundation is already two Yards high, and shall be finished by the end of June next, with granaries and all other Conveniences…And I trust his Majesty will allow of the Charge, being so necessary, and for so good a Purpose' (Knowler 1740, Vol. I, 131–2; McCarthy 2008, 29; Howarth 1997, 198).

105   Howarth 1997, 207. The personal rivalry between Wentworth and Jones is discussed in Williamson 2012, Chapter 14.

106   Hawkins 1844, 141; see Appendix 3.

107   Maguire 1974, 11. Both Brereton and Ware were impressed by the size of Strafford's stable block (which if still the same building as shown by Robinson) measured some 140ft by 50ft (42.7m by 15.2m) and, according to Brereton, possessed stalls that were approximately 18ft (15.5m) high under the lofts: 'it is a double stable, there being a strong wall in the middle, to either side whereof stand the horses' heads. Thirty horses may stand at ease on either side, the stalls being very large; these are exceeding high, at least five or six yards, and very near the same breadth'. The stables were also technically advanced, particularly with respect to the flooring. Whereas wooden planks and cobbles were common into the seventeenth century, neither was ideal with planks proving dangerously slippery and cobbles an uneven surface difficult to clean. Instead, Holland Bricks or clinkers, set on edge, were used for flooring in the stables being 'as easy to walk upon as to lie upon'. These bricks were made of Holland earth, as used in paving in Holland and which Brereton considered 'harder and more durable…than our clay' (Hawkins 1844, 141; see Appendix 3).

108   Carpenter 2003, 140. New stabling at the castle is briefly mentioned 'In a diary of events in Ireland from 1685 to 1690', HMC *Ormonde*, ns, VIII, 1920, 374; McParland 2001, 94.

109   Knowler 1740, I, 131–2.

110   CSPD, 1673, 571; Loeber 1980, 57. Stephens was appointed Governor of the Castle in 1661 and appears to have been still living in 1667, the year before his widow claimed the expense of the building. Letters Patent containing a Grant of the office of Governor of Dublin Castle to Sir John Stephens, knight. Bod. Lib. Carte MS 43, 66 (IAA, EMcP files); Gilbert 1885, 54.

111   The depiction of this diagonal end wall in 1843, as a thick 'wedge' may well support the possibility that the structure incorporated some medieval fabric. It should be noted that Phillips' survey (NLI, MS 3137) shows the diagonal line clearly and as though corrected from an earlier right-angled line that is still faintly evident.

112   Lawlor 1923, 43–4; Lawlor 1928, 50–2.

113   BL Stowe Ms 214, 166; CSPD, 1673–4, 198. Lawlor, without the benefit of the Dartmouth plan, suggested a different location for the chapel, proposing a free-standing building depicted by Speed, located further to the west and closer to the Bermingham Tower (Lawlor 1923, 51–2).

114   Confirming the earl of Arran's own account, another eyewitness to the fire in 1684 remarked how it had 'likewise destroyed the Chappel, the King's drawing room, the Presence [Chamber], and the great Dining Room so that that Row is quite burnt, from the Great Door and Stairs of the Castle eastward, to the Closet, the Secretaries, Office, and all the other offices below, with the lodgings over them, (viz. Where the young Lady lay) are all blown up'. B.R., *A True and Particular Relation of the Fire which happened in the Castle of Dublin in Ireland* (1684) in Gibney 2006, 19; see Appendix 5.

115   With the old chapel within the state apartments having been destroyed as a consequence of the fire, all that is clear is that sufficient provision for a chapel had already been made after the fire for it to be taken over in 1687 by Tyrconnell for Roman Catholic service. Its new location east of the Record Tower can readily be confirmed in the 1680s plans for the new state apartments (BL, map K Top 53/19e) where, on the ground plan, an opening in the east end of the arcade is marked as leading 'to ye chappel'. A building extending south from the tower is also evident in Robinson's 1683 plan of the Lower Yard (NLI, MS 2436) 'range of buildings east of Gunners Tower' and Philips' 1685 surveys. Its location, as noted by Dunton in 1697, is further confirmed by the plans of 1698 to extend the state apartments eastwards to the Record Tower, where a passage through the Record Tower is proposed to connect the apartments directly with the chapel (TNA, MPD1–188); see Appendix 7.

116   Loeber 1980, 66.

117   Lennon 2008, 37. Thomas Denton's account goes on to state: 'This part lyes below the cast[le] upon a rill call'd the Miln-pool, which watereth all the suburbs on the south & east sides & falls into the Liffy at Temple Barr.' See Appendix 6. While Lawlor discounts the likelihood of the chapel having been established here by this time, the challenges of the site mean that excavation work may have been commenced well in advance of building – the demolition of the chapel in 1806 revealed that the foundations had been laid on piles of hazel wood 23 feet below the surface – or is it more likely that this was a misinterpreted archaeological feature? Also perhaps of relevance here is Wentworth's earlier reference that within the castle 'there is not any stable but a poor one, and that made of a decayed church, which is such a prophanation as I am sure his majesty would not allow; besides there is a decree of Exchequer for restoring it to the parish whence it was taken' (Knowler 1740, Vol. I, 131). Notwithstanding the discussion at n.115 above, it may be reasonable to propose that the building shown by de Gomme on the site of the present Chapel Royal, was Wentworth's 'decayed church' adapted as stables; perhaps then its representation by Phillips reflects its abandoned, ruined state before the new chapel was built? (Lawlor 1928, 46–8).

118   Lawlor 1928, 50.

119   Carpenter 2003, 140.

120   TNA, T1/176, 92 (IAA, EMcP). It is not exactly clear whether or not the chapel range was ever extended according to Burgh's plans, nor indeed is the nature of its intended use known. In reporting on the progress of works at the castle in 1714, apart from the Treasury (for which only groundworks had commenced) and the armoury ('covered, but not floored, nor the windows put in') the only other buildings related to the Lower Yards, mentioned by Burgh, and by then finished were 'the new kitchens and offices depending on it, together with the coal yards and sheds…[and] one range of stables'.

121   CSPI, 1601–3, 411; (NMS, DCCI).

122   This reference derives from a lease of 1578 and made to George Ardglas, the newly appointed housekeeper of the castle, and also included a 100ft square (9.3m square) parcel against the north wall of the castle 'all anciently crown property'. There is also a reference in 1578 to a little garden or piece of land before the Castle of Dublin, parcel of the possessions of the monastery of St Thomas the Martyr, Dublin granted by the Crown to Thomas, earl of Ormond and Ossory. *Fiants Eliz.* 3416; *Fiants Eliz.* 3309; 13th DKR, Appx. IV, 94 (NMS, DCCI).

123   Knowler 1740, I, 131–2

124   *ibid.* See also reference in 1660 (CSPI 1600–62, 139) to Sir Henry Talbot having contracted with the earl of Strafford to surrender 'certain valuable lands adjoining Dublin Castle' 'in exchange for 1,000 acres in the then intended plantation of Connaught'. Another of May 1661 (CSPI 1600–62, 327) relates to parcels 'of land and two mills adjoining Dublin Castle' owned by the earl of Cork, demised by him to Alderman Barry and afterwards 'sold to the E of Strafford and thrown into the garden of the Castle'.

125   Hughes 1940, 2, 90.

126   HMC *Ormonde*, ns, VIII, 1920 – compare with the treatment of the bowling green at Oxmantown and the layout of St Stephen's Green.

127 McNeill 1931, 53–4, but see also Carpenter 2003, 140 and Maguire 1985, 16; see Appendix 7.

128 McParland 2001, 94.

129 Ibid. citing Bod. Lib. Ms Rawlinson D71 'A Tour Through Ireland, in seven letters', 25. See also Carpenter 2003, 139. James Butler (1665–1745), 7th earl of Ossory, succeeded his grandfather, the 1st duke of Ormond, in 1688, his father having died in 1680.

130 NLI, MS 2524, 1705 inventory at McParland 2001, 94.

131 NLI, MS 41582/1. Grimaldi, who had made his London debut in December 1708, was esteemed in Dublin as 'the most celebrated singer that ever was known', tickets for his performances during this time cost 'two crowns apiece'.

132 HMC Ormonde, ns, VIII, 245. This letter from the Surveyor General Thomas Burgh to Ormond's secretary, Edward Southwell also refers to 'the new closet in the Castle' as finished. Various works to the castle in the period 1705–7 are also found at TNA, WO55/ 1984 (IAA, EMcP).

133 Barnard 2003, 216–17. Loeber 1981, 34–5 and mentioning evidence (citing NLI, MS 992, 61) for proposed repairs to the castle in 1704 by Ormond, costing £1,037 6s.

134 Loeber 1981, 31–9.

135 TNA, SP 63/371, 1–4 where Burgh's patent as 'Engineer of all Fortifications' is dated 10 July (12 Wm. III) (IAA, EMcP). Dunlevy 2002, 15.

136 An Act of Parliament in 1697 (9 Wm III c.4, I.) provided the finance, raised from tobacco duties, to initiate a campaign of barrack building (O'Dwyer 2002, 110; Dunlevy 2002, 8–15; McParland 2001, 92).

137 The Surveyor General was not, however, responsible to parliament, as the post was held by patent, and at times this proved problematic until resolved between 1759 and 1763 (McParland 1995, 91–9; O'Dwyer 2002, 111–13).

138 Casey 2005, 27.

139 Payment to Burgh in 1703 is recorded in CSPD, 1703, 21–3. The provision of stables for the Horse Guard and move to the barrack ground in 1705 is found at BL Add. Ms, 9716, 201–2 (IAA, EMcP). However, it is unclear how this related to the existing Horse Guards' accommodation near the Council Chamber on Essex Quay, and the location of the 'barrack ground' referred is not identified. It may relate to temporary accommodation at the Royal Barracks while existing structures off Dame Street were rebuilt. The location of the Horse Guards in 1673, beside the Poddle, south of the Council Chamber is identified as 'Life Guard' on de Gomme's survey where the site of the stables and yards corresponds exactly to the site of the Horse Guard yard shown on John Greene's 1721 survey, copied 1755 by Roger Kendrick – DCA, WSC 654; reproduced HTA Dublin II, Map 11. Burgh's building of the riding house in the castle yard is at TNA, SO1/15, 296; payment to Burgh of some £1,200 for these works as well as repairs to the Council Chamber is at JH of C, II, clviii, while a payment to Burgh of £400 in 1706 for rebuilding stables for Horse Guards is also recorded at TNA, T14/8, 427. An 'Account of Thomas Burgh for fortification and buildings' (1705–07) is at TNA, WO55/1984 (IAA, EMcP).

140 HMC Ormonde, ns, VIII, 294–5; see also TNA, T1/126, 30 (IAA, EMcP).

141 TNA, SO1/15, 578–9 (McParland 2001, 94). The warrant issued in March 1710 granted £3,000 towards buying land and making the new entrance. TNA, T14/9, 201–2 (IAA, EMcP). On 18 July 1710 Wharton 'sent over an address of the Irish House of Commons asking that…300l. to be paid for buying in certain houses on Cork Hill to enlarge the way into Dublin Castle'. CTB 1708–1714 (1879), 191: CXXII, 53. R. Ingoldsby in a letter to E. Southwell, dated 20 Jan. 1711, states 'the 3,000 pounds for making the way to the Castle is in the Vice-Treasurer's hands'. NLI, MS 698, 55–6.

142 HMC Ormonde, ns VI, 421.

143 The proposal is detailed in DCA, Gilbert MS 195, containing 'an account of the proceedings of the House of Commons about enlarging the passage on Cork-Hill & into her Majesties Castle of Dublin' and related maps. See also TNA, T14/8, 201–2; T14/9, 2 (IAA, EMcP).

144 TNA, T14/9, 201–2 (IAA, EMcP).

145 DCA, Gilbert Ms 195.

146 ibid.

147 ibid.

148 Molesworth's sale of land in 1710 required for the approach to the castle is found at RD, 7/100/1812.

149 The plan shows the alignment guided by the fronts on the west side of the passage, and to extend as far as 'Doran the Joyner's house' on the east side of Rathborne's holding. The ground behind Rathborne's holding including the yard behind the coffee house, and evidently extending into the castle ditch, are noted as belonging to Lord Cork. Another plan in the same hand purports to show the individual businesses which occupied the affected properties. These include along the east side of the existing passage – 'Gunsmiths', 'Alehouse' and 'Tom's Coffee House' which adjoined a 'Perewigmaker' which fronted Castle Street, adjoined in turn by 'The Toyshop' a woollen drapers and 'The Barbers'. In 1677 there was reference to two little shops by the drawbridge, one possessing two small rooms and selling bottled drink, the other a barber's shop. HMC Ormonde, ns, IV, 31.

150 TNA, T1/247, 77 (IAA, EMcP). Petition of J Rathborne – undated but forwarded to the Lords of Treasury on 11 Jan. 1723. A later document of 1724 relates how in return Rathborne was to receive 'all the ground over which the present passage to the Castle leads' as far as the castle wall, in addition to the site of 'Tom's Coffee House'. As part of this he gained 'the two Stone Towers adjoining to the Gate of the Castle and the ground on which the…Towers now stand…with Liberty to build thereon unto the Castle Wall'. The agreement detailed that the 'street or Passage' was to be made at the queen's expense and to be 'vaulted from the end of such new passage to the Castle wall and to be paved and fitted for public use'. CTP, Vol. 6 (1889), 258.

151 DCA, Gilbert Ms 195, 9, 12. Its location suggests it was a defensive feature built outside the castle ditch, possibly as part of works in 1577.

152 NA/ PRO T1/247/78, 79 (IAA, EMcP), Sol. Gen. report of 17 Feb 1721: 'the two towers (near the Castle Gate) stand twenty feet in front and fifty feet in depth'.

153 TNA, T1/247, 77 (IAA, EMcP). Petition of J Rathborne – undated but forwarded to Lords of Treasury on 11 Jan. 1723: The change is explained 'whereby that side of the Castle which lyes next to Castle street was to be brought about twenty five feet nearer to the street that it now is, which could not be done without encroaching in the ground intended to be conveyed to your petitioner, twenty five feet in depth and fifty feet in length'. This is likely to have come about as plans for the north range were developed, which as built (and confirmed by the evidence from modern excavations) projected well beyond the curtain wall. It may also have been related to the need to find a suitable site for the Treasury building. 30th DKR (1898), 53.

154 TNA, T1/247, 78, 79 (IAA, EMcP), Sol. Gen. report of 17 Feb 1721. However, a few years later in 1724 Rathborne complained that although 'he had pulled down his houses & c. to carry out the arrangement…there was due…£1198 17s 6d by the non-conveyance of the ground to him'. CTP, Vol. 6 (1889), 258.

155 McParland 2001, 94.

156 NLI, MS 41582/1. Certain progress on establishing these redoubts was made, and after asking whether 'a convenient corner of the Park may not be set apart for that service…' a site associated with the Royal Hospital was selected, but ultimately this too proved unobtainable. As late as 1714 Burgh reported: 'The two powder magazines are not begun; the ground on which they were… appointed to be built is in a field belonging to the Royal Hospital where the magazines would stand dry, be at a convenient distance from the city and near a body of 400 men entertained by the Crown who have arms and are disciplined and would be a great security against the magazines being surprised. This ground could not be conveyed by the Governors of the Hospital, it being granted for the use and benefit of the Hospital only and made inalienable and incapabale of ever coming to the possession of the Crown'. HMC Ormonde, ns, VIII, 294–5; see also TNA, T1/126, 30 and T1/176, 92 (IAA, EMcP). Ultimately a warrant to build the Magazine Fort in the Phoenix Park was not issued until 1734, its design attributed to John Corneille, 2nd engineer to the Board of Ordnance. In July 1735, £2325-8-4½ was allowed for the magazine according to a plan 'laid-down and contrived' by Corneille. TNA, T14/12, 40 (IAA, EMcP); see also McParland 2001, 137,140.

157 The warrant for building an arsenal, approved during Wharton's tenure in April 1710, is referenced at CTP, 1708–1714 (1879), 174, CXXI, 31; the 'copy of rule, orders and instructions' at p. 186, CXXII, 16; p.197, CXXIII, 10 relates to payments for 'Ordnance Stores at the Arsenal'. See also TNA, T14/9, 169, 170 (IAA, EMcP). The warrant for the arsenal was accompanied by an estimate (a very substantial £31,850-5-6) by Burgh which refers to excavating '4,321,376 solid feet of earth dug from moat to form ramparts, 896,000 solid feet of earth dug from moats for 4 ravelins, another 281,760 solid feet of earth dug in various places'. See also McParland 2001, 95–6. In relating his concerns about the abuse, Ormond stated that the work had stopped after it was revealed that more than £1,200 had been 'misspent' out of some £2,900. In making his proposal he suggested 'direction for plans…ought to be given' to ensure 'no time might be lost" CTP, 1708–1714 (1879), 226–7, CXXVI, 30.

158 NLI, MS 698, R. Ingoldsby to Ormond, 18 Nov. 1710.

159 NLI, MS 698, R. Ingoldsby to Ormond, 26 Dec. 1710.

160 TNA, TI/176, 92 (IAA, EMcP). Costed at approximately £3,989 it was about £670 more expensive than the Treasury. In referring to the Upper Yard, Ingoldsby may simply have included that part of the Lower Yard west of the, then still exposed, Poddle river. An explanation that seems likely given that de Gomme showed the old magazine on the lower, eastern side of the water course which presumably contributed to the damp and rust issues.

161 NLI, MS 41582/1.

162 Based on an account of the fire found at NLI, MS 41580/29, [Alderman] Robert Curtis, Dublin, to Mrs Bonnell (his 'cousin'), 17 Apr. 1711. In describing the damage Curtis reported that only '18 books of the Land Surveyor's…were saved, which will be very mischievous to the kingdom. Captain Pratt got away all his books and papers (and what little money there was in this very poor Treasury), and so did the Pells, and [the] Chamberlains…lost some papers, but I thank God of no great consequence. Had there been any wind stirring, that side of Essex Street could not have escaped.' A few months later it was also reported 'we suffer an irretrievable loss from the Down Survey, which was burnt at that time'. NLI, MS 41582/1.

163 NLI, MS 698, ff. 60–2, Richard Ingoldsby to Edward Southwell, 31 March 1711. For clarity, the original spellings have been corrected. While it is difficult to know how well-informed Ingoldsby was in architectural matters, Southwell certainly was as an active, knowledgeable, and well-travelled patron who had already employed John Vanbrugh to rebuild Kings Weston, and who would become a benefactor to Colin Campbell's Vitruvius Britannicus, earning from him praise as the 'Anagaranno of our Age' (Downes 1987, 342–3). On 11 March 1712, Archbishop King wrote to Southwell, separately, to say that as the duke of Ormond will need good engineers, 'What if he should carry Captain Burgh with him, I persuade myself that he knows more, will be more faithful and diligent than any his Grace will meet with, if it would be made worth his while. He was Coehoorns [Menno Baron van Coehoorn, Dutch Engineer) disciple, who had a great value for him'. TCD, 750/4/30v (IAA, EMcP files).

164 See n.149 above.

165 Ibid. Sir Richard's sister Barbara married in 1713 William Smyth, who looked after Ingoldsby's family and affairs, and whose sister Mary had married Thomas Burgh in 1700.

166 NLI, MS 41582/1.

167 CMLP, 24 May 1711, J. Pulteney to Dawson.

168 NLI, MS 41589/3. In the same source it was also noted that work had commenced on the library at Trinity College, and that 'Burgh is to go away next week, but this is not certain'.

169 McParland 2001, 96, citing BL, Add. MS 38160, 53. While there remains a possibility that removing the tower may also have been related in some way to the works associated with the new passage, it should be noted that £10,000 was granted in the same month as part of the £20,572-14-0 associated with building the Council Chamber (£3,317-7-9) with the remainder allocated to the offices of the receiver general and commissary general (£3,710-23); the armoury (£3,999), and the two powder magazines at Kilmainham (£7,486-4-0). TNA, T14/9, 260–1 (IAA, EMcP).

170 The other offices related to the receiver general, auditor general, commissary general, Registry of Deeds and the Barrack Board (McParland 2001, 96). Estimate for Council Chamber, armoury etc. 1712 is at TNA, T14/9, 260–582; estimates are also to be found at JH of C, II, cclv-cclvii (IAA, EMcP).

171 30th DKR, App. I, 53.

172 Ibid.

173 Ibid.

174 From its description in 1585 as a five-storied structure with a spiral stairs on one side, and the little that is suggested in Francis Place's distant view, there is no true impression of the appearance or condition of the Powder Tower at the time of its demolition; used to store gunpowder when the castle fire broke out in 1684, its protection was the reason for Lord Arran's use of 'controlled explosions' and so while his actions were effective in preventing greater disaster, the extent to which the tower may have been damaged or undermined at the time is not known. Ultimately it was taken down to a height of about 6m above the bedrock, which forms its foundation, and leaving, at most, about a metre of the tower above the original, lowest floor level (Lynch and Manning 2001, 195).

175 This much is apparent from the necessity to rebuild the north-east portion of the Cross Block in 1742, and again in the 1790s. The problems with subsidence certainly seem to have endured, and in 1961 the decision was taken to demolish and rebuild the entire east Cross Block. See pp 246 .

176 TNA, T/176, 92–3 (IAA, EMcP).

177 Ibid, which provides the detail for much of the following section.

178 Ibid. Without referring here to the 'Treasury' explicitly Burgh simply lists the offices together under the single estimate of £3,710:2:3. He does, however, refer to it later as 'the Treasury and other publik offices'.

179 Ibid. It is possible that covering the watercourse was prioritised with the armoury to mitigate the issue of damp that had contributed to the unsuitable conditions in the previous magazine, and which had caused Ingoldsby to complain that 'the ground being so very low and moist…our small arms cannot be preserved from rust'. NLI, MS 698 ff 29–30.

180 Ibid.

181 TNA, T14/9, 582 (IAA, EMcP).

182 For example, as late as 1720 estimates were produced concerning the accommodation of the Trustees of the Linen Manufacture 'in the east building' and in October 1721 estimates were received relating to 'work to be done in the garrets over the offices in the Lower Castle Yard'. It seems that only in November 1722 were estimates provided 'for fitting up offices for the Treasury in the New Building in the Lower Castle Yard'. McParland 2001, 98, citing TNA, SP63/372, 133; SP63/373, 50 (IAA, EMcP).

183 With their tall proportions and segmental pediments characteristic for this date, the doorcases – except for the easterly one – were differently disposed according to Thomas Sautelle-Robert's early nineteenth-century view (Fig. 3.63) and an 1829 plan by William Murray, although the position of the westerly doorcase in the engraving does not agree with the plan.

184 McParland 2001, 98.

185 However, see BL Eg. Ms 917, 214–5 (IAA, EMcP) concerning Thomas Burgh's slightly earlier 1710 'draft for the Magazine for the Arms' devised as a long range comparable in scale to the Treasury. The designs are endorsed as 'No.5' which perhaps indicates the level of consideration being given to the scheme; the proposed location of the building can be qualified by the following inscription 'Plan of an Armoury projected for ye place where now the Guard Room is in the Castle of Dublin'. It is not clear whether this draft relates in any way to the one referred to by Ingoldsby, and sent to Ormond's secretary, Edward Southwell in Jan. 1711. NLI, MS 698, 55–6.

186 TNA, TI/176 (IAA, EMcP). Burgh had explained that 'the timber and walls will be greatly damaged if the covering them [sic] be long delayed'.

187 McParland 2001, 99. See also McDowell 2003, esp. 4–12.

188 The location of kitchens here is further confirmed by the 1606 Wattson and 1673 Dartmouth plans (Figs 1.15, 2.1), and kitchens and servants' hall are suggested together at this location in an outline plan attributed to Robinson (Fig. 3.8). See also Manning 2017–18, 149, noting that the location of kitchens in the tower is likely to have posed a fire hazard and so possibly accounts for a fire recorded there in 1758. Here it is also stated that the 'use of one storey of the Bermingham Tower as a kitchen appears to have continued up to the demolition of the tower in 1775'. The state kitchen continued to occupy the lowest level through the nineteenth century.

189 Euclid Alfray's 1767 plan indicates that the central arch of the west Cross Block led through to the 'Coal hole sheds and other conveniencys' and as it is shown leading to a yard it is possible these, with part of the west range formed part of Burgh's new kitchen in 1714. It is also quite conceivable that the kitchens built by Burgh at this time actually relate to the site later identified as the 'Chief Secretary's kitchen', which were essentially located only at basement level, adjoining the west end of the Treasury block. NMS, Xerox copy of 1828 William Murray plan, annotated with notes by C. Manning. See also n.459 below.

190 TNA, TI/176, 92–3 (IAA, EMcP).

191 Manning 2017–18, 149–50.

192 TNA, T14/9, 635 (IAA, EMcP). One for the House of Lords was also included in the payment.

193 Ibid, 582. Between 1721 and 1723 estimates were submitted for accommodation relating to the auditor general, the Treasury and the ordnance 'in the New Buildings in the Lower Castle Yard'; and again in 1725 for the chamberlains of the exchequer in the Lower Castle Yard, and, while not explicitly included in Burgh's original programme of work in 1714, an estimate for the Provost Marshal's house 'at the back of the Castle of Dublin' exists for 1725. CMLP, 10 May 1721; 17 Oct 1721; 16 Nov. 1722; 25 Feb. 1723 (NMS, DCCI). An account of work undertaken 1712–4 is also found at TNA, T1/308, 108 (IAA, EMcP).

194 TNA, SO1/16, 140; SP63/374, 427 (IAA, EMcP).

195 TNA, T1/308, 108, 16 June 1738 (IAA, EMcP).

196 Ibid.: 'in ye year 1717 ye Surveyor General directed ye said work to be further proceeded on which was done accordingly in ye year 1724 ye balance due to ye severall tradesmen and for ye work finished & set up pursuant to ye Surveyor General's direction was then cleared off'. The sum due to Whinnery was £6-7-9.

197 The problem of encroachment into the castle ditch, and its condition are likely to have affected any plans to advance the north ranges between 1712 and 1726, as well as the failure to achieve adequate provisions for a new entrance. 6th DKR App., 27. In 1719 Sir John St Leger submitted a petition to the Lords Justices alleging injuries to his house adjoining the castle of Dublin, by workmen acting under the Surveyor General. CMLP, 9 Dec. 1719. That the Under Secretary's office and accommodation was already well established by 1727 could be implied from the estimate for repairs prepared that year. CMLP, 22 Mar. 1727. A further reference to necessary repairs is dated 1749. CMLP, 19, 21 Aug. 1749 (NMS, DCCI).

198 In effect it was the newest structure on the perimeter wall of the medieval castle having collapsed in 1624 (presumed to have been weakened by an explosion at Wood Quay in 1596) it was rebuilt, apparently at the expense of Lord Cork whose property was adjoining, his association also contributing to the naming of Cork Hill (Lynch and Manning 2001, 187).

199 Ibid.

200 McParland 2001, 97.

201 NA OPW/5HC/1/61 Euclid Alfray, Plans of Dublin Castle, 1767 – *Lower State Floor; Upper State Floor*. The extent to which the entire east Cross Block was rebuilt by this time is now impossible to say as the block was entirely rebuilt in the 1960s without the original interiors or fabric having been recorded. The 1742 rebuilding involved 'taking down with great care 1200 feet of Architrave

frieze & cornice'. While there are no corner fireplaces (a characteristic of early-Georgian building practices) evident on the first level in 1767 in any of the rooms, some of the ground-floor rooms in the north-east corner have the later, more commonplace, central breast type. However, it should be noted that the north-east range (Chief Secretary's Office), which can be ascribed to Arthur Dobbs' work in 1742, has corner fireplaces on both levels. Brooking's depiction of the north end of the west Cross Block shows it terminating in a narrow gable, unlike the south end where the block has been returned to accommodate an entrance and staircase; a similar arrangement at the north end was eventually in place by 1767, presumably built as part of the Under Secretary's accommodation, whenever that may have been, but probably before 1749. Other internal changes in the west range are less discernible, though most rooms (on both levels and despite certain opening up of the cross wall) retain early type, corner fireplaces. The present chimney pieces, of various dates and styles, are not original, some perhaps part of Victorian alterations but most seem to have been either re-installed or introduced as part of extensive refurbishment in the late twentieth century – as with the 1960s rebuilding of the east range, the original interiors were not formally recorded as part of this work.

202 See McParland 2001, 93.

203 The rooms beyond the small entrance lobby and staircase, at the junction of the south and west ranges, accommodated a large scullery at a slightly lower level, next to the Berminghan Tower on the west side; beside this there was a 'passage' with a large cistern leading to the main 'English' kitchen in the tower (at a higher level), equipped with stoves flanking the entrance and a large fireplace opposite, cut into the south wall between two windows. A further flight of steps led into the western tower projection, where the room for the clerk of larder was located, with the 'French' kitchen directly beside it. The first cook's room, a deep, narrow chamber with a corner fireplace, lay at the west end of the colonnade, accessed directly off the entrance lobby.

204 McDowell 2003, 7.

205 Although the steward was the more senior, the roles were not always clearly defined, at least according to one early-nineteenth-century observer: 'the Steward was the man that did the work, the Comptroller more assisting in the pageantry of the Court, but very often the Comptroller was the man conversant with business and the roles should be reversed' (McDowell 2003, 7–8).

206 Presumably, Lord Warkworth, Hugh Percy 1742–1817, eldest son and heir of the 1st duke of Northumberland, Lord Lieutenant in 1763.

207 In 1767 it was labelled as 'Mr Secretary Waite's Office', a reference to Thomas Waite (1718–80), who served 1747–77.

208 17th DKR, 24; CMLP, 10 Aug. 1720 (NMS, DCCI). Although Lord Sunderland appointed Baillie Upholsterer to the Government in 1716, his accounts would seem to imply that he had been employed at the castle from at least 1714. Baillie's repairs at the castle, and the supply of furniture to it were recorded in 1717. CTP, 1714–1719 (1883), CCXII, 35. In 1719 Baillie was paid just over £500 for 'furnishing the Castle of Dublin, and the house of Chapelizod'. Ibid., CCXXI, 46.

209 In 1717 Thomas Burgh reported to the Treasury 'on certain goods' supplied to the castle including '493 yards of matting for the Council Chamber'. CTP, 1714–1719 (1883), CCXII, 18. For detail of the layout of the Council Chamber in the mid-nineteenth century see the plan at OPWT, E000528 U16–14.

210 TNA, SP 63/384, 70 (IAA, EMcP).

211 Severens 1992–3, 3.

212 It is worth noting that even across the water the Surveyor General of the King's Works, Sir Thomas Hewett, could complain in 1724 that the job brought 'nothing but repairs' and 'no prospect of fine new buildings' (Downes 1998, 395; Colvin 2005, 492–3; 745–6).

213 Colvin 2005, 745; McParland 2001, 105–12; 203–5.

214 McParland 2001, 203.

215 See, for example, Cornforth 1970, 343–4. Craig having ambiguously written in 1964 that the designer of the Bedford Tower was 'possibly Pearce, though I think not' he did later include it in his list of 'candidates for buildings in some way connected to Pearce' (Colvin and Craig 1964, L. Craig 1996, 33. McParland 2001, 105).

216 *Ibid.* In so far as human associations can be reasonably used as circumstantial evidence to support ideas of stylistic fidelity or an artistic inheritance (whether acquired directly simply by practice and experience on site or from a deeper personal loyalty), there may be some relevance in the knowledge that close connections existed between many of the leading personnel involved in these public buildings, including for example George Ensor, clerk of works to Arthur Jones Nevill, the Surveyor General from 1743–52, and whose father Job Ensor had been employed as a carpenter on the building of Pearce's Parliament House. For the significance of such connections see O'Dwyer 1996–7, 7–23.

217 Cornforth 1970, 343.

218 A series of plans from the Elton Hall collection, now in the Victoria & Albert Museum, London have been associated with the castle, listed as 'Plans showing alterations to buildings at the rear of Dublin Castle' and include only one 'plan for a new Office' that can with absolute certainty be identified with the castle buildings – E.2124:60-1992 (on verso, pencil drawing of candle sconce) (Colvin and Craig 1964, Cat. No. 60, Plate lxvii a). It is not clear which of the remaining drawings (E.2124:61-1992 Plans showing alterations to buildings at the rear of Dublin Castle; E.2124:68-1992 Plan of part of a large building, possibly Dublin Castle; E.2124:91-1992 Designs for alterations for buildings at the rear of Dublin Castle) relate to the two other designs illustrated in Colvin and Craig 1964, clv; Cat. Nos. 61 & 91; Plate lxvii b & c. Both relate to the same section of building, one that seems to share some affinities with the Chief Secretary's block. The plans (unseen, and outside the resources of this study) would repay study as one of them, perhaps signficantly, shows a proposal for a skewed passage formed as a colonnade through the building, suggesting the designs were concerned with creating a new entrance to the Upper Yard.

219 Dobb's professional abilities as an architect may reasonably be questioned in the absence of evidence of training or earlier career. For example, Craig describes him as a 'gentleman and political economist rather than an architect' (Craig 1952, 166). For more recent discussion of some of the issues around this see McParland 2001, 101; O'Dwyer 2002, 111.

220 At the time of Pearce's death it was recorded that 'all the portico from the architrave up, roofing and ceiling same, part of the Voluta columns, and the whole pavement under the colonnade, the levelling of the same with the steps of the pavement in the area in front of the portico, and iron palisades are yet to be finished', H of CJ, Ireland, v.6 cited in Clarke 1958, 42. It was substantially complete only by 1739, 'except The Iron Rails' (McParland 2001, 188).

221 Neville may have acted as an assistant to Dobbs, before 1743, and Dobbs supported Neville when he was charged with embezzlement while in office (Clarke 1958, 101).

222 BL, Add. MS 38671 (IAA, EMcP). Jones assumed the maternal surname Nevill (or Neville) in anticipation of his succession *c*. 1750 to Furness, the Kildare estate of his uncle, Richard Nevill.

223 Casey 2005, 540; McDonnell 1991, 20–1; Maguire 1985, 37. After his tenure as Surveyor General, Nevill's continuing interest in architecture can be demonstrated in his subscription to two of the most significant Irish architectural books of the eighteenth century – Aheron 1754 and Payne 1757. In 1757, he had his drawing room at No.14 Rutland Square decorated after the works of Pietro da Cortona in the Palazzo Pitti in Florence, executed by Jacob Ennis, an Irish artist, whose recent trip to Italy had been sponsored by Nevill (Ingamells 1997, 339).

224 Kelly 2012, 73–7.

225 O'Dwyer 2008, 107–9. Myers held the office jointly with his son Graham from 1777 until his death in 1783. The younger Myers had resumed the post of architect in 1793, in lieu of others, and held it jointly with John Gibson from 1799 until 1801, when Myers died (O'Dwyer 2002, 131–4).

226 Cooley may have had a role in devising plans for the Lower Yard (Fig. 3.34) – see that section at p.198-200 .

227 Upon his appointment as architect, Waldré's salary as painter ceased and so he was obliged to devote his attention to buildings, thereafter much occupied with the rebuilding of the Commons Chamber in the Houses of Parliament, destroyed by fire in February 1792.

228 IAA, EMcP files citing Walsh 1973, 30; McParland 2001, 102. There was some acknowledgement at this time that the castle had 'for several Years...been rebuilding', and while not yet finished 'according to the plan', it was expected to result in a 'palace not to be exceeded by many sovereign Princes Courts' (A Citizen of London 1732, 8–9). One later eighteenth-century history of Irish theatre refers to the 'great support the duke of Dorset gave the stage whilst Lord Lieutenant' and clearly supported more private productions, as for example when in January 1732, the *Distressed Mother* was played in the Council Chamber with viscounts Mountjoy and Kingsland among the 'persons of quality of both sexes' who played the parts. It was remembered that the chamber was 'fitted up in the most elegant stile...the chambers and passages were illuminated with wax...and the whole was conducted with the greatest regularity and decorum' (Hitchcock 1788 I, 75–6).

229 For Mrs Delany's description of the castle in Sept 1731/2 see Llanover 1861–2, Vol. I, 289, 299, 309, 337, and for her later visit in 1751, see Vol. III, 51–2. Some indication of the 'Establishment of the Duke of Dorset's Household' at the castle in 1731, including list of servants and their positions, lists of weekly allowances for wine, beer, candles, coal and charcoal and well as a 'list of entertainment money for a year' is found in the Nottingham Archives, DD/P/6/3/77.

230 The duke's own account is found in Anon. 1824, Vol. II, 33–5 with a full transcript given at n.262 below; for an elaborate description of the duke's ball see *Dublin Evening Post* 30 Oct–3 Nov 1733, while reference to the splendour of decoration in October 1733 is found at TNA, SP 63/396, 91(IAA, EMcP).

231 However, O'Dwyer (1992) argues for it as a work by Joseph Tudor. See also detailed discussion at n.262 below.

232 Llanover 1861–2, Vol. I, 337.

233 For discussion of the decoration of the hall in 1731, and the question of whether the painted view attributed to Van de Hagen may in fact relate to the duke of Dorset's second term as Lord Lieutenant, see O'Dwyer 1992, esp. 150–5 and further consideration by McParland 2001, 100–2. More recent discussion is found in Doderer-Winkler 2013, 46–50. The hangings were offered to the Office of Public Works in the 1990s but the offer was declined. Information from The Lord Sackville, November 2015. For the eventual sale of the hangings from Knole to a private collector in the late 1990s, see Loos 2007, 71–4.

234 Colvin and Craig 1964, LXVII, a, b & c.

235 Cornforth 1970, 344. In February 1737, the issue of rebuilding the state dining room in the south range (and other apartments) was raised, and this was followed in March 1741 with a plan and estimates for the pulling down and rebuilding of certain parts of Dublin Castle, a scheme later endorsed by Chesterfield as 'absolutely necessary'. CMLP, 14 Feb 1737; CDC 3495, 23 March 1741; CDC 3513, 20 May 1742; CDC 3524, 5 June 1742. In July 1738 estimates were also submitted to the Lords Justices for work at the Horse Guards (presumably on Essex Street) CMLP, 31 July 1738 (NMS, DCCI).

236 A reference by Dobbs to plans by Burgh for a new passage into the castle, dated 1713, is at TNA, T1/290, 27 (IAA, EMcP). Estimates 'for making the new passage from the Blind Quay into the Castle of Dublin' are referenced in CMLP for 29 July 1718 and 18 June 1722. On 29 Dec. that year Burgh had reported to the Lords Justices on the proposal to purchase land adjoining the castle gates. The Articles of Agreement with John Rathborne for widening passage into the castle are again referenced in KQL, 23 March 1723. In June 1725 Burgh reported on John Rathborne's petition for fulfilment of his agreement, KQL,15 June 1725. A year later £208.10.00 per ann. was granted to Rathborne 'till lands be conveyed in lieu of others from him' to make the new passage, KQL 23 April 1726. Twenty years after it had first been proposed, Burgh was still concerning himself about the 'new entrance to the Castle' by sending copies of reports relating to it to the Chief Secretary, CMLP, 3 Jan 1730 (all from NMS, DCCI).

237 Dobbs's estimate for the new entrance, dated February 1738, was prepared by his deputy John Wilkinson. See TNA, SO. I/18, 285–6; T14/12, 124, 125 (IAA, EMcP).

238 Although it was sometimes believed that one of the towers had been incorporated within the new building (Cornforth 1970, 458) this theory can be completely discounted. However, it should be noted that none of the excavations between 1985 and 1987 concerned the site of the gatehouse, nor were any associated features discovered in the vicinity other than a short section of the curtain wall to the west (between it and the Cork Tower, under the façade of the former Under Secretary's apartments – later, the Children's Court) and to the north, the truncated base of the causeway and the drawbridge pit. Further west of the gatehouse a 15m section of the curtain wall (under the former Chief Secretary's apartments) was also excavated (Lynch and Manning 2001, 187–95).

239 The 1712 consideration of the site occurs in 30th DKR (1898), 53, while the renewed interest in the site can be traced to 1733. In December 1735 Dobbs sent a report to the duke of Dorset, concerning the memorial of Joseph Gascoyne relating to a site 'formerly part of the estate of Charles, late Earl of Burlington' which he agreed to allow to 'be exchanged and made use of for a new intended passage or entrance into [Dublin] Castle' (CTP, Vol. 3 (1900), 57–62. This source also refers to an earlier petition of Gascoyne's, sent to the duke of Dorset and dated October 13, 1733). See also 'Memorial of Joseph Gascoyne, with report of Att. & Solr. Gen. in reference to ground taken by the Crown for the new entrance to the Castle' (CMLP, 23 Sep. 1735). Payment in relation to the 'new way' is found at KQL, 7 March 1737. £160.13.7 ¼ paid to Dobbs for new passage also appears at KQL, 17 Dec. 1737. Settlement with Gascoyne over the ground taken for the new passage appears not to have been resolved for some time. In March 1738 the Lord Lieutenant was warranted to compensate Gascoyne, in the amount of £1237 2s. 6d., for the non-performance of its agreement (CTP, Vol. 3, (1900), 470–75; see also CMLP, 9 August 1741). In 1743, £574.0.8 ¼ was paid to Joseph Gascoyne for rent of ground and opening of the passage (KQL, 17 May 1743). A year later he submitted a petition, claiming rent due to him for the same (CDC 3722, 10 May 1744). Formal legal agreement appears not to have been entered into until later again. On 8 August 1745 Lord Chesterfield wrote to the Lords Justices from London, approving the Gascoyne lease. A year later the Gascoyne 'Lease to the Crown forever' was found to be defective for want of the royal seal affixed to a counterpart. NA M2446; 1A.36.8; NA 1C., 1 1697–1798, 12 April 1746 (NMS, DCCI).

240 The site had become part of the yard associated with the 'Barbadoes' or 'Two Toms Coffee House' which in 1712 had been considered as a possible site for the new Treasury, when £1,200 was offered to Lord Cork for it. 30th DKR (1898), 53. See also n.242 below.

241 The source for this is a later memorial, dated 26 April 1745, between J. Gascoyne and including plan signed by A.J. Nevill. While the total of £84 per annum is mentioned in the memorial, Gascoyne appears to have been paid the sums of £119.13.10 and £95.11.4 in the years 1745 and 1746 respectively for rent of ground near the castle(KQL, 23 July 1745; 29 April 1746).

242 It is not clear whether the Lucas Coffee House precisely represents the former 'Barbadoes' or 'Two Toms Coffee House' recorded here in 1712. Lucas's Coffee House occupied the former Cork House 'the city's only Stuart house in the grand manner' which having been temporarily lost to the family during the Crowellian period was reclaimed and reoccupied as a residence. However, by 1670 it had been divided up to accommodate a coffee house and museum, with apparently the exchange built in the garden (formerly part of the graveyard of St Mary del Dam), and made 'convenient with buildings erected on pillars to walk under in foul weather' (Barnard 2003, 36; McCullough 1989, 22, 60). Cork House itself survived somewhat longer and 'was finally demolished by the Commissioners for widening the streets leading into the Castle'. 30th DKR (1898), 53. See also DCA, WSC 329.

243 The earlier map of November 1741 (NMS copy, of a map attached to 'letters patent, George II to Gascoyne, dated 20-1-1742') was prepared by Arthur Dobbs's deputy, John Wilkinson. It shows a narrower plot of ground measuring 103ft by 22ft (31.4m by 6.7m) (at its widest) which it describes as 'the ground which is to be conveyed to Joseph Gascoyne adjoining the new passage...'. The second survey 'An exact map of a Lott of Ground taken by the Crown from Joseph Gascoyne, Esq' shows the enlarged plot (NMS copy. The original bears A. Jones Nevill's signature and was attached to a 'conveyance Gascoyne to Geo. II 21.9.1745').

244 CMLP, 1 April 1738. Along with the efforts required to progress this new passage in the 1730s, there were also efforts to resolve the issues still outstanding over the earlier attempts to open a passage, with reference to a provision 'to free and discharge the establishment of Ireland from the payment of £208 10s per annum payable to John Rathborne…under directions of George I of date 1723–4, March 23 for non-execution of an agreement heretofore made with said Rathborne for other ground for the purpose of making the said new passage'. In 1751, John Rathborne's earlier agreement resurfaced yet again when Rathborne Mills petitioned the duke of Dorset for settlement of claims relating to the land adjoining to the castle gate that had been taken from J Rathborne. CMLP, 13 Nov 1751.

245 £592 was authorised to pay for this work and by August 1741 the entrance was completed. For payments for the work see JH of C, IV, clxii; TNA, SO1/19, 182 (IAA, EMcP). Of the £598-3-6 eventually paid to Dobbs, £47 related to 'the two side walls and peers [sic] over the new passage' and £20 to 'a large Gate framed and lined, and two doors at each side of the said gate'. TNA, T14/12, 122, 124–5 (IAA, EMcP).

246 Referring to the visible section of the eastern block between the two entrances into the castle, the 'Plan for Opening and Widening a Principal Avenue to the Castle' in 1757 refers to 'a handsome colonade or a piazza betwixt said two gates, &c &c'. The proposed arrangement is shown on the earlier plan of January 1753 (Fig. 3.29). For the arrangement of bollards at this time see view of Sackville Street and Gardiner's Mall c. 1750 after Joseph Tudor. For a wider discussion of covered walk or 'piazzas' see Montague 2007, 225–45.

247 Ultimately, the earlier removal of the Powder Tower now allowed the Record Tower to close the vista, as indeed the 1757 scheme (Fig. 3.28) envisaged, though it is incorrectly named as the Birmingham Tower.

248 TNA, T1/308, 114–7 (IAA, EMcP).

249 CDC 3549, 31 July 1742 concerning the Royal Warrant for payment of £2800-18-1½ for 'pulling down' this part of the castle. See also CDC 3602 (n.d., though from the period 1741–5) concerning Lord Duncannon's (Chief Secretary 1741–5) request for an estimate relating to the cost of pulling down a certain portion of the castle (NMS, DCCI).

250 TNA, T1/308, 114–7 (IAA, EMcP). The length of cornice is quite considerable bearing in mind that the entire length of the north elevation of the north-east block was just over 100ft (30.5m), suggesting that a sizeable portion of the Cross Block must have been rebuilt as part of these works.

251 Loeber 1980, 48; 1981, 82–3. The site is clearly indicated on de Gomme's 1673 survey. In 1682 some of the officers sought improvements to the conditions, although it is not clear whether or how these were ever addressed (HMC Ormonde, 14, App. 7, 367–8). Stables for the Horse Guard were among the works undertaken by Thomas Burgh in 1705, though the location and arrangements for them at this time is confused. CSPD, 21–3-1703; BL Add. Ms, 9716, 201, 202; at TNA, SO1/15, 296; T14/8, 427; T1/322, 21; NA 1A-35-58; JH of C, II, clviii (IAA, EMcP). It may be that the Horse Guard was partly or temporarily accommodated at the castle, and certainly by 1725 the Horse Guard stables were again identified with the Essex Street site, off Dame Street, according to John Greene's survey (DCA, WSC654, as copied by Roger Kendrick in 1755). Also in 1725 an estimate was prepared concerning repairs to the Horse Guard, Dublin, but the location is not specified. CMLP, 11 Feb. 1725 (NMS, DCCI).

252 At the same time Chesterfield enclosed the Surveyor General's estimate for building a stable, hay loft and granary for fourteen horses in the timber yard, beside the riding house. NA M2446, 17 April 1746. Further related references concern £5205-4-7 for building in 1746. KQL, 22 April 1746. See also Royal Warrant for paying A.J. Nevill for works & repairs. CDC, 3933 26 April 1746. A more specific Royal Warrant 'for payment of the expense of certain buildings to be erected for the Horse Guards at Dublin' is found at CDC, 3939 13 May 1746 (all NMS, DCCI).

253 DCA, WSC 537/2; 162/2

254 See n. 290 below.

255 253 TNA, T1/322, 14 (IAA, EMcP).

256 TNA, T1/322, 14 (IAA, EMcP). NA M2446, 35, R. Liddell to J. Belcher, 18 May 1745 (NMS, DCCI), and PRONI, T3019/631, Liddell to Belcher, 16 May 1745. McParland 2001, 103.

257 NA M2447), 8 March 1745: Memorial of A.J. Nevill to Lord Chesterfield concerning the state of the castle buildings. The estimate for rebuilding £5205-4-7. See also entry for 18 May 1745; CDC 3886, 18 May 1745; CMLP, 8 March 1746; KQL, 22 April 1746; CDC 3933, 26 April 1746: Royal Warrant for paying Nevill for works and repairs (all NMS, DCCI).

258 While the upper floor of the new west range was given a dormer storey matching the south-east range, a more refined modillion cornice was introduced rather than the bolder bracketed cornice originally used on the Robinson and Molyneux range. The contrast is recorded both by Tudor in his view of 1753, and by James Malton's of 1792; see Appendix 8. Building operations at the castle were usually planned so as to be completed during the eighteen months or so while the Lord Lieutenant was in England – that is between April in an even-numbered year and September of the next year. This meant that the work initiated by Chesterfield would have to be completed by the autumn of 1747. A warrant for the first £2,000 of Nevill's estimate was issued on 5 May 1746. The detailed estimate suggest that plans had already been prepared. Progress payments recorded in the Irish *Commons Journal* reveal that Nevill was simultaneously building a new stable block for the Horse Guard at the recently opened entrance from Cork Hill. *Commons Journal*, Vol. IV, pt. II, p. cclxxix. The warrant was issued on foot of a King's Letter of 22 April 1746. TNA, T14/12, 484 (IAA, EMcP).

259 Baillie 1967, 177 and discussed in O'Dwyer 1992.

260 While O'Dwyer accepts the entrance as Paine's work, Fenlon suggests that it is earlier, related to Lord Wentworth's works at the castle in the 1630s, based on a stylistic comparison with the frontispiece at King's Manor York (Fenlon 2011, 209–12).

261 The ceiling – from its rendering on the Castle Sheet – seems suggestively comparable to some of the main rooms at Chesterfield House (demolished) in London, which Isaac Ware had built for Lord Chesterfield 1747–9, but in fact was part of Francis Johnston's 1820s major repairs to the room (McCarthy 2017; Campbell 2017).

262 The question of whether the hall in its present form was 'purpose-built or adapted from an earlier structure' is dealt with comprehensively by O'Dwyer (1992), even if the question is not fully resolved, with further careful analysis of the matter offered by McParland 2001, 100–2. The earliest visual sources for the room are two painted views: the first is usually attributed to William Van der Hagen, and depicts the State Ball of 1731 during Dorset's first lord lieutenancy, though this attribution has been challenged, with an alternative ascription to Joseph Tudor, so as to represent a later event in 1750s during the duke's second term as Lord Lieutenant. The second view relates to the 'Inaugural Investiture of the Knights of St. Patrick in 1783', captured by John Keyse Sherwin, in a contemporary oil sketch (Fig. 3.38) and in subsequent engravings made between 1793 and 1803. There is virtually no close correlation between the room as depicted in each view, other than perhaps similar proportions and the use of tiered seating along the sides and of a columnar screen across at least one end, though the earlier view shows fluted Ionic columns, and the later view, a fluted Corinthian order. The flat ceiling of the earlier view contrasts with the coved ceiling shown in 1783, corresponding with the present interior. Neither view indicates the presence of windows

along the south wall, and in fact Sherwin's view might even be misconstrued to suggest the room was toplit (although feasible before Vincenzo Waldré's paintings were inserted), though from at least 1767 (Fig. 3.19) the present window arrangement can be confirmed. The fact that some details were altered between the oil sketch and the engraved view means that the reliability of the view as an accurate record is somewhat diminished. For example, where the outline of a window appears to be suggested in the oil sketch, there are no windows indicated at all in the engraved views. As a 1731 view, the painting (accepting the Van der Hagen attribution) seems perfectly compatible with Mrs Delany and Dorset's description of Pearce's efforts. The discovery of canvas drops at Knole that so closely correspond to those shown in the painting, at the very least connects the painting to a scene presided over by the duke of Dorset (Knole being the Dorset seat, with further confirmation given by the survival of the painting in the family's possession, owned in recent times by a branch of the Sackville family). These accounts also confirm that the ball was held in an old room, as the duke of Dorset indicated in his resolve 'to make use of the old hall, which had long been disused and very much out of repair' by covering the walls 'with canvas painted in perspective'. From this O'Dwyer concludes (p.151) 'Pearce, therefore, can be credited only with the decorations, not the structure', yet from Dorset's letter to the countess of Suffolk, written from Dublin Castle in November 1731, and given below, it is clear that the room must have needed major repair (its poor condition confirmed also in 1724 when a ball for the prince's birthday was held in the Council Chamber):

…*I should not do justice to Captain Pearce's genius, if I did not give you some account of the ball-room that he fitted up for this night's entertainment – the usual place was thought too little, and therefore it was resolved to make use of the old hall [Footnote: a fine room in Dublin Castle, now called St. Patrick's Hall; which ever since the Duke of Dorset's repair, has been employed on the state occasions of the Irish court, and particularly on those connected with the Order of St. Patrick'], which had been long disused and very much out of repair; however he so contrived it, that I think I never saw a more beautiful scene: I am sure you won't think that an improper expression, when I tell you that the walls were all covered with canvas, painted in perspective; the space was a large one, but it was so contrived as to make it look as big again; there were your arches, your pyramids, your obelisks, and pillars of all orders and denominations: in short, there were all those things that your fine folks talk on now-a-days; and the lights were so perfectly well disposed, that, upon my word, it had the most surprising fine effect. Some jokers were of opinion that our room might be better than our company but they were perfectly convinced to the contrary, when they saw how it was filled* (Anon. 1824, Vol. 2, 33–5)

In examining the basis of O'Dwyer's rejection of the 1731 view (that it appears to show a hall wider and higher than anything that could have existed here before the present hall, and so must be a later view depicting a ball during Dorset's second viceroyalty), McParland argues that it is unsafe to rely on the evidence of an artist's view serving to record an event for posterity rather than provide an accurate or reliable building survey – some naivety must be assumed based on the artist's intention to give a sense of the occasion, rather than its true specifics. As evidence of this, the dimensions of the surviving hangings (that these are not strictly identical to those in the painting supports the agrument that the precision of the detail in the painting cannot be relied on – there is also (apart from Delany's mention of Pearce) strong evidence that the hangings were the responsibility of the Surveyor General's office) suggest that the hall in which they originally hung was not nearly as tall as the present one (c. 25ft (7.6m) compared to 38ft (11.5m)). There is also disagreement in respect of the columnar screen: the Ionic columns represented in the painted view – and in accepting the relative veracity of the view, likely only to have existed at one end (unless removed by the artist for convenience) – are difficult to relate to the representation of the room on later plans by Alfray (Fig. 3.19) and Penrose. Whereas Alfray does suggest columns that are integrated with screen walls, McParland argues that these would have been too narrow to reach the ceiling (they do, however, compare in scale to the half-round columns shown in the Presence Chamber), and therefore must have existed instead to support (and decorate?) the tiered seating. In support of the theory it is pointed out that both the seating and the columns have disappeared on Penrose's plan; however, the columns of the, then old Presence Chamber have also been omitted though these did exist – Penrose merely giving the essentials of the plan (for example he didn't include the canopies of state as Alfray did), and the screens in the hall are indicated at either end (Fig. 3.24). The question therefore must, for the present, remain an open one.

263 Llanover 1861, Vol. III, 51–2.

264 TNA, T14/13, 31–2 (IAA, EMcP).

265 O'Dwyer 1992, 164. Here it is stated that the carver John Houghton was employed on Chesterfield's additions, as well as works in the ballroom and Council Chamber for the Birth Night celebrations in 1749, but without any reference to nature of the work, or the source. The surviving overmantel for the Presence Chamber installed by 1751 has been attributed to Houghton, but according to Kennedy, Houghton's name is not among the craftsmen listed for payments relating to fitting up the castle to receive the duke of Dorset in 1751 (Kennedy 1999, 86; Glin and Peill 2007, 71, 72–4).

266 TNA, T14/13, 31–2 (IAA, EMcP). See also CMLP, 19 August 1749, Isaac Dance to Mr Wilkinson concerning repairs needed in the domestic apartments in the castle (NMS, DCCI).

267 McParland 2001, 104–5; accounts in the J of H C., Vol V, p. ccxxxvi confirm that the ceiling of the Presence Chamber dates from 1750–1.

268 Letter to Colley Cibber, 17 November 1748 (Victor 1761, Vol. II., 215–18). See also NLI, MS 41,591/1: William Smyth, Dublin, to Ralph Smyth, 2 Nov. 1751: 'There was more splendour and finery at the Castle than ever appeared in this kingdom on the Birthday: Miss Gardner [sic], Miss Foster and Mark White's daughter the three finest ladies, who outshined most of the rest. ...'. Although Isaac Ware is suggested as the possible architect for Chesterfield's work by O'Dwyer, this is not supported by any documentary evidence, the strength of the suggestion based largely on his employment by Chesterfield in London, and his qualification, both as a neo-Palladian and as secretary to the English Board of Works. However, Nevill was in fact an engineer and architect and is likely to have been familiar with, and possessed, Ware's published works, including The Plans, Elevation and Sections of Houghton in Norfolk (1735) to use for example as the source for the chimney piece and overmantel formerly in the 1750 Presence Chamber (and its probable sculptor, John Houghton, is equally likely to have been familiar with Ware's publications) (O'Dwyer 1992, 160–4; Kennedy 1999, 86–7; The Graphic 14 April 1888, 405; Glin and Peill 2007, 71, 72–4). Furthermore, as Nevill was issued monies for the works (NA M2446, 68-69) it is reasonable to assume the design was entirely conceived and carried out by the office of the Surveyor General and if not Nevill himself, his clerk of works, George Ensor was suitably competent, just as with Eyre (whose background, like Burgh's, included military engineering) whose work at the castle is closely associated with Joseph Jarratt. And it may be noted that in 1771 it was stated that Nevill in order to 'hide his own Ignorance...was forced to retain a celebrated Carpenter whom he consulted on all Occasions' (Hibernian Journal, 14–17 June 1771 cited by McParland 2001, 219, n.85; see also Craig 1992, 167-8). It is also worth remembering the earlier disquiet caused by efforts to introduce plans from outside in Burgh's time, and it would occur again with plans for a new chapel from Gandon. Concerning the completion of the works to the north range, Nevill did assert in 1750 that he 'drew a plan for the Rebuilding and finishing that part of the Castle' (TNA, T.I/337,95, IAA, EMcP). Certainly his complaint in 1749, that as Surveyor General, 'now engaged in so many works that all my time is taken up, and by which I neglect my private affairs' would seem to accord with the extent of works then underway at the castle (PRONI, T3019/1317).

269 Although there is reference to the creation of 'pieces of machinery' and the exhibition of 'paintings designed and painted by the celebrated Mr. [Joseph] Tudor', the statement was corrected in a later issue saying 'that through misinformation it was represented...that the decorations exhibited at His Majesty's Castle on the Birth Night had been designed by Mr. Joseph Tudor, since which he [the Editor] hath been informed that Mr. Tudor only executed the Design given to him from the office to which the ordering and conducting that affair belonged' (Strickland 1913), Vol. II, 463).

270 TNA, T.I/337, 95 (IAA, EMcP).

271 TNA, T.14/13, 31-2 (IAA, EMcP).

272 PRONI, T3019/1579, T Waite to E Weston, 17 May 1750, and TNA, T.I/337, 95, 96 (IAA, EMcP).

273 PRONI, T3019/1579; TNA, T. 14/13, 31-2; T.I/337, 95,96 containing a detailed estimate for building the Bedford Tower (IAA, EMcP).

274 Salmon 2013, 316–18. One might even detect an attempt to establish a close identity between the Dublin building and Kent's building by the inclusion of two Venetian windows in the original estimates for the Bedford Tower (McParland 2001, 106). Severens (1990, 29) also argues that the Dublin composition was 'based generally' on the Horse Guards design. It was natural that London would be looked to for inspiration for suitable architectural models at a time when attitudes and fashions were frequently measured against those of London (McParland 1972, 4–5, quoting John Bush, who in 1769 refers to 'the inhabitants of this metropolis, whose dress, fashions, language and diversions are all imported from London').

275 Not shown in Brooking's view, the precise date of the north-west wing has not been established, though its existence before the Bedford Tower might be implied by a reference in 1749 concerning repairs needed in the 'second Secretaries office and apartments'. CMLP, 21 Aug. 1749 (NMS, DCCI).

276 A drawing of a doorcase (RIBA Library SB42 [157]), attributed to the Venetian designer Antonio Visentini (1688–1782) and associated with one of the Basadonna Palazzi in Venice, bears very close comparison with the Dublin gateways and may be a possible source, though the means by which this design could have been transmitted to Ireland is not known (McParland 2001, 106–9).

277 McParland 1972a, 2–3.

278 33 Geo. II, C15, cited in McParland 1972a, 6, n.15. Here (p.8) Semple is named as the 'probable author' of the original scheme while referencing NLI, Map 16.G.49/6; however, see also DCA, WSC 329.

279 The earlier scheme of 1753 shows a street of 46 feet, not on a straight alignment with the bridge, but veering slightly east to align with the space between the Treasury and the east range – intending perhaps to create a vista with the surviving Record Tower.

280 DCA, WSC 329.

281 Montague 2007, 237–40.

282 CDC, 53083, 1 Jan 1758; CDC, 5294, 3rd Jan 1758; KQL, 26 Jan 1758. A further grant was allowed in 1762 as works on Parliament Street were completed. KQL, 24 Feb. 1762 (NMS, DCCI).

283 After Semple's scheme was rejected at least one other scheme was considered, involving a less ambitious design planned by a surveyor named Purfield. As with Semple's, the proposals included removing the 'curious Equestrian Statue' of George I from its position on Essex Bridge' and making it the centrepiece of a new square. See DCA, WSC 94; 162; 499; 537. The background to the competition for the Exchange is discussed in detail by McParland (1972b).

284 See DCA, WSC 499 – undated, but ante 1769 – which, for example, shows in the centre of the, by then redundant, square the 'pedestal for the statue of his Majesty which faces Parliament Street and Castle Street'. The later state of Rocque's map (1769–70) shows the square, named after Bedford (Lord Lieutenant 1757–61); Lennon and Montague (2010, 53) believe that the 'new square involved the clearance of a complete block of houses' explaining that 'traces of the removed lines from Rocque's original engraving can still be discerned on this version of the map'. However, see DCA, WSC 162/2, where the map (which closely relates to WSC 88/1, and dated to 1764), predating the Royal Exchange, refers to 'lotts for building houses or an Exchange' and shows proposals for a reduced 'Parliament Square' measuring '229 feet by 116 feet' while making it clear that the site was then still occupied by 'old buildings'. The map was signed by Gorges Edmond Howard (1715–86) 'regr. to the Passage Trustees', solicitor and writer who his biography claims 'was active in promoting structural improvements in Dublin'. ODNB, Vol. 28 (1891), 21–2. See also McCullough 1991, 4.

285 DCA, WSC 113

286 In his description and assessment of the scheme, McParland notes only WSC 90, yet refers to 'a circular *place* at the junction with George's Street' which is present not on WSC 90, but only WSC 113. It is possible his description conflated the detail from both plans (McParland 1972, 10, his description deriving from J *of* HC, viii, 2 Jan 1772).

287 While Thomas Cooley might reasonably have had a hand in at least one of the schemes (WSC 90), especially in the context of his success in winning the Royal Exchange competition in 1769, Thomas Penrose (who succeeded Cooley in 1782 as Clerk and Inspector of Civil Building) seems more likely, being known to Conyngham, and having been involved at this time at Slane Castle (most likely in his role as agent to James Wyatt, see Martin-Robinson 2012, 161. And, significantly, a decade later Penrose was tasked by the commissioners 'to lay down a Plan of the several Grounds surveyed, so as to lay down different Streets. Making Dame Street Eighty feet wide' (McParland 1972, 10).

288 McCullough 1989, 75.

289 McParland 1972, 7. The average width of Dame Street east of George's Lane was 25ft (7.6m).

290 From Scalé's plan it does not appear that the Horse Guard accommodation was significantly impacted upon by the erection of the new Exchange, other than the rebuilding of the office range around this time. See for example DCA, WSC 88 and especially WSC 105 by Barker (*c.* 1766?) which indicated 'part of the Horse Guard which is to be given up for the Exchange' along with an additional strip as well as the proposal to move back the front of the offices, thereby widening the passage to the castle. WSC 499 shows the Horse Guard offices projecting well into the passage (but less so on WSC 537), which if accurate, will certainly have necessitated complete rebuilding to bring its facade in line with the end wall of the Chief Secretary's office, as represented on Scalé's map. WSC 209 is endorsed by Thomas Cooley and the date 1777 (and further inscribed on verso by T. Sherrard with the date 1814) and showing the site of the Exchange, indicates a narrow strip of ground on the south boundary of the Exchange – part of the site of the Horse Guard stable that was 'granted to the Guild of Merchants by the Commissioners of the Barrack Board'.

291 DCA, WSC 105, by Jonathan Barker, probably *c.* 1766; WSC 92 and WSC 94 are related surveys of 1766 by Barker also showing the various plots.

292 The structure is first clearly indicated on Henry Chaigneau's 1801 plan (Fig. 3.62), then shown as two separate blocks. By 1828 it had become a more irregular assemblage.

293 McParland 2001, 110–12.

294 Maguire 1985, 29.

295 Ibid.

296 Ibid, 30. Eyre's account shows the building cost some £6,500 to erect, only marginally less than the estimates prepared by Nevill for the works to the north range in 1750. IAA, MS 86/149.

297 Transcript excerpt from Wesley's Journal, 1767, IAA, EMcP.

298 TNA, T.I/354, 48–50 (IAA, EMcP); IAA, Jarratt Album Ms 84/51.

299 TNA, T.I/367, 48; T.14/13, 311; T.I/376, 58 (IAA, EMcP).

300 TNA, T.14/13, 315 (IAA, EMcP).

301 IAA, MS 84/51.

302 Eyre's accounts also survive recording payments to Jarratt for labourers' work and 'for overseeing'. Eyre acc. Book IAA, MS 86/149, 119, 134.

303 Transcript excerpt from *Freeman's Journal*, 1775, IAA, EMcP.

304 TNA, SO/1/23, 249; JH of C, 8, ccclvi (IAA, EMcP).

305 Manning 2017–18, 149–50.

306 RCPRI 1815–29, I, 448.

307 Manning 2003, 94.

308 Connolly 1995b; Manning 2017–18, 149. For Eyre's repairs to the tower in 1758, see TNA, SO 1/21, 132; /23, 249 (IAA, EMcP).

309 O'Dwyer (2008, 108–9) suggests that the treatment of the supper room in 1775 represents the first employment of Gothic Revival architecture in a state building in Ireland, but if its remodelling in the 1720s adopted correct late-medieval details, then it is fair to say that elements of Gothic Revival or perhaps Survivalism had in fact already been employed at the castle some fifty years earlier (Manning 2017–18, 151).

310 O'Dwyer 2008, 108–9. Despite the accepted date for the works, Casey (2005, 356), however, offers a tentative attribution to Thomas Penrose and certainly in stylistic terms it could reasonably be the work of either man, though knowledge of Penrose's oeuvre is limited, his recorded designs rather scarce and difficult to assess, or indeed to separate from those of Wyatt (Martin-Robinson 2012, xi, 112–13; 204 et passim). Purely on stylistic grounds, the decoration of the supper room can be compared favourably with the details in design by Cooley for the episcopal throne in St Patrick's cathedral in Dublin, signed and dated 1775. Similar in terms of delicacy and detail are the conjoined cusped pointed arches employed on the gallery fronts at St Patrick's with those on the supper room cornice. The continuous tall lancet arches decorating the spandrels of the throne can be related to those on the fireplace frieze, as can the quatrefoils in roundels and the cusped pointed arches in the door panels of the tower. Dating from 1773 and 1774 a portfolio of drawings for parish churches by Cooley preserved in Armagh Public Library offers further comparison with the details employed in the supper room. These include thin switch-line tracery bars in the heads of windows (and tympana) and the attenuated pointed arches to door frames with recessed orders. Cooley's pupil Francis Johnston would develop this motif of tall pointed-arch door surrounds, employing heavy continuous rolls in place of square sections.

311 This work also affected the small waiting room to the north, and the adjoining staircase. The name is modern and derives from the framed Wedgwood reliefs of the Labours of Hercules by John Flaxman, along with two others, acquired for the room in 1952 when two plaster reliefs, representing Night and Day, *c.* 1815, by Berthel Thorvaldsen (1770–1844), were also transferred here (Kennedy 1999, 100–1).

312 The principal evidence, reports from contemporary newspapers, describe in limited detail the extent of interior remodelling instigated by the marquess of Buckingham, focusing principally on the conversion of the Battle-Axe Hall to an 'Audience Chamber' which, besides the installation of a new throne canopy and possibly the introduction of the surviving, ersatz pilasters, included the addition of grisailles overdoors of the Four Seasons, commissioned from Peter de Gree, at whose death in 1789 on nearby Dame Street, just one – Autumn – had been finished (*Freeman's Journal*, 27–9 Nov. 1788 (IAA, EMcP); Strickland 1913, Vol. II, 276). See also a view of the room reproduced in *Walker's Hibernian Magazine*, January 1795 in which it seems one of the grisailles is depicted and so the others, if installed, were possibly completed by Waldré. For a recent, detailed account see Campbell 2017, 47–93, and citing as the main sources *Faulkner's Dublin Journal*, 18–20 Sept., 30 Oct.–1 Nov., 24–27 Nov. 1788; *Freeman's Journal*, 20 Sept., 28 Oct. 1788; 27–29 Nov. 1788; *Dublin Evening Post* 18 Sept. 1788. It is not clear how the old Presence Chamber was subsequently used, though evidently it was still utilised for state occasions and perhaps intended as an additional drawing room, besides the 'great Drawing-room'. *Saunders Newsletter*, 22 May 1789. The former drawing rooms adjoining it to the east became private dining rooms – named respectively on Penrose's plan an 'Eating Room' and 'Breakfast Room'. In the sequence of rooms in the south range, the former state bedchamber in the centre had by 1789 become a dressing room, with the bedchamber relocated to the smaller, former Lady Lieutenant's dressing room. It should be noted that the private apartments of the Lord Lieutenant were subject to constant change as each new incumbent adapted the room uses to their own personal requirements and preferences.

313 NLI, MS 13,034, 4–5; Excerpts from *Freeman's Journal* for 1775 (IAA, EMcP).

314 Lord Harcourt was himself knowledgeable in architecture, and so must have been an interested patron, with O'Dwyer drawing attention to the fact that the combination of oval (Wedgwood Room) and circular rooms together at the castle, has a certain consonance with the complexity of spaces employed together at Harcourt's Oxfordshire seat, Nuneham Park (O'Dwyer 2008, 108–9).

315 Galloway 1999, 11–38.

316 In the context of the grisailles commissioned from Peter de Gree for the new 'Audience Chamber' (Throne Room) in 1788, it is not known whether those of the hall were perhaps also by him, or entirely part of Waldré's work. See n. 312.

317 IAA, EMcP.

318 *Saunder's Newsletter* 20 May 1789; an even more detailed account is given in the same paper, two days later.

319 Kennedy 1999, 19–23.

320 *Faulkner's Dublin Journal*, 2–4 April 1776 where in a notice from the Barrack Office, Dublin Castle, it was stated that 'the commissioners were 'ready to receive proposals for building an attic story on the east and north-east side of Dublin Castle' with a 'plan & bill of scantling' available 'to be seen at this office'. By 1779 Thomas Adderley, Commissioner and Overseer of the Barrack and Public Works from 1769, and Treasurer to the Barrack Board from 1772 had received monies for erecting 'an attic story on part of the east side of castle' J H of C, 10, vi (IAA, EMcP).

321 NA/SPO 516/94, 8 (IAA, EMcP).

322 Supported by the evidence from excavation, it appears that Burgh's work on the north range extended only to the provision of a staircase, occupying a bay to the west of the main Cross Block, at the northern end. This seems to be confirmed in Brooking's vignette. This section was taken down and rebuilt in the 1740s and extended to the new castle entrance by Arthur Dobbs.

323 O'Dwyer 1981, 110. See also Walker 1788, 94, in which there is illustrated a small woodcut view of 'Ward-robe Tower of Dublin Castle' (Fig. 3.82) and the explanatory note on p.172 says this 'drawing was made from the windows of the upper Treasury, by Mr. A. Cooper, in the year 1782. The range of little buildings that appear to cover the base of the tower have been lately removed'.

324 JRSAI (1898), 69–70, quoting *Dublin Evening Post*, 3 September 1793.

325 Maguire 1985, 31, referring to the 1962 survey (OPW file A6:33/6), says evidence of these timber piles was revealed, used to support the three bays adjacent to the Record Tower.

326 JRSAI 28 (1898), 69–70.

327 Lynch and Manning 2001, 176 citing NA OP/94/8. See DCA, WSC maps 329 (1757); 92 (n.d.); 94 (1766); 499, 537 (c. 1760).

328 NA/SPO OP/94, 8; WO 78-1154 as cited in Breen e), 11. It is difficult to relate these descriptions to the buildings and it is noteworthy that in Alfray's plan, the Chief Secretary's block is shown with the fireplaces of the four rooms on each floor, grouped together in the corners, served by a central stack. This form still survived in the southern section of the east range into nineteenth century – as well as in the west range – which would seem to confirm that it was principally the northern half of the eastern range that was rebuilt by 1800; compare OPWT early-nineteenth-century plans endorsed BV and BX. Whereas by 1789, in Penrose's plan, the two easterly rooms have been opened into one room with a breasted chimney, while the former east staircase has been extended, projected north to form a longer room with a new staircase formed beside it, against the north wall. It is possible that this was the problematic staircase wall referred to.

329 ibid.

330 Breen c), 34, citing MacLysaght 1939, 403–4.

331 A Citizen of London 1732, 13.

332 TNA, SO.1/15, 296. Payment to Burgh for repair works at castle in 1705 (about £1,200 in all) also included expenses towards the riding house. JH of C, II, clviii (IAA, EMcP).

333 Privy Council Papers 1640–1707, DCA, Gilbert Ms 205, 73–4; 1705. TNA, SO.1/15, 296 (IAA, EMcP).

334 Worsley 2004, 283, n.1.

335 Ibid, 69

336 Quoted in Maguire 1974, 11.

337 While private riding houses were usually attached to an open ménage for outdoor activity and display, the restricted site in the Lower Yard appears to have made this impossible and it is likely that Burgh's riding house in effect replaced an open ménage (Worsley 2004, 67–8).

338 Ibid, 68, 180–1. A riding house, though smaller in scale, was an integral part of the stable provisions as proposed in the 1770s scheme for the Lower Yard (Fig. 3.34), and indeed as a building type was retained when a new riding school by Jacob Owen was built nearby in 1837, replacing Burgh's building. Owen's riding house was demolished in the 1960s (O'Dwyer 2002, 152; McCarthy 2008, 32).

339 Brooking, however, shows – incorrectly, perhaps – a strictly rectilinear L-plan, implying there was a structure set against the western boundary wall, without suggesting the skewed alignment of the wall that is evident on Rocque's and subsequent surveys.

340 In 1749, Anthony Garmonsway wrote to the Surveyor General A. Jones Nevill informing him that repairs were required in the riding house (NMS, DCCI citing CMLP, 3 Apr 1749); a later reference of 3 July 1752 to a Memorial of Colonels of Horse & Dragoons for a riding house in Dublin, may not relate to the castle. CDC 4581.

341 The dimensions of 86ft by 40ft (26m by 12m) are known from other eighteenth-century examples (earl of Hertford's, 1728; Grenadier Guards, Gt. Portland St., 1752). When the Irish-based architect Christopher Myers designed a cavalry riding house in 1773, it measured 90ft by 40ft, but generally ratios of 3:1 seem to have been preferred (Worsley 2004, 160–6; 180–1).

342 NLI, MS 2789 f46, Reading's map was copied by Brownrigg & Co. The map needs to be used with some caution as it seems that some of the references relate to the uses in 1804, and not necessarily of 1769 – for example, the Surveyor General's house is labelled as 'Ordinance Office & Ingineer's Office', a use not known before 1800.

343 By 1817 the open yard at the west end had been built upon to provide a residence, then associated with the 'Keeper of the Civil Offices'. A small ancillary structure, a boiler house with a small yard attached, are also evident as projections on the north side of the riding house. Longfield, NLI, MS 2790, f.54.

344 While based on Essex Street, it is possible they were given temporary accommodation within the castle, which might explain the references to their move (back?) to the barrack ground. The Horse Guard were entirely brought into the castle complex in 1746. See n.348 below. Payment to Burgh in 1703 is recorded in CSPD, 21-3-1703. The provision of stables for the Horse Guard and move to the barrack ground in 1705 is found at BL Add. Ms 9716, 201, 202; while a payment to Burgh of £400 in 1706 for rebuilding stables for Horse Guards is also recorded at TNA, T14/8, 427 (IAA, EMcP).

345 TNA, T1/176, 92–3 (IAA, EMcP).

346 Ibid, 92.

347 Ibid, 92–3.

348 NA M2446, 71–2: Chesterfield to the lords of the Treasury, 17 April 1746. Lord Chesterfield in dealing with the ruinous condition of the Horse Guards buildings on Dame Street, had forwarded proposals by the Surveyor General for 'a stable, hay loft and granary for 14 horses for the end of his Majesty's riding house in the timber yard adjoining the riding house', a description which would in fact seem to locate the proposed building closer to the riding house, either as the range of buildings along the boundary east of the riding house, or the stables present by 1769 along its south side. See also NLI, MS 2789, 54; NAI, *Calendar of Irish Correspondence Vol. 1 1697–1798* (NMS, DCCI). On 13 May 1746 a Royal Warrant was issued 'for payment of the expense of certain buildings to be erected for the Horse Guard at Dublin' CDC 3939 (NMS, DCCI); see also McParland 2001, 98, 103.

349 Undated and unreferenced photographic copy of a plan of the Lower Castle Yard, showing Palace Street Gate and Stables, late eighteenth century (NMS).

350 TNA, SO.1.23, 33 refers to two houses to be built in the stable yard in 1762 and, perhaps concerning the same proposals, NA/ PRO T14/14, 312 refers to Lord Halifax's orders in the same year for two houses to be built in the Lower Yard. In the late eighteenth-century survey, the block associated with the riding master's house is shown with four separate elements, the easterly one obviously a building, set in front of it and the adjoining stables, evident also on DCA, WSC 389 (1801) and Sherrard's 1802 survey (Fig. 3.65), but not on DCA, WSC 187.

351 Besides the maps associated with Reading (1769/1804), Chaigneau (1801) and Longfield (1817), it also appears on a late eighteenth-century survey, on William Murray's 1829 survey (NMS copy) and the Ordnance Survey's *Castle Sheet* (revised 1843).

352 By 1829 (Fig. 3.67) the northern wing is shown divided by a closely spaced series of horizontal walls, presumably representing a series of latrines over the Poddle.

353 Nichols 1779, Vol. III, 295.

354 *Ibid.* As well as responsibility for the 'inspection of the King's Lodgings', ensuring they are properly serviced, the groom porter was also charged with providing for cards and gaming, and adjudicating in disputes.

355 Malton 1799; Anon., 1896, 48. See also Lawlor 1923, 34.

356 Lawlor 1923, 54.

357 Brewer 1825–6, Vol. I, 63–5.

358 *Dublin Evening Post*, 19 August 1790.

359 BWM, Book 1, 26 Aug 1803 (IAA, EMcP).

360 *Dublin Evening Post*, 19 August 1790, which refers to 'The new Chapel, intended to be built in the Castle garden' without any further detail, only the wish 'for the sake of the public character, that some taste may be exhibited in the edifice.

361 *Dublin Evening Post*, 3 Sept. 1793, as quoted in JRSAI 28 (1898), 70.

362 McParland 1985b, 106, noting that the Dublin Evening Post, 22 Sept. 1791 announced that the project had been abandoned.

363 TNA, T14/13, 238. Drawings for the building dated 19 July and 12 August 1756 are at NA/ PRO T1/367/48–51. O'Dwyer 2002, 114 and n.24, 168 citing a letter from Eyre to W.G. Hamilton of December 1761 in Eyre's Letter Book in IAA. O'Dwyer (2002, 115, Plate 5) illustrates the carriage arch on the north side of the main façade. The view of the Lower Yard by Thomas Sautelle-Roberts is taken from the house, its garden railings shown in the foreground. The narrow front garden is shown attractively planted on the 1843 Ordnance Survey, suggesting it had increased from the narrow area shown on Chaigneau's 1801 map. In an undated Wide Streets Commissioners' proposal for the Lower Yard (Fig. 3.34) a house for the Surveyor General was proposed on the chapel site, part of a symmetrical composition with the ordnance office (to the east) projecting from a newly planned chapel set on a north–south alignment with a bowed south end.

364 As noted, at least two other houses were built in the Lower Yard in 1762. See n. 350 above.

365 As noted above, it is unsafe to assume that eighteenth-century use is correctly identified on the copy of Reading's original survey, but certainly this use can be confirmed in 1801 on Chaigneau's map, and again on Longfield's 1817 survey; the building is neither detailed nor identified on William Murray's 1829 surveys.

366 Breen c), 34

367 There are intractable difficulties with the sources for the provision of ordnance stores in the early eighteenth century, whereby documents contain various references to erecting variously, a magazine, armoury, arsenal and stores, but without always clarifying how these uses relate to one another, or whether actually intended as the same or different building proposals; that difficulty is further compounded with the contemporary building of a fortified arsenal in the Phoenix Park (abandoned), and by the existence, before 1756, of a store house on the west side of the garden (although it does seem this was principally used for 'camp equipage'). For example, in 1711 (KQL, 15 March 1711, NMS, DCCI) there is reference to building an 'arsenal', while Thomas Burgh at this time generally seems to refer to the 'Magazine', and while this term is not used in any of the later surveys there is reference to repairs being needed in the 'Magazine Guard' in 1749 (CMLP, 19 April 1749, NMS, DCCI). In 1721 estimates relating to 'raising yard walls belonging to the Stores of War at Dublin Castle', and a further estimate for 'work to be done at the Stores of War in Dublin' seem likely to refer to the stores on the western side of the garden rather than the armoury, but some uncertainty must remain (CMLP, 25 Feb. and 7 April 1721, NMS, DCCI). See also n.372 below.

368 HMC *Ormonde*, ns, VIII, 294–5; see also TNA, T1/126, 30 (IAA, EMcP).

369 HMC *Ormonde*, ns, VIII, 294–5.

370 *ibid*; Burgh's plans for a magazine or armoury at the castle are found at BL e.g. Ms 917, 212, 214–15 (IAA, EMcP); see also McParland 2001, 140–1; 222, n.152.

371 McParland 2001, 140–1.

372 HMC *Ormonde*, ns, VIII, 294–5; TNA, T1/126, 30; T1/176,92–3; T14/9, 169 (IAA, EMcP). See also McParland 2001, 96, 137, 140. In 1714, accounts (TNA, T1/176/92–3, IAA, EMcP) show the larger expense of £3,989-5-8 'for the Armoury' which Burgh reported 'is covered, but not floored, nor the windows put in'. In the V&A, Elton Hall Collection, there are several plans (not examined for this study) by Burgh's successor, Sir Edward Lovett Pearce showing alterations to buildings at the rear of Dublin Castle (V&A Ref: E.2124:60, 62; 68; 91-1992), and at least one of these to a building on the arsenal site. In August 1742, Arthur Dobbs submitted a memorial, accompanied by plans and estimates for 'the building of a New Armoury…in [the] old artillery yard adjoining the Garden of Dublin Castle' and in October payment of the cost, £1,883.16.5, was approved and work evidently had progressed towards completion in June 1744 (CDC 3556; 3566; 3777; 3751; 3758, NMS, DCCI). Dobbs's reference to an armoury in the artillery yard has compounded the already existing confusion of identification resulting from the existence of both an arsenal and armoury in the Lower Yard. For example, in referring to the arsenal site Casey (2005, 360) states: 'An Armoury was built on the site in 1710 to Thomas Burgh's design and was subsequently extended in 1730s and 1740s by E.L. Pearce and A. Dobbs. While the floor plan does not correspond to Burgh's surviving design, it is difficult to believe that such an old fashioned building would have built from scratch in the 1730s.' In 1782 the architect Samuel Sproule was engaged to 'fit up the Arsenal in the Lower Yard for the Purpose of the National Bank' but this was not executed (*Faulkner's Dublin Journal*, 10–12 Dec, 1782, IAA, EMcP; see also DLOP 28 Feb. 1783, Samuel Sproule to David La Touche – Valuation of ground in Lower Castle Yard where the Arsenal stands, for the purpose of the Bank of Ireland, NMS, DCCI). In 1796 Bryan Bolger measured stone work at the armoury on behalf of Frederick Darley (NA Brian Bolger Papers 1A/58/128) and it seems probable that this refers not to the arsenal but to the armoury shown on Rocque's plan.

373 However, on Chaigneau's and Sherrard's 1801 surveys, the range is shown reduced in size, no longer an L-plan and with no trace of the former armoury at the east end.

374 Brooking shows the quadrant walls as though buildings existed behind, extending to the eastern Cross Block, whereas Rocque provides a more accurate representation. The west end of the southern (armoury) range was, according to Rocque's survey, aligned with the west end of the Treasury block. Further west, the space is shown as vacant, but was in fact the location of the ice house – partly submerged in the angle between the Record Tower and the Cross Block. The structure was presumably an eighteenth-century construction and is clearly evident here on early nineteenth-century surveys; by then it was enclosed by a castellated wall, seen for example in Petrie's 1830s view of the castle (Fig. 3.66). It survived into the twentieth century.

375 An estimate for the repair of the 'Armourer's House in Lower Castle Yard' in 1725 could relate to this building. CMLP, 26 Oct 1725 (NMS, DCCI).

376 See n.372 above. Casey does not take into account the evidence for a separate armoury, as shown on Rocque. This building is accepted as Burgh's building by McParland (2001, 98), who does not, however, discuss the arsenal.

377 This was done by taking an area from the armoury – see Henry Chaigneau's 1801 survey – though Sherrard in the same period simply highlights the front range which is labelled 'Barrack', and William Murray's 1829 plan shows it as an L-plan 'dwelling'. In Chaigneau's survey the building appears to have been divided east–west by a passage and the courtyard is not indicated. The courtyard is understood to have been roofed in by Jacob Owen as part of works undertaken in the early nineteenth century (Casey 2005, 360).

378 CMLP, 25 March 1724, mentions 'Mr. Westland for bricks' (NMS, DCCI).

379 CMLP, 7 April 1721; 25 July 1722; 23 December 1725; 15 July 1727

380 See TNA, T1/376, 56–9; T1/379, 73,74 (IAA, EMcP). Eyre's memorial, plan and estimates for the new laboratory, dated 8 Dec 1757, are recorded at CDC 5285 (NMS, DCCI). The payment of £405-8-4 to Eyre for the building is located at TNA, T14/13, 311 (IAA, EMcP).

381 On 21 July 1764 Waite wrote to say that the Lords Justices ordered an enquiry to be made by the Master General of the Ordnance (NMS, DCCI, no further ref. given). The explosion was also reported in *Faulkner's Dublin Journal*, 7 July 1764: 'Dublin Castle 6 o'Clock Tues fire…in laboratory in Lower Castle Yard… gunpowder…whole building blown up…'.

382 That the 'Ball Room' (St Patrick's Hall) and Bermingham Tower seem to have borne the brunt of the explosion suggests that the laboratory had been built just north of the store house, a space that formed a forecourt behind quadrant screen walls and gateway. In August 1769 Sir Robert Wilmot wrote to Thomas Waite concerning the costs of repairs at the castle and erecting a gate in the Lower Castle Yard (NMS, DCCI citing DLOP). A warrant for rebuilding the roof of St Patrick's Hall and for building the gate in the Lower Yard is found at TNA, SO.1.23, 249 (IAA, EMcP). Although not certain, it seems reasonable to connect these works with the damage caused by the explosion in 1764. Although the present Ship Street Gate is dated to 1807, an equally substantial predecessor is evident in 1801 (Chaigneau), so that the reference to building a gate may relate to the entrance to the store house complex, evident in much the same form in Chaigneau's survey though with a structure (guard house?) present behind the eastern quadrant.

383 TNA, T1/176/92.

384 DCA, WSC 92, possibly of the 1760s.

385 DCA, WSC 329, printed map of 1757 which shows the proposed widening of Castle Lane; also WSC 94/1 dated 1766 concerns the sale of lots in advance of widening Castle Lane. Casey (2005, 360) states the entrance was built by Eyre in 1756. Breen (d), 9), however, states it was built in 1769.

386 Salmon 2013, 316–18. In the ambitious 1770s scheme for Dublin Castle (WSC 90), even the stables might be seen to have aspired to some of the grandeur of composition that had been invested in the Royal Mews at Charing Cross.

387 The block between Palace St and George's Lane was apparently rebuilt in 1782 (McCullough 1989, 75).

388 Salmon 2013, 316–18.

389 O'Dwyer 2002, 135 and n.82. The survey is located at TNA, MPH 202 (1) and inscribed 'No 2 Castle Yard'. It appears to be a copy of Chaigneau's July survey as it is signed (in lower left corner) 'David Robinson 4th September 1801'. O'Dwyer also refers to Porter and Watson 1889, Vol. 3, 140 which implies that the purpose of Chaigneau's survey is expanded upon there.

390 Since the abolition of the office of Surveyor General in 1763 and the creation of two architectural posts connected with the Barrack Board, the situation becomes even less straighforward after 1798. James Cuffe (Lord Tyrawley from 1797) was appointed head of the Barrack Board in 1796, and from 1799 was given direct charge of barracks, therefore from this time the Barrack Board and Board of Works ceased to have any responsibilty for barracks, its duties related only to civil buildings. Confusingly the name of the organisation did not change, so that in effect there was an ongoing division of responsibilities within the organisation whereby the military work was now overseen solely by Lord Tyrawley (as Barrack Master General) whereas civil remained under the control of commissioners (but who were also headed by Tyrawley) (O'Dwyer 2002, 109–75; 131–4).

391 McDowell (2003, 18–19) notes that while 'the political and social importance of the viceregal court may have somewhat declined…according to the first post-Union viceroy, Hardwicke, there was no diminution in the numbers attending Castle functions'. And while for peers, the centre of power shifted to London 'many county families were content with the less expensive and for them probably more sociable Dublin season'.

392 O'Dwyer 2002, 135.

393 The board, however, continued to operate under the old patent granted to the Barrack Board and Board of Works. The military functions were now the concern of the Barrack Department which continued under Lord Tyrawley – named as Chief Commissioner of Barracks and Deputy Barrack Master General. However, only in 1806 was the Board of Works granted its own office accommodation, separate from the Barrack Department (O'Dwyer 2002, 135).

394 Earlier thoughts about rebuilding the castle chapel were revealed when the *Dublin Evening Post* in August 1790 suggested that a 'much wanted' new chapel was to be built in the castle garden – probably not literally in the garden, and more likely somewhere alongside and related to the site of the existing chapel. In September 1791 the same paper reported that plans for the chapel had been abandoned. Having been revived by the Chief Secretary's request to Gandon, the idea was again postponed until 1807 (McParland 1985b, 97–8; 106; 203).

395 ibid, 203 citing BL, Add. Ms 35733, 312, Gandon to an unidentified clergyman (20 March1802) in which the architect reveals his pleasure with 'his Excellency's Approbation' of the designs.

396 McParland 1985b, 149.

397 ibid, 106

398 ibid, see also IAA, EMcP, referencing SPO 527/188/2 as a source for Gandon's plans for the Treasury and chapel.

399 Lawlor (1923, 57) records that Gandon's designs for the chapel were then extant, but these have since been lost. Without Gandon's designs it is not possible to assess the extent to which they may have influenced Johnston's own designs. It is likely, as McParland (1985b, 106) suggests, that Johnston would have had the opportunity to study Gandon's designs.

400 Hart's career at the castle closely coincided with Johnston's and in the years after Johnston's death he was no longer employed by the board and sought the post of clerk of works to Trinity College Dublin. IAA, EMcP.

401 NA SPO CSO/RP 1827/335 (IAA, EMcP).

402 McDowell 2003, 1–53, esp.7–12; for the size of the household during the marquess of Anglesea's lord lieutenancy (1828–33) see the viceregal household accounts at PRONI, D619/33/1A1.

403 The map, dated 1801, is published in Sherrard 1802. Another version of the map is dated 1802.

404 To some degree, this would have revived the idea present in the earlier proposal of the Wide Streets Commissioners discussed above, based on DCA, WSC 90 (Fig. 3.34).

405   In one case, an arched passageway leads to a laneway or mews lane running behind several houses and parallel to the castle garden. This lane terminated immediately north of a Methodist chapel built on the site of a large garden plot, recorded in 1756. The curious step back in the northern boundary of the chapel suggests it is honouring an earlier boundary.

406   NMS copy of letter from J D'Olier, 6 May 1802, original at SPO OP142/7. Breen e), 46.

407   A Rental of houses and premises to be sold pursuant to a decree of his Majesty's Court of Exchequer…the 12th day of February 1802 (1802, NMS copy). The rental comprised more than half the premises within Cole Alley and Hoey's Court, listing Nos 1–8, represented by most of the houses on the west side; Nos 14–15, which flanked the entrance from Castle Street; Nos 17–22, which occupied the middle of the east side; Nos 7 and 8, which adjoined St Werburgh's churchyard, were listed as new houses, their leases having commenced in 1793 and 1798 respectively. Significantly perhaps, John D'Olier is named as the original tenant of No. 18 in 1766, a premises on the west side, abutting the castle boundary.

408   NMS copy of letter from J. D'Olier, 6 May 1802, original at SPO OP 142/7. Breen e), 46.

409   St Werburgh's vestry book, 22 August 1803, 328.

410   Breen e), 46 citing NA PW/I/1/2/1/1, 149, Lynch and Manning 2001, 177, 198, giving NA OP 185/7 as the source for D'Olier's purchasing activity and demolition of houses.

411   Breen d), 46 citing NA PW/I/1/1/1, 365–6; 404; 421–2; PW I/1/2/1/1, 247ff.

412   Lynch and Manning 2001, fig. 5, copy in NMS, original at NA PWI/1/2/I/I. See also 'Map of holding on the N side of Cole Alley, the property of Miss Bond, let to Wm Malone by Brownrigg & Co' NLI, 21 F 52/022.

413   Lynch and Manning 2001, fig. 5, copy in NMS, original at NA PWI/1/2/I/I; St. Werburgh's vestry book 22 August 1803, 328. On the vestry's valuation of Minister Money lost, and based on a tax of around 12d. in the £ valuation, it would suggest that the average valuation of houses in Cole Alley was £12. This was within the £10–£20 valuation bracket which included the largest number of houses in the parish. A vestry record for 1722 also mentions two small tenements in Cole Alley recovered by the parish. This might suggest a variety rather than strict uniformity of houses in the former Alley. St Werburgh's vestry book 4 January 1722, 33. Examining the width of the house plots in Cole Alley, there were eleven or more houses with a plot width of between 16ft (4.9m) and 17ft (5.2m), with two narrower at 13ft (3.9m). Four further plots ranged in width between 18ft (5.5m) and 27ft (8.2m), and two more at 32ft (9.7m) might have had a similar appearance to 9 Hoey Court.

414   There was a 7ft-wide (2m-wide) passage into Hoey's Court towards the southern end of the lane.

415   St Werburgh's vestry book 22 August 1803, 328.

416   Ibid. Compensating the owners of houses in Cole Alley, Silver Court and Castle Street which were incorporated into the castle precincts also raised the argument that the parish of St Werburgh's should be compensated for the loss of parochial income 'from the injury sustained by the Parish in consequence of a refusal of this Board to Grant an adequate remuneration for the Ministers Money, Parish Cess and other dues which arose out of houses in Cole Alley and Castle Street that had been taken down for the defence and security of the Castle…', St Werburgh's vestry book 1780–1859, 19 January 1807. The matter was raised again in May 1807 when the commissioners conceded that compensation was due while stating its position that 'the valuation made by Mr D'Olier' represented 'the most eligible terms that could be procured from the circumstances of the case'. The properties and their valuations are given as: 'An old house and lot of ground on the east side of Cole Alley worth £20 p.a. and valued at 20 years purchase. £400-0-0; Two old houses on the West side of Cole Alley worth £65 per an: and valued at 15 years purchase. £975-0-0. Making together the sum of £1375-0-0.' BWM, Book 2, 6 February 1807. See also entry for 16 May, 1807, recording a representation 'in reference to Governments Order of the 27th March last respecting the Claim of the Minister and Church Wardens of Saint Werburgh's Parish for parochial Taxes on Houses taken down for the security and Improvement of Dublin Castle'.

417   See n. 407 above concerning John D'Olier as original tenant of No. 18 Cole Alley in the eighteenth century.

418   Lynch and Manning 2001, 197, where 'structural elements from a timber-framed house' (though the implication is that these were perhaps reused here) and evidence for 'a substantial stone-built house' were found 'on the edge of the moat, close to its north-west corner'.

419   The elevation of the west side of Cork Hill as captured in Shaw (1850) might give some idea of the appearance of the south side of Castle Street. There, tall narrow houses, some five storeys over basement had a shop front to the ground floor. These were one, two and three bays wide. As depicted in 1850 they have lost projecting signs and other ornaments and also may have former Dutch-type gables built up and levelled off.

420   Breen e) 47, citing PROI [NA] PW I/1/2/1/1, 314.

421   It is not, however, clear whether this plan was made before or after the wall and passage were made, but it does appear to concern itself largely with the proposals to build 'small tenements' and a school-house on the south side of the passage.

422   Breen, d) 47, citing NA OP 249/2. The works do not appear to have been commenced before April 1806 when there were discussions about the repaving of Castle Street and the necessity of the street level after these works to 'meet the effect' of 'the new buildings to be erected for Government'. Breen, 47, citing NA OP 230/13.

423   Breen, d), 47, citing PROI [NA] PW I/1/2/1/1, 401. Henry Chaigneau's plan of 1801 shows a substantial square building (though it could represent two buildings together) on this site that are rendered as part of the castle. TNA, MPH 202. Reference to Johnston's plans for the gate, guard house and curtain wall are found in BWM, Book 2, 10 March 1807 (IAA, EMcP).

424   The wall was complete by September 1807 and the passage described as 'recently opened' in April 1808. NA/SPO OP 249/4; PW I/1/2/1/1, 401, both cited in Breen d) 47.

425   Casey 2005, 361.

426   See n.413, n.416.

427   St Werburgh's vestry book 1780–1859, 133: 6 May 1788: '…committee to examine the state of the Steeple and Bells and report their opinion thereon'; 143: 1 March1789: 'Resolved that the proposal of Mr Alex Roche & co for Repairing the Spire & Steeple be complied with & immediately put into execution on condition of his giving security of keeping it in repair for seven years.'

428   St Werburgh's vestry book 1780–1859, 426: 21 May 1810.

429   Johnston proposed to use baulks of timber internally within the spire, modelled on Sir Christopher Wren's solution to supporting the spire of Salisbury Cathedral (Warburton, Whitelaw and Walsh 1818, I, 501). The cost of repair was estimated at £592 compared to Robbins' estimate of £450 to take it down.

430   Hughes 1889, 33. Hughes noted that 'there lingered for generations a feeling that pressure had been at work somewhere'.

431   McParland 1985b, 106, 203. Casey (2005, 358) and Hill (2015, 39), on what basis is unclear, suggest that Gandon's involvement came to an end due to cost-cutting. It does appear that Gandon struggled to get paid for his efforts and was forced to submit a series of petitions.

432   However, reference to Gandon's plans for the Treasury and chapel are found at NA/SPO 188, 2 (IAA, EMcP).

433   Breen e), 48, citing TNA, PW I/1/1/2, 38.

434   Ibid. Believing that the works at the Treasury would be complicated, and therefore expensive, it was indicated that they should be carried on progressively by the board's tradesmen.

435   BWM, Bk 2, 12 May 1807. Johnston's letter, read to the board, named the occupants as George Oakes and James Wilson.

436 Casey 2005, 358.

437 McParland 1969, 103–7; Casey 2005, 359; Hill 2015, 43–9.

438 This was first suggested by Richardson (1983, Vol. I, 53).

439 *Lines on seeing Swift's head over one of the doors of the Castle Chapel Dublin* were published in *The Morning Chronicle* 23 Aug. 1813.

440 *Ibid.* Johnston followed the auditory church model of nearby St Werburgh's and St Anne's (both early eighteenth century) in having a narrower space for the chancel. However, Johnston marks the space off far more dramatically than in these, then century-old, exemplars. The chancel is one bay deep and set off from the nave by a slight narrowing and lowering of the space. The side walls step into a second set of grouped shafts. These carry a second transverse rib and the vault drops down slightly here. The chancel arch formed in this way is decorated with ogival arches as well as some startling figures.

441 Brewer 1825–6, Vol. 1, 63; Richardson 1983, Vol. I, 56–7; Hill 2015, 46–7.

442 Richardson 1983, Vol. I, 56–7, quoting Clarke (1962, 80) and Britton 1807–27, Vol. I, where the chapel of seven plates were used to illustrate King's College chapel. A detailed and extensively illustrated essay on Henry VII's chapel at Westminster was given in Britton (1807–27, Vol. II, 9–51).

443 Anon., 1896, 48.

444 Lucey 2007, 91.

445 *Ibid.*, Plate 156; NA Bryan Bolger Papers/Public Buildings, measured work, 'Plastering & Stucco Work done…in the Quarter ending 5th Day of July 1812 per Geo. Stapleton – Vice Regal Chapel'.

446 Stewart continued to be employed at the chapel up to 1825, when he had a falling out with Johnston over the carving of the Wellesley arms. His correspondence respecting his work at the chapel is at NA/SPO 558AAE/984/2 (IAA, EMcP).

447 NA Bryan Bolger Papers/Public Buildings, measured work, 'Carpenters work at New Chapel, Castle Yard by Arthur Battersby'. In 1815, after the completion of the chapel, Battersby continued to carry out work, with several payments recorded in respect of his 'jobbing account Castle Chapel'.

448 NA Bryan Bolger Papers/Public Buildings 'Bills of Board of Works for Quarter ending 10 Oct. 1812'. As well as brick work, the bricklayer A. Kerfoot was also responsible for stone work, which in the first quarter of 1810 included 574 loads of ashlar. John Dwyer is also named for stone cutting work on the chapel.

449 NA Bryan Bolger Papers/Public Buildings, various bills. Lucey 2007, 90.

450 Henry VIII, Edward VI, Elizabeth I, and William III (Richardson 1983, 61).

451 NGI, 2455, see also Plan of the Chapel Royal, 13 Jan 1863 (OPWT, E000519 U16-11).

452 The account referred specifically to 'The sanctuary, very clearly marked… and not flanked by galleries, with its large substantial altar, painted window, carvings albeit armorial, seats placed sedile-fashion, to the north and south, and massive rails, is really of a very religious aspect. The members of the choir are placed in a regular chorus cantorum of two sides, standing antiphonally in the body of the chapel'. The 'iconographic opulence' also drew attention: 'The amount of imagery throughout this chapel is one of its remarkable features, and may be interpreted in various ways. It is certainly a fact that all these figures, the half bust of S. Peter for instance, do not seem in the spirit of the popular religion of Irish 'Protestant' platforms'. C.E.S., 'Some notes from Ireland', *Ecclesiologist*, xiii, (Oct. 1852), 305, quoted in Richardson (1978, Vol. I, 59).

453 *The Dublin Builder* (1 June 1860), 274–5 where it says 'It may not be amiss to add, that though this work bears the impresse of English paternity, it is in reality not so, but is essentially an Irish work, in all its departments'. An engraved view by George Hanlon shows the pulpit in position. See also Plan of the Chapel Royal, 13 Jan 1863 (OPWT, E000519 U16-11).

454 At a meeting of the Commissioners of the Board of Works, Friday 10 March 1807.

455 Brewer 1825, 63.

456 Penrose's plan only represents the principal (first) floor. RCPRI 1813–15, Plates XIX–XX: Record Tower: south view drawn by W. Flavelle and sections and floor plan by Francis Johnston, engraved by James Basire and printed 14 July 1813.

457 This building is evident in Rocque (Fig. 3.11) and is shown as a modest two-storied structure in the late eighteenth-century topographical view of the Lower Yard (Fig. 3.54). Johnston granted it battlements as part of the works to remodel the tower.

458 BWM Bk 2, 10 March 1807.

459 The 1986–7 excavation in the area of the Chief Secretary's kitchen concluded it was of uncertain date, but possibly by Darley and showed that 'the basement area continued around west end of original Treasury'. NMS, Xerox copy of 1828 William Murray plan, annotated with notes by C. Manning. This could be interpreted to suggest that it was part of an earlier foundation for the Treasury, the one objectionable to Burgh before the present site was settled upon. However, the excavation also revealed that the base of the Powder Tower was retained here and represents a solid construction – retained as perhaps too troublesome to remove, or intended that it could be used as foundation, just as the Cork Tower had been. Perhaps it was ultimately decided not to excavate any further in 1712 when it was realised that the area was prone to flooding, as it still is. See Lynch & Manning 2001, 194: '…once the arches [in the city walls] were blocked up…in about the fourteenth century, the only water source would be derived from natural springs, ground water and seepage from the Poddle… High tides remain an issue here and at present water is pumped out once it reaches a certain level.' It was further confirmed by excavation that Darley's buildings extending the Chief Secretary's accommodation over the north moat of the medieval castle, had been built on poor foundations using timbers bolted to granite blocks, and that these had 'developed structural problems' and ultimately with the adjoining 1840s ranges were demolished, despite the early-eighteenth-century portions having had good foundations (Lynch and Manning 2001, 169, 178).

460 The arrangement of the screen wall, as shown in Sautelle-Robert's view, is also confirmed by an undated, unsigned early nineteenth-century plan. OPWT, E000480 U16-1.

461 Casey 2005, 358.

462 Owen's block was demolished and completely rebuilt in the 1990s, retaining only the external architectural character of the original.

463 BWM Bk 1, 31 July 1802 (IAA, EMcP).

464 NA/SPO 516/84/8 (IAA, EMcP).

465 BWM Bk 2, 19 July 1808 (IAA, EMcP).

466 *Faulkner's Dublin Journal*, 24 April 1776.

467 For example, the plasterer and stuccodore George Stapleton was employed in the Upper Yard on works related to the visit, with Thomas Hart, the clerk of works, also involved in overseeing unspecified improvements here, and at the viceregal lodge in the Phoenix Park. NA/Brian Bolger Papers 1A/58/127-8 (IAA, EMcP).

468 CSORP/1824/1884 - 10,628 which contains Johnston's proposals and estimates and on which all the following excerpts are based.

469 CSO/RP/1824/1884.

470 The works also involved replacing the stuccowork to the main ceiling. BWM 24 June 1824; 20 Jan. 1825; 19 May 1825; 30 March 1826; (IAA, EMcP); NA/SPO CSO/RP 1825/11. A description of the ceiling of St Patrick's Hall is found in the entry for 8 June 1826 (IAA, EMcP).

471 NA/SPO CSO/RP 1826/13,687 (IAA, EMcP), two years earlier Johnston had provided estimates for the 'probable expense of furniture &c required in the State Drawing Rooms in Dublin Castle', listing the following expenditure: state drawing room (£1,948:17:1), the Presence Chamber (£149:16:0) and dining room (£316:2:6). NA CSORP/1824/1884 - 10,628; NA CSO/RP/1826/551.

472 Murray 2004, 63, 202, 218.

473 NA CSORP/1824/1884.

474 Casey 2005, 353.

475 An undated early-nineteenth-century plan shows the open arrangement of the entrance. OPWT, E000508 U16–8. Another is referenced (IAA, EMcP) at BL Add. Ms 31,323 (microfilm p.744). By 1829, the present wooden sentry boxes had been inserted to flank the central intercolumniation. Ground plan of the Upper Yard by William Murray, January 1828. OPWT, E000505 U16–7.

476 Owen 1848–9; NA/SPO CSO/RP 1839/64-8732 (IAA, EMcP). See also O'Dwyer 2002, 152 and for a more recent, in-depth discussion see Hickey 2017.

477 The entrance was still represented as the westernmost bay, though by 1843, according to the Ordnance Survey (Fig. 3.37 – Castle Sheet), it seems to have been moved to the centre bay.

478 See NA CSO/RP/1818/362: Thomas Keck of Stephen's Street Dublin to Robert Peel, Chief Secretary requesting 'a situation in any part of the world' and citing his father's loyal service during 1798'; in 1827 Mr Keck is listed as Keeper of the Civil Office. HC, Sessional Papers, Vol. 15, 1 (1825–7), 18 and again in 1831 in *Finance Accounts of the United Kingdom* Vol. XXVI (6 December 1831–16 August 1832), 14; in 1833 he is named as Chief Office Keeper and Clerk of Disbursements. Several rooms in the Upper Yard (north-east corner?) are ascribed to 'Miss Keck'; see detail of plan in NMS copies.

479 A later survey dated 1913 (OPWT, E000486 U16–3), shows the 'Parlor' and kitchen occupying the western end.

480 In 1801 Chaigneau's plan showed the farriers yard at the north-west corner, immediately west of the Palace Street gate, and extending directly behind the aide-de-camp's house, with access off Dame Lane.

481 The stabling in this range was detailed by Murray as belonging to the private secretary (three boxes), aide-de-camp (four boxes), chamberlains (three boxes), and first aide-de-camp (six boxes).

482 NLI, MS 2790 f46. Henry Chaigneau's 1801 survey labels the house as 'Late Surveyor General's House given up to Lieutenant Littlehales as the Military Secretary'. TNA, MPD1-188.

483 OPWT, E000505 U16–7, undated early-twentieth-century drainage survey, signed E. Griffith.

484 In 1829 Major Henry Charles Sirr's stable adjoined the coach house with a connecting internal doorway.

485 See also OPWT, E000528 U16–14; E000505 U16–7.

486 O'Dwyer 2002, 152.

487 See survey (after 1843 – unreferenced, undated surveys, copies in NMS – author's refs. 20140812_160207) showing the old stables labelled as 'Household stables' and the castellated range as 'State Stables'.

488 Casey 2005, 360.

489 Although Johnston himself included the Quarter Master General's and Adjutant General's office among the buildings he designed at the castle (Anon. 1963, 3), there remains the possibility that the redevelopment of this entire area was overseen by the chief engineer (O'Connor and O'Regan 1987, 11).

490 This relates to the offices on Ship Street, known latterly as Block M, occupied by the Registrar of Friendly Societies in the 1990s, but unfortunately the building was completely gutted in 1997 and no record remains.

491 The block is labelled as a store house on Rocque's map. On Chaigneau's 1801 survey part of it is still referred to as 'Old store', with the remainder divided between a temporary stable and laboratory, the upper part of the latter serving as a 'temporary barrack'. It presumably was fully adapted as a barrack after this date.

492 Johnston confirms that the building had been erected before 1820 (Anon., 1963, 3).

493 A later survey of Leitrim House is at OPWT, E000492 U16–4.

494 Barnard 2000, 256–61.

495 Cornforth 1970, 287.

496 Falkiner 1904, 24.

497 Casey 2005, 349.

498 The loss of the old Presence Chamber by fire in 1941 was mitigated somewhat by the reconstruction when three important eighteenth-century stucco ceilings were salvaged from Dublin houses for reuse here, including one by Bartholomew Cramillion, and the Apollo ceiling from Arthur Jones Nevill's Tracton House, installed in a room specially created for it, achieved by moving the new state drawing room west, extended into the place of Nevill's old Presence Chamber.

Appendices
Edited by Conleth Manning

Appendices
Descriptions of Dublin Castle 1585–1792

Appendix 1
Towers of the Castle of Dublin (Perrot's Survey, 1585)[1]

The tower on the east side of the castle gate. In primis: In the lower room there are three spicks, the first flanking the gate, the second northward over the end of the bridge, the third flanks the wall between it and the north-east tower. In the second room there are three spicks standing in the same sort and in the upper room three in like manner.

The north-east tower. In the lower room there is but one spick, which flanks the north wall to the great gate. In the second room there are two spicks and two windows, whereof the first flanks the wall towards the gate, the second scours the gardens northward, the third being a spick scours the gardens eastward, the fourth flanks the east wall, being the garden wall. In the third room there are three windows, the first scouring north-west, the second north-east, the third flanks the garden wall. In the fourth room there is but one window opening into the north. In the fifth room, which is your lordship's chamber, there are two windows, the one east and the other north, and in the stairs going up the same tower there are five spicks, which do all flank the north wall towards the castle gate.

The south-east tower. In the lower room there are four spicks. The first flanks the castle wall next the garden, the second scours the gardens to the eastward, the third scours south and by east, the fourth the wall on the south side towards the middle tower. The second room, one window and three spicks standing as before. In the upper room there is one window and a spick there flanking the garden wall, and the other the south wall.

The middle tower on the south side. In the lower room there are three spicks. The first scours the wall towards the south-east tower; the second scours the orchards southwards; the third flanks the south wall towards 'Bremeghams' tower. In the second room there are three windows standing as the aforesaid spicks. In the uppermost room there is one window, which opens to the south, and between that same middle tower and the south-west tower in the castle wall there are nine or ten spick holes and small windows.

The south-west tower. In the lower room there are three spicks. The one flanks the south wall to the middle tower; the second to the garden southward; the third westward along the town wall joining to the same. In the second room, being the kitchen, there are two spicks and a window standing as the spicks in the room before. In the third room, one window opening into the east. In the fourth room, two windows, whereof one is stopped up with brick and opens into the west and the other into the south-east. Adjoining to the same there is a little square tower, which has three spicks in the middle room, one scouring the gardens southward, the other into the town westward, the third flanks the west wall towards the north-west tower. In the upper room there are four spicks, whereof two scour the gardens southward, the third into the town westward, the fourth flanking the wall to the north-west tower.

The north-west tower. In the dungeon there is never a spick. In the second room there are three spicks, one flanking the west wall to the square tower, the second scours into the town north-west, the third flanks the north wall towards the castle gate. In the third room there are four

---

1 TNA SP 63/121, fo. 226. As published by Gilbert 1889–1944 with spelling and punctuation modernised and with one correction as noted by Duffy in this volume.

spicks. The first flanks the west wall to the square tower, the second into the town west, the third north and the fourth flanks the north wall towards the gate. In the uppermost room there is one window full north.

The tower on the west side of the castle gate. In the lower room there is one spick that is stopped up, which flanks the north wall towards the north-west tower. In the second room, one spick standing in like sort. Between both towers over the gate, one window and a spick.

The number of spicks and windows that are on the outside of the castle, four score.

Over the gate there 'wanteth' (needs to be) a murdering hole and a portcullis and over the garden door the wall is very thin and weak, by means there has been, as I think, a murdering hole and portcullis, and now there is none. The north-east tower, the south-east tower and the middle tower unto 'Brimejame' his tower in all the battlements of the walls and towers there is neither spick nor loop and, if it shall seem good to your lordship, for that the castle wall is weakest in the south side, by means of the hall windows and other windows, with privies and such other works as have been of late years, that you would cause to be strongly ditched on that side from 'Brimejam' his tower round about the garden to the north-east tower. As regards the platforms, I think your lordship has taken order for them already.

Appendix 2
The survey of Dublin Castle in 1624[2]

Dublin Castle: An estimation made the 5th of April 1624 by Thomas Pynnock and Thomas Gray, masons, for the pulling down of the great tower standing west-north-west being 63 foot high, which makes 3 perches at 21 foot the perch, and the compass thereof being taken in the middle of the wall is 124 foot, making 6 perches for the circumference. And the thickness of the wall is ten foot.

	£
For the pulling down of the tower and laying the stones in place may cost by estimation	080 00 00
The tower will contain 1600 perches, which for the workmanship only at 2s. 6d. the perch will cost	200 00 00
Every perch of work will require 2 barrels of 'roache' lime, which at 9d. the barrel being 3200 barrels will cost	120 00 00
Every barrel of lime will require 2 barrels of sand, which at 3d. the barrel to be laid in the place to be wrought, being 6400 barrels will cost	080 00 00
For digging of stone sufficient for this work may cost by estimation	045 00 00
For the stone itself and bringing it home may cost	090 00 00
For scaffolding	025 00 00
For 'ankers, dogges and spikes' may cost	025 00 00
For 100 stone stairs rough hewn at 3s. 4d. the piece	016 00 00
For timber and planks for one platform and five floors may cost by estimation	100 00 00
For taking up of the lead, which must be all new cast and wrought, may cost by estimation	050 00 00
For cleansing the moat from all rubbish and the mud, which [is] in great abundance, may cost	060 00 00
Suma	891 00 00

Nicholas Pynnar, T.P. and Thomas Graye, masons

---

2   As printed in Falkiner 1904, 39–40, with spelling modernised, where the original source is given as: S. P. (Ireland), vol. ccxxxviii. Pt. i. No. 37, I.

	£
There is also in divers of the towers (which because the names of them are not known, we do set down in general their defects) a great deal of wall and parapet that is fallen down and some so riven that it must be taken down, which will be in all 213 perches and for the workmanship of all this with stone, lime and sand will cost 8s. each perch as is hereunder specified and this will amount unto by estimation	085 08 00
There is a great deal of stonework must be pulled down and the stones to be saved and laid in place may cost by estimation	005 00 00
The tower called Bremagems Tower wants no stonework but it has no platform, which is a place fit for a piece of artillery. This is 41 foot long and 24 foot wide, and this may cost by estimation	024 00 00
The lead of this tower must be taken up and new wrought which may cost by estimation	030 00 00
There is a little tower standing south, which also has no platform and is very needful to have a piece of artillery and this may cost by estimation	014 00 00
The lead also of this must be taken up and new wrought, which may cost by estimation	025 00 00
For 'ankers, dogges and spikes' to fasten in the walls, which for want of these formerly has been the cause of the ruin of these walls and this may cost by estimation	025 00 00
All the outside of the castle wall towards the south and the west is weather-beaten and in the west end there is a crack from one tower to the other and must be pinned both in that place and some others and this may cost by estimation	250 00 00
Suma	458 08 00

There must be for every perch of work 2 cart loads of stone, which costs	3s.
For 2 barrels of roach lime	18d.
For 4 barrels of sand	12d.
For workmanship per perch at	2s. 6d.
Suma	8s.

Nicholas Pynnar, T.P. and Thomas Graye, masons

Appendix 3
A description of Dublin Castle by Sir William Brereton (1635)[3]
Hence I went to the castle, wherein my Lord Deputy resides, within which are both the Houses of Parliament, whereof I took a view: much less and meaner than ours. The Lords' house is now furnished with about sixty or seventy armours for horse, which are my Lord Deputy's: this is a room of no great state nor receipt. Herein there sat the first session about eighty lords; not so many the latter.

The Commons House is but a mean and ordinary place; a plain, and no very convenient seat for the Speaker, nor officers. The Parliament men that sat in this house were about 248. There are about 30 or 32 shires, which send 60 or 64 knights for the shire, the rest are burgesses.

Here in this castle we saw the council chamber, wherein stands a very long table, furnished with stools at both sides and ends. Here sometimes sit in council about 60 or 64 privy councillors. Here we saw the hall, a very plain room and the dining room, wherein is placed the cloth of estate over my Lord Deputy's head, when he is at meat. Beyond this is the chamber of presence, a room indeed of state; and next unto this is there a withdrawing chamber, and beyond that a pretty, neat, short gallery, which leads to the council chamber; this was lately built by my Lord Falkland, whilst he was here deputy; the lower part of it is built arch-wise and very gracefully, so that it is a great ornament to the castle, about which there are very high walls and of great strength, and a drawbridge which is pulled up every night.

The command which this castle has over this city is from some of the leads and towers above on the top of the castle, whereupon there is ordnance planted; and one fair brass

---

3   As printed in Falkiner 1904, 380–1.

piece of ordnance is placed in the court before the gate. Parker committed a forfeiture here in taking out the stopple, for which he was seized upon, and I paid 6d to redeem him. Here my Lord Deputy has lately erected a gallant, stately stable, as any I have seen in the king's dominions; it is a double stable, there being a strong wall in the middle, to either side whereof stand the horses' heads. Thirty horses may stand at ease on either side, the stalls being very large; these are exceeding high, at least five or six yards and very near the same breadth; no planks made use of, but Holland bricks placed upon the edges, whereon the horses lie and you walk; these as easy to walk upon as to lie upon and these are made of Holland earth, which is harder and more durable much than our clay; with these the streets are paved in Holland.

July 11. We went to Sir Thomas Rotheram (who is a privy councillor), who used us respectively and accompanied me to the castle and showed me the courts of justice, which are conveniently framed and contrived, and these very capacious – the Star-Chamber, the Chancery, the King's Bench and Common Pleas – these rooms as useful as ours in England, but there is not such a stately structure or hall to walk in as Westminster Hall.

Appendix 4

A description of the Castle of Dublin by Robert Ware (1678)[4]

The castle of Dublin is a fortress and citadel of the greatest importance in the kingdom of Ireland; and had been so happy in the late rebellion of Ireland to be almost the only conservatory of the English and English interest. It is fortified with strong and high-raised walls contained within the compass of its ancient circumvallation. You enter the great gate from the city by a drawbridge between two towers of each side joining to a bridge.

The gate is furnished with portcullises; it is also attended by a Constable, Gent[leman] Porter and Guarders, besides a strong guard of the Royal Regiment. Before the gate is always placed a great piece of artillery of a dreadful aspect to such as should attempt to force an entrance into that fort. The wall extends itself equally on all sides in height except the surmounting of the gate towers and the Bermingham's Tower. From the gate tower on the right hand reaches a curtain parallel to Castle Street and unto the tower of late called Corck Tower upon this occasion viz. this tower on the first day of May (1624) about nine of the clock in the forenoon suddenly fell to the ground, the which being

built so high as to the place where the Boyle's arms are now fixed. Richard, the opulent first earl of that name anno 1629 undertook the finishing thereof at his own proper cost and charge; in the accomplishment thereof he disbursed £408.

From this tower the wall of the said citadel is continued in one curtain as far as to join unto the tower called Bermingham's Tower, which is the stateliest, highest and strongest tower in this fortress. This tower is celebrated not only by the name of its noble founder, but also by the custody of the ancient records of the kingdom, there being an established maintenance for the keeping of them in this place. The right honourable the Lord Viscount Lanesborough being the present patentee for the keeping of them there.

There be two other towers but of less dimension between this and the Guardrobe Tower, where the king's royal robe, the cap of maintenance and other furniture are kept and preserved by a patent officer, who had a competent salary for this employment.

Another curtain reaches from the last-mentioned tower to the North Tower near Dames Gate (in this tower until of late was kept the ammunition belonging to his majesty's store). The wall is continued hence unto the tower on the left hand as you enter into the great gate of the castle.

I have now finished the towers and curtains of the castle and as you enter thereinto you may be pleased to take notice that the constable of the castle holds the tower on each side of the castle gate for the custody of his majesty's prisoners. This castle was built (at least the most part thereof) in the time of Henry Loundres, archbishop of Dublin, his government. It is furnished with great ordinances planted on the platforms of the several towers thereof.

Thus you see this citadel well fortified against all emergencies being as commodious for its own defence as it is convenient to succour the city, though it was somewhat stronger when it was encompassed and fortified by the flowing of the sea round about it.

Let us now look upon it as it is the king's court and palace as you make your entrance into the court you may behold the beautiful form of a fair building, unto which you may ascend by a noble staircase lately erected in the time of the duke of Ormond's government under our royal sovereign Charles the second since his most happy restoration.

The next thing considerable is the dining room lately re-edified and raised to a stately height together with all the upper part of the building proportionably thereunto by the earl of Essex.

---

4 Extract from 'The History and Antiquities of Dublin collected from authentic records and the manuscript collections of Sir James Ware, Knt., By Robert Ware son of the learned Antiquary, 1678.' (Gilbert Ms. 74, Dublin City Library and Archive, Pearse Street). Transcribed by J.B. Maguire. Checked against original and spelling and punctuation modernised. Printed here with the permission of Dublin City Library and Archive.

The next part of the palace contiguous thereunto is the Chamber of Presence, the lobbies and the chambers thereunto appertaining which, being an ancient structure, is thought to want reparation or rebuilding, and no doubt therefore but the earl of Essex his noble design to have repaired it had he continued longer will be accomplished by his grace, who now happily governs this kingdom, if he shall see it necessary and conducing to his majesty's honour.

From this building towards the gate, extends itself a stately structure on your left hand as you pass from the gate to the palace door, erected in the time of the Lord Deputy Falkland, borne upon pillars in the nature of a piazza, a stately long gallery and many other places of convenience for the chief governor and his family. (In margin: This gallery [was] built anno 1624).

Contiguous unto this structure is another ancient piece of building, wherein upon the ground is a chapel, over which is a stately drawing room built in the time of Sir Henry Sidney his government, whose arms are placed thereon. (In margin: The chapel built by Sir Henry Sidney anno 1567).

Hereunto on the place of an old decayed building was lately raised a stately and convenient structure contained within these walls by the earl of Essex whereon are fixed the king's arms, and underneath his own coat of arms, in memory of his name. In this apartment are the Lord Lieutenant's private lodgings and the rooms thereunto appertaining much more noble and convenient than formerly they have been. (In margin: The late addition that was built by Arthur earl of Essex anno 1674).

I have now described the front with such other buildings as are contiguous thereunto on the left hand of your entrance into the palace. On the right hand are the hall, on the ground, the kitchen and other places belonging to the offices below stairs reaching as far as Bermingham's Tower.

Now hereunto on the right hand was an ancient structure built after the form of a church, raised upon several stately pillars, in the lower part whereof was kept his majesty's store, but the powder by god's admired providence was removed thence by order of that circumspect governor of Ireland the Lord Roberts a very short time before the fire, which happened in the time of Lord Berkley his government, the occasion and original thereof is yet unknown, destroyed the said storehouse and upper loft of that famous building, wherein was anciently kept his majesty's courts of justice and also were held both houses of parliament until the wisdom of the state thought fit to free the castle from so great a concourse of people as usually frequented that great assembly and to hold the last parliament at Chichester House. The roof and lofts of this building being burnt as aforesaid the most part of the walls with the arches were demolished in the time of the earl of Essex his lieutenancy

and the stones thereof disposed of by him towards the building of Saint Andrew's Church. (In margin: A description of the late storehouse in the castle of Dublin, which was burnt in 1671).

This great structure, though built in the form of a church, was anciently called the hall of the castle and has aisles thereunto belonging covered with lead until the time of King Edward the 4th, who caused the same to be sold by the Treasurer of Ireland for repair of the said structure as appears by the statute *anno Secundi Edwardi Quarti*, wherein are these words: 'Whereas the castle of the king, our sovereign lord, of the city of Dublin, in which the courts of our sovereign lord are kept is ruinous and like to fall to the great dishonour of our said sovereign lord, whereupon the premises considered, it is ordained by authority of the said parliament that forty shillings yearly to be taken and received of the issues and profits of the Hanaper of our sovereign lord of his Chancery of Ireland, and forty shillings yearly to be received of the issues and profits of his Chief place, and forty shillings yearly to be received of the issues and profits of his Common place, and three pounds yearly to be received of the issues and profits of his Exchequer in his said land, and twenty shillings yearly to be received of the issues and profits of the Masters of the Mint for the time being and the same to be delivered yearly to the Clerk of the Works of the said castle for the time being, and that he shall account yearly before the Barons of the Exchequer of the king of Ireland according to the ancient form and that all the leads of the aisles of the hall of the said castle be sold by the Treasurer of Ireland to make and repair the said hall.'

If the reader shall doubt of the keeping of the courts of justice in the castle to the later days of Queen Elizabeth he may be confirmed in the truth hereof by the story, which I am now to relate.

Adam Loftus, archbishop of Dublin and Lord Chancellor of Ireland in the time of Sir John Perrott's government [was] sitting publicly in the high court of chancery in the castle of Dublin, whilst there were public animosities between the deputy and him. The Chancellor's secretary, being then a suitor unto the daughter of the Lord Deputy's secretary and having thereby opportunity and permission to resort unto their lodgings, he found the closet door of the Lord Deputy's secretary lying wide open. The Deputy's secretary being at that time suddenly called to answer some occasions of business that his lord and master had for him, he espied spread upon the secretary's desk a large sheet of paper fairly written whereupon his curiosity tempting him to acquaint himself with the contents thereof, he drew near to a closer view, and there read in capital letters the title of an accusation in the name of articles against his lord, the Lord Chancellor of Ireland. He thereupon snaps up the said articles and immediately repairs to his master the Lord Chancellor there sitting in the Chancery within the castle, presenting them unto him folded up in the form of a petition, beseeching his grace to take the same into immediate consideration, or that otherwise the intended ruin of the petitioner would hardly be avoided. The Chancellor at first reproved him for his unreasonable address in the solemn hearing of a cause. Notwithstanding he had received a check he continued his instance with greater importunity and thereby his grace conceiving it to be a matter of extraordinary importance, received the paper and by the title informed of the scope thereof, he read the same seriously over once or twice, and thereupon he returned it to his secretary directing him to return it back again, assuring him that the party who was concerned should receive a suitable and seasonable answer, he returned with the paper unto the lodgings of the Lord Deputy's secretary, who being still detained in business with his lord was not yet returned. So that the Chancellor's secretary left these articles of pretended treason in the place where he found them without any notice that he had either taken or seen them. The Lord Chancellor, being a person of great sagacity and wisdom, soon takes occasion to arise, and repaired to his own house where having imprinted in his memory the whole matter suggested in the before specified articles, he forthwith drew a letter to Queen Elizabeth a full satisfactory and distinct answer to every of them. He also wrote concerning the same to the Lord Cecil and other ministers of state then most prevalent at court, which he sent that very afternoon by his said secretary into England, the wind as if it had been bribed to serve the turn of the one and to disappoint the other, just serving to convey him over, immediately chopped about to the contrary, so that the Lord Deputy's packet having not been in readiness to take the opportunity, which the Lord Chancellor's secretary made use of, was stopped on this side so long before a passage could be gained into England, that before its departure letters of approbation were returned to the Chancellor both from the queen and the lords of the council too large to be inserted here as also a sharp letter from the queen to the deputy reproving him for so groundless an attempt against his Chancellor, and thus the matter of accusation ceased.

I have proceeded perhaps too far in digression upon this point. [I] shall therefore desire the reader to turn his face with me to that side of the buildings, which are on the same side with the great gate, where he may behold, on the right hand as he goes out of the palace, the place of the Council Chamber, and what other rooms belonged thereto, of late converted into an apartment for the lodging of such persons of the Chief Governor's household as are consigned thereunto. And on the other side of the gate he may place his eye on the Constable's lodgings, very much beautified and reduced to the better accommodation of modern contrivance in the time of the duke of Ormond's first government after his majesty's happy restoration and also the apartment built of brick in the time of the earl of Strafford, for the accommodation of Sir George Radcliff, Bart., who was then not only a member of the Privy Council but also received a salary of £500 per annum for his assistance to the earl of Strafford in matter of law, he being as eminently knowing in the affairs of state as he was learned in the laws, having been Attorney General of the Presidency of York before his coming into Ireland, which office he managed with great applause and dexterity.

Next to this apartment are other more ancient brick buildings in the same range under the castle wall, which were built in the time of King James and are now within a portal adjoining to Cork Tower.

There were until of late two sally ports or postern gates lying open: the one towards Sheep Street, the other towards the Castle Yard, but that towards Sheep Street was closed up by order of the duke of Ormond, upon occasion of the conspiracy of Warren and Jephson, who designed to make their treasonable entrance into the castle by the surprise of that port, since which time it has been stopped against all passage out or in to the castle. The other postern gate is still open, but secured by a constant guard, which will permit you to descend thence into the Stable Yard, where you may take delight in seeing the great horse ridden and managed by the rules of the best horsemanship and martial skill. There also you may behold large stately stables of an elegant contrivance built in the time of the earl of Strafford, as also a place designed for a mint and other offices for the forging of arms and other uses appertaining to the stores there, [which] also were built in the time of that vast minded governor, [and] a great storehouse for the keeping of all furniture belonging to war. The office for the ordnance is now kept at the issuing out of the said last mentioned postern gate. And I have now no more to say regarding the castle in this place, or what appertains thereunto, than that there passes through the Stable Yard a full stream of water issuing out of the castle gardens, which plentifully serves to all uses belonging unto the horse there kept and to the several artificers and persons who minister to public uses in that place. And to tell the reader as I pass from the castle to the city, by authority of parliament 18 Ed: 4 Cap. 11. that the prior of Kilmainham was to build the castle bridge.

Appendix 5

A true and particular relation of the fire which happened in the castle of Dublin in Ireland [1684][5]

There is no place so secure, nor person so careful, that are not subject to the contingencies that daily attend on human affairs, especially such as happen by fire, when that powerful enemy gets the mastery. Troy, that resisted the war-like foe for ten years, could not withstand the fire so many hours, nor all its (titular) deities defend it from the flames. We have had many fatal examples of late years in England, especially in London, nor has the Royal Palace, nay hardly His Majesty's own bed-chamber, escaped, notwithstanding the vigilance of the guards, and the more peculiar hand of providence over him.

His excellency the Earl of Arran, a gentleman of approved trust and loyalty, His Majesty's Deputy in the Kingdom of Ireland, resided in the Castle of Dublin, where on the 7th. instant there happened such a fire as almost totally consumed the castle, etc., a true relation whereof take as follows:

Dublin, April the 7th 1684

Sir

This morning, about half an hour after one of the clock, broke out a most dreadful fire in the Castle, which is thought to have begun in the Lord Deputy's dressing-room, by the beam of the room going under the room, which taking fire, become immediately so outrageous, that my lord himself was in great danger of being destroyed. In fine, (though, God be thanked, not one person is hurt, yet) it has consumed all the new brick buildings, (viz.) the Queen's drawing room, my Lord's own apartment, and the Lady's apartments, wherein my Lady Duchess has received very considerable loss, to the value of several thousand pounds, in rich furniture etc. It has likewise destroyed the chapel, the King's drawing room, the Presence, and the great dining room; so that row is quite burnt, from the great door and stairs to the castle eastward, to the very corner of the wall. As for the other row, the long gallery, my Lord's closet, the Secretary's office, and all the other offices below, with the lodgings over them, (viz. where the young Lady lay) are all blown up. The conflagration was so fierce and devouring, that there is nothing of the castle left (within the walls) but the hall, kitchen and cellars; that is as to the palace: the out-lodgings (such as they are) are still standing, though defaced.

You may, by this sad relation, easily imagine the splendour of our court; but the consternation of the people cannot well be thought; for the Tower of the Magazine, (which has in it at least 2000 barrels of powder) was greatly endangered, the fire coming within 20 yards of it; which, as it would have destroyed half the town, so questionless many thousands of the inhabitants must inevitably have perished.

Amidst the horror and alarm of drums beating, trumpets sounding, and people running about distracted they knew not whither, in the dead of the night, I (your friend and servant) knowing my service could be but small, and that I should but add one to the crowd, with what expedition I could, got me ready, and away with my coach to the *Strand*, where, from half an hour after two, till the fire was quite out, (which was full three hours after) did I tower it all alone, out of the reach or danger of the fire.

My Lord Deputy is removed to *White-Fryars*, where he remains till *Chappelisard* be in order, where he will then reside, he having sustained no small share in this loss. All the papers both of his closet, and the Secretary's office under him, were saved before that apartment was blown up.

> I am, Sir,
> Yours, etc.
> B. R.

Appendix 6

Description of the castle by Thomas Denton (1687-8)[6]

Dams-gate, now called Damaskgate: this leads to Corkhill, where on the left hand there is a little exchange, like Exeter Exchange. A little higher on the left hand is Castle Street, on the south side whereof stands the king's castle, on high, strongly fenced with ditches, towers and an armoury or store house built by Henry Loundres, archbishop 1220. It is not large, nor beautiful; it was lately burnt, but rebuilt again. This is the most considerable street in the town, where the richest merchants, goldsmiths, mercers and other tradesmen of eminent dealing dwell; and also the most taverns, in respect of the lord deputy's court and of the courts of justice not far from hence.

Castle-gate is the third gate on the backside of the castle leading into the city, within which there is a courtyard where 1,000 men may be drawn up. On the north side stands the king's stables and on the south side a new Popish chapel and small priory for Dominican friars. This part lies below the castle upon a rill called the Miln-pool, which waters all the suburbs on the south and east sides and falls into the Liffy at Temple Barr.

---

5   A pamphlet published in 1684. Text transcribed and spelling modernised from photographic image of pamphlet published in Gibney 2006, 19.

6   Lennon 2008, Appendix A, p. 37.

Appendix 7
Description of the castle by John Dunton (1698)[7]

Another of my inquisitive rambles is to the castle, the place of residence of the chief governor. It is encompassed by a wall and dry ditch, over which is a drawbridge and within that an iron gate, opposite to which in the inner court are two brass field pieces planted, as also some others on top of one of the towers; and yet it is no place of great strength, I mean such as is able to endure the battery of great guns, though it can command all the city from its towers. It has a handsome guard house for the soldiers and other rooms for the officers, for a foot company with three commissioned officers daily mount the guard, and whenever the government go out or come in they are received with colours flying and drums beating as the king is at Whitehall, and indeed the grandeur they live in here is not much inferior to what you see in London if you make allowances for the number of great men in court there. The building is handsome without much magnificence on the outside; you enter the house up a noble stairs and find several stately rooms, one of which is called the presence chamber and has a chair of state with a canopy over it. One part of the house stands over a large stone gallery supported by several pillars of stone.

At the back of the house lies a broad terrace walk the length of the building, the walls covered with greens and flowerpots. From hence, on a stone arch over a little river, you descend by two spacious pair of stone stairs into the garden, which is handsomely laid out into grass plots with green and gravel walks, and at the north side there are two rows of flourishing lime trees, beneath which lies another grass walk. This garden was made by that great man the Lord Sidney, now earl of Rumney, when he was chief governor.

To the castle belongs an officer called the Constable of the Castle, who receives prisoners of state when committed, as the Lieutenant of the Tower does. To the north side lies the chapel to which the Lord Galway goes constantly every morning to prayers, and at his return spends some time in receiving petitions, which he answers with all the sweetness and readiness that any petitioner can wish for in so great a man.

Next the chapel is the office of the ordnance, near which the king's gunsmiths and armourers work. Before these buildings lies a large piece of ground called the stable yard, on one side of which are the king's stables which, as they are not extraordinary, so they are in no way despicable, but convenient and big enough; in this yard two companies of foot parade every morning, one of which mounts the town guard and the other that of the castle. The little river which I now mentioned runs here, on the other side of which stands the coach houses, and [the] biggest hay stacks that ever I saw.

Appendix 8
Description of Dublin Castle by James Malton (1792)[8]

The Castle of Dublin, the residence of the Lord Lieutenant of Ireland, is a considerable, and on the whole, a very respectable pile of building; situated on the highest ground, and now, in or about the very centre of the city. It is divided into two courts, termed the upper and the lower; the Upper Court is principal and contains the state and private apartments of the chief governor and his suite; and, although the buildings wear an appearance of age, yet from their uniformity, the spaciousness of the court, and fine display of the north side, it has an air of grandeur superior to what is observable in any of the courts of Saint James's, the royal palace of London.

The annexed plate, is a view of the Upper Court, from the gateway at the east end. The form of the court is a quadrangle, two hundred and eighty feet long, by one hundred and thirty feet broad: the buildings around being uniform, the architecture and effect of the whole, may be judged from the view, as it exhibits more than half. The near gateway, on the right hand, is the principal entrance from the street; over it, is an excellent statue of Justice; on the other gate, corresponding, is a statue of Fortitude. The colonnade, on the opposite side, is the chief approach to the apartments of the viceroy, to which is access by a broad flight of stairs, rising in the middle of a lobby at the end of the colonnade. These apartments occupy the whole of the south side, and part of the east end. In this court are also the apartments and office of the principal secretary of the Lord Lieutenant, the war, and other necessary offices to the government. The building between the gateways, supporting the tower called Bedford Tower, is appropriated to the use of the Master of the Ceremonies, and aid-de-camps of the chief governor, behind which, to the street, is the principal Guard House. The gallery over the arches is for the state musicians on gala days.

---

7   Dunton 2003, 139–40.

8   Malton 1799, text accompanying the plate of the Upper Yard, Dublin Castle by James Malton (Fig. 3.58).

The private apartments, for the use of the viceroy, can neither boast of much elegance or great convenience; nor have the presence or council chambers, much to recommend them to notice, beside the usual ornaments of state. The Presence Chamber is over the colonnade and was formerly the Yeoman's Hall; the throne and canopy are covered with crimson velvet, richly ornamented, with gold lace, and carved work, gilt. From a rich stucco ceiling hangs an elegant glass lustre, of Waterford manufactory, purchased by the late Duke of Rutland, when Lord Lieutenant, on his visiting that city, which cost two hundred and seventy-seven pounds. The object that commands a principal attention, is the ball-room, or Saint Patrick's Hall, as it is called. This is stately, spacious apartment, eighty-two feet long, forty-one feet broad, and thirty-eight high; it has been newly fitted up, and decorated, since the institution of the Knights of Saint Patrick in 1783, begun by command of Earl Temple, now Marquis of Buckingham, when chief governor. The paintings are excellent, particularly of the ceiling, the flat of which is divided into three compartments: an oblong rectangle, at each end, and a circle in the middle. In one of the rectangles is represented Saint Patrick converting the Irish to Christianity in the fifth century; in the other, King Henry II, seated under a canopy, receiving the submissions of the Irish chieftains, who attended to do him homage on his arrival in Ireland in the year 1172. In the circle is an allegorical representation alluding to the present happy and flourishing state of the country from the two preceding events and recent favours granted by his present majesty, George III, who is therein represented, supported by liberty and justice, the whole designed with a greatness of composition, correctness of drawing and brilliancy of colouring, as will do lasting honour to Mr. Waldre, the artist who executed them. Around the ceiling, to the cornice of the room, is a deep cove, richly painted by the same artist; in it are some devices, wherein great judgement is displayed in managing the perspective effect from below, where the appearance is fine and perfect. At each end of the room is a gallery for the musicians and spectators. To the rear of the apartments of the viceroy is a small lawn with walks adorned by trees and shrubs called the Castle Garden, to which is communication, from the building, by a large flight of steps, from a terrace before the garden front, which is a regular, and not inelegant, piece of architecture, all of stone.

The Lower Court, from the neglect which is shewn it, has a very inferior appearance; it is larger than the upper, but very irregular. In this court, on the north side, is the Treasury, Hanaper, Register, and Auditor General's offices, forming a range of indifferent brick buildings, with a terrace before them, owing to a great descent in the ground. The Ordnance office, at the east end, is a more modern and better building, likewise of brick. Here is also an arsenal for the stores and an armoury, containing arms for forty thousand men, with some cannon and mortars, beside guardhouses, riding house, stables and accommodation for several petty officers and other necessary requisites, which buildings make no appearance worthy of particular description. The private chapel of the Lord Lieutenant is in this court to the south, the external appearance of which and internal decorations appear very little consistent with its attachment to a royal palace. There is a passage to it, from the apartments of the viceroy, through a round tower called the Wardrobe Tower, the only remaining one of the original construction, which obtained its name from being the repository for the royal robes, the cap of maintenance and other furniture of state.

The lieutenancy of Ireland is the first government under the crown and has an income annexed of twenty thousand pounds per annum to support the station with becoming dignity. The viceroy is appointed a body guard consisting of a captain, two subalterns and sixty privates, with a subaltern's guard of horse.

Over the west end of the upper court, seen in the view, appears the steeple of Saint Werburgh's Church, situated in a street of the same name. In it is a seat for the Lord Lieutenant, the castle being in the parish.

The Castle of Dublin was originally built as a citadel of defence and place to deposit the royal treasure in the reign of King John, about the year 1205, but in the reign of Queen Elizabeth in 1560, in addition to its original uses, it was made commodious for the reception of the Lord Lieutenants, or chief governors of Ireland, there to hold their courts and was first occupied by that great patron of Ireland, Sir Henry Sidney, from which time, it has continued the residence of the chief governor, gradually altered and enlarged, as found necessary, until the whole face has been almost totally changed, and now, scarcely a vestige remains of its pristine state.

Bibliography
Abbreviations

Abbreviations

BL	British Library.
Bod. Lib.	Bodleian Library, Oxford.
BWM	Board of Works Minute Books, National Archives of Ireland.
CoA	College of Arms, London.
NMS, DCCI	Card index of historical references to Dublin Castle compiled by Thaddeus Breen *c.* 1986, National Monuments Service Archive.
DCA	Dublin City Archives.
HMC	Historical Manuscripts Commission, London.
IAA EMcP	Irish Architectural Archive, Edward McParland files, Acc. 2008/44.
NAI	National Archives of Ireland.
NGI	National Gallery of Ireland.
NLI	National Library of Ireland.
OPWT	Office of Public Works Library, Trim.
PRONI	Public Records Office of Northern Ireland.
RD	Registry of Deeds, Dublin.
RIA	Royal Irish Academy.
SPO	former State Paper Office, now National Archives of Ireland.
TCD	Trinity College Dublin.
TNA	The National Archives, Kew.
V & A	Victoria and Albert Museum, London.
WSC	Wide Streets Commission.

Abbreviated published references

AClon	*The annals of Clonmacnoise, being the annals of Ireland from the earliest period to A.D. 1408 translated into English A.D. 1627 by Conell Mageoghagan*, (ed.) D. Murphy (Dublin, 1896).
AFM	*Annals of the Kingdom of Ireland by the Four Masters*, (ed.) J. O'Donovan, 7 vols (Dublin 1851).
AI	*The Annals of Inisfallen*, (ed.) S. Mac Airt (Dublin 1951).
ALC	*The annals of Loch Cé: a chronicle of Irish affairs from A.D. 1014 to A.D. 1590*, (ed.) W.M. Hennessy, 2 vols (London, 1871; reprinted Dublin, 1939).
APC	*Acts of the Privy Council of England: A.D. 1542–[June 1631]*, 46 vols (London 1890–1964).
ASC	*The Anglo-Saxon Chronicle. A collaborative edition, volume 3*, (ed.) J.M. Bately (Cambridge 1986).
AT	'Annals of Tigernach', (ed.) W. Stokes in *Revue Celtique* **16** (1895), 374–419; **17** (1896), 6–33, 119–263, 337–420; **18** (1897), 9–59, 150–97, 267–303, reprinted in 2 vols (Felinfach 1993).
AU	*Annals of Ulster*, (ed.) W.M. Hennessy and B. MacCarthy, 4 vols (Dublin 1887–91). *The annals of Ulster (to AD 1131)*, (eds) S. Mac Airt and G. Mac Niocaill (Dublin 1983).
Cal. Fine rolls	*Calendar of the fine rolls […], 1272–[1509]*, 22 vols (London 1911–62).
Cal. misc. inq.	*Calendar of inquisitions miscellaneous: (Chancery) [1219–1422]*, 7 vols (London 1916–69).
Cal. pat. rolls	*Calendar of the patent rolls...1232–[1509]*, 53 vols (London 1891–1971).
Cal. Wells D. and C. MSS	*Calendar of the manuscripts of the Dean and Chapter of Wells*, vol. 1 (London 1907).
Carew MSS	*Calendar of the Carew manuscripts preserved in the archiepiscopal library at Lambeth, 1515–1624.* 6 vols (London 1867–73).
CDI	*A calendar of documents relating to Ireland, 1171–1307*, (ed.) H.S. Sweetman, 5 vols (London 1875–86).

Chartae Chartae, Privilegia et Immunitates: being transcripts of charters and privileges, to cities, towns, abbeys, and other bodies corporate…1171 to 1395 (Dublin 1889).

CIRCLE A calendar of Irish chancery letters, c. 1244–1509, (ed.) P. Crooks (https://chancery.tcd.ie/).

Close rolls Close rolls of the reign of Henry III, 1227–72, 14 vols (London 1902–38).

CMLP Calendar of Miscellaneous Letters and Papers pre 1760

CS Chronicum Scotorum, (ed.) W.M. Hennessy (London 1866).

CSPD Calendar of state papers preserved in the Public Record Office, domestic series, 1547–1695, 81 vols. (London 1856–1972).

CSPI Calendar of the state papers relating to Ireland, 1509–1670, 24 vols (London 1860–1912).

CSPI rev. ed. Calendar of state papers Ireland. Revised edition, (ed.) M. O'Dowd et al. (London and Dublin 2000–).

CTB Calendar of Treasury Books Vol. 22, 1708–14, (ed.) W. A Shaw (London 1952).

CTP Calendar of treasury books, 1660–92, 9 vols (London 1904–31).

DKR First [etc.] report of the deputy keeper of the public records in Ireland. (Dublin 1869–).

DMLBS Dictionary of medieval Latin from British sources (http://www.dmlbs.ox.ac.uk).

eDIL The electronic dictionary of the Irish language (based on Dictionary of the Irish language based mainly on Old and Middle Irish materials (Dublin 1913–76)) (http://www.dil.ie/).

FAI Fragmentary annals of Ireland, (ed.) J.N. Radner (Dublin 1978).

Fiants The Irish Fiants of the Tudor Sovereigns, 4 vols (Dublin 1994). Originally published in DKR between 1875 and 1890.

HC Sessional Papers House of Commons, Sessional Papers, Vol. 15, 1 (1825–7)

HMC Dartmouth The manuscripts of the earl of Dartmouth, 3 vols (London 1887–96).

HMC De L'Isle Report on the manuscripts of Lord De L'Isle and Dudley preserved at Penshurst Place, 6 vols, (London 1925–66).

HMC Egmont Report on the manuscripts of the earl of Egmont, 2 vols (London 1905–9).

HMC Layborne-Popham Report on the manuscripts of F.W. Layborne-Popham (London 1899).

HMC Ormonde Report on the manuscripts of the marquis of Ormonde. 3 vols (London 1895–9).

HMC Ormonde ns Calendar of the manuscripts of the marquess of Ormonde, new series, 8 vols (London 1902–20).

HMC RCHM First [etc.] report of the Royal Commission on Historical Manuscripts (London 1870–).

HMC Salisbury Manuscripts of the Most Hon. The Marquis of Salisbury, 24 vols (London 1883–1976).

JH of C Journals of the House of Commons of the Kingdom of Ireland, 19 vols (Dublin 1796–1800).

L. & P. Ric. III–Hen. VII Letters and papers illustrative of the reigns of Richard III and Henry VII, (ed.) J. Gairdner, 2 vols (London 1861–3).

L. & P. Hen. VIII Letters and papers, foreign and domestic, Henry VIII, 21 vols (London 1862–1932).

MIA Miscellaneous Irish annals (A.D. 1114–1437), (ed.) S. Ó hInnse (Dublin 1947).

ODNB Oxford dictionary of national biography: in association with the British Academy: from the earliest times to the year 2000 (Oxford 2004).

OED Oxford English dictionary. Oxford.

Pat. rolls Patent rolls of the reign of Henry III, 1216–25, 6 vols, (London 1901–13).

RCPRI Report from the Commissioners… respecting the Public Records of Ireland, 3 vols (London 1815–29)

S.P. Hen. VIII State papers, Henry VIII, 11 vols (London 1830–52).

Bibliography
Books, articles and theses

A citizen of London 1732 *A description of the city of Dublin*. London.

Aheron, J. 1754 *General treatise of architecture*. Dublin.

Airy, O. (ed.) 1890 *Essex Papers. Vol. I. 1672–79*. Camden Society ns 47. London.

Allott, S. 1974 *Alcuin of York: his life and letters*. York.

Andrews, J.H. 1983 The oldest map of Dublin. *Proceedings of the Royal Irish Academy* **83C,** 205–37.

Anon. (ed.) 1824 *Letters to and from Henrietta, Countess of Suffolk and her second husband, the Hon. George Berkeley from 1712 to 1767*, 2 vols. London.

Anon. 1896 Castle chapel, *The Irish Builder and Engineer* **38,** 48–51.

Anon. (ed.) 1963 A letter from Francis Johnston, *Quarterly Bulletin of the Irish Georgian Society* **6,** 1–5.

Bagwell, R. 1909–16 *Ireland under the Stuarts and during the interregnum*, 3 vols. London and New York.

Baillie, H.M. 1967 Etiquette and the planning of State Apartments in Baroque palaces, *Archaeologia* **101,** 169–99.

Ball, F.E. 1900 Monkstown Castle and its history, *Journal of the Royal Society of Antiquaries of Ireland* **30,** 109–17.

Ball, F.E. 1902 The battle of Rathmines, *Journal of the Royal Society of Antiquaries of Ireland* **32,** 246–56.

Ball, F.E. 1913 Extracts from the journal of Thomas Dineley, or Dingley, Esquire, giving some account of his visit to Ireland in the reign of Charles II, *Journal of the Royal Society of Antiquaries of Ireland* **44,** 275–309.

Barnard, T. 2000a The viceregal court in later seventeenth-century Ireland. In E. Cruickshanks (ed.) *The Stuart courts*, 256–65. Thrupp Stroud. Gloucestershire.

Barnard, T. 2000b Introduction: the Dukes of Ormonde. In T. Barnard and J. Fenlon (eds), *T he dukes of Ormonde, 1610–1745*, 1–54. Woodbridge.

Barnard, T. 2003 *A new anatomy of Ireland, the Irish Protestants 1649–1770*. New Haven and London.

Barry, J. 2009 Derricke and Stanihurst: a dialogue. In J. Harris and K. Sidwell (eds), *Making Ireland Roman: Irish Neo-Latin writers and the republic of letters*, 36–47. Cork.

Barry, J. and Morgan, H. (eds) 2014 *Great Deeds in Ireland: Richard Stanihurst's De Rebus in Hibernia Gestis*. Cork.

Belcher, T.W. 1866 *Memoir of Sir Patrick Dun*. Dublin.

Berger, R.W. 1973 Review of Wolfram Prinz, *Die Enstebung der Galerie in Frankreich und Italie*, *Art Bulletin* **55,** 459–60.

Berry, H.F. 1890–91 The water supply of ancient Dublin, *Journal of the Royal Society of Antiquaries of Ireland* **21,** 557–73.

Berry, H.F. 1902 Sir Peter Lewys, ecclesiastic, cathedral and bridge builder, and his company of masons, 1564–7. In *Ars Quatuor Coronatorum: being the Transactions of the Lodge Quatuor Coronati*, no. 2076, 4–22. London.

Berry, H.F. 1907 Notes on a statement dated 1634, regarding St Thomas' Court and St Katherine's churchyard, Dublin, *Journal of the Royal Society of Antiquaries of Ireland* **37,** 393–6.

Berry, H.F. (ed.) 1914 *Statute rolls of the parliament of Ireland, first to the twelfth years of the reign of King Edward the Fourth*. Dublin.

Bhreathnach, E. 1998 St Patrick, Vikings and Inber Dée – longphort in the early Irish literary tradition, *Wicklow Archaeology and History* **1,** 36–40.

Biddle, M., Clayre, B. and Morris, M. 2000 The setting of the Round Table: Winchester Castle and the Great Hall. In M. Biddle (ed.), *King Arthur's Round Table: an archaeological investigation*, 59–101. Woodbridge.

Blair, J. 1993 Hall and chamber: English domestic planning, 1000–1250. In G. Meirion-Jones and M. Jones (eds), *Manorial domestic buildings in England and northern France*, 1–21. London.

Borenius, T. 1943 The cycle of images in the palaces and castles of Henry III. *Journal of the Warburg and Courtauld Institutes* **6,** 40–50.

Boyle, E. and Breatnach, L. 2015 *Senchas Gall Átha Clíath*: aspects of the cult of Saint Patrick in the twelfth century. In J. Carey, K. Murray and C. Ó Dochartaigh (eds), *Sacred histories: a festschrift for Máire Herbert*, 22–55. Dublin.

Bradley, J. 1992 The topographical development of Scandinavian Dublin. In F.H. Aalen and K. Whelan (eds), *Dublin city and county from prehistory to present*, 43–56. Dublin.

Bradley, J. 2007 Sir Henry Sidney's bridge at Athlone, 1566–7. In T. Heron and M. Potterton (eds), *Ireland in the Renaissance, c. 1540–1660*, 173–94. Dublin.

Brady, C. 1994 *The chief governors: the rise and fall of reform government in Tudor Ireland, 1536–1588*. Cambridge.

Brady, C. (ed.) 2002 *A viceroy's vindication: Sir Henry Sidney's memoir of service in Ireland, 1556–78*. Cork.

Brady, C. 2012 'Viceroys? The Irish Chief Governors, 1541–1641'. In P. Gray and O. Purdue (eds), *The Irish Lord Lieutenancy: c. 1541–1922*, 15–42, Dublin.

Bray, W. (ed.) 1850 *Diary and correspondence of John Evelyn, F.R.S., … To which is subjoined the private correspondence between King Charles I and Sir Edward Nicholas, and between Sir Edward Hyde, afterwards earl of Clarendon, and Sir Richard Browne*, 4 vols. London.

Brewer, J.N. 1825-6 *The beauties of Ireland*, 2 vols. London.

Britton, J. 1807-27 *The architectural antiquities of Great Britain*, 5 vols. London.

Brown, D.F.J. 2016 The archbishop and the citizens of Dublin during Hugh de Lacy's rebellion, 1223–4. In S. Duffy (ed.), *Medieval Dublin XV*, 253–63. Dublin.

Buckley, L. and Hayden, A. 2002 Excavations at St Stephen's leper hospital, Dublin: a summary account and an analysis of burials. In S. Duffy (ed.), *Medieval Dublin III*, 151–94. Dublin.

Campbell, C. 1715–25 *Vitruvius Britannicus or the British Architect containing the plans, elevations and sections of the regular buildings both public and private in Great Britain*, 3 vols. London.

Campbell, M. 2017 'Sketches of their boundless mind': the Marquess of Buckingham and the Presence Chamber at Dublin Castle, 1788–1838. In M. Campbell and W. Derham (eds), *Making Majesty: the Throne Room at Dublin Castle, a cultural history*, 46–93. Newbridge.

Campbell, T.P. (ed.) 2007 *Tapestry in the Baroque, threads of splendour*. New York.

Carpenter, A. (ed.) 2003 *Teague Land: or a merry ramble to the wild Irish (1698) by John Dunton*. Dublin.

Carroll, F. 1953 The ancient name of the Poddle. *Dublin Historical Record* **13**(3/4), 155–7.

Carte, T. 1735–36 *An history of the life of James Duke of Ormonde, from his birth in 1610, to his death in 1688*, 3 vols. London.

Casey, C. 2005 *The buildings of Ireland: Dublin.* New Haven and London.

Charles-Edwards, T.M. 2013 *Lebor na cert and clientship.* In K. Murray (ed.), *Lebor na cert: reassessments,* 13–33. Irish Texts Society Subsidiary Series, 25. London.

Clark, W.S. 1955 *The early Irish stage: the beginnings to 1720.* Oxford.

Clarke, A. 1999 *Prelude to restoration in Ireland: the end of the commonwealth, 1659–1660.* Cambridge.

Clarke, D. 1958 *Arthur Dobbs Esquire, 1689–1765.* London.

Clarke, H.B. 1977 The topographical development of early medieval Dublin. *Journal of the Royal Society of Antiquaries of Ireland* **107**, 29–51; reprinted in idem (ed.), *Medieval Dublin: the making of a metropolis,* 52–69. 1990. Dublin. Irish Academic Press.

Clarke, H.B. (ed.) 2002 *Dublin, part I, to 1610.* Irish Historic Towns Atlas No. 11. Dublin.

Clarke, H.B. 2004 Christian cults and cult centres in Hiberno-Norse Dublin and hinterland. In A. MacShamhráin (ed.), *The island of St Patrick. Church and ruling dynasties in Fingal and Meath, 400–1148,* 140–58. Dublin.

Clarke, H.B. 2009 Cult, church and collegiate church before c. 1220. In J. Crawford and R. Gillespie (eds), *St Patrick's cathedral, Dublin: a history,* 23–44. Dublin.

Clarke, K. 1962 *The Gothic Revival.* London.

Cleasby, R. and Vigfusson, G. (eds) 1874 *An Icelandic-English Dictionary, based on the ms. collections of the late Richard Cleasby. Enlarged and completed by Gudbrand Vigfússon. With an introduction and life of Richard Cleasby by George Webbe Dasent.* Oxford.

Clover, H. and Gibson, M. (eds) 1979 *The Letters of Lanfranc, archbishop of Canterbury.* Oxford.

Cole, H. (ed.) 1844 *Documents illustrative of English history in the thirteenth and fourteenth centuries.* London.

Collins, A. (ed.) 1746 *Letters and memorials of state,* 2 vols. London.

Colvin, H.M. (ed.) 1963 *The history of the king's works, volumes I and II, the Middle Ages.* London.

Colvin, H.M. 1975 *The history of the king's works, volume III, 1485–1660 (part I).* London.

Colvin, H.M. 1982 *The history of the king's works, volume IV, 1485–1600 (part II).* London.

Colvin, H. 2005 *A biographical dictionary of British architects 1600–1840.* 3rd edition. New Haven and London.

Colvin, H. and M. Craig (eds) 1964 *Architectural drawings in the library of Elton Hall by Sir John Vanbrugh and Sir Edward Lovett Pearce.* Oxford.

Connolly, P.M. 1978 *Lionel of Clarence and Ireland, 1361–1366.* Ph.D. thesis, University of Dublin.

Connolly, P. 1994 An attempted escape from Dublin Castle: the trial of William and Walter de Bermingham, 1332. *Irish Historical Studies* **29**, 100–08.

Connolly, P. 1995a "Devices made by magic": an attempted escape from Dublin Castle in 1332. *History Ireland* **3**(1), 19–23.

Connolly, P. 1995b The medieval Irish Plea Rolls – an introduction. *Journal of the Irish Society for Archives* **2**(1), 3–12.

Connolly, P. (ed.) 1998 *Irish exchequer payment, 1270–1446.* Dublin.

Connolly, P. 2008 "The head and comfort of Leinster": Carlow as the administrative capital of Ireland, 1361–1394. In T. McGrath (ed.), *Carlow: history and society,* 307–29. Dublin.

Coope, R. 1986 The "Long Gallery": its origins, development, use and decoration. *Architectural History* **29**, 43–72, 74–84.

Cooper Walker, J. 1788 *An historical essay on the dress of the ancient and modern Irish.* Dublin.

Corish, P.J. 1976a The Cromwellian conquest, 1649–53. In T.W. Moody, F.X. Martin and F.J. Byrne (eds), *A new history of Ireland, iii, early modern Ireland, 1534–1691,* 336–52. Oxford.

Corish, P.J. 1976b The Cromwellian regime, 1650–60. In T.W. Moody, F.X. Martin and F.J. Byrne (eds), *A new history of Ireland, iii, early modern Ireland, 1534–1691,* 353–86. Oxford.

Cornforth, J. 1970 Dublin Castle – I, II and III. *Country Life,* **148**, 284–7, 342–5, 458–61.

Coughlan, T. 2003 Excavations at the medieval cemetery of St Peter's church, Dublin. In S. Duffy (ed.), *Medieval Dublin IV,* 11–39. Dublin.

Coxe, H.O. (ed.) 1841–4 *Rogeri de Wendover chronica; sive, flores historiarum,* 4 vols. London.

Craig, D.V. 1984 *The memoranda roll of the Irish exchequer for 3 Edward II.* Ph.D. thesis, University of Dublin.

Craig, M. 1952 *Dublin 1660–1860.* Dublin.

Craig, M. 1970 New light on Jigginstown. *Ulster Journal of Archaeology* **33**, 107–10.

Craig, M. 1996 The quest for Sir Edward Lovett Pearce. *Irish Arts Review* **12**, 27–34.

Crawford, J.G. 2005 *A star chamber court in Ireland: the court of castle chamber, 1571–1641.* Dublin.

Cromwell, T. 1820 *Excursions through Ireland.* London.

Curran, C.P. 1977 The architecture of the Bank of Ireland: part I, The Parliament House 1728–1800. *Bulletin of the Irish Georgian Society* **20**, nos 1 & 2, 3–36.

Davies, O. and Quinn, D.B. (eds) 1941 The Irish pipe roll of 14 John, 1211–1212. *Ulster Journal of Archaeology,* 3rd series, **4**, supplement, 1–76.

de Beer, E.S. (ed.) 1955 *Diary: now first printed in full from the manuscripts belonging to Mr. John Evelyn,* 6 vols. Oxford.

Derricke, J. 1581 *The image of Irelande with a discouerie of vvoodkarne…Made and deuised by Ihon Derricke, anno 1578 and now published and set forthe by the saied authour this present yere of our Lorde 1581. for pleasure and delight of the well disposed reader.* London.

Derricke, J. 1985 *The image of Irelande with a discoverie of woodkarne by John Derricke 1581.* Belfast.

Devon, F. (ed.) 1837 *Issues of the exchequer; being a collection of payments made out of His Majesty's revenue, from King Henry III to King Henry VI inclusive.* London.

Doderer-Winkler, M. 2013 *Magnificent entertainments, temporary architecture for Georgian festivals.* London.

Dolley, M. 1966 *Hiberno Norse coins in the British Museum.* London.

Dolley, M. 1973 The forms of the proper names appearing on the earliest coins struck in Ireland. In F. Sandgren (ed.), *Otium et Negotium: studies in onomatology and library science presented to Olof von Feilitzen,* 49–65. Stockholm.

Dolley, R.H.M. and O'Sullivan, W. 1967 The chronology of the first Anglo-Irish coinage. In E. Rynne (ed.), *North Munster studies: essays in commemoration of Monsignor Michael Moloney,* 437–78. Limerick.

Downes, K. 1987 *Sir John Vanbrugh.* London.

Downham, C. 2000 An imaginary Viking-raid on Skye in 795?. *Scottish Gaelic Studies* **20**, 192–6.

Downham, C. 2003–4 The Vikings in Southern Uí Néill to 1014. *Peritia* **17**, 233–55.

Downham, C. 2011 Viking identities in Ireland: it's not all black and white. In S. Duffy (ed.), *Medieval Dublin XI,* 185–201. Dublin.

Duffus Hardy, T. (ed.) 1833–44 *Rotuli litterarum clausarum in Turri londinensi asservati, 1204–1227,* 2 vols. London.

Duffus Hardy, T. (ed.) 1835 *Rotuli litterarum patentium in turri Londinensi asservati, 1201–1216.* London.

Duffus Hardy, T. (ed.) 1837 *Rotuli Chartarum in Turri Londinensi Asservati, Pars I. Ab anno MCXCIX ad annum MCCXVI,* vol. 1. London.

Duffy, S. 1992 Irishmen and Islesmen in the kingdoms of Dublin and Man, 1052–1171. *Ériu* **43**, 93–133.

Duffy, S. 1998 Ireland's Hastings: the Anglo-Norman conquest of Dublin. In C. Harper-Bill (ed.), *Anglo-Norman Studies XX: Proceedings of the Battle Conference,* 69–85. Woodbridge.

Duffy, S. 2005 A reconsideration of the site of Dublin's Viking Thing-mót. In T. Condit and C. Corlett (eds), *Above and beyond: essays in memory of Leo Swan,* 350–61. Dublin.

Duffy, S. 2014 The saint's tale. In S. Booker and C.N. Peters (eds), *Tales of Medieval Dublin,* 7–17. Dublin.

Duffy, S. and Mytum, H. (eds) 2015 *A new history of the Isle of Man, volume III: the medieval period 1000–1406.* Liverpool.

Dumville D. 2005 Old Dubliners and New Dubliners in Ireland and Britain: a Viking Age story. In S. Duffy (ed.), *Medieval Dublin VI,* 78–93. Dublin.

Dunlevy, M. 2002 *Dublin barracks: a brief history of Collins Barracks, Dublin.* Dublin.

Dunlop, R. 1913 *Ireland under the commonwealth: being a selection of documents relating to the government of Ireland from 1651 to 1659,* 2 vols. Manchester.

Dunton, J. 2003 *Teague Land: or, a merry ramble to the wild Irish (1698).* Edited by Andrew Carpenter. Dublin.

Dyche, T. and W. Pardon 1750 *A new general English dictionary,* 6th edition. London.

Ellis, S.G. 1998 *Ireland in the age of the Tudors, 1447–1603: English expansion and the end of Gaelic rule.* London and New York.

Ellis, S.G. 2019 Siegecraft on the Tudor frontier: the siege of Dublin, 1534, and the crisis of the Kildare rebellion. *Historical Research* **92**, no. 258, 705–19.

Essex, Arthur Capel, earl of 1770 *Letters written by His Excellency Arthur Capel, Earl of Essex, Lord Lieutenant of Ireland, in the year 1675: To which is prefixed an historical account of his life.* London.

Etchingham, C. 1996 *Viking raids on Irish church settlements in the ninth century.* Maynooth.

Etchingham, C. 2000 Episcopal hierarchy in Connacht and Tairdelbach Ua Conchobair. *Journal of the Galway Archaeological and Historical Society* **52**, 13–29.

Etchingham, C. 2010 The battle of Cenn Fúait, 917: location and military significance. *Peritia* **21**, 208–32.

Etchingham, C. 2017 Clontarf 1014: military significance, external dimension and outcome. In S. Duffy (ed.), *Medieval Dublin XVI,* 122–43. Dublin.

Eyton, R.W. 1878 *Court, household, and itinerary of King Henry II.* London.

Falkiner, C.L. 1904 *Illustrations of Irish history and topography mainly of the seventeenth century.* London.

Falkiner, C.L. 1904/1905 The parliament of Ireland under the Tudor sovereigns: with some notice of the speakers of the Irish house of commons. *Proceedings of the Royal Irish Academy* **25**, 508–41.

Fenlon, J. 1996 *Ormond Castle*. Dublin.

Fenlon, J. 2000 Episodes of magnificence. In T. Barnard and J. Fenlon (eds), *The dukes of Ormonde, 1610–1745*, 137–59. Woodbridge.

Fenlon, J. 2001 *The Ormonde picture collection*. Dublin.

Fenlon, J. 2003 *Goods and chattels: a survey of early household inventories in Ireland*. Dublin.

Fenlon, J. 2010 'Woven frescoes': tapestry collections in seventeenth-century Ireland. *Irish Architectural and Decorative Studies* **13**, 114–29.

Fenlon, J. 2011a 'They say I build to the sky': Thomas Wentworth, Jigginstown House and Dublin Castle. In M. Potterton and T. Herron (eds), *Dublin and the Pale in the Renaissance c. 1540–1660*, 207–23. Dublin.

Fenlon, J. 2011b Moving towards the formal house: room usage in early modern Ireland. *Proceedings of the Royal Irish Academy* **111C**, 141–68.

FitzGerald, W. 1915 The sculptured stones from the bridge of Athlone, built in 1567, now in the crypt of the Science and Art Museum, Dublin. *Journal of the Royal Society of Antiquaries of Ireland* **45**, 115–22.

Flanagan, M.T. 1989 *Irish society, Anglo-Norman settlers and Angevin kingship*. Oxford.

Flanagan, M.T. 2017 After Brian Bóruma: the high-kingship and the kings of Connacht. In S. Duffy (ed.), *Medieval Dublin XVI*, 218–48. Dublin.

Foyle, J. 2002 A reconstruction of Thomas Wolsey's Great Hall at Hampton Court Palace. *Architectural History* **45**, 128–58.

Frame, R. 1982 *English lordship in Ireland 1318–1361*. Oxford.

Galloway, P. 1999 *The most illustrious order, the Order of Saint Patrick and its knights*. London.

Gibbons, M and Gibbons, M. 2008 The search for the ninth-century *longphort*: early Viking-Age Norse fortifications and the origins of urbanization in Ireland. In S. Duffy (ed.), *Medieval Dublin VIII*, 9–20. Dublin.

Gibney, J. 2006 Restoration Dublin in the Ireland of its time c. 1660–1700. *History Ireland* **14**(3), 15–20.

Gibney, J. 2009 Capel, Arthur earl of Essex. In J. McGuire and J. Quinn (eds), *Dictionary of Irish Biography*, s.n. Cambridge.

Gilbert, J.T. 1857–8 The castle of Dublin. *Dublin University Magazine* **49** (1857), 259–71, 515–28; **50** (1857), 105–13, 247–54, 297–308, 610–22; **51** (1858), 248–55.

Gilbert, J.T. 1861 *A history of the city of Dublin*, 3 vols. 2nd ed. Dublin.

Gilbert, J.T. 1865 *History of the viceroys of Ireland: with notices of the castle of Dublin and its chief occupants in former times*. Dublin.

Gilbert, J.T. (ed.) 1884 *Chartularies of St Mary's abbey, Dublin; with the register of its house at Dunbrody, and annals of Ireland*, 2 vols. London.

Gilbert, J.T. (ed.) 1885 *The manuscripts of the marquis of Ormonde, the earl of Fingall, the corporations of Waterford, Galway etc.* HMC Tenth report, Appendix, Part V. London.

Gilbert, J.T. (ed.) 1889 *Register of the Abbey of St. Thomas, Dublin*. London.

Gilbert, J.T. (ed.) 1889–1944 *Calendar of ancient records of Dublin*, 19 vols. Dublin.

Gilbert, J.T. (ed.) 1897 *Crede mihi: the most ancient register book of the archbishops of Dublin before the Reformation now for the first time printed from the original manuscript*. Dublin.

Gillespie, R. 2009 Reform and decay, 1500–1598. In J. Crawford and R. Gillespie (eds), *St Patrick's cathedral, Dublin: a history*, 151–73. Dublin.

Girouard, M. 1978 *Life in the English country house: a social and architectural history*. New Haven and London.

Girouard, M. 2009 *Elizabethan architecture: its rise and fall, 1540–1640*. New Haven and London.

Glin, Knight of, and J. Peill 2007 *Irish furniture*. New Haven.

Goodall, J.A.A. 2004 A medieval masterpiece: Herstmonceux Castle, Sussex, *The Burlington Magazine* **146**, no. 1217 (Aug. 2004), 516–25.

Goodbody, R. 2014 *Dublin, part III, 1756–1847*. Irish Historic Towns Atlas No. 26. Dublin.

Gowen, M. 2001 Excavations at the site of the church and tower of St Michael le Pole, Dublin. In S. Duffy (ed.), *Medieval Dublin II*, 13–52. Dublin.

Grossart, A.B. 1886–88 *The Lismore papers. First [and second] series*, 10 vols. London.

Haliday, C. 1969 *The Scandinavian kingdom of Dublin*. Shannon.

Handley, S. 2004 Cotton, Sir Robert Bruce, ODNB, s.n.

Hardy, T.D. (ed.) 1833–44 *Rotuli litterarum clausarum in Turri Londinensi asservati [The close rolls kept in the Tower of London]*, 2 vols. London.

Harris, W. (ed.) 1747–50 *Hibernica: or, some antient places relating to Ireland*, 2 vols. Dublin.

Harris, W. 1766 *The history and antiquities of the city of Dublin*. Dublin.

Hawkins, E. (ed.) 1844 Travels in Holland, the United Provinces, England, Scotland and Ireland 1634–5 by Sir William Brereton. In *Remains historical & literary connected with the Palatine counties of Lancaster and Chester published by the Chetham Society*, vol. 1, Manchester.

Hayden, A.R. 2011 *Trim Castle, Co. Meath: excavations 1995–8*. Dublin.

Hemmeon, M. de W. 1914 *Burgage tenure in mediaeval England*. Cambridge, Mass.

Hickey, G. 2017 'Quite like a palace': the Presence Chamber at Dublin Castle 1838–1911. In M. Campbell and W. Derham (eds), *Making Majesty: the Throne Room at Dublin Castle, a cultural history*, 94–131. Newbridge.

Hill, J. 2015 'A stile more suited to vice-regal splendor': the building of the Chapel Royal, 1807–14. In M. Campbell and W. Derham (eds), *The Chapel Royal, Dublin Castle: an architectural history*, 39–53. Trim.

Hitchcock, R. 1788 *An historical view of the Irish stage*, 2 Vols. Dublin.

HMSO 1975 'The King's Manor'. In *An Inventory of the Historical Monuments in City of York, Volume 4, Outside the City Walls East of the Ouse*, 30–43. London. British History online https://www.british-history.ac.uk/rchme/york/vol4/pp30-43 [accessed 21 July, 2021].

Hogan, E. (ed.) 1881 *Words of comfort to persecuted Catholics: written in exile, anno 1607; Letters from a cell in Dublin Castle and diary of the Bohemian War of 1620 by Henry Fitzsimon; illustrated from contemporary documents, correspondence of Irish Jesuits and government officials*. Dublin.

Hogan, E. 1894 *Distinguished Irishmen of the sixteenth century: first series*. London.

Holinshed, R. 1577 *The Chronicles of England, Scotlande, and Irelande. Conteyning, the description and chronicles of England, from the first inhabiting vnto the conquest, the description and chronicles of Scotland, from the first originall of the Scottes nation, till the yeare of our Lorde, 1571, the description and chronicles of Yrelande, likewise from the firste originall of that nation, vntill the yeare 1547. Faithfully gathered and set forth*, 2 vols. London.

Holinshed, R. 1586 *The description and historie of England, The description and historie of Ireland, The description and historie of Scotland: first collected and published by Raphaell Holinshed, William Harrison, and others: now newlie augmented and continued (with manifold matters of singular note and worthie memorie) to the yeare 1586. by Iohn Hooker aliàs Vowell Gent and others*, 2 vols. London.

Holinshed, R. 1808 *Holinshed's chronicles of England, Scotland, and Ireland. In six volumes. Vol. vi, Ireland*. London.

Holland, K. 2011 The Sidney Women in Ireland, c. 1556–1594. *Sidney Journal* **29**(1–2), 45–68.

Holm, P. 2015 Manning and Paying the Hiberno-Norse Dublin Fleet. In E. Purcell, P. MacCotter, J. Nyhan and J. Sheehan (eds), *Clerics, kings and Vikings: essays on medieval Ireland in honour of Donnchadh Ó Corráin*, 67–78. Dublin.

Horwood, A.J. (ed.) 1879 The manuscripts of Sir Harry Verney, Bart., at Claydon House, Co. Bucks. *Seventh report of the Royal Commission on Historic Manuscripts*, Appendix, 433–509. London.

Howarth, D. 1997 *Images of rule: art and politics in the English Renaissance, 1485–1649*. Basingstoke.

Hudson Turner, T. 1851 *Some account of domestic architecture in England from the Conquest to the end of the thirteenth century*. Oxford.

Hughes, J.L.J. 1940 Dublin Castle in the seventeenth century: a topographical reconstruction. *Dublin Historical Record* **2**, 81–97.

Hughes, J.L.J. 1960 *Patentee officers in Ireland 1173–1826*. Dublin.

Hughes, S.C. 1889 *The church of S. Werburgh*. Dublin.

Hull, C.H. (ed.) 1899 *The economic writings of Sir William Petty*, 2 vols. Cambridge.

Ingamells, J. 1997 *A dictionary of British and Irish travellers in Italy, 1701–1800*. New Haven and London.

Jackson, V. 1958–9 The inception of the Dodder water supply. *Dublin Historical Record* **15**, 3–41; reprinted in H.B. Clarke (ed.), *Medieval Dublin: the making of a metropolis*, 128–41, Dublin. 1990.

Jaski, B. 1995 The Vikings and the kingship of Tara. *Peritia* **9**, 310–51.

Johnston, D.B. 1977 Richard II and Ireland, 1395–9. Ph.D. thesis, University of Dublin.

Johnston-Liik, E.M. 2002 *A history of the Irish Parliament, 1692–1800*, 6 vols. Belfast.

Jones, I. 1727 *The designs of Inigo Jones consisting of plans and elevations for public and private buildings*. London.

Joyce, P.W. 1869 *The origin and history of Irish names of places*, 3 vols. Dublin.

Kelly, E.P. 2015 The longphort in Viking-Age Ireland: the archaeological evidence. In H.B. Clarke and R. Johnson (eds) *The Vikings in Ireland and beyond: before and after the battle of Clontarf*, 55–92. Dublin.

Kelly, E.P. and O'Donovan, E. 1998 A Viking longphort near Athlunkard, Co, Clare. Archaeology Ireland 12(4), 13–16.

Kelly, J. 2012 Residential and non-residential Lords Lieutenant – the viceroyalty 1703–90. In P. Gray and O. Purdue (eds), The Irish Lord Lieutenancy c. 1541–1922. 66–96. Dublin.

Kennedy, R. 1999 Dublin Castle art: the historical and contemporary collection. Dublin.

Kenny, C. 1995 Kilmainham: the history of a settlement older than Dublin. Dublin.

King, C.S. 1906 A great archbishop of Dublin, William King D.D., 1650–1729. London.

Kinsella, S. 2011 Colonial commemoration in Tudor Ireland: the case of Sir Henry Sidney. Sidney Journal 29(1–2), 103–41.

Knowler, W. (ed.) 1739 The Earl of Stafforde's letters and dispatches, 2 vols. London.

Lawlor, H.J. (ed.) 1908 A calendar of the Liber Niger and Liber Albus of Christ Church, Dublin. Proceedings of the Royal Irish Academy 27C, 1–93.

Lawlor, H.J. 1923 The chapel of Dublin Castle. Journal of the Royal Society of Antiquaries of Ireland 53, 34–73.

Lawlor, H.J. 1928 The chapel of Dublin Castle. Journal of the Royal Society of Antiquaries of Ireland 58, 44–53.

Leclerq, J. (ed.) 1962–92 Recueil d'études sur saint Bernard et ses écrits, 5 vols. Rome.

Lennon, C. 2008 Dublin Part II, 1610 to 1756. Irish Historic Towns Atlas No. 19. Dublin.

Lennon, C. and Montague, J. 2010 John Rocque's Dublin, a guide to the Georgian city. Dublin.

Llanover, Lady (ed.) 1861–2 The autobiography and correspondence of Mary Granville, Mrs Delany, 6 vols. London.

Lodge, J. (ed.) 1772 Desiderata curiosa Hibernica: or a select collection of state papers; consisting of royal instructions, directions, dispatches, and letters…, 2 vols. Dublin.

Loeber, R. 1980 The rebuilding of Dublin Castle: thirty critical years, 1661–1690. Studies: An Irish Quarterly Review 69, 45–69.

Loeber, R. 1981 A biographical dictionary of architects in Ireland 1600–1720. London.

Loeber, R., Dickson, D. and Smyth, A. (eds) 2012 Journal of a tour to Dublin and the counties of Dublin and Meath in 1699. Analecta Hibernica 43, 47–67.

Loos, T. 2007 Date with destiny. Art & Auction Feb. 2007, 71–4.

Lucey, C. 2007 The Stapleton Collection, designs for the Irish neoclassical interior. Tralee.

Lydon, J.F. 1966–7 Three exchequer documents from the reign of Henry III. Proceedings of the Royal Irish Academy 65C, 1–27.

Lydon, J.F. 2016 Dublin and the Scottish threat, 1315–18. In S. Duffy (ed.), Medieval Dublin XV, 277–92. Dublin.

Lynch, A. and Manning, C. 1990 Dublin Castle – the archaeological project. Archaeology Ireland 4(2), 65–8.

Lynch, A. and Manning, C. 2001 Excavations at Dublin Castle, 1985–7. In S. Duffy (ed.), Medieval Dublin II, 169–204. Dublin.

Maas, J. 2008 Longphort, dún, and dúnad in the Irish annals of the Viking period. Peritia 20, 257–75.

McCarthy, P. 2008 Stables and horses in Ireland, c. 1630–1840. In Y. Scott (ed.), The Provost's house stables. Building & environs, Trinity College Dublin, 28–71. Dublin.

McCarthy, P. 2017 Trophys and festoons, the lost Presence Chamber, 1684–1788. In M. Campbell and W. Derham (eds), Making Majesty: the Throne Room at Dublin Castle, a cultural history, 22–45. Newbridge.

McCormick, T. 2018 Restoration Politics, 1660–1691. In J. Ohlmeyer (ed.), Cambridge History of Ireland, volume 2, 1550–1730, 96–119. Cambridge.

McCullough, C. and Crawford, W.H. 2007 Armagh. Irish Historic Towns Atlas No. 18. Dublin.

McCullough, N. 1989 Dublin, An urban history. Dublin.

McCullough, N. 1991 A vision of the city: Dublin and the Wide Streets Commissioners. Dublin.

McDonnell, J. 1991 Irish eighteenth-century stuccowork and its European sources. Dublin.

McDowell, R.B. 2003 Historical essays 1938–2001. Dublin.

McEnery, M.J. and Refaussé, R. (eds) 2001 Christ Church deeds. Dublin.

MacLysaght, E. 1939 Irish life in the seventeenth century. Cork.

MacLysaght, E. (ed.) 1944 Commonwealth state accounts Ireland, 1650–1656. Analecta Hibernica 15, 229–321.

McMahon, M. 2002 Early medieval settlement and burial outside- the enclosed town: evidence from archaeological excavation at Bride Street, Dublin. Proceedings of the Royal Irish Academy 102C, 67–135.

McNeill, C. 1921 New Gate, Dublin. Journal of the Royal Society of Antiquaries of Ireland 51, 152–65.

McNeill, C. 1931 [Irish material in the] Rawlinson manuscripts (Class D). Analecta Hibernica 2, 44–92.

McNeill, C. 1934 Harris: Collectanea de rebus Hibernicis. Analecta Hibernica 6, 248–450.

McNeill, C. (ed.) 1943 The Tanner letters. Dublin.

McNeill, C. (ed.) 1950 Calendar of Archbishop Alen's register, c. 1172–1534. Dublin.

McNeill, T.E. 1997 Castles in Ireland: feudal power in a Gaelic world. London.

McParland, E. 1969 Francis Johnston, architect, 1760–1829. Quarterly Bulletin of the Irish Georgian Society 12, 61–139.

McParland, E. 1972a The Wide Streets Commissioners: their importance for Dublin architecture in the late 18th – early 19th century. Quarterly Bulletin of the Irish Georgian Society 15, 1–32.

McParland, E. 1972b James Gandon and the Royal Exchange Competition, 1768–9. Journal of the Royal Society of Antiquaries of Ireland 102, 58–72.

McParland, E. 1985a Royal Hospital, Kilmainham, Co. Dublin. Country Life 177, no. 4577, 1260–3, 1320–4.

McParland, E. 1985b James Gandon: Vitruvius Hibernicus. London.

McParland, E. 1989 Edward Lovett Pearce and the parliament house in Dublin. The Burlington Magazine 131, no. 1031 (Feb., 1989), 91–100.

McParland, E. 1995 The office of the Surveyor General of Ireland in the eighteenth century. Architectural History 38, 91–101.

McParland, E. 2001 Public architecture in Ireland 1680–1760. New Haven and London.

MacShamhráin, A. 2016 Swords and district: the political and ecclesiastical background, fifth to twelfth centuries. In S. Duffy (ed.), Medieval Dublin XV, 39–63. Dublin.

Maguire, J.B. 1974 Seventeenth century plans of Dublin Castle. Journal of the Royal Society of Antiquaries of Ireland 104, 5–14.

Maguire, J.B. 1985 Dublin Castle, three centuries of development. Journal of the Royal Society of Antiquaries of Ireland 115, 13–39

Malton, J. 1799 A picturesque and descriptive view of the city of Dublin. London.

Manning, C. 1998 Dublin Castle: the building of a royal castle in Ireland. Château Gaillard 18, 119–22.

Manning, C. 2003a Excavations at Roscrea Castle. Dublin.

Manning, C. 2003b The Record Tower, Dublin Castle. In J.R. Kenyon and J. Knight (eds), The medieval castle in Ireland and Wales: essays in honour of Jeremy Knight, 72–95. Dublin.

Manning, C. 2010 Arms and the man:…armorial plaques erected by Sir Henry Sidney. Archaeology Ireland 24(1), 8–11.

Manning, C. 2014 Dublin Castle. In R. Moss (ed.) Art and architecture of Ireland, vol. I, medieval c. 400–c. 1600, 346–8. Dublin, New Haven and London.

Manning, C. 2017–18 'But you are first to build a tower' – the Bermingham Tower, Dublin Castle. Ulster Journal of Archaeology 74, 145–54.

Marillier, H.C. 1927 The Mortlake horses. The Burlington Magazine for Connoisseurs 50, No. 286, 12-14.

Marstrander, C. 1915 Bidrag til det norske sprogs historie i Irland. Kristiana.

Martin-Robinson, J. 2012 James Wyatt 1746–1813, architect to George III. New Haven.

Meyer, K. (ed.) 1906 The triads of Ireland. Dublin.

Mills, J., Wood, H., Langman, A.E. and Griffith, M.C. (eds) 1905–56 Calendar of the justiciary rolls…of Ireland… [1295–1314], 3 vols. Dublin.

Mills, J. and McEnery, M.J. (eds) 1916 Calendar of the Gormanston register from the original in the possession of the right honourable the viscount of Gormanston. Dublin.

Molyneux, C. 1820 An account of the family and descendants of Sir Thomas Molyneux Kt. Chancellor of the Exchequer in Ireland to Queen Elizabeth. Evesham.

Monck Mason, W. 1819 The history and antiquities of the collegiate and cathedral church of St Patrick, near Dublin, from its foundation in 1190, to the year 1819. Dublin.

Montague, J. 2000 The impact of some secular cathedral cloisters and their patrons on developments in English architecture before 1300. M.A. dissertation, History of Art, University of Warwick.

Montague, J. 2006 The cloister and bishop's palace at Old Sarum with some thoughts on the origins and meaning of secular cathedral cloisters. Journal of the British Archaeological Association: the medieval cloister in England and Wales 159, 48–70.

Montague, J. 2007 A shopping arcade in eighteenth-century Dublin: John Rocque and the Essex Street 'piazzas'. Irish Architectural and Decorative Studies 10, 224–45.

Montague, J. 2012 John Ogilby's map of London (Fag. portfolio XV, no. 1), in W.E. Vaughan (ed.), The Old Library, Trinity College Dublin, 1712–2012, 72–6. Dublin.

Montague, J. 2014a Lighthouses. In R. Loeber, H. Campbell, L. Hurley, J. Montague and E. Rowley (eds), *Art and architecture of Ireland*, vol. iv: *architecture: 1600–2000*, 157–9. Dublin, New Haven and London.

Montague, J. 2014b Theatres from the seventeenth to the nineteenth century. In R. Loeber, H. Campbell, L. Hurley, J. Montague and E. Rowley (eds), *Art and architecture of Ireland*, vol. iv: *architecture: 1600–2000*, 486–9. Dublin, New Haven and London.

Morgan, H. 2007 The messenger in John Derricke's "Image of Irelande" (1581). *History Ireland* **15**(1), 6–7.

Morrin, J. (ed.) 1861 *Calendar of the patent and close rolls of Chancery in Ireland, of the reigns of Henry VIII, Edward VI, Mary and Elizabeth*, vol. 1: *1514–1575*. Dublin.

Morrin, J. (ed.) 1863 *Calendar of the patent and close rolls of Chancery in Ireland of the reign of Charles I. First to eighth year inclusive*. London.

Morrissey, J.F. (ed.) 1939 *Statute rolls of the parliament of Ireland…twelfth and thirteenth to the twenty-first and twenty-second years of the reign of King Edward the Fourth*. Dublin.

Moss, R. 2014a Materials. In R. Moss (ed.) *Art and architecture of Ireland*, vol. i, *medieval*, 21–2. Dublin, New Haven, London.

Moss, R. 2014b Cathedrals: administration and function. In R. Moss (ed.) *Art and architecture of Ireland*, vol. i, *medieval*, 158–9. Dublin, New Haven, London.

Moss, R. 2014c Athlone Bridge, in R. Moss (ed.) *Art and architecture of Ireland*, vol. i, *medieval*, 387–8. Dublin, New Haven, London.

Moss, R. 2014d Appendix 1B: fine metalworkers, in R. Moss (ed.) *Art and architecture of Ireland*, vol. i, *medieval*, 532–8. London, Dublin, New Haven.

Moss, R. 2015 "The chapel of the king in the castle of Dublin": the Dublin Castle chapel before 1807. In M. Campbell and W. Derham (eds), *The chapel royal, Dublin Castle: an architectural history*, 29–37. Trim.

Mullen, A. 1682 *An anatomical account of the elephant accidentally burnt in Dublin on Fryday June 17 in the year 1681 sent in a letter to Sir Will. Petty*. London.

Murphy, M. 1995 Balancing the concerns of church and state: the archbishops of Dublin, 1181–1228. In T. Barry, R. Frame and K. Simms (eds), *Colony and frontier in medieval Ireland: essays presented to J.F. Lydon*, 41–56. London and Rio Grande.

Murray, P. 2004 *George Petrie (1790–1866), the rediscovery of Ireland's past*. Cork.

Nelson, E.C. 1991 "Reserved to the fellows": four centuries of gardens at Trinity College Dublin. In C.H. Holland (ed.), *Trinity College Dublin and the idea of a university*, 185–222. Dublin.

Nicholls, K.W. 1972 Inquisitions from 1224. *Analecta Hibernica* **27**, 103–12.

Nichols, J. (ed.) 1779 *A supplement to Dr. Swift's works*, 3 vols. London.

Nichols, J.G. (ed.) 1867 *History from marble. Compiled in the reign of Charles II by Thomas Dingley, gent*. London.

Nicolas, H. (ed.) 1834–7 *Proceedings and ordinances of the privy council of England, [1386–1542]*, 7 vols. London.

O'Connor, C. and O'Regan, J. (eds) 1987 *Public works: the architecture of the Office of Public Works 1831–1987*. Dublin.

O'Conor, K., Brady, N., Connon, A. and Fidalgo-Romo, C. 2010 The rock of Lough Cé, Co. Roscommon. In T. Finan (ed.), *Medieval Lough Cé: history, archaeology and landscape*, 15–40. Dublin.

O'Conor, K. and Naessens, P. 2012 Pre-Norman fortification in eleventh- and twelfth-century Ireland. *Château Gaillard* **25**, 259–68.

Ó Corráin, D. 1974 Royal fortresses and military fortifications. In B.G. Scott (ed.), *Perspectives in Irish archaeology: papers presented to the 5th annual seminar of the Association of Young Irish Archaeologists held in Dublin, November 1973*, 68–71. Belfast.

O'Donovan, E. 2008 The Irish, the Vikings, and the English: new archaeological evidence from excavations at Golden Lane, Dublin. In S. Duffy (ed.), *Medieval Dublin VIII*, 36–130. Dublin.

O'Dowd, M. (ed.) 2000 *Calendar of state papers, Ireland, Tudor Period 1571–1575*. Dublin and Kew.

O'Dwyer, F. 1981 *Lost Dublin*. Dublin.

O'Dwyer, F. 1992 The ballroom at Dublin Castle – the origins of St Patrick's Hall. In A. Bernelle (ed.) *Decantations, a tribute to Maurice Craig*, 148–67. Dublin.

O'Dwyer, F. 1996–7 Making connections in Georgian Ireland, *Bulletin of the Irish Georgian Society*, **38**, 6-23.

O'Dwyer, F. 2002 Building empires: architecture, politics and the Board of Works 1760–1860. *Irish Architectural and Decorative Studies* **5**, 108–175.

O'Dwyer, F. 2008 In search of Christopher Myers: pioneer of the Gothic revival in Ireland. In M. McCarthy and K. O'Neill (eds), *Studies in the Gothic Revival*, 51–111. Dublin.

Ogilvie, S. 2011 *Institutions and European trade: merchant guilds, 1000–1800*. Cambridge.

O'Keeffe, T. 2009 Dublin Castle's donjon in context. In J. Bradley, A. Fletcher and A. Simms (eds), *Dublin in the medieval world: studies in honour of Howard B. Clarke*, 277–94. Dublin.

O'Keeffe, T. 2015 *Medieval Irish buildings, 1100–1600*. Maynooth research guides for Irish local history: number 18. Dublin.

Olley, J. 1991 Sustaining the narrative at Kilmainham. *Irish Arts Review Yearbook 1991–1992*, 65–72.

Ó Néill, J. 2004 Excavations at Longford Street Little, Dublin: an archaeological approach to Dubh Linn. In S. Duffy (ed.), *Medieval Dublin V*, 73–90. Dublin.

Orpen, G.H. (ed.) 1892 *The Song of Dermot and the Earl*. Oxford.

Orpen, G.H. 1907a Athlone: its early history, with notes on some neighbouring castles. *Journal of the Royal Society of Antiquaries of Ireland* **37**(3), 257–76.

Orpen, G.H. 1907b Motes and Norman castles in Ireland. *English Historical Review* **22**(86), 228–54, 440–67.

Orpen, G.H. 1911–20 *Ireland under the Normans*, 4 vols. London (reprinted in one volume, Dublin, 2005).

Owen, J. 1848–9 An account of the mode adopted for raising the roof of the Presence Chamber, Dublin Castle. *Transactions of the Institution of Civil Engineers of Ireland* **3**, 32–4.

Palgrave, F. (ed.) 1835 *Rotuli Curiae Regis: Rolls and records of the court held before the king's justiciars or justices*, 2 vols. London.

Parker, J. 1957 A staircase by Grinling Gibbon., *The Metropolitan Museum of Art Bulletin* new series, **15**, no. 10 (June 1957), 228–36.

Payne, J. 1757 *Twelve designs of Country Houses*. Dublin. (Title page gives author as 'a gentleman').

Perros-Walton, H. 2013 Church reform in Connacht. In. S. Duffy (ed.), *Princes, prelates and poets in medieval Ireland*, 279–308. Dublin.

Phelan, S. 2010 The bank, the ditch and the water: Hiberno-Norse discoveries at Church Street and Hammond Lane. In S. Duffy (ed.), *Medieval Dublin X*, 165–97. Dublin.

Pigot, J. 1824 *City of Dublin and Hibernian Provincial Directory*. London.

Porter, W. and Watson, C. 1889 *History of the Corps of Royal Engineers*, 2 vols. London.

Power, R. 1986 Magnus Barelegs' Expeditions to the West. *Scottish Historical Review* **66**, 107–32.

Power, R. 2005 Meeting in Norway: Norse-Gaelic relations in the kingdom of Man and the Isles, 1090–1270. *Saga-book: Viking Society for Northern Research* **29**, 5–66.

Prendergast, J.P. 1886 *The vice-royalty of Ireland and the vice-regal court, historically vindicated*. Dublin.

Purcell, E. 2015 The first generation in Ireland, AD 795–812: Viking raids and Viking bases?. In H.B. Clarke and R. Johnson (eds), *The Vikings in Ireland and beyond: before and after Clontarf*, 41–54. Dublin.

Quinn, D.B. 1941 Guide to English financial records for Irish history, with illustrative extracts, 1461–1509. *Analecta Hibernica* **10**, 1–69.

Quinn, D.B. 1993 The re-emergence of English policy as a major factor in Irish affairs, 1520–34. In A. Cosgrove (ed.), *A new history of Ireland, II: medieval Ireland 1169–1534*, 662–87. Oxford.

Rady, J., Tatton Brown, T. and Bowen, J.A. 1991 The archbishop's palace, Canterbury: excavations and building recording works from 1981 to 1986. *Journal of the British Archaeological Association* **144**, 1–60.

Reeves-Smyth, T. 2004 Irish gardens and gardening before Cromwell. In J. Ludlow and N. Jameson (eds), *Medieval Ireland: the Barryscourt lectures, I–X*, 100–43. Kinsale.

Richardson, D.S. 1983 *Gothic Revival architecture in Ireland*. New York.

Richardson, H.G. and Sayles, G.O. 1961 Irish revenue, 1278–1384. *Proceedings of the Royal Irish Academy* **62C**, 87–100.

Robinson, A.T. 1994 The history of Dublin Castle to 1684. Ph.D. thesis. National University of Ireland.

Ronan, M.V. 1926 *The Reformation in Dublin, 1536-38*. London.

Ronan, M.V. 1940 Lazar houses of St Laurence and St Stephen in medieval Dublin, in J. Ryan (ed.), *Féilsgríbhinn Eóin Mhic Néill: essays and studies presented to Professor Eóin Mac Neill*, 480-89. Dublin.

Round, J.H. 1920 The staff of a castle in the twelfth century. *English History Review* **35**, 90–7.

Rule, M. (ed.) 1884 *Eadmeri Historia novorum in Anglia*. Rolls Series, London.

S., C.E. 1852 Some notes from Ireland. *Ecclesiologist* **13**, 305.

Sabine, E.L. 1933 Butchering in mediaeval London. *Speculum* **8**, no. 3, 335–53.

Salmon, F. 2013 Public commissions. In S. Weber (ed.), *William Kent, designing Georgian Britain*, 315–63. New Haven and London.

Sayles, G.O. (ed.) 1979 *Documents on the affairs of Ireland before the king's council.* Dublin.

St John Brooks, E. 1933 The grant of Castleknock to Hugh Tyrel. *Journal of the Royal Society of Antiquaries of Ireland* **63**, 206–20.

St John Brooks, E. (ed.) 1936 *Register of the hospital of S. John without the Newgate, Dublin.* Dublin.

St John Brooks, E. 1935–7 Unpublished charters relating to Ireland, 1177–82, from the archives of the city of Exeter. *Proceedings of the Royal Irish Academy* **43C**, 313–66.

Severens, K. 1990 Emigration and provincialism: Samuel Cardy's architectural career in the Atlantic world. *Eighteenth century Ireland* **5**, 21–36.

Severens, K. 1992–3 A new perspective on Georgian building practice: the rebuilding of St. Werburgh's Church, Dublin (1754–59). *Bulletin of the Irish Georgian Society* **35**, 3–16.

Shaw, D. 2006 Thomas Wentworth and monarchical ritual in early modern Ireland. *Historical Journal* **49**, 331–55.

Shaw, H. 1850 *New city pictorial directory 1850.* Dublin.

Shelby, L.R. 1964 The role of the master mason in mediaeval English building. *Speculum* **39**(3), 387–403.

Sherrard, T. 1802 *Extracts from the minutes of the Commissioners…for making Wide and Convenient Ways, Streets, and Passages, in the City of Dublin.* Dublin.

Simms, J.G. 2009 The war of the two kings, 1685–1691. In T. Moody, F.X. Martin and F.J. Byrne (eds), *A new history of Ireland III*, 478–508.

Simpson, L. 1999 *Director's findings: Temple Bar West.* Temple Bar Archaeological Report, no. 5. Dublin.

Simpson, L. 2000 Forty years a-digging: a preliminary synthesis of archaeological investigations in medieval Dublin. In S. Duffy (ed.), *Medieval Dublin I*, 11–68. Dublin.

Simpson, L. 2002 Historical and topographical survey. In M. McMahon, 'Early medieval settlement and burial outside the enclosed town: evidence from archaeological excavations at Bride Street, Dublin'. *Proceedings of the Royal Irish Academy* **102C**, 67–70.

Simpson, L. 2004 Excavations on the southern side of the medieval town at Ship Street Little, Dublin. In S. Duffy (ed.), *Medieval Dublin V*, 9–51. Dublin.

Simpson, L. 2005 Viking warrior burials in Dublin: is this the longphort?. In S. Duffy (ed.), *Medieval Dublin VI*, 11–62. Dublin.

Simpson, L. 2006 *Dublin City: walls and defences.* Dublin. Dublin City Council.

Sims-Williams, P. 1991 The submission of Irish kings in fact and fiction: Henry II, Bendigeidfran, and the dating of The four branches of the Mabinogi. *Cambridge Medieval Celtic Studies* **22**, 31–61.

Singer, S.W. (ed.) 1828 *The correspondence of Henry Hyde, Earl of Clarendon and of his brother, Laurence Hyde, Earl of Rochester*, 2 vols. London.

Smirke, E. 1845 On the hall and round table at Winchester. *Proceedings at the Annual Meeting of the Archaeological Institute*, 44–80.

Smyly, J.G. 1945 Old Latin deeds in the library of Trinity College, I. *Hermathena* **66**, 25–39.

Stanihurst, R. 1577 'Description of Irelande' in *Holinshed's Chronicles of England, Scotland and Ireland.* London.

Stanihurst, R. 1979 A treatise containing a plain and perfect description of Ireland. In L. Miller and E. Power (eds) *Holinshed's Irish Chronicle.* Dublin.

Stewart, I.H. 1989 King John's recoinage and the conference of moneyers in 1208. *British Numismatic Journal* **59**, 39–45.

Strickland, W.G. 1913 *A dictionary of Irish artists*, 2 vols. Dublin and London.

Stubbs, W. (ed.) 1867 *Gesta Regis Henrici Secundi Benedicti Abbatis*, 2 vols. Rolls Series. London.

Stubbs, W. (ed.) 1868–71 *Chronica Magistri Rogeri de Houedene*, 4 vols. Rolls Series. London.

Swan, L. 1983 Enclosed ecclesiastical sites and their relevance to settlement patterns of the first millennium AD. In T. Reeves-Smyth and F. Hamond (eds), *Landscape archaeology in Ireland.* BAR. British Series, vol. 116. Oxford.

Swan, L. 1985 Monastic proto-towns in early medieval Ireland: the evidence of aerial photography, plan analysis and survey. In H.B. Clarke and A. Simms (eds), *The comparative history of urban origins in non-Roman Europe*, 77–102. British Archaeological Reports (International Series) 255 (i). Oxford.

Sweetman, H.S. (ed.) 1875–86 *A calendar of documents relating to Ireland, 1171–1307*, 5 vols. London.

Thornton, A. 1875 *The autobiography of Mrs. Alice Thornton, of East Newton, Co. York.* Durham.

Thurley, S. 2003 *Hampton Court: a social and architectural history.* New Haven and London.

Tighe, J. 1988 An early Dublin candle maker. *Dublin Historical Record* **41**, 115–22.

Todd, J.H. (ed.) 1867 *Cogadh Gaedhel re Gallaibh: the War of the Gaedhil with the Gaill.* Rolls Series. London.

Townshend, D. 1904 *The life and letters of the great earl of Cork.* London.

Turner, T.H. 1851 *Some account of domestic architecture in England from the conquest to the end of the thirteenth century with numerous illustrations of existing remains from original designs.* Oxford.

Twiss, H.F. 1920 Some ancient deeds of the parish of St Werburgh, Dublin, 1243–1678. *Proceedings of the Royal Irish Academy* **35C**, 282–315.

Usher, R. 2008 Reading architecture: St Andrew's Church, Dublin, 1670–1990. *Visual Resources* **24**(2), 119–32.

Usher, R. 2012 *Protestant Dublin, 1660–1760: architecture and iconography.* London.

Veach, C. 2014a *Lordship in four realms. The Lacy family, 1166–1241.* Manchester.

Veach, C. 2014b King John and royal control in Ireland: why William de Briouze had to be destroyed. *English History Review* **129**(540), 1051–78.

Victor, B. 1761 *The history of the theatres of London and Dublin from the year 1730 to the present time*, 2 vols. London.

Walker, J.C. 1788 *An historical essay on the dress of the ancient and modern Irish.* Dublin.

Wallace, P.F. 2000 Garrda and airbeada: the plot thickens in Viking Dublin. In A.P. Smyth (ed.), *Seanchas. Studies in early and medieval Irish archaeology, history and literature in honour of Francis J. Byrne*, 261–74. Dublin.

Walsh, C. 2012 The excavation of an early roadway and Hiberno-Norse houses at the Coombe. In S. Duffy (ed.). *Medieval Dublin XII*, 113–37. Dublin.

Walsh, P. (ed.) 1948–1957 *The life of Aodh Ruadh O Domhnaill*, 2 vols. Irish Texts Society Vols XLII and XLV. London and Dublin.

Walsh, P.G. and Kennedy, M.J. (eds) 2007 *William of Newburgh. The history of English affairs, Book II.* Oxford.

Walsh, T.J. 1973 *Opera in Dublin 1705–1797: the social scene.* Dublin.

Warburton, J., Whitelaw, J. and Walsh, R. 1818 *History of the city of Dublin*, 2 vols. London.

Ware, I. 1735 *The plans, elevation and sections of Houghton in Norfolk.* London.

Ware, J. 1705 *The antiquities and history of Ireland.* Dublin.

Watts, J.L. 2002 Looking for the state in later medieval England. In P. Coss and M. Keen (eds), *Heraldry, pageantry and social display in medieval England*, 243–67. Woodbridge.

Whaley, D. (ed.) 2009 Arnórr jarlaskáld Þórðarson, Þorfinnsdrápa 23. In K.E. Gade (ed.), *Poetry from the Kings' Sagas 2: from c. 1035 to c. 1300*, 257–8. Skaldic Poetry of the Scandinavian Middle Ages 2. Turnhout.

White, N.B. (ed.) 1941a *The Reportorium viride of John Alen, archbishop of Dublin.* Analecta Hibernica **10**, 173–222.

White, N.B. (ed.) 1941b *The annals of Dudley Loftus.* Analecta Hibernica **10**, 225–38.

White, N.B. (ed.) 1943 *Extents of Irish monastic possessions, 1540–1541.* Dublin.

White, N.B. (ed.) 1957 *The 'Dignita Decani' of St Patrick's cathedral, Dublin.* Dublin.

Wilde, W.R. 1861–4 Statement on the presentation of certain antiquities. *Proceedings of the Royal Irish Academy* **8**, 324–30.

Williams, B. 2001 The Dominican annals of Dublin. In S. Duffy (ed.), *Medieval Dublin II*, 142–68. Dublin.

Williamson, T. 2012 *Inigo's Stones: Inigo Jones, royal marbles and imperial power.* New York.

Wilson, T. 1713 *An account of the foundation of the Royal Hospital of King Charles the Second.* Dublin.

Woods, A. 2013 The coinage and economy of Hiberno-Scandinavian Dublin. In S. Duffy (ed.), *Medieval Dublin XIII*, 43–69. Dublin.

Woolgar, C.M. 1999 *The great household in late medieval England.* New Haven and London.

Worsley, G. 2004 *The British stable.* New Haven and London.

Bibliography
Pamphlets, Newspapers/magazines and Manuscripts

Pamphlets and Newspapers/magazines

A true and particular relation of the fire which happened in the castle of Dublin in Ireland, B.R., 1684. (See Appendix 4)

The secret intrigues of the Romish party in Ireland, licensed 14 Aug 1689.

Great news from the port of Kingsale in Ireland; giving a true account of the arrival of Admiral Herbert; of his taking the same place and of King James; of his grace Duke Schomberg's landing and other material occurrences, licensed 19 Aug 1689. (NLI Thorpe Collection of Pamphlets No. 644).

Dublin Evening Post 30 Oct–3 Nov 1733

Dublin Evening Post 18 Sep 1790

Dublin Evening Post 19 Aug 1790

Dublin Evening Post 22 Sep 1791

Faulkner's Dublin Journal 7 Jul 1764

Faulkner's Dublin Journal 2–4 Apr 1776

Faulkner's Dublin Journal 24 Apr 1776

Faulkner's Dublin Journal 10–12 Dec 1782

Faulkner's Dublin Journal 18–20 Sep 1788

Faulkner's Dublin Journal 30 Oct–1 Nov 1788

Faulkner's Dublin Journal 24–27 Nov 1788

Freeman's Journal 1775

Freeman's Journal 20 Sep–28 Oct 1788

Freeman's Journal 27–9 Nov 1788

Hibernian Journal 14–17 June 1771

Mercurius Politicus 29 Dec 1659–5 Jan 1659 [1660]

Morning Chronicle 23 Aug 1813

Saunders Newsletter 20–22 May 1789

Walker's Hibernian Magazine Jan 1795

The Dublin Builder 1 June 1860

The Graphic 18 April 1888

Manuscripts

Dublin National Monuments Service Archive

Breen Thaddeus Breen, Dublin Castle Building History, a) To 1500; b) 1500–1600; c) The Seventeenth Century; d) The Eighteenth Century; e) Since 1800. (Unpublished typescript, *c.* 1986)

DCCI Dublin Castle Card Index of historical references (compiled by Thaddeus Breen *c.* 1986)

Ó hEochaidhe 1962 An account of the archaeological investigations carried out at the Cross Block, Dublin Castle, November 1961 – February 1962. Prepared by: M. Ó hEochaidhe, Asst. Inspector, National Monuments Branch, Office of Public Works, 10 Hume Street, Dublin. Deireadh Fómhair [October], 1962. (Photocopied typescript with line drawings and photographs)

Historical plans and maps. Large folder with photocopies of historical plans, illustrations and maps relating to Dublin Castle (mostly collected by Thaddeus Breen *c.* 1986).

Dublin City Library and Archives (DCA or DCLA)

EL Expired leases

Gilbert Coll. MSS. 74–76, 'The history and antiquities of Dublin, collected from authentic records and the manuscript collections of Sir James Ware, by Robert Ware, son of that learned antiquary, 1678. With a transcript of the same'.

Gilbert Coll. MS. 195, various documents related to improvements to Dublin Castle, in 1710.

Gilbert Coll. Ms. 205

WSC Wide Streets Commission 88/1

WSC Wide Streets Commission 90

WSC Wide Streets Commission 92

WSC Wide Streets Commission 94/1

WSC Wide Streets Commission 105

WSC Wide Streets Commission 113

WSC Wide Streets Commission 162/2

WSC Wide Streets Commission 187

WSC Wide Streets Commission 209

WSC Wide Streets Commission 329

WSC Wide Streets Commission 389

WSC Wide Streets Commission 499

WSC Wide Streets Commission 537

WSC Wide Streets Commission 654

Irish Architectural Archive, Dublin (IAA)

84/51

86/149 – see Eyre's Letter book below

EMcP Edward McParland files, Acc. 2008/44

Eyre's Letter Book - Eyre's MS. letter book, 1756–65, and 'General Accompt', 1752–1762, are both referenced at IAA, Acc. 86/149.

National Archives of Ireland (NAI)

NAI, *Calendar of Irish correspondence Vol. 1 1697–1798*

NAI, PROI D19722

NAI, RC 8/28

NAI, OPW/5HC/1/61 (Euclid Alfray plans)

NAI, Wyche 1/1/14. Letter from William Ellis to Sir Cyril Wyche, Chief Secretary to the Duke of Ormonde, 1676–82

CMLP Calendar of Miscellaneous Letters and Papers pre 1760

KQL Index to Kings' and Queens' Letters Vol. 1 1649–1852

Many other references to manuscripts in the National Archives of Ireland are second-hand references from researchers like Breen and McParland working in the 1960s to 1980s when the State Paper Office (SPO) was still housed in the Record Tower in Dublin Castle and the Public Record Office of Ireland (PROI) was housed at the Four Courts. These offices have since been amalgamated as the National Archives of Ireland (NAI) located on Bishop Street, Dublin, and the manuscript referencing systems have been updated. In some cases the old references were to temporary boxes and have no validity in the present referencing system. Where this problem arises, the second-hand references are placed first and match those in the notes. This is followed by an indication of the nature of the manuscript, if known, in round brackets. Where the present reference is known it is added in square brackets even when only the collection or group of manuscripts could be adduced.

NA 1A-35-58 (Horse Guard housed off Dame St in 1660s) [NAI, M 2449 (Orrery Papers)]

NA 1A.36.8 (Lease of land at new entrance to castle) [NAI, Deed (mixed box M / D / T/ C)]

NA 1C., 1 1697-1798, 12 April 1746 (New entrance to castle)

NA/SPO 188

NA/SPO 516/84/8

NA/SPO 516/94

SPO 527/188/2 [NAI, OP 527/188/2]

NA/SPO 558AAE/984/2 [NAI, OP 558AAE/984/2]

NA Bryan Bolger Papers 1A/58/1 [NAI, Bryan Bolger Papers or TCD?]

NA Bryan Bolger Papers 1A/58/128 [NAI, Bryan Bolger Papers, Public Buildings]

NA Bryan Bolger Papers/Public Buildings [NAI, Bryan Bolger Papers, Public Buildings]

NA CSO/RP/1818/362 [NAI, CSO/RP]

CSO/RP/1824/1884- 10,628 [NAI, CSO/RP]

NA/SPO CSO/RP 1825/11 [NAI, CSO/RP]

NA/SPO CSO/RP 1826/13,687 [NAI, CSO/RP 1826/551]

NA SPO CSO/RP 1827/335 [NAI, CSO/RP 1827/323]

NA M2446 [NAI, M 2446]

NA M2447 [NAI, M 446?]

NA M2549 [NAI, M 2549]

NA/SPO OP/94 [NAI, OP/94]

SPO OP 142/7 [NAI, OP 142/7]

NA/SPO OP 165 [NAI, OP 165]

NAI, SPO OP 165:12 [NAI, OP 165/12]

NA OP 185/7 [NAI, OP 185/7]

NA OP 230/13 [NAI, OP 230/13]

NA/SPO OP 249/4 [NAI, OP 249/4]

NA PW/1/1/1 (OPW Minute Books 1802-65) [NAI, OPW 1/1/1/2-10]

NA PW1/1/2/1/1 (OPW Letter Books 1802-93) [NAI, OPW 1/1/2/1-11]

PROI PW 1/1/2/1/1, 314 [NAI, OPW 1/1/2/1?]

NA/SPO WO78-1154 [TNA, MPH/1/203/1-5]

NA, Wyche MSS 1/14 [NAI, Wyche 1/1/14]

NA, [Wyche MSS] 1A/41 [NAI, Wyche 1/1/14?]

NAI, Wyche MSS, 2/142, ff. 1–4, 'Inventory of the King's Goods in the Castle of Dublin', May 1693 [NAI, Wyche 2/1/142]

National Library of Ireland (NLI)

NLI, MS 21F 52/022

NLI, MS 392. Thomas Dineley, 'Observations in a voyage through the kingdom of ireland'.

NLI, MS 698

NLI, MS 992

NLI, MS 2327, f. 111 'Remaining due to workemen, and for Materialls used in the Repaireing his Ma.ies Castle of Dublin &c the 18th of October 1662'.

NLI, MS 2436.

NLI, MS 2487, f. 125. 'An Estimate of what is at present very needfull to bee Repaired in & about his Ma.ies Castle of Dublin besides the Powdar Tower, and the 2 stores &c.'.

NLI, MS 2528

NLI, MS 2524

NLI, MS 2554

NLI, MS 2656 (18)

NLI, MS 2789

NLI, MS 2790 (Longfield)

NLI, MS 13034

NLI, MSS 3137(3) & MS 2557(1): 'A draught of Castle of Dublin at present' [1685], two maps:

NLI, MSS 41563–41603

NLI, MSS 41582/1 and 41582/29

NLI, MS 41589/3

NLI, 1959TX, 54

Registry of Deeds, Dublin (RD)

7/100/1812

Representative Church Body Library, Dublin

P0236/05/01 St Werburgh's Vestry Minute Books 1720–80

P0236/05/02 St Werburgh's Vestry Minute Books 1780–1859

Royal Irish Academy, Dublin (RIA)

MR/17/B/3

24 G 4

Trinity College Dublin (TCD)

TCD, MS 543/2/14 Manuscript list of mayors and bailiffs of Dublin, I Henry V to 26 Henry VIII (1413–1534).

TCD, MS 750/4/30V

TCD, MS 772

TCD, MS 2062

Office of Public Works Library, Trim, Co. Meath

E000480 U16-1

E000486 U16-3

E000492 U16-4

E000505 U16-7

E000519 U16-11

E000508 U16-18

E000528 U16-4

E000528 U16-14

E000558 U16-7

Public Record Office of Northern Ireland, Belfast (PRONI)

D619/33/IAI

T689

T3019/631

T3019/1317

T3019/1579

British Library (BL)

Add. 4760

Add. 9716

Add. 41803

Add. 21135

Add. 31323

Add. 35733

Add. 35933

Add. 38160

Add. 38671

Add. 72414

Add. 72856

Eg. 917

Map K Top 53/19d–i

Stowe 204

Stowe 205

Stowe 209

Stowe 213, f. 308. October 13, 1673, letter from the earl of Essex to his brother.

Stowe 214

College of Arms, London

CoA MS PH 15174 William Betham, Repertory to the rolls of the exchequer, vol. V: 1 Henry V to 39 Henry VI.

The National Archives, Kew

TNA, E101/233/23

TNA, E159/184

TNA, E364/34/1

TNA, E403/561

TNA, MPDI 1-188

TNA, MPH1

TNA, MPH 202(1)

TNA, PW I/1/1/2

TNA, SO1/11

TNA, SO1/15

TNA, SO1/16

TNA, SO1/18

TNA, SO1/19

TNA, SO1/21

TNA, SO1/23

TNA, SP 63/121

TNA, SP63/371

TNA, SP63/372 and 373

TNA, SP63/374

TNA, SP63/384

TNA, SP63/396

TNA, T1/51

TNA, T1/126

TNA, T1/176

TNA, T1/176/92

TNA, T1/247

TNA, T1/290

TNA, T1/307/48–51

TNA, T1/308

TNA, T1/322

TNA, T1/337

TNA, T1/354

TNA, T1/367

TNA, T1/376

TNA, T1/379

TNA, T14/4

TNA, T14/8

TNA, T14/9

TNA, T14/12

TNA, T14/13

TNA, T14/14

TNA, Works 31/20

TNA, WO55/1726

TNA, WO55/1984

NA/SPO W078-1154 [TNA, W078/1154?]

Oxford, Bodleian Library (Bod. Lib.)

Aslim. G12

Carte MS 39

Carte MS 40

Carte MS 43

Carte MS 50

Carte MS 52

Carte MS 53

Carte MS 169

Carte MS 215

Carte MS 220

Carte MS 232

Rawlinson D71

**Royal Institute of British
Architects Library**

SB42

Victoria and Albert Museum (V & A)

E2R4:60-1992

E2124:60

Nottingham Archives

DD/P/6/3/77

Staffordshire Record Office

'The Ground plott of the Castle of Dublin, with
y.e thicknes of y.e Walls, Parapets and Battlements,
with the Out-lines of the Severall Buildings therein
Contained. Anno 1673'. This map is part of the
manuscript collection of the earl of Dartmouth,
housed in the Staffordshire Record Office.

Index

Compiled by Julitta Clancy